Edward Jenner

1749–1823

Richard B. Fisher

Edward Jenner

1749–1823

André Deutsch

First published in 1991 by
André Deutsch Limited
105-106 Great Russell Street
London WC1B 3LJ

ISBN 0 233 98681 2

Printed in Great Britain by
St Edmundsbury Press, Bury St Edmunds, Suffolk

C004101726

To Don

Contents

Lord Bacon complains of biographical literature of his day. He says that actions both great & small, public & private, sho'd be so blended together as to secure that genuine nature & lively representation, which forms the peculiar excellence & use of biography.

Edward Jenner

Notes begin on page 293, where they are identified by page number and a key phrase. For example, the reference for Sir Francis Fust's letter on page 1 appears on page 293 as follows:

'*1*   'I hope he will live . . . .': Revd Stephen Jenner, Correspondence and papers. . . .

List of Illustrations

8. The Temple of Vaccinia built by Robert Ferryman in the garden of the Chauntry. Photograph provided by the Jenner Museum.

9. Stephen Jenner drew and described his great uncle about 1820. Original in the Jenner Museum.

The eighteenth-century lancet displayed between Chapter numbers and Chapter titles is reproduced from a drawing supplied by the Wellcome Institute Library, London. Vaccinists and variolators would have used a similar instrument.

Chapter 1

Gentry
1749

Edward Jenner observed his birthday on 17 May although in the year of his birth, 1749, the Old Style calendar was still in use, and the actual date was eleven days earlier. 'I hope he will live to be a comfort to you and Mrs Jenner, and Supply in some measure the Loss of your former Son', wrote Edward's godfather two weeks later. 'I have enclosed Sent you two Guineas to be disposed of as you se propper, a perquisite I always give on the Like occasion'. At the bottom of this generous and kindly note, Sir Francis Fust of Hill Court, four miles south of Jenner's home at Berkeley in Gloucestershire, wrote his newborn godson's correct birth-date, 6 May.

This child survived. Judging both by the ideals of Christian charity and obligation which shaped his upbringing and by the sheer number of lives he preserved, Edward Jenner deserves to be recognized as one of the giants of human history. He introduced vaccination against smallpox – 'the speckled monster', in his own graphic phrase – a killer perhaps superior even to the Black Plague in the decimation of villages and cities, rich and poor, armies and navies, rulers and ruled. Those whom smallpox left alive, it almost always disfigured and frequently blinded. According to one contemporary authority, two thirds of the applicants for relief at the London Hospital for the Indigent Blind in St George's Fields were victims of smallpox.

Its full horror can perhaps be distantly imagined from a textbook description published by Dr Robert John Thornton in 1803:

There is no disease, that the medical writer has to describe, which presents a more melancholy scene than the *natural Small-pox*, as it very frequently occurs.

When the physician is first called to the bedside of the patient, he is enabled at once to form a probable conjecture as to the approaching disorder,

1. From the frequent sighings and sobbings of the person labouring under an anxiety he is unable to express.

2. By pains felt in the region of the stomach, with an inclination, but generally an inability, to vomit.

3. By the racking and frequent shooting pains along the back and loins.

4. A general lassitude and aching of every limb.

5. A most unpleasant sensation of cold, not relieved by any external warmth.

6. A continued drowsiness, and disinclination to take food.

Then succeed

7. Heat.

8. Thirst.

9. An inflamed eye.

10. Restlessness, or a constant inquietude.

11. The pulse is quick and hard.

12. Convulsions now come on in children, and

13. Violent sweating in adults.

Such are the symptoms which usher in this dreadful foe to the human race, which now manifests itself,

14. By many speck-like spots, resembling flea-bites, which appear first on the face, and upper parts of the body, and afterwards invade the whole trunk, look angry, create pain, and gradually elevate themselves above the skin, taking on the appearance of pimples.

15. By the fifth or sixth day, these are converted into pustules, containing a transparent fluid, and each has an accompanying inflammation around.

At this period of the disease,

16. The throat becomes inflamed and is painful.

17. The breath is hot and foetid.

18. Swallowing is difficult.

19. The voice hoarse.

20. In adults there comes on a salivation, and

21. In infants a diarrhoea.

On the seventh day,

22. The eye-lids swell, and are glued together, and the patient has both the sensation and apprehension of the loss of sight.

On the eighth day,

23. The aqueous fluid of the pustules is changed into thick pus.

24. And the effluvia now issuing from the patient is highly noisome and infectious.

25. Or, instead of a yellow pus, or matter, only ichor is produced, which erodes deep, and ends in mortification of the parts.

26. Often, purple spots appear in the spaces surrounding the eruption, which forebodes the approaching catastrophe.

27. Often, profuse haemorrhages of thin corrupt blood pass off by the several outlets of the body.

28. The human face divine, bereft of every feature, then exhibits the most distressing sight, being one mass of corruption; and, at this time, should sleep kindly come in to appease his miseries, it is disturbed and short, and he frequently wakes with a start, as if roused by some dreadful apprehension; but more generally the sleepless nights are passed in tearing off this mask of humours, which from a dark brown changes to a black, and each morning presents a horrid scene of gore mingled with corruption.

To behold the poor tortured victim muffled, resisting, and finally overcoming every artifice to prevent him tearing his flesh to pieces, is the most melancholy sight which the fond mother can witness. Bystanders no longer recognize the temper or features of the lovely infant. Happy if he escapes without actual loss of vision, and the dimples of the cherub cheek not furrowed into deep seams and unsightly pits. Parents at such a moment would willingly compromise every external grace for the possession of life. But fate yet hangs suspended on a thread. The swelling of the face abates.

29. The limbs in their turn become tumified.

30. The fever, which has remitted somewhat of its first violence, recurs, from the matter absorbed, and the poor tortured victim undergoing a second conflict more dreadful than the first, with weakened powers of resistance.

31. Most commonly from between the 14th to the 17th day (one out of three or four usually dying of the natural small-pox) finds a release from his miseries by the Arrow of Death, now esteemed as a kind Deliverer, instead of the Horror of the Human Conception.

32. Or if Nature should come off victorious, how scarred! how each bone protrudes through the skin! how the limbs totter! how fretful the temper! how emaciated the countenance! how sunk the eye! how livid the flesh!

Perhaps even then the Destroyer has still accomplished his work, and the patient, too early congratulated, sinks under

1. A lingering consumption,
2. Or he is eaten away by slow corroding ulcers, commonly called the king's evil, or scrophula.

When the World Health Organization announced the disappearance of smallpox in 1980, it signalled an 'unprecedented event in human history; the deliberate worldwide eradication of an important human disease'. It also celebrated the realization of Jenner's dream.

He was a country doctor familiar with the local old wives' tales, especially the belief that an unsightly but harmless disease of the cow's udder and teats called cowpox, when it infected the finger of the milkmaid, gave her lasting protection against the dreaded smallpox. But cowpox was uncommon, even amongst the prosperous herds of the Vale of Berkeley, and there was a further problem: more than one recognized variety of cowpox exists, but only one assures safety. Jenner's ability to distinguish 'true' from 'spurious' cowpox is one of those miracles of precise and detailed observation that characterized his real genius. Because of these difficulties with cowpox, Jenner realized that it was not enough to wait for people to catch it accidentally, nor was the disease sufficiently widespread to make it possible for everyone to be infected by fluid taken directly from the blisters on a cow. Indeed, cowpox has probably occurred only amongst herds in Britain and Western Europe; it was unknown in Eastern Europe, Asia, Africa and the Americas. The answer, Jenner realized, was to transfer the infected contents of a cowpox blister or vesicle from one human being to another.

He was forty-seven years old when he performed the first successful person-to-person vaccination. Therein lies the crucial fact of Jenner's life: prior to that experiment and its immediate aftermath, he was a successful country doctor with landed interests which assured his status as a member of the ruling English gentry. After 1796, or more precisely, 1798 when he announced the discovery, Jenner was catapulted on to the world stage, a stage no less real than it is today, despite the existence of only one news medium, the written word, travelling only as fast as the fastest horse could gallop. For the remaining twenty-six years of his life, until his death in 1823, Jenner devoted himself to elucidating the techniques essential to successful vaccination and to promoting its acceptance as the best hope for the eradication of smallpox. Though he never travelled beyond British shores nor north of a line roughly drawn between Cheltenham and London, Jenner became the recognized saviour of the French, Spanish, Germans, Italians and Russians, the Hindus, Muslims, Buddhists and Chinese, the new Americans as well as the old, of the citizen and the subject, of presidents and kings – everywhere, that is, but within his native land. When in the early years of the nineteenth century Vienna enjoyed almost total freedom from smallpox thanks to an intelligently conceived vaccination programme, London still suffered as many as seventeen hundred deaths a year from that disease alone.

Such a life is bound to reveal interesting continuities and stresses. He had to adjust a private past to the public present. His wife and children and all the other members of a large, closely knit clan had to be placed in a new perspective focused through Jenner's acceptance that a myriad strangers needed him too. This conflict between his duty to his family and his duty to vaccination, as he saw them, dominated his life during the crucial decade and a half following his discovery. His naïveté produced foolish mistakes in tactics which diminished his influence and actually impaired his

effectiveness as a propagandist, especially after the mistakes became allied
with an uncharacteristically stubborn refusal to accept that vaccination did
not give most people permanent protection. Yet throughout his life, he never
flinched from the responsibility of what he believed he had accomplished.
Whether as son and brother, husband and father, landlord, magistrate or
undoubted scientific genius, Edward Jenner practised the real if modest
virtues of courage, hard-headedness, honesty and compassion.

In the beautiful Vale of Berkeley and the nearby southern Cotswolds
Jenners were as thick on the ground as the dormice whose nests formed
the first collection made by eight-year-old Edward. There was a Samuel
Jenner, Bookseller, of Stroud, and a Josiah Jenner Jordan, Merchant, of
Gloucester, with both of whom Edward probably dealt. Jenners also lived in
Worcestershire, Wiltshire and Oxfordshire and in East Anglia – though any
connection between these widely separated families must have been remote
– but the Gloucestershire Jenners were probably the most numerous.

Edward Jenner believed there was a connection with 'Kenelem Jenour
of Much Dunmore in the Country of Essex, Esq. . . Created a Baronet
by Charles the First on July 30, 1628.' He based his belief in part on
the arms of Jenour: 'Azure, a cross valie between three fleur de lis, or. . .
The trifling difference from the arms now in use in Gloucestershire denotes
another branch of the same family.' His friend, the Reverend Thomas Dudley
Fosbroke who wrote histories of Berkeley and Cheltenham, differed, spelling
the ancestral surname Genor and incidentally describing quite a different coat
of arms. In the same section of a sort of commonplace book kept sporadically
during his later years Jenner dwelt on the family past, recalling the motto of
his grandmother Davies's family, *Vive ut Vivas* or, roughly, 'Live life to the
full'. Genealogy was not one of his hobbies, however; he left it to Fosbroke
to sketch the family tree.

Edward's branch of the Jenners originated around a village called Standish, in rich farm land about eight miles by road from Berkeley. Its isolated
church claims to have housed for one night the twisted corpse of Edward II,
murdered at Berkeley Castle the day before, on its way to burial in Gloucester
Cathedral. That was in 1327. Today in the cool shade of its churchyard lie
the gravestones of nineteenth-century Jenners. The first Jenner listed by
Fosbroke, Stephen, died about 1667. He was a baker, as was his eldest
son, also Stephen, who moved a few miles to Slimbridge and died there
about 1727. *His* eldest son, Edward's grandfather, also a baker at Slimbridge,
married Mary Davies. This Stephen died young, only a year after his father,
but Mary outlived him by thirty years and must have known her youngest
surviving Jenner grandson quite well. She had other grandchildren named
Phillimore by a daughter.

These bakers appear to have prospered. They were able to buy both the lease- and freeholds of parcels of land in and around Slimbridge and Berkeley, added to which their wives brought property as parts of their dowries. Land was of course the only true wealth in eighteenth-century England. Many of the parcels described in elegant but barely readable courthand legalisms on the stiff parchment indentures are very small indeed, scarcely larger than a city garden. But there was no better assurance of their owners' respectability.

After about 1600 and until the end of the war with France in 1815, these tiny parcels and customary rights were under attack by enclosures and other acts of rationalization which aimed to enlarge the fields under cultivation. At first enclosures reflected primarily the tendency towards scientific agriculture which began in England, though by the end of the period soaring cereal prices inflated by wartime demand energized the movement. Between 1801 and 1803, Edward Jenner's nephew, the younger William Davies, noted in his diary several meetings with Commissioners appointed by Parliament to oversee enclosures on behalf of the landlords seeking them. On 18 June 1803, he: 'Rode to Slimbridge Met there Mr. John Clarke, who valued the Lands given up under the Enclosure Act to Lord Berkeley from my Father, and from my Father to Lord Berkeley. – ' When Edward Jenner's immediate forebears were acquiring property, however, not only were the plots of land intermixed in a crazy quilt of ownership and use, but only those with intimate local knowledge could hope to unravel local quarrels.

It was not only that land provided food and therefore rents, but also that the entire social structure rested on the individual's relationship to land. If he had some, he counted; if he had none, he did not, although it must be admitted that by 1749, when Edward entered the world, Englishmen who had amassed fortunes in banking and commerce could claw their way to aristocratic rank by appointment or marriage. Baking, socially necessary though it was, however, did not guarantee respectability.

Stephen Jenner, Edward's father, was born in Slimbridge in 1702. Unlike his forebears, he went up to Pembroke College, Oxford, to be educated as a clergyman. A cousin, Reverend Thomas Jenner, whose family still lived at Standish, was then also at Pembroke, although he later became the President of Magdalen and a Doctor of Divinity. Stephen probably left Oxford in 1724. During that summer, his father wrote enclosing £14 to 'discharge every thing and Leave nothing unrepaid. . . is [as?] to horsis to Carry you and your Cases send what you can by Child', presumably a servant. A month earlier, Stephen's brother-in-law, John Phillimore, assured him that he and his wife, Stephen's sister, Mary, 'shall be Glad to see yoo In ye Contry'. Stephen left Oxford with an MA degree and the ecclesiastical title of Clerk.

Meanwhile, the student had apparently fallen in love. There is another letter from his sister Deborah who was then living in Bristol. On 28 November 1720, she wrote: 'the beauty you admire at Bristol, desires her service to you, with due thanks for, as she says undeserved praise, but I agree with your opinion, I assure you time have not [deranged?] her charming features, I am very glad my dear you have so commodious a living.' This is a little confusing because as an undergraduate, aged eighteen, Stephen would not have been expected to have a job, let alone a living. Perhaps he had already become tutor in the family of the Earl of Berkeley, a position he certainly held later in the decade, and one often available to an intelligent Oxford student. In any case the girl in question was almost certainly Sarah Head, daughter of the Reverend Henry Head, Prebend of Bristol Cathedral and vicar of Berkeley. The Reverend Henry could well have arranged the tutorial position with the Earl if he approved his candidate son-in-law. Prudence, the watchword of the eighteenth-century gentry, demanded a long engagement before a mere student and tutor could hope to marry, however.

In 1825, Stephen was appointed by the Bishop of Gloucester as curate of the parish church of Coates, a village in the Cotswolds between Stroud and Cirencester. This lowest rung on the Church ladder of preferment still did not offer adequate security to Stephen and Sarah, though a curacy certainly satisfied the needs of many other clergymen, young and not so young, then and later. But Sarah's father, the Reverend Head, died in 1728, the same year as Stephen's father. On 22 August 1729, Thomas Jenner wrote:

Dear Cousin, I am oblig'd to You for ye last good news, In wch (let me assure You) I take a very particular pleasure. I both give you joy; and am also persuaded, it is not ye less for ye difficulties, you have met with. The greater hazards one has pass'd thro', ye Relish of Victory is ye sweeter; Especially too, when a man's own heart approves ye Uprightness of ye measures taken in order to seek Victory.

We do not know all of these hazards, but at least one must have been the appointment by the Earl of Berkeley, whose gift the living was, of a man named Ralph Webb to succeed Henry Head as vicar of Berkeley. Again, events are murky, but Webb stayed less than a year, whereupon Stephen Jenner was presented to be the new vicar.

On 8 August 1729, Stephen's mother addressed a letter to him at 'ye Reverd Mr heads to ye left at Cranfordbridge in the County of Middlesex'. This gentleman was Sarah's brother and rector of Cranford, also a living in the gift of the Earl of Berkeley. Stephen was no doubt settling with them both the terms and, perhaps above all, the date of their forthcoming marriage. Six days later he was inducted into the church at Berkeley, but it was to be more than two months before he actually came to live there. On 1 September, Stephen thanked cousin Thomas for his 'kind expressions of Joy upon ye score of Berkeley', but complained sharply that the clerical substitute Thomas had promised to supply to conduct the services at Berkeley during Stephen's absence had been slow to arrive.

The marriage settlement between Stephen Jenner and Sarah Head consists of three full-sized parchments, each about two feet by three, and has four parties: Stephen's mother, Mary Jenner, and himself; Henry Head, Sarah's brother, and Edward Smith, clerk of Berkeley church; William Davis of Slimbridge and Edward Saniger of a nearby farm by that name, both Jenner relatives; and Sarah herself. Davis and Saniger are there as trustees for the terms of the settlement, which is designed to assure that Sarah and her children will have the benefit of Stephen's property should he predecease her. Mary Jenner, as widow of Stephen senior, still receives rents from and controls some of the property. The document specifies certain pieces of land belonging to Stephen junior that are excluded from the 'joint property' agreement but could not be alienated without everyone's approval. Stephen also received £700 in cash, of which £300 was immediately returned to Henry Head and Edward Smith to be invested in land or securities for the benefit of Stephen and/or Sarah, their heirs and assigns. This tortuous and complex document is remarkably modern in its intention to protect the rights and physical well-being of the future Mrs Jenner. Its humanity is manifest in a final clause requiring that any later legal acts under the settlement be so arranged that the parties and their heirs 'be not obliged to travail or go for the doing thereof from the place or places of his or their most usual abode or habitation'. The settlement is dated 9 September 1729. The couple were married at St Catherine's Hospital, London, by Sarah's brother who was the Master.

I know of neither portraits of Stephen Jenner nor descriptions of his physical appearance, but in his letter of congratulations the Reverend Thomas Jenner offers us hints about Stephen's character. He appears to have coveted the Berkeley vicarage for some time. His determination may reflect in part the unusual polity of the town itself.

Berkeley had a stable population of about two thousand in some five hundred houses throughout the eighteenth century, although it lost inhabitants during the first quarter of the nineteenth, perhaps as a result of enclosures. 'It is seated on a hill and hill side,' wrote one 'ancient authority', 'though not of the greatest, and from hence it beholds *Cotteswold* Hills, the Forest of *Dene*, the River *Severne*, and the City of *Gloucester*.' Today the Severn view is interrupted by the concrete bulk of the recently decommissioned atomic power station on the river shore half a mile from the town. Berkeley Castle, a small, walled medieval structure, hunches near the hilltop to the south-west of the town, but the church stands at the highest point, separated by fifty yards from its lonely tower. The church was probably built as a parish church by the first Lord Berkeley between a 'Prebendal Church' and the castle. The former has disappeared, its site marked only by the tower which was itself erected, or at least restored as recently as 1756, after Stephen Jenner's death. But what gave Berkeley its special character amongst the small towns in the neighbourhood such as Stroud and Cirencester was its government: Berkeley had been created a borough under the later Roman emperors, and had its own mayor and council. Though he lived cheek-by-jowl with the town, the principal landlord, the Earl of Berkeley, gained no special authority by his eminent position, in theory at least.

Stephen Jenner's interest in the Berkeley living no doubt also emerged from the fact that the parish of Berkeley included four valuable tithings: Ham, Hinton and Alkington which surrounded the borough itself. In other words, the incumbent could anticipate a very reasonable income. Stephen's tithe accounts include also his income from his own estates. In 1733 he owned a house and orchard at Cambridge which he had bought from Josiah Smith, Butcher. It was let to one Richard Williams at £8 a year, but in 1737 Stephen sold the property to Williams for £120. He paid £180 to one John Summers, 'now Schoolmaster of ye Free School at Cam', for a ninety-nine-year lease of a property called Dayhouse Mead, which he rented to the Widow Cox at £18 a year. In 1744, Stephen paid land taxes on parcels at Halmer, part of Hinton, a place called Falfield, another called The Hill which he described as eight acres near Hamfield, plus 'a little meadow of 2 acres near it also'. Two years later, he noted in his tithe accounts: 'exchang'd Ladyday, 1746, with ye Earl of Berkeley, a Quarter part of Oldmore & Ground call'd mead. . .' for 'an other Ground at Hinton adjoyning to my Barrows. . .call'd High Cross' which had belonged to the Earl. Whether it tardily describes this exchange or another one, there is in the Gloucester County Record Office an indenture between Stephen and the Earl of Berkeley dated 2 May 1753, giving details of Stephen's land which lay in Berkeley adjacent to the Earl's and the latter's in Hinton adjacent to some already held by Stephen. In addition to these estates, by 1751 Stephen also paid land taxes on the rectory at Rockhampton, the Shoulder-of-Mutton Ground at Ham, for which he was paid £7 a year rent, and Suglands in Hinton, rent: £56-15 per year. Part of the Hinton lands belonged to Sarah's mother, Mary Head, who died in 1739, and to her son, Henry. Stephen Jenner paid the taxes on these properties, collected the rents and acted as agent for his in-laws, for no fee. It was part of his family responsibility, just as years later Edward's nephew, the Reverend William Davies, was to serve his uncle as unofficial business manager over a period of thirty years.

Stephen's duties also included the poor of Berkeley. Each year at Christmas from 1744 to 1746, he gave fifty-one souls (including one James Phipps who was probably the grandfather of Edward's first experimental vaccinee) forty-five pig cheeks, six beef dinners and a penny each. Christian charity did not reflect soft-headedness, however. Although the churchyard had been let to one Daniel Latch who received all the grass in exchange for cutting it and paying rent of £1-6 a year, Stephen noted that on 3 August 1753 he 'Recd all rent for ye Church Yard to Ladyday 1753 From wch time ye Parish have agreed to allow me 27 Shillings a year & I am to cut ye Weeds.'

His prosperity can be demonstrated by the purchase in November 1744 of the right to the living of Rockhampton, a parish about four miles south of Berkeley, for 'ab 396–0–0', a huge sum of money. The incumbent rector, Thomas Willis, died four years later and Stephen took his place. It was not unusual in the eighteenth century for a Church of England clergyman to hold more than one living. In the event Rockhampton proved of great benefit to his family.

His worldly achievements to the contrary notwithstanding, Stephen Jenner felt himself able to say to his parishioners: 'we must not judge of our own selves by the success we gain in this world. But the God of all Wisdom and knowledge cannot be deceived.' As a clergyman, he was probably no worse than the thousands of his contemporaries. In 1732 he became a deacon. In that same year, he first made use of a sermon that had been written by Thomas Jenner, and later employed others by his cousin for more than one service. It was a common practice. Sermons lasted an hour or more. They were frequently written down not only for their better initial delivery but so that they could be repeated or borrowed or, in a few exceptional cases, published and sold. One of Stephen's sermons, which he called 'The Dangers of Sin', he preached soon after his induction at Berkeley and eleven times thereafter at both Berkeley and Rockhampton. Whether these repetitions reflected his taste or that of his flock cannot be said with certainty.

In theory sermons were directed to the whole congregation, but in practice Church of England clergy seldom bothered to address themselves to the illiterate majority of their parishioners. This was certainly one of the major reasons why Dissenting sects enjoyed the success they had. Dissenters too were for the most part university-educated men, but because their messages tended to be much more fundamentalist, their language was often more accessible than that of the established clergy. For example, in 1747 Stephen Jenner preached about the sacraments, dealing in particular with 'the things appointed for Sacrifices':

> 1st There were Beasts, as Sheep, Oxen, Turtles etc. and these were called *Victims*. Next, the Fruits of ye Earth, as Bread, Salt, Incense; These were call'd Immolations. Then Liquors, as Blood Wine, Oyl; and these were call'd Libations. But all these were comprehended in ye Single Sacrifice of the Law of Grace (viz) the true Body and Blood of Christ. It was, we find, instituted under ye Laws yt men shd offer Sacrifices of ye Fruits of their Cattle & of their Ground. . . .

Enthusiasm became a term of abuse within the Church of England, in part as a reaction against the fanaticism of the previous century. The result was a decline in church attendance which continued unabated until about 1830. In any case, Stephen Jenner's religious attitudes were balanced by a most desirable sense of humour. About 1747, he was sufficiently shocked when an acquaintance at Oxford, Dr Obodiah Walker, turned Papist, to write in his commonplace book:

Old Obodiah Sang Ave Maria
And so will no I ah!
Why ah?
Quia
I had rather be Fool I ah
Than Knave Obodiah.

There may well have been a Free School for the Berkeley poor for many years, but in 1736 Thomas Jenner replied to his cousin's request by recommending a young man named Williams, whose mother had Gloucester connections, to be the new schoolmaster. A year later Stephen asked for more substantial assistance for the school from Magdalen College, presumably because Thomas was President. Thomas replied, politely and at length, that their own building programme was absorbing all their funds. However, there were also school land rents which supported the school and were administered by the vicar. He was responsible for the organization of the Berkeley Lecture Sermons. Two series of these took place in alternate years. One consisted of seven sermons on every Wednesday during Lent given at Berkeley, Wotton, Cromhall, Tortworth, Dursley and Thornbury, all parishes nearby. The other consisted of seven sermons delivered on the first Wednesday of each month from May through November at the same places, presumably by the local clergyman. It seems that Thomas Jenner left £14 a year toward maintenance of yet another series of lectures by one Richard Tyler of Bristol. Stephen Jenner was one of the trustees of his cousin's bequest.

In 1739 this busy and respected local figure became a freeman and burgess of the city of Gloucester. At the same time the Earl of Berkeley and his secretary, William Young, were similarly honoured. Unfortunately, I have found little detail of Stephen Jenner's private social life. The shortage of data adds lustre to five brief and otherwise ordinary diary entries during April and May 1747 in one of his commonplace books. In the first, three ladies called at Berkeley. Later in April, 'my wife & I & Molly, at Ld Fr Fust's'. Lord Francis became young Edward's godfather. Molly may have been Mary Head, Sarah Jenner's sister. On 17 May, 'Mr Lowes preach'd at Berkeley', and three days later he recorded 'a Large Company of Gentlemen & Ladies at Mrs. Hoopers', Stephen's sister, Deborah. Finally, another visitor to Berkeley, a Miss Nanny Jenner; she may have been a niece of Thomas's. Not a very rich haul, though even these few entries indicate a quiet and ordered life which evidently did not lack conviviality.

In the same year Stephen built a 'Cyder House' at the vicarage adjoining the stables, at a cost of £9-11. The old Berkeley vicarage itself was torn down many years ago. No description of it survives from this time, but on 6 February 1792 the *Glocester Journal* carried an advertisement offering the house with its gardens, pastures and fish-pond to let. The ground floor contained two parlours, a vestibule, kitchen, two pantries, cellar and brewhouse, no doubt the name now given to the Cyder House. There were five bedrooms 'with convenient closets', as well as garrets above. It seems unlikely to have been much altered, despite changes in its occupants in the intervening years.

There, Sarah gave birth to nine children. Mary was baptized on 29 December 1730, doing honour in her Christian name to both her grandmothers. Next came a boy, Stephen, baptized 19 April 1732. Eighteen months later a boy was baptized Henry who died, aged two and a half. Sarah was already pregnant again, and on 25 November 1736 this child too was baptized Henry, and survived. A second daughter was christened Sarah on 14 August 1738. Within the family she was called Sally, probably to reduce, however slightly, the confusion that must have arisen when someone called out 'Sarah' or 'Stephen' or 'Mary'. Anne was baptized on 30 March 1741. Two years later on 19 October 1743, a fourth son was named Edward. At the age of five he too died. He was buried on 22 April 1749, and poor Sarah gave birth to another son exactly two weeks later. Christened Edward on 26 May, he is the subject of this biography.

A careful count through the preceding paragraph will reveal that Edward was the eighth child of whom six were to survive into adult life. Mary, who had just passed her nineteenth birthday, no doubt had charge of the household. Even given that the loss of two children in childhood was by no means exceptional amongst their parishioners and friends, the sensations of sorrow felt by the parents at this rapid succession of burial and birth, though modified by Christian resignation, can scarcely be imagined. There were more to come.

Chapter 2

'a distemper named the Cow Pox'
1750–1772

The summer after Edward was born, his eldest brother, Stephen, went up to Oxford. Like his father, Stephen matriculated at Pembroke College as a Commoner, but in July a year later he became a Demi, a scholar, at Magdalen. At this time perhaps in celebration, the young student made a trip to the metropolis; on the inside front cover of a new notebook he wrote: 'S Jenner July 23d 1750 – Londini – 10d'. Appropriately, the book later contained his tithe account.

His father continued to keep track of Stephen's expenses. In August 1752, 'Gave him 20s to new ruffled shirts a pr riding Stockings 3s–', and the next year he paid bills for upholstery to a Mr Clarke of Covent Garden. Meanwhile, the vicar of Berkeley faced the additional expense of his second son, Henry, matriculating at University College, although he too became a Demi at Magdalen, thanks no doubt to the influence of Thomas Jenner. The next January, his father bought Henry 'a Bed bolster & pillows 1-1-6/ [?] pd Feathers at 8d 1: 16: 2 a pr of Blankets & under one 13s–6/ a Grate Cloaths & a Hat & Wig etc 8£ Teaspoons 10/6/ etc etc etc 5£10s'. Keeping two young gentlemen at Oxford was not to be done on the cheap.

Edward would have been about four when Henry joined Stephen at the university, and he may have remembered their holidays at the vicarage. But almost certainly the little boy's firmest early recollections were of the tragedies now approaching. On 17 April 1754, his father signed an agreement appointing a new churchwarden at Rockhampton in a hand that was not only palsied but actually non-cursive. In October his mother gave birth to a sixth son, Thomas, who was christened on the 8th and buried on the 9th. The next day Sarah Jenner died, aged forty-six. Almost exactly two months later on 9 December, Stephen Jenner followed her. He was just fifty-two.

Before he was six years old, Edward was orphaned. His brothers spent most of their time living at an important place called Oxford – or perhaps Magdalen. For the present he was fortunate to be left in a household of sisters: Mary who was twenty-four, Sarah sixteen and Anne thirteen. It seems likely that, in overcoming their own grief, they spoiled him.

The family's finances must have been much altered. Stephen's tithes ceased, of course. A new vicar, Reverend George Charles Black, was presented by the Earl of Berkeley in January. Five years before, he had succeeded Henry Head as rector of Cranford. Stephen's will has not been discovered, but an account book kept mainly by his eldest son indicates that his property was divided amongst his surviving children more or less even-handedly. At the end of 1757, Mary Jenner and the Reverend Black were married. In their marriage settlement, Stephen and Henry paid £850 to their new brother-in-law. By 1760 Stephen was signing the churchwardens' accounts as the rector of Rockhampton. His father's immediate successor at Rockhampton, a Reverend Edwin Smith, resigned in 1757.

Young Edward was sent away to school. In 1757, aged eight, he was enrolled in the Wotton-under-Edge Grammar School, a Free School for local boys whose families could do without their labour but not pay their fees. Wotton is a long, narrow market town picturesquely stretched along the valley of the Little Avon River. Its grammar school had been endowed in 1384 by Lady Katherine Berkeley, an ancestor of the Earl, and the family continued to exercise its influence over the school. Not being local, Edward boarded with the headmaster, the Reverend Mr Thomas Clissold.

Perhaps because there was an outbreak of smallpox in the town, or amongst Edward's schoolfellows, it was decided that he was to be inoculated with the disease by a local surgeon, Mr Holbrow. In any case Jenner was one of several to undergo the treatment. It began with a preparatory period lasting six weeks during which, according to his friend Fosbroke,

> He was bled, to ascertain whether his blood was fine; was purged repeatedly, till he became emaciated and feeble; was kept on very low diet, small in quantity, and dosed with a diet-drink to sweeten the blood. After this. . .he was removed to one of the then inocula-
> , tion stables, and haltered up with others in a terrible state of disease, although none died. By good fortune the Doctor escaped with a mild exhibition of the disease.

But the effect of 'this barbarism of human-veterinary practice' 'was this – as a child, he could never sleep, and was constantly haunted by imaginary noises; and a sensitivity too acutely alive to these and sudden jars has ever since subsisted.' Although Fosbroke's disapproval was no doubt honest enough because, as a confirmed vaccinist, he understood the dangers of smallpox inoculation, the practice was still common in many parts of England in 1821 when he wrote.

To the modern patient, variolation stands as one of the most astonishing medical interventions ever invented. The word is a nineteenth-century crea-tion derived from *variola*, the Latin name for smallpox, to match vaccination, derived from *vaccina*, the Latin name for cowpox. It simply meant injection of some of the pus from a smallpox vesicle into the body of a healthy person. The idea was that because catching smallpox was almost inevitable, and because it was believed that if you survived you were permanently secure against it, better to give the disease intentionally when the individual was healthy, usually during childhood. The great Arab physician, Avicenna, has been credited with discovery of the technique, but there is no hard evidence. Variolation was also practised in China and India, albeit by sniffing dust from the scabs on drying smallpox lesions rather than by inoculation. Most writers agree that it was imported to Constantinople late in the seventeenth century by Circassian traders carrying goods from Persia and China. The first report to reach England appears to have come from an East India Company trader in Amoy named Joseph Lister in a letter dated 5 January 1700, to Dr Martin Lister, a fellow of the Royal Society. It described the powdered-scab technique. In 1714 Dr Emanuel Timoni of Constantinople published a treatise in English on smallpox inoculation which appeared in London the next year. Neither of these events produced any recorded effects.

Variolation came to England thanks to the endeavours of a remarkable woman, Lady Mary Wortley Montagu. She had been a great beauty when she married Wortley, a baronet of no particular distinction, but smallpox had done for her what it did to millions of others: left her alive but disfigured. Then Wortley was appointed English Ambassador to the Turkish Porte in Constantinople. In 1717 Timoni along with the Embassy surgeon, Charles Maitland, attended Lady Mary at the birth of her second child, a daughter. From Timoni she learned about variolation, and when her husband was absent 'at the Grand Vizier's camp near Sophia', on her own initiative and with considerable courage she had her first child, a boy, 'engrafted'. The infant girl could not be inoculated because her nurse had not had the smallpox. The variolated disease was just as infectious as the natural smallpox, and the poor nurse had two further disabilities: she was an adult and variolation was reserved for the young, and she was a servant.

Lady Mary wrote to her friend Sarah Chiswell about what she had done, describing the procedure in some detail. But it was not until she herself returned to England that variolation began in earnest there. Charles Maitland left the Embassy in Constantinople and took up practice in Hertford. Early in 1721, Lady Mary called him in to inoculate her daughter. During her recovery, three doctors from the Royal College of Physicians were allowed to visit her. For the first time, information about smallpox inoculation appeared in the newspapers.

In England success for a new medical technique could be almost immediately secured if royalty supported it. Seventy-five years later the Jennerians profitably used the same method to promote vaccination. The news of Lady Mary Wortley Montagu's daughter reached Princess Caroline of Wales, who, in the meantime, had cautiously determined to test variolation before allowing it to be used on her own children. Six prisoners at Newgate were induced to volunteer in return for their freedom. All were variolated, and all recovered. The Princess was still not quite satisfied, perhaps because the prisoners were adults, but that spring of 1722 an orphan child of St James's parish went through the inoculated smallpox safely. On 22 April, two of the royal daughters were engrafted, and survived.

Despite royal approval and the support, albeit reluctantly, of Sir Hans Sloane, President of the Royal College of Physicians and later of the Royal Society, variolation did not prosper. In 1726 Lady Mary's correspondent, Sarah Chiswell, died of smallpox. A mere handful of the wealthier citizens availed themselves of the technique. Statistics are notoriously unreliable even after Edward Jenner's lifetime, not only because the mathematics of their use remained uncertain but, more fundamentally, because the sources from which they were collected were so inadequate. The poverty of basic counting techniques will become clearer when we use the London Bills of Mortality to try to find out what was happening to smallpox in the metropolis in the new century after the introduction of vaccination.

During the first years of variolation, according to one account, 638 people were inoculated between 1721 and 1728, the actual number varying from time to time with the incidence of smallpox. Of these people twelve died. John Baron, Jenner's first biographer, said that up to 1735, 845 went through the technique, of whom seventeen died. Based on these figures, the death rate was roughly 1 in 50, a figure which agrees with one of the estimates made by the Royal Society at the time. Natural smallpox was believed to kill from 1 in 5 to 1 in 8. In fact, in severe outbreaks the death rate could be as high as 40 per cent. Variolation undeniably saved lives, but in addition to the fact that it was not without risk, the procedure was expensive. As it was practised on Edward Jenner, it took two to four weeks to prepare the patient, ten to fourteen days while the disease took its course, and another month to convalesce. During much of this time, he was in no condition to work. Later, when attempts were made to give the poor free variolation, they could seldom afford the time. The London Smallpox and Inoculation Hospital opened in 1746 to provide a refuge while the patient went through the disease, but most people lacked even this amenity and went home to infect family and friends.

After the first experiments, therefore, variolation fell into neglect. Meanwhile, it had been practised amongst West African tribesmen who became the victims of the American slave trade. In 1706, Cotton Mather, a Puritan clergyman at Boston, discovered that Onesimus, one of his slaves (probably from the Gurumanche tribe of what is now Burkina Faso), had been inoculated, along with several others, by the tribal doctor. Mather introduced the practice in Massachusetts, whence it spread to the other colonies. From Charleston, South Carolina, it was reintroduced to England, but with an important difference. Instead of taking the pus from a smallpox victim, the serum from an inoculation vesicle itself was used to inoculate the next person. In other words, the Americans had begun to practise what might be called arm-to-arm variolation. Using this procedure, furthermore, the risk seemed to decline.

In 1754 the Royal College of Physicians announced its formal support for variolation. Though the practice, involving as it did an incision, was principally the preserve of surgeons, approval by the more prestigious physicians lent it great weight. Within the next few years it changed radically, however, from the aggressive and time-consuming intervention by bleeding and diet that young Jenner had experienced to a much more benign procedure. These changes are credited to a surgeon-apothecary named Robert Sutton who practised in Debenham, Suffolk. He began by making a much smaller, shallower incision than had previously been used, and by taking the smallpox matter from the pustules of people who had only mild doses of the disease. He reasoned that the less he interfered the better for the patient, but, without knowing it, he reduced the risk of infecting the wound, a not infrequent cause of complications that could be fatal.

Sutton was assisted by his two sons, Robert and Daniel, until about 1760, when Robert established himself as an inoculator at Bury St Edmunds and Daniel underwent a brief apprenticeship in surgery at Oxford. Daniel returned to his father's practice at Debenham and introduced further modifications of variolation. Both men almost certainly were aware that Robert's practical non-interference originated in the contributions of one of England's greatest doctors, Thomas Sydenham. A century before, Sydenham had asked, 'How is it that so few of the common people die of this disease compared with the numbers that perish by it among the rich?' In addition to the fact that 'many of the poor simply die unnoticed,' Sydenham argued that only the rich could afford the prevailing treatments involving warmth, heavy blankets, the exclusion of light and air and a diet rich in bread and hot drinks. He believed in the miasmatic theory, which attributed smallpox, among other diseases, to harmful gases or effluvia exhaled by cesspits or unaired sick-rooms, but Sydenham's great contribution was his insistence on the observation of clinical details in order to understand the illness. The best treatment for smallpox was none at all. The patient should be kept cool by opening windows and using only those blankets the weather required. By these means, he may have added to the patient's comfort and possibly reduced the incidence of secondary infections even if, as he seems to have recognized, he could do nothing to alter the course of the disease itself.

The Suttons found it easy to add Sydenham's cool therapy to their other modifications. They obliged their patients to remain outdoors exposed to the air, recommended exercise and shortened the preparatory period – changes which were very popular with the patients themselves. During the eruptive period, cooling medicines were used. The Suttons also had the wit to anticipate one of the most serious criticisms of variolation, especially after the introduction of vaccination: that if they were not rigidly quarantined, an expensive and almost unenforcible precaution before people understood the causes of contagion, patients with inoculated smallpox could spread the disease. The Suttons recommended the variolation of whole communities whenever possible.

In 1763 Daniel Sutton opened his own inoculation house at Ingatestone in Essex because the village was the first stage stop on the Essex Great Road to Harwich, perhaps the most important embarkation point for the continent then because of the Hanoverian connection. It was also convenient for London but outside the jurisdiction of the new College of Surgeons, of which Daniel was not a member. He was enormously successful, inoculating almost fourteen-thousand people in the first two years. In-patients were charged between £3-15 and £7-35, though the fee to a rich patient might be as high as £20; but the poor were treated free – when there was room for them, one suspects. Medically, the practice was equally successful: a contemporary authority, Sir George Baker, physician to the King, claimed that the death rate was 1 in 2800. Later it was claimed that five died out of forty thousand, the equivalent of 1 in 8000. A modern writer puts the death rate at about 12 per cent, still undeniably an improvement over the natural disease.

Daniel Sutton knew that he had a gold-mine and did his best to keep his methods secret. He himself did not publish until 1796, the very year in which Jenner made his crucial experiment, but by this time elements of the practice were widely known. Sutton's secrecy and sense of commerce, acceptable though they were in his age, provide the backdrop for Jenner's contrasting behaviour.

, The Suttons had a number of important rivals in England and on the continent. Dr Thomas Dimsdale studied surgery at St Thomas's Hospital and settled in a practice at Hertford. After taking a medical degree from Aberdeen, he began to practise variolation using the Suttonian methods. In 1768 when Daniel Sutton refused an invitation to go to St Petersburg to inoculate the Empress Catherine the Great of Russia, Dimsdale accepted. She made him a baron and paid him a fee of £10,000 plus £500 a year for his lifetime. A Dutch doctor, Jan Ingenhousz, was recommended to Maria Theresa of Austria by George III. His rewards for successfully inoculating Her Majesty are not known, but he later crossed swords with Jenner over vaccination.

The Suttonian method itself may have been the major reason for the continued expansion of variolation in the latter half of the eighteenth century. Not even the death from smallpox of George III's eighth son, Prince Octavius, following his inoculation by another successful practitioner,

William Bromfield, seems to have slowed progress. In London the Smallpox
and Inoculation Hospitals cared for the poor during the natural disease and
after variolation. Indeed, after 1743 the London Foundling Hospital made
inoculation mandatory for all the children it admitted. In Gloucester on
Jenner's doorstep, a smallpox hospital opened in 1768; it had given free
inoculations to 4829 people by the end of 1771, and variolated more than a
thousand more during the next quarter, with only one death. The *Glocester
Journal* carried advertisements for variolators throughout these years, and
reported that the Chancellor's prize for English verses for 1772 would
be awarded to the Oxford undergraduate who wrote the best poem on
the subject, 'The Beneficial Effects of Inoculation'. About 1782, twenty
Liverpool medical men formed a society to inoculate the poor in their own
homes. As late as 1793 a leading London doctor, John Haygarth, published
A Sketch of a Plan to Exterminate the Casual Small-Pox from Great Britain. It
involved systematic inoculation throughout the country, isolation of patients,
an inspectorate decentralized into districts, a system of fines and rewards, and
of course prayers every Sunday. Haygarth's use of the word 'exterminate' in
the smallpox context was to be revived by the Jennerians a decade later.

Lay people, particularly the clergy, were also asked to variolate. George and
Henry Jenner, sons of Henry Jenner, Edward's second brother, variolated
309 people in Berkeley in 1795, with no fatalities. Henry was a surgeon, and
George, a clergyman, had had some medical training. Both later assisted their
uncle. While he was qualified only as a surgeon, Edward Jenner variolated
when necessary, and in an emergency he fell back on the practice at least once
after committing himself to vaccination. Lay inoculation, free inoculation of
the poor, the risks and benefits of variolation – all foreshadow controversies
that arose again with vaccination. But already in 1757, when he was eight
years old, Edward Jenner had become aware that for all its unpleasantness
and danger, medicine possessed a means which doctors believed could
reduce the risk from smallpox, a means which did not apply to the plague,
leprosy, syphilis or the many dreadful disorders now known to be forms of
tuberculosis.

All the signs indicate that Edward had left the Reverend Mr Clissold's
household by the end of his first school year. Fosbroke wrote that Jenner
was under the care of 'an eminent physician, the late Dr. Capell' while he
was being taught at the Wotton-under-Edge Free Grammar School. The
disturbed state of his health may provide all the explanation necessary for
his early departure, but surely his headmaster, who was then aged about
forty himself, would have sympathized and tried to induce Edward to stay.
The decision to leave must have come from the boy and his family, especially
Mary and Stephen.

In 1758 when he was nine, Edward went to Cirencester to become a

boarding student under the tutelage of the Reverend Dr Washbourne, a
gentleman who 'respected proficiency in the classics', according to John
Baron. Washbourne became headmaster of the Cirencester Grammar School
in 1765, long after Jenner had left. There Edward confronted Latin and
Greek, probably for the first and almost certainly for the last time in his life.
He learned no other languages, admitting to a friend that he knew 'nothing
but my Mother Tongue'. A few years later Jenner claimed that although he
remembered little of either, he had 'obtained a tolerable proficiency in the
Latin language, and got a decent smattering of the Greek'. With religion,
they were the necessary preparations for Oxford. We are told that he spent
his free time collecting fossils from the hills around the ancient town. The
evidence of his later life convinces me that the fossils meant much more to
him than the classics.

Among Washbourne's other boarding students at Cirencester young
Edward also found friends, some of whom remained close for the rest
of their lives. Caleb Hillier Parry was the son of the local Presbyterian
minister and later a doctor in Bath. Charles Brandon Trye's father was
rector of Leckhampton near Cheltenham. The son became a successful
surgeon in Gloucester. Both were younger than Jenner, but probably
his academic contemporaries. At Cirencester he also met John Clinch,
who became a clergyman and settled as a missionary to the Indians in
Newfoundland.

Not even Baron, whose sycophancy can become wearing, claims that
Edward was a scholar, certainly not a classicist – the only kind of formal
education then available to an English gentleman. Perhaps the boy was
spoiled, being the youngest, and lazy. He seemed serious enough about
fossils, the nests of dormice and other collections that he began in these
early school years, but these were looked upon by his elders as avocations,
not the stuff of serious education. I think Edward simply did not wish to
follow his brothers to Oxford. Today, we would say he lacked motivation.
He left the Reverend Mr Washbourne after between two and three years,
probably during the summer of 1751 when he was twelve.

What was to be done with the boy? Considering his interest in the
physical world, it could have been Edward himself who suggested surgery.
More probably, it was a family friend, one of the two surgeons in Berkeley,
or possibly even the Earl himself; or the idea of a medical career could have
originated with his brother Stephen, then senior dean of arts at Magdalen. No
more information has been found to explain the choice of surgeon–teacher,
but Mr John Ludlow of Chipping Sodbury accepted the thirteen-year-old
boy as an apprentice. Edward became the first member of his family to enter
medicine, and he seems to have taken to it. He remained with Ludlow for six
years.

From the standpoint of history, perhaps the most interesting part of this apprenticeship occurred towards its end. 'About the year 1768,' wrote a younger friend of Jenner's in 1817, '. . .he learnt that there was a report, rife in the dairies, of a distemper named the Cow Pox, which infested the teats of milch cows, and infected the hands of the milkers, being sometimes a preventive of the Small Pox.' This is the earliest date assigned by any of his contemporaries to Jenner's interest in cowpox, and the information no doubt came from Jenner himself.

In fact we know very little more about these six years. That he satisfied Ludlow's requirements appears to have been as certain as that Ludlow satisfied his. At the end of the apprenticeship, Edward would have been entitled to set himself up to practise surgery. No further qualification was required in the countryside, although in order to practise surgery in London or Edinburgh it was necessary to pass examinations set by the respective Companies or their successors, the Colleges of Surgeons, not then 'Royal'. In London various private medical schools existed to teach anatomy, therapeutics and surgery. These schools can be said to have included the large hospitals like Guy's and St Thomas's, which were actually private foundations. But none of them could give degrees. Physicians, that is, Doctors of Physic, might also be trained as apprentices in private schools at this time, but in England and Wales the designation 'doctor' could only be obtained by men who took a degree in 'physic' from Oxford or Cambridge, or bought the degree from a Scottish university. To practise medicine as a doctor in London, the man had to pass examinations in physic and the classical languages set by the much older Royal College of Physicians of London. Women did not enter these or any other professions – excepting, rarely, the Dissenting churches. In 1782, as a result of these restrictions, 117 doctors were resident in London and forty in all the rest of England and Wales. There were in addition 625 surgeons and apothecaries in London, and about 4400 outside. Apothecaries learnt their trade as apprentices in the same manner as surgeons, and in London became members of the Society of Apothecaries. Because all four of the important Scottish universities could teach both physic and surgery and award a degree of Doctor of Medicine to the successful student, the profession tended to be rather better trained north of the border.

That Edward Jenner's apprenticeship in surgery was extended well beyond the average is yet another aspect of his educational career which lacks clear explanations. If my estimation of the reasons for his entering surgery are correct, however, then the decision to continue his education probably arose with him. Practice as such interested him less than theory, experience less than knowledge. Fortunately, his private income permitted him to choose.

According to one of his late-nineteenth-century opponents (for vaccination continued to be controversial within the medical profession well into this century), John Ludlow's son and partner had studied in London with John Hunter, the greatest surgeon of his time and one of the handful of eighteenth-century scientists who believed that knowledge grew only out of experiment and observation. Authority was never to be trusted unless the assertion was based on the evidence of the senses. Hunter was then chief surgeon at St George's Hospital, where Edward formally enrolled as a student. During the autumn term 1770, Hunter began to take boarding pupils, and Edward was probably the first.

Jenner appears to have had no other tutor at St George's, not a major teaching hospital at the time, but he did attend medical lectures beside those of John Hunter. Probably that same year he enrolled in a private school on Great Windmill Street operated by Hunter's elder brother, Dr William Hunter. William had come to London from Glasgow in 1740 already possessed of a medical degree, opened his school (on Jermyn Street), and made so great a success of it that about the time of Edward Jenner's birth he had induced his younger brother to come down from their home village near Glasgow as his assistant. John was then twenty, possessed of only a poor elementary education and no prospects. In London he learned like any of William's students while tending the cadaver, from the demonstration anatomical models, the museum of anatomical preparations preserved in suitable media, and from the laying out of his brother's instruments before a dissection. More formally, he studied surgery at St Bartholomew's and St George's. After twelve years as William's assistant, there were quarrels and the younger brother became a military surgeon during the mid-century war with France. Returning in 1763, John set up his own surgical practice, and became a Fellow of the Royal Society two years later on the basis of his research into the temperature of animals, and a member of the Company of Surgeons. Meanwhile, William's school maintained a reputation for excellence. He was appointed Physician Extraordinary to the Queen.

The syllabus that Edward followed at Great Windmill Street consisted of two courses 'read every winter, one from the beginning of October to the middle of January, the other from the end of January to the middle of May.'

> 1. The first lectures give the history, the uses, and the best method of conducting the study of anatomy.
> 2. Then the nature and uses of the similar and constituent parts of the body are explained, to convey a general knowledge of the body, and its operations in this order: blood, arteries, veins, lymphatics or absorbents, glands, nerves, muscles, bones, and their appendages.

> After which the particular anatomy is taken up in the following order:

> 3. The bones.

4. The muscles in a fresh subject [i.e., a cadaver].
5. The male organs in the same.
6. The different fresh joints in the same.
7. The viscera and female organs in a fresh subject.
8. The organs of sense and integuments in a fresh subject.
9. The brain and nerves in a fresh subject.
10. The diseases of bones.
11. The diseases of the viscera.
12. Chirurgical diseases more particularly, and the operations of surgery explained and performed upon a fresh subject.
13. The anatomy and physiology of the gravid uterus and foetus.
14. The diseases peculiar to the sex.
15. Of pregnancy and parturition.
16. Of the disorders and management of women in childbed.

This straightforward listing was followed by an advertisement, as accurate as it was instructive:

The advantages of this school are various:

1. The long experience of the lecturer.
2. The great convenience of the several apartments, which were planned and built on purpose for anatomical studies.
3. But above all the inestimable treasure of preparations, and especially of diseases, which the museum contains, and which are introduced into the lectures, such as no teacher was ever possessed of before.

Jenner evidently felt that there was sufficient variety in William Hunter's instruction to warrant a second helping. A certificate signed by Hunter on 15 May 1772 states 'that Mr Edward Jenner, Surgeon, hath diligently attended Four Courses of my Anatomical and Chirurgical Lectures.' He was wise to have done so; like any other teacher, Hunter would have varied his presentations from year to year by using new preparations and grappling with new clinical discoveries such as the changes in variolation methods.

No doubt under John Hunter's guidance, Jenner took advantage of other lecture courses in medicine. Between 7 and 10 a.m., Monday to Saturday, for three terms from the autumn of 1770 to December 1772, he attended classes on chemistry, physics and materia medica, the minerals and plants used to make medicines in those days. The lectures were given in his house on Essex Street off the Strand by Dr George Fordyce, a Scotsman who was then physician at St Thomas's Hospital. 'The Theory and Practice of Midwifery' Jenner studied with two eminent male midwives, Thomas Denman and William Osborne. Denman, from Bakewell in Derbyshire, had learnt surgery at St George's Hospital, London, and obtained his MD from

Aberdeen in 1763. He served the Middlesex Hospital as midwife. Osborne, his junior partner, was a Londoner who had also studied at St George's. He had begun teaching with Denman in 1770, the year in which Jenner joined the course. Denman and Jenner remained friends not least because Denman became a defender of vaccination during the controversies of the first decade.

All of these lectures cost money, of course. Jenner probably paid John Hunter £100 a year, which would have included his bed and board. A fee had to be paid to register at St George's, and in theory payment would have been repeated every six or twelve months, but Jenner seems to have registered only once, in October 1770. Presumably he paid a fee to the private medical schools for each course he attended, four to William Hunter, three to George Fordyce and four to Drs Denman and Osborne.

To keep Edward in London and to pay for his medical education cost no less than a similar period at Oxford, and a great deal more than the fees paid to the Reverends Clissold and Washbourne and to Mr John Ludlow. Clearly, any decline in disposable family income following Edward's father's death almost twenty years before had been reversed. Happily, it is not necessary to guess. From 1760 until his death in 1797, his eldest brother, Stephen, kept family accounts on behalf of Henry, Sarah and Edward. Henry had been married in 1762 and was chaplain to the Earl of Ailesbury and the Dowager Countess of Elgin. In 1770 Sarah married Hopewell Hayward of Birmingham, but she was widowed four years later. Mrs Black, Mary Jenner, was widowed in 1776. The youngest daughter, Anne, married the Reverend William Davies while Edward was still at Sodbury in 1766. Apparently, Mary and Anne, or their husbands, managed their own inheritances.

Edward's income from rents was about £19-12 a year from 1770 to 1773. In 1771 he sold lands at Ham Fields just south of Berkeley for £150. His Aunt Deborah Hooper gave him £21, perhaps as a twenty-first birthday present when he went to London in 1770. The accounts list non-rental income of £7-5 from 1770 to 1773, in addition to which Stephen loaned him a total of £98-6-6. For these three years Edward's income, including loans, came to about £335. His outgoings were typically about £2-14-7 per year for rents and land taxes, roughly £1-6 annually to pay poor-rates and tithes, and rather more erratic miscellaneous expenses which included the following bills or drafts sent to London:

30 Sept., 1771	£90
4 Febr., 1772	20
10 June, 'Pd by Mr Hickes in London'	21
1 Sept., 'Pd by Mr Davies in London'	10-10
9 Oct.,	25
9 Nov.,	30

(Mr Hickes was a friend of his father's from a nearby village, Eastington, and Mr Davies was Edward's brother-in-law, husband of Anne and rector of Eastington.)

These meticulous accounts give us more than the details of how Edward Jenner paid for a far better medical education than he could have obtained at Oxford in those years. They provide an insight into the domestic management of a family of Gloucestershire gentry. This class governed England along the lines that they managed their properties. They paid their way out of the incomes God and good management gave them, paid their taxes, tithes and poor-rates, and expected the rest of the world to acknowledge their security if not their superiority. Edward Jenner received a better than average education not just in medicine but also in the duties, rights and privileges of his station.

My assertion that Jenner's London training bounced him ahead of his fellow medical students at Oxbridge or even the Scottish universities reflects my modern bias in favour of what we call scientific medicine. This works on the principle that there is no absolute truth but only an approximation which must be tested and revised by experiment and observation. It had evolved slowly in all fields of knowledge, as absolutism bolstered by the dead hand of religion fragmented under the corrosive action of free trade, sponsored by commercial capitalists interested in a return on their risky investments. What good was authority if it impeded commerce, especially when kings and popes often depended on the cash that commerce produced? But in the sciences, and especially medicine, these new attitudes had created very little of practical value before the middle of the eighteenth century. Indeed, variolation was perhaps one of the first therapies introduced without the sanction of medical authority which actually saved lives. The emergence of a new science, chemistry, significantly advanced thinking about medicine. Disease might be a consequence of chemical errors which could be put right. Under the influence of John Hunter, Jenner achieved a mind-set consistent with such a theory of medicine. Observation and experiment formed his mental machinery.

In addition to the professional knowledge and experience that he acquired while he lived in John Hunter's house, Jenner expanded both his cultural horizons and his friendships. During his first year his co-boarders were John Kingston, who had qualified as a regimental surgeon some years earlier, and William Guy of Chichester. Two later presidents of the Royal College of Surgeons were also fellow house-students: Henry Cline became the first man in London to use vaccination. Everard Home advised Jenner against formally submitting his first paper on vaccination to the Royal Society, but remained a supporter throughout the difficult years. Yet almost certainly Home burned all of Jenner's letters to Hunter along with many of the research notes on which Hunter's papers had been based – some believe because he had used them without acknowledgement to support his own work. He was Mrs Hunter's brother and Hunter's executor.

Mrs Hunter had been Anne Home, a Scottish poet said to have been admired by Burns. She and John Hunter were married in London during the summer of 1771. Her poem, 'My mother bids me bind my hair', was later set to music by none other than Haydn, who became a friend of the family during his visits to London. She maintained a salon to which artists and writers were invited, though she was especially fond of music. Young Edward had learned to play the flute and violin in Berkeley and was presumably a welcome guest when his schedule allowed.

Hunter started his first dissections at 6 a.m., working until breakfast at nine. He saw patients until noon, and during the afternoon unless there was work to be done at the hospital. Dinner was at 4 p.m. Hunter wrote or dictated to his pupils or assistants often until midnight. Jenner's day must have been largely governed by that of his tutor.

Soon after he came to Hunter's house, he told the surgeon about cowpox and its reputed role as a protective against smallpox. Before he left two years later, he had also shown Hunter a drawing of the typical vesicle caused by cowpox on the finger of a milker. Hunter mentioned Jenner's observations to others, including Dr Thomas Beddoes of Bristol who was also Hunter's student about ten years later. Beddoes acknowledged Hunter's information in a book of his own, published before Jenner's discovery was made public.

Of much greater interest at the time, probably to Jenner as well as to those responsible for his future, was the return to England in July 1771 of Captain Cook aboard his ship *Endeavour*. It had sailed almost three years before on a voyage of scientific exploration which took it around the world. The *Glocester Journal* noted not only the ship's safe reappearance in the Downs off Southampton, but also the arrival in London of its chief botanist, Joseph Banks, and his assistant, Daniel Solander of the British Museum. They had returned with thousands of specimens, most of them never before seen in Europe and, of course, entirely unclassified, in addition to hundreds of drawings by the ship's artist, Sydney Parkinson. That winter Banks urgently wanted the collection catalogued. John Hunter, who knew Banks from the Royal Society, recommended his pupil, Jenner, who had the necessary intelligence and experience in anatomical presentation. In order to classify some species, he had to use his skills as a dissector on tender and delicate plant organs. Banks seems to have been pleased. Certainly, his continuing friendship guided some of Jenner's later work and assisted his admittance to the Royal Society after Banks became the longest-serving president that august body has ever had.

John Coakley Lettsom, a Quaker physician with a successful London practice who supported Jenner faithfully until his death in 1815, originated the report that early in 1772 Banks solicited Jenner to accompany him in some capacity on Cook's forthcoming second voyage around the world in the *Resolution*. Banks was again to be the chief scientific officer, assisted by Solander, the artist Zoffany, and the physician James Lind. Jenner told Lettsom and others that he had refused 'partly guided by the deep and grateful affection. . .for his eldest brother. . .and partly by an attachment to the rural scenes and habits of his early youth.' If this is true, and there seems no reason to doubt Jenner's word, it was certainly a profoundly revealing decision. Of course, something depends on what precisely Banks offered. James Moore, Assistant Director of the National Vaccine Establishment and Jenner's constant informant after about 1811, refers to 'one of the literary associates'. Banks's correspondence at the time fails to mention Jenner, or any other literary associate, but as President of the Royal Society he was in a position to have heard about Lettsom's statement, made to the Medical Society of London thirty years later, and to have denied it if it was not true.

In the event neither Banks nor his named colleagues accompanied Cook on his second and final circumnavigation, but Edward Jenner had already refused. He was no adventurer. At that time his ambitions for conquest extended only to the esteem of his neighbours and peers. More invitations were to follow, not least one from Hunter himself; these too Jenner refused.

Perhaps it was this very placidity that pleased John Hunter. He recognized competence, skill, and intellect. Hunter more than most men did not suffer fools lightly, and died partly because of a fury aroused by one such colleague, but Jenner was no fool. A modern curator of the Hunterian Museum in the Royal College of Surgeons of England asserted that Jenner 'was probably the closest friend that Hunter ever made. . . . their relationship was one of great confidence and mutual respect.' In his turn, Jenner called Hunter the 'dear man'. He loved and admired the rough Scotsman and did his best to aid and protect him. Despite the disappearance of Jenner's contributions to it, their correspondence over the next twenty years provides most of the evidence we have about Jenner's activities. It even contains the key to the motive force that converted the quiet country surgeon into a thrusting experimenter and publicist.

Chapter 3

Romance
1773–1788

After more than two years under the direct supervision of John Hunter, Edward Jenner, aged twenty-three, returned to Berkeley with better qualifications than any other surgeon for miles around. Not only had he satisfactorily completed a six-year apprenticeship, but young Ned, as his family called him, had attended lecture courses by several of the leading teachers in London, not least the bluff and choleric surgeon in whose home he lived. The intimacy that grew up between the city and the country surgeons reflected their mutual interest not only in the art of doctoring but more especially in the acquisition of knowledge through observation and experiment, vocations which certainly did not occupy much of the time of the average eighteenth-century medical man, surgeon or physician, rural or urban.

Despite the ancient gulf between physicians and surgeons, in the country they tended to do very much the same things. Mr Jenner attended the disturbed digestions, skin eruptions and pulmonary disorders of his neighbours, perhaps their most common complaints, as well as their inflammations and fevers. He prescribed herbs and minerals from the accepted pharmacopoeia in concoctions that he had learned or, in a few cases, invented. Of course he variolated the children of those who wished it, especially when there was a smallpox outbreak in their neighbourhoods. Perhaps the skill that he practised least often was surgery itself, the use of knives being all but interdicted by the surgeon's enemies, infection and pain. By and large he charged fees for his services related to the distances his patients lived from Berkeley, which meant that the vast majority of those he attended were families of shopkeepers and professional men, the aristocracy and the gentry like himself. Jenner treated people in Gloucester, and after he established a second home there, in Cheltenham. He went as far south as Thornbury, east to Dursley and west to the river Severn. In other words, he practised throughout a region of about four hundred square miles. He travelled on horseback, regardless of weather. On one occasion early in 1786 he suffered severely from the intense cold when he had to make the ten-mile ride from Berkeley to Kingscote to visit a patient.

> The ground was deeply covered in snow, and it blew quite a hurricane, accompanied with continual snow. Being well-clothed, I did not find the cold make much impression upon me till I ascended the hills, and then I began to feel myself benumbed. . . .my face and my neck was, for a long time, wrapt in ice. There was no retreating and I had still two miles to go. . . .As the sense of external cold increased, the heat about the stomach seemed to increase. I had the same sensation as if I had drunk a considerable quantity of wine or brandy. . . .
>
> . . .My hands at last grew extremely painful, and this distressed my spirits in some degree. When I came to the house I was unable to dismount without assistance. . . .Rubbing my hands in snow took off the pain very quickly. The parts which had been most benumbed, felt for some time afterwards as if they had been slightly burnt. . . .
>
> One man perished a few miles from Kingscote, at the same time, and from the same cause.

How many people Jenner treated it is impossible to say, but the number of his patients seemed to vary in proportion to the time he had available.

The question fundamental to an understanding of Edward Jenner in these early years of his independence is how much time he had for doctoring. He was a singularly fortunate young man. His income as a landowner, if it could not supply all his needs, nevertheless assured him both security and a social position. His London education provided lasting connections in the metropolis. Inclination, training and his continuing association with Hunter, moreover, gave him an incentive to dabble in research. Because for the next two decades Jenner made no clear choice of a road along which he would stride, both his posthumous critics, their attitudes influenced perhaps by Victorian vocational single-mindedness, and his contemporary friends, thought they had a case to answer. His friend Fosbroke, for example, complained that Jenner blended 'activity of mind with indolence of person, and habits of procrastination' and 'showed rather the want of discipline and regularity in earlier days, than any inaptitude for a more sustained and severe study.' Indeed, Edward saw the mote in his own eye: 'of all the ill habits a man may fall into, indolence is the most difficult to get rid of. I for one am a sad example of the truth of this position', he wrote in 1789 to his Cirencester schoolfriend, John Clinch, now in Newfoundland. Yet, like any one of us, he looked into the mirror each morning and said, today I will pay a call on neighbour X, discuss her digestion with Lady Y or butcher hedgehogs for Mr Hunter. The weight he gave these three strands in his life, the medical, the social and the experimental, depended not on any life-plan – nothing could have been more foreign to him – but on events.

First among these events was the availability of a housekeeper to make a home for him. His brother Stephen never married. Edward's friends, Edward Gardner and Thomas Fosbroke, agreed that Stephen was an amiable man. Fosbroke called him 'virtuous', and Gardner wrote that he was quiet and modest with 'excellent sense'. Like his fellow countrymen, Stephen appreciated the good life: 'I fought my way thro' Venison & Wine yesterday without much fatigue,' he wrote to his brother-in-law, William Davies. By 1773 this paragon of the eighteenth-century priesthood had become rector of Rockhampton, a few miles south of Berkeley, and in September he was instituted to the rectorate of Fittleton, a parish about fifty miles to the east in Wiltshire where he remained as pastor for sixteen years until his death. Early the next year Stephen resigned the rectorate at Rockhampton and presented it to his brother, Henry. Meanwhile he had also become the perpetual curate of Stone, a village between Rockhampton and Berkeley. Although his flocks grazed elsewhere, Stephen continued to live in Magdalen, where Edward 'was extremely happy' for some time in 1769 or 1770.

In 1773, however, Stephen settled again in Berkeley in a house he owned there. A few years later he acquired adjacent property on a ninety-nine year lease from the Earl of Berkeley, on which stood a cottage that Stephen was to demolish to make way for a new house. Whether he then moved into the new house the records do not reveal, but for fifteen years until Ned's marriage, the eldest brother maintained an establishment in Berkeley for the two of them.

At about the time that Edward returned from London to Stephen's house, he met Edward Gardner, a somewhat younger man who made his living as a wine merchant in the lovely village of Frampton-upon-Severn, but considered himself a poet. He and Jenner shared many interests including the beauties of the Severn plain, the pastoral poetry characteristic of the period and, of course, a glass of wine. In later years Jenner confided to Gardner matters both personal and professional which there is no record he told anyone else. It was Gardner who provided John Baron with a portrait of the twenty-five-year-old Jenner:

> His height was rather under the middle size, his person was robust, but active, and well-formed. In dress he was particularly neat, and every thing about him showed the man intent and serious, and well prepared to meet the duties of his calling.
>
> When I first saw him it was on Frampton Green. . . .He was dressed in a blue coat and yellow buttons, buckskins, well-polished jockey boots, with handsome silver spurs, and he carried a smart whip with a silver handle. His hair, after the fashion of the times, was done up in a club, and he wore a broad-brimmed hat.

Clearly, the subject of this sketch was no enemy to fashion, a matter of greater interest to young gentlemen in Georgian England than even to their ladies, whose manner of dress was most rigorously confined by their female elders. Compare any of Jane Austen's heroines, perhaps especially Emma Woodhouse, to the younger men around them. Edward Jenner's manners had been polished in London, if not by the blunt and poorly educated John Hunter certainly by his wife. He enjoyed the leisure of the country, and with his musical abilities was welcome in many drawing-rooms. He participated in a catch club that met in the neighbouring village of Cam and liked to sing in company, sometimes ballads of his own composition. One of these, undeniably a Jennerian product, began

> Come all ye bold Britons who love to be jolly
> And think that Starvation's a very great folly,
> Let's sing of the thing wch so much we admire,
> A good foaming pot, Boys, of Ladbroke's Entire.
> Derrydown
> Tis bright as a ruby, & brown as a berry,
> It makes the Heart light, and the countenance merry
> From eve until morn one might quaff & not tire;
> A Feast that neer cloys us is Ladbroke's Entire.
> Derrydown.

For yet another of the accomplishments of the young Georgian gentleman might well be poetry.

Edward's gift, such as it was, may have been encouraged by Anne Hunter. Two of her poems survived amongst his papers. There is also his copy of a six-line poem, 'On a late defeat at Gloucester', which he ascribed to Andrew Marvell. The prevailing pastoral forms undoubtedly pleased him most in these early years. 'Address to a Robin' stands out:

> Come, sweetest of the feather'd throng,
> And sooth me with thy plaintive song;
> Come to my cot, devoid of fear,
> No danger shall await thee here;
> No prowling cat with whisker'd face
> Approaches this sequester'd place;
> No school-boy, with his will[ow] bow,
> Shall aim at thee a murd'rous blow;
> No wily lime-twig e'er molest
> Thy olive wing or crimson breast;
> Thy cup, sweet bird, I'll daily fill
> At yonder cressy bubbling rill;
> Thy board shall plenteously be spread
> With crumlets of the nicest bread.

And when rude Winter comes & shews
His isicles & shivering snows,
Hop o'er my cheering hearth & be
One of my peaceful family.
Then sooth me with thy plaintive song,
Thou sweetest of the feather'd throng.

'To a Lady – with a Woodlark' begins inconsequentially with a familiar phrase:

So, sweetest of the feather'd throng.
To her who sings so well;
Improve by Chloe's matchless Song
All others to excel.

Amongst these early songs, 'By a Negro after being severely beaten for Stealing a bit of bread' is atypical:

If, when me nothing had to eat,
For stealing bit of bread,
Black Man you so severely beat,
And whip till almost dead;
What Punishment's to Massa's due?
From Guilt can he be free?
Who, when he bought poor Negro, knew
That white man steal a me.

The poem is also unique in that it is Jenner's single known comment on the white-hot contemporary issues of black slavery, still not uncommon in Britain up until the end of the eighteenth century, and the African slave trade then dominated by British captains.

Judging by their relative frequency, he preferred epitaphs and epigrams. They can be punchy, clever, and above all are brief. Among the early examples is 'To a Fellow Sportsman who upbraided the Author with being a bad shot.'

Why thus abuse me, mighty Sirs,
And jeer me with your taunting Slurs?
You're only joking – sure.
Each breast with Horror wd. be fill'd,
Heavens! to think that I Had kill'd
Whose Province 'tis to cure

A few years later he responded to another issue of the day with an eight-line 'Epigram':

Since the French are such Atheists, how comes it to pass

That of late they are all grown so fond of a <u>Mass</u>?
By a Mass in <u>Vendee</u> they lay waste ev'ry Acre,
Converting their Mass for a dreadful <u>Mass</u>-Acre,
'By the Mass,' they shall not British Valor allay!
Our Troops shall instruct them for Mercy to pray.
They shall find, if their Rashness approaches our Coast,
Oppos'd to their Mass, ev'ry Briton a <u>Host</u>!

'To Mrs J on her dismal dream the night before she went to Bath – '
reflects his more usual vein of warmth and affection:

When Fancy at midnight's disposed for a ramble
She often will steal to our pillows to gambol.
Then laugh my dear Kate at her <u>Tale of the Hearse</u>
What she whispers in dreams happens just the reverse.
And <u>sure as you're there</u> she has chosen this path
<u>To heighten the pleasures you'll meet with at Bath</u>.

Whether or not his fancy helped to dispel what must have been a frightening
dream, especially for a woman then in the early stages of tuberculosis, this
poem suggests how much Jenner enjoyed using poesy, doggerel or just wit.
Although he found less time for frivolity as the years passed, the epigrams
never dried up entirely. During the early years of the new century, Dr John
Coakley Lettsom, Jenner's great defender in the vaccine cause, proposed a
subscription to erect a monument to John Howard, the prison reformer who
had died in 1790. In his diary Jenner wrote:

Why Lettsom bid the sculptur'd Pillar rise
To him whose name's familiar in the Skies,
And on the Earth will never be forgotten,
Until old TIME himself be dead and rotten?

Later his humour became more waspish, but the pleasure he took in these
short rhymed couplets suggests to me that his mind enjoyed creation at least
as much as observation. There were twelve lines in 'Epitaph on an Ass', an
early effort beginning:

Beneath this huge hillock here lies a poor creature,
So easy, so gentle, so harmless his nature,
On earth by kind heaven he surely was sent,
To teach erring mortals the road to content. . . .

Edward was a countryman blessed with health and humour, which he
liked to spread around. Excursions through the countryside, like singing,
eating and drinking, enlivened his days and evenings. He thought nothing of
riding twenty or thirty miles with friends of a morning. One of his favourite
spots was Barrow Hill, a rise of about a hundred feet from the flat Severn

plain, near the end of a tongue of land with the village of Frampton at its base that causes a slow westerly curve in the river. 'Of the delightful scenes, which the varied prospects of this country afford,' said the *Glocester Journal* on 21 July 1788, 'none are deemed equal to Barrow Hill, in the parish of Arlingham. The windings of the Severn, the diversified objects of hill and dale, all combine to render the view from this spot complete.' Jenner agreed.

Baron, the respectful first biographer, claimed that Jenner 'had a particular dislike for cards, both because they interfered with a much more instructive employment of time, and often led to evils of a much more serious nature.' Yet there can be no doubt that games of chance were being played in his brother's house. His brother-in-law, the Reverend William Davies, lists his winnings and losings between 1781 and 1786 in his household accounts, amounts such as 7s, 2s 6d, and 2s 11d in different years, but including 3s 6d paid to Edward Jenner on 14 August 1786. Jenner was brought up to good company and pleasure. Had he been accused of dilettantism in the eighteenth-century sense of amateurism, he would have concurred, but had he been thus arraigned in the later sense of trifling he might have denied it with more or less grace, depending on the accuser. Nor did his interests stop with music and poetry.

In his first surviving letter to Jenner, Hunter offered to sell him an oil, 'a small landscape of Barretts of cattle and herd. I gave 5: 7: 6 it is one of his 8 guinea pictures you shall have it or not as you please. I have one of the same size that I bought of him some time ago.' Edward pleased to have it. Hunter was a collector with catholic taste. He owned pictures by Titian, Rubens, Canaletto, Le Nain, Zoffany, Reynolds, Van Dyck, Teniers, Cuyp, Routhenbourg, Ruysdael, Van Goyen, Stubbs and Wright of Derby. A few years later Hunter sent Jenner a landscape with figures by 'Bassani' 'as a remembrance of the trouble' Edward had had with some blackbirds for his friend. The fate of another painting by Barrett and Stubbs, 'The Landscape by Barret, and a Horse frightened at the first seeing of a Lion by Stubbs' is unknown. On another occasion Hunter wrote that he had 'bought the print of wright viz the Smiths which is his best. there is one more I would have you have Sir Jos Reynolds of count Hugolino, it is most admirable and fit only for a man of taste. . .there were some good Heads,' he adds, which he tried to buy for Edward; 'unluckily there were some that saw their merit as well as I. . . .Pictures seem to be rising again.'

Hunter's shopping for his former student also extended to candlesticks, but he failed to buy for Jenner anatomical preparations from a collection made by the late William Hewson, at one time William Hunter's partner, because 'They all went so dear.' These acquisitions and near-misses reveal the several levels not only of the friendship between Hunter and Jenner, but also of their personalities. Jenner seems to have bought only one more picture by a major artist after Hunter's death, perhaps because he no longer had an agent in London whom he could trust. The single exception is a painting by Inigo Jones listed in the inventory of his Cheltenham house made for his executors. Unfortunately, the rest of the inventory for both Cheltenham and Berkeley consists primarily of '3 paintings, 2 drawings, 3 prints', though with the addition of drawings by his great-nephew, Stephen Jenner, and two paintings by one Pearce, possibly a connection of his Berkeley lawyer, Thomas Pearce. Jenner's aesthetic interests were sufficiently powerful to prompt his material support for young poets and artists after he himself had achieved eminence.

The purchases of pictures and other items that he found for Jenner played a very minor role in Hunter's letters. These were mainly devoted to research he wanted his ex-student to do for him, or to specimens for his growing museum that Jenner might find in the fields around Berkeley and along the banks of the Severn. The very first letter encourages Jenner's proposed observations: 'on the Cuckow and upon the breading of toads, be as particular as you possibly can; If you can pick me up anything curious, and prepare it for me do it; either in the flesh or fish way.'

Hunter's demands continue in very much the same importunate, semi-literate vein until Jenner's marriage in 1788, after which the letters take on something of the tone of equals conversing rather than mentor and student. Edward sent him an unidentified bird and 'two young animals which I imagine to be guinea-pigs', but he wanted 'a large Porpass for either Love or Money.' That neither Hunter nor Jenner distinguished between porpoises and whales, in language at least, appears from Hunter's later response: 'The large Porpois I would have coarsly strip'd & the Bones put into a cask and sent. the young one if not too large put into spirits to be able to inject it. If the Breasts of the old one were taken off and put into the cask among the spirits I should like it.' Hunter certainly knew that the animals were whales, however; he recorded them as 'the Delphinus Delphis or Bottle-nose Whale'. A few days later he acknowledged receipt of the shipment. 'The bubby's of this are as flat as a pancake but I have injected the Ducts. Was the milk sweet. could you save some of it but two drops to see if it grows sower.' Hunter was fully aware that his demands took time and some money to meet. With regard to some 'Black birds nests Let me know the expense you are at for I do not mean that the picture [the one by Barrett and Stubbs] is to go for any of it only for your trouble'.

He was even more importunate about the research he wanted Jenner to carry out for him. At the time Hunter was pursuing the puzzle of animal warmth. That all mammals are warm-blooded had been recognized for centuries, but it was by no means clear why. Men like Joseph Priestley and Antoine Lavoisier, Jenner's contemporaries, were beginning to associate newly discovered elements like oxygen with events inside the body such as breathing. The idea that we inhabit chemical factories in which many of the reactions release heat could emerge only very slowly. Hunter's training included almost no chemistry, though Jenner's generation had become aware that some medicines might cure diseases by correcting chemical mistakes. Vaccination, for example, only 'took' if it led to obscure chemical changes in the body. Hunter's interests, however, were limited to the fluctuations in temperature which could be associated with events such as eating, digestion, sleeping and hibernation.

Hedgehogs are among the few British animals that hibernate. Common creatures in almost any country region, they were rare city dwellers, so Hunter urged Jenner both to supply living specimens and to experiment himself.

> I Have rec'd my Hedge Hogs. If you have time see their natural winter haunts, and in the very cold weather, run the Thermometer into the anus and observe the heat, then open the Belly by a small hole and pass the Thermometer down towards the pelvis and observe the Heat; then towards the Liver or Diaph: and observe the heat open the chist between two ribs, and obserf the heat. you may do all this in a very few minutes. observe the fluidity of the Blood, by comparing it with another, that has been keep'd warm for some days.

Clearly Hunter knew that Jenner would accept his instructions without rancour – and carry them out, what is more. Some years later when he had turned his interest to colour vision, Hunter thanked Jenner for some observations and continued: 'I want you to pursue the enquiry considerably further; and to give you an Idea of what I mean, I'll first premise that there are in Nature but three Colours; Viz: Red, Blue and Yellow. . . .'

Far from resenting Hunter's intrusion on his time, Jenner asked for more, and occasionally caught Hunter with no specific requests. '. . .I do not know well what to set you about. If you could make me some expt on the increased heat of inflammation I should be obliged to you.' He then described manipulations with an ass and a dog no less brutal than those called for on hedgehogs, and, elsewhere, on bats and blackbirds. Notions of animal suffering lay even further in the future than modern chemistry.

When Hunter was studying the 'heat of inflammation', young Edward was almost thirty and unlikely to have seen himself as Hunter's research assistant. Yet the pedagogical benefits that continued to accrue from Hunter were material. For example, Hunter not only gave him the task of measuring animal heat but supplied the means of doing so, a thermometer of his own engineering.

> The Thermometer is a very useful one when understood, you will observe a scratch upon the glass stalk; perhaps about 2 inches from the globe which is the freesing point. put o or naught, which is upon the Ivory scale two degrees below the scratch, then o becomes the thirthy

degree, and the scratch being two degrees above it stands at the freesing point: then from that count upwards. or if the cold is below 30 then put no 1 or no 2 or 3 at the scratch and count down. Every no is 10 degrees.

He warned Edward to 'take care you do not brake your Therm: in the Dogs chist'. For five years the fragile instrument seems to have survived, but then: 'you very modestly ask for a Thermometer I will send you one, but take care that those damned clumsy fingers do not break it also.' Was it a joke, Hunter's heavy-handed irony meant really to pay a compliment for the many months of meticulous care that had conserved the original thermometer? Or was it Hunter's customary bluntness?

Jenner's posthumous antagonists used the remark to castigate his alleged inadequacies as a vaccinist, arguing that his awkwardness with the lancet made his claims even less dependable. Apart from the logical uncertainty of their argument, they ignored Jenner's insistence that success was to be judged only by observing the pustule that followed vaccination, not the technique of the operative. I know of no other evidence, furthermore, that he was excessively clumsy or suffered more than the usual lack of coordination in everyday actions. Toward the end of his life after an illness that may have entailed a mild stroke, he complained of a nervous disinclination aroused by certain sounds, but never mentioned any loss of manual or indeed pedal dexterity, which might have been expected had his movements ever worried him in health.

Hunter also put the cat amongst the pigeons by a dictum in one of his earliest letters. 'I thank you for your Expt on the Hedge Hog,' he wrote, probably during the summer of 1775; 'but why do you ask me a question, by the way of solving it. I think your solution is just; but why think, why not trie the Expt. Repeat all the Expt upon a Hedge Hog as soon as you receive this, and they will give you the solution.' Again, Jenner's posthumous opponents seized upon Hunter's 'why think, why not trie the Expt' as evidence of laziness and general unreliability in matters scientific. They disregarded the relationship conveyed by the whole tone of these letters between the master and a favourite pupil.

Indeed this very letter begins with regrets that Edward has rejected Hunter's offer of a partnership. Hunter wished to expand his teaching into his own school of anatomy and natural history, but he needed cash. The partnership was to acknowledge Jenner's contribution of £1000 to the venture, as well as his participation as Hunter's assistant. Jenner's refusal is usually attributed to his determination to remain in Berkeley, added to which he now felt beholden to his brother, who had settled there to make a home for them both. I think these thoughts must have weighed heavily in his decision, aided and abetted perhaps by the fact that he might have obtained £1000 only by selling property or going into debt. Hunter responded: 'I own

I suspected it would not do; yet as I did intend such a scheme, I was inclinable to give you the offer.' Even if, as some said, he had first made the offer to Daniel Ludlow, the son of Edward's former master, Hunter's high valuation of Jenner cannot be doubted. Criticism reflected his recognition of Edward's genuine and unusual talent and his affection.

Nor was Hunter's estimate unique. Soon after Jenner returned to Berkeley, the University of Erlangen offered him the degree of Doctor of Physic, probably to entice him to join its faculty of medicine. Jenner refused the degree. At about the same time,

> He happened to dine with a large party at Bath: something was introduced at the table which required to be warmed by the application of the candle; and doubts were expressed by several persons present, whether the most speedy way would be, to keep the flame at a little distance under, or to immerse the substance into it. Jenner desired the candle to be placed near him, and immediately put his finger into the flame, suffering it to remain some time; next he put his finger above it, but was obliged to snatch it away immediately – *'This Gentlemen,' said he, 'is a sufficient test.'*

According to the Quaker physician, John Lettsom, who first recorded Jenner's recollection of this incident in 1804, the next day a General Smith (possibly Sir John, 1754–1837) offered Jenner a medical appointment in India 'which would assure him, in the course of two or three years, an annuity of 3000l.' An anonymous contemporary biographer said that the offer actually came from Warren Hastings, but does not say whether this controversial gentleman was also present at the candle-lit supper. Wrote Lettsom, 'The offer was referred to his brother; and our Jenner, from his attachment to him, declined it.'

Certainly Edward Jenner wanted his contemporaries to believe that affection, duty and a strong sense of place governed his decisions. Three career refusals, at least, he had given – in response to Banks's suggestion that he might join Cook's second expedition, Hunter's offer of a partnership and the Indian proposal. I think he was telling the whole truth. Any doubt I might feel about the wisdom of his decisions stems in large measure from my own attitude toward the value of travel, an attitude probably no older than the romantic wanderlust of Lord Byron, who died about the same time as Jenner but in rather different circumstances. Jenner's love for Berkeley and the life he led there strikes us as complacent, even smug, but we are very different people: products of an age of individuality and adventure. To us, rejection of travel is inconsistent with scientific imagination. Exploiting one's opportunities symbolizes success. *Roots* recalls an idealized, dead past useful only for transmutation into money. But to Jenner, roots symbolized the source of life, of inheritance, without which nobody could grow and expand. Even in an age of imperial growth, Jenner's determination to stay put expressed the fundamental strength of his class.

Curiously, his love of place never effected a meeting with Hunter outside London. In November 1777 towards the end of a restful holiday in Bath, Hunter wrote that he and Mrs Hunter would like to call on Jenner at Berkeley. Unfortunately, the letter failed to arrive, and they 'did not chuse to come without an answer as it was possible you might not be at home.' Two years later Anne Hunter wrote because her husband was napping and she did not want to miss the post: they were again in Bath because of his ill-health. For some reason Jenner was unable to visit them there.

Of course, he was well occupied. In addition to his social life and the experiments he conducted both for Hunter and in his own right, Jenner had an expanding medical practice. Hunter's letters refer to patients whom Jenner had sent to him or about whose cases Jenner wanted advice. Evidently Hunter's two letters on colour vision were prompted by a blind patient of Jenner's who regained his sight, thus providing a subject whose new perceptions of colour might give answers about how they were perceived. In three letters probably written at the end of 1775 and the beginning of 1776, Hunter answered Jenner's inquiries about a boy with a fungus on the skull that seemed to be affecting his brain. He strongly urged no action at all, arguing that it would go away. Jenner replied that the fungus was the brain itself, though without his letter it is impossible to guess how he knew or what he meant. In the event Hunter expressed doubt and advised: 'if it is Brain let it drop off, if it is Fungus let it either drop or waste off therefore be quiet and think yourself well of[f], that the boy is not dead.' Unfortunately, the outcome is unknown.

Occasionally Jenner consulted other medical men. For example, he had been treating an elderly clergyman, Thomas Hodges, who lived in nearby Arlingham. Apart from the role played by age, the nature of Hodges's illness is lost, but it may have been angina pectoris, a heart disease in which a temporary shortage of oxygen or of some other essential chemical in the heart muscle causes severe pain. Jenner himself published original observations on this serious condition a few years later, but in his patient's interest at the end of 1783 he wrote to Dr William Heberden, an authority on this very new subject. He had probably met Heberden through Hunter. In any case Heberden replied that Hodges's local doctor was in a better position to advise Jenner, though he recommended certain cathartics and a bland diet. Hodges died early the next year. Jenner's willingness to seek the advice of this established London acquaintance suggests that he put his patients' welfare above his own limited knowledge, exhibiting a certain humbleness which remained even in the face of the self-justification that often poisoned the post-vaccination years.

Young as he was, Jenner had attracted the attention of his surgical colleagues. One of the junior surgeons at the Gloucester Infirmary, Charles Brandon Trye, had not only known Jenner at Cirencester but had also been a Hunter student. Trye may have been the immediate source of the urgent request sent to Jenner that he make the sixteen-mile journey to perform an emergency operation. Both of the senior surgeons at the Infirmary had been indisposed when a patient named Bailey had been brought in with a hernia needing immediate surgical relief. According to Fosbroke, the patient vomited during the operation, ejecting intestines on to the table. Jenner replaced them, completed the task, and Bailey lived another twenty years.

That Edward Jenner was well reputed amongst his colleagues reflects not only his educational history but also his sociableness. He had maintained his friendship with the Ludlows, father and son, and met them from time to time at the Ship Inn, now a thriving Trust House Hotel on the outskirts of Alveston between Berkeley and Bristol. All three were members of an informal drinking and dining club which included medical men from Winterbourne, Frenchay, Hinsbury, Bristol and Wotton-under-Edge. Perhaps the man who most interested Jenner was his neighbour, a Mr Fewster of Thornbury. Fewster had been either a pupil or a partner of the variolator, Daniel Sutton, possibly both. In 1765, almost fifteen years before, he had presented a paper, never subsequently published, on 'Cow Pox and its Ability to Prevent Smallpox' to the Medical Society of London. Not surprisingly, the subject was often discussed by the assembled medical drinkers at the Ship Inn, to the point where, except for Jenner and Fewster, they began to resent it. The good John Baron blames it all on his hero: Jenner 'often recurred to the subject. . .at length it became so distasteful to his companions that. . .they threatened to expel him if he continued to harass them with so unprofitable a subject.' Although it never came to that, in time the club languished. Jenner called it the Convivio-Medical Society to mark the contrast in emphasis with the more scientifically committed Medico-Convivial Society which he helped to form a decade later. Fewster, who was not a member of the second group, became one of Jenner's earliest supporters, practising the new vaccination himself and publicly recognizing Jenner's priority. 'As a proof' of his appreciation, Jenner wrote in December 1803, 'I myself proposed him as an honorary Member of the Royal J. [Jennerian] Society in London.' Indeed, Jenner's ability to maintain early friendships contrasts with the difficulties that seemed to plague relationships originating after the defence of vaccination became central to his life.

Meanwhile, however, his social life led inexorably to romance. Again, the only hard evidence of this is to be found in Hunter's letters, another indication of the closeness between them. Important though it is, the date of Hunter's first reference is uncertain, but it was probably 22 June 1778.

'I was told the other day that you was married, and to a young Lady with a considerable portion. I hope it is true, for I do not know any body more deserving of one, let me know whether it is so or not.' Sadly, it was not true. On 25 September, Hunter wrote:

I own I was at a loss to account for your Silence, and I am sorry at the cause. I can easily conceive how you must feel, for you have two passions to cope with viz that of being disappointed in Love and that of being defeated, but both will wear out, perhaps the first soonest. I own that i was glad, when I heard that you was moored to a woman of fortune; 'but let her go never mind her'. I shall imploy you with Hedge Hogs. . . .

The instantaneous response of any biographer worth his salt to such a challenge is to hare off in pursuit of the object of Jenner's disappointed affections. For better or worse, the search has produced only negative results. Amongst the possible local heiresses married during the first few months of 1778, one finds Eleanor Clutterbuck of Eastington, Judith Excell of Wotton-under-Edge, Elizabeth Pearce of Stone, Edith Saniger and Elizabeth Williams, both of Berkeley, all women whose surnames appear in other Jenner connections, if only amongst Edward's later vaccinees. Meticulous though such exploration may have been, it produced nothing beyond whatever satisfaction comes from leaving no stone unturned. The identity of Edward's beloved remains hidden. Perhaps the answer lies in another direction, one sanctioned by the realities of the eighteenth century's hardheaded approach to marriage as well as by nineteenth-century romance.

On 6 March 1788, exactly a decade later, Edward Jenner married Catherine Kingscote in Kingscote parish church. They were married under licence, an ecclesiastically accepted alternative to the tripart swearing of banns then required by the Church. Licences were usually granted either to those who wanted to be married in a hurry or to couples who considered the publicity surrounding banns undesirable. In the case of the Jenners, there seemed no particular urgency, but the second explanation would have suited the status of the bride. She was 'sister to Robert Kingscote, Esq; of Kingscote' and of sufficient importance for her marriage to be noticed in the *Glocester Journal*. As the duplication of the family name in the name of the village and the parish implies, the Kingscotes were eminent freeholders of ancient pedigree. One of Catherine's aunts had married the Duke of Suffolk. Another brother, Thomas, married the sister of Sir John Rous MP, later a supporter of vaccination. A sister married the banker, Robert Ladbroke. Respectable though the Jenner family no doubt was, its members had made no marriage connections with half as much glamour and resplendence.

When they were married, Edward was almost thirty-nine but Catherine was barely twenty-seven. Almost certainly he had known Catherine for at least five years, since his balloon flight to Kingscote in 1783 – of which adventure, more below. Quite possibly, they had known each other much longer. Both socially and professionally, as the freezing January journey in 1786 indicates, Edward had contacts with the Kingscote family, including its eligible female members. But in 1778, Catherine was only seventeen. Regardless of his family and his friendship with Hunter, little known outside the medical world, Edward was nobody in particular. Not only did he lack a personal fortune, but what was there about the young man to make an anxious elder brother consider him a suitable lover for his youngest sister? Young surgeons were fairly thick on the ground, and the Hunter connection meant little in Kingscote circles.

One possible explanation for Jenner's disappointment and defeat, then, consistent with the mores of his time, is that he had fallen in love with his wife-to-be and been rejected by her guardian brother. Nevertheless, because she had attached herself to him too, they endured an unrecognized engagement lasting more than ten years. Fosbroke describes their first meeting thus:

> After he had discovered the benignant influence of green colours in melancholy, he was called to a lady in that case. For her he selected a retirement in a small valley among beech woods. . . .she recovered. In the ivied cottage which she occupied, Jenner formed the foundations of a union with this lady, whose life was a personification of virtue, and whose claims of family were suited to gratify the most ambitious mind. . . .

The paucity of real data in this eyewash indicates that Jenner told Fosbroke very little of the truth. The one person who may have known whether the object of Jenner's unrequited love in 1778 was Catherine Kingscote or some other girl was his close friend Edward Gardner. In 1783, five years after the unhappy affair, Edward wrote twice to Gardner. In the first letter he said:

> I am jaded almost to death, my dear Gardner, by constant fatigue: that of the body I must endure; but how long I shall be able to bear that of the mind, I know not. Still the same dead weight hangs upon my heart. Would to God it would drag it from its unhappy mansion! then with what pleasure would I see an end of this silly dream of life.

The second is dated 8 April, and goes on: 'As for myself, the same stream of unhappiness is still flowing in upon me; its source seems inexhaustible; but there is a soothing consolation in it; all little disquietudes are sunk or washed away. I feel their influence no more.' Unfortunately, the originals of these two letters have not been found. Is this mere fashionable melancholy, or could it mirror Catherine's depression, and for the same reason? In other words was there a first love, followed by a second, or were Edward and Catherine simply proving the permanence of the bond that was eventually accepted by her brother and solemnized by marriage?

[42]

Dr Baron may also have been told the truth by his hero, but he too is ambiguous: 'Jenner appears to have experienced some disappointment in his affections,' he wrote before 1827. In fact not until the august *British Medical Journal*, celebrating the centenary of the first vaccination in 1896, stated unequivocally that there had been a first love affair did the story enter subsequent biographies. The *BMJ*, furthermore, linked the unhappy event to 'Jenner's future mistrust of the fair sex. . . .', a statement for which I can find no justification whatsoever. True, the gossipy Fosbroke says that Jenner frequently spoke of 'the defect of reflection in women'. Jenner himself commented on the role of women 'as a medium of conveyance of a sum of money from a father to a husband – or as a plaything', and wrote to another friend: 'How wonderfully constructed is the female mind; and we as well confess, while we are about it, the male too.' If the known facts do reflect the truth, Jenner is more likely to have resented the role of a dragon-like brother who nevertheless stirred him up to play St George.

In February 1783, about the time he wrote the letters to Gardner, Jenner completed his first sustained prose composition, a remarkable 'Essay on Marriage'. 'That Man is naturally born with Inclinations for Pleasure and happiness is a Maxim that cannot be controverted, to pass our lives with Content is the sole end of Education and diligence. . . .,' he began. Compare this opening line to that which introduced the vital paper on vaccination fifteen years later: 'The deviation of man from the state in which he was originally placed by nature seems to have proved to him a prolific source of diseases.' Let no one doubt that Jenner was a child of his age. He may not have read Rousseau, but the ringing words of the American Declaration of Independence had been printed in the *Glocester Journal*.

'The most prevailing passions in the human breast are love and Ambition, the first exists in our Very Nature, the other in the Child of Custom & Education,' he continued in his 'Essay on Marriage'. 'Marriage is undoubtedly the ultimate View of Love', moreover, even though it entails abridgement of freedom. The choice of a wife may be dictated by love, ambition or avarice, but gold should not be the standard for judging a woman. Though that standard be called Prudence, it 'converts the Baseness of a vicious principle into a Virtue.' True Prudence is 'to follow the dictates of Reason and Nature unseduced by Custom and uninfluenc'd by Ambition'. Believing wealth is essential to happiness is to succumb to pride, which 'can make another the mere Engine to gratify its Sordid Dispositions.' Such wrong motives are due to the teachings of parents, but a new way must be found: '. . .no one has Ventur'd to oppose what be called <u>Notions of Romantic Love</u> to maxims which they dignify with the names of Reason and Prudence'. Older people, parents, religious folk, 'all those. . .who make others miserable for the gratification of their own inordinate pride, let them consider whether this

[43]

Corresponds with the purity of their professions'. Some seek the ' "whistling of a Name" ', distinctions of 'Birth. . .good Family. . . .the ridicule of one person enobling Another is sufficiently obvious, and the impious pride of ancestral distinction is severely to be condemn'd. . . .we all must be equal in the Eyes of that Being who shaped us as we are – '.

'Reason and Nature alike informs us that we ought to follow the effusions of our own hearts in this most important Concern of Life.' He was not recommending poverty, he wrote, but a person of some property should be free to choose his wife. Such a marriage has its own reward in gratitude, love and generosity. Any sensible man seeks advice, of course, but ultimately he must follow his heart if that advice directs him along 'a path to Misery.' Seldom has a man of thirty-three utilized philosophy more overtly to plead his cause. There is no indication whether anyone else read his manuscript until I did in the middle months of 1988, but why should we not believe that he brought it to the girl he loved, perhaps in her 'ivied cottage', and that they shared its righteousness? In any case the 'Essay' lends strong support to my belief that Edward fell in love with Catherine when she was very young, that her brother not surprisingly forbade the marriage in 1778, but allowed it to go ahead ten years later.

Edward had begun to prove himself. Added to the determination of the couple themselves, his London connections, friendly intercourse with the local medical 'faculty', as they called themselves in those days, limited successes as a physician and surgeon, and his growing prestige in experimental science must have influenced Robert Kingscote. Simultaneously, it seems, Jenner attracted professional attention as a chemist, a botanist and an ornithologist while, locally, he shone as a respectable adventurer.

Soon after his reports to Gardner about his own melancholia, Jenner undertook his most spectacular experiment. The notion originated with two brothers, paper-makers of Annonay near Lyons, named Montgolfier. From the behaviour of clouds, the Montgolfiers conceived the idea of a paper bag filled with smoke that might fly. Toward the end of 1782, they made their first tests, followed on 5 June 1783 by a successful, very public unmanned ascent. Barely two months later, the physicist, J. A. C. Charles, filled a balloon prepared by two more brothers, Roberts by name, with hydrogen gas which rose to three thousand feet above the Champs de Mars and soared for fifteen miles in the vicinity of Paris. Naturally, the reports of these flights were published in British papers. Although the fact went unrecorded by the author of the article on 'Aeronautics' in the impeccable eleventh edition of the *Encyclopaedia Britannica*, the first such flight on this side of the Channel was organized by Edward Jenner with the assistance of the Earl of Berkeley.

The motive seems to have been the joy of doing it, combined of course with the spirit of scientific research. Jenner wrote to his medical friend, Caleb Hillier Parry, in Bath: 'Please to send me by return of Mr. Marklove half a yard of such Silk as you may think most fit for the purpose. I have got some oil ready.' Urging Parry's attendance at the forthcoming ascent, he added: 'Perhaps your Patients may suffer you leave them a day. – Remember the Peer looks a little yellow sometime.' Probably using the hydrogen-making method adopted by Charles in Paris, iron filings in sulphuric acid, the balloon was filled with hydrogen in the great hall of Berkeley Castle and flew to a place called Symond's Hall. Attached to the balloon was a celebratory poem by Edward Gardner. Jenner then organized a second flight which began at Kingscote, undoubtedly in the presence of the Kingscote family. No further aeronautical experiments have been discovered, however, and Jenner almost certainly never flew himself.

Ballooning was no doubt excellent medicine for melancholia and for the elevation of his status, considering the role of the Earl of Berkeley, but it was not Jenner's line. Being a chemical transaction, making the hydrogen gas came closer to his usual interests. In this same momentous year, 1783, he had published anonymously *Cursory Observations on Emetic Tartar*. This eight-page pamphlet, much shorter than the 'Essay on Marriage', described a purified chemical but did not give the method of producing it. Emetic tartar is also called antimony potassium tartrate. In Jenner's day it was used to cause vomiting because the release of matter from the gut was supposed to combat fever. Then, variations in the purity of this drug, like many others, were unpredictable. It was and still may be manufactured by dissolving antimony in wine, where the antimony combines with tartar in the wine. Jenner had elaborated a technique for purification that gave consistent results. Naturally, he sent the pamphlet to Hunter, who replied:

> I have a great deal to say about it. First, do you mean to take out a Patint? Do you mean to advertise it? or do you mean to let it take its chance. I approve of it much, and will do all in my power to promote the sale, but I would advise you to give it a new name expressive either of the composition or of its virtues in the body viz sal antim: or sal sudorif: or sal antim: sudorif: I would also desire you to burn your Book for you will have all the world making it.

This was probably the first time Jenner was advised by another medical man how to capitalize on his labours, but it was certainly not the last.

Jenner must have cavilled, because Hunter wrote a month later: 'I love a new name so well, that I could have wished it had been christened. Mr Jones [a shopkeeper, possibly a bookseller, known to Hunter] informed me that there was a man of some fortune making expts with the same view, he may hit on some method better than the present, and which may or may not be as good as yours. . . .' He asked for several copies of the pamphlet to send to his acquaintances. His next letter (the one which also refers to

Jenner's 'damnd clumsy fingers') begins, 'I am puffing off your Tartar as the Tartar of all Tartar, and have given it to several Physicians to make trial, but have no account yet of the success, had you not [better] let a Book seller have it to sell as Glass of Oxford did his magnesia; Let it be call'd Jenner's Tartar Emetic, or any bodys else you please.' Hunter's irritation with what he considered to be Edward's impracticality is evident, but he persisted. By this time a new element had entered the calculation. Jenner must have asked whether a fuller description of the purification technique might enable him to become a Fellow of the Royal Society. 'I am affraid it will be now too late for this year publication,' Hunter replied; 'but put it to paper. your paper must be publish'd before you can think of being a member and then we still stirr for you. . . .'

In the event, the enlarged paper was published almost a decade later in the first volume of a new publication by a new medical organization. The process involved mixing antimony and tartar (in wine), pouring on boiling water, filtering, letting the mixture stand to allow crystal formation and reliquifying with boiling water twice more. Jenner made no attempt to identify the purified emetic tartar as his own or to keep any corner of the process secret.

Meanwhile at the behest of Joseph Banks, now President of the Royal Society, he undertook a series of experiments between February 1780 and June 1782, testing the value of human blood as a manure. First, he took the serum, the pale viscous liquid separated from the coagulated red solids (blood cells and other formed elements, but Jenner would not have known that), from forty ounces of blood and poured it over a square foot of grass. Two months later, he noted, the grass was rich and green. In a second experiment he placed mustard seeds on layers of wool in three saucers. One he wetted with water; a second with blood serum; and a third with the coagulated part mixed into the serum. The seeds in saucer one sprouted, whereas the others became mouldy and died. At the same time using other saucers he found that in a mixture of equal parts of serum and water, some seeds sprouted while others died. If the mixture consisted of one part serum and two parts water, the seeds sprouted and flowered. He also used a mixture of whole blood mixed with wood ash and chalk around the roots of a polyanthus. The plant flowered but then suddenly withered and died. The final horticultural experiments began with four peach trees, two of which were manured using animal dung in the usual manner, and two just watered. Not surprisingly, the manured trees grew better than the other two. He then took four young currant bushes of the same age planted in pots. The first was manured with the coagulated part of the blood, and the surface was covered with garden mould. Pot two received equal parts blood and mould, and the surface was covered with mould. Pot three was covered with mould and wetted with serum twice, at intervals of about six days. Pot four received mould only. All four pots were placed beside an east-facing wall in April 1782. Six weeks later, the bush in pot one was dead; in pot two, nearly dead; in pot three, sickly, though two weeks later it had recovered; and pot four, healthy. These experiments may well have been connected with Banks's interest in the gardens of the King's newly acquired house and estate at Kew, but Jenner delayed his report on them until 5 June 1787, writing: 'I recollect that I promis'd to send you an Account of some Experiments made on Vegitables with animal manure. I wish they were more worthy your Observation. A Person engaged in business can't conduct these matters as he would wish; his pursuits are too often interrupted.'

This interesting letter begins with an account of another experiment which Jenner had promised to Banks 'When I had the honour of waiting on you in London in the Spring' of 1787. He now passed on the account from an acquaintance who had brought together a dog fox and a terrier bitch. The animals copulated three times, but the bitch did not become pregnant. Jenner promised further experiments. None has come to light.

Behind their mutual interest probably lay the paper, 'Observations tending to show that the Wolf, Jackal and Dog are all of the same Species', read to the Royal Society on 26 April 1787 by John Hunter. But from Jenner's standpoint, it is the last paragraph in this long letter to Banks which contains the vital message:

> By a letter from Mr. Blagden [secretary of the Royal Society], I have the pleasure of being inform'd my Observations on the Cuckoo are order'd for Publication in the Phil: Trans: I shall pursue the Subject during the Summer & hope to have the honour of presenting you with another paper in the Autumn; & also a paper on the exciting cause to migration in Birds.

The paper on bird migration remained unpublished until after Jenner's death. After some vicissitude, though, the cuckoo was to be the instrument enabling Edward to fulfil two ambitions: fellowship of the Royal Society and marriage.

Banks replied on 7 July 1787, thanking Jenner for his observations on plant manures and the story about the fox and bitch: 'In consequence of your having discovered that the young cuckoo, and not the parent bird, removes the eggs and young from the nest in which it is deposited,' he continued, 'the council thought it best to give you a full scope for altering it ['Observations on the Natural History of the Cuckoo'] as you shall choose.' The cuckoo exercised the special interest of naturalists because of its unique nesting habits. Instead of building its own nest, laying and hatching its eggs in the usual way, the cuckoo lays its eggs in the nests of various birds, particularly the hedge sparrow, and depends on the foster-parents to hatch them. The chicks of the foster-parents, furthermore, are thrown out of their nests and allowed to die, leaving the cuckoo chick in possession not only of the nest but also of all the food supplied by the foster-parents. Such remarkable parasitism raises a number of questions: for example, why should the cuckoo almost alone amongst animal species desert its own young, and how are the 'rightful' chicks removed from their parents' nest? These were questions Jenner had set himself to answer.

We know from Hunter's letters that the cuckoo puzzle intrigued him and that Jenner's interest dated back at least to his return to Berkeley in 1773. In an undated letter to Dr Hickes of Gloucester, he proposed 'to run over the Ph. Trans: to see what has been sd. on Cuckoos. That is my present Hobby – . . .Daines Barringtons acct I have seen in an old Review. . . .this Subject has puzzled Philosophers in every Age from the days of Aristotle.' Like all of Jenner's research, this work progressed very slowly, interrupted no doubt by his experiments for Hunter, his other interests, his practice and his social life. A decade later, during his recovery from melancholia, Edward took on his sixteen-year-old nephew Henry, son of his second brother (also Henry), to assist him with his observations. Baron wrote that most of the hedge sparrow nests Jenner was observing were located on a farm belonging to his aunt Deborah Hooper at Clapton, three miles from Berkeley. Henry was engaged to make the six-mile circuit of the nests each morning, and to report developments to his uncle. Baron also said that Jenner prepared his paper for publication at the home of a friend, Henry Hicks, who lived at Eastington, several miles from Berkeley in the opposite direction, and it was Baron who implied that Henry, being a lazy boy, failed either to make accurate observations or to report fully, or both.

In any case Jenner sent his first paper, the one mentioned in his letter to Joseph Banks, to Hunter for submission to the Royal Society. It stated that the foster-parents themselves ejected their young to make room for the cuckoo, offering no explanation for such peculiar behaviour. Perhaps it was this lack of a rational explanation that caused him to pursue the matter further, even after submitting his paper. When during June 1787 he once again watched hedge sparrow nests occupied by cuckoo eggs, he made his own observations closer to home.

17.   Saw a Hedge Sparrows Nest at Mr Bromedges with two Hedge Sp: in it just hatched, two Eggs not hatched & a Cuckoo just hatched.
18.   In the morning early there were four Hedge Sparrows & the young Cuckoo in it – Abt noon it contained the Cuckoo & one Sparrow only & at night the Cuckoo was left alone in the Nest. . . .25.   . . . .Put a Cuckoo 8 days old into Hedge Sparrows Nest which had a Cuckoo in it abt. the same age. About half an hour afterwards one of the young ones was turned out & found alive on the ground under the Nest. . . .9 [July] a nest containing two hedge sparrows and a newly-hatched

cuckoo. . . .Fastened a piece of lead on the Cuckoos Legs in such
a way that He cant throw out his fellow Nestlings.

The results of these new observations were unexpected and highly controversial.

Jenner concluded that the real villain was the cuckoo chick. This tiny
creature, scarcely larger than the chicks of the rightful owners, began almost
immediately to hoist any other object in the nest, occupant or egg, on to its
back and to manoeuvre it upwards to the edge whence it was pitched out to
more or less immediate destruction. The foster-parents seemed to disregard
the behaviour. What is more, Jenner discovered by dissection that the cuckoo
chick's back contains a slight declivity between the wings sufficient to provide
a purchase for its enemy object. Then, about the twelfth day after hatching,
this declivity disappears. The bird's back begins to look like that of any other
species, including adults of its own. So startling were these assertions that
some naturalists refused to accept them. Jenner's observations were proven
correct only in 1921, after the introduction of motion pictures.

In his notes he had recorded that two cuckoo hatchlings in one nest was
one too many. 'The contest was very remarkable. The combatants alternately
appeared to have the advantage, as each carried the other several times to
the top of the nest, and then sunk down again, oppressed by the weight
of its burden; till at length, after various efforts, the strongest prevailed.'
Here indeed is an example of what the grandson of Jenner's friend, Erasmus
Darwin, referred to seventy years later as 'survival of the fittest'.

Why had Jenner missed it all the first time? It is pointless to blame
young Henry. For whatever reason, Edward had not completed his observations properly before he drafted the original paper. In the later version
he wrote, '. . .supposing from the feeble appearance of the young cuckoo
just disengaged from the shell that it was utterly incapable of displacing
either the egg or the young sparrows I was induced to believe that the old
sparrows were the only agents in this seeming unnatural business.' At least
he had had the honesty to admit his own doubts, and then to act upon them
by undertaking further observations, but it is hard to avoid the conclusion that
he had behaved very unwisely, perhaps in haste to satisfy Robert Kingscote.

The paper contained two more original observations, however. Seeking
differences between the cuckoo's eggs and those of the foster-parents, the
sizes and colourings of which tend to blend, Jenner found that the cuckoo
egg was always heavier. By dissection and observation, he also cast doubt
on the prevailing theory that the reason for the cuckoo's peculiar egg-laying
behaviour was anatomical: the cuckoo was said to have a covering over its
large stomach so thin that nesting might rupture it. Jenner found no percep-
tible difference between the stomach cavities of cuckoos and other birds. He
suggested a new theory, based on the migratory behaviour of cuckoos, which

is now accepted. The birds arrive in England about mid-April and depart during the first week in July, a period of roughly eleven weeks. The time required for incubation, hatching and feeding up to independence can be as much as fifteen weeks, added to which cuckoos may produce more than one egg over a period of several days. The only answer, from the standpoint of the cuckoo, is to hijack the nests and instincts of other species.

On 27 December 1787, the revised paper was again sent to Hunter with a formal request that he present it to the Royal Society. It was read on 13 March 1788, exactly a week after the Jenners' long-anticipated marriage. Almost a year later, on 25 February 1789, Jenner was elected a Fellow of the Royal Society. In addition to Hunter, he was supported by Charles Blagden, who had been born at Wotton-under-Edge, and by Sir William Watson. A physician and variolator himself, Watson became a staunch defender of Jennerian vaccination.

Perhaps even more because of its false start, 'Observations on the Natural History of the Cuckoo' confirmed the scientific capabilities that both Hunter and Banks had seen in Jenner. Both men had spurred him on, Hunter with continuous intensity for almost two decades. The great diversity of their interests seems to have dovetailed with Jenner's eager willingness to delay his own development. Too many avenues lay open, and, of course, he had a living to earn. As he wrote to Banks: 'A person engaged in business cannot conduct these matters as he would wish; his pursuits are too often interrupted.' What concentrated his mind was a love affair, or more precisely, a brother's prudent interference with mere romance.

Chapter 4

Immortalizing James Phipps
1789–1796

Three years before his marriage Jenner bought Chauntry Cottage, a large, handsome house with a garden surrounded by high brick walls that separate it from Berkeley churchyard to the east and the park surrounding Berkeley Castle to the north. It had belonged originally to the Chauntry Priest of St Andrew's Altar in the parish church, having been built for that worthy under licence from Richard II in 1380 by Lady Katherine Berkeley, who also endowed the Wotton-under-Edge Grammar School. Jenner bought it for £600 from Jane Hicks, a relation of the Earl of Portland according to Fosbroke. The house had been Georgianized by Jane's family, the Westons of Berkeley, and the new owner laid out the garden afresh. Both Catherine and Edward considered the comfortable house and varied garden with its wide square lawn as their real home for the rest of their lives.

There, Edward Robert Jenner was born on 24 January 1789. Two months later John Hunter wrote: 'Dear Jenner I wish you Joy, it never rains but it pours. Rather than the brat should not be a christian+. I will stand godfather. for I should be unhappy if the poor little thing should go to the Devel. because I would not stand Godfather. I hope Mrs Jenner is as well. and that you begin to look grave now you are a father.' Below in Jenner's hand is a note: '+Poor Edward! EJ', probably added after his first child died, aged twenty-one, of tuberculosis.

In May 1788, two months after his marriage, Jenner and his friend from Cirencester schooldays, Caleb Hillier Parry, now a doctor in Bath, had converted what had been a gentlemen's evening out into a new medical society. There were three other members – Dr John Heathfield Hickes of Gloucester and later Bristol, Thomas Paytherus, surgeon of Ross, later London, and Daniel Ludlow of Sodbury, the son of Jenner's first tutor in surgery. According to Baron, the first biographer, Henry Hicks of Eastington in whose house Edward had written his original paper on the cuckoo and no relation of Dr Hickes, was a frequent visitor because he lived on the direct road from Berkeley to Rodborough where the new society met at the Fleece Inn. Like the old Convivio-Medical Society, this one was 'at first instituted and has now twice met for the purpose of conviviality'. Its new regulations extended its function 'to the more important end of improvement in the different branches of science connected with medicine and surgery'. To demonstrate its serious purpose, furthermore, regulation 13 declared: 'That as a principal part of the view of this Society is the mutual communication of knowledge without fear, reserve, or any other authority, than that of truth, no new members shall be admitted for these seven years to come whose age exceeds 40 years.' No wonder Jenner later called it the Medico-Convivial Society. Formally named the Medical Society, it met sporadically for about five years, but the idea survived. More than a century later the *British Medical Journal* said that the Gloucestershire Medical Society was probably the oldest known provincial medical society.

The regulations specified meetings on the first Wednesday in June, the last in July and the second in September. Members paid not only for their meals and drinks, but also fines: half a guinea for late arrival and a guinea for missing a meeting. Original papers were acceptable in any of six categories: anatomy, physiology and pathology; descriptions of diseases, especially from the evidence of dissection; preparations and choice of medicines; effects of medicines, and other forms of treatment; new therapies, and new uses for old ones; and the improvement of surgical instruments. The regulations laid down rules for the submission of written papers and their eventual publication by the Society.

In the event, no publication appeared. Yet the members heard sixteen papers in the three years from July 1788: five by Parry, four by Jenner, three by Hickes, one each by Paytherus and Ludlow and one by Hickes and Jenner. Parry, who had been selected as the first President, opened the initial meeting with a discussion of the manner of making medical inquiries – how the medical man should ask questions of his patient in order to elicit useful information – a subject that has never ceased to fascinate and infuriate both partners in the relationship. He continued with a paper on the dissection of a case of angina pectoris. In 1799 Parry published a book, *An Inquiry into the Symptoms and Causes of the Syncope Anginosa, Commonly called Angina Pectoris*. He wrote about the Medical Society: 'the influence of the heart on the animal œconomy had often been the subject of discussion. . . .it was suggested by Dr. Jenner, that the Angina Pectoris arose from some morbid change in the structure of the heart, which change was probably ossification, or some similar disease, of the coronary arteries.' Jenner's first contribution to the Society, on 29 July 1789, was a paper on heart disease following rheumatism, actually a case of mitral stenosis, hardening and malfunction of one of the heart valves. In the manuscript that remains, he wrote, 'the Symptoms arising appear to be very different from those which shew themselves in Angina Pectoris.' Chest pain is the same in both, but the obstruction affects the brain, a symptom not seen in angina, because the impedence of blood flow causes it 'when the motion becomes accelerated [to] be accumulated in the Vessels of the Head so as to compress the Brain – '. This was a guess which is not far off the mark, but the evidence from the dissection, while not the first of its kind, may have been the first observation brought to the attention of this group of medical men.

In his book Parry acknowledged the importance of Jenner's earlier dissections to the understanding of angina. He published a vivid letter from Jenner answering questions he had put to him:

> The first case I ever saw of Angina Pectoris, was that in the year 1772, published by Dr. Heberden with Mr. John Hunter's dissection. There, I can almost positively say, the coronary arteries of the heart were not examined. Another case of a Mr. Carter at Dursley, fell under my care. In that, after having examined the more important parts of the heart, without finding anything by means of which I could account either for his sudden death, or the symptoms preceding it, I was making a transverse section of the heart pretty near its base, when my knife struck against something so hard and gritty, as to notch it. I well remember looking up to the ceiling, which was old and crumbling, conceiving that some plaister had fallen down. But on a further scrutiny the real cause appeared: the coronary's were become bony canals. Then I began a little to suspect. Soon afterwards Mr Paytherus met with a case. Previously to our examination of the body, I offered him a wager that we should find the coronary arteries ossified. This, however, proved not to be exactly true; but the coats of the arteries were hard, and a sort of cartilagenous canal was formed within the cavity of each artery, and there attached, so however as to be separable as easily as the fingers from a tight glove. We then concluded that malorganization was the cause of the disease.

Jenner continued that at this time, he realized, 'my valued friend, Mr. John Hunter, began to have the symptoms of Angina Pectoris'. During 1777 Hunter had been ill, and when he went to Bath in September for a rest, Jenner had hoped to visit him. He felt unable to discuss his diagnosis with Hunter not only because it would cause serious distress to his much loved master, but probably also because he felt unsure. Instead, he wrote to Heberden giving him many of the details he later gave Parry and asking his advice with respect to Hunter. Unfortunately, this important letter appears never to have been sent. He also told Parry that his worry about the effect of the diagnosis

> prevented any publication of my ideas on the subject, as it must have brought on an unpleasant conference between Mr. Hunter and me. I mentioned both to Mr. Cline and Mr. Home my notions of the matter at one of Mr. Hunter's Sunday night meetings; but they did not seem to think much of them. When, however, Mr. Hunter died, Mr. Home very candidly wrote to me, immediately after the dissection, to tell me I was right.

The only paper presented by Paytherus to the Medico-Convivial Society also dealt with a case of angina. During that same meeting, 28 July 1790, Jenner read a report about 'a case of Hydatids in the kidneys, successfully treated by the Essential Oil of Turpentine.' An hydatid is a cyst, a small envelope of tissue containing watery liquid. Unless the fluid contains pus, indicating an infection, or the cyst causes discomfort or some malfunction, it would usually be ignored today. Jenner and his contemporaries associated hydatids with both tuberculosis and certain tumours because they could see a similarity in the appearance of hydatids, tubercles and encysted tumours.

Jenner believed with Hunter that because they moved when removed from dissected tissue, hydatids were alive. 'When the natural History of this Insect is better understood,' he wrote in his commonplace book, 'we shall be able to divide the Genus into Species.' He saw an analogy with growths on plants which he called vegetable tumours: 'The oake-Apple, the gall Nut, the mossy excresence on the wild rose, with many other substances (all of which evidently owe their origin to the Intrusion of an Insect). . . .'. Although insects may produce some of these plant growths, they can also be caused by virus infections. Jenner had dissected the lungs of a tuberculous cow and described the tubercles, one of which contained hydatids, leading him to the conclusion that cysts develop into hydatids and hydatids into tubercles. He also inferred 'that encysted Tumours in general are Hydatids', adding some years later: 'All Tumors truly cancerous seem to arise from Hydatids.' He had observed hydatids on the face and neck of his baby son, although they contained no fluid, he said, and about the same time 'on Mrs Jenner's Lip'. Both Edward junior and Catherine Jenner later died of tuberculosis. Sadly, there is a good chance that the mother infected her infant, but their cysts almost certainly reflect some other condition.

In July 1790 Jenner reported to the Medico-Convivial Society the case of James Merrett, aged twenty-two, who suffered from severe pain in his kidneys and bladder 'accompanied with a total suppression of Urine for a short time; when something would seem to give way & presently after the Skin of a broken Hydatid would be discharged with a stream of Urine.' The poor man probably suffered from stones, which had irritated the kidney tubes, causing products of inflammation to appear in the urine. 'I now discovered the Substances that came from him to be Hydatids,' said Jenner, who looked with nothing but his naked eye. 'They are of a globular form & of various sizes from that of a small pin's head to that of a Pea.' He had tried the usual therapy, warming the nether regions, to no avail. 'As it is an opinion pretty generally received that Hydatids are Insects, it occurd to me that Oil of Turpentine might be so introduced into the System as to destroy them. . . .' The patient took the new medicine and seemed to improve. 'For this last fortnight he has omitted the use of his Medicines supposing himself quite well, but he is now put upon the use of the Turpentine again.'

Jenner apparently sent a copy of this paper to Hunter, who replied in December: 'I have just now forgot the case of the Hydatids. but if there was any thing that struck me I dar say it is laid by They are frequently in the Kidnies. but I should doubt your oil of Turpentine having any merit in bring them away.' He agreed they are alive, however: 'My reason for supposing them animals is because they move after they have been extracted I have taken them out of the Head or brain of a sheep, and they have contracted in difft. parts. . .when put into warm water.' The subject of hydatids continued to interest Jenner, and he does not appear to have made any substantive changes in his opinions about them in later years, but I have found no more records of observations from his patients.

At the end of this letter on hydatids, Hunter wrote: 'How does Mrs Jenner do? dar you bring her to London?'; and a year later: '. . .I have been informed that Mrs J has been extremely ill.' Catherine Jenner's health seems never to have been robust. Doubtless the melancholia of which Fosbroke wrote derived in part from physical weakness. Whether the marks of the disease that finally killed her were evident when she was married no one knows, but in those days the slight breathlessness and weakness of early tuberculosis were easily overlooked. The illness that prompted Hunter's inquiry could also have been attributed to the late effects of childbirth. Unfortunately, this is all we know of the day-to-day Catherine shortly after her marriage, except that toward the end of 1789, when Edward junior was about ten months old, she was staying with her brother at Kingscote.

This minor biographical item takes on importance because it led Edward senior to participate in a remarkable experiment in inoculation. On 18 July 1790, just before a paper by Ludlow and Jenner's contribution on hydatids, Dr Hickes reported on 'an eruptive dis[ease] which has lately spread itself thro many parts of Glostershire, and which is known among the common people. . .by the name of the Swine Pox.' At the September meeting of the Medical Society, Hickes and Jenner together presented further details. The disease was observed in a girl at Kingshill, Dursley, on 9 December 1789. She had returned a few days before from Kingscote, where she had been nurse to infant Edward. Because there was a possibility that the former nurse had smallpox, and that Edward was therefore at risk, his father inoculated him on 17 December with matter from the girl's pustules. At the same time and with the same matter he inoculated two girls, servants to Revd Furnell of Kingshill who had also been exposed. Jenner reported to Hickes: 'The two young women who were inoculated at King's-hill with the swine-pox matter sickened on the 9th day after its insertion into the arm. . . .a few pustules or rather little eminences appeared which did not suppurate – They very much resembled the eruptions in the case of Edward Jenner. . . .' All three were later inoculated with smallpox with no effect, showing the putative swinepox inoculation had provided protection. According to Baron, furthermore, Edward junior was variolated again in April 1791, when he showed a mild reaction, and a year later Jenner sought to make sure his son was safe. Unlike cowpox, swinepox lacked local lore as a smallpox preventive. Curiously, in 1810 when the antivaccinists trumpeted his use of variolation to protect his own children, Jenner wrote to a supporter: 'My two eldest children were inoculated for the Small-pox, before I began to inoculate for the cow-pox', failing to mention the swinepox inoculation. Had he forgotten it? Another explanation seems more likely.

Dr Hickes reported to the Medical Society that there had been an outbreak of swinepox in Gloucester Infirmary, where he had first observed the disease. It was considered so similar to smallpox that many doctors believed it was not a distinct disease. 'Upon the whole,' he said, 'we may conclude that if it be not the small-pox, it certainly is a disease which renders a person. . .much less likely to receive the infection of the small-pox. . . .' By the end of the decade, Jenner also believed that he had actually inoculated Edward junior and the two servant girls with a mild form of smallpox. To a Mr Fry, surgeon at Dursley, he wrote about the swinepox, 'This was the mild variety of the Small Pox'. The disease persisted in the neighbourhood of Kingscote for about a year, until roughly the time Hickes read his paper, and then disappeared. Further to confuse the matter, Hickes added that at nearby Stroud, it was 'called by the common people some times the pig-pox, but more frequently the cow-pox – '.

Nor were Hickes and Jenner alone in their confusion. Cowpox, swinepox and a pox-like infection of horses' heels called 'grease', were of course animal diseases. All three could infect humans, and when that happened, they became hard to distinguish. What is more, symptoms resembled human disorders, notably smallpox, but also chicken-pox and measles. Eighteenth-century physicians had not observed the distinctions amongst the most prominent symptoms of the human diseases, the rashes, which their twentieth-century successors used for diagnosis: for example, the universal appearance of white spots inside the cheeks of people about to develop a measles rash; and the tendency of the smallpox rash to appear all at once, concentrated on the extremities, whereas the chicken-pox rash spreads slowly from a concentration on the trunk outwards. Dr William Heberden had read a paper 'On the Chicken-Pox' to the Royal Society, published in 1768, which was supposed to distinguish clearly between that mild affliction and smallpox, but all of these diseases were classified as eruptive fevers, and because of smallpox, all of them caused alarm. In the face of uncertainty, it was customary to variolate the patient. If nothing happened, the previous disease had been smallpox; if smallpox developed, then it had been chicken-pox or measles. Later, when a previously vaccinated patient developed a rash and fever, the only proof of its nature acceptable to both the vaccinists and their opponents was to inoculate a child known not to have had smallpox with the contents of a pustule from the rash in question.

All pox diseases, including swinepox and 'grease' or horse-pox but excluding chicken-pox, are caused by a member of the orthopox virus family. Chicken-pox is caused by a herpes virus; as most of us will remember, it cannot be prevented by vaccination. The orthopox virus family is united by one characteristic: 'that infection with one member will confer specific immunity to the other members.' Pox diseases also infect sheep, cats, goats, molluscs, rabbits, canaries, monkeys, camels, buffalos and more besides. Back in 1813 a British resident of Bushire in Persia wrote to another Briton in Bombay that in Persia cowpox was widely known as a protection against smallpox, but that it was more commonly caught from sheep. Indeed, cowpox is not primarily a disease of cows, 'but may be a disease of rodents which occasionally infects cows, man, and other mammals'.

The ultimate irony, however, is that by the time between the two world wars that technological advances had made possible identification of viruses, the virus found in the vaccines then being used bore no more than a family resemblance to all of the others associated with pox in one species or another, including humans – and cows. Called 'vaccinia' because it is found only in vaccine, this pox variant is known by the scientific name: *Poxvirus officinalis*. In the opinion of Derrick Baxby, the English virologist who has done more than anyone to unravel the mystery of which pox viruses were actually being used by medical men during the early years of vaccination, 'vaccinia virus may derive from a now extinct poxvirus of horses and possibly other animals, including small rodents.' As we shall see, Jenner's first controversy arose from his assertion that cowpox originated when cows were infected with the horse disease, grease, by milkers who had previously tended the infected horses. But if unexpectedly he should now be proven right about that less important detail, what evidence is there that he was actually using cowpox matter as a preventive of smallpox? Argument began after accidental contamination of cowpox lymph in 1799, and continues to this day. Because no one can look at the inocula then being used, the question is ultimately unanswerable. Jenner himself always believed that his preventive was the cowpox 'virus', a word which he used to mean an infectious principle rather than specific particles, about which he knew nothing. Yet he later experimented successfully with matter from the greasy heel of a horse. On one occasion before the crucial experiment of 1796 with cowpox, moreover, he inoculated with what he at first believed to be swinepox, albeit some people called swinepox 'cowpox'. Although all the pox viruses induce immunity against all the others, this multiplicity of potentially usable vaccines was misunderstood, and proved time and again to be dangerously misleading to both Jenner and his contemporaries.

The swinepox incident probably served to restore Jenner's priorities. Because of Hunter, he later said, as well as the relative rarity of the disease amongst his patients, he felt unable to pursue the interesting subject of angina pectoris. Hydatids continued to interest him too, but they could be neither prevented nor cured, whatever their connections with tubercles and cancer. At both the June and July meetings of the Medico-Convivial Society in 1792, Jenner reported case histories. The first concerned a 'Boy that passed an extraneous substance into the Bladder and another Case of the sudden absorption of the fluid from an Hydrocele', water filling a fairly large internal cavity. Incidentally, the remaining 'Transactions' of the Society show no meetings during 1791, only two during the next year and one in June 1793. Bound with the 'Transactions', however, is an interesting fragment in Jenner's handwriting:

> We hear that an eruptive Disease has lately spread thro many parts of the County of Gloc in its appearance very similar to the small pox, but generally called by the People of that County Swine or Pig-Pox. It is there believed that this Disease acquired either in the natural way or by inoculation, is capable of preserving the Patient from the infection of the small-Pox – It is with pleasure we announce to the Public that the Members of the Medical Socy. who meet at Rodbor', have for some months past been engaged in an experiment enquiring into the nature of the disease, the result of which will appear in the 1st Vol. of their mem. which they propose publishing in the course of the ensuing Year.

Probably dated from 1790, this reads like the draft of an advertisement to appear in the *Glocester Journal*. No doubt it failed to appear because Jenner and Hickes became convinced that they had been variolating using a mild form of smallpox after all. The only really suitable candidate for protection against smallpox appeared to be cowpox.

After years during which he had occasionally discussed the cowpox disease with Hunter, who mentioned it in his lectures, and with lay friends like Gardner, Jenner had taken to London with him early in 1788 drawings of cowpox pustules on milkers' hands. He had shown them to Everard Home and others. The gradual spread of medical interest that originated with Jenner is illustrated by a letter dated 15 April 1794 from Dr Haygarth of Chester, the man who had urged a general programme of variolation to stop smallpox, to Dr Richard Worthington. Jenner probably met Worthington in London, and they became close friends, particularly after Jenner began to practise in Cheltenham in 1794. Worthington was soon to be instrumental in shaping the published version of Jenner's first and most important vaccination book. He had evidently written to Haygarth about Jenner's interest in cowpox. Haygarth replied expressing many doubts and urging that 'no reliance will be placed on vulgar stories.' Meanwhile in London, Dr Joseph Adams, another of Hunter's auditors, had learned about the cowpox preventive in discussions with Hunter's student, the surgeon Henry Cline, and had mentioned the phenomenon in the first edition of his influential book, *Observations on Morbid Poisons, Chronic and Acute*. For various reasons, Jenner's own attempts to understand cowpox continued slowly.

On 7 July 1792, the academic senate of St Andrews University in Scotland conferred the degree of Doctor in Medicine on Edward Jenner of Berkeley, Surgeon. The degree was purchased by a gift to the university which was accompanied, in the case of St Andrews, by a letter of recommendation from two doctors certifying that the 'candidate for the degree of Doctor in Medicine, is a gentleman of respectable character, that he has received a liberal and classical education, that he has attended a complete course of lectures in the several branches of Medicine, and that from *personal knowledge* we judge him worthy of the honour of a doctor's degree in Medicine.' Jenner's recommendation was signed by his two old friends, Caleb Parry and John Hickes. All of the Scottish universities had begun the practice of selling degrees under similar circumstances during the eighteenth century. It was a response, of course, to pressure from south of the border arising out of the monopoly of the degree exercised by Oxford and Cambridge. Not until a Royal Commission had condemned the system in 1830 did the Scottish universities abandon it, but by that time the University of London and several teaching hospitals had broken the Oxbridge monopoly.

Dr Baron says that Jenner decided to obtain an MD, 'The fatigues of general practice [including surgery] having become irksome'. He was already being called 'Doctor' by his family and friends, and three years earlier he referred to himself as a physician, not a surgeon, in a long letter to Revd John Clinch in St John, Newfoundland. However, Jenner never hid his diffidence. He wrote to Clinch:

A man must be guided by his own genius; indeed, without a good portion of this a physician must ever cut a poor figure; and if he should be a man of fine feelings he must often be subject to unpleasant sensations within himself. Something new is for ever presenting itself – neither books, lectures, nor the longest experience are sufficient to store his mind with the undescribable something a man of our profession should possess.

Later in the same letter, he added: 'For it is by appearances. . .not from a real knowledge of things, that the world. . .form a judgement. A look of significance, a peculiar habit, and a very scanty acquaintance with the human machine, will make a man pass current for a great physician.' His humility is no less real than the quest for status that the degree unquestionably conferred.

In fact his practice seems to have changed very little. Happily, there is direct, detailed evidence in the form of a visiting book, which also lists fees received and outgoings day by day for the entire year 1794. This windfall is repeated only once, in 1803, when his brief fling in London can be usefully contrasted with the country practice. Of course, there was another important difference: by 1803 he was famous.

On 2 January 1794, having advanced ten guineas to Mrs Jenner, he visited a patient in Stroud where he had evidently been called in as a consultant. His fee was three guineas. Almost every day he rode somewhere to call on a patient. On the 9th, it was a Miss Jones closer to Berkeley; he assisted her surgeon with a trepanning, a serious operation to relieve pressure on the brain by making a small hole in the skull. Needless to say, he saw Miss Jones frequently during the coming months. On the 20th, he prescribed for Mrs Niblet in Thornbury, having begun the day nearby in Whitminster and then ridden to Dursley, a round trip of about twenty miles and in January. Lord Berkeley paid him a fee of £20, and he received two years' rent amounting to twelve guineas on the 29th. Prescriptions, consultations and minor operations fill the days. On 31 March, he gave advice to a coachman of Lord Ducie, another local landowner; 'the last time,' he noted cryptically. In May outgoings included three guineas to the Gloucester Infirmary. On the 19th, he received £1-12-3 from a patient named Whithorn for thirty-six calls and going with him to Bath, including the cost of a chaise. Doctor and patient made the journey again four days later. Perhaps Jenner was consulting Caleb Parry. A few days later he 'applied Leeches etc' to a patient in Uley. The longest break in his busy schedule that year lasted six days, between 4 and 10 September. He also appears to have made no visits on 12 August, the day his second child, Catherine, was christened.

On 27 October, Jenner removed a growth from the face of his brother-in-law, Revd William Davies, who came to Berkeley from Eastington for the operation. A month later, Jenner performed further minor surgery for William, who recorded in his household accounts that he paid Edward five guineas and his nephew, Henry, two guineas 'for his Attendance at the Operation'.

Henry Jenner, now a surgeon and apothecary, had again become his uncle's assistant. On 6 June 1794, he was paid an advance of £10 against his salary. He had been apprenticed professionally to his uncle, after which he followed partially in Edward's footsteps by spending much of the year 1792 in John Hunter's household. Although his name appears in a list of the household made by Hunter's seventeen-year-old apprentice and secretary, William Clift, all the others outside the family except Henry are designated 'Pupils'.

Could it be that Henry was there solely because of Hunter's friendly response to Jenner's wish that his nephew benefit from observing the great man? Henry also had an opportunity to work on botanical specimens for Joseph Banks, and he was made a Fellow of the Linnaean Society. On 13 December 1792, Henry married Susannah Pearce of Stone, daughter of the lawyer, Thomas Pearce, and received a dower of £1300. At the age of twenty-five he seems to have been an ideal assistant. Yet unexceptionable though Henry's career had been, he was to become a source of serious concern to his aunt and uncle.

Jenner's most eminent local patients were the members of the Berkeley family. Hunter wrote to him about one of them, Frederick Berkeley, a younger son of the Earl, who had consulted Hunter about 'being lame of one leg I think the left'. Berkeley was returning to the castle, and Hunter recommended sea-bathing as 'the only preventive I know' for what he feared might be a nascent lumbar abscess.

The letter was dated 12 August 1793. Two months later Hunter collapsed at St George's Hospital, London, and died of coronary heart disease. It is said that he lost his temper in an argument with colleagues during a committee meeting. Jenner had feared he was unaware of his condition, but Hunter had written: 'My life is in the hands of any fool who cares to upset me.' To his pupil, admirer and friend, Hunter's death must have been an emotional shock as well as a professional loss, but it may also have freed Edward, now aged forty-four. He had still to make the quantum leap from cowpox, the accidental protector, to cowpox, the transmissible preventive. In Hunter's mighty shadow, would he have had the incentive or the time?

Jenner's last recorded appointment during the busy year 1794 was with a Mrs Purnell on 10 December. Soon afterwards he became ill himself with what was then called typhus. It was probably typhoid fever, a very serious contagious disease carried in foul water but not distinguished from typhus until after Jenner's death. Mrs Jenner had evidently suffered from the disease earlier, and indeed it was quite common. Jenner himself had had 'the dreadful fever' in 1786 and again two years later when he thought it was associated with a cold. But the attack at the end of 1794 was especially severe. Dr Parry attended him five times all the way from Bath. Dr Hickes came from Gloucester five times, and Ludlow from Sodbury as many. 'My medicine is the Cascarilla bark,' he wrote to a medical friend, W. F. Shrapnell of Gloucester. This is not quinine of course, but a laxative; neither could have been of much use. Henry's wife, sister and infant daughter were also ill, and a servant girl in Henry's house died. Jenner believed he had been afflicted by 'the venomed arrow' while attending Susannah Jenner, but that he might have thrown it off 'had it not been for a dreary, wearisome ride over mountains of ice'. Evidently it was a winter to remember, according to the Revd William Davies senior:

A severe Frost began Xmas Eve 1794 & lasted to January 16th 1795 when a sudden & rapid Thaw from a deep Snow commenced which occasioned the largest Flood January 27 in the Meadows opposite the Parlor Windows I ever remember. . . .January 28th. a very hard Frost which continued to Febry. 8th. when there was another thaw accompanied with a twenty Hours Rain which produced a second great Flood. [The vicarage at Eastington was built on bottom land near a small river. Flooding was probably not a problem on Berkeley's hilltop site.]

Henry was too busy with his own household to see to his uncle, and then fell ill himself, but his brother George, almost alone in the family, escaped and was able to look after Edward. After a month the fever left him 'so feeble that I think a great matter has been achieved when I quit my bed for an hour or two, and hobble across my chamber.' Recuperation took weeks, although by March the Revd Nathaniel Thornbury of Avening, fifteen miles from Berkeley, could congratulate him on his recovery. In April he was able to ride to Frampton with William Davies junior, and early in May he and Mrs Jenner visited her brother along with William and his mother.

That summer of 1795, the Jenners took a house in the spa town of Cheltenham, eight miles north of Gloucester. At first it was probably intended as a family holiday and diversion. Everyone needed a change from the rigours of cold, disease and medical practice. Only slowly, almost as an afterthought, like so many of the actions which shaped his life, did Cheltenham become Jenner's second home, the source of a second practice of major financial and social import.

Twenty years later William Cobbett wrote that Cheltenham

is what they call 'a watering place;' that is to say, a place, to which East India plunderers, West India floggers, English tax-gorgers, together with gluttons, drunkards and debauchees of all descriptions, female as well as male, resort, at the suggestion of silently laughing quacks, in the hope of getting rid of the bodily consequences of their manifold sins and iniquities.

Though the town fathers might not have welcomed the description, preferring to call attention to the waters which had provided Cheltenham's *raison d'être*, Cobbett was as always applying only the smallest distorting lens. For example, as to 'East India plunderers', Warren Hastings, from an old Cheltenham family, was acquitted on 23 April 1795 of various frauds and misuses of power after a trial lasting seven years, causing 'great rejoicing' in the town. Cheltenham had long been a fashionable resort for local people. Each year the *Glocester Journal* published week after week the names of the arrivals for the season. On 26 August 1782 they included Mr Kingscote, and Jenner's Berkeley relative,

Mr Phillimore. Then in 1788 George III visited the town, staying in Bays Hill Lodge belonging to Lord Fauconberg. He was convalescent from a stomach disorder and spasms, which may have been early symptoms of the mental disorder that shortly overtook the poor man. Whatever the circumstances, the presence of the King made the town. Members of the Berkeley clan as well as more of the gentry like the Jenners settled there for several months every year.

Although Cheltenham now served a valuable purpose, aiding in his recovery from a debilitating disease, Jenner's enjoyment of society always required time and attention. Indeed, even his marriage into the Kingscote family reflects this side of his personality, though Catherine seems to have shared his sociability only very partially. She was a religious woman, apparently with few friends, and one is inclined to the view that Edward and probably her children (though direct evidence is lacking) were the only other interests in her life. She certainly ran a house where her husband's needs and preferences prevailed. 'Dined and spent the day at Dr. Jenner's with a large party,' noted William Davies junior in his diary, on 6 September 1792. On various other occasions young William dined or drank tea with his uncle, often with other guests. About a year after the large party, he mentions being invited to share a haunch of venison, for William Davies the apogee of culinary bliss. Occasionally, he reports having dined with Dr Jenner and one or both of his other Jenner uncles at his father's house. His aunts are not named. Dr Baron, who knew Mrs Jenner, attributes her absences to her poor health. No doubt it played a role.

The younger Reverend Davies took his friend, Thomas Fosbroke, to dine with his uncle on 20 June 1793, probably the occasion on which Jenner made the acquaintance of one of his earliest and more eccentric chroniclers. It was Davies's first meeting with Jenner after a lapse of four months, denoting Jenner's absence from Berkeley, either at Kingscote or possibly in London. That the pattern of his relations with Fosbroke had been established quickly is revealed under the heading 'Mr Fosbrokes Acct' in Davies senior's household accounts: 'Novr. 22. [1794] Dr. Jenner lent Mr. Fosbroke 2.2.0'.

Jenner's social life apparently extended beyond the Medico-Convivial Society, furthermore, to a club in Berkeley also attended occasionally by William Davies junior. Davies first mentions it in February 1792 and then occasionally during the next three years, referring once to 'Dr. Jenner's Ladies Club'. Could this have been a mixed-sex social gathering, rare indeed in the eighteenth century except in the home or at a heavily chaperoned grand occasion such as a ball? Where did this club meet? Did Catherine Jenner attend? Young Davies's laconic references provide no answers.

From 22 March 1792, when William Davies jr wrote: 'Dined at Dr. Jenner's' until long after his uncle's death, he kept a telegraphic daily diary of his comings and goings. During most of these years, he performed many of the functions of an estate manager for his uncle. Davies recorded the more pedestrian, country side of Jenner's social life, along with his family attachments – an important factor in his motivation for refusing opportunities in London and overseas.

In the late autumn of 1795 the Jenners returned to Berkeley, shortly to face one of those unforeseeable family tragedies. Edward's nephews, Henry and George, had an elder brother, Stephen, who was an officer on a troopship, the *Catherine*. She was headed for the West Indies when she was wrecked off Portland Bill in a storm, with the loss of all aboard. Edward heard the news almost at once from W. F. Shrapnell, surgeon to the South Gloucester Militia then stationed at Weymouth.

As his health improved after typhoid fever, Edward began to enter Cheltenham society, with credit to his purse as well as debits. In September 1795, he wrote to his nephew William: 'I pick up a few Fees – Mrs J has puff'd me too high in her Letter – However, Fortune has shewn me the Countenance of George the third thirteen times since this day se'ennight.' 'Famous!' Jenner went on. 'This was owing to a coincidence of Events that cannot from the nature of things be lasting.'

What can he have meant? The answer must be circumstantial, but at this time news of Jenner's involvement in a spectacular murder case would have been circulating. The trial took place in Gloucester in mid-April 1796, but the murder itself had been perpetrated exactly two years before. In the early hours of 17 April 1794, a messenger from the landlord of a small cottage at Swanley on the Bristol Road called on Henry Jenner to come at once. Henry found a middle-aged man named William Reed with bleeding scalp wounds and severe stomach pains. After binding the man's head and giving a purgative, Henry left, promising to return the next day.

William Reed had been travelling from his home in Poole with his much younger wife, Mary, her brother James Watkins, and a medical student named Robert Edgar. Mrs Reed had married for money. Probably soon after the wedding, she had begun to give Reed poison. Feeling ill, he had made a will leaving Mary £6000. Her brother, Watkins, suggested that he could induce Edgar to marry her, and brother and sister apparently decided to murder Reed together. The deed could not be performed in Poole, however, because all but Edgar were known there, and the circumstances of the wedding may well have been a subject of local gossip. Reed was induced to embark on a journey to Bristol along with his wife, her brother and her putative lover, during which the brother was to finish him off in exchange for £200. The unlikely party stopped at Swanley the night of the 15th. Mary prepared poisoned soup for Reed, who was then beaten by Watkins with a broomstick. The same thing happened on the next day, but this time the landlord took fright and called a doctor, Henry Jenner.

When Henry left the cottage, Mary Reed put her husband to bed again and told her brother to finish the job. Reed died, but apparently from the poison. Thus, Henry found him on the 18th. He gave some of Reed's vomit to a dog, which promptly died. At the same time he asked his uncle to analyse the stomach contents. Edward found both arsenic and mercury. He too sacrificed a dog in the search for justice. Charles Brandon Trye, surgeon at the Gloucester Infirmary, was called in for a second opinion and agreed Reed had died of poisoning. Thereupon Mrs Reed and James Watkins fled. Edgar told all to the authorities. An inquest reached a verdict of wilful murder. Watkins shot himself, but Mary Reed was eventually arrested by Bow Street runners, the private-enterprise predecessors of the Metropolitan Police. She was tried and found guilty at Gloucester Assizes, Edward Jenner being amongst those who testified for the Crown.

The trial of Mary Reed took place a bare month before Jenner laid a much firmer foundation for his eternal fame. He had been observing cowpox for years. He had even perceived the distinction between true cowpox and what he called 'spurious cowpox', which could explain why some of those who contracted cowpox nevertheless caught smallpox later. Although there is no evidence that he experimented with cowpox from the animal, he had certainly tried inoculation with what he believed was swinepox from the animal, though he later changed his mind. One of his problems was the uncertain supply of animals with any of the pox-like diseases, let alone cows with cowpox. The disease regularly disappeared for extended periods from the dairies of the Vale of Berkeley. At some time, perhaps while he was convalescing in Cheltenham, Jenner realized that if cowpox was ever to be a useful preventive of smallpox the protective substance had to be transferable from human to human in the same way that smallpox was transferred in variolation. He had to conduct an experiment to see if such a transfer worked. Edward Gardner certainly knew about the plan in advance. Henry and George Jenner probably did, and it would be surprising if other members of his family – Catherine and her brother Robert Kingscote, Stephen Jenner and Mary Black, both living in Berkeley, Anne and William Davies in nearby Eastington, William Davies junior and his brothers, Robert and Edward – were not also among those who knew the drift of Edward's thoughts. In fact in view of Jenner's aversion to secrecy and love of conversation, the knowledge probably spread to Parry, Hickes, Paytherus, Ludlow, Trye and beyond. Perhaps the idea of inoculating for cowpox with the contents of a human cowpox pustule actually came from one of them. Though no one else claimed it, we shall never know for sure. The point is that in full knowledge of what he was attempting, Jenner did something about it.

Jenner saw no ethical barrier to the experiment. Inoculation against smallpox had been enshrined in medicine if not in the public's heart.

John Hunter had even inoculated experimentally against syphilis and gon-orrhoea, no doubt permanently infecting his unsuspecting subjects. Cowpox was usually a mild disease. Its most prominent symptoms were the inflamed spots or pustules about the finger joints and at their tips. They tended to be circular with edges higher than their centres, and a bluish colour. If they were scratched, pustules might develop elsewhere on the body, and the sores that remained healed slowly. Swellings might appear temporarily in the armpits. The person might have a quickened pulse, fever, lassitude, some joint pains and headache, and she might vomit. But it all passed fairly quickly. No one knew of any deaths from cowpox.

Even before the crucial experiment, Jenner had been collecting cases of milkmaids and cowherds protected against smallpox by cowpox that they had caught accidentally from the animals they handled. On 7 May 1796, his friend W. F. Shrapnell wrote to Jenner about a monument to his nephew, Captain Stephen Jenner, the erection of which he was supervising. His letter continued:

> I do not believe Dr Gravess knowledge of the Cowpox much more than what Major Tenet communicated to him which were of course your Ideas, but I shall prevent him from making any thing publick untill after your paper appears however, he has just published a pocket conspectus of the Pharmacopoeas with the doses, accent, etc a very useful book, worth the attention of a Country apothecary or any one to refer too, occasionally, –

Legend to the contrary notwithstanding, the donor of the cowpox lymph, a young woman named Sarah Nelmes, was the daughter of a prosperous farmer at Breadstone, a hamlet within Berkeley parish. According to my gossipy late colleague, Paul Saunders of Cheltenham, the local church has four Nelmes family tombs with armorial bearings, a sign of landownership and some wealth. Nevertheless, in May 1796 Sarah had contracted cowpox through a thorn scratch on her hand while milking cows belonging to her master, possibly her father.

'The more accurately to observe the progress of the infection, I selected a healthy boy. . .', Jenner wrote in the book that announced his work on vaccination. James Phipps was about eight. His father was a landless labourer who often worked for the Jenners. For generations the family had lived in Berkeley, probably on the edge of poverty. Their births, marriages and deaths are chronicled in the parish records, and as early as 1745 Stephen Jenner, then the vicar, paid 2s to a James Phipps for beef on behalf of his father-in-law, Mr Head. On 14 May 1796, this Phipps' grand- or great-grandson held out his left arm so that Dr Jenner could make two incisions, 'each about half an inch long'. Using the point of a clean lancet dipped into the pale liquid that had seeped from an incision in the pustule on Sarah Nelmes's hand, he placed the lymph in the incisions on the boy's arm.

After about four days, some redness appeared around the incisions, and four or five days later two pustules with reddish raised edges and a bluish sunken centre rose over the sites, 'much the same as when produced in a similar manner by variolous matter' – one of several statements in the *Inquiry* that were to cause Jenner much future trouble. James suffered only the mildest lassitude and fever for a day or two, and was well again.

On 1 June, according to William Davies junior, 'My Uncle Dr. Jenner & his family left Berkeley this day for Cheltenham – they return'd Decr. 7.' William's next entry concerning his uncle, dated 20 August, reads: 'My Uncle Dr. Jenner came from Cheltenham this day & left Berkeley in the morning.' On 19 July, however, Edward wrote to Edward Gardner:

> As I promised to let you know how I proceeded in my Inquiry into the nature of that singular disease the cowpox & being fully satisfied how much you feel interested in its success, you will be gratified in hearing that I have at length accomplish'd what I have been so long waiting for, the passing of the vaccine Virus from one human being to another by the ordinary mode of Inoculation.
>
> A boy of the name of Phipps was inoculated in the arm from a Pustule on the hand of a young Woman who was infected by her Masters Cows. Having never seen the disease but in its casual way before, that is, when communicated from the Cow to the hand of the Milker, I was astonish'd at the close resemblance of the Pustules in some of their stages to the variolous Pustules. But now listen to the most delightful part of my Story. The Boy has since been inoculated for the small pox which as I ventured to predict produc'd no effect. I shall now pursue my Experiments with redoubled ardor.

The letter was written at Berkeley. There is a PS: 'You wd. have heard from me sooner had I not expected to have seen you.'

James Phipps had been variolated on 1 July. Jenner would have waited at least fourteen days, known to be the incubation period for smallpox, before he could have felt certain that the variolation would not 'take', and he wrote to his friend very soon afterwards. But why should this important visit to his country home have escaped the attention of the meticulous William Davies? In August a month later, he noted a visit lasting overnight, less than a day. Yet he omits a stay of almost three weeks. Other entries in his diary prove that Davies was himself present in the neighbourhood during June and July. One explanation, suggested by Jenner's behaviour nine years earlier in preparing his original draft of the paper on cuckoos, is that his attitude to research could be casual to the point of irresponsibility. In 1787 he had accepted unchecked the observations of his nephew, Henry. In 1796, if the evidence of the Gardner letter and the Davies diary is to be accepted, he returned to Berkeley briefly, perhaps without the knowledge of William Davies, only after the variolation had been performed and the negative results noted, probably by the same Henry Jenner, to see for himself. During that brief stay he wrote to Gardner whom he had expected to see earlier in Cheltenham, not in Berkeley.

In professional terms he was well within his prerogatives to have acted in this manner. Physicians by and large did not variolate. No physic, in the eighteenth-century meaning of the word, was involved, so that variolation was left to surgeons and apothecaries. Fortunately for Jenner, and mankind, Henry had not slipped up this time. James Phipps's lack of reaction to variolation was caused by a successful vaccination – the first one performed by the transfer of fluid from one person to another. It seems extraordinary that Jenner would not have wished to do the variolation himself and to observe his patient during this crucial test of his theory. Yet if he did not, the explanation lies not only in the medical mores of the time, but in Jenner's mental bent. The letter to Gardner begins by highlighting 'my Inquiry into the nature of that singular disease the cowpox', an intellectual exercise. Although he ends by proposing to pursue his 'Experiments with redoubled ardor', he was now defending a theory: that cowpox transmitted from human to human would prevent smallpox. As with his insistence on similarities between the smallpox and cowpox pustules, also a feature of this significant letter, Jenner could appear maddeningly casual about details while gliding flexibly from one generalization to another. Conversely, he could stick at some seemingly minor practical detail and lose the wood amongst the trees. Perhaps even now, in the dawn of greatness, his central flaw, a lack of perspective judgement, serrated the horizon like a mountain range.

Chapter 5

'To the King'
1796–1800

On 13 September 1796, Joseph Farington, member of the Royal Academy and a copious diarist, noted his first meeting with Edward Jenner, then on a visit to London. A fortnight later, 'Dr. Jenner shewed us some lines which the Revd. Dr. Steevens gave him as having been written by Gray as part of his Elegy in a country Church Yard, but were omitted.' Jenner was probably staying with his brother-in-law, the banker Robert Ladbroke, but what his business in London was, we can only speculate. Satisfied with the import of his vaccination of Phipps, Jenner had, I believe, taken an early version of his *Inquiry* to London to submit for publication in the *Philosophical Transactions* of the Royal Society through its President, Sir Joseph Banks, with the support of Everard Home. Banks asked Lord Somerville, President of the Board of Agriculture, to read the manuscript. Somerville in turn showed it to 'Mr Dolland, a surgeon, who resides in a dairy county remote from this,' said Jenner, and Dolland confirmed the thesis that cowpox protects against smallpox. Nevertheless, almost certainly because of the paucity of experimental proof in the original paper, Sir Joseph decided against publication, advising that Jenner 'ought not to risk his reputation by presenting to the learned body anything which appeared so much at variance with established knowledge.' Although when the *Inquiry* appeared it contained several more cases of vaccination, cowpox disappeared from the dairies of the Vale of Berkeley between mid-1796 and the spring of 1798. There seemed little Jenner could do for the moment.

By early October he was back in Cheltenham with his family. They remained until 7 December, returning to Berkeley to face one of the coldest winters in years. On Christmas Day, according to the Revd. William Davies senior, the thermometer at Stroud registered 12 degrees and at Oxford in the Observatory, zero Fahrenheit. Soon after Christmas Jenner took his family back to Cheltenham because of the weather, while he himself moved into Berkeley Castle. Lady Berkeley was suffering repeated haemorrhages after childbirth. For ten years she and her family had been Jenner's patients, so that he felt compliance was essential when the Earl begged him to stay close to her.

This was in fact Lady Berkeley's first legitimate child. She had been the Earl's mistress since 1785, and her first child had been born the next year. Mary Cole, daughter of a Gloucester butcher, had met her lover and future husband, then aged forty, through her sister. The nature of their liaison was widely known in Gloucester and especially in Berkeley where, according to one modern writer, Catherine Jenner 'alone, of all the villagers, openly disapproved.' If that is true, it could be another reason why Catherine and her two children returned to Cheltenham when Edward moved temporarily into the castle.

Nature, perhaps unhindered by Dr Jenner, pulled Lady Berkeley through. She and the Earl had been married in London on 16 May 1796, but upon the Earl's death it would transpire that he had caused the Berkeley parish register to contain a forged record of a marriage dated 1785. The subsequent hearing on the Berkeley inheritance before the House of Lords required Jenner's reluctant attendance and testimony. Meanwhile, the Countess had borne the Earl four more children. She outlived him by thirty-five years.

By staying in Berkeley Edward could also attend Stephen Jenner, his eldest brother. After an illness lasting about eight weeks, Stephen died on 23 February 1797. His loss must have been a great blow. Stephen had provided a home for them both for a decade and a half after Edward returned from studying with John Hunter. Judging from the account books that remain, Stephen husbanded their landed property and no doubt stood emotionally *in loco parentis*. By comparison their middle sister, Sarah, was a stranger. After her marriage she had settled in Birmingham, where she had died in 1786. The Revd Henry Jenner, the middle brother and father of Henry and George, died at Burbage a year after Stephen. For the three who remained, Mary Black living out her widowhood in Berkeley, Anne Davies in nearby Eastington, and Edward, there was now a long respite from death.

Stephen had been the perpetual curate of Stone. On 24 August 1797 that living was presented to William Davies junior, Anne's son, whose diaries provide the skeleton for Jenner's life in Gloucestershire.

Shortly after Stephen was buried in Berkeley church, Mary Black wrote to a cousin, Elizabeth Hodges: 'The Doctor & Mrs. Jenner are as well as can be supposed in these times of affliction, their dear children are very well, a further increase expected about the end of next month.' Indeed, Robert Fitzhardinge was born on 4 April 1797, earlier than his aunt had expected. Although his first name again commemorated the Kingscote connection, his second was the Berkeley family name. The first major event in the infant's life took place a year later. On 12 April 1798, soon after cowpox had again appeared near Berkeley, Robert was one of four children to be vaccinated by his father. Jenner noted in the *Inquiry* that of the four, only Robert's did not take. However, he did not repeat the inoculation, and later that year in Cheltenham the baby was exposed to smallpox. Again there was no cowpox immediately available, so Jenner took the one remaining sensible precaution: he had Robert variolated. In May 1803 one Revd Dr Ramsden of Grundisburgh, Suffolk, revealed this alleged secret to an assembly at Cambridge University. Despite attempts by Jenner and his partisans to publicize the actual sequence of events, antivaccinists continued to trumpet the Ramsden version as proof that even Jenner distrusted vaccination when it came to his own.

During that March 1797, soon after Stephen's burial, Jenner spent a few days at Rudhall near Ross, the home of a Cheltenham friend, Thomas Westfaling. Richard Worthington, John Hickes and Edward Gardner were also invited, and Jenner's friend, Thomas Paytherus, then practised at Ross. He wanted these gentlemen to form an ad hoc editorial committee on the *Inquiry*, now eighteen months late, as it were, because of Banks's decision. The fact that there were two or more very similar original manuscripts may be explained by the number of people whom Jenner asked to read and criticize the paper in a limited time. One of these was dated on the title page by the author, 'Berkeley, March 29, 1797', but it contains a dedication in the form of a letter, also from Berkeley, to Dr Caleb Hillier Parry dated 10 July, something more than three months later. Now it is possible that a copy was sent to Home for Banks during this period, but both of the manuscripts contain changes indicating that the Royal Society was no longer being considered as publisher. For example, the phrases 'on the Minds of this Society' and 'to the satisfaction of this learned Body' have been crossed out. I think that during the March meeting his friends advised him, in light of the doubt Banks had expressed, to publish privately. An advertisement in the *Glocester Journal* on 21 August announced early publication of 'An Enquiry into the Natural History of a Disease known in some of the Western Counties of England, particularly Glocestershire, by the name of the Cow-Pox; with observations on Inoculation, and on the Origin of the Small Pox. By Edward Jenner, M.D. F.R.S.' That version never appeared.

In August Catherine Jenner took her children to Cheltenham, where Edward followed her the next month. Their stay seems to have been unusually short because Dr and Mrs Jenner with Edward and Catherine went to London for two months in mid-October, staying again with Catherine's sister and brother-in-law, the Ladbrokes. The baby, Robert, remained 'at home to protect the Family Mansion', his father wrote to a friend. All thought of the cowpox seems to have disappeared. Not even the ubiquitous Farington reported sighting the good doctor that autumn. Baron failed to notice this trip, suggesting either that Jenner considered it unimportant or that he preferred not to mention it. There are several possible reasons. Mrs Jenner had been unwell following Robert's birth. Perhaps the purpose of the trip was to consult a specialist such as Jenner's former instructor in midwifery, Thomas Denman. Another possibility concerns young Edward, now approaching his tenth birthday. Edward had not yet been sent to school and may have been somewhat retarded mentally. Three years later, after the Jenners had settled in London the first time, he went to a well known school run by Revd John Evans in Islington. Jenner could have used the journey at the end of 1797 to look into schools for the lad. The stay would also have given him a chance to seek out and make arrangements with a publisher for the *Inquiry*, when it was completed. Indeed, John Nichols, a printer in the City who lived in Islington and was soon to become an active propagandist for vaccination, may have introduced Jenner to John Evans. With the concurrence of his friends, especially Richard Worthington, he had decided not only to publish privately but also to extend the vaccination experiments in accordance with Banks's strictures, as soon as cowpox lymph again became available. This hiatus must have been frustrating, and it would also have been embarrassing. Possibly he avoided more social contact with professional colleagues than the minimum required by courtesy.

By 4 December, the family were reunited in Chauntry Cottage. William Davies dined and drank tea with them on the 4th and again on the 7th, 13th and 14th. On the latter occasion, 'My Cousins Catherine & Robert Fitzhardinge were admitted into the Church.'

In February three cases accidentally infected with grease came to Jenner's attention. From one of these, Thomas Virgo, on 16 March 1798, Jenner vaccinated a five-year-old boy named John Baker, who developed all the symptoms of cowpox. However, Baker could not be variolated because he 'was rendered unfit for inoculation from having felt the effects of a contagious fever in a workhouse, soon after this experiment was made.' What this meant, Jenner admitted in his second paper, was that the child died of a workhouse fever. Antivaccinists toward the end of the next century criticized Jenner for having neglected to mention this fact in the *Inquiry*, and maintained that the fever was a result of *erysipelas*, redness of the skin, which was caused by the vaccination, thus explaining his reluctance to admit the whole truth. In fact if the fever was *erysipelas*, it could have been the result of the vaccination only in the sense that bacteria on the lancet or the child's skin produced the disease. Even more likely was it that Baker had contracted one of the common workhouse fevers caused by throat or gut infections, typhoid or any of several other disorders which eighteenth-century medicine could not always distinguish. Indeed, even those who later criticized Jenner's lack of candour in this case had not the full benefit of the germ theory of disease, which remained controversial until the 1890s.

Of greater interest is the silence of his contemporaries about the child's death. Not even the most virulent antivaccinists mentioned it during Jenner's lifetime. His opponents combed through his writings looking for faults. Perhaps they overlooked this case because such unexplained deaths also occurred after variolation, the only competing treatment to protect against smallpox, and no one considered the event or the reporting of it notable.

John Baker was case number 18 in the *Inquiry*. Virgo and the two other farmhands, William Wherret and William Haynes, were collectively number 17. Cowpox had also developed on the same farm. According to Jenner's theory, which may in fact have been correct, the cowpox had come from the horses via the hands of Virgo and his colleagues. On the same day that Jenner inoculated John Baker with lymph from a horse's heel, he inserted cowpox material into the arm of case 19, William Summers, aged about five and a half. Again the symptoms of cowpox developed. William was later variolated by Henry Jenner and remained healthy. From the pustule on Summers's arm on 28 March Jenner took material to vaccinate another child, William Pead, who went through the cowpox, and in the course of time variolation, with no effect. William Pead provided lymph for the inoculation on 5 April 1798 of seven-year-old Hannah Excell, as well as several other children and adults. Curiously, not only did Jenner fail to name them; he did not even count them, possibly because both Edward and Henry Jenner were preoccupied by the death the day before of Edward's brother, Henry's father. On the other hand Hannah Excell, case 21, was recorded because cowpox lymph from her arm was to have an important career. She developed pustules which Jenner said were like those seen after smallpox inoculation, but she was not variolated.

Immediately the lymph from Hannah Excell became available, Jenner inoculated four more children. John Marklove, aged a year and a half, Mary Pead, aged five, and Mary James, aged six, all developed cowpox. Both John Marklove and Mary James had pustules that seemed to become inflamed, worrying Jenner so that he applied a caustic to them. A caustic irritates or burns the skin, like alcohol or iodine, and was used to stop inflammation before it caused damage or spread to other parts. It works because it acts as an antiseptic against the bacteria that cause inflammation. Jenner's anxiety was all the greater because he feared that if the vaccination became more inflamed than a variolous inoculation, it would count against his new theory. In fact he soon stopped using caustics, also called 'escharotics', for two reasons: they caused the patient much more discomfort than the itching of the vaccination itself; and, as Jenner soon realized, the inflammation accompanying the pustule was a normal part of the process. The red aureole that surrounds the vaccination pustule is caused by the virus, but it may often have grown worse because of bacterial infection. These facts were of course unknown to Jenner, but the parents, who had to cope with the wailing of their children when sore arms were made even more painful by the doctor's salve, no doubt deterred him from applying it.

The fourth child inoculated immediately with matter from Hannah Excell was Robert Jenner, aged eleven months. His vaccination did not take. All four children were grouped together in the *Inquiry* as case 22. There was to be one more vaccination using the lymph from Hannah Excell.

The final case in this first pamphlet on vaccination was a seven-year-old named J. Barge, who was vaccinated with material from Mary Pead, developed cowpox and was variolated by Henry Jenner, who used the same smallpox matter on an unprotected patient. J. Barge was protected by his vaccination, but the other patient developed 'the Small-pox in the usual regular manner.' Edward Jenner summarized: 'These experiments afforded me much satisfaction, they proved that the matter in passing from one human subject to another, through five generations, lost none of its original properties, J. Barge being the fifth who received the infection successively from William Summers, the boy to whom it was communicated from the cow.'

Moving now with unaccustomed dispatch, Jenner left Berkeley for London on 24 April with Mrs Jenner and Catherine. That night they stopped at Cirencester, and the next at Benson. On the third afternoon the party, which probably included three servants – Jenner's man Richard, Mrs Jenner's maid and a nurse for the child – reached the home of Mrs Jenner's sister, Mrs Ladbroke, in Pall Mall. It had been an unusually slow journey, thanks perhaps both to the size of the party and to Mrs Jenner's health. Normally, the coach journey from Berkeley to London required about thirty-six hours, including an overnight stop at a town mid-way such as Oxford. Unless the traveller was rich enough to maintain his own coach and horses, or willing by himself to brave the weather and risk the well-being of his own horse, he used the scheduled coaches that criss-crossed England. By the end of the century, travel was common for the middle class and the gentry. We tend to the view that before the invention of the motor car, if not the railway, everyone stayed very much at home. But even Jane Austen's most conservative landowners went to London or Bath or called on friends in different parts of the country. Jenner's contemporary, the Revd James Woodforde, travelled back and forth between his Norfolk parish and his former Somerset home once or twice a year for fifteen years. William Davies courted his wife-to-be in Chepstow on the other side of the then unbridged lower Severn. His father had gone to London the year before for surgical treatment by Jenner's friend from Hunterian days, Henry Cline. Not only Members of Parliament but those on the political fringes like Wilkes and Cobbett travelled widely by public conveyances. And on this occasion, Jenner was eager at last to present his new evidence to his medical colleagues.

Why then did he take Mrs Jenner, considering the alleged delicacy of her health? Catherine seemed to like London. Whatever her lack of stamina in Berkeley and Cheltenham, she seemed able to cope with the rigours of London society. She and Edward had, after all, returned to Berkeley only four months before. A few years later William Davies came to London in connection with the House of Lords hearings into the Berkeley peerage scandal. With his usual precision, he noted: 'My dear Wife during her stay in London went to the Opera, Covent Garden Theatre, Miss Linwood's Exhibition, Somerset House, Exhibition of Water Colors, Do. of the Society of Arts, Ashley's Theatre, China Manufacturies, Panorama (Siege of Flushing) etc. . . .' Unfortunately, Catherine Jenner's movements are by no means so well charted, but she now felt able and apparently eager to accompany her husband.

The couple stayed almost three months. Jenner had brought three items of immense professional importance: the revised manuscript of the *Inquiry*; some meticulous coloured drawings of the cowpox pustule, both as it occurred in nature on cows' teats and human hands, and as a result of vaccination; and vaccine lymph from Hannah Excell dried on a quill. It was the first experiment in the transportation and delayed use of vaccine. He had two major objectives: to get the *Inquiry* published and, using the material he had brought, to demonstrate vaccination to his medical colleagues in the metropolis. In the latter purpose he failed completely. During his stay, said Baron, he was 'unable. . .to procure one person on whom he could exhibit the vaccine disease.' He left the quill containing the dried lymph undisturbed with Henry Cline, then surgeon to St Thomas's Hospital. At the end of July, about two weeks after the Jenners had left Pall Mall for Cheltenham, Cline decided to use it on a patient of his. The child 'had some affection of the hip joint, and it was thought that the counter-irritation excited by the cowpox might prove beneficial'. For that reason, the inoculation was made on the affected hip rather than the arm. Though the hip was not helped, Cline decided to test the cowpox by variolating the patient. He resisted the infection, and Cline, who had read Jenner's manuscript, became a firm partisan of the new therapy.

Nor was the *Inquiry* published during the Jenners' stay. Although the dedication to Caleb Parry was dated 21 June at Berkeley, it was actually rewritten in London. The author himself did make arrangements for publication with the firm of Sampson, Low on Berwick Street in Soho, but the pamphlet did not appear until 17 September, 'Price 7s.6d. in Boards', according to the advertisement in the *Glocester Journal*.

The full title of the published volume, *An Inquiry into the Causes and Effects of the Variolae Vaccinae, a Disease discovered in some of the Western Counties of England, particularly Gloucestershire, and known by the name of the Cow Pox*, was longer and more exact than earlier titles. Jenner invented the Latin name, *Variolae Vaccinae*. It means 'smallpox of the cow'. He did not believe that it was actually smallpox because it did not cause smallpox in humans, but he was firmly of the opinion that it was related to smallpox and so could properly be called 'smallpox of the cow'. Because the *Inquiry* was a learned treatise, he translated the phrase into Latin. As in the case of his incomplete candour with regard to the death of John Baker, this invention accorded with the medical mores of his time and raised no objections amongst even his opponents. Eighty years later it outraged the antivaccinists, who interpreted the phrase as an effort to deceive.

Vaccinae or in its nominative feminine form, *vaccina*, is of course the origin of the words 'vaccine' and 'vaccination'. Although I have used 'vaccination' in relating Jenner's early experiments, the word was not invented until 1803 by Richard Dunning, a surgeon in Plymouth who supported Jenner's work. 'The useful terms "vaccination and to vaccinate" are undoubtedly yours,' Jenner wrote to Dunning. At the organizational meeting of the Royal Jennerian Society on 19 January 1803, Benjamin Travers said: 'A new species of Inoculation has at length been providentially introduced by our countryman, Dr. Jenner'. In the minutes of the RJS Medical Council dated 6 October, ten months later, the word 'vaccination' appears for the first time. Before 1803 and for many years afterwards, the Jennerian therapy was called 'cowpox inoculation', 'vaccine inoculation', 'cowpoxing' and, occasionally, 'vacciolation'. In the United States, cow-pock came to be identified with spurious cowpox, the true variety being called 'kine-pock', an additional confusion born perhaps of the fact that the disease is not native to North America. Appropriately, the great Louis Pasteur determined our broad and technically incorrect use of 'vaccination' many years later, at the time he introduced inoculation against rabies. He proposed that despite the fact that the cow no longer had anything to do even with preventing smallpox, let alone with the rabies vaccine, all inoculations designed to protect against a disease should be called 'vaccinations' in honour of Jenner.

The *Inquiry* began with the usual eighteenth-century attempt to place disease in God's scheme for mankind. Jenner then proposed that horse grease was the origin of cowpox. He considered the relationship between grease, cowpox and smallpox, noting that when grease infects humans, its symptoms 'bear so strong a resemblance to the Small Pox, that I think it highly probable it may be the source of that disease', though as with cowpox, not the disease itself. In a footnote at the end of this introductory section, he described a cowpox-like infection that did not give protection against small-pox. Only on the penultimate page of the *Inquiry* did he refer to 'the *true* and not the *spurious* Cow-pox', with another footnote directing attention to the earlier note. I intend to enlarge on these and other speculative passages because they are the causes of the controversy that surrounded Jenner for the rest of his life, but first they should be seen in the context of the *Inquiry* as he brought them to the public's attention.

The last seven cases beginning with James Phipps were experimental vaccinations, several of which were variolated to test the efficacy of the new therapy. The first sixteen cases, on the other hand, were people who had accidentally caught cowpox or, in two instances, grease. Case 1, Joseph Merret, was then under-gardener to the Earl of Berkeley, but back in 1770 when he was servant to a nearby farmer, Merret had transmitted grease to the cows and caught the disease himself. Twenty-five years later he had been variolated with his family but had resisted infection. Case 2, Sarah Portlock, had had cowpox twenty-seven years before. She resisted cowpox inoculation. Case 3, a local tradesman named John Phillips, had had cowpox forty-three years before he was tested with vaccination. Case 4, Mary Barge, had cowpox and nursed smallpox patients repeatedly, with no illness herself. Case 5 was Mrs H., 'respectable Gentlewoman' of Berkeley who had had cowpox when young. She resisted both natural smallpox and variolation. Case 6 involved a Berkeley farmer named Baker, two male servants and two dairymaids. An outbreak of cowpox occurred on the farm in 1796, but only one of the five, Sarah Wynne, caught the disease. Later that year all but Sarah caught smallpox. Jenner subsequently variolated Sarah, moreover, but with no effect. A similar set of circumstances applied in Case 7, William Rodway, the only person on another Berkeley farm who caught cowpox in 1796 and later escaped the smallpox. Case 8 was Elizabeth Wynne, aged fifty-seven, who may have been a relative of Case 6. She had had cowpox thirty-eight years before, remained healthy after Jenner variolated her in 1797, but caught cowpox a second time in 1798. Jenner reported her second illness in support of his belief that although cowpox protected against smallpox, it did not prevent a recurrence of cowpox. He overlooked another possibility – that cowpox did not bestow lifelong protection. Perhaps this oversight was understandable in light of the nearness in time of Elizabeth Wynne's variolation.

Case 9, however, confirmed his belief: 'Although the Cow Pox shields the constitution from the Small Pox, and the Small Pox proves a protection against its own future poison, yet it appears that the human body is again and again susceptible of the infectious matter of the Cow Pox'. William Smith had cowpox in 1780, 1791 and 1795 though he had withstood casual smallpox during the same years and twice resisted variolation in 1795. Case 10: Simon Nichols had cowpox in 1782, and experienced no effect from variolation by Jenner. Case 11: William Stinchcombe, similar. Case 12: an unspecified number of paupers in a nearby village, apparently all women, were variolated by Henry Jenner. Eight had had cowpox, and remained healthy. Thomas Pearce, Case 13, caught grease and resisted repeated variolation by Edward Jenner six years later. Case 14, James Cole, had a similar history. Case 15, Abraham Riddiford, also caught grease from a horse, but twenty years later caught smallpox, although the case was mild. Jenner took this as evidence that the horse-pox was not a sure protection against smallpox unless it had first passed through a cow. Again, he saw no significance in the passage of time. Cases 1, 2, 3 and 9, among others, explain why.

In the remaining pages of the *Inquiry*, Jenner was concerned to demonstrate the advantages of vaccination compared to variolation, because 'notwithstanding the happy effects of Inoculation. . .it not very infrequently produces deformity of the skin, and sometimes, under the best management, proves fatal.' On the other hand, 'I have never known fatal effects arise from the Cow-pox.' Secondly,

> It is an excess in the number of pustules which we chiefly dread in the Small-pox; but in the Cow-pox, no pustules appear, nor [thirdly] does it seem possible for the contagious matter to produce the disease from effluvia, or by any other means than contact, and that probably not simply between the virus and the cuticle, so that a single individual in a family. . .might receive it without the risk of infecting the rest, or of spreading a distemper that fills a country with terror.

This third advantage implied that people in the same room or the same house were not at risk simply from breathing the same air as the vaccinated patient, and probably not even by touching him. 'The first boy whom I inoculated with the matter of Cow-pox [James Phipps], slept in a bed while the experiment was going forward, with two children who never had gone through either that disease or the Small-pox, without infecting either of them.' In the smallpox, of course, both effluvia – essentially the air breathed by the patient, though also the air that surrounded him – and touching the patient, were believed to guarantee infection. And so they did. The virus was carried in exhaled water droplets so that anyone in the same room breathed them in, and the skin, covered by eruptions, was bathed in virus-laden lymph and pus. Finally, medical men believed that, in those predisposed to it, smallpox whether acquired naturally or by variolation was a cause of scrofula, a widespread affliction now recognized as tuberculosis of the skin. Cowpox was not. If they could be sustained as the evidence accumulated, these were mammoth advantages.

'Thus far have I proceeded in an inquiry, founded, as it must appear, on the basis of experience,' Jenner concluded; 'in which, however, conjecture has been occasionally admitted in order to present to persons well situated for such discussions, objects for a more minute investigation. In the mean time I shall myself continue to prosecute this inquiry, encouraged by the hope of its becoming essentially beneficial to mankind.' This was not just another pious wish added to improve the public perception of a new idea. Jenner's eagerness to publish his great, innovatory pamphlet demonstrates his sincerity.

Just as it appeared, Jenner's old friend Henry Cline, backed by the express authority of the King's physician Sir Walter Farquhar, advised

Jenner that if he would move his practice to London, he would be guaranteed £10,000 a year. If he had preferred to keep the nature of vaccination a secret, as the Suttons and Dimsdale had tried to protect their new method of variolation, he could have made a fortune, as they had. He could have avoided the vicissitudes that arose immediately in London when others began the experiments he had called for; and because wealth and greatness do much more than reasonable arguments to awe the generality, he might vastly have improved the quality of his later years. But it was the story of the emetic tartar all over again, with Cline playing the role of Hunter. John Baron has given the surviving part of a letter Jenner wrote from Cheltenham on 29 September, immediately after the *Inquiry* was published. It was addressed to an unidentified medical friend in London who had urged upon him the same course as Cline had suggested. The language is too high-flown for our tastes, but I cannot doubt its genuine feeling:

> Shall I, who even in the morning of my days sought the lowly and sequestered paths of life, the valley and not the mountain; shall I now my evening is fast approaching, hold myself up as an object for fortune and for fame? – Admitting it as a certainty that I obtain both, what stock should I add to my little fund of happiness?
>
> My fortune, with what flows in from my profession, is sufficient to gratify my wishes; indeed so limited is my ambition and that of my nearest connexions, that were I precluded from future practice I should be enabled to obtain all I want. And as for the fame what is it? a gilded butt, for ever pierced with the arrows of malignancy. The name of John Hunter stamps this observation with the signature of truth. . . .On the one hand, unwilling to come to town myself for the sake of practice, and on the other, fearful that the practice I have recommended may fall into the hands of those who are incapable of conducting it, I am thrown into a state that was at first not perceptible as likely to happen to me. . . .
>
> How very few are capable of conducting physiological experiments! I am fearful that before we thoroughly understand what is cow-pox matter and what is not, some confusion may arise; for which I shall, unjustly, be made answerable. . . .

He perceived the potential conflict between his preference for the country and the need to navigate his newly launched vessel through uncharted shoals. But what had that conflict to do with his decision four years later to petition Parliament for the compensation he now spurned?

Jenner realized that the 'conjectures' to which he referred at the end of the *Inquiry* arose in the largest part from lack of knowledge about cowpox and about the best techniques for handling the cowpox lymph. He had tried to describe precisely the techniques he had used and to generalize his admittedly limited experience with cowpox so as to restrict the scope of his conjectures, but he was prepared for the worst. Others would certainly deviate from his procedures, new as they were, with what results? The remarkable thing about the *Inquiry* is that it contains so much of the system as it finally emerged, having been born full-blown from the head of Jenner, so to speak.

First amongst the conjectures was the grease theory. The importance Jenner assigned to his epidemiological hypothesis is a reflection of medical thinking at the time. Today, the cause of an infectious disease is recognized to be a specific germ, but prevention may well involve knowing where the germs came from to infect us. Eighteenth-century doctors saw the same connection between epidemiology and prevention but, without our clearcut knowledge of cause, it was only occasionally of use to them. For example, epidemiology seldom prevented smallpox, but it did much to control cholera after John Snow observed the spread of that disease around a Soho water pump in 1848. To prove Jenner's theory, it was necessary only to show that cows could be infected under controlled circumstances – that is, intentionally.

Various experiments were undertaken, the earliest perhaps by Dr William Woodville, physician to the London Smallpox and Inoculation Hospitals. His attempts to infect cows with grease failed. On the other hand a London veterinary surgeon, Thomas Tanner, son of a veterinarian in Stroud who was well known to Jenner, was reported to have succeeded. Much more important experimental support for Jenner came from the work of an unnamed Yorkshire surgeon assisted and reported by a colleague, Dr John Loy. In one experiment they transferred grease from a horse to a cow and thence to a child; in another, from a horse to a child and thence to a cow. But they also had failures, which may have arisen from the undoubted existence of at least two kinds of horse-pox, the equivalent of true and spurious cowpox. In March 1803 Jenner reported Loy's evidence to his earliest continental supporter, Dr Jean De Carro. De Carro replied that his friend, Dr Louis Sacco of Milan, had also succeeded in producing true cowpox with grease from his own horse and that of a neighbour. Not only was such anecdotal evidence bound to be inconclusive, but also criticisms of the theory were widespread. Jenner made no mention of grease in his third and fourth pamphlets on vaccination, dated 1800 and 1801. Baron said he 'corrected' his views, but I have seen no evidence for this. He dropped them. In any case Jenner's epidemiological concern was curious because he had no wish to prevent the spread of horse-pox, or more especially cowpox, a fact that he soon perceived himself. Indeed, the revival based on modern virology of Jenner's theory by Dr Derrick Baxby of Liverpool University is a fine irony.

Jenner's thesis was that 'the Cow-pox protects the human constitution from the infection of the Small-pox'. It implied that grease and
cowpox were not the same disease as smallpox, although they must be
somehow related. 'It seems as if a change, which endures through life,
has been produced in the vessels of the skin; and it is remarkable too,
that whether this change has been affected by the Small-pox, or the Cowpox, that the disposition to sudden cuticular inflammation is the same on
the application of variolous matter.' In other words, testing by variolation
produces the same quick eruption after vaccination or variolation. During
1799 evidence arose that cowpox might be accompanied by eruptions,
although only in cases where the patient had been 'contaminated' with
smallpox. Jenner reasserted his position in his third pamphlet: smallpox
virus, he said, 'being the original, the latter [cowpox] the same disease
under a peculiar, and at present an inexplicable modification.' They are
the 'same diseases under different modifications,' he continued. 'The axiom
of the immortal Hunter, that two diseased actions cannot take place at the
same time in one and the same part, will not be injured by the admission of this theory.' This assertion of the similarities amongst the kinds
of pox created no massive problems for Jenner's contemporaries. Many
had observed for themselves. What worried them all, not least Jenner,
were questions like these: Smallpox inoculation always protects (and is
seldom fatal), but though safe enough cowpox can fail. How do you know
when cowpox assures protection and when it does not? Is it really true,
as Jenner asserted in the *Inquiry*, that cowpox causes no eruptions? And
above all, as time passed, is it true that the 'change. . .endures through
life'? These are practical clinical questions. The first two quickly took
over from problems of epidemiology and nosology. The third, though it
was implicit in several of the *Inquiry* cases, became an issue only as the
years passed.

As to the first, whether the patient was really safe, Jenner had to
explain the widely recognized fact that not everyone who had had cowpox
escaped smallpox. Many of his contemporaries, including his old friend Mr
Fewster of Thornbury, believed that such variability depended somehow on
the constitutions of the patients; that is, some people were more subject to
smallpox infection than others. Such a theory is not only untestable but,
from Jenner's standpoint, it could defeat everything he aimed to achieve.
Nowhere have I found evidence that he recognized these flaws in the old
theory, but to deal with the apparent inability of cowpox to give universal
protection, he advanced two arguments: that there are two kinds of cowpox,
true and spurious, and that the vaccine lymph itself may deteriorate if it is
improperly stored. In the published *Inquiry* he was somewhat circumspect
about the two kinds of cowpox, dealing with them in footnotes and actually
separating the names, 'true' and 'spurious', from their descriptions. Yet the

description of a true cowpox pustule on the cow is important because it soon was recognized as the best evidence, when the human pustule took on a similar appearance, that the vaccination had taken. The spurious pustules, Jenner wrote, 'are always free of the bluish or livid tint so conspicuous in the pustules in that disease. No erysipelus [redness] attends them, nor do they show any phagadenic disposition [tendency to become ulcerated] as in the other case, but quickly terminate in a scab without creating any apparent disorder in the Cow.' In the earlier versions of the *Inquiry*, very much the same material appears in the text, but without the adjectives, 'true' and 'spurious'. Why the author demoted this important distinction to a footnote, I cannot say; perhaps he and his friends decided that one more controversy might be diminished by this editorial sleight-of-hand. Unfortunately, the decision reflects Jenner's continuing attitude to a subject on which it was impossible to produce any conclusive experimental evidence. It was his observation against that of his detractors; his word against theirs. Had he known what we know – that there are four or five different infections of the cows' teats only one of which is cowpox – but of course he did not.

In his second pamphlet on vaccination Jenner used the term 'spurious cowpox' to cover four different circumstances: the use of matter from a spurious pustule on the cow's teat, the use of putrefied matter, the use of matter from a pustule that has degenerated into an ulcer, and the use of horse lymph that has not passed through the cow. The first is, of course, the definition of 'spurious', bringing together the two footnotes in the *Inquiry*. In *Further Observations on the Variolae Vaccinae or Cow Pox*, however, he described not just one spurious vesicle or eruption on cows' teats but several. The last circumstance was part of the grease theory.

, Jenner discussed the danger of using putrefied lymph, the second circumstance in which a spurious disease might be produced, in the *Inquiry* in connection with variolation, but only in the second pamphlet explicitly warned that the same danger could affect vaccine lymph. His observations of putrefied matter show how sophisticated medical knowledge could be, despite the missing key supplied by the germ theory.

A Medical Gentleman. . .frequently preserved the variolous matter . . . on a piece of lint or cotton, which in its fluid state was put into a vial, corked and conveyed into a warm pocket; a situation certainly favourable for speedily producing putrefaction in it. In this state (not unfrequently after it had been taken several days from the pustules) it was inserted into the arms of his patients, and brought on inflammation of the incised parts, swelling of the axillary glands [i.e., glands in the armpits], fever, and sometimes eruptions. But what is this disease? Certainly not the Small-pox; for the matter having from putrefaction lost or suffered a derangement in its specific properties, was no longer capable of producing that malady. . .and many, unfortunately, fell victim to it [smallpox] who thought themselves in perfect security.

Spurious cowpox arising from matter taken when the vesicle had passed its prime was not mentioned in the *Inquiry*, but Jenner now recognized that the lymph must be taken before the vesicle had begun to deteriorate. The importance of this stricture increased during the early years of the new practice, as experience mounted. If the lymph was taken too early, Jenner perceived, it would not contain the protective element; if it was taken too late, the protective element would have been dissipated or diminished but the vaccination would cause infections. By late 1801, Jenner had concluded that the best time to take lymph was between the fifth and eighth days after vaccination, 'or even a day or two later, provided the efflorescence [redness] be not then formed around it'. In this window of time the matter acquired its maximal value. That is for us to say, before the fifth day the lymph in the vaccine pustule contained too little cowpox virus to produce the desired immune response; after the eighth day, the pustule, an open wound in the skin, would almost certainly have become contaminated with inimical bacteria and the cowpox virus would have declined or disappeared. Writing a few years later, Thomas Creaser, a surgeon of Bath, pointed out that the second pamphlet 'supplies the single deficiency (as it refers to practice) in his Inquiry, by directing practitioners to use of recent Vaccine Virus'.

In his eagerness to assure the safety of patients, Jenner strove to elucidate every circumstance that could enhance or endanger successful vaccination. His worries about lymph storage and the best time to take the lymph were familiar because they had concerned variolators for half a century. It was easy to avoid the use of horse-pox lymph, and the grease theory was suspect anyway. But the notion that there were two kinds of cowpox was something else again. The first attack came from Dr Jan Ingenhousz, physician to the Austrian Emperor and a noted variolator, who read the *Inquiry* while he was the guest of the Marquis of Lansdowne at Bowood Park near Calne, Wiltshire. He proceeded to make some inquiries of his own amongst the neighbouring farmers, and wrote to Jenner in October 1798 that he had discovered people who had had the cowpox but then caught smallpox. One such unfortunate had passed smallpox on to his father, who had died. Ingenhousz also questioned Jenner's assertion that putrefied matter had occasionally been used by variolators. Jenner replied by distinguishing between what he now called 'perfect' and 'imperfect' cowpox. Ingenhousz rejoined that no such distinction was known. He refused to countenance Jenner's sensible proposal to publish their correspondence. It was an oddly bad-tempered exchange, due both to the self-esteem of the continental court physician on the one hand and the oversensitivity of the English country doctor on the other.

In 1806 a more persistent critic, John Birch, wrote, 'I cannot understand this doctrine; it seems contrary to the general Laws of Nature; she has given us a genuine but no spurious Small Pox; a genuine but no spurious Measles.' How pleasant for the biographer smugly to note that modern science has proven Jenner more attuned to 'the general Laws of Nature' than the opposition, but how irrelevant. Introducing a new therapy at the end of the eighteenth century, Dr Jenner had begun to realize that techniques were at least as important as theories. Lacking some vital element of evidence, theories might well be wrong, but pragmatic experience was hard to fault. He did not abandon the theory of spurious cowpox as he did the grease theory, but as the source for vaccine increasingly became the arms of those who had been vaccinated rather than the cows' teats, he could safely shift attention to the vesicle and storage. Again, there is no evidence that Jenner perceived what he was doing, but nevertheless he dropped references to the spurious cowpox as a disease of the cows' teats distinct from true cowpox. In 1807 the Royal Jennerian Society, its Medical Committee presided over by Jenner, set forth the causes of spurious pustules. They

> may be occasioned not only by matter taken from a spurious pustule, but also by matter taken from a genuine vesicle at too late a period; or by that which has been injured by keeping, exposure to heat, or otherwise. They may also be occasioned by using rusty lancets in inoculating; – by rude and unskillful methods of performing the operation; or by the genuine vesicle having been destroyed at an early stage. . . .

Even more explicit was the report to Parliament by the Royal College of Physicians in 1807, after they had interviewed dozens of practitioners about vaccination, including Jenner:

> Some deviations from the usual course have occasionally occurred, which the author of the practice has called spurious cow-pox, by which the public has been misled, as if there were a true and a false cow-pox, but it appears, that nothing more was meant, than to express irregularity or difference from that common form and progress of the vaccine pustule from which its efficacy is inferred.

As he allowed the emphasis to shift from theory to practice, Jenner's answer to the question, How can you judge whether vaccination has assured protection?, became a matter of experience. Providing it was handled properly, taken at the right time and injected with suitable precautions, he maintained cowpox lymph continued to protect against smallpox no matter how many times it was passed from arm to arm. His early experiments provided the evidence, and the theory was challenged only by those who disapproved of vaccination, root and branch. It had also the history of variolation to support it. Jenner said in his third pamphlet:

> Whether the nature of the virus will undergo any change from being farther removed from its original source, in passing successively from one person to another, time alone can determine. That which I am using has been in use near 8 months, and not the least change is perceptible in its mode of action. . . .

The Quaker physician and pro-vaccinist, John Coakley Lettsom, wrote, 'the vaccine fluid has been conveyed from one patient to another in seventeen hundred subjects, in succession, with undiminished efficacy'.

Because arm-to-arm propagation was the major source for vaccine throughout Jenner's life, and until late in the century, the theory that the vaccine retained its strength from generation to generation was immensely important. That it is unsound emerged only after arm-to-arm propagation had ceased to be the paramount source of vaccine, but in this instance modern science did not wholly confirm Jenner.

At the time, however, and for the immediate future, the details provided in the first three pamphlets satisfactorily answered the question of how one was to determine whether a vaccination had been successful. The controversy over whether cowpox caused eruptions analogous to smallpox arose early in 1799, caused increasingly violent disagreement for a year or two, and then was amicably resolved in Jenner's favour. It was not simply an argument about the symptoms of cowpox; at bottom it was about the risks involved in inoculating an animal disease into humans – an issue that persisted, if only on the lunatic fringe. While the argument about eruptions lasted, not only was it very worrying to the cause of vaccination, but indirectly it might be said to have given rise to the first public body to promote and conduct vaccination.

During most of this period Jenner was in Gloucestershire. From the time he went to Cheltenham in July 1798 to the end of November, there was again a cowpox drought. According to his nephew William Davies, on 30 November Jenner and his family 'this day return'd to Berkeley from Cheltenham.' However, Edward seems to have travelled ahead of Catherine and the children, probably because he had been told that cowpox had appeared in a herd at Stonehouse, near Eastington. He took matter on 26 November and the next day vaccinated two children of his friend, Henry Hicks of Eastington. Baron noted that Hicks was the 'first gentleman' to encourage the vaccination of his own children. Excepting Robert Jenner, all of the previous subjects had been farm labourers, their children, or workhouse inmates. With matter from Stonehouse dried on a quill, Jenner inoculated Susan Phipps, James's young sister, on 2 December. Her case and that of Mary Hearn, a twelve-year-old vaccinated from Susan's arm, were reported in *Further Observations*. Jenner had considered it necessary to use a caustic on Mary Hearn.

The vaccination practice had now an opportunity to spread locally. A Stroud surgeon, Mr Darke, also took matter from Susan Phipps to use on an unspecified number of his own patients. A local colleague named Hughes wrote to Jenner about five of Mr Darke's patients, three daughters of a Revd Colborne, his servant, William King, and Mr Darke's servant, Thomas Vick. The results were variable: Vick and the two older children responded to variolation with cases of mild smallpox, but King and the youngest child suffered only local reactions. The variolations were all carried out a bare seven days after the vaccinations, however, by which time the body's immune response would only have begun to appear. A third Stroud medical man, Mr Thornton, obtained his own fluid from the Stonehouse herd. In a family called Stanton, Thornton inoculated the father and four children. The father's failed to take, and the children all developed inflammation. Thornton variolated the children, producing mild disease, but the father resisted the smallpox. The Stanton cases may demonstrate that the father had been immunized by some earlier illness, and certainly revealed the common experience that in those cases where smallpox did follow vaccination, for whatever reason, the disease was almost always mild.

Toward the end of 1798, the definitive action on vaccination left Edward Jenner in Berkeley and moved to London. First in the metropolitan field after Henry Cline was Dr George Pearson, physician to St George's Hospital. Pearson was an almost exact contemporary of Jenner's. He had studied medicine in Edinburgh, had practised for ten years in Yorkshire, and now taught chemistry as well as medicine. Pearson is said to have introduced the word 'nitrogen' into the English language. In September Jenner wrote to Pearson from Cheltenham acknowledging the proofs of a book. Their 'perusal. . .has afforded me great pleasure, both from the handsome manner in which you mention my name, and from the mass of evidence which has poured in from different countries in support of the facts which I so ardently wish to see established'. *An Inquiry concerning the History of the Cow Pox. Principally with a View to Supersede and Extinguish the Small Pox* was published in November. With commendable industry Pearson had collected observations as widely as possible, denying any 'expectation of participating the smallest share of honour, on the score of discovery of facts. The honour on this account, by the justest title, belongs exclusively to Dr. Jenner'. His literary style, remarkably for his time, makes modern bureaucratic gobbledygook read like Shakespeare. He had sent out dozens of letters asking nine questions: whether those taking cowpox accidentally were protected against smallpox (most respondents said yes); whether inoculated cowpox had a similar effect (yes); whether the disease produced by inoculation with cowpox is the same as disease from arm-to-arm inoculation (yes, quoting only Jenner's *Inquiry*);

whether it was possible to catch cowpox more than once, but not to catch smallpox (most doubted); whether a person who had had smallpox could still catch cowpox (doubtful); whether cowpox could be transmitted only through breaks in the skin (yes); whether cowpox could produce a severe disease which was nevertheless not dangerous (probable – Mr Fewster of Thornbury thought so, and doubted the need for vaccination); whether cowpox promotes other diseases in people disposed to them, as it was believed smallpox did (not proven); and finally, whether smallpox may occur if, after vaccination, the patient suffers local inflammation without constitutional symptoms (probable). In view of the paucity of evidence, then consisting exclusively of Jenner's own published cases, Pearson seems to have been conducting a kind of public opinion survey of medical men familiar with the *Inquiry*. It showed their support for Jenner's work and provided the dash of favourable publicity that fertilizes any new thing.

Meanwhile, Jenner was writing *Further Observations* at Berkeley. In the New Year he went to Cheltenham, probably without his family and for less than a month. What lay behind this brief stay the available evidence does not reveal; possibly he had patients there who required his attention.

On the day Jenner went to Cheltenham, 25 January, Dr William Woodville, physician at the London Smallpox and Inoculation Hospitals, sent him important news. Five days earlier, the veterinarian, Thomas Tanner, had found cowpox in a dairy belonging to a Mr Harrison on Gray's Inn Lane near the hospitals. The next day Woodville accompanied Tanner to the dairy and took matter from a cow with which he vaccinated six in-patients. On the 22nd, Woodville returned to the dairy, and with matter from the hand of a milker he inoculated two more men. That same day he called on Sir Joseph Banks, George Pearson and Dr Robert Willan, physician to the London Public Dispensary and a specialist in diseases of the skin. Woodville asked them to join him on the following day at Harrison's dairy, along with Lord Somerville, President of the Board of Agriculture, Sir William Watson, a prominent variolator, and others. Woodville brought along a copy of Jenner's *Inquiry* so that the illustrations of pustules could be compared to those on the cows before them and on two or three of the milkers, as a means of confirming that Woodville had been using true cowpox. The learned gathering agreed that he had.

Between 21 January and 10 March 1799 Woodville vaccinated two hundred people, plus another four hundred or so by May. From the standpoint of protecting them against smallpox as demonstrated by subsequent variolation of a large number, the series provided vaccination with its first major clinical success. All of the influential figures who accompanied Woodville to Mr Harrison's dairy became early converts. Yet for a time it appeared that the reverse might be the case, that vaccination had fallen at the first hurdle.

Jenner replied to Woodville's letter to 'suggest the immediate propriety

[87]

of inoculating [i.e., variolating] those who may resist the action of the cow-pox matter, and may have been exposed to the variolous contagion at the hospital.' His prescience was greater than anyone realized. Of Woodville's cases, 60 per cent developed generalized eruptions, this in spite of Jenner's assurance that cowpox did not produce eruptions. There was even one death following vaccination, and although it was later shown to have been the result of another infection, the antivaccinists kept the unfortunate memory alive. The first case of generalized eruption was one of the patients inoculated directly from the cow. Other than Jenner, no one seemed to appreciate that 'variolous contagion at the hospital' might affect the results.

On 15 February Pearson reported to Jenner what had been going on, but, despite the eruptions, 'Dr W and myself conclude that the inoculated cowpox, as far as we have seen in at least fifty cases, is a slighter disease than the inoculated variola [smallpox], and that it is not probable there is any danger to life from it.' Enclosed in Pearson's letter was thread imbued with matter from one of Woodville's in-patients, Ann Bumpus, aged twenty, who had been vaccinated with matter taken from another patient without eruptions. Two days after Pearson sent the thread to Jenner, Ann Bumpus developed a smallpox-like rash, but it cleared fairly quickly and had no serious complications.

With the matter from Ann Bumpus Jenner vaccinated his great-nephew Stephen Jenner, Henry Jenner's son, aged three and a half, and a four-year-old named James Hill. Stephen had a slight eruption on his body, but it was the vaccination pustule itself that concerned his uncle. He applied a caustic which controlled the pain and swelling within ten minutes. James's vaccination took, with no problems or complaints. Jenner used matter from young Hill successfully to inoculate two more of Henry Hicks's children, as well as servants and employees in Hicks's 'manufactory' at Eastington, eighteen in all. An unspecified number were variolated, with the usual negative results. Jenner reported these cases in *Further Observations* and speculated on why the arms of those inoculated in the country were more likely to become inflamed than patients in London. He could see no other answer than the difference in the air. The generalized eruptions Pearson had reported did not seem to concern him, as though he had not connected them with his warning to Dr Woodville.

Pearson had also taken matter from infected cows in a dairy at Marylebone fields, with which he began to inoculate in his private practice. With this matter and probably also with lymph from patients in the Smallpox Hospital, Pearson prepared two hundred threads which he posted to a like number of correspondents in a circular letter asking them to try out the new therapy and report back their results.

His letters were posted in mid-March. On the 21st, Jenner left Berkeley to take up residence for three months in lodgings in Norfolk Street. Both his nephew, George Jenner, and his friend, Thomas Paytherus who was now practising in London, had written to him about Pearson's circular letter as well as about a public lecture on vaccination that Pearson had delivered. They evidently perceived a danger that, despite his earlier self-effacement, Pearson was staking an unjustified claim. Whether these pleas carried more weight with Jenner than his natural curiosity and concern about what Woodville was doing, to say nothing of his desire to oversee publication of the second pamphlet, no testimony of his reveals. In any case, Woodville received the first reported call that Jenner made after he arrived in London.

Further Observations on the Variolae Vaccinae or Cow Pox was published in early April 1799 with a dedication to Caleb Parry dated from Berkeley, though like the dedication in the *Inquiry*, it too was probably written after Jenner got to London. He explained the limited number of additional cases by referring readers to Pearson's *Inquiry*, which 'produced so great a number of attestations in favour of my assertion that it proves a protection to the human body from the Small Pox, I have not been assiduous by seeking more', confusing attestations with experimental evidence. He aimed to 'enforce the precaution suggested in the former Treatise on the subject, of subduing the inoculated pustule as soon as it has sufficiently produced its influence on the constitution', by using caustics.

Within a few days of publication his friend, Thomas Tanner, discovered cowpox on a farm belonging to a Mr Clark in Kentish Town. Jenner said that he took some of the matter himself 'immediately' to Berkeley, where he stayed for less than a week. Though he no doubt sought an opportunity to be reunited with Catherine, albeit briefly, the probable explanation for this short, tiring journey arises out of what he had discovered during his conversations with Woodville about the matter from Ann Bumpus that he had used in February and March. Matter from some of those patients had been passed on to an Eastington doctor, J. R. Marshall, for use in his practice, and some had also been left with his friend Hicks. Vaccination, like variolation, was a very simple procedure, which in theory at least required no special qualifications. Despite his horror of malpractice, Jenner encouraged lay vaccinators, especially amongst his female patients and friends. All of this matter was now suspect, and despite the evidence that on the whole it had not caused eruptions amongst Jenner's patients, I think he may have wanted to replace it as soon as possible. On the day he returned to London, however, Dr Marshall wrote that he had inoculated 107 people. 'I had no intention of extending the disease further than my own family, but the very extensive influence which the conviction of its efficacy in resisting the Small Pox has had upon the minds of the people in general, has rendered that intention nugatory'. This is the first sign of any public attitude, favourable or unfavourable, to the new therapy.

Dr Marshall went on to do 316 more vaccinations between April and

September 1799, 211 of which went through subsequent variolation, all with no effect. In a later letter he reported what could have been a disaster but happily proved to be merely instructive. Marshall had taken matter on a clean lancet from a patient with severe smallpox, and then accidentally had used the same lancet two days later to take vaccine with which he inoculated a woman and her four children. 'In three days I discovered the mistake', but fortunately, the family developed only cowpox and later withstood variolation.

William Woodville's *Report of a Series of Inoculations for the Variolae Vaccinae. . .with Remarks and Observations on this Disease, considered as a Substitute for the Small-Pox* was published in late May or early June, probably before Jenner returned to Berkeley. Woodville had no doubt whatsoever about the effectiveness of cowpox as a preventive of smallpox. Whereas Jenner had stressed the similarity between the cowpox pustule and that caused by the inoculated smallpox, Woodville noted their differences. His second original contribution was experimental evidence that human cowpox could be inoculated back into the cow.

About a quarter of Woodville's patients had had some sort of eruption after vaccination, but upwards of four hundred had later been variolated and none had had smallpox. As to those who had had eruptions, he believed then that the cowpox itself was at fault. The lancets he had used to initiate the series from the cow in January had been freshly ground to remove any contamination from previous use. He had variolated some patients within a few days of vaccination and had taken lymph from the vaccination vesicle for use in other patients, but 'before the constitution could be affected by the variolous matter, and during the time that both inoculations were merely local diseases'. Woodville believed that 'in respect to their local action' smallpox and cowpox continued separately and distinctly. Even though Jenner must have discussed these findings with Dr Woodville, if indeed he had not read the *Report* in manuscript before he left London, there is no record that he responded in any way at this time to the account of eruptions. Perhaps he had been distracted by Woodville's statement, based on his own attempts to transfer it directly, that the vaccine disease was not derived from the horse.

Woodville himself modified what he had said about the eruptions within days of publication. He wrote to the *Medical and Physical Journal* on 13 June: 'I have observed, that the result would probably have been more favourable, if the matter used for communicating the infection, had been taken from those only, in whom the disease proved to be very mild.' Of 310 cases of cowpox, 39 had had an eruption that suppurated or developed pus. Of these 39, 19 had been among the first hundred vaccinated, 13 amongst the second hundred and 7 only amongst the third hundred. These patients had been vaccinated after the *Report* had been written, when Woodville had begun to use matter only from those with little or no signs of disease. 'This information. . .leads to a conclusion widely different from that published in the "Reports",' he concluded.

Later in June, not long after Jenner had left London for Berkeley, Dr Pearson took steps to establish the first institution to promote vaccination, by vaccinating the poor free of charge and supplying matter to those in London and elsewhere in the country who wished to try vaccination. The Duke of York agreed to become a patron along with several medical men, and one of the officers was Lord Egremont. Pearson naturally became head of the London Vaccine-Pock Institution.

The Jenners made their annual migration to Cheltenham early in August. About this time Dr Joseph Marshall of Eastington wrote to Jenner. He had read Woodville's *Report*, and now called attention to his own quite different experience. 'He says that the generality of his patients had pustules. It certainly seems extremely extraordinary, that in all my cases there never was but one pustule'. Marshall had used some of the lymph supplied by Woodville from his patient, Ann Bumpus, as well as the fresh matter which Jenner had brought to him from the cows at Kentish Town.

Jenner communicated Marshall's experience to Woodville, who replied: 'The cow-pox inoculations certainly go on very successfully here, but we cannot, like Dr. Marshall, boast that our cases have never been attended with eruptions.' He added that Francis Knight, a former Gloucestershire surgeon now in London, had had similar results. Jenner had mentioned Knight in the *Inquiry*, among others familiar with cowpox, and had received an acknowledgement from Knight about a year before. Knight had also asked for fresh cowpox matter, but it was during a period in which the disease had disappeared. He had probably succeeded in obtaining matter from Woodville's trials. With it he vaccinated the Duke of Clarence's mistress, Mrs Jordan, and two of their children. Jenner wrote at once to Knight, who replied that he had taken matter from one of the Duke's children for use on a ten-year-old girl from a village where there was smallpox. She seemed to develop that disease, but recovered without serious effects. There the puzzle of Woodville's eruptive cowpox stood for several months, until Jenner had completed his third pamphlet.

Despite the war with France and Holland, copies of Jenner's *Inquiry* had reached medical men in Geneva, Hanover and Vienna during the first half of the year 1799. The long and bitter military struggle paralleled and obviously affected the history of vaccination, as it did every other aspect of European and American life. On land the course of British arms was consistently disastrous, not least because the Prime Minister, William Pitt the Younger, depended on alliances with various combinations of Russia, Prussia and Austria, which looked powerful on paper but were in fact disunited, badly led and underfunded. British naval strength prevailed at sea and had the power to prevent the much feared invasion. In October 1803, Jenner wrote from Cheltenham to a literary friend, the bibliophile Thomas Frognall Dibdin, suggesting that Dibdin's new poem be printed on 'paper. . .thick enough for cartridge-paper for the soldiers of the invading Corse. . . .the volunteers of this place were marched into a meadow yesterday afternoon for the second time since their enrollment. I was struck with astonishment. They marched and performed a variety of pedestrian evolutions with as much adroitness as veterans.'

Stalemate ensued for almost a decade, while Napoleon kept a stranglehold on Western Europe. It was his attempts to break out, first in Spain and then in Russia, which so weakened the French that the Grand Alliance could finally prevail. With the exception of about eighteen months of peace from late 1801 to May 1803, this military backdrop for the unfolding personal concerns of millions lasted almost twenty years.

Although the first translation of the *Inquiry* was into German, completed in about six months by Dr Ballhorn of Hanover, Jenner began his enormous continental correspondence with Dr Jean De Carro, a twenty-nine-year-old Genevois educated in Edinburgh. He had settled in Vienna because of political upheavals in his native city, and performed his first vaccinations in May 1799 with matter from threads sent by Pearson. He first wrote to Jenner in September. De Carro had been unable to find cowpox near Vienna and asked Jenner for fresh matter to be sent to him through the office of the Foreign Secretary, Lord Grenville, to the office of Mr Stratton, Secretary of the British Legation in Vienna. Jenner sent the dried matter with a covering letter from Berkeley toward the end of November, and reported, 'in this Island the numbers inoculated with vaccine virus already exceed five thousand.'

The next month he received a request through the wife of a British military attaché in Berlin from none other than Princess Louisa of Prussia for vaccine matter. This he dispatched immediately, with a covering note containing the same statistic he had sent to De Carro.

In England, nine people were vaccinated in Manchester in April 1799, probably with matter sent by Pearson. Typical of the wave of enthusiasm, particularly outside of London, was the experience of one W. Finch, a minister of St Helen's, who had inoculated a child with a lancet from a fellow clergyman of Finmere, Oxfordshire, on 17 November 1799. From that child Finch vaccinated 713 up to 6 February 1800. Twenty had been variolated subsequently, with no effect.

But the year 1799 also saw the beginnings of doubt in Britain. First in the field seems to have been Dr Thomas Beddoes of Bristol, who knew Jenner as a younger neighbour. Their mutual friend, Dr Thomas Hickes, had reported to Jenner in October 1798 that Beddoes thought the *Inquiry* satisfactory, but on 25 February Beddoes told a German medical writer, Hüfeland, that 'the facts which I have collected are not favourable to his opinion that cowpox gives complete immunity from the natural infection of smallpox', adding that experiments were then in progress at the London Smallpox Hospital. The next day Jenner wrote to Beddoes himself. His older colleague was assembling *Contributions to Physical and Medical Knowledge*, published in Bristol later in the year. Two of the letters he intended to include, from Charles Cooke, a Gloucester apothecary, and E. Thornton, the Stroud surgeon, were critical of cowpox inoculation. Beddoes had sent their manuscripts to Jenner asking for his comments. Jenner thanked Beddoes for his 'candour', said that *Further Observations* was then ready for the press, and asked that the public withhold judgement 'until the whole of the facts and the consequent rational deductions shall be laid before them.' Beddoes added Jenner's letter to his volume.

In July the organ of the English gentry, *Gentleman's Magazine*, carried an article signed 'Candidus' which attacked 'a *bottle-conjuror's* history' that 'could not fail to excite ridicule', but without explaining why. *Gentleman's Magazine* seemed to have permanently entered the opposition with a favourable review of a pamphlet entitled *Reflexions on. . .the Caesarean Operation. To which are added. . .Experiments on the supposed Origin of the Cow-Pox*. The author, a Manchester clergyman named W. Simmons, had experimented with three children and three cows. He claimed that all six had been given smallpox afterwards!

Simmons's curious practice of adding *obiter dicta* to a medical pronouncement was common even in the publications of medical men. Indeed, such was the first antivaccinist pronouncement of Jenner's most inveterate professional enemy, Dr Benjamin Moseley. A friend of Nelson, Moseley was for thirty years physician to the Royal Medical Hospital, Chelsea. Like Jenner, whose contemporary he was, Moseley had been trained as a surgeon, but he then practised in Jamaica, returning to take his MD from St Andrews. Unlike Jenner, he also became a licentiate of the Royal College of Physicians of London. He had written important treatises on tropical diseases and on coffee, and in 1799 published *A Treatise on Sugar. with Miscellaneous Medical Observations*. Amongst the latter are some remarks on 'Cowmania': 'Can any person say what may be the consequence of introducing the *Lues Bovilla, a bestial* humour – into the human frame. . . ? Who knows, besides, what ideas may arise. . .from a *brutal* fever having excited its incongruous impressions on the brain? . . . the doctrine of engrafting distempers is not yet comprehended by the wisest men. . . .' *Lues Bovilla* was Moseley's Latin reply to *Variolae Vaccinae*, for 'lues' means syphilis. He was suggesting that this 'bestial humour' might well be animal syphilis. A review of the *Treatise on Sugar*, signed 'P', probably Pearson, states that 'The account Dr. Moseley gives of the *yaws* is more sober and interesting' than his account of cowpox;

but Moseley's Latin, like Jenner's, imposed a lasting imprint. Scientific techniques at the time could not prove that while Moseley was talking nonsense, Jenner had spoken the truth. Only experience could tell.

Yet every experience required interpretation. So it was with the eruptions suffered by so many of Woodville's vaccination patients at the beginning of the year. After Jenner's prescient reply to Woodville's first letter about these events in January, he had withheld his fire. When at last he did attempt an explanation, it was part of his late November letter sending vaccine matter to Dr De Carro in Vienna:

> . . .on the 5th day after the Cowpox Virus had been inserted into one arm, the variolous virus was inserted into the other, in those whose eruptions resembled those of smallpox; & thus, in my opinion, the two diseases became blended. The Pustules, as the disease made its progress from one Patient to another soon began to decrease in number, and now they are become quite extinct. . . .How extremely curious & singular is this Fact! Does it not tell us that the Cowpox is the original disease, the Smallpox a Variety & being the weaker is driven off by the stronger? or is the latter assimilated by the former?

Because Jenner was writing the third pamphlet at the same time, it contains essentially the same explanation. *A Continuation of Facts & Observations Relative to the Variolae Vaccinae* appeared in the second part of 1800. That Jenner then believed that the pamphlet completed his new system appears in its conclusion: now that the cowpox inoculation has been proven by Woodville's work as well as his own, 'May I not with perfect confidence congratulate my country and society at large on their beholding. . .an antidote that is capable of extirpating from the earth. . .the severest scourge of the human race!' But it explained eruptions while not getting to grips with their source. Only in January 1800, after having been asked by the *Medical and Physical Journal* to comment on an advance copy of an article in the same journal by George Pearson 'concerning the Eruptions resembling the Small-Pox, which sometimes appear in the inoculated Vaccine Disease', did Jenner reassert his original warning that patients entering the Smallpox Hospital for vaccination might be infected accidentally; '. . .at present, I very much suspect, that where *variolous pustules have appeared, variolous matter has occasioned them.*'

Meanwhile, Woodville maintained that cowpox was not contagious if it was confined to the vesicle itself, 'but where it produces numerous pustules upon the body the exhalations they send forth are capable of infecting others in the same manner as Small Pox.' He followed up his original *Report* with a pamphlet, *Observations on the Cow-Pox*. Unwisely, it attacked Jenner gratuitously, in an eighteenth-century manner which though common enough was not Woodville's style. In the same pamphlet, moreover, he added: 'I readily admit that they [the eruptions] have been and still continue to be the effect of some adventitious cause, independent of the Cow-pox.' What then could have been the 'adventitious cause'?

Any answer must take into account the case of Ann Bumpus. From her arm vaccine matter had been sent to Jenner at Berkeley, but despite the generalized eruptions that she suffered, neither Jenner's patients nor patients vaccinated with the same matter by Dr Marshall developed any significant outbreaks. Yet it seems certain that patients being vaccinated in the Smallpox Hospital were being infected with smallpox. Of course, different combinations of physical circumstances may have affected different patients. For example, accidental smallpox infection could have occurred one or more days before or immediately after vaccination. The most likely explanation in Ann Bumpus's case may not apply to other patients, but she at least may have been infected with smallpox near enough in time to her vaccination so that the latter alerted the immune system before the smallpox virus could reach maturity in her body. Smallpox takes about two weeks to incubate. One twentieth-century authority on smallpox wrote of the Jenner-Woodville controversy, 'Much, if not most, of this smallpox was due to simultaneous infection by the normal respiratory route, but it would appear that if a mixed variola-vaccinia lymph is used [as might have been the case with that taken from Bumpus], it will yield vaccinia on human propagation rather than variola.' In short, Jenner had been right and Woodville wrong – at first.

Perhaps the most independent contemporary medical observer of the dispute was Dr Joseph Adams, who became physician to the Smallpox and Inoculation Hospitals after Woodville's death in 1805. He later wrote: 'The controversy. . .ended in both parties admitting that about the end of the second or commencement of the third week. . .scattered eruptions will appear having all the properties of the original vesicle.' In our terms, the disputants had begged the question. In theirs, they accepted their mutual good faith: Jenner, knowing that Woodville supported vaccination, modified his assertion that cowpox never caused eruptions. Woodville had to admit that in a variolous atmosphere contagion might occur, but much modified by vaccination. In the end, they were both right. Happily, they were reconciled through the mediation of Dr Lettsom, like Woodville a Quaker, Dr Valentin of Nancy who visited London during the spring of 1803 to meet Jenner, and Dr William Saunders of Enfield, with Lettsom a founder of the Medical and Chirurgical Society and its first President. Jenner tended to treat his pronouncements on vaccination like a dog with a bone but, coaxed by a degree of rationality and goodwill on the part of the opposition, he was not without give.

The quarrel with George Pearson that erupted almost simultaneously, however, growled and rumbled without let or resolution because it involved Jenner's status and his claim to priority. There was no medical difference between the parties. On 2 December 1799, Pearson called a formal organizational meeting to inaugurate the Institute for the Inoculation of the Vaccine-Pock. Eight days later he wrote to Jenner in Berkeley asking him to 'be an extra[ordinary?] corresponding physician' to the Institution. 'No expense is to be attached to your situation except a guinea a year as a subscriber, and indeed I think you ought to be exempt from that, as you cannot send any patients'. At the very least Pearson had been guilty of a massive haemorrhage of tact. Stiffly, Jenner replied on 17 December:

> It appears to me somewhat extraordinary that an institution formed upon so large a scale, and that has for its objective the inoculation of the cowpox, should have been set on foot and almost completely organized without my receiving the most distant intimation of it. The institution itself cannot, of course, but be highly flattering to me, as I am thereby convinced that the importance of the fact I imparted is acknowledged by men of the first abilities. But at the same time allow me to observe that if the vaccine inoculation, from unguarded conduct, should sink into disrepute (and you must admit, Sir, that in more than one instance its reputation suffered) I alone must bear the odium. . . .
>
> At the present crisis I feel so sensibly the importance of the business that I shall certainly take an early opportunity of being in London. For the present I must beg leave to decline the *honour* intended me.

It was not an absolute refusal, but Jenner had been shocked into action. Pearson really did seem to wish to arrogate to himself the captaincy of the ship. On 28 January 1800, Jenner left Catherine and the children at Chauntry Cottage, and travelling with Dr Hickes by way of Bath, reached London three days later. It would be reasonable to suppose that he had wanted to consult Parry. This time he lodged in Adam Street off the Strand.

Jenner's first business was with Lord Egremont. Probably as early as June 1799, Egremont had become one of the patrons of the Vaccine-Pock Institution. He was ideally placed to influence the future of that institution, and because of Jenner's contribution to the health of the Petworth people, a suitable person to hear Jenner's doubts about Pearson. As soon as he arrived in London, therefore, Jenner wrote proposing that he be allowed to come to Petworth.

The third Earl, George O'Brien Wyndham, maintained his Sussex estate at Petworth as an examplar of progressive agriculture and a refuge for artists. Among the greatest was J. M. W. Turner. Mr André, a surgeon at Petworth, had inoculated fourteen people there with matter he had obtained from George Pearson, but all of them had had eruptions. Lord Egremont wrote to Jenner about the failures. Jenner replied with an account of what he believed had taken place in the Smallpox and Inoculation Hospitals, explaining the results of André's vaccinations, and sent some of his own store of lymph. In a second letter he offered to send his nephew, Henry, to do the new vaccinations. The offer was considered unnecessary, but forty vaccinations were undertaken, all of them successful. They included the fourteen original patients, suggesting that Pearson's vaccine had not worked.

Pearson must have been kept informed, perhaps by Egremont himself. On 11 February 1800, Mr Brande, chairman of the committee organizing the Vaccine-Pock Institution, was authorized to call on Dr Jenner to 'make what alterations he pleased in the plan of the Institution, &. . .if any of the officers were not agreeable to him, there was not one who was not willing to resign.' Then on 15 February, accompanied by his brother-in-law Robert Ladbroke, probably one of Egremont's bankers, Jenner went to Petworth. He stayed nine days, during which he vaccinated some two hundred people, but the principal purpose of the visit was of course to discuss the new Institution. Nothing is known about what was said or whether anyone else was present. I think it probable that Egremont, who had acted in complete good faith, would have tried to win Jenner over, but that Jenner's objective would have been to demonstrate that Pearson was not the proper person to organize such an institution.

The day after Jenner had returned to London, the Duke of York invited him to an interview. His earlier contacts with royalty had been no more than those of the average citizen with something to sell. A copy of the *Inquiry* had been inscribed to the Prince of Wales. Some time in February 1799, moreover, he had been introduced to the Duke of Clarence, with whom he discussed the Vaccine-Pock Institution. Accompanied by the surgeon, Francis Knight, he met the Duke of York on 1 March. The Duke said that he had recommended vaccination to those units of the army under his command, and therefore had been willing to give his patronage to Pearson's Institution.

Jenner remained adamant in his refusal to join the Institution, no matter what adjustments were offered to accommodate him, but we do not know what these adjustments entailed. Baron wrote that 'the conduct of the individuals who framed the institution proved that the cause of vaccination could not be safely committed to their hands'. That Jenner believed this, I do not for a moment doubt. Nor could he forgive Pearson for not having consulted him from the outset. That failure seemed to justify his conviction that Pearson intended to grab a priority which was not his to claim.

The first *Report* of the Vaccine-Pock Institution observed that when Jenner had finally rejected their proposals that spring, he also 'at last said, it was thought best, that there should be no Institution.' John Julius Angerstein, one of the founders of Lloyds, a noted art collector and, with his family, a friend of the Jenners in Cheltenham, refused to have anything to do with the Institution because of what he considered to be Pearson's blunders. Of greater significance, however, was the decision, reported to

Jenner during an interview on 17 March with Egremont, that he and the Duke of York would withdraw their support.

Meanwhile greater events had ensued. In a letter from Berkeley before Christmas 1799, Jenner wrote to Edward Gardner in London. 'Great news from St James's. The King has sent me a very civil message, so you will produce a page to wait upon his majesty and express the obligation.' Early in March when all had been arranged, he wrote to W. F. Shrapnell: 'What will you give for a sight of me all in velvet, girt with a sword too? What a queer creature is a human being!' What an ambivalent creature was Edward Jenner, but one can imagine his sense of pride and his pleasure when the audience took place on 7 March. The Earl of Berkeley presented his neighbour to the sovereign, who gave his permission that the forthcoming second edition of the *Inquiry* should be dedicated to him. The replacement of the original dedication to his friend Parry by the new dedication, 'To the King', confirmed the country doctor's achievement socially and politically.

Chapter 6

Ten Thousand or Twenty?
1800–1802

Before the end of March 1800, Edward had been received by the Prince of Wales at Carlton House with 'marked respect', according to Dr Baron. The Queen's chamberlain, the Earl of Morton, presented Jenner to Her Majesty at St James's Palace on 27 March. Queen Charlotte was a kindly woman whose intention would have been both to honour this interesting man and to encourage acceptance of a system of which her husband's physician, Sir Walter Farquhar, approved. She and all her children had long since been variolated against smallpox. Indeed, her eighth son, Octavius, had died of the inoculated smallpox almost seventeen years before. The promise of security with safety would have had strong personal meaning to her.

Neither were Jenner's professional services required by the Prince of Wales or any other members of the royal family. On 26 May 1808 the Princess of Wales wrote to her doctor, Matthew Baillie, asking 'that Dr. Jenner would receive little William any morning before Thursday – and that after that Dr. Jenner would call on the Princess to see what progress the inoculation makes.' William was 'her little Protégé'. Although there is no direct evidence, Jenner no doubt vaccinated the child. Like his presentation to the King, the reception at Carlton House had important political overtones. The Prince's scandalous lifestyle contrasted sharply with the placid domestic virtues exemplified by his parents. Inevitably, an unhappy conflict evolved between father and son. The family differences took on national political significance during George III's first battle against mental disease in 1788 and 1789, when his eldest son as possible regent became a focus for the disparate opposition to the Pitt ministry. Although Pitt, and the King, seemed firmly in the saddle at the beginning of 1800, the Prince of Wales removed any doubt that Jenner's triumph had unanimous Establishment applause.

These marks of royal favour may have been the additional incentive Jenner needed to settle in London for at least part of each year. The Pearson row gave an immediate reason for taking up residence. Nor would the need for Jenner's steadying hand over the politics and science of vaccination disappear with the apparent neutralization of Pearson's Vaccine-Pock Institution. A year before, Henry Cline had urged this course on him for personal financial reasons, but now Jenner saw that there might well be broader social and medical ends to be served. To these he could respond.

Before the end of April 1800 he had moved from lodgings into a house on New Bond Street near the home of his west-country friend, Thomas Paytherus. Mrs Jenner and the children joined him there probably in time for his fifty-first birthday. On 30 April, Edward wrote a long letter to William Davies junior, giving him various instructions. One of his parcels of land, Shoulder-of-Mutton Ground, had been in the family for three generations. He thought it should be mowed this year. William was to inquire of Mr Pearce, the lawyer, what had happened about an affair that Jenner thought had caused a 'Mr B', possibly a younger Berkeley, 'to have entirely cut me.' The letter suggests that he intended his nephew to take charge of his local business affairs.

On another note, he told Davies: 'George [Jenner, brother of Henry] went Saturday to Colchester to prepare the way for my going. We shall inoculate about two thousand people, but unfortunately I find they have almost all of them to a man got the Itch. Shd. I catch it, could not your father furnish me with some good old family Receipt for curing it?' Jenner had been asked by the Duke of York to vaccinate the 86th Regiment. In the event he could not go just then, for unknown reasons, and George undertook all the vaccinations. Jenner arrived on 2 May to find that only one child had been successfully vaccinated. The men had by that time recovered, however, and Jenner tried again, but with little more to show for it. This experience provided his first evidence that skin eruptions such as the itch could disrupt vaccination. On the other hand, the lymph used had recently arrived in London from a farm at North Nibley, a Cotswold village between Berkeley and Kingscote, sent by Thomas Tanner's father, Robert. It was said to have been taken from cows inoculated with grease. Jenner also gave some to Mr Wachsel, surgeon to the Smallpox Hospital in London. No records exist of Mr Wachsel's results with it, and Jenner seems not to have considered that the vaccine itself could have been the cause of his Colchester failures.

With this extension of his practice in hand, Jenner replied immediately to a letter in the May issue of the *Medical and Physical Journal* from Richard Dunning, the Plymouth surgeon who later invented the word 'vaccination'. Dunning had written to Drs Jenner, Pearson and Woodville asking eight questions about vaccination. The cowpox inoculation, Jenner replied, 'taking the result of a great number of cases, appears to me, to be a disease as much milder than the inoculated small-pox, as that disease is milder than the casual small-pox.' No evidence had yet come to light that the cowpox could be communicated by effluvia. Providing that the vaccine lymph was good and the process complete, the person 'is ever after secure from the small-pox.' Although vaccine pustules might resemble the pustule caused by variolation, vaccination never produced 'a small pox-like pustule.'

Cowpox leads to no other diseases and may actually help scrofula. In short, Jenner had nothing new to add following the publication five months before of his third pamphlet. Only in one respect, the degree of resemblance between the smallpox and cowpox pustules, had he modified the statements published first in the *Inquiry*.

Others rallied to the flag. Thomas Denman, Jenner's former instructor in midwifery, wrote to the *Medical and Physical Journal* in March that following the directive of the Duke of York, a regiment of the Gloucester militia numbering about a hundred men had been vaccinated and then ordered to clean and move into barracks previously occupied by troops who had had smallpox. Not one case of smallpox occurred in the new regiment. Denman also published a letter commending vaccination that he received from Lord Derby in May. In the same issue of the magazine, Charles Cooke, the Gloucester apothecary whose doubts had been published along with Jenner's reply by Dr Thomas Beddoes the year before, now acknowledged the value of vaccination though he believed it should be practised only by qualified practitioners.

Baron said that the Navy accepted vaccination at the end of 1800, thanks to a recommendation by Sir Gilbert Blane, Physician-in-Ordinary to the Prince of Wales, previously physician to the fleet and the man who introduced lime juice to ward off scurvy in the British Navy. Blane must share the credit for vaccination in the Navy with Dr Thomas Trotter, then physician to the fleet stationed at Plymouth, where he was a colleague of Richard Dunning's. One of the journals that opposed vaccination criticized Trotter's action in July 1800.

In February 1800 'the Managers of the Publick Dispensary of Edinburgh established a Vaccine Institution at that Charity. . .for the gratuitous vaccination of the children of the poor'. Within four years four thousand had been vaccinated at the Institution, and many more in their homes. However, impressive as these figures may have seemed to those involved in the operations, they are less than cheering when seen in the light of a population greater than sixty-six thousand at the time. If a third of the total were children under twenty-one, a conservative estimate, a thousand vaccinations a year could do little to stop epidemic smallpox.

The number of the poor who accepted free vaccination from the institutions established for that purpose remained very low. Entrenched class prejudices on both sides largely account for the repeated failures of well-meaning charities to reach out widely into the population, and later in the decade the opposition managed to win over part of the popular press, especially the caricaturists, by the graphic absurdity of its claims. Despite Jenner's appreciation of the importance of favourable newspaper publicity, neither he nor his professional friends understood clearly what was happening. The war had greatly increased the cost of food. At the same time the shortage of meat and cereals stoked the enclosure movement, throwing thousands of people off land they had used customarily but not legally. Added to these factors was the absence of any coherent opposition to the ruling gentry that might have expressed some of the frustration of the poor. The threat of bloody revolution, moreover, only confirmed the Establishment's paranoia. The poor and illiterate, especially in London, sullenly rejected gifts from their social superiors out of perversity as well as fear.

Only when compulsion could be combined with enlightened self-interest did matters improve. One of the most dramatic examples was reported by Robert John Thornton, then a young doctor working in the wilds of West-morland on the estate of the Earl of Lonsdale. The Earl was a stocking and carpet manufacturer employing 'an hundred orphans. . .from the Foundling Hospitals of London and York' who were 'instructed in labour by the super-intendent, Mr. Bloom'. On 4 October 1800, Thornton vaccinated not the orphan operatives but Mr Bloom's four-and-a-half-year-old grandson. His next vaccinees were the seven children of the innkeeper in the nearby village of Lowther, but then a village child who had carried mushrooms for sale from Lowther to Penrith contracted smallpox. On orders from the Earl, who had a linen manufactury in the village, Thornton vaccinated all four hundred inhabitants. Needless to say, the smallpox did not spread. Soon afterwards he vaccinated 110 people from nearby villages in one morning, and completed about a thousand vaccinations in the neighbourhood within a few weeks. In November Thornton sent a charged lancet to Dr Heysham of Carlisle for his infant granddaughter. The lymph failed to take. After three more failures, Thornton adopted more direct means: 'I agreed with the parents of one of the villagers, who had the pustule in the proper state, to set out on horseback, for Carlisle, with his child, Mary BROWN, a girl only five years old. . .and immediately upon reaching Carlisle, after a journey of twenty-six miles, *nine* persons were inoculated from her by Dr. Heysham'. Brown's expenses were paid, and he received 15s 6d in gifts from Heysham, as well as a payment from Thornton which he at first refused.

At the other end of the social scale, Jane Austen wrote to her sister on 20 November 1800 that she had attended a dinner party after which her host and hostess 'alternately read Dr. Jenner's pamphlet on the cow-pox.' Which of the three pamphlets then published, she does not say, but such determination to be informed must have been unusual even then.

No doubt there was room for much public confusion. The Vaccine-Pock Institution continued to insist that the 'variolous-like eruptions during the Vaccina in the year 1799 and 1800. . .could not be satisfactorily explained'. In May 1800, the period covered by the first *Report*, its author, George Pearson, summarized his experience to date. Cowpox, he wrote, could be inoculated into cows, it did not originate from grease, it could be passed on only once and by inoculation, and it could not be caught after smallpox.

Jenner would not have been seriously disturbed by these assertions. Either they agreed with his position, or they were not central to the argument. The occurrence of eruptions after vaccination was another matter, however, and Pearson also wrote in a report for the *Medical and Physical Journal* that two kinds of eruption could occur, one 'probably the same as the Small-pox' and the other resembling smallpox but much milder. Independent testimony demonstrates how Pearson's remarks disturbed the public:

> Such was the terror inspired by the first reports of vaccine inocula-
> tion in London, together with the falsehoods propagated with great
> industry by certain artful and ambitious men, that it was in danger
> of being laid aside, had not more favourable reports by other prac-
> titioners, and a testimonial recommending the practice, signed by a
> considerable number of the most eminent physicians and surgeons in
> the metropolis, appeared in the medical journals, and other respectable
> channels of information.

The signatures in question were collected by John Ring, a surgeon at St Thomas's Hospital who had studied with both the Hunters. Ring was a poet and classicist and above all a medical journalist. Although he and Jenner may have met before, Jenner first wrote to thank Ring for attacking Dr Benjamin Moseley's ill grounded remarks about 'Cowmania'. From 1799 for fifteen years he wrote millions of words in defence of Jennerian vaccina-tion. Ring was Jenner's publicist, loyal and uncritical, in a symbiosis that could only end badly. In 1811 Jenner wrote to Baron about 'poor John Ring' whose 'derangements', he said, were due to 'mental irritation of the most painful kind'. Ring's increasingly intemperate attacks on those with any doubts at all about vaccination had at last convinced even Jenner that his support had become a liability. Yet he had encouraged Ring to throw up the defensive earthworks which Jenner himself was either too fastidious or too preoccupied with his worldwide correspondence to undertake. He also knew that Ring had personally vaccinated more individuals than anyone else in England. 'He vaccinated vast numbers of the poor,' wrote James Moore, then Assistant Director of the National Vaccine Establishment, 'and distrib-uted to the friends and enemies of the Vaccine both lymph and sarcasms with equal liberality.' After his remarks to Baron, Jenner's letter two years later asking Moore to find out why Ring has 'broken off his correspondence with me near a twelve month' seems a trifle naïve.

Ring's principal instrument for collecting signatures in defence of vacci-nation was an advertisement in the *Morning Herald* for 19 July 1800, although he also used his professional contacts wherever possible. By August he had the signatures of thirty-three physicians and forty surgeons. The doctors included Thomas Denman, Denman's sons-in-law, Matthew Baillie and Richard Croft; John Lettsom, Robert Willan, Thomas Bradley and Robert

Thornton. Amongst the surgeons were Thomas Paytherus, Henry Cline, the young Astley Cooper, James Moore and men such as John Abernethy and William Blair, who became active in the Royal Jennerian Society. All of the signatories – and there were thirty more by January 1801 – were Londoners, because Ring's object was to display the support of powerful figures in the medical establishment of the capital. They signed a declaration that 'those persons who have had the cowpox are perfectly secure from the infection of the smallpox. We also declare that the inoculated cowpox is a much milder and safer disease than the inoculated smallpox.' Similar declarations were later issued by the medical faculties of York, Leeds, Chester, Durham, Ipswich and Oxford.

After six momentous months, Jenner left London for Berkeley on 23 June 1800. He must have known not only the nature of the report Pearson was about to publish in the *Medical and Physical Journal*, but also that Ring had begun work on the testimonial to vaccine inoculation. Although it may be true that Jenner returned to Gloucestershire because he needed money and could capitalize quickly on his practice in Berkeley and Cheltenham, he seems to have departed in some haste. Catherine and the children stayed on at New Bond Street for the present. He may have wanted to be away before Ring's advertisement appeared, to avoid both the donkey-work and the whiff of controversy. His friends may have advised that with the aura of royalty so near, it would be better to maintain an Olympian reserve while the troops engaged in battle. I think he had also realized that nothing was to be gained in the eruptions argument with Woodville and Pearson without more experience of vaccination on both sides.

In any case, he travelled with George Jenner and his servant, Richard. They slept at Buckingham the first night, and the next day dined with William Fermor of Tusmore near Oxford. Fermor was a gifted dilettante and landowner whose formal education seems to have been limited, although he had been awarded the degree of Doctor of Civil Law by Oxford in 1792. He and Jenner had met in Cheltenham during the summer of 1798. At first sceptical about cowpox, Fermor nevertheless asked George Jenner to stay with him at Tusmore and to undertake vaccinations of local people. In May 1800 Fermor published a pamphlet in support of vaccination based on 326 cases of whom 173 had been challenged by variolation, with no effect. He had also shown some of George Jenner's cases to Sir Christopher Pegge, then Reader in Anatomy at Oxford, to Dr Wall, Professor of Chemistry, to Dr Williams, Regius Professor of Botany, and to Mr Grosvenor, surgeon to the Radcliffe Infirmary. After his dinner with Fermor, Jenner went on to reach Oxford the same evening. The next day he met these four eminent medical men as well as the Vice-Chancellor of the university, Dr Marlow. All five later signed the testimonial supporting vaccination.

During this brief visit Jenner was shown some people who had been recently vaccinated, including a child who was the patient of one of Mr Grosvenor's students. Out of this incident a vaccination *cause célèbre* was to develop. In September 1801 William Fermor wrote to Jenner inquiring about four children in one family who had had smallpox after vaccinations. Jenner recalled that he had seen only one of these siblings and had pronounced the vaccination 'insecure, from the appearance of the arm'. As these cases became part of the ammunition of the antivaccinists, it emerged that the mother had failed to act on Jenner's advice to have this child revaccinated. Naturally the story evolved through repetition until it asserted that Jenner himself had performed the vaccinations, and if not Edward Jenner then his nephew George.

Jenner arrived in Berkeley on 27 June. William Davies called the next day, no doubt on business. Two days later Jenner visited his friend Henry Hicks at Eastington and dined there with young Davies and Fosbroke, and the next morning Davies rode to Gloucester to pay his uncle's land taxes. On 10 July, Jenner took up residence again in Cheltenham, where his family joined him at the end of the month.

Baron reported that during his periods of residence, Dr Jenner offered free vaccination to the poor of Cheltenham 'who thought fit to apply at stated periods'. Individual families could apply, and parish officers often sent along groups of those who would accept the new preventive. One parish had held back until this summer of 1800, when their children were suddenly brought forward in large numbers. It seems that smallpox had recently ravaged the parish, while neighbouring parishes where people had taken advantage of free vaccinations escaped. The cost of coffins for paupers became so burdensome to the parish that the churchwardens 'compelled the people to avail themselves of Dr. Jenner's kind offer.'

In August, Jenner received an important letter from Count de la Roque, a Frenchman who had been resident in London when the *Inquiry* was published. He had translated the pamphlet in January 1800, and it had already gone through three impressions. De la Roque said he had now also translated *Further Observations*. Prompted perhaps by an earlier reference to Jenner's work in a new book on variolation by Valentin and Desoteux, the Institut National and the École de Médecine had established a joint committee to look into vaccination. A Dr Colladon of Geneva, who had been in London, returned home through Paris and brought lymph which he had probably obtained from Pearson. Trials made at Le Salpêtrière failed. Meanwhile the committee had sent one of its members, Dr Aubert, to England where he met Woodville and Pearson, and spoke frequently to Jenner himself. Then in April an institute for the promotion of vaccination was established in Paris with the support of Lucien Bonaparte, Minister of the Interior. Two months later the *Journal de Paris*, published by the government, reported thirty vaccinations with new matter from Pearson, but possibly because of a very hot summer in Paris that lymph, as well as some sent from Geneva, was lost. Dr Woodville, 'having little to lose in England,' wrote James Moore a decade later, 'set out for France on a vaccine adventure.' In Boulogne Woodville inoculated three children and left instructions with an English physician, Dr Nowell, to send vaccine matter from the arms of these children to him in Paris. There he again demonstrated proper techniques, and the fresh lymph seems to have been preserved. A year later the *London Medical Review* noticed *Sur la Vaccine* by a Dr Careno just published in Vienna, which embraced 'this opportunity of congratulating Dr. Jenner on the success of his labours.'

The exigencies of war provided both incentive and opportunity for English medical men to extend the use of vaccine matter. Jenner's neighbour, Dr J. R. Marshall of Stonehouse, sailed at the beginning of July 1800 with letters from the Duke of York to the military governors in the Mediterranean, directing them to introduce vaccination into their garrisons forthwith. He was accompanied by Dr John Walker, Marshall's schoolfellow in Cockermouth, along with William Woodville. Walker had begun his career as a blacksmith with his father. In the 1780s he became an engraver in Dublin, a self-described Quaker who was never actually admitted to the Society of Friends, a schoolmaster and the author of a geography and gazetteer. In 1794 he entered Guy's Hospital as a student, and took an MD at Leyden five years later, during which time, wrote his biographer, he had been 'supported by the lady to whom he was afterwards married.' During the winter of 1799 he took his bride to visit friends at Stonehouse, including Marshall, and met Jenner. On 3 July 1800, Jenner wrote to Walker from Berkeley: 'I am extremely happy to find that you are to accompany Dr. Marshall in his very important tour, not only on account of [y]our known integrity, but from your knowledge of the subject he is engaged in'. Together Marshall and Walker vaccinated British military personnel in Gibraltar, Menorca and Malta. They may have been the moving force behind a Jennerian Institute that was established on the island of Malta about this time.

Walker went on to Egypt with the expedition led by Sir Ralph Abercrombie. Dr Marshall returned to England during 1802 via Naples and Palermo. The *Inquiry* had been published in Italian toward the end of 1801, and some opposition had developed in the two states from those who considered smallpox to be God's will. Marshall wrote to Dr Jenner from Paris in January that during the previous year smallpox had caused eight thousand deaths in Palermo. The Church, therefore, seemed not to share the antivaccinist view. 'It was not unusual to see in the mornings of the public inoculation at the Hospital a procession of men, women, and children, conducted through the streets by a priest carrying a cross, come to be inoculated. . . .the common people expressed themselves certain that it was a blessing sent from Heaven, though discovered by one heretic and practised by another.' While he was in Paris, Marshall, accompanied by George Jenner, attended a dinner in honour of Edward Jenner given by the official Vaccine Committee during the brief period of peace.

At the time of the French dinner, Jenner was in London immersed in his petition to Parliament, of which more in a moment. He must have felt fairly confident, in light of the information he received in his correspondence, that the cause advanced on the continent without his presence. From north Italy Dr Louis Sacco wrote in October 1801 that he had been appointed Director of Vaccination for the new Napoleonic state, the Cisalpine Republic, with its capital at Milan. Sacco was perhaps the first medical man to enforce vaccination as an official policy. About a year later, he sent Jenner via Dr Woodville cowpox lymph from a Lombardy herd, the earliest recorded example of such a reciprocal gift.

At the end of 1800 one Don Francesco Piguilem brought vaccine from Paris to Madrid. Translation of the *Inquiry* into Spanish was announced in the *Madrid Gazette* on 3 May 1801, and Jenner was elected an honorary member of the Royal Economical Society, the first of his foreign honours.

Vaccine sent to Geneva by Dr De Carro in Vienna unfortunately caused some smallpox deaths. Later, according to Jenner, George Pearson implied that he – Jenner – had exported spurious vaccine to Geneva. Of course, he denied 'this malignant design', and asked his friend Dr Marcet to write to his continental contacts correcting Pearson's new calumny. By January 1801, however, fifteen hundred citizens of the Swiss city had been successfully vaccinated, and a campaign had the support of the Protestant clergy who handed out leaflets at baptisms recommending vaccination.

Vaccination began in the German states during 1800, thanks principally to Dr Ballhorn's translation of Jenner's *Inquiry* in Hanover. Opposition emerged in Frankfurt and Berlin. A Dr Ehrmann of Frankfurt published an article arguing that cowpoxing could not succeed, but his influence was eliminated by his suicide. The Berlin situation was complicated by anti-Semitism. A Jewish banker and physician named Hertz asked Dr Wolf, another Jewish doctor, to vaccinate his two children. Wolf opposed vaccination and variolated the children. Both of them died. Wolf's prosecution for murder no doubt helped the cause of vaccination. Of much greater practical value to the people of Berlin, however, was the successful vaccination of Princess Louisa with matter sent by Jenner at the end of 1799. The King established an inoculation institute in his capital and in 1802 recommended vaccination throughout Prussia.

The Austro-Hungarian provinces of Bohemia and Moravia received vaccine from Count Francis Hugh de Salm, who had visited Jenner in London. Bohemian priests read the names of smallpox victims from their pulpits and urged parents to vaccinate their children. The sister of the King of Poland, then no more than a region divided amongst Russia, Prussia and Austria-Hungary, lived in Vienna, where she met De Carro and was instrumental in bringing vaccination to the people of her dismembered homeland. In October 1801 vaccine was sent from Breslau in Pomerania, part of Prussia, to Moscow. So successful were the first vaccinations that the Dowager Empress Maria sent Jenner a diamond ring worth about £1500. 'It consisted of a cluster of brilliants, with a very large one in the centre,' wrote his friend Dibdin; 'the whole sat in an oblong, and, to an English taste, old-fashioned way. We could never prevail upon its owner to wear it, except upon the birthday of one of his children.' The covering letter from Maria having been in French, Edward replied in the language of European culture.

Holland was then also an enemy country. Vaccination was not introduced until early 1801. In March Dr L. Davids of Rotterdam, who translated the *Inquiry* into Dutch, wrote to Jenner that the cowpox had come, 'just at the time the small-pox made ravages through the whole country; but thank God not one is infected after the vaccine.'

The situation in Denmark was even more favourable. Probably through an introduction from their mutual friend Jean De Carro, Jenner met Dr Alexander J. G. Marcet, also a Genevois, who had studied medicine at Edinburgh and established a practice in London. Marcet knew scientists in various European cities and obtained vaccine matter from Jenner in 1801 which he sent to Copenhagen. Success with this batch inspired the Danish King to appoint a committee on vaccination. After his usual delay, caused by the volume of his correspondence – 'I am now so far behind hand, that full forty Letters lie before me unanswer'd.' – Jenner thanked Marcet for a paper from Copenhagen about smallpox in cows, and cited another case that seemed to him to prove the origin of cowpox in horse-pox. The Danish committee reported favourably in December. The King accepted the report and backed its recommendations. Indeed, Denmark banned variolation and made vaccination compulsory in 1803, one of the first countries to do so, with the result that smallpox disappeared entirely there.

From Denmark vaccination spread to Sweden, where it enjoyed similar acceptance. Only in Vienna, where De Carro had first introduced the Jennerian sword on the continent, was there a hitch. After supporting a Viennese ordinance requiring vaccination in 1802, the Austrian government reversed itself, probably as a result of reports of failures. During 1803 De Carro wrote to Marcet that it was prohibited to give notice of free vaccinations for the poor, to perform such services and indeed to publish accounts of successes. Vaccination was confounded with variolation, De Carro said. This surprising setback was reversed at least by 1808, when vaccination was again required in Austria.

About the time that Jenner returned to Cheltenham in July 1800, De Carro was introduced in Vienna to the parents of Lady Elgin, wife of the British Ambassador to the Ottoman Porte in Constantinople. It was a meeting pregnant with significance for the spread of vaccination, because Mr and Mrs Nesbit reported De Carro's enthusiasm to their daughter and her husband. Lord Elgin asked De Carro for vaccine and had his own child vaccinated successfully. From the young Elgin's arm, in the usual manner, vaccination began in Constantinople, in Corinth and in Athens.

In March 1801 Lord Elgin received a request for vaccine from Jonathan Duncan, Governor of Bombay, who suggested it be sent via Baghdad and Bussore. For some reason Elgin delayed until September, and that vaccine failed. A second consignment was dispatched, with which Dr James Short established cowpox at Baghdad early in 1802. Shortly thereafter, Mr Milne, a surgeon and the British Consul at Bussore, using matter from Baghdad, vaccinated some forty people including crew members of the *Recovery*, headed for Bombay. Finally on 14 June 1802, Dr Helenus Scott of the East India Company in Bombay vaccinated Anna Dusthill, the three-year-old daughter of a servant to a Captain Hardie: 'from her alone, the whole of the matter that is about to be sent all over India was at first derived.'

Jenner had tried several times to send matter by ship to the East, the first aboard the *Queen*, an East Indiaman that was lost at sea in 1799. He was twice called in by Lord Hobart, the Secretary of State, because of an epidemic that had broken out in Ceylon. Finally he proposed that twenty recruits who had not had smallpox be placed on a ship bound for India with a surgeon to attend them, one of the volunteers having been vaccinated before sailing so that the vaccine could be passed from arm to arm during the voyage. Hobart rejected the proposal, whereupon Jenner determined to put up £1000 to equip a vessel himself, but the successful transmission of the lymph that had originated with De Carro intervened.

In August 1802 some of the Bombay vaccine matter was used to vaccinate in Trincomalee. From there it spread from arm to arm around Ceylon. The successful programme of vaccination on the island has been credited to the Medical Superintendent-General of the colonial government, Thomas Christie, who himself inoculated two thousand in the Colombo district in one month. By 1808 no smallpox was reported from Ceylon, with the exception of two or three cases near the northern port of Gallée, imported by boat from the Maldivian coast of Bengal.

From Ceylon vaccine was carried up the west coast of India by the British Navy. The Governor-General of India, the Marquis of Wellesley (later the Duke of Wellington), published an order in council commending Dr John Fleming of the Medical Board, Captain Anderson of the ship *Hunter*, Dr James Anderson at Fort St George and some other doctors for 'the successful introduction of Dr. Jenner's discovery.' At first vaccination seemed to be spreading amongst the Indians without hindrance. 'The Brahmins finding this preservative had originated from the cow hastily adopted it and thus the sacred benefits of this animal have been happily realized,' wrote a surgeon in Bedford, basing his information on a letter he had had from Jenner. Brahmin goodwill disappeared quickly, however, when the inoculators amongst them found that the customary 'slight offering to an idol' which passed through their hands ceased with vaccination. 'It was boldly asserted. . .that the Vaccine could answer no good purpose, because none of the water of the Ganges was mixed with it; and. . .without this additive, even Small Pox inoculation was ineffectual.' This difficulty proved to be surmountable when Lord Wellesley offered to double the income that inoculators received from variolation, if they would adopt vaccination. At the end of 1806, Dr George Kier, Superintendent-General of Vaccine Inoculation at Bombay, wrote telling Jenner that he estimated five thousand lives had been saved in Bombay alone. Nevertheless, the size and poverty of India, perhaps exacerbated by the priorities of British rule, meant that the subcontinent was among the last regions to be freed of smallpox.

The remaining sphere of British influence at the beginning of the nineteenth century, the New World, benefited from being nearer to the homeland than India – a matter of days rather than weeks – and from a climate less likely to hasten putrefaction. At the end of 1798 Jenner sent vaccine dried on threads to his friend the Revd John Clinch in Trinity, Newfoundland. Clinch vaccinated his own children and about seven hundred local people, the first to do so in North America.

At about the same time that Dr Jenner sent vaccine to Clinch, Dr John Lettsom posted a copy of the *Inquiry* to his friend and co-religionist, Dr Benjamin Waterhouse, Professor of the Theory and Practice of Physic at Harvard University. Born in Newport, Rhode Island, in 1754, Waterhouse had begun his medical apprenticeship there, but had sailed to England on the last ship to leave Boston in March 1775. In London, he lived and studied with his mother's cousin, Dr John Fothergill, who also taught Lettsom. Waterhouse went to Edinburgh, took his MD at Leyden in 1780, and returned to Newport in 1781. In March 1799 he published a short account of the *Inquiry* in the *Columbian Sentinel*, and soon afterwards addressed the American Academy of Arts and Sciences on the subject. John Adams, then President of the United States, was also President of the Academy.

Not until July 1800, however, did Waterhouse obtain vaccine. It had been sent to him by Dr Haygarth, now at Bath, who had it from Jenner's stock. Daniel Waterhouse, aged five, was the first United States citizen to be vaccinated, but three more Waterhouse children and three servants quickly followed. Waterhouse had his son Daniel variolated at the Smallpox Hospital near Boston, with no effect. His next move was most un-Jennerian.

He determined to retain a monopoly of the vaccine practice by keeping details secret and offering franchises to fellow practitioners. Among the first was Dr Lyman Spalding, a recent Harvard graduate then practising at Portsmouth, New Hampshire, and there may have been at least three others in Boston, Amherst and Hampton. Waterhouse intended to ask a fee of $5 for each vaccination, but finally accepted $150 from Spalding and sent him vaccine matter. The monopoly lasted one more month! By mid-October 1800 several New England doctors had received vaccine from England. Waterhouse believed that in view of the pains he had taken – though what pains neither he nor his biographer explained – and the risk to his reputation, he should keep vaccination 'under his own eye until the practice is more firmly established by the public opinion.' It might have been better had he succeeded for a little longer.

According to Baron, some Americans bought pieces of the shirt sleeves of patients stiffened with the purulent discharge from an ulcer following vaccination, and soaked the threads in water to obtain matter. One sailor on a ship from London bound for Marblehead, Massachusetts, was thought to have cowpox, but inoculation with matter from his pustules spread the smallpox. Waterhouse had written to Jenner describing these disasters and asking for new vaccine. Jenner's reply arrived in March 1801. Waterhouse sent some of this matter to the new American President, Thomas Jefferson, whom he had supported politically. Because Jefferson was a Virginian, Waterhouse asked his help in introducing vaccination to the southern states. The President entered into the scheme enthusiastically, despite the failure of Waterhouse's first two shipments to him. With the third and the help of his sons-in-law, he vaccinated some two hundred of his Virginia neighbours. Impressed by the difficulty of transporting vaccine, Jefferson designed a special two-part bottle consisting of an inner phial containing the matter, which was immersed in a larger bottle filled with water to prevent overheating. According to a letter from Waterhouse to Jenner, the President arranged for vaccine to be provided for some American Indian tribes, 'and the interpreter. . .took a copy of the directions for conducting the process I had transmitted to the President'. The Plains Indians had suffered severely from smallpox outbreaks from the Gulf of Mexico to the Dakotas. An embassy under the leadership of Little Turtle came to Washington in December 1801 to meet Jefferson, who told him about the new therapy. The Indian introduced vaccination amongst his own people. Later, Jefferson wrote to Jenner personally, assuring him 'that mankind can never forget that you have lived.'

Edward corresponded directly with the Abenaqui tribe of Canadian Indians. On 11 August 1807 he sent his pamphlets 'For Chief of the Five Nations'. In November they replied with a string of wampum and an address of thanks signed by ten chiefs: Two Pointed Arrows, Two Wampum Belts, Clear Sky, Feather on His Head, Moving a Tree with Brush and Planting It, A Town Destroyer, Raven, Belt Carrier, A Disturber of Sleep, and Fish Carrier.

The career of Benjamin Waterhouse continued to be profoundly affected by his espousal of vaccination. During 1801 he wrote to Lettsom about a fraud perpetrated by some medical students who claimed they had produced cowpox by inoculating cows. Since cowpox is not native to America, their announcement was on the face of it important. Apparently Waterhouse accepted the story when he wrote to Lettsom, only realizing the truth sometime later. I find this puzzling, because according to an anonymous article dated April 1802 in the *London Medical Review*, cowpox had been 'discovered' at about the same time, May 1801, in three places: Sheffield, Massachusetts, and Goshen and Danbury, Connecticut, by three local doctors. That anyone should accept the sudden appearance of a previously unknown disease in three different communities without the most careful checking no doubt testifies to the power of wishful thinking.

At the end of May 1802, because doubts had been expressed, Waterhouse asked the Boston Board of Health to set up an inquiry into vaccination. The Board adopted the practice in principle, and later the same year satisfactorily tested nineteen vaccinated boys by variolation.

Waterhouse continued a friendly correspondence with Jenner, but his relationships with the Boston doctors deteriorated. Although he had ceased to charge for vaccinations, the early attempt at monopoly returned to plague him. He was subjected to constant sniping from his medical colleagues. In 1806 he published a broadside attacking the Massachusetts Medical Society. Three years later he was forced to resign his lectureship in natural history, and in 1812 Harvard dismissed him. Not until late in the century was his work on behalf of vaccination recognized. Meanwhile, in February 1802 vaccine lymph had been shipped from England to Charleston, South Carolina, providing a new American centre for the spread of vaccination.

Despite setbacks such as the strange reversal of the Austro-Hungarian government, which appear now to have been minor whatever their impact at the time, vaccination advanced everywhere. In Britain, except for cavils by George Pearson and the singular virulence of Benjamin Moseley, there appeared to be no opposition worthy of the name. Jenner's study, whether in Berkeley, Cheltenham or London, became increasingly the hub of a network of correspondence, receiving data from around the world and broadcasting data, instructions and propaganda in reply. If the names of the correspondents – Waterhouse, Curier, Coloumb, Delambre, Fried, Sacco – are for the most part forgotten, Jenner understood that without their practical efforts, the Jeffersons and the Marias of Russia would have remained silently ignorant. William Wilberforce, MP and would-be liberator of black slaves, noted some time later that there was 'no man who is so much inquired after, by Foreigners, when they arrive in this country.' Little wonder that Jenner told Henry Addington, then Prime Minister, 'that it would be my fate to be Vaccine Clerk to the World', an expression that he seemed to like because he is said to have repeated it often.

Jenner met Addington in order to obtain the essential support of the Prime Minister for a petition to Parliament requesting compensation from the Treasury for the 'expense and anxiety' he had incurred. The petition seemed to him the logical outcome of his earlier refusal to contemplate secrecy. When he had taken the opportunity to establish a practice in London, afforded by his presence there to assure the proper conduct of vaccination, he had been frustrated by his very openness. The people who could pay him had their own doctors, who were perfectly capable of following Jenner's simple directions. Of those who did not, many must have felt they ought not to impose on the time of so important a gentleman for an operation that could be performed by the apothecary. Thus, Jenner's attempt to establish a London practice cost him a great deal of money, because at the same time his income from Berkeley and Cheltenham naturally declined. Faced with these hard facts, his friends, medical men like Cline and Lettsom and political supporters like the Berkeleys, now agreed that he ought to apply for public compensation.

Jenner returned to London from Cheltenham on 6 November 1800. Although it would be more than a year before he began to do something about it, I think the idea of a petition was already a gleam in his eye. He settled again in New Bond Street. Part of his intention must have been to write his fourth pamphlet, again answering criticisms, bringing details of the practice up to date, and for the first time summarizing his own priority in the introduction of vaccine inoculation. In particular he began by calling attention to the commencement of his interest 'upwards of twenty-five years ago', or some time after he left Hunter's board to return to Berkeley. *The Origin of the Vaccine Inoculation* was published on 6 May 1801. It is very short, scarcely a thousand words, but its completion had many interruptions.

Soon after he arrived in London, Jenner fell ill. Again it seems to have been typhoid fever, but this time the effects were less severe. By 20 December he was well enough to attend a party given by Lord and Lady Spencer at their house in London. There Jenner was asked to explain the theory and practice of vaccination to a number of political figures, including Lord Lucan, Lady Spencer's brother; Lord Macartney, first British Ambassador to China and governor of the newly acquired territory of the Cape of Good Hope, but now retired; Mr Greville (probably Henry), a friend of Sir Joseph Banks; and Lord Campden, who held various offices under Pitt and was also Chancellor of Cambridge University. This may have been the beginning of a fairly well orchestrated campaign to precede the application to Parliament for compensation.

He found time, however, to take the children to see the illuminations in honour of the Queen's birthday on 19 January, and the next day he took Edward junior to Mr Evans's school in Islington. Jenner was also standing *in loco parentis* to the son of his Newfoundland friend, Revd John Clinch. The young man was 'very well at Mr Moore's', and, according to Jenner, wanted to become a bookseller. Mr Moore may have been the apothecary, however, whose partnership with John Savory occupied premises on New Bond Street. Perhaps Clinch junior was an apprentice in the house, an arrangement for which Jenner could have been responsible, and the remark about bookselling might easily have been persiflage. A warehouse, along with a shop of some description, occupied the ground floor of the Jenners' house on New Bond Street.

On 23 January Jenner wrote an informative letter to Lady Berkeley, who had probably inquired about his plans:

> Notwithstanding the immense importance of evidence before me in support of the effect intended for Parliamentary consideration, yet your Ladyship may be assured I am industriously seeking for more; indeed it already begins to flow in from all quarters. On this account, I will be bound for it, no blame shall lie at my door, the Committee will have at their command all the medical Men in Town, & from them they may learn enough to remove all that nonsense which has crept into the brains of some of the sceptical. They may, if they please, trace this to all its sources; & I hope they will trace it; & then it will appear to have sprung either from jealousy; as at Gloster – from Envy, as at Bristol; & from stupidity, as half the country over.

The letter leaves no doubt that the campaign was under way. He concluded that he expected Lady Berkeley would be in London by the time his petition was admitted. The changes in administration then planned, including the accession to office of George Tierney and Sir Benjamin Hobhouse, would not affect his chances. Both men joined the Addington government the next year. The letter is also remarkable because of its incoherence, as though it had been written under much mental pressure. Existing evidence provides no clear explanation. Not even the causes of complaint at Gloucester and Bristol are known, although they may have been, respectively, Cooke the apothecary, and Beddoes who perhaps seemed to be dragging his feet. I am inclined to believe that Lady Berkeley, though she was genuinely eager for Jenner to prosper, could be a trifle imperious, and that the object of her concern was still not absolutely certain that his proposed petition could be morally justified.

On 20 February Edward received his first material recognition from a group of Englishmen. Dr Trotter, physician to the fleet at Plymouth, wrote to him enclosing a gold medal presented on behalf of the medical officers of the Navy. In April he attended a meeting of a society founded by John Hunter and another of Jenner's instructors, Dr Fordyce, the Lyceum Medicum Londiniense, and was elected a fellow.

Amidst all the signs of acceptance and success, however, stumbling blocks arose. On 19 June 1801 he wrote to a medical friend in Suffolk about some vaccination problems, but he concluded with a PS: 'My Parliamentary affair is put off to the next Session – Perhaps it may be all for the best.' Pitt had resigned in March because of his quarrel with the King over the government of Ireland. The loss of a chief minister whom he trusted no doubt contributed to a recurrence of George III's madness, and for about three months government almost ceased to exist. Jenner and his correspondents would have been alive to these 'greater' issues, and I believe Jenner was glad not to be caught up by events that might have given his petition short shrift.

At the end of July the family travelled together from London to Cheltenham. Mrs Jenner returned to Berkeley with the children, leaving Edward in Cheltenham where he remained alone until the end of November. It was probably during this season that he met Thomas Frognall Dibdin, a bibliophile who became Jenner's admirer and, occasionally, his amanuensis. Dibdin then lived in Worcester and moved to London two years later. It is also recorded that on 4 September 1801, with his friend Henry Hicks, Jenner attended the Theatre Royal, Cheltenham, for a performance in honour of the Prince of Wales. Because there is no evidence that he went to the theatre before or afterwards, Jenner's interest on that unique occasion may have been more political than dramatic. Even so, Catherine Jenner's absence is unusual.

So shadowy a figure is she because of the paucity of evidence that I can only guess at the reasons. In the midst of a politicking letter about the petition, probably written from Berkeley to Jenner in London in early January 1802, the Duchess of Berkeley introduced a quite surprising paragraph:

> I have a long letter from Mrs Jenner by this nights post, I am fearful of hurting her feelings were I to answer it as my Heart and Soul seem to dictate, and yet it would grieve me extremely could I for a moment think you would ever adopt any system but that you were raised up in, what would your Brother Stephen have felt had he thought R. Hill was to be an associate in your Family or any of his sect – restrain the enthusiasm of Mrs Jenner if possible, or when your Children grow up they will be all Preachers –

R. Hill was no doubt Rowland Hill, a Methodist minister with a congregation at Newington Butts in south London and a summer residence at Wotton-under-Edge, probably his birthplace. That he was no common convert to Methodism may be judged from his marriage in 1789 to Mary Tudway, sister of the MP for Wells. Hill also became an early supporter of vaccination, and vaccinated many of his parishioners himself. Indeed, so effective was Hill's championship of the cause that the redoubtable Benjamin Moseley attacked him personally in a scurrilous pamphlet, *An Oliver for a*

Rowland; or, a Cow Pox Epistle to the Reverend Rowland Hill. A suggestion of its flavour can be sniffed from the knowledge, apparently widespread amongst literate persons two centuries ago, that Rowland was the legendary son of Charlemagne, and Oliver his companion. What is more, the Reverend Hill replied in kind with *A Rowland for an Oliver.* Neither pamphlet much advanced the understanding of vaccination.

Evidently Catherine Jenner felt disillusioned by the Church of England. If she did, she was scarcely unique even amongst people of her own class. What is more, she had reason: her health was very poor. During the period of their courtship, unrecognized early signs of tuberculosis and the frustration of her affection for Edward almost certainly produced a bout of melancholia. As early as 1792, the Jenner family were concerned about her. 'We are very happy to hear by letter just receiv'd from Mary [Black] that Mrs. Jenner is so much better,' wrote the Reverend Henry Jenner to William Davies senior. Five years separated her first child from her second, and her third, born three years later when she was thirty-six, was her last. In May 1803 she was recovering from the flu, 'but I trust, if the wind wd but blow from a more general quarter, She would soon get rid of her Cough, which at present is very troublesome,' Edward wrote. A few months later she was, if anything, worse: 'Mrs Jenner is much reduc'd by her late long & severe illness,' her husband told a family friend: 'but I trust she is now clearly convalescent.' Toward the end of the year he wrote to his favourite sister, Anne Davies: 'My dear Wife on the whole gains ground. She rides gently on a quiet Pony when the weather will permit – You talk of her trotting round the Town of Berkeley with you. I have no objection provided you bring a Horse. It will be rather a singular expedition. Could not one contrive to get a Penny by it?' The note of levity reflects Jenner's gratitude that Catherine was better again. But he knew well enough that it could not last, and so did she.

Other factors may have stirred what Mary Berkeley called her 'enthusiasm' – a grave religious misdemeanour in the Established Church. To Catherine, who had experienced Cheltenham society even before her marriage, its shallowness may have surpassed its charms. She lacked Edward's practical incentives for mixing socially as well as professionally with their neighbours. Although it was her duty to accompany her husband and to maintain a home for him, perhaps in the middle of 1801 when he was preoccupied with his petition, she felt she must have solitude and the comfort of a more active vision of God than the Church of England offered her. Perhaps there was even a difference between husband and wife about the petition itself, concerning his moral justification for seeking financial reward. Might not Catherine have held consistently to Jenner's former view that because he had enough to get by on, the power to serve mankind was reward enough? If there was a domestic clash, however subdued, it passed. When many years later she wrote to her brother-in-law, William Davies, 'My good Man desires his best affections', she stated no more than the simple truth of her marital relationship. Yet a rift in 1801 could have acted to enhance her search for religious comfort.

Nothing overt seems to have happened as a result of Lady Berkeley's unexpected intervention. Catherine and her husband may have had a word. He might well have pointed out that whatever her doubts, he had committed himself to the course he was following and could not withdraw. In any case she must have agreed that the promotion of vaccination was the true object, and there was little doubt that if his financial petition succeeded, that cause would be immensely strengthened. He had probably sensed that the Duchess of Berkeley was also saying, this is the wrong time for a lapse from orthodoxy, and passed the warning on to Mrs Jenner without revealing its source. If it was not enough simply to invoke the Kingscote family name against religious deviancy, moreover, perhaps Jenner sought the help of her sister, Mrs Ladbroke, and her brother Robert.

Catherine remained within the Church of her fathers, but her religious commitment did not diminish. She is said to have founded and taught in the Berkeley Sunday School. Obviously she was engaged in good works for the poor. At the end of 1805 Edward wrote to William Davies senior from Cheltenham about the monument to Stephen Jenner, then being sculpted by Charles Manning. After proposing some initial lines for the inscription, he said: 'Mrs Jenner will add the remainder.' Her contribution was sonorous but sound; it concluded: 'may our good and gracious Lord of his infinite mercy grant that when our Bodies, and the Bodies of those belonging to us are entomb'd – our never dying Tombs may dwell with Him. . . .' Her correspondence was peppered with religious asides. In one letter from Berkeley to her sister-in-law Anne Davies in Eastington, she acknowledged a scrapbook prepared by William's younger brother, Robert, 'wch. contains many great and important Truths in wch. I most heartily coincide & as heartily pray that every body belonging to us may be sensible of.' 'We are very busy in preparing for our journey next Tuesday – may we all be as earnest in preparing for our grand journey out of this World!' Inasmuch as Jenner remained in Berkeley, she may have been taking the children with her to Cheltenham. The preparations included arranging for the Davieses to take 'poor dear Clinch & sending him to school', probably a younger brother of the boy who was staying with Mr Moore in 1800. Her reading included books of a suitable nature: in November 1812 she sent William Davies senior her copy of 'Grosvenor's Mourner, or the afflicted relieved'. He had recently lost his wife. 'This valuable Book in my opinion possesses irrisistable consolations, & most ardently do I hope that you may peruse it with the same comfortable & soothing experience which I have repeatedly done.' She acknowledged a shipment of Bibles from Charles Murray, Secretary to the National Vaccine Establishment, but unfortunately does not mention their destination. Her faith was the small change of her life, always in her pocket for the benefit of her friends, her family and herself.

With so little evidence to build up a picture of Catherine Jenner, it would be unforgivable to omit a letter that she wrote to Anne Davies about some of the common cares of child-rearing. Both she and Anne had sons named Robert, but this Robert seems to have been a foster-child or possibly the Clinch boy.

> Robert pays you a visit tomorrow & I flatter myself you will think his health is <u>much mended since you</u> parted with him at Berkeley & I am convinced he has likewise acquired no small portion of strength. As I am so <u>sincerely & warmly</u> interested concerning his welfare I shall not apologize for dictating to you concerning the Diet etc. which is so necessary my little Friend should strictly adhere to & I can with truth assure you that I have ever found the smallest hint exacts the most <u>cheerful compliance</u>. he does not lie in Bed late in a morning. his Breakfast is Chocolate with dry bread, or <u>very weak</u> Tea with a moderate quantity of Bread & Butter. if he <u>really</u> feels a want of something he takes a Bunn or bits of Bread & Butter before dinner. at dinner he don't eat more than one third part (<u>or less</u>) of what he did when he first came & what will give you great pleasure to hear he has almost subdued that <u>ravenous</u> way of eating & I dare say in a little time (if not Corrupted) he will eat as genteel as a <u>fine Lady</u>. he scarsely half the Bread which he us'd with his dinner. & <u>no Cheese</u> unless a bit of soft. <u>very weak</u> Tea in the afternoon & of course but little Bread & Butter – only a glass of wine & water after dinner & if possible <u>no fruit</u>. supper, Bunns or bits of Bread & Butter & in Bed between nine and Ten. if it is convenient for Robert to ride, it will afford him great benefit as well as pleasure. . . .I imagine he will be very happy to pay you all a visit at Easton. & I beg you will keep him as long as you think proper but hope you will not forget how <u>glad</u> I shall <u>always</u> be with his Company here. . . .

> [PS] Robert has been <u>quite</u> free from all complaints a long time. The flatulency which used so painfully oppress him is <u>entirely</u> subdued. . .

Her intimacy with her sister-in-law was such that she felt she could be very explicit without being rude. Perhaps more amusing is the degree to which her husband's professional manner had by this time rubbed off on her. Self-assertion was no doubt one way that she found to cope with his occasional preoccupation. Perhaps the threatened religious revolt in 1801 was another, but it was addressed to another woman, and to a strong woman of whom she supposedly disapproved. Ill though she was, Catherine Jenner must have been a source of certainty and security to her husband when he chose. Incidentally, in 1820 after Catherine was dead, Rowland Hill actually preached in Berkeley church, an event that may have had more to do with the disgrace of the incumbent vicar of Berkeley than with a victory for Methodism.

The Duchess of Berkeley's response to the letter from Catherine Jenner was subordinate to her report on the campaign in support of Edward's petition for a grant from Parliament. Her husband had told her that Lord Bathurst could be depended upon, which surprised her, but she had written to her brother-in-law, Admiral Berkeley, about Bathurst. Her letter was not delivered, which she attributed to the fact that Jenner had many 'tho' feeble' enemies. She warned about naming names if there was any danger that letters could be intercepted. She had also asked Henry Hicks and Colonel Kingscote their opinion of a letter from Jenner's Gloucester neighbours to the London papers. Inasmuch as no such letter appeared, they may have advised against it.

The enemies to whom she referred were probably political rather than medical, members of the House of Commons who might vote against Jenner, or unfriendly peers with influence albeit no vote on the matter in hand. On 1 November 1802, months after the parliamentary grant, Jenner wrote in a similar vein to Lady Berkeley, abetted by Catherine. 'Respecting Letters & my present uncommon caution about them, I shall draw up a certificate which shall be signed by Mrs. Jenner.' To which was appended: 'This is to certify that my Husband Dr. Jenner is become extremely careful of every letter he receives from his Correspondents. Witness my hand Cath. Jenner.' Despite the note of guying, their mild paranoia – a verbal anachronism only – reflects the state of politics without parties.

Government tended to be conducted by intrigue because the Establishment was so small that its interests were largely interchangeable. Fewer than 1 per cent of the population were entitled to vote, and of those not more than one in twenty-five could vote freely. The remaining twenty-four cast their ballot publicly as they were expected to do. Internal groupings within the electorate reflected family allegiances based on both blood and alliance; clientage, which meant some legal or economic relationship; and, of less importance, parties. Government was conducted not by a party but by a more or less permanent group of servants chosen by the King from amongst those who could assure him of parliamentary support for his measures. A Cabinet consisting of heads of administrative and judicial departments could be said to exist after 1784, but collective responsibility developed only during the Victorian era. The idea of a Prime Minister emerged slowly from the practical role played by the Chancellor of the Exchequer as adviser to the King. In these circumstances opposition had about it a sense of disloyalty, if not of overt treason. There was no constitutional role for an opposition party. The Foxite Whigs who opposed Pitt were both unpopular and discredited. They had nothing whatsoever to

Edward Jenner 1749–1823

do with Pitt's resignation in 1801. After nineteen years in power and in the midst of a war with France that he was losing, Pitt resigned because the King opposed his modestly liberalizing measures for the government of Ireland. Henry Addington, who replaced Pitt briefly and was Chancellor when Jenner's petition was presented, had been Pitt's friend and protégé. Although he certainly did not support Charles James Fox, some of Fox's partisans such as Tierney and Hobhouse joined his government. Without a unifying political institution like a party, the maintenance of a majority on any one issue depended on favours and horse-trading.

Jenner himself admired Fox, whom he had met at Cheltenham. Yet to say that he was a Whig, as some have done, is wrong. He was a country gentleman, and a professional man. He voted for Admiral Berkeley to continue as his Member of Parliament because they were neighbours, and Jenner knew that he and George Berkeley saw eye to eye. His notions of government contain no surprises:

1. Every state, from the nature of things must be considered as a Democracy – out of this for the conveniency of the General Mass of Population grows a King. The King as a compensation for the arduous situation he has engaged in is rewarded without the trouble of seeking for it, with all those things which are suppos'd most conducive to him or happiness – wealth & power. As the machine of Government wd. be too complex for one human body to manage he is allowed to call in the assistance of other men – These are therefore called his Majesties Servants of his Ministry & are splendidly supported by the [?] People.

2. The Prince has no right to appoint whom he pleases for his Ministers.

Jenner wrote these notes in a diary he kept sporadically about ten years after the events of 1802, but they demonstrate that he understood pretty well the system with which he was dealing.

He dated the Duchess of Berkeley's letter January 1802. Early the previous November he had written to her that he was awaiting a call from Mr Addington to come to London. He enclosed certificates supporting vaccination from the two British commanders in the Mediterranean, General Hutchinson and Lord Keith, to whom Drs Marshall and Walker had been responsible, 'as it may facilitate the introduction of the subject to anyone you may wish to convert'. And he asked Lady Berkeley to apply for support to the two MPs for the county – her brother-in-law, Admiral Berkeley, and the Marquis of Worcester – because 'an application from me wd. be indecorous.'

The Berkeleys did much more than that to organize the political support he needed. They took the view that Parliament would respond to an indication of the esteem in which Jenner was held by his neighbours, a visible price-tag

showing his worth, and of course that of vaccination too. The Earl placed an
advertisement in the *Glocester Journal* asking for contributions to raise money
for a testimonial for Jenner in the form of a service of silver plate. On 18
November 1801, he wrote asking the Duke of Beaufort, perhaps the leading
local magnate, to contribute. The Countess, assisted by Henry Hicks and
the Reverend Thomas Pruen, an old friend of Jenner's, organized the list of
subscribers and ordered the service, suitably inscribed, from a London silver
merchants. It was not delivered until the end of 1803, when the account was
paid by William Davies junior. Jenner was very proud of the service. He left
it to his son, Robert, in his will, but specified that upon Robert's death it
would be returned to the trustees, who were to deal with it as an heirloom.
Pieces from it are now to be seen in the Jenner Museum at Berkeley.

On 30 November William Davies 'dined and drank tea' with his uncle at
the Chauntry. Jenner remained in Berkeley about two weeks, during which
he seems to have read and corrected the proof of his *Instructions for Vaccine
Inoculation*:

> Let the vaccine fluid be taken, for the purpose of Inoculation, from
> a pustule that is making its progress regularly, and which possesses
> the true vaccine character, on any day from the fifth to the eighth, or
> even a day or two later, provided the efflorescence be not then formed
> around it. . . .
>
> To obtain the virus, let the edges of the pustule be gently punctured
> with a lancet in several points. It. . .should be inserted upon the arm
> about midway between the shoulder and the elbow, either by means
> of a very slight scratch, not exceeding the eighth part of an inch, or
> a very small oblique puncture.

There follows a paragraph on the appearance and progress of the pustule
through stages 'commonly completed in fifteen or seventeen days.'

> A single pustule is sufficient to secure the constitution from the
> small-pox; but as we are not always certain the puncture may take
> effect, it will be prudent to inoculate in both arms, or to make two
> punctures in the same arm, about an inch and a half asunder, except
> in very early infancy, when there is a great susceptibility of local irri-
> tation.

After brief attention to treatment of the sore if, for example, the scab
is rubbed off, he continues:

> Vaccine virus, taken from a pustule, and inserted immediately in
> its fluid state, is preferable to that which has been previously dried;
> but as it is not always practicable to obtain it in this state, we are
> compelled to seek for some mode of preserving it. Various means
> have been suggested, but from the test of long experience, it may

be asserted, that preserving it between two plates of glass is the most eligible. . . .

The virus, thus preserved. . .may easily be restored to its fluid state by dissolving it in a small portion of cold water, taken up on the point of a lancet. . . .

The vaccine fluid is liable, from causes apparently trifling, to undergo a decomposition. In this state it sometimes produces what has been denominated the spurious pustule. . . .

This paragraph, the longest in the leaflet, describes in considerable detail the appearances of spurious pustules produced by various causes of decomposition. Testing by re-inoculation or variolation should be used whenever there is any doubt. Constitutional symptoms like fever and headache may occur.

If the effluvia of the small-pox have been received into the habit [body] previously to the inoculation of the vaccine virus, the vaccine inoculation will not always be found to stop its progress, although the pustule may take its advances without interruption.

The lancet used for the inoculation should always be perfectly clean. After each puncture, it is proper to dip it into water, and wipe it dry. . . .

The preservation of vaccine virus upon a lancet, beyond the period of a few days, should never be attempted. . . .

The leaflet, signed 'EDWARD JENNER', consists of a single sheet printed on one side. It was meant to be posted where the practitioner could consult it paragraph by paragraph.

Its publication at this time had much more to do with Jenner's dilatory writing behaviour and his insistence on repeated corrections to proofs than with the campaign. In September, he had written to his friend Fermor at Tusmore that 'incessant interruptions' had impeded completion of the *Instructions*. Curiously, he called it a 'fourth paper' when it was the fifth, apparently a simple case of miscounting.

Dr and Mrs Jenner and the children returned to New Bond Street on 9 December. Always before they had passed Christmas at Berkeley, but the anticipated summons from Addington had arrived. Because the petition involved a grant of money, ministers had to agree, and because the Army and Navy had benefited from vaccination, Jenner's friends thought an officer might present the petition; but this meant that Pitt, still the most powerful figure in the House of Commons, also had to approve. There was much work to be done. On 12 January 1802, Jenner had the requisite interview with Addington. He then employed a solicitor, a Mr White, to draw up the formal petition.

In February the Physical Society at Guy's Hospital heard a

> paper on the cow-pox. . .which has occupied much attention. The theatre, for three or four nights, has been unusually crowded, and members have gone away for want of room. The paper contains a good account of the rise and progress of the discovery, but nothing new on the subject. The full attendance was owing to the presence of the illustrious discoverer, and of several eminent practitioners who have actively propagated it.

Jenner was named an honorary member of the Society, which included Henry Cline, J. C. Lettsom, William Woodville, Robert Willan, Everard Home, John Ring and John Walker. A month later the Medical Society of London presented their testimonial. Jenner had been a member for a decade. The Suffolk Society of Surgeons was the first of the county medical societies to honour him, followed closely by the Benevolent Medical Society of Essex and Hertfordshire. Further recognition came from abroad. He was made corresponding associate of the medical societies of Tours and Paris, the timing no doubt in part a recognition of the unaccustomed state of peace between France and Britain. In May 1802, moreover, Jenner was named a Fellow of the American Society of Arts and Sciences in Massachusetts.

The Reverend John Clinch was in England at this time. I assume that he and Jenner met to discuss not only Clinch's life in Newfoundland but his success with vaccination there, and Jenner's current business before Parliament. On 2 February, furthermore, Jenner was supposed to stand up as godfather at the christening of Edward Gardner's child. William Davies junior acted as proxy.

The formal document required for presentation of his claim had now been completed. In the first paragraph it opened a new controversy: '. . .your petitioner having discovered' that cowpox can be inoculated from the cow to man 'with the singularly beneficial effect of rendering through life the persons so inoculated perfectly secure from the infection of the Small Pox', 'did not wish to conceal the discovery. . .but immediately disclosed the whole'. It was to prove an unfortunate formulation, but it reveals that at the beginning of 1802 Jenner knew nothing of those earlier experiments which George Pearson was to introduce into the forthcoming parliamentary hearings. The claim also suggests his confusion about his own role, which only the threat posed by Pearson forced him to clarify. In his report of the hearings George Jenner promoted a more accurate image: '. . .the practice of which Dr. Jenner asserts himself to be the original inventor, is, the inoculation from one human being to another, and the mode of transferring, indefinitely, the vaccine matter without any diminution of its specific power'. He 'threw the first light upon' 'the whole business'. Looked at from our perspective, it may seem unimportant whether Jenner 'discovered' cow-to-human inoculation or human-to-human, but from the standpoint of his contemporaries familiar with variolation, the folk wisdom about cowpox and the fact that Jenner was asking for money from the public purse, it was important to know.

Financial support from the Treasury for inventors was infrequent, but scarcely unknown. Indeed, in his speech opposing the amendment which would have given Jenner £20,000 instead of the £10,000 originally proposed, Addington said that there were two reports concerning grants to individuals before the House at the same time, one dealing with vaccination and the other with a discovery which 'saved human beings from the perils of shipwreck'. It was also pointed out during the debate on Jenner's petition that £5000 had been granted to a Mr Stevens 'for a solvent of the stone, which has been found to be inefficacious.' Few ailments are more painful than kidney stones, and the promise of a miracle solvent – unfulfilled to this day – raised immense hope. Parliament had also become involved in grants to John Harrison for a chronometer accurate enough to determine longitude at sea, after the Board of Longitude, having awarded Harrison its prize, failed to pay him the money. These grants expressed the nation's appreciation for practical contributions to her welfare at a time when neither science nor commercial enterprise were well enough organized to do the job. Today Jenner might have received a grant from the Medical Research Council or from a major pharmaceutical manufacturer. In 1802 it was left to Members of Parliament, non-scientists to a man, to separate nutritious wheat from fraudulent chaff.

The petition went on to point out that Jenner had broadcast the knowledge and techniques of vaccination throughout the world, and that the new therapy had saved lives in the British Army and Navy; 'That the said inoculation hath already checked the progress of the Small Pox, and from its nature must finally annihilate that dreadful disorder'; and that because of the 'great expense and anxiety' that the petitioner has suffered as a result of the interruptions in his professional life, he asks the House for 'such remuneration as to their wisdom shall seem meet.'

William Wilberforce was asked to move the petition in the House of Commons, but found it inconvenient for reasons that his letter does not make clear, although he assured Jenner of his support. He also warned that the deadline for petitions – in effect private members' bills – for the present session was rapidly approaching in mid-February. At that point the lawyer had not finished his work, an explanation for the delay that might not have satisfied the House. When the petition was moved by Sir Henry Mildmay on 17 March 1802, it began:

A petition of Edward Jenner, Doctor of Physic, was presented to the House and read. . .and that the Petitioner with a view to obviate doubts which of late were falsely represented to have arisen in a foreign Country respecting the efficacy and certainly of the vaccine Inoculation, and thereby to enable himself with better confidence to solicit the favourable attention of the house, was induced to delay his application till after the time limited by the house for receiving Petitions of a Private nature was elapsed; and therefore praying that leave may be given to exhibit a Petition. . . .

I am not aware of any material 'doubts' raised abroad at the beginning of 1802, and believe they were a cover for another of Jenner's procrastinations.

In any case, the petition was accepted. Addington told the House that the King approved the request in principle, and it was referred to a Committee of the House chaired by Admiral Berkeley. The Committee sat for the first time on 22 March and heard witnesses for a little more than a month.

Jenner was among the first to be called. That he had prepared himself for the hearings is demonstrated by a letter written on 10 March to Dr James Currie of Liverpool. In 1797 Currie had proposed an inoculation against 'typhus', probably typhoid fever, about which Jenner wanted information to present to the House of Commons. Evidently he proposed to show that the vaccine therapy was not unique, thus reducing for laymen the strangeness of the idea that a disease could be prevented. Perhaps he had in mind Hunter's inoculation experiments, but like the inductions about grease and the existence of spurious cowpox, this too was a brilliant perception so far ahead of its time that it lacked any real evidential foundation. To more immediate purpose, Jenner had had detailed drawings of the vaccine pustule made by Captain Charles Gold of the Royal Artillery to support his petition. But despite his efforts to organize himself for the ordeal, his testimony was a disaster. 'He himself was called in,' wrote his friend James Moore fifteen years later; 'but, from singular diffidence, was incapable, even with preparation, to give an oral testimony in public of what he thoroughly knew. He therefore delivered to the Committee a written statement'. If Jenner objected to this description, the record does not reveal it. The light Moore casts is unexpected and striking.

On the one hand, Jenner had no difficulty in meeting the demands of a social occasion at which he was asked to explain vaccination, as at Lord Spencer's party early the previous year. He seemed perfectly comfortable in person-to-person discussions, or in small groups, whether of laymen and women or medical men. Yet he never made a speech about vaccination, nor did he read any of the papers he presented to medical bodies. Almost unintentionally, Baron revealed Jenner's tongue-tied shyness on a public platform. He described an anniversary dinner of the Royal Jennerian Society, which always took place on Jenner's birthday. In 1807 the Duke of York took the chair. 'Though Jenner felt a peculiar dislike to exhibitions of this kind, he seems to have been much gratified with the events of this day. Dr. Lettsom and the Rev. Rowland Hill energetically supported vaccination. Jenner, too, on his own health being drank, spoke with much delicacy and propriety.' His diffidence was no pose. 'I am by accident, you know, become a public character; and having the worst head for arrangement that ever was placed on a man's shoulders, I really think myself the most unfit for it,' he wrote to his friend Richard Worthington at the end of 1809. As is so often the case, self-doubt could produce wit. Rowland Hill is said to have introduced him thus: ' "Allow me to present to your lordship my friend, Dr. Jenner, who has been the means of saving more lives than any other man." "Ah!" replied Jenner, "would that I, like you, could save *souls*!" ' Diffidence coloured his personality, but not in monochrome. Its contrasting hue was the stubborn self-righteousness that led to the quarrel with Woodville, destroyed the Royal Jennerian Society and may have cost him a knighthood.

Those who appeared to support the petition included the Duke of Clarence, the Earl of Berkeley, Lord Rous, Edward Gardner and thirty-one medical men, including the King's physician, Sir Walter Farquhar, who said: 'I think it the greatest discovery that has been made for many years.' Jenner's former teacher, Dr Thomas Denman, addressed the Committee, as did his sons-in-law; Dr Richard Croft, who became the King's physician, said: 'I doubt not but it will ultimately cause the small-pox to be remembered only by name.' Dr Matthew Baillie, physician to St George's Hospital, believed '*it is the most important discovery that has ever been made in medicine*'. Dr Lettsom emphasized the opportunity Jenner refused:

> . . .considering the apparent incredibility of this new practice to common observation, and the secrecy with which the Suttonians monopolized the inoculation of the small-pox. . .I think fully that Dr. Jenner might have exclusively kept the new practice to himself for a long period of time. . . .

Mr Ring, Mr Cline and Sir Everard Home also were among the supporters of the petitioner. On this occasion the Royal College of Physicians and the College of Surgeons were not consulted.

The Committee heard six voices question Jenner's originality or the value of his contribution. John Birch, Ring's surgical colleague at St Thomas's, said with candour unmarred by scientific hesitation that cowpox inoculation was 'a subject he had not much attended to, as he did not like it'. Dr William Rowley, physician to the Marylebone Infirmary and the Queen's Lying-in Hospital, a newcomer to the opposition, described the cases of the four Oxford children allegedly vaccinated by Jenner. Benjamin Moseley was actually called after Jenner suggested to the Committee 'the propriety of examining him', but added nothing new to his previous comments. Mr Robert Keate, Surgeon-General of the Army, appeared only to confirm that he had delivered certain papers questioning Jenner's priority to Dr George Pearson, and Mr Thomas Nash of Shaftesbury told the Committee how he had come by the papers in question. The evidence from Keate and Nash, like almost all the data presented by Dr Pearson, would have been irrelevant had Jenner not claimed in his petition to have discovered cowpox inoculation.

Pearson gave evidence twice. On the first occasion he dealt with Jenner's alleged priority. Between 1799, when he affirmed that Jenner deserved all the credit for the introduction of vaccine inoculation, and 1802, he had unearthed at least five and possibly six prior claimants. First was a Mr Downe who had stated to Pearson that he was the discoverer of cowpox inoculation, but could provide no evidence. Then, Reverend Herman Drew of Abbotts, Dorset, informed Pearson that about thirty years before he had written to Sir George Baker, physician-in-ordinary to George III and nine times President of the Royal College of Physicians, about the cowpox experiments of Mr Nicholas Bragge of Axminster. Bragge said his documents had been destroyed by fire, but Drew told Sir William Elford, a member of the Committee hearing evidence on Jenner's petition, that 'sheets of paper' had been sent to Sir George, who would have tried cowpox inoculation but could not find an infected cow. Sir George denied any recollection of the incident. Apparently Drew also wrote to Pearson about a Benjamin Jesty (though he called him Justin). Pearson received two more communications about Jesty, from Dr R. Pulteney of Blandford, who called the man Justins, and Mr W. Dolling, an inoculator at Chettle. Jenner knew Dolling and had sent him a copy of the *Inquiry*, which Dolling had acknowledged with a note of thanks, affirming the truth of Jenner's evidence. He had made no mention of Jesty.

Benjamin Jesty farmed near Yetminster, Dorset. He and two of his servants had had cowpox. In 1774 during a smallpox outbreak, he took his wife and two small sons to a neighbouring farm where the herd had the disease. He scratched their arms with a needle and rubbed in matter from pustules on the udders. Although the children recovered without incident, Mrs Jesty was very ill. She too pulled through, but apparently during her illness the villagers treated Jesty like a witch, abusing him both verbally and physically. The incident became one he preferred to forget – until, that is, he was taken up by Pearson's Vaccine-Pock Institution, which brought him to London, his first and only visit to the metropolis, and awarded him a gold medal.

On 26 April 1802, Thomas Nash (some spell it Naish) appeared before the parliamentary Committee at the suggestion of Dr Pearson. Nash said that he had been inoculated by his father, a surgeon, in 1781. He believed his father had used cowpox. His mother had given papers covering the experiment to her brother, a Dr Battiscombe. The brother had neither opened nor examined them when he returned them in 1795 or 1796 to his nephew, Thomas. Thomas had passed them to Robert Keate, who had informed Pearson. Extracts from these papers showed that the elder Nash had inoculated about sixty people from the cow, of whom forty had been protected. That was the evidence laid before the Committee; but about eighteen months later, Thomas Creaser, a surgeon and vaccinist, received a letter from Mr Pew, a surgeon who had practised at Shaftesbury before moving to Sherborne. He supported Creaser's opinion that at least two of Nash's patients had been variolated after they had had cowpox. Pew also wrote that Nash had not cowpoxed his son, Thomas, but variolated him.

On two occasions during the coming years Mr Pew turns up again in the history of Edward Jenner. In 1808 or 1809 he published *Observations of an Eruptive Disease Which Has Lately Occurred in the Town of Sherborne, Dorset, after Vaccination*, which was highly favourable to vaccination despite its occasional failures. Then in June 1816 a French periodical, the *Journal de Pharmacie et des Sciences*, reported that toward the end of the last century a Mr James Ireland of Bristol had travelled to Montpellier, taking with him Mr Pew. Pew had met the Protestant minister of Montpellier, Jacques-Antoine Rabaut-Pomier, who had told him about a disease of cows, *la picotte*, which might prevent smallpox. Back in England, Pew was said to have reported this news to Jenner. I have found no evidence that Jenner ever commented on the report.

Dr Pearson presented three even less well authenticated candidates for the role of pre-Jennerian inoculators of cowpox: Mrs Rendell, wife of a Whitchurch farmer near Lyme, inoculated herself and her three or four children about 1780; an unnamed apothecary of Windsor, known to a Dr Lind of that town, had vaccinated his apothecary son; and Peter Platt, a tutor of Schönwaide, Holstein, vaccinated his three children. Although Pearson seemed to be drawing cowpoxers out of the walls, all of them may have done what he reported before Edward Jenner vaccinated James Phipps on 14 May 1796. I exclude Pew, who did not claim to be an inoculator. Most medical men in the south-west of England and a great many farmers, milkmaids and other lay persons knew the cowpox tale. It may well have been known in those parts of the continent where cowpox existed. I find it much harder to believe that imaginative people, medical or laymen, who were understandably terrified of smallpox, would not have tried cowpoxing their loved ones than that they did. Person-to-person variolation was even more widely known than the cowpox story, but no one before Jenner seems to have attempted it with cowpox. In fact, Pearson offered no evidence on earlier arm-to-arm passage, perhaps because Jenner's petition did not specifically mention it. Yet Jenner was the first to vaccinate arm-to-arm, in order to determine experimentally whether the lymph produced in the pustule held its protective property from generation to generation. In other words, he first consciously used vaccination not only to protect patients but also as an experimental paradigm. In the best tradition of his friend and mentor, John Hunter, he combined medicine *with* science, clinical practice with detailed observation and data collection, from all of which he drew generalizations. Even more to the point of the parliamentary hearings, Jenner first publicized vaccination as the best available defence against smallpox.

During his second examination by the Committee, Pearson made several points bearing indirectly on Jenner's priority. He presented evidence that he and Woodville had vaccinated far more people than Jenner had, thus providing the real demonstration of its efficacy. He said that they had shown that the use of caustics to control the vesicle was unnecessary, that not only did cowpox protect against smallpox but also, contrary to Jenner's view, that smallpox prevented cowpox, and that grease was not the origin of cowpox. Pearson also claimed that he and Woodville discovered the 'safety of infant inoculation'. That was not true. In the *Inquiry* Jenner recorded the vaccination of an infant of six months, and of his own son, then eleven months old. In *Further Observations*, he wrote that he had asked Henry Jenner to vaccinate an infant born twenty hours before. The child later resisted variolation. Significantly, Woodville associated himself with none of Pearson's claims.

Jenner never forgave Pearson. At the beginning of 1805 he wrote to Caleb Parry, 'Since my return from Cheltenham, I have had a pretty close correspondence with P. but to no purpose; it began and ended in sparring. He is one of those extraordinary Beings who never committed an error. In future I shall request H.[enry Jenner] to be his correspondent – I have done.' Indeed, given Woodville's silence on matters in Pearson's testimony that concerned him, Pearson's motives can only be suspect. Thomas Creaser, the Bath surgeon and pro-vaccinist, wrote: 'if Dr. P. could atchieve his grand design of appearing as the efficient author of Vaccination, we should hear no more of its failures or imperfections'. He may have been influenced by the fact that, with Woodville, he had experimented far more widely than Jenner. Almost equally certainly, Pearson wanted to get back at Jenner for causing the Duke of York and the Earl of Egremont to withdraw from the Vaccine-Pock Institution. Although that body continued to function with Pearson in a leading role, he seems to have lost interest in the vaccine controversy after about 1806. From my perspective, of course, Pearson's thoroughness and hard work once again provided immense amounts of useful data, this time about the early history of cowpoxing, that neither Jenner nor anyone else collected. The irony is that he did so only because of Jenner's incautious claim.

Partly no doubt because, true or false, it was a convenient shorthand, members referred throughout the parliamentary hearings to the 'author of this Discovery', this 'matchless Discovery', 'his discovery of Vaccine

Inoculation' and 'this most incalculably valuable discovery'. By and large they were responding to medical opinion throughout the country, as well as to the Committee proceedings. As early as September 1801, half a year before the Committee first sat, the physicians, surgeons and apothecaries of Bath had approached Parliament for a suitable reward to be made to Dr Jenner. During the debate, Dr Beddoes of Bristol expunged his earlier sins by publicly proposing a 'National Subscription' to supplement a parliamentary grant which he believed would be too small. Unwittingly, John Birch attended an anniversary dinner at Guy's: 'What was my surprise. . .to find, that the sole business of the meeting was to begin a canvas for names to a petition to Parliament, in support of Dr Jenner's bill? it was presented to me and I refused to sign.' The tide at the time was unstoppable.

Admiral Berkeley fell ill shortly before the hearings ended, but the chair was taken by another member, Mr Banks, who drew up the Report. It was submitted to the whole House on 6 May and debated on 2 June (the House sitting as a Committee of Supply). Admiral Berkeley began the debate, pointing out that the Committee acknowledged Dr Jenner's priority as 'the original inventor' of 'the inoculation from one human being to another, and the mode of transferring, indefinitely, the vaccine matter'. The Committee had recommended a grant of not less than £10,000, and Admiral Berkeley moved the Report to be approved. Sir Henry Mildmay then moved an amendment increasing the grant to £20,000. Sir James Erskine Sinclair, supporting the motion, argued that Jenner had spent at least £6000 pursuing and presenting his inquiries. If the House considered £20,000 too much, he suggested £15,000. John Courtenay pointed out that vaccination could be said to have saved the lives of forty thousand men who would bring into the exchequer about £200,000 in their lifetimes. Therefore, Dr Jenner was entitled to £20,000. A few others spoke on both sides, but the makeweight was the Chancellor of the Exchequer, then Henry Addington, who acknowledged the importance of the Jennerian contribution and concurred in the Committee recommendations. The amendment was lost by a vote of 59 to 56. 'The difference of ten and twenty thousand pounds tho' of great consequence to an individual receiver, amounts not to one farthing apiece to the Public; and that for insurance against the most frightful & most fatal of human diseases,' wrote Thomas Creaser soon after the event. No record has been found of Jenner's comments.

The House then passed the original motion. Jenner's brother-in-law, William Davies, noted in his household accounts:

> June 2 1802 Dr. Jenner had a Reward from Parliament by an unanimous Vote for the most important Discovery that perhaps was ever made of preventing the Ravages of the small Pox by introducing Vaccine Inoculation. Ten thousand Pounds
>
> £10000/0/0

Not only did the Reverend Davies perceive accurately Edward's contribution, the introduction of vaccination, but he also appreciated how very large a sum of money it was, perhaps approximately two million 1990 pounds.

Chapter 7

Royal Jennerian Society
1802–1803

Jenner probably sat for his first formally commissioned portrait during the parliamentary hearings. The artist, James Northcote RA, had been born in Devonport and was known to members of the Plymouth Medical Society. One of the Society's founders, Richard Dunning, persuaded Jenner to sit for Northcote, the greater part of whose twenty-five guinea fee was paid by another of the founders, Dr Rensmett, out of his own pocket. Edward was not wildly enthusiastic about the result, according to a letter he wrote to John Lettsom in 1804, though he did approve 'a fine engraving of this by a young man of the name of Saye' (that is, William Say).

In the Northcote painting, which still hangs in the Plymouth Medical Society hall, Jenner is seated, his right arm resting on the *Inquiry* open at a page of drawings illustrating the progress of the vesicle. He is dressed with some care in knee breeches, a full coat trimmed with a fur collar, waistcoat and stock. The figure appears to be full but not fat. The face is round with soft eyes and mouth, large lips, a pronounced aquiline nose, prominent but orderly eyebrows and well trimmed dark hair. He was then fifty-three, but çould have been as young as forty.

Jenner preferred the portrait painted by Sir Thomas Lawrence about six years later. On 23 October 1808, he wrote to his friend Thomas Pruen, 'Lawrence catches the very soul of a Man.' He added, figuratively, 'I never saw myself before on Canvass.' 'Many catch the mind in portrait painting but L– catches the soul,' he confided to his notebook. In the engraving by W. H. Mote, the face is smoother and appears even younger than in the Northcote portrait. He is again seated, dressed even more formally and with his hair windswept in the Romantic mode. In neither portrayal does the face appear other than benign and untroubled.

The subject of these representations indicated his preferences but not his reasons for them – as which of us can when confronted with a likeness? Perhaps Jenner saw in the paintings, as I do, the description of him written by Dibdin at this time: 'I never knew a man of a simpler mind or of a warmer heart, than Dr. Jenner. I never knew a man who, being in the road, as he was,

[132]

to incalculable wealth, despised it all for the benefit of his fellow creatures'. In other words, I think the portraits underestimate if they do not flatter the man, emphasizing his Christian charity and humility but neglecting the complex self-doubt and deep personal worry about the dangers that can arise with any new medical treatment. They portray the squire which most doctors at the time wanted to be. The underside of his character Jenner tended to hide from himself. He described the dreamer he believed he was:

> While the vaccine discovery was progressive the joy I felt at the prospect before me of being the instrument destined to take away from the world one of its greatest calamities, blended with the fond hope of enjoying independence and domestic peace and happiness, was often so excessive that in pursuing my favourite subject among the meadows, I have sometimes found myself in a reverie.

In Jenner's day 'reverie' had a fantastical sense beyond mere day-dream. Coleridge at the same time wrote about the opium-based reverie which underlay 'Kubla Khan'. This poetic Romanticism was embodied in the Lawrentian view of Dr Jenner.

On 17 February 1805, when the waves of success had just begun to break across the shoals of opposition, he wrote to Robert Ferryman, 'Vaccination draws upon me for near £500 per annum. It would be intollerable but for the incalculable happiness the world derives from my labours'. Then a new theme enters:

> I look upon myself as having been much neglected for what predeceser of mine ever conferd so great a favor on his Country. . . .I don't say this vauntingly – I trust there is nothing ostentatious about me, but concurring circumstances urge me to contend for something which appears to be a kind of tribute due to me.

The happiness of discovery has been extended from himself to the world, an objective and defensible evaluation. The assertion of neglect is new, surprising and hardly justified, excepting that Jenner now visualizes a 'tribute due to me'. Not money, I believe, despite the costs of which he complains, but something else. An honour, perhaps a knighthood? During young manhood the reward for success was the woman he loved. Though essential, she was extraneous to the achievement, which almost fell at the first hurdle because he had neglected his own acute observational skills. In the earth-shattering case of vaccination, where was his extraneous reward?

About the time the Lawrence portrait was painted, Jenner wrote in his notebook under the heading: 'From the Life of Sir Isaac Newton'

> Notwithstanding the extraordinary honors that were paid him, he had so humble an opinion of himself that he had no relish of the applause wct. was so deservedly paid him; & he was so little vain & desirous

of glory from any of his works, that he, as it is well known, would have let others run away with the glory of those inventions, wct. have done so much honor to human nature, if his friends and countrymen had not been more jealous than he, of his and their glory.

The language of the author he is quoting is convoluted and Jenner's use of it unrefined, but I think he believed that his friends should recognize both his claims and the reward they deserved without prompting from him. If, as seems likely, he was comparing himself to Newton, what he neglected was the reason for their self-doubt and humbleness. I leave Newton scholars to deal with Newton, but Jenner was far too humble to rise above his profound sense of responsibility for the fact that if vaccination did go wrong, the patient died. Obviously he could not express this contradiction; it could damage the case for vaccination. But it was always there, underlying timorous feelings of neglect as well as the powerful demands for recognition that he tried to suppress. An anonymous reviewer of Baron's biography caught the substance of Jenner's doubt exactly:

> . . .nothing could exceed his anxiety when his experience of vacci-
> nation had not led to any positive and satisfactory conclusions, lest
> the promulgation of the practice should prove injurious, by inducing
> parents to forego the advantages of small-pox inoculation, and thus
> expose their children to the natural disease.

As the opposition emblazoned failures, real and alleged, Jenner's heartfelt and justifiable need for recognition ballooned. A grant of £10,000 bought only temporary relief.

After Parliament had done its duty, however, Jenner began negotiations to purchase the lease of a house on Hertford Street. His decision to abandon rented accommodation indicated that he considered himself committed to a practice in London. Arrangements for the purchase and necessary refurbishment took the rest of the year 1802. Meanwhile, the family continued to live at 136 New Bond Street.

On 28 April 1802, Jenner had written to Henry Hicks that he had inoculated the son of Lord Holland, Charles James Fox's brother. At the time he saw the event as a step toward gaining support for his petition. Nor could he neglect his wider responsibilities. W. T. Cobb, a correspondent in Banbury, asked for and was sent vaccine matter, one of many such requests. In the letter to Hicks, Jenner reported that Catherine 'had had a most violent fever, but not typhus.' Happily, she was much recovered. 'I have taken a box for Mrs J. and the child [probably Catherine] at Bayswater. . . .Tomorrow night we are all a blaze here. The preparations going forward in every street are unexampled. I have just seen one in which Billy P[itt]. cut a conspicuous figure'. The illuminations and tableaux no doubt celebrated the signing of the peace treaty.

[134]

During this year, furthermore, Jenner had the doubtful pleasure of learning that the Smallpox Hospital at St Pancras had begun to substitute vaccine for variolous inoculation, and 'with a sort of pious fraud, they administered it to many who inconsiderately preferred the Small Pox, and thought they were receiving that Species of Inoculation'. Three years later the hospital authorities stopped this wildly unethical behaviour amongst out-patients, with the result, only then becoming predictable, that smallpox deaths in London greatly increased. From the beginning of 1799 to the end of 1806, however, the Smallpox Hospital carried out 20,323 vaccinations, certainly more than any other public institution in Britain. No more than twenty people contracted smallpox after vaccination, of whom either two or three died.

Even commercial variolators saw the error of their ways. Mr Thomas of Daventry had kept three houses for patients who came to him for the old therapy. He wrote to the *Medical and Physical Journal*: 'to my very great disappointment, I found the Vaccine-pock so safe and mild a disease. . .that I became a convert. . .and in a very short time [was] compelled to shut up my Inoculating Houses'. Jenner's reverie had become flesh.

In early August 1802 the Jenners returned to Berkeley for a few days. There Edward received a visit from a Dr Franck of Vienna, who bore an introduction from a London connection, Dr Babington. There was also time for a family gathering at Eastington. Mrs Jenner, the two eldest children and Mrs Black 'dined and spent the day' with William and Anne Davies. Robert was probably at school, and Edward senior may have already left for Cheltenham. Very little has been recorded about that season. For the time being, the politicking had ended. Among the family connections in Cheltenham was a young unmarried gentleman named Witts, who recorded that on 6 November 'Dr. & Mrs. Jenner, the inventor of the Vaccine Pox. . .rendered our Evening very agreeable.' Six weeks later Witts assisted Jenner at a vaccination. By 1 December he was settled again in Berkeley, where he remained through January.

On 3 December Benjamin Travers, probably the brother of a London sugar merchant, Joseph Travers, convened a meeting in Joseph's factory on Queen Street off Cheapside. Those attending were Dr William Hawes, one of the founders of the Humane Society and a friend of J. C. Lettsom, Joseph Leaper and John Addington, both surgeons and among the signatories of Ring's manifesto in support of vaccination two years earlier. Lettsom had been expected, but had not turned up. The gentlemen met 'for the purpose of considering the propriety of estab-lishing an Institution for promoting universal Vaccination with a view to the extinction of the Small Pox'. Because of Lettsom's absence as well as the fact that Jenner was not in London, it was agreed to call a later meeting. Addington was deputed to write informing Jenner of the proceedings.

Jenner replied from Berkeley on 10 December. He had, he said, just returned with his family 'after an absence of some years'. I assume he meant they had settled for an extended stay, because they had certainly been there in August. Though the news of an inoculation institution was very welcome, Jenner told Addington, he wished to remain where he was for the present. 'I have written to my Friend Dr Lettsom and requested him to have the kindness to be. . .my Representative.' With similar encouragement from Jenner in a letter to Benjamin Travers, a second meeting was called for 16 December. No doubt in part because it met at the City Coffee House in Cheapside, it was much better attended. With Travers again in the chair, the founders were joined by Dr Lettsom, Dr William Bradley, editor of the *Medical and Physical Journal*, John Ring and nine other medical men and City businessmen. Among those who wrote in support of the plan for the institution were John Gurney, the banker, and William Wilberforce. The principal business was the establishment of a committee chaired by Lettsom to prepare an address to the public. Lettsom proposed that the organization be called the Jennerian Society, and the meeting adjourned for one week.

At the third meeting two days before Christmas at the City Coffee House, the address was approved, with some modifications. It called attention to the estimated forty thousand Britons killed annually by smallpox. Not only had variolation proven ineffectual, but 'by spreading the contagion, [it] has considerably increased its Mortality.' Dr Jenner's 'new species of Inoculation' 'proves an effectual preservative', as the House of Commons had now agreed. An organization to promote the diffusion of the new practice in the metropolis sought the support of 'The enlightened, the benevolent, the opulent'. Joseph Leaper and Richard Nicholls, a printer, were added to the drafting committee, which was now charged with preparation of regulations for the Jennerian Society. Again the meeting was adjourned for a week.

In light of the quarrel with Dr John Walker which was to destroy the Royal Jennerian Society, the claim in 1816 that 'The idea of the formation of a vaccine institution in London. . .originated with Dr. Walker' demands attention. It appeared in a history of the Society, either written by Walker or approved by him before publication, which described his work in Malta and Paris without mentioning Dr J. R. Marshall, who had been his superior. On his return to London, Walker was given hospitality by Joshua Fox, a surgeon and one of those who attended the second and third meetings of the new Society. On 29 December, according to this document, Dr Walker wrote to offer his services. In other words, not even this inspired history substantiates the startling claim with which it begins. Indeed, if anyone is to be credited with having originated the idea of a vaccine institution, it must have been George Pearson.

Certainly, Jenner maintained no such priority. He seems, rather, to have taken a comfortable back seat in Berkeley, while the careful orchestration built up with his blessing. The fourth meeting of the organizers took place in Queen Street on 30 December. It heard a letter from Jenner which was not included in the minutes, although Walker's letter does appear. Walker also attended this meeting, which directed the chairman, Benjamin Travers, Lettsom and Nicholls to ask the Lord Mayor to take the chair at a public meeting to be called by advertisement at the London Tavern in Bishopsgate.

A meeting on 6 January 1803 in Queen Street called itself 'General' and appears in a new minute book separate from the Board of Directors', indicating some evolution in the organizational planning. In other respects there were no changes. Travers took the chair, and the business concerned the forthcoming public meeting. On the same evening the meeting, now confusingly minuted as a Board of Directors, approved the language of a newspaper advertisement and of individual invitations to support the new institution. The Lord Mayor had agreed to act as chairman of the public organizational dinner on 19 January. The minutes list seventy-six signatories to the advertisement, led by the Duke of Clarence and four peers – Berkeley, Egremont, Darnley and Somerville. Four MPs include George Berkeley and Wilberforce. Three City aldermen are followed by the name of John Julius Angerstein, the financier. Then begins the list of doctors, now including Sir Walter Farquhar, Sir Gilbert Blane, Robert Willan, and James Sims and Alexander Marcet of the Medical Society. The surgeons include the young Astley Cooper, and there are the names of printers and business people from the City. Not a bad beginning for a project that was just a month old.

The public meeting achieved the same standard of success, in that it was large and that it obtained an excellent launch in the newspapers. Jenner was quite clearly biding his time in Berkeley, but he wrote thanking the Lord Mayor, the Duke of Clarence, the Duke of Bedford, Admiral Berkeley and 'other Noblemen and Gentlemen' for the 'particular notice. . .confer'd upon me.' The Lord Mayor, J. J. Angerstein and Benjamin Travers were named trustees for the Society, and authorized to receive contributions on its behalf. In addition, the meeting approved an organizing committee composed in the main of those who had undertaken the task so far. This committee met under the chairmanship of Angerstein a week later at the London Coffee House on Ludgate Hill. It resolved to invite the King and Queen to become patron and patroness and their children, vice-patrons. The Duke of Bedford was to be asked to become President (he agreed), and fifty-two vice-presidents were proposed. They included the Archbishops of Canterbury and York, the Bishops of Durham and London, a clutch of peers, the Prime Minister, Mr Pitt, Charles James Fox, Richard Brinsley Sheridan (because of his position as an opposition MP rather than as a playwright), Samuel Whitbread, Sir Joseph Banks and, of course, Dr Edward Jenner. This glittering assembly reflected not only the stapling of the Royal Jennerian Society, as it became when the King and Queen accepted, to the Establishment but also a large and, it was hoped, permanent reservoir of funds.

The meeting of 26 January established two more bodies, a Board of Directors of twenty-four non-medical persons and a Medical Council, a division of responsibility which many of those involved were to live to regret. Nowhere have I found an explanation for this structure. In part it must have been an acknowledgement of Jenner's preferences. On 2 February, the day he arrived in London, the Board appointed him to head a subcommittee 'to prepare a plan to carry the object of this Society into effect'. Its other members were Lettsom, Addington, Denman, Bradley, Hawes, Travers, Ring and Joseph Leaper. I doubt that Jenner would have wished to take the responsibility for administration, disbursements and fund-raising which became the natural preserve of the directors. On the other hand, he would have demanded a position that placed him in control of the Society's vaccination operations. Therefore, he became President of the Medical Council, which consisted of twenty-three more doctors and surgeons including Farquhar, Ring, Denman, Bradley, Everard Home, Cooper, Cline, Willan and, of course, Lettsom. At a board meeting the following week the Medical Council was expanded by sixteen, including Blane and Marcet, and Lettsom was made Vice-President. The Board of Directors itself included three bankers, Robert Barclay and Robert and Felix Ladbroke, two printers, William Phillips and John Nicholls, various other businessmen and the Reverend Rowland Hill. Angerstein and Travers as Vice-Presidents were *ex officio* directors too.

Jenner himself attended his first board meeting on 10 February. This meeting heard that the royal family had graciously agreed to become patrons and patronesses. The minutes also note that Charles Murray, a young lawyer, offered himself as one of the secretaries of the Society. Thus began an association which continued for the rest of Jenner's life.

Although it is not clear that Catherine accompanied him, Edward had arrived in London on 2 February after an overnight journey from Berkeley. He settled at once in the Hertford Street house. For the first and last time after 1794, Jenner's visiting book for the period has survived. It begins on 2 February with a call on a Mrs Russell Palmer at 20 Curzon Street and peters out on or about 13 March. Yet, such as it is, it proves that Jenner seriously sought to establish a practice in London. On 3 February he made five calls, including one to Lord Bute on South Audley Street. Bute's name appears several times along with Lord Darnley, Lord Gosford, Lord Westmorland, Lord St Helens and various other members of the aristocracy. In mid-February he saw a Mr Hunter, possibly John Hunter's son, and 'BP. of London', presumably the Bishop. On the next day a long list of names includes Wilberforce and both Admiral and Lord Berkeley. These calls (or callers) may have been political rather than medical. On the same day,

Thursday 16 February, he saw 'Mrs. Kingscotes Sister', probably a sister of Robert's wife. Perhaps the only member of the Lower Orders to figure in the visiting book is 'Ld. St Asaph's Servt.', whose fee would have been paid by his lordship, as would those of Lady St Asaph and the 'Three Children of Lord St Asaph' who were treated in March. The last pages of this tantalizing memo pad contain three separate items, each on a page by itself: 'An Essay on the Method of studying natural History [possibly] Byth: Kentish'; a list:

> Duke of Clarence
> Mr Knight
> Croft
> Lord Berkeley

and 'Mem: – House Tax & Window Tax – 2 Houses only to be paid for if 3 are occupied – '. The book title undoubtedly reflects Jenner's continuing interest in geological and fossil collections. The list has no explanation; Knight and Croft are medical men. And the final item indicates that, like all of us, Jenner, who occupied houses in Berkeley, Cheltenham and now London, was happy to note a legitimate way of reducing his taxes.

Why did he not maintain the visiting book? The immediate cause was probably a bout of flu, or what he called 'the prevailing Epidemial Catarrh' in a letter congratulating De Carro on his successful transmission of vaccine to Bombay. Jenner was reported ill by the Medical Council minutes on 17 March due to the 'generally prevailing sickness', causing the Council to delay its vaccination instructions, the address to the public and a reply to the Earl of Hardwicke, Lord Lieutenant of Ireland, who had asked for advice on how to obtain and preserve vaccine matter. The illness lasted more than a fortnight: on 6 April, he wrote to Dr Marcet, 'since I saw you [probably at a meeting of the Medical Society at Guy's on 24 February] the abominable Influenza has been sticking its Harpy claws deeper and deeper into my Chest.' 'We have all had it – Mrs Jenner and the Children have weathered the storm rather better than myself.' Yet it cannot be the whole explanation for discontinuing his appointments book when there is no evidence that the practice dried up or the appointments stopped.

Not least because of his biographer, Baron's, reticence, the underlying cause is obscured. At first he was perhaps depressed following his illness, but disillusionment gradually set in, laced by dislike of London. On 8 March 1803, before falling ill, he wrote to a Cheltenham friend and patient, T. Cobb, 'Honours certainly fall in showers upon me, but Emoluments fall off.' People went to him once for vaccination, but thereafter it was cheaper to take their children to a domestic surgeon or apothecary. 'They clearly shew the fallacy of Mr. Addington's prediction, who express'd a confidence in my soon remunerating myself by the numbers who would flock to me for Inoculation.' The complaint is a reprise of the melody from 1801. 'Honors most certainly fall down upon me in abundant showers,' he wrote to his Berkeley lawyer, Thomas Pearce, two weeks later, 'but Honor wont buy Mutton – ' 'Elated and allured by the speech of the Chancellor of the Exchequer,' Jenner wrote in what appears to have been a memorandum to Baron long after the fact, 'I took a house in London for 10 years, at a high rent, and furnished it; but my first year's practice convinced me of my own temerity and imprudence'. Does this mean that the calls recorded in the visiting book were in fact 'loss leaders' or, perhaps, even worse, more political than medical? Or does it mean that Jenner could not be bothered to persist against the competition of the metropolitan medical establishment? He worked from Hertford Street from 2 February to the end of July 1802, not a 'first year's practice' but half that. In Berkeley he had been for years a big fish. Even in Cheltenham, through his wife's connections and those of the Berkeleys, he had achieved local success well before national acclaim. Why should he bother with London, where he had to run fast merely to stand still? Eighteen months later he wrote to an 'intimate friend', according to Baron: 'The London smoke. . .is too apt to cloud our best faculties. I don't expect to risk the injury of mine. . . .That the public has not the smallest right to expect it of me, no one will deny.' Again, the whining note that seems so out of place except in a man dissatisfied not with his achievement but with his recognition.

Some of his supporters continued to blame his naïveté. Benjamin Travers wrote to Jenner in February 1804: 'your liberality and disinterestedness every one must admire. . .but you are sadly deficient in worldly wisdom.' Yet Travers and Baron, who quoted the letter, to the contrary notwithstanding, Jenner was no Holy Fool. Two quite worldly situations prompted Jenner's letter to Thomas Pearce, written just after his illness. He thanked Pearce for 'your investigations respecting the Premises in the Lane.' Two dilapidated cottages had belonged to the 'late Edward Cornock', whose wife had been the daughter of a Walter Gardner. The Cornock descendants were apparently willing to sell the cottages, and Jenner thought that all the Gardner descendants were dead. He suggested that Pearce check further, but 'If you shd. not think there was much risk in the purchase, I would proceed; for Berkeley (next to the Parson's Ditch) has not a greater nuisance to complain of than the Tottering Cottages in question.' They looked like a good proposition. In a postscript the astute writer added, 'What a blow Harry Addington gave to the Funds Thursday – I fear he wont do for us much longer.' A month later Pitt was back. Addington became Lord Sidmouth and returned to a well deserved obscurity. Jenner's prescience may have been heightened by his understandable annoyance that Addington had effectively blocked the doubling of his grant. In any event his naïveté seems to have been partial, most in evidence perhaps when he had to make decisions based on his ability to command public gratitude.

Other explanations for the interrupted record in the visiting book are possible. For example, in the welter of correspondence that filled his study, a slim notebook could easily have got lost.

Meanwhile, the Royal Jennerian Society adopted by-laws and regulations. A governor must have paid one guinea a year, five guineas in one payment or left the Society a legacy of £20 or more. Both the Board of Directors and the Medical Committee were to consist of governors. Each would appoint its own secretary. The regularity of meetings and of appointments was specified, with a General Court or general meeting given ultimate authority. London would be divided into twelve districts with an inoculation centre in each. The regulations also specified that an Annual Festival was to be held on Edward Jenner's birthday.

The Medical Council met for the first time on 23 February, with Dr Denman in the chair. With Lettsom, Ring, John Addington and two others, Jenner was appointed to a committee to prepare the Society's address to the public. At its next meeting a week later, Jenner, Ring and Addington were asked to cooperate with the directors' printing committee. Jenner and Ring were appointed, together with Addington and C. R. Aikin, to a third subcommittee charged to draw up the vaccination instructions. The Board of Directors met simultaneously, a technique frequently adopted to assure smooth communication between the two autonomous bodies, and appointed committees to consult with and seek support from various groups. Jenner was placed on the committee assigned to call on the Church of England and the Kirk of Scotland. On 29 March he accompanied other members to a meeting with the Archbishop of Canterbury, who 'had not yet had sufficient time to determine as to the proper measures'. The Church never gave vaccination its formal blessing, but it remained friendly and encouraged individual clergymen to help in any way they could. John Birch later took credit for this lack of wholehearted commitment. He said that the Archbishop had sent 'a respectable Clergyman' to obtain Birch's views and that gentleman had reported them back to his Grace. In this instance Birch may well have been right.

Jenner was also deputed by the Medical Council, along with Drs Denman and Bradley, to join three directors who were to confer with two officials, Lord William Bentinck and Lieutenant-Colonel Henry Clinton, about to sail for India, on the best means for promoting the Society there. Jenner was ill at the time, and it is not clear whether he was able to accompany the delegation.

This same meeting approved the delayed reply to the Lord-Lieutenant of Ireland on the 'mode of obtaining and preserving the genuine Vaccine matter.' Jenner and Ring signed the letter, which was probably drafted by Ring.

When fluid matter can be procured, it is always to be prefered; especially when the Small Pox prevails. . .Some persons who are to be Inoculated may be conveyed to the place where a Vaccine patient resides; and the fluid may be transferred Immediately from arm to arm: or a person who has the Vaccine affection, may be conveyed to any place where the practice is to be Introduced, and a considerable number may daily be Inoculated from that single source.

But when it is impracticable to obtain fluid matter there are various modes of transmitting it in a dry state. When it is to be used within two or three days, a lancet is a proper vehicle; but if it is not used within some such period, the lancet rusts. . . .This has been one of the most common causes of the numerous errors committed in Vaccine Inoculation. The Vaccine fluid is much more aqueous than the Variolous. . . .

Many safe and effectual methods of preserving Cow-Pock matter, have been devised. . . .Some of the most common are, the taking it on thread or glass, and suffering it to dry. . . .These methods are entitled to some degree of approbation; but they are attended with a great consumption of matter which is important in an affection, where that article is so sparingly produced.

. . .Lancets have been made of Gold, Silver, Platine [platinum], and Ivory; which. . .have been employed for the transportation of Vaccine virus with advantage.

Another mode. . .is to take the fluid on a quill shaped like a tooth-pick. . . .At the time of Inoculation, a puncture is first to be made with a lancet; then the point of the quill is to be inserted, and held in the part half a minute, or more. . . .

To render the instrument the more portable, it may be made out of a slender portion of a quill, stopped with white wax. Sealing wax is unfit for the purpose. The heat necessary for melting it may decompose the matter.

Another method is, to take the matter on a small bit of Ivory, shaped like the tooth of a comb; and pointed at the end like a lancet. This may be called a Vaccinator. . . .

Vaccine virus ought not to be taken after the areola begins to be extensive; nor to be dried before the fire; nor in any other way to be exposed to much heat.

Much progress had been made by meticulous observation and clinical experiment since Jenner's *Instructions for Vaccine Inoculation* were published two years before. But not all Jenner's experience led to such useful results. He had first noticed the apparent disruption of the vaccination process by skin eruptions when George Jenner had vaccinated the Chelmsford regiment. In February 1803, he wrote to Marcet that on a person with a 'scabby Face, especially if it be accompanied with Tinea Capitis [ringworm] or papilous [skin] eruptions', the vaccine vesicle 'will never contain limpid matter, but throughout all it's stages its Contents will be purulent – '.

A month later a letter to De Carro was even more speculative:

> Don't you observe that in Cases of Tinea Capitis and also in some erup-
> tive Cases, that the Pustule is often purulent, as in Small-pox. . . .It
> often happens that obstinate cutaneous affections are quickly dissipated
> by the magical touch of the Vaccine Lancet. A new action is excited
> in these Eruptions by the agency of the Vaccine Fluid – the original
> morbid action cannot be resumed, & thus it necessarely happens that
> the disease must terminate; at least thus I reason upon it – '

Now he seems to be saying that although eruptions prevent successful
vaccination, he has observed that they may themselves be cured by vaccine
matter. Considering the frequency of skin disorders in a population where
neither rich nor poor understood the benefits of bathing, such a discovery
could hardly be undervalued; but Jenner never repeated the theory.

At a meeting in mid-March the directors learned that the Royal Jennerian
Society had received its first substantial contribution, £500 from the Corporation of London. The Board decided to announce the donation in press
advertisements. It designated the Bank of England and the East India Company as suitable recipients for memorials requesting funds, and approved
an approach to the latter. The minutes of 7 September 1803 record a gift
of £100 from the Company, the only other large donation noted. In April
the proprietors of Sadlers' Wells, a popular 'resort' just north of the City,
offered 'a free benefit there for the Society', but the Board declined with
thanks 'for the present'.

The Board had asked a committee of the Medical Council to locate a
central house or headquarters for the Society, to house a resident inoculator
and the office of the Secretary to the Board of Directors, Charles Murray, as
well as meeting-rooms and inoculation quarters. It also asked this committee
to locate premises for the twelve inoculation stations, at not more than £50
rental per year each. At a meeting on 17 March, the Medical Council sought
authorization to contract for a house at 14 Salisbury Square, off Fleet Street.
Jenner, who was absent from the meeting, had recommended premises in
Chatham Place which the Council considered less suitable. A week later
the Society signed a lease for eight years at £105 annual land tax plus £300
purchase money, exclusive of fittings.

The first meeting, the Board of Directors', took place at the new Central
House on 31 March. Until a Resident Inoculator could be appointed, it
asked six members of the Medical Council each to agree to act as inoculator
on one day of the week between 10 and 11 a.m. Dr Walker, for example,
was scheduled for Wednesdays. At the same time, the Medical Council set
up a committee including Jenner, who was still absent, to receive and
vet applications for the important post of Resident Inoculator. He would
have responsibility for carrying out vaccinations at Central House and for

supplying vaccine to the stations when they were unable to obtain it from their own patients, and for maintaining a vaccine store from which he could supply requests from provincial practitioners. The high public image of the Society that everyone hoped to maintain, furthermore, meant that the vaccine it supplied had to be effective.

Inoculations by the Resident Inoculator and at the twelve inoculation stations throughout London were to be free to 'persons of all ages' between 10 a.m. and 3 p.m. every weekday. The Society adopted the common practice of charity dispensaries in all British cities. Patients had to be sent along by a contributor or official of the Society. They could not just turn up, although in practice inoculators themselves admitted someone who arrived without the required written notice. Nevertheless, to poor and uneducated people, the implied restriction could be daunting. Follow-up examinations were also free, but the patient had to return 'three or four times or oftener if desired' to the place where the vaccination had been done. This too could be a deterrent. Inoculation hours were, of course, working hours. It was seldom easy for a woman with children at home to bring her vaccinated youngster twice, let alone several times. No doubt the arrangements were better than nothing for those who could be induced to make use of them, but the world was not designed to meet the needs of the Lower Orders.

The Medical Council postponed selection of the Resident Inoculator for a month so that the position could be advertised. It fixed the salary at £200 per year plus 'House Rent Coals and Candles', and the successful candidate would be allowed to carry on some private practice. The Council received four applications, one of whom, a Dr Aberdour, withdrew before the vote. Dr William Domeier, a German by origin, had the recommendations of the Dukes of York and Cumberland. The other two were members of the Medical Council, Dr Joseph Leese and Dr Walker. The election by the Council took place on 28 April. Leese had six votes, Domeier ten and Walker twenty-seven. Voting was secret, but it is reasonable to assume that Jenner and the other members of the vetting committee such as Ring, Aikin and Marcet voted for Walker.

The Society issued its first two publications in April 1803. The first was a single sheet showing a *Comparative View of the Natural Small Pox Inoculated Small Pox and Inoculated Cow Pox in their effects on Individuals and Society*. Twenty thousand of a 'small' size were printed, and five thousand larger sheets suitable for posting. The second, an 'Address to the Public', contained a list of subscribers and an appeal for funds. The original draft approved by the directors had been rewritten by the Medical Council after delays caused by Jenner's illness. However, five thousand were printed in May for distribution to subscribers, members of both Houses of Parliament and the Corporation of London. Copies were also offered at a shilling to the public.

Jenner had taken the chair on three occasions at Council meetings in March and April, demonstrating his commitment to the details of Society business, despite his own preferences. In May he was appointed with Lettsom and Ring to represent the Medical Council in discussions with three directors on the election and privileges of honorary and corresponding members of the Society.

On 17 May the Society held its first Annual Festival, a dinner for three hundred at the Crown and Anchor in the Strand. The Earl of Egremont took the chair. Jenner was there. 'I was all but overcome by the tumultuous Plaudits of an Assembly met to celebrate my Birth day,' he wrote to William and Anne Davies. 'Firmer nerves than mine would have been shaken on such an occasion.'

Early in June the Board of Directors appointed a committee to concert with Jenner an approach to government which would seek reimbursement for his own expenditures on postage and a franking privilege for his vaccine mail. Nothing came of this initiative, but with Jenner's help the Society itself was more fortunate. On 7 July he joined a small group which called on the Postmaster General about franking privileges. They were granted at the end of 1803, to be reviewed in six months.

The Society's General Meeting on 15 June heard reports of its progress. Already more than eleven hundred inoculations had been performed, and vaccine matter had been supplied to 450 applicants. Subscriptions stood at £3226-2. Similar societies had been established in Plymouth Docks, thanks to Richard Dunning, and at Exeter and Doncaster. Within the next few years free vaccine institutions appeared across the land. In Somerset and Sussex they were called the Jennerian Society and Institution, respectively. Both had royal patronage. In Edinburgh, Liverpool and some other cities existing voluntary bodies took over the dispensing of free vaccinations. This haphazard structure went through many superficial alterations, but remained fundamentally unchanged until the National Health Service became a reality.

Despite the undoubted successes of the Royal Jennerian Society, its two heads were already at odds. Some of the directors disapproved of the election of John Walker as Resident Inoculator and the appointment of his friend, Mr Fox, as Secretary to the Medical Council. The General Meeting of 15 June had to adjudicate, and it voted in favour of the Council's actions. Jenner attended this meeting. In the light of his support for Walker, I assume that he voted with the majority.

An absurdly trivial quarrel between the Board and the Council simmered throughout June and July. The Medical Council had ordered large blank books to be made up for use as registers of inoculations, distribution of vaccine and any anomalous cases. The Board, not the Council, had to authorize expenditures, and asked for information about these blank books. After a lapse of two weeks because of the absence of John Addington, who was in charge of the order, Addington questioned the size of one book and said the costs 'much exceeded the expectations of the Council'. The Board officially doubted that they were needed at all, and the Council replied by suggesting they could be used for something else. The Board appointed another three-man committee to find a use for them, and there the matter ended as far as the minutes were concerned.

Jenner attended three of the four Council meetings at which these weighty tomes were discussed. The last, on 21 July 1803, coincided with a board meeting which authorized the printing of twenty-six thousand handbills for distribution by the inoculating stations:

Preservative against the Small Pox

At this Season of the Year when the Small Pox is very prevalent and fatal, the inhabitants of this parish are hereby informed that the Station of the Royal Jennerian Society for the Extermination of the Small Pox is at No.   where all persons are inoculated gratis And that the hours of Attendance are from   to

Thirteen stations were now in operation. The first ten opened for business on 15 May. The Hoxton station operated from the Methodist Sunday School, and the one in Drury Lane from the Methodist School House. Surry Chapel Station in St George's Fields used the Revd Rowland Hill's schoolroom rent-free. The stations at Great Castle Street, Oxford Market, Marylebone, and 6 Whitehart Court, Castle Street, Kings Mews, Westminster, were commercial rentals. Dr Jenner was the 'Superintending Physician'. At the outset, stations sought to operate with a staff of four – two physicians and two inoculators who were usually surgeons. Original assignments included Dr Woodville in Rotherhithe, Dr Willan in Southwark, Drs Babington and Marcet at Golden Lane, Drs Sims and Blane at Ratcliff, Dr Hawes at Bishopsgate and Dr Lettsom at Surry Chapel. Mr Ring attended at Marylebone, Messrs Addington and Aikin at Bishopsgate and Mr Dimsdale at Drury Lane. As the weeks passed many of these assignments became rather more honorary than active, but the charitable spirit at the outset is evident. Up to 20 August, they performed 2701 inoculations. Almost a quarter of these were done at the Surry Chapel station. Marylebone followed with 215, Bishopsgate 170, Hoxton 158, Rotherhithe 130, Ratcliff 100, and in descending order Golden Lane, Maze Pond in Southwark, Clerkenwell, John Street, Mile End, Drury Lane and Westminster, with two only.

Obviously, the stations were not attracting overwhelming support from a grateful population. Nevertheless, in 1803 a report from the Finsbury Dispensary, Clerkenwell, noted 'that the prejudices of the poorer classes. . .are gradually declining; they embrace with avidity the good which is presented to them.' The Medical Council was less sanguine and considerably more realistic in February 1804: 'It appearing that a small proportion of the poorest class participate of the benefits of this Institution, the consideration of such measures as are necessary to be adopted to induce them to accept it is recommended to the next Meeting.' The Council noted that changing the locations of stations which were deemed too expensive or to have attracted too few vaccinees had not helped. The Society was already offering vaccine matter free to medical practitioners throughout the country. In March 1805 the General Meeting heard that the Society had performed 6924 vaccinations during the past twelve months in all of London. In roughly the same period 145,840 vaccinations had been performed in Madras, and in Paris sixty thousand had been vaccinated in the preceding three months. The Board asked the Council to consider 'whether some additional Plan may not be adopted to visit the poor at their own habitations with the offer of vaccine Inoculation.' It was an approach which John Ring used with considerable success in his own practice, and it was also done in Nottingham. So profound was class distrust and mutual ignorance that the problem could only get worse. Jenner himself wrote to Dr De Carro on 30 March 1803: 'In London my practice is limited to the higher orders of Society – In the Country, I can always find little Cottagers on whom I can introduce vaccine Virus in any form.' He was in fact only thanking De Carro for a charged ivory lancet, but it is obvious he looked upon 'little Cottagers' as laboratory animals with souls.

The Medical Council meeting of 21 July was to be Jenner's last for nearly two years. He probably remained in London for the presentation of the Freedom of the City on 11 August. In 'a Gold Box of the value of one hundred Guineas' lay the elegant certificate. In September at the instigation of Dr Hawes, the Royal Humane Society made Jenner an honorary member.

The Jenners left Hertford Street never to return. They had settled again in Cheltenham by 14 August. He began to revive his practice immediately. In September Joseph Farington, then visiting Cheltenham, noted that the portrait painter, John Hoppner, was Jenner's patient and that he 'has recommended Him to rub in Mercury for his Liver complaint.' For the next few weeks the record is singularly blank. The family returned to Berkeley in December, where, on the 6th, William Davies junior 'Dined and drank tea', or in other words spent the day with his uncle. According to Davies's diary, they had not met since the previous January. Now Jenner had evidently determined to remain in Gloucestershire. The Hertford Street lease was to be sold, and he intended to concentrate on his immense correspondence and his lucrative practice.

Chapter 8

. . . so large, so temperate, and so consistent . . .
1804–1807

The decision to sell the Hertford Street lease and to leave London indefinitely marks a watershed in Jenner's life. Since 1799 he had tried, very much against the grain, to meld politics and medicine into a hand that would assure both a win for vaccination and a living that matched his status as a Public Figure. Everyone – all his friends – claimed it should be possible. Even the Prime Minister had held out the hope that private practice would effectively double his parliamentary grant. In fact he had earned about £350 per year from vaccination in London, and had accumulated an estimated deficit of nearly £6000 in four years. The threat of personal bankruptcy must have seemed very real to a small west-country landowner bred to husband scarce resources for reinvestment in property, the only true wealth. '. . .I have to thank my stars that I have a little farm or two in Glostershire, where I shall at once repair, quit doctoring, and turn ploughman,' he wrote to Richard Dunning when the parliamentary grant still seemed to hang in the balance. The statement may be a little overdramatic, albeit in the mould of the Lawrence portrait Jenner admired, but his departure fifteen months later enacted the sentiment.

I have found no evidence to show how sudden the decision was. Certainly his departure for Cheltenham in early August 1803 fits the pattern of previous years. Both for social (including political) and for financial reasons, the annual visit began when the season was at its height. But exactly when he made up his mind to sell the Hertford Street lease, no doubt the crucial decision, the record does not reveal. Of course it could have been as early as the bout of flu in the spring. Perhaps he preferred not to mention it to Baron nor to keep the documents. It must have seemed a confession of failure. The decision to spend half of each year in London had been wrong. Both the medical and the financial objectives had failed. Or so it may have seemed at the end of 1803. Yet if that were true, even Jenner must have realized when he took time to reflect that however unsuccessful his London practice, vaccination had struck down roots which could never be extirpated. It was here to stay,

[148]

a permanent part of the medical armoury not only in Britain but throughout the world. Parliament had approved it, the King had given his name to its support. There remained a small matter of popular lack of enthusiasm which a tiny minority of medical men would soon exploit, but in 1803 even George Pearson had been relatively quiet, and William Woodville volunteered his services as an inoculator to the Royal Jennerian Society. Perhaps the fact that Jenner did *not* give up doctoring when he moved back to the country indicates that in his heart he knew what he had achieved. In any case, he needed the money from doctoring.

Could he have won the vaccination battle from headquarters at Berkeley? Sir Walter Farquhar, Henry Cline and Lady Berkeley, among others, thought not. Jenner thought not too, and in that at least he was right. His audiences with royalty, his call on the Prime Minister, his presence in London society, all exerted political force. Whatever his moral doubts about the application for money, it was a facet of the jewel Respectability, no less integral than the medical evidence that vaccination worked, and a good deal more flashy. So while he was there in London, was it not at least sensible to practise his profession? Until the cost began to eat away his substance, it was.

In Cheltenham his practice had always been circumscribed by the presence of a number of other medical men. The town was, after all, a spa where people came to take the waters for their health. But in Berkeley during the quarter-century he had practised there, Jenner had had the field pretty much to himself. After four years his former practice had been taken over by two doctors, one of whom was his nephew, Henry. To re-establish himself in his home town took some time, but here his fame undoubtedly worked to his advantage.

By contrast with its immediate predecessors, 1804 was a quiet year divided between Berkeley and Cheltenham. In January and June the younger Reverend William Davies administered the sacrament to Mrs Jenner at Berkeley. He ate dinner and drank tea with the Jenners and 'a large party' on 3 February at the Chauntry. They met again in March, then twice in May, the second occasion being Edward's fifty-fifth birthday. The Royal Jennerian Society had asked Jenner to attend their Annual Festival at the Crown and Anchor on the day, but Catherine's health had been Jenner's excuse. On this birthday, furthermore, his brother-in-law, Reverend William Davies senior, noted that his youngest son, Edward, 'went to Berkeley to consult his Uncle – '. The note following was dated four days later: 'Edward gave his Uncle Dr. Jenner a Cow Calf out of his Cow – Five Weeks & 4 Days when the Dr. sent for her. – Recd Cow Feb. 24'. Of such events was the new rhythm of Jenner's life composed.

On 7 June, when he administered the sacrament to Mrs Jenner, William Davies also attended 'the Masonic Lodge in the Eve.' This is the first reference in William's meticulous diary to his own and his uncle's Freemasonry. When Jenner became a Mason, I have not discovered. It could have been at almost any time after he had begun to establish himself as a country practitioner, in the decade between his apparent rejection by Catherine's brother and their marriage, after his marriage but before his move to London, or it could have been an integral part of his return to the country in 1804. If he had joined before 1804, Edward had probably introduced William Davies to the order; otherwise, the nephew could have introduced his eminent uncle. Baron maintained total silence on the subject, probably not least because he too was a Mason and therefore committed to the principle of secrecy. The Berkeley Lodge consisted of the local professionals and shopkeepers. William Davies appears to have been its only Church of England clergyman and Jenner its only doctor until Henry Jenner joined some years later. The Berkeley family do not seem to have been local members, if they were Masons at all. There was also in Berkeley a Royal Arch Lodge of which both Jenner and William Davies were members.

Great Britain may have been the source of freemasonry. The organization had been consolidated early in the eighteenth century, and had been dominated by the royal family since the Duke of Cumberland had become Grand Master in 1782. In predominantly Catholic countries such as France and even in Ireland, Masonry tended to be anti-Catholic and antimonarchist. In France, indeed, atheism became an acceptable element in the lodges, though in Britain such a development was anathema. Theoretically, any believer in one God could become an initiate. Practically, members were largely communicants of the Established Church, at least in England, though not in Ireland or North America.

Berkeley was probably a Christian lodge in the sense that Dissenters were acceptable. Jenner himself, perhaps under Catherine's influence, tended toward religious tolerance. Probably about the time that George III was preparing to accept Pitt's resignation because the First Minister stubbornly supported a degree of Catholic emancipation in Ireland, Jenner wrote to his friend the Revd Thomas Pruen: 'I wish I cd transfer the malady to the Hides[?] of some of those who made all this idle Bustle about the Catholic Question. They shd not have it sparingly – '. At that time his impatience may have been exacerbated by the delay the change of government imposed upon his petition for a parliamentary grant. Many years later under no such pressure, he wrote in his notebook, 'If a Catholic peer, as it has been said, does not regard an oath by an heretic, why does he not boldly enter the House of Peers, take the oath & his seat? The answer is clear, his conscience keeps him out, and thus the objection is answered.' He understood the danger of religious conflict to the state, no doubt because he had experienced it at home. Again he wrote to Pruen at the end of 1809:

I dread the consequence of the Contest which is to take place in the ensuing Sessions, between these people [Methodists] & the Bishops. I know nothing more likely to upset our tottering State. From the nature of the human mind, religious conflicts must necessarily be more furious than others. . .the Man who draws the Sword in defence of Religion feels the highest impulse, because he fights, as he conceives, under the Banners of Heaven.

In so far as Jenner's personal God can be separated from the Thirty-nine Articles, He seems to have been the construction of a practical theist.

How often do we say 'this is bad weather – too much rain has fallen this month – the frost has been too long, too severe season.' But this cannot be. The weather may be inconvenient for the designs of man, but must always be in harmony with the designs of God, who has not only this planet, our Earth, to manage, but the universe.

The whole creation is the work of God's hands. It cannot manage itself. Man cannot manage it, therefore, God is the manager.

God's design is expressed in the laws of nature: 'To an observer of those divine laws which harmonize the general order of things, there appears a design in the arrangement of this sylvan minstrelsy,' he wrote in his paper on bird migration. This expression of what might be called natural religion appears in all ages, especially amongst those who cannot or wish not to imagine Orderliness without an Ordering Power. Jenner's educated contemporaries, scientists, artists and politicians alike, commonly viewed disorder as aberrant, evil, the devil's work – a perception that has been almost totally turned upside down from his time to ours. Even Coleridge, the embodiment of a new antistatist individualism, perceived the unity of experience rather than its diversity: of an admired schoolteacher, he wrote: 'I learnt from him, that Poetry, even that of the loftiest and, seemingly, of the wildest odes, had a logic of its own, as severe as that of science; and more difficult, because more subtle, more complex, and dependent on more, and more fugitive causes.' Jenner, who was trained neither in philosophy nor literature, expressed an analogous logical universality: 'The highest powers in our nature are our sense of moral excellence. The principle of reason & reflection, benevolence to our fellow creatures & our love of the Divine Being.' The universe astonished not because of its originality but because of 'the arrangement of this sylvan minstrelsy'.

Freemasonry embodied these rational values in the convivial atmosphere of a gentlemen's club enriched by symbols and mystery. The lodge might have been a Church where everyone shared the priesthood. Seen in this light, surely it would have been more surprising if Jenner had remained aloof from the order, especially in 1804 (whenever he had joined it).

Edward Jenner 1749–1823

In August the *Medical and Physical Journal* gave pride of place to Jenner's long article, 'On the Varieties and Modifications of the Vaccine Pustule'. It was his first publication since the *Instructions for Vaccine Inoculation* at the end of 1801, and the first extended work on vaccination by its author to appear in a medical journal. Jenner had enlarged it from letters and conversations in the six months after settling again in Berkeley. Most recently, he had concluded a long letter to an unnamed Leipzig correspondent with observations on these eruptions. 'Varieties' 'in the character of the Vaccine Vesicle,' he began,

> may undoubtedly be excited, but whenever they appear we should be cautious not to perpetuate them by inoculating from such a source. Were we to attend to the Maxim (a Maxim I Have endeavourd strenuously to enforce) of always inoculating from a Pustule perfectly characterized, on some early day of its formation and not after the Areola is formd, Varieties would scarcely ever appear; never, I believe, unless the process of inoculation was ill conducted, or upon a skin under the influence of some previous affection. . . .there are many cuticular diseases which do not impede the action of the Vaccine Virus, but there is one. . .which (especially in its recent state) almost always alters the natural order of its progress, and this is Tinea Capitis. . . .a spurious or imperfect pustule is the consequence and the Constitution receives no security. . . .This disease (the Tinea Capitis) either in its genuine state or under some of its modifications, is not uncommon among some of our poor Cottagers. . . .what I have mentioned is more frequently the source of spurious Pustules, and of deception among inexperienced Practitioners than all the rest put together. . .

Tinea capitis, ringworm, had been classified by Robert Willan under psoriasis as an herpetic disease, a group of diseases with similar eruptive symptoms. Inasmuch as the notion of an infectious agent existed amongst medical men only in the vaguest sense and might refer to the air as well as particulate matter, the use of the word 'herpetic' did not imply a cause. The word 'virus' was in common use, but it too meant a vague infectious principle. Jenner never used it in the context of herpetic eruptions. 'I am greatly deceived,' he wrote to Robert Ferryman in February 1805, 'if it will not be found that most of these affections of the skin which have been called irritative, such as scaly Tetter, ring worm, etc, have not their origin in simple Herpes. The itch of course is an exception.' Psoriasis was then also called 'tetter'. Then, as now, its cause was unknown.

In his paper, Jenner explicitly followed Willan's classifications. The prior existence of an herpetic disorder definitely endangered the patient's security following vaccination. Apart from observation, Jenner's rationale for this theory was John Hunter's precept that two similar disorders – similar, that is, symptomatically – could not coexist in the same patient. The precept

[152]

was wrong; but, as in this case, it seemed to fit the facts because without an understanding of cause, cause and effect were often confused. Vaccination might fail for all the reasons Jenner understood plus the passage of time, but it could not have failed because the patient had caught a dirt-born infectious agent such as ringworm or an herpes virus.

He made two other significant points, neither of them wholly new but both clarified here. He insisted on revaccination if the practitioner had any doubt about the pustule, and he wrote: 'the herpetic and some other irritative eruptions are capable of rendering variolous inoculation imperfect, as well as the Vaccine.' Evidence that variolation might also fail was to become an important theme in the defence of vaccination against its critics. For example, later in 1804 John Ring wrote a reply to the first of many practitioners who reported cases of smallpox after vaccination. Even after smallpox inoculation, he said, patients developed symptoms such as fever, pustules, inflammation and suppuration, either because of a second variolation or from exposure to natural smallpox. About a year and a half after Jenner's paper appeared, Willan wrote to him that he had an hypothesis 'Respecting the principle, by which the human frame, when under the influence of Herpes, is often rendered insusceptible of the *contagion* of Small-pox'. What was true of smallpox might also be true of cowpox. Willan intended to publish his hypothesis 'at some future day', but seems never to have done so.

Doubts about the adverse influence of herpetic disorders evidently surfaced early. In January 1805 Jenner complained to Dibdin that his paper was 'by far the most useful that has appeared since my first Pamphlet came out. But how remarkable – interesting, extremely interesting as it is, it does not seem to have excited the smallest sensation among medical men.' To John Walker he admitted: 'My paper on Herpes is unpopular, I find; I am sorry for it.' The reason was obvious. In a report on the medical year 1805 in Newcastle-upon-Tyne, Dr J. Wood said: 'My experience warrants me in concluding that the presence of *herpes* neither prevents nor lessens the security usually obtained by vaccination.'

In this case Dr Wood and many of his colleagues were right. Jenner's observations, based on what must have been a misinterpretation of the vaccination failures at Chelmsford, were wrong. According to a modern textbook, 'There is no evidence that other diseases interfere with the development of vaccinia', the virus which gives immunity in vaccination. With regard specifically to skin diseases, 'it is advisable to postpone vaccination, not because sepsis will interfere with vaccinial growth, but because there is a danger of spreading' the skin infection. Jenner can scarcely be blamed for his ignorance of modern virology, however, and it was not his way to abandon his observations because others disagreed. The mounting need to explain vaccination failures, real and alleged, furthermore, provided motivation for a bias in his judgement. The same forces operated to produce his subtle and unacknowledged redefinition of spurious cowpox in these years.

He never abandoned the conviction that herpetic eruptions could interfere with vaccination. In 1818 he complained to Baron: 'It is unaccountable, but not one of my correspondents seem to know anything of the impediments arising from the presence of Herpetic Lymph, tho' I have said so much about it.' Two years later for the first time he added 'Dandriffe' to the list. In his circular letter of 1821, he stressed that the size of the outbreak was irrelevant: 'a speck behind the ear which might be covered by a split pea, being capable of disordering the Vaccine Vesicle.' Sore eyelids could also be classified as an herpetic eruption. 'In short, every disease of the skin, which may be called *serous*, or one that sends out a fluid capable of conversion into a scab, has the power of exerting this modifying and counteracting influence'. Thus Jenner concluded yet another paragraph in the history of ideas that failed.

In the same month that saw the publication of his paper on herpes eruptions, August 1804, Jenner left Berkeley for the first time in eight months, returning to Cheltenham with his family. Although they had been living in the town for extended periods each year since 1796, Jenner had settled for rented accommodation. During their first season they occupied part of a building opposite a chemist's shop in the High Street, but he then leased a house at 8 St George's Place. The street runs into the High Street, and number 8 was the end house farthest from that thoroughfare in a new terrace. It had been built by the proprietor of an adjacent livery stables, a Mr Lambert, who leased the entire terrace to a Cheltenham practitioner, Dr Minster. Minster is said to have occupied number 7. Dr Thomas Newell was at 1 St George's Place and a Dr Fowler at number 6. With two more doctors on Manchester Walk, a lane connecting St George's Place to the parish churchyard, the neighbourhood had a highly medical flavour. The terrace gardens were separated from the shady churchyard by a high brick wall, but the first-floor sitting-rooms overlooked the green perspective. Today, though the church and its restful graves remain, the red-brick Georgian houses have disappeared. The High Street is a wilderness of concrete boxes, and fashionable Cheltenham has moved several hundred yards north-west. Perhaps appropriately in light of its original owner, the terrace site is largely occupied by a driving school. Catherine was to die at number 8 in 1815, whereupon Edward retired permanently to Berkeley. He owned the Cheltenham house when he died, however, and left it to his son, Robert. It had been bought during the 1804 season. 'So great has been the scramble for Houses in this favorite haunt of the great & opulent,' he wrote to Robert Ferryman in February, 'that I have been obliged to be a buyer in order to secure a place to hide my little Head in.'

So surprising is the fey reference to 'my little Head' that I was taken aback. I assume it reflects the relationship between Jenner and the remarkable Reverend Robert Ferryman (1753–1837). In his twenties, Ferryman became chaplain to the Margrave of Ansbach, who later married the Earl of Berkeley's sister. Perhaps the most notable aspect of his chaplaincy is the fact that Ferryman was not admitted to the priesthood until 1796. Meanwhile, he had returned to England and settled in Gloucester, where he opened the Museum of British Quadrupeds and Birds in Berkeley Street in July 1789. He had collected and preserved the specimens himself, in the best tradition of British amateurism. The following year, according to the *Glocester Journal*, the Duke of Gloucester visited the museum along with the Bishop and other clergy.

By 1793 its creator was living in Hammersmith and then at Drayton in Middlesex, where he was consulted by Thomas Paytherus, probably in relation to what we would today call a survey of the house Paytherus bought in Bond Street. In 1795 he went to sea briefly with Admiral Berkeley, but the next year he lived for a time with the Jenners during their first summer at Cheltenham. When and how he had met Jenner, I do not know, but I imagine they were introduced by one of the Berkeleys before 1790, and that Paytherus called on Ferryman's skills as a result of a suggestion by Jenner. At some time between 1796 and 1804, furthermore, Ferryman designed and supervised the construction of a folly in the south-west corner of Jenner's garden. It was a rustic room, roughly eight feet by six and seven feet high, built of logs and with a wooden roof, a small hearth in the wall opposite the door and no windows. In the literary style of an *ancien régime* delineated by Angelica Kauffmann, Fosbroke described it as 'a refuge for faun or dryad or Arcadian deity'. Jenner, who used the room once a week as a vaccination station for the local poor, named it the Temple of Vaccinia, thus reinforcing the form of expression in his February letter to its architect.

When Ferryman was admitted to the priesthood, he was living at Iping in Sussex with the Earl of Egremont. Some time thereafter while he was staying with the Duke of Bedford, he vaccinated three hundred people at Woburn Abbey. Clearly he was a man of great but unregulated capacity, with a manner which won him impermanent entrée into high places. After a friendship of thirty years, Jenner summed him up thus:

> I have just got a letter from Ferryman. He says if he could get a Curacy he wd relinquish his Post at Halifax. . . .
> What a strange jumble of intellect does this unfortunate man possess. How much he has mistaken himself, & put that in front which should have been in the background. He is preeminent (in my opinion) as a landscape Gardener & by pursuing that for the benefit of others, he might have enriched himself – but he must become an architect & be hanged to him, ruin himself & those who were heedless enough to employ him.

Ferryman had taken a position as curate in Halifax, Nova Scotia, possibly to escape his wife. After years of marriage and raising several children, the couple had separated angrily.

Jenner's strictures on his friend's abilities as a builder eventually gave way. A few years later he suggested to a friend of his daughter's that Catherine might profit from Ferryman's architectural skills. She had married and settled in Birmingham, where she was thinking of erecting cottages

> in the skirts of the Town. How clever it would be if they could get a magical touch from the Wand of Ferryman. When he first came among us thirty years ago, the Gloucestershire mind had not advanced far enough to feel the force of his Pencil. . .straight lines and angles were better relished than swells and hollows. Taste is either a very coy Nymph, or she has few Lovers.

Jenner was then an old man with the privilege of unknowingly changing his mind, a common trait made the more acceptable because his expressive language reveals a command of metaphor that had improved with time.

Ferryman was only one of the Renaissance characters whom Jenner befriended and promoted. He proposed to pay for the paper to assist publication of Thomas Frognall Dibdin's poem, *Vaccinia*, though it never saw the light. Dibdin and Thomas Fosbroke were of the next generation, but Ferryman was Jenner's contemporary. Christopher Anstey, who was some years older and best known for his *New Bath Guide*, later illustrated by Cruikshank, wrote a Latin 'Ode to Jenner' in 1804. John Ring's translation appeared in a pamphlet, all proceeds from the sale of which went to the Royal Jennerian Society. Jenner and Anstey may never have met, but Jenner was certainly acquainted with Robert Bloomfield, the poet best known for *The Farmer's Boy*, illustrated by Bewick. Bloomfield dedicated a poem to Jenner and the RJS. 'Do me the favour,' Jenner wrote gratefully, 'to accept a silver ink-stand, into which the enclosed may be converted if you will call upon Rundell & Bridge, Ludgate Hill, and use my name. I should like the following plain engraving on it. – "Edward Jenner, M.D. to Robert Bloomfield".' Jenner recorded a visit in 1808 from the immensely popular Scottish poet, Thomas Campbell, but there is no evidence of a continuing friendship. Fosbroke said that Jenner also knew Thomas Moore, the Irish poet who is best remembered today as the author of *Lalla Rookh*, and Samuel Taylor Coleridge. Coleridge knew Dr Thomas Beddoes of Bristol well, but doubtless there were other connections between Jenner and the great poet. In October 1811, in a pencil note about various matters to his old friend Thomas Pruen, Jenner wrote: 'His [Coleridge's] offer to me was very important; not less than to bring out a series of Essays on Vaccination in the Courier.' The *Courier*, a London evening paper, regularly published Coleridge, but the proposed essays never appeared. Perhaps inevitably, Fosbroke saw in those connections the evidence of a generous patron: '. . .he was not only fond of having "a batch of geniuses about him," but if he saw "signs of true genius with empty pockets," he was foremost in supplying its needs. He said, "I have often found these men up to their chin, but I would never let them sink below." ' There is ample evidence that Jenner could be kind and generous, as he had been to Fosbroke himself, but it is worth repeating that he was no fool. Fosbroke may have noticed that almost every one of these poets and eccentrics contributed or proposed to contribute to the advancement of vaccination. Yet it was Fosbroke who also quoted a Jennerian remark with a different flavour: 'I show everything to my friends but my back.'

The steely fury with which he met what he considered to be ignorant and ill informed opposition demonstrates his hard-headedness. If there is good reason to doubt the contribution made by his verbal weaponry to the ultimate victory of vaccination, its importance to Jenner during his later years cannot be overstated. So paramount was the war effort that some of the casualties included loyal generals like Sir Lucas Pepys, President of the Royal College of Physicians. But if Jenner went too far, it was because the logic of public safety from smallpox demanded the same selflessness that had characterized his behaviour from the outset. Unfortunately, fanaticism is always naïve and inevitably self-destructive.

The opposition to vaccination was based on evidence that it did not always work, that some people caught smallpox after they had been vacci-nated. Antivaccinists were quite prepared to accept that vaccination assured protection to most people, but they maintained that whereas smallpox inocu-lation could not fail because it was not possible to contract smallpox twice, vaccination could and did fail. When the animal origin of cowpox was added to the failure rate, opponents argued, the case against vaccination was over-whelming. Until somewhat later they did not question the positive benefits of cowpox inoculation: that it did not spread disease and that people could work after vaccination. Most antivaccinists accepted that cowpox caused no deaths, but they also denied that deaths might follow properly conducted Suttonian variolation. Had the facts they alleged been proven, vaccination could not have succeeded. In reply, therefore, the Jennerians had to show that oppo-sition practitioners had misinterpreted specific cases. Either the patient had measles or chicken-pox rather than smallpox or, if he or she had smallpox, it was caused by prior infection as in the London Smallpox Hospital cases. At first Jenner and his supporters took it for granted that unless the vaccine lymph itself was faulty, vaccination always succeeded. They reasoned from analogy: cowpox was akin to smallpox. Smallpox inoculation always worked providing the inoculum was efficient. QED. Slowly, it began to dawn on both sides not only that in some cases smallpox had followed variolation, but indeed that a few caught natural smallpox twice. At the same time, the Jennerians realized that when smallpox did follow either variolation or vaccination, it was probably never fatal. Finally, the Jennerians had the relatively simple task of demonstrating that variolation could cause fatal smallpox.

From about 1805, a minority of antivaccinists began to interpret data to prove that vaccination actually caused disabilities and death. These were extremists driven into a corner by their failure to win the more reasoned argument. Their graphic claims gave them entrée to the popular press. The one weapon denied to both sides was statistics; both the art and the science of counting were newborn infants: the first decennial census had been conducted in 1801. For this reason as much as any other, Jenner refused to the end to accept that the risk of smallpox after vaccination increased in direct proportion to the time elapsed.

In 1808 Dr Richard Reece published *A Practical Dictionary of Domestic Medicine*. Dr Reece disapproved of vaccination. In an entry on 'Cow-pox' he listed the antivaccinists known to him: Dr Moseley, first to enter the field, Dr William Rowley of Oxford, John Birch, William Goldson of Portsea, George Lipscomb of London, Mr Steward – who may be Thomas Stewart, surgeon, of Plymouth, though in 1800 he favoured vaccination – and Dr Clutterbuck, who was probably Mr Clutterbuck. He had reported the alleged fatality following vaccination at the Smallpox Hospital in 1801. Reece also listed Dr Thomas Mott Caton, and a Mr Roberts, but he omitted Mr W. R. Rogers (Roberts?), a junior to Birch at St Thomas's, and, most surprisingly, Dr R. Squirrell whose real name was John Gale Jones. Several antivaccinists published for the first time after Reece's *Dictionary* appeared: two Browns, Thomas of Musselburgh in Scotland and a London surgeon, Dr Charles Maclean of London, and, arguably, Richard Walker of Oxford. If Messrs Steward and Roberts are included, the published antivaccinists number fifteen, of whom eight – Moseley, Rowley, Birch, Goldson, Lipscomb, Squirrell, Maclean and Thomas Brown – carried the most weight. From the articles cited in the Notes to this paragraph alone, moreover, it can be seen that frequent claims by the antivaccinists that they were ignored by the medical press were hard to justify.

William Goldson was the first of the new wave of critics, practitioners whose experience had often been acquired after Parliament had accepted Jenner's claim in 1802. On 29 March 1804, Goldson read a paper to the quarterly meeting of the Portsmouth Medical Society describing eight cases of smallpox occurring after vaccination. His central concern was the length of time that vaccination could be expected to protect the patient, given that one of his cases had been vaccinated only a few months before becoming ill. Soon after presenting his evidence orally, Goldson published a pamphlet containing the same material, a common enough procedure amongst medical men at the time. He addressed it to the 'Directors of the Vaccine Institution', by which he later said he meant the Royal Jennerian Society, and his language was mild-tempered and informative. Within weeks John Ring replied with *An Answer to Mr. Goldson, proving that Vaccination is a Permanent Security against the Small-Pox.* Not the least striking aspect of this effusion is its length, about forty thousand words, and the speed with which it must have been written. Ring was certainly not unique in his astonishing fluency. Pearson in the early days of vaccination, Birch, Moseley and, indeed, Goldson poured out language unceasingly in the style then current, each sub-clause and qualification receiving full verbal attention. Ring perhaps surpassed them all in the vaccination controversies of the first fifteen years, for sheer volume. It was logorrhoeic warfare possible only to people who had nothing like radio or, worse, television to distract their attention.

Ring's first aim was to show that Goldson was mistaken: either his vaccinations had not taken or his patients had not had smallpox but some other eruptive fever, possibly chicken-pox. Even if he had been correct in detail, despite the fact that Goldson had reported observations whereas Ring made assumptions, his central argument was wrong. He and his colleagues, including Jenner of course, argued by analogy from examples in Jenner's early papers, especially the *Inquiry* and *Further Observations*, that time had no effect. It does, but years of experience were required to validate that discovery. In any event, Goldson's cases were far too recently vaccinated to have been affected by any time-based loss of protection, so that Ring's assumptions about his mistakes may well have been right.

Unfortunately, Ring's strong, vituperative language fixed the ill-tempered tone of an increasingly angry debate. Jenner may have had some moral excuse for his often scathing but seldom published comments about the opposition. Ring had only the dangerous conviction of the fanatic and, it should be said, the customary forms of expression used by his profession in public arguments. Until well into the twentieth century, the medical press often conducted the search for clinical and scientific truth in language that might have embarrassed football hooligans and lager louts. In part, practitioners hoped to hide their common ignorance by shouting.

However, Ring succeeded in eliciting a reply from Goldson, *Some Recent Cases of Small Pox subsequent to Vaccination.* This pamphlet is much longer and less closely reasoned than the first one, and although Goldson had not yet mastered the art of invective, he was trying: 'I hope it will teach him [Ring] a little more moderation, and learn him in future to be more correct himself, before he accuses others of ignorance in the practice [of vaccination].'

Jenner himself entered this particular arena only on a matter of detail, in a letter to Richard Dunning dated 23 December 1804: '. . .it has been represented to me, that Mr Goldson once wrote to me, and that I did not answer his letter. This is not true. He wrote a very civil letter to me during the sitting of the committee on the affair of Clarke the marine [one of Goldson's cases]. . . .This letter I answered almost immediately; and enclosed one of my papers of instructions for vaccine inoculation.' His letter to Dunning was written from Berkeley, but I do not know when the Jenners returned from Cheltenham at the end of the 1804 season. On 23 October, Edward had dined with the Mayor and William Davies junior at the White Lion in Berkeley. Laconic as always, Davies gives no further details. It is the last entry to mention his uncle until 6 December, however, and probably indicates that Jenner had come to Berkeley for some special purpose, possibly the installation of a new Mayor, that official being elected annually.

On 1 January 1805 William Davies junior ate breakfast with the Jenners, an unusual event for New Year's Day. In England, however, it was an ordinary day, and there may have been accounts to be gone over. Even Christmas, before the Victorian age, was no more than a religious feast day. Stephen Jenner and Parson Woodforde alike fed the poorest of their flock – and kept careful records of what they spent. The week-long festival of buying, eating and drinking had yet to begin its evolution. A week later, when William Davies breakfasted again at the Chauntry, his business was in part at least to give the sacrament to his aunt.

Professionally, Edward's concern remained the antivaccinists. 'All the Petty opposition to vaccination might have been prevented if my Friends had but attended to my early requisitions, which they certainly have not – "guard the public thro' the Newspapers" was always my cry,' he wrote to Dibdin. Though this letter appears to be the first written evidence of his cry, it was to be frequently repeated. Jenner knew that the medical press might win the minds and hearts of the practitioners but, without compulsion, the popular press alone could advance the cause of cowpox inoculation amongst those who needed it most. Conscious of the potential though he was, Jenner never published in the newspapers himself. He doubted his own ability to express himself clearly for the layman. 'You don't like my style when I write for the public eye, nor do I,' he was to write to James Moore, Assistant Director of the National Vaccine Establishment, in 1810;

> but I cannot mend it, for I write then under the impression of fear. . . .My great aim is to be perspicuous, and I got credit for succeeding in the papers I sent out; but some of the others might be more obscure through my taking pains with them. . . .

On the other hand, he determined about this time to try a popular pamphlet which would be anonymous. The use of anonymity by both pamphleteers and writers for the newspapers was very common. It allowed the author a latitude which he felt his name and position forbade, if a *nom de plume* did not simply protect him from the laws of libel or treason. Medical journals published anonymous articles as often as other publications. On 4

February 1805, Jenner sent Dibdin in London a draft of such a pamphlet. He suggested details of format and asked for advice on a printer. 'As I so much wish for secrecy, this will require your attention.' He asked Dibdin to remind him of 'the names of any Men of consequence who have figured on the Vaccine side', though he has listed them in the pamphlet only by their initials. This pamphlet has never been identified.

Amongst Jenner's papers, however, I have found a draft in his hand dated at Cheltenham, 27 December 1805:

> It has been a question often agitated among the Friends of Vaccination, whether or not (as it is obvious the practice must ultimately be universally adopted) it would be prudent to notice the malignant efforts of those persons who have given a temporary check to its progress?
>
> If the base & unfounded assertions, & insinuations they have spread abroad by a variety of means, but principally thro the medium of Pamphlets were treated by the british public, with the contempt they deserve, there would of course be no necessity for exposing their falacy, but unfortunately that is not the case. Among a numerous class of the Community they certainly have obtained credit, and the consequence has been severely felt in the Metropolis, as is evinced by the following Facts. The numbers of Patients vaccinated there during the present year (1805) have been less than in the former year. The numbers variolated have comparatively increasd during that period; consequently, as a great proportion of these patients are exposed full of infection in the public streets, having no where else to seek the open air, the unwary passengers become infected, & the smallpox has raged with such fury (and is still raging) that it is computed no less than 6000 persons have perishd from this disease in London and its Environs. This is a melancholy consideration. It strikes me that this growing mischief may speedily be put an end to, and the designs of its atrocious authors completely frustrated by collecting into one clear point of view that Mass of evidence in favor of vaccination which this Town of Cheltenham & neighbourhood can readily produce. The leading objections advanced by its adversaries are comprised under the following Heads
>
> 1st.   That it does not afford the promised security against the infection of the Smallpox.
>
> 2d.   That it is a loathsome disease – that it excites Scrofula [tuberculous swellings beneath the skin, especially of lymph glands; known as 'the King's evil' because of the belief that the King's touch could effect a cure] & other diseases which either terminate fatally, or prove highly injurious to the Constitution.
>
> . . .My first inoculations commenced here so long since as the 9th of June 1799, & from that time to the present, they have gone on in annual succession, so that since the period of its commencement, many thousands have been vaccinated, of all age's from the earliest Infancy to

eighty years – of all Constitutions – in all kinds of weather the Climate affords – In sickness as well as in health – Women in every stage of pregnancy – the Mechanic and the Husbandman, in the midst of their busiest employments, neither rarely finding any hindrance even for an hour during its progress. . . .No new diseases of any sort or kind has been seen or heard of. No Ox-faced boys or mangy Girls. Herpetic Eruptions that common infantile appearance, which has been so craftily held up as a Bugbear to frighten the ignorant & the timid, have not occurred more frequently among the vaccinated, than those who have not been vaccinated. And what is far beyond all other considerations, great numbers of these persons have been repeatedly exposed to the contagion of the smallpox in its most malignant stages, without effect, in any one instance. Many have suffered this exposure after the lapse of several Years from the time of Vaccination; & suffered it repeatedly; and no inconsiderable number have been vaccinated with perfect success many days after the fullest exposure to smallpox contagion. . . .

Although it was signed with the initials 'EJ', the draft is marked '[unfinished]'. Clearly, it was not meant to be anonymous. Even more clearly, it was a straightforward defence based on the author's practice. On all of these counts, it is unlikely to have been the manuscript sent to Dibdin in February.

A second, undated, fragment seems an even less probable candidate. It is also in Jenner's hand:

. . .I lately made a digression out of Fleet Street into Salisbury Square to reconotre the Central-house of the Jennerians, the centre I suppose they mean of corruption. There I perceived two Persons standing upon the steps, one of whom I was confident belong'd to the Gang, as he frequently uttered a word that sounded like Vaccination. . . .They were looking over and reading something together which I should have thought has been your Book (for what else have the Jennerians now to think of?) but that neither of their Countenances was at all Chop-fallen. . . .I took another turn round the Square, and pondering, thought they might have dissipated their gloominess for a moment with one of those no-meaning, paltry squibs Lampoons that B– [Bradley?] admits into his Journal, respecting you; much to his disgrace by the way. . . .These may not be Jennerians, thought I, but really Squirrel-ists and perhaps that identical paper is the Doctors grand work epitomized for general distribution. What seemed to confirm me in this suspicion was my distinctly hearing one of them whom the Quaker [Walker?] called Joseph [Leaper?] exclaim in tones of exaltation 'This will do John, this will do – This will knock up all our Enemies – it comes ad rem, ad hominem – it comes home to mens business & bosoms. . . .'

The story-telling style began to be applied to vaccination in October

1806, with the publication of Benjamin Moseley's *An Oliver for a Rowland*, the scurrilous attack on the Reverend Rowland Hill. Whether this was the book to which Jenner referred is unclear, because several other antivaccinist tracts had also appeared.

'R. Squirrell MD' entered first with *Observations Addressed to the Public in General on the Cow-Pox, Showing that it originates in Scrophula*. The title states Squirrell's ostensible case: that cowpox in humans is the scrofula, a conclusion reached entirely by deductive reasoning. However, 'R. Squirrell MD' was a practising apothecary and, as such, had been employed to variolate patients, a treatment that was also practised by surgeons but rarely by physicians. His pamphlet argued that apothecaries and surgeons 'are the only men in this country possessing any claim to a real judgement' about variolation; '. . .these are the only men who are qualified, and could be justified in making any alteration. . .in the practice.'

An Examination of That Part of the Evidence Relative to Cow-Pox, which was Delivered to the Committee of the House of Commons, by Two of the Surgeons of St. Thomas's Hospital was published at about the same time anonymously, although the author, W. R. Rogers, was identified as the addressee of a letter from John Birch added to the pamphlet. Rogers mounted a more standard attack by listing cases where smallpox had occurred after vaccination. However, he enlarged the indictment: 'The first fatal case which was made public was a patient in Islington; the arm ulcerated, and the patient died. . . .' He named three more fatalities, one of them from Dr Squirrell, and went on: 'These cases were as favourably palliated and as ingeniously excused as they could be; but it is admitted *that each patient was punctured by a lancet injected with what is called cowpox; each arm so punctured became inflamed and ulcerated, and each patient died.*' Rogers was expressing a widespread fear. It was up to the vaccinists to prove that something other than vaccine caused the septicaemia that probably killed these unfortunate patients, but no one then knew how to explain infections. The vaccinists could counsel cleanliness, but in an age that found bathing a nuisance if not physically impossible, the chances were legion of dirty fingers scratching an itching vaccination scab. They were forced back on dubious statistical proofs which left doubters unconvinced and worried.

Rogers introduced a new theme, with the case of a five-month-old girl who developed large purple knobs on her forehead and arms within a year after vaccination: 'this case, I think, clearly demonstrates a *new disease of the skin*'. The little girl undoubtedly provided a clinical foundation for all of the deformities later ascribed to vaccination.

The most graphic evidence of this kind was the work of Dr William Rowley in *Cow-Pox Inoculation No Security against Small-Pox Infection*. As the title indicates, Rowley's principal interest was also to prove that vaccination was fallible and therefore untrustworthy. He cited 218 cases of vaccination failures, and further inflamed the debate by noting: 'From motives of liberality and professional delicacy, it was thought most honourable not to *immediately* publish the names of the respectable gentlemen vaccinators. . .in the many disastrous cases that appear'. He added that 'if any anonymous abuse or scurrility be permitted in the reviews. . .from the irritated parties' he would publish all of the names. Variolation worked perfectly well. 'Why leave a certainty for an uncertainty?' His 'Oxfaced Boy' and 'Mange girl' were by-products, so to speak. The former was a child who had developed swellings about the head and some displacement of hair, which may have been symptoms of a serious nutritional disorder such as vitamin deficiency. The little girl, too, had a scurfy skin that could have been caused by dozens of factors in her environment, though not by the vaccine itself. An imaginative artist, given his lead by the author, injected a bovine quality into his portraits of these cases. From them grew the famous and influential caricatures by Gillray and others, showing people turning into cattle under the ministrations of Dr Jenner and his colleagues.

Rowley also introduced a new note into the debate. 'There is no danger in natural Small Pox,' he argued, 'if skilfully treated. . . .' This is patent nonsense, and Rowley must have known it. Not only was he a practising physician, but he also wrote that 'The Small Pox is a visitation from God'. You cannot have it both ways: if God meant smallpox to be a Malthusian depopulator, He could not also make it safe and treatable – nor had He. Rowley's passive fatalism naturally infuriated Jenner, the man who had made medical activism possible. 'I could pardon this kind of logic in a superstitious <u>old woman</u>,' he wrote to Robert Thornton, 'but the <u>anile</u> doctrine of its being <u>impious</u> to attempt the removal from our land of any disease, productive of death and misery, in a Physician of the present day, and this in a professed <u>friend</u> to Small-pox inoculation, excites the risible muscles and would not, indeed, be credited'. The motives of the opposition were indeed very mixed.

John Birch himself introduced the Malthusian argument in favour of smallpox, in a pamphlet, *Serious Reasons for Uniformly Objecting to the Practice of Vaccination*. To it was appended an article from the *Gentleman's Magazine* which had driven the Royal Jennerian Society Medical Council to conduct its own inquiry into the practice of vaccination in Britain during the latter part of 1805. The report found that most cases of alleged vaccination failures were 'unfounded or grossly misrepresented', but 'admitted. . .that a few cases' involved patients 'who had apparently passed through the cowpox'. However, the fifteenth item in the conclusions (there were twenty-two altogether) said that 'scarcely any' failures had been reported in the Army or Navy or from the Empire; almost all failures came from London and its vicinity. In *Serious Reasons* Birch objected that the names of the twenty-five-member Medical Council subcommittee had not appeared in their report. Much more apropos was his complaint that the report used 'ambiguous expressions' such as 'a few cases' and 'apparently passed through the Cow Pox'. He was right, but not without sin himself.

Thornton's sensible reply containing Jenner's outburst against Rowley was published in July 1806, and did more than many pro-vaccination tracts effectively to ring the alarm. Apart from his reasoned answers to specific charges, Thornton revealed the extent of opposition attempts to arouse public opinion. He called attention to 'Dr. Rowley's *placards* stuck up at every *urinal* place in the metropolis and its neighbourhood.'

MORE PROOFS AGAINST COW-POX.
440 Cases.
ANTI-VACCINARIAN SOCIETY,
FOR RECEIVING, CORRECTING, AND PUBLISHING THE
DANGEROUS AND DESTRUCTIVE EFFECTS OF
COW-POX,
WITHOUT ANY REWARD WHATEVER TO MEMBERS. . . .

Apparently, some of Jenner's correspondents felt that the only answer to what they considered to be blind stupidity, not to say criminal incitement, was legislative fiat. To one Wiltshire MP, T. J. Estcourt, who was also a patient, Jenner replied on 13 March 1805: 'Coercion, in a state like this, is out of the question; but I have a scheme made out, which would (or I greatly deceive myself) answer all the intended purposes.' The 'scheme' is lost, but it could have been his first thoughts on a bill so to regulate variolation as to limit rigorously its availability.

During the early months of 1805 Jenner remained quietly at Berkeley. On 23 February, he and Mrs Jenner dined with his sister and brother-in-law, Reverend William Davies senior. With his nephew, the junior Reverend Davies, he attended Masonic lodge meetings on 4 February, 4 March, and 1 and 11 April. The decision to return to London had already been taken, however, by the time he wrote to Estcourt on 13 March; he agreed to 'wait upon you' there in about six weeks. He reminded Estcourt of his promise to mention Jenner's 'situation' to Lord Sidmouth, the former Prime Minister Addington. 'Did you forget me?' he asked. 'I am driven to a Corner, and obliged (thro' losses and expenditures) to sustain a burthen of near £500 per annum'. In June 1804 he had told an 'intimate friend', according to Baron: 'The Treasury still withholds the payment of what was voted to me two years ago'. When he did finally receive the money later that year, nearly £1000 had been deducted to pay fees and taxes. Three years later Jenner drew up the following balance sheet as part of a 'Statement for those Parliamentary friends' who would support his second claim for services rendered:

[For the years 1799–1802]

Establishment at Berkeley	£500
Establishment at Cheltenham	500
Do. at London, including Carriage, House rent, loss by furniture, Journeys, etc.	1,400
Total for four Years	£9,600
Expenses attending Printing, Postage, etc Pr. Annum £200	800
	10,400
Total receipts during the above four Years at £900 per Annum	£3,600
Actual loss up to the Year 1802	£6,800
Five Years' subsequent expenditure including everything, at £2000 pAn.	£10,000
Five Years' receipts at £900 pr. An.	4,500
	£5,500
Total Loss (Carried forwd)	£12,300
Grant of Parliament [1802]	10,000
Apparent net loss	£2,300

With pressures such as these to drive him, the old doubts about his moral right to ask for money seem to have been permanently quashed. Jenner left his family at Berkeley and returned to the capital on 9 May 1805. He stayed at 27 Great Russell Street. The next day he had an interview with Lord Egremont. According to Baron, it was the Earl who suggested a second application to Parliament.

The wheels of influence again began to turn. On 30 May the Board of the Royal Jennerian Society appointed a committee to inquire into Dr Jenner's out-of-pocket expenditures related to vaccination. Benjamin Travers reported for the committee that Jenner's losses due to diminished practice, added to his costs, amounted to about £800 per year. Meanwhile, the people of Britain, the Army, the Navy and the Empire had all benefited from his discovery. The Board thereupon appointed a new committee to continue the investigation. Neither Jenner nor anyone else seemed to have questioned this peculiarly personal role of a public charity. Had they done so, the answer would no doubt have pointed to Dr Jenner's unique importance in fulfilling the Society's purpose. The mores that suppressed the question are more important, however: English gentlemen constituted a club, with various specialist subcommittees. One was the House of Commons. Another, the Lords. A third, the Royal Jennerian Society. Obviously, a club has old members and new, rich and relatively less rich. The fundamental rule of any club is to acknowledge and, where necessary, reward the membership of any man who knows and abides by its rules of precedence and procedure. Nor is this club meant to be a mocking metaphor but a reasonably accurate description of British upper-class morphology – in the early nineteenth century.

The banker J. J. Angerstein, one of the vice-presidents of the RJS, raised the matter of Jenner's financial embarrassment with the Duke of Devonshire. The Duke replied that he had spoken to one of the royal dukes, the Prince of Wales, 'and Morpeth, and they will all do what you think best; but Morpeth has undertaken to make inquiries whether it is not possible to bring it again before Parliament. He thinks if that could be done, it would be more satisfactory than any subscription. I desired him to find out how Mr Pitt [again Prime Minister] was *really* inclined on the subject'. Evidently Pitt did not stand unalterably opposed. Jenner wrote:

> During my residence in town in the summer of 1805, Lady Crewe happened in conversation to tell me how much Lord Henry Petty wished for a conference with me on the vaccine subject, and that [s]he would like to bring us together. We met at her villa in Hampstead; and went so fully into the matter, that his Lordship, convinced of the injury I had sustained, expressed his determination to bring something forward in the ensuing session. Before this session arrived, Mr. Pitt died; and Lord Henry Petty became Chancellor of the Exchequer. In the early part of the present year (1806), I again saw his Lordship; and found that his ardour in my cause had suffered no abatement. This was soon after proved by his Lordship's motion in the House.

On 11 June, Dr Lettsom invited Jenner to his office for tea. He asked him to bring 'Whatever memorial or memoranda you have'. Lettsom had no doubt gathered other influential men. Along with Beddoes in Bristol, he had independently proposed that a subscription be raised for Jenner before the first parliamentary grant had been approved. The RJS Board itself seemed to be pursuing a similar course in May, but Lettsom's tea-party may now have been organized in part to direct everyone's attention to the parliamentary procedure.

Lettsom's note also asked Jenner to bring 'your Brother too, if in town'. Neither of Jenner's brothers was still alive in 1805, but perhaps Lettsom meant William Davies or a Kingscote brother-in-law. Whether the tea took place is not recorded but, three days later, Jenner along with Catherine, Mrs Black '& 3 children dined' at Eastington with the elder Davieses. A month later Davies senior went to Berkeley for three days 'to consult Mr. Pearce

[167]

respecting Dr. Jenner's Legatees.' This is odd, because Jenner's will was drawn up several years later, after Pearce was dead. William Davies junior seems not to have been directly involved in these events, furthermore, although he dined and slept at the Chauntry several times in both June and July, including the days his father spent in Berkeley, and he breakfasted there with his uncle on 19 June. I doubt that he was being excluded. On the other hand I imagine that, at Jenner's behest, the older generation was being consulted on the disposition of his property. Perhaps there was some passing thought about personal bankruptcy, in order to shame the nation to attention.

According to the minutes of the Medical Council, Jenner attended the meetings of 4 and 15 July 1805, but soon afterwards he left London for Cheltenham, where he remained through Christmas 1805 and the New Year. In late January and early February the entire family was again laid low by the flu. By the middle of the month Jenner himself was much better, and his eleven-year-old daughter, Catherine, was well enough to act as his amanuensis, the first of many such occasions. She wrote to reassure Charles Murray, Secretary to the Board of Directors of the RJS.

February 1806 saw the birth of a new medical magazine, the *Medical Observer, or, London Monthly Compendium of Medical Transactions*. The stock-in-trade of this quarterly journal was to expose quackery in medicine. For the first year or two its contents consisted principally of lucid descriptions of various medicines, both new and old, then being offered to the public without prescription under trade names. It had been as one of these that Hunter had urged Jenner to introduce his emetic tartar twenty years before. Not all of the compounds were common frauds, but the *Medical Observer* sought to offer proof that many of the claims for them were at least mistaken. For example, 'Schweppe's Soda water' might settle the stomach but could not prevent dyspepsia. More than a year passed before the periodical noticed vaccination. A long article, 'Of the Practice of Medicine in Great Britain', allotted four pages to a critique of the report on the practice just completed by the Royal College of Physicians of London, but even then, 'The Editors cannot discover any connexion between Cow-pox and Quackery.' For the next four years, however, until it ceased publishing, the *Medical Observer* harried vaccination and the vaccinists at the top of its well developed lungs, usually with the voices of leading opponents like Moseley and Birch.

Though he did later reply briefly to one charge in the magazine, Jenner had little to say specifically about it. Voices opposing vaccination worried him collectively. On 23 February 1806, he wrote from Cheltenham to Richard Phillips, a London printer of radical political views and publisher of the *Monthly Magazine*, who was also a subscriber to the Royal Jennerian Society. Jenner thanked Phillips for a favourable review of the vaccination literature which had appeared in the January *Monthly Magazine*, before putting an editorial suggestion of his own:

> In the Med: & Phys: Journal there are a great number of very excellent Papers relating to the subject of Vaccination. There they lie, as it were entomb'd, as far as regards the public Eye. This Publication being entirely medical, meets the medical Eye only. . . .What think you? At the present hour when the arch Imposter Moseley & his Dupes, Rowley, Squirrel & the rest, have so deluded the Metropolis, might not these Papers be easily form'd into a Volume that would be gladly received. . . .

No doubt about it, Jenner understood the power of the media and the role of a publicist in a cause.

The first certain indication that the family had returned to Berkeley is William Davies's diary entry dated 17 March: 'drank tea with my uncle Dr. Jenner. Attended Lodge.' On 17 April, Jenner noted in his own commonplace book that he was 'Godfather to Mr Hickes' son Thomas'. Toward the end of the month a coincidence brought the London medical establishment to Berkeley for a visit that must have been very nearly unique. Jenner learned that Dr Joseph Adams, now physician to the London Smallpox Hospital, was staying in the neighbourhood. At the same time grease had appeared on a local farm, followed by cowpox. Adams had been sceptical of Jenner's theory about the origin of cowpox, but Jenner still clutched it to his breast. He invited Adams to spend a night at Berkeley, and the next day introduced him to Mr Tanner, the veterinarian, at the farm. Adams took some of the cowpox matter to London with him to compare its effectiveness with that which 'has been four or five years inserted only in the human subject, but no difference could be perceived.' Adams apparently took no interest in the grease outbreak.

By the beginning of May, Jenner must have realized that his retirement was about to end again. Two powerful motives compelled his return, however temporary, to London. The first in time and no doubt in importance to him were events which might lead to a second parliamentary grant. The second was a more immediately pressing problem, the apostasy of John Walker, over which he could exercise direct influence by his presence. He addressed a letter to Alexander Marcet from 46 Greek Street, Soho, on 30 May, but was living at 27 Great Russell Street a month later. By the end of this stay in August 1806, he was living at Great Rupert Street, Bedford Square, presumably at no. 108, the home of Thomas Paytherus. He may have changed London accommodation after his short visits to Berkeley.

With Jenner's support, John Walker had been elected to the position of Resident Inoculator by the Royal Jennerian Society in 1803. The first hint of difficulty arose when the Secretary, Charles Murray, received a letter dated

24 February 1804, from a John Bedwell of Carshalton. Bedwell had applied to Walker at the Central House to have his wife and child vaccinated before they returned home, because smallpox had appeared in Carshalton. Walker had said that he would vaccinate free only during the prescribed hours, but that for a fee of a guinea each he would vaccinate them immediately. Bedwell chose to go to a practitioner he knew who directed him to the Bloomsbury station of the RJS, where the vaccinations were done free. Bedwell expressed his 'grateful acknowledgement' to the Society. Walker, though, had been hired with the understanding that he could undertake private practice, and the RJS Board acknowledged at a meeting on 29 March 1804 that he had acted correctly. Mr Bedwell attended the meeting.

No further complaints against Walker disturbed the Society until 5 October 1805, and then, indeed, it was the Resident Inoculator himself who charged, in a letter to the Medical Council, that Charles Murray had been opening his letters and changing the destinations on packages of vaccine matter prepared by Walker for dispatch to practitioners. Then Walker backtracked. The Medical Council minutes for 7 November note that Walker 'did not wish the letter to be considered as an accusation against Mr Murray, only as a hint for future regulation.' Nevertheless, Murray angrily replied that Walker had refused to discuss his allegations before a joint committee of the Board and the Council, but had proceeded then to write his letter of 5 October. What is more, Walker had blamed Murray for delays in shipments caused by Walker's own interference. Walker in turn replied that Murray's hostility to him was diverting the Society from its essential business. The minutes for the Medical Council meeting that received this long reply acknowledged Walker's 'zeal and diligence' as an inoculator 'together with the correctness with which he has conducted his inoculations', and assured him of 'the confidence of the Council.' The Board of Directors, meanwhile, had assigned to a subcommittee the task of redefining and clarifying the jobs of the Secretaries to the Board and the Medical Council.

Whereas the time-honoured dodge of appointing a committee could have limited the damage due to this local conflagration, the Walker fire had spread much further. Central to it was the 'correctness with which he has conducted his inoculations', but in order to measure accurately the dimensions of this major issue, I must introduce briefly one of those embarrassing conflicts of personality that always seem so irrelevant to men of goodwill. Walker's origins were deeply plebeian. He was a rough soldier who had risen through the ranks intellectually as well as financially. He had become a Quaker in dress, language, and presumably worship. After an uncertain beginning, he had contracted a proper marriage. Such a man might be expected to fight hard to prove his professional respectability, on the one hand, and be impatient of advice from the 'Quality', like Jenner, on the other. Toward his charity patients, moreover, he evidently saw no reason to display the bedside manner which Jenner and the medical establishment took as a matter of *noblesse oblige*. His biographer describes with evident approval Walker's entrance at a vaccination station:

> The first thing that Dr. Walker looked to, when entering the room, was the table on which he expected to see his books. If any mother had put the child's bonnet, pelisse, or any other person, his hat thereon, they were immediately swept away to the floor. If any woman stood in the way, he pushed her back, and would make her, if much irritated, stand up in the corner, as if she were a naughty child. He then. . .gave a short, but very potent, address to the mothers on the protection afforded by the vaccine inoculation. . . .the director then issued the order for the children's names, places of habitation and age to be told. . . .the parents very often muttered. . . .This disturbed Dr. Walker very much. He often made the offending woman spell her child's name ten or twelve times over, adding at the conclusion, 'Now, thou wilt learn to speak plain.'
>
> . . .the next process. . . .was to obtain some vaccine ichor for the purpose of vaccinating the children, not as yet protected. Here often was a great struggle. . . .The few mothers that had the courage to bring back their children for examination were frightened. . . .Someone perhaps attempted to fly; Dr. Walker leaped to the door, and barricadoed it with his body, saying, 'Thou foolish woman, if thou wilt not do good to others, I will bless thy little one,' and forthwith drew his lancet. . . .The screams of the terrified child, the complaints of the excited mother. . .did not intimidate the courageous soul of the director.

Direct comparison with the Jennerian bedside manner is not possible because Edward Jenner never manned a London inoculation station. Although for many years he vaccinated his neighbours free of charge in his Temple of Vaccinia, later in life he curtailed the practice. 'I am ashamed to send you so many patients,' he wrote to Rowland Hill. 'Your own kindness and attention to the poor and successful efforts on their behalf greatly augments the number of petitioners to me for a recommendation to you. The bearer is Snell, a decent youth.' He perceived the village poor as his charges. 'You pass by these little Children as *weeds*,' he was reported as having said to a friend; 'I treat them at least as *vegetables*.' The only record I have found of his dealings with a patient concerns a peer. 'Lord Carbery did me the honor to consult me,' he wrote to a Suffolk patient in 1801. 'After our conference I told his Lordship freely what I thought of his habits (which he confessed to me) & their final consequences, which I endeavord to place before his Eyes in so frightful & horrid point of view, that I hope a due impression will be made & that he will step back from the dangerous Precipice on which he stands.' The mind boggles at the cause of this medical rebuke, but note that his lordship was above rather than below his doctor in the social scale.

In any event Walker, even less than Jenner, was a part of the medical establishment. In the storm that now broke, influential lay members of the Board of Directors gave Walker shelter, whereas in the end the Medical Council supported Jenner.

The quarrel began in the pages of the *Medical and Physical Journal*. In September 1804, Walker wrote a letter to the editors describing how he took vaccine matter from the very early vesicle, as soon as a scab formed over it, by puncturing the sides of the pock. He had even removed the scab, wiped out the pus forming beneath it, and then taken vaccine from punctures in the raised edges. The relative violence of this approach was contrary to the instructions issued by the Royal Jennerian Society, which were in turn an elaboration of Jenner's *Instructions* of 1801. The most relevant passages were these:

> Matter may be taken from a genuine vesicle at any time, from its commencement till the areola begins to spread. . .but never after the areola is formed.
>
> It is to be taken by small superficial punctures, made in several parts of the vesicle with the point of a lancet introduced horizontally. Time should be allowed for the fluid to exude. . . .If necessary very slight pressure may be applied. . .to quicken the discharge.
>
> Great caution must be observed in this process; or violent inflammation, and extensive ulceration may sometimes ensue.

The core of the dispute was the degree to which a direct attack on the vesicle as opposed to the recommended gradualist approach endangered the success of a vaccination. John Ring replied to Walker that he was engaged in a hazardous experiment, and Dr Dunning of Plymouth published a newspaper article which also questioned Walker's procedures. Walker had replied briefly to Ring, but his answer to Dunning in the May 1805 issue of *Medical and Physical Journal* introduced an important new argument:

> From the constant demands for matter, at the Central House, I am daily obliged to break down the pocks at all stages, from the first formation till they have almost acquired their full dimensions. The matter collects again, the pocks bear their characteristic form, and the parents are assured that their children are perfectly protected.

In the same communication Walker quoted a letter from Jenner dated 16 April 1805:

> I destroyed the pustule completely on the eighth day, before the areola began to form, by the application of a bit of caustic; but on

putting my patients to a test. . .they were found secure. . . .How then can puncturing the pustule at any period destroy its influence on the constitution. . . .Do we not see the pustule resume its character after it has been opened on an early day and exhausted, or nearly so?

At this juncture, early in 1805, Jenner did not appear to be worried by Walker's procedures. In this letter, however, although he commented on a single interference with the vesicle, he did not consider either multiple interventions to take vaccine or the extreme procedure of removing the scab, wiping out the pus and taking vaccine from the edges.

Dunning's extended reply in the next issue of the *Medical and Physical Journal* expressed genuine alarm.

. . .we beg leave to call earnestly to the Doctor's recollection the very prominent situation which he fills; and at the same time to request him. . .immediately and henceforward to discontinue the unwise and unwarrantable custom in the Central house of *breaking down pocks, at all stages. . .or that he will not continue to assure the parents of children who have been so treated that their children are always secure.* . . .

Dr. Jenner has no where authorized such *breakings down*, such *lacerations* of the vaccine vesicle; he has, I believe, admitted that sometimes, the *accidental rupture of the vesicle may destroy its preventive powers.* . . .

. . .I have said. . .that *all the effects* of the process of vaccination. . .*are not completed before nor at this stage* (the eighth day) *of the vesicle, where this has been. . .repeatedly ruptured.* . . .

Dr. Jenner's experiments, therefore, with caustic on the eighth day of the vesicle. . .are. . .without the least application. . . .

For about six months controversy ceased in so far as the *Medical and Physical Journal* was concerned. Then in March 1806, just as the dispute with Murray ended, Walker wrote a letter of comment on the more conservative practice of Dr James Clarke, physician to the Vaccine Institution in Nottingham. In it a footnote appeared:

In the numbers which it continually falls to my lot to inoculate, it is generally extremely easy to determine by the eye when the effect is complete; but, when the pock has been ruptured, and even almost obliterated, if I can feel, about the tenth day, a degree of hardness and tumefaction [looking like a tumour or new growth] about the inoculated part, I find in people of every colour that the protection is complete; and without such inflammation I suspect that the effect is never perfect.

This was heresy indeed. As Ring put it in reply: '*If no case can be secure without induration* [where the centre is sunken while the edges are raised] *or tumefaction,* it by no means follows that the converse of this proposition is true, and that every case is secure, when either induration or tumefaction occurs.' Jenner put this footnote at the centre of his charges against Walker in his letter of 10 July threatening to resign from the Medical Council if Walker remained. For it had come to that.

On 4 June 1806, at a regular General Meeting, occasionally called the General Court, Dr Denman moved and Dr Jenner seconded a motion to accept the minutes of the previous meeting on 26 March, excepting those minutes relating to the election of new directors. The motion held that for technical reasons the elections had been improperly conducted. A Solomon would have had difficulty in judging the accuracy of the charge, but anyone could see that Denman, Jenner and their supporters believed that the newly elected directors were a pro-Walker faction. The General Court defeated the motion by 26 votes to 25. Thereupon, twelve subscribers led by Jenner and Denman called for a special meeting of the General Court on 18 June 'for the purpose of enquiring into the state of the Society. . . .' Duly assembled, this special meeting set up a committee chaired by Angerstein and including Jenner, Denman, Dr William Bradley and Paytherus to put forth proposals on reorganization. The subscribers now realized that the division of authority amongst a lay Board of Directors, a Medical Council and a mixed subscribers' General Meeting tended to diminish efficiency. As to Walker, by a vote of 158 to 6 the 18 June meeting supported the original motion of 4 June, but a protest against the proceedings signed by several subscribers appeared in the minutes.

In his diary for 23 June 1806, William Davies junior wrote that he 'dined with' his uncle at Berkeley. For some reason Jenner had returned briefly to Berkeley, despite events in London.

He must have felt doubly pressed when on 2 July the new Lord Chancellor, Lord Henry Petty, at last introduced the debate that might lead to a second parliamentary grant. It was in fact 'the subject of vaccination' that he brought before the House, 'both on Dr. Jenner's account, and the cause of vaccination itself. Its progress had been much obstructed in our own country in consequence of the numerous prejudices which had been excited against it; and smallpox was again becoming prevalent.' Petty now proposed that the Royal College of Physicians be asked to set up an inquiry into the practice, and report to the House of Commons. The yea vote was unanimous. Now, Jenner had to bide his time yet again, until the late spring of 1807.

Meanwhile, it seemed apparent to parliamentary supporters of vaccination such as William Wilberforce that Jenner deserved a further reward. At dinner and tea in Wilberforce's home on 19 July and again two days later, Jenner's losses and his disinterestedness were discussed. According to Mr Bernard, as Joseph Farington referred to Sir Thomas Bernard, a surgeon and friend of Jenner's, Petty favoured a pension of £1000 a year for life plus £6000 compensation for expenses already incurred. The conversation rehearsed the stories of Jenner's unselfishness, and the party concurred in their admiration.

The day after the Chancellor had reintroduced his business to the House, Jenner found himself unable to attend a meeting of the Medical Council, but he wrote twice to Thomas Paytherus. The first letter stated 'my opinion that Dr. Walker is incompetent to discharge the duties' of Resident Inoculator, and the second asked Paytherus to find a letter along these lines that he had written to Ring in March. He also demanded Walker's dismissal, or, he insisted, he would resign as president of the Council. Paytherus must have read the letters to the meeting because they appear in the minutes. Jenner did attend the next meeting of the Council on 7 July. It was adjourned, after some discussion of the charges against Walker, to allow him an opportunity to reply. The continuation on 17 July received a formal charge from Jenner, who attended: 'That he has from time to time published dangerous and absurd doctrines. . .respecting Vaccination; and uniformly resisted various admonitions on this subject which were repeatedly given him by myself and others.' Walker's reply is long and detailed, but perhaps the central points are these:

> To Dr. Jenner's charge of my publishing doctrines, dangerous and absurd, I reply I am ready to defend them; and if in the defence, I shall have to shew, that some of his own doctrines are, only, hypothetical or erroneous, the true interests of vaccination, I hope may profit. . . .
>
> On the subject of my practice you will with pleasure observe, as trustees of the Medical affairs of the Society, and with that high respect for the experience and successful practice of Dr. Jenner; which we must all entertain, that my practice, perfectly agrees with and fully confirms many of the most valuable of his observations.

Walker knew perfectly well that, with Jenner against him, he had no real chance. Within the limits of decency, he tried to be conciliatory. The Council approved a resolution that Walker had 'deviated from the practice of vaccination enjoined in the printed instructions of the Medical Council', and passed the whole matter to a Special General Court, the second in as many months. The call was signed by Jenner, Lettsom, Ring, Marcet, John Addington, Paytherus, Richard Croft and seven others.

A very well attended Special General Court met on 25 July. William Smith MP took the chair, and there were 167 subscribers present including Edward Jenner and a 'J. A. Jenner', probably George Jenner, but neither Benjamin Travers, the founder, nor Joseph Leaper. Walker inserted into the minutes a further statement, which indicates that his opponents had sought a clumsy compromise: 'I refuse the offer of 100 Guineas of the Society's money, together with their so highly flattering testimonial. I cannot, by a resignation tacitly acknowledge to be true all the calumnies raised against me. . . .' Walker had hoped to send this letter to the governors in advance of the meeting, but a copy of the subscribers' list was refused to him unless he paid for it. Dr Denman put the motion that Walker should be dismissed, and James Moore, soon to become Assistant Director of a new National Vaccine Establishment, seconded. An amendment introduced by William Lewis and seconded by Thomas Hardy supported Walker because 'his opinions and practice were well known'. The amendment was passed by 73 to 70. Thereupon, twenty-four subscribers including Jenner called for a ballot on the original resolution at a further meeting on 8 August. An anonymous pro-vaccination pamphlet published in 1808 claimed that the meeting had been packed with thirty new subscribers, who voted for the amendment.

To any remotely independent and rational observer, it was obvious that the Royal Jennerian Society was tearing itself to pieces. Sir Joseph Banks wrote to Walker on 3 August offering a proxy vote in his favour because 'I think the conduct of some of the members of the Jennerian Society towards you is much too severe'. Such interventions were to no avail. On 4 August Jenner refused to take the chair at another special meeting of the governors, called for the next evening to decide whether the ballot scheduled for 8 August was 'authorized by the Regulations of the Society'. His letter to Marcet began: 'Another Flag of Truce has been sent here, Suspecting a [undeciphered], I ordered it back to the Enemys Camp.' Three hundred and seventy-one attended the meeting. Of the 353 who voted, 228 said the ballot was authorized by the regulations. The Jenner faction had won the battle.

Three days later, on the 7th, Jenner chaired a Medical Council meeting. It heard a letter from John Walker dated 2 August. He argued that he had been cleared of all wrongdoing by the General Court of 25 July, and that the forthcoming ballot was illegal. But then his tone changed:

> It would be supposing you capable of cruelty or of a thoughtless inattention to the tenderness always due to those who are directly in our power, to believe that you could unite with a set of men long since determined to ruin a much injured individual; however such men may have succeeded to warp the judgement of one most eminent character, to counteract the known mildness of his disposition.

Walker's suggestion that Jenner had been used by evil forces was even more interesting than his unexpected appeal to the spirit of *noblesse oblige*. Was it an ill judged, last-ditch attempt to win over the prime mover, or did he really believe it? If he did, the malign men must have been led by Ring and Dunning, with Lettsom, Marcet, Denman, Paytherus, Angerstein and William Smith in the vanguard. But there is no evidence to support the supposition. If Jenner came relatively late into the attack, it was because he had been rusticating in Berkeley, and because the five- or ten-thousand word pamphlet produced at breakneck speed with a minimum of research and an eye for the well turned epithet was simply not his style. In his *History and Practice of Vaccination* published in 1817, James Moore suggested another motivation for the quarrel. The Quakers, he said, by and large backed Walker, who claimed to be one of them. Episcopalians, Dissenters and Freethinkers opposed him. Lettsom, of course, was a Quaker, but perhaps he was merely the exception. I am not convinced, because I can see no connection between religious dogmas and the arguments or the personalities involved. The class differences and the related schism between the City and professional men who made up the Board of Directors, and the medical men, seems a much more obvious cause. Yet even here there were exceptions, notably J. J. Angerstein, the banker who gave Jenner his unqualified backing. In the end, however, Jenner himself must bear the responsibility for what happened. He could have used his influence for conciliation. That he did not reflects his genuine worry about the vaccination failures being reported and his proper concern that the vaccinators adhere to the safest procedures that experience recommended. On the other hand, Walker too had had experience in the Army as well as amongst the London poor. His mistake was to challenge the new 'Vaccine Establishment'. Until Jenner came to London in May 1806, Walker could have modified his language in the interest of job security and organizational peace. Then was the time for conciliation and 'flags of truce'. After Jenner began making public pronouncements, it was too late. And another factor: Walker chose the very moment that Jenner's stock rose again amongst the power-brokers to challenge him. Walker's bad timing, added to a native insensitivity, inflamed Jenner's distrust of London, his anti-organizational bias and his scientific fears. Like a small boy, he determined to keep all his toys beneath his own hands.

The quarrel arose from, and was sustained by, differences in clinical practice. From the standpoint of assuring the viability of the vaccine fluid, there was little to choose between the two sides. At the centre of the dispute was the problem of incidental inflammation, which could at the least cause pain and, in the extreme, prove fatal. Jenner urged as little interference and manipulation as possible. The vesicle was an open wound and could allow great mischief to enter the body. In part because he needed more vaccine to carry on his duties as Resident Inoculator and in part, no doubt, because of his experience in the field, Walker saw no reason to mollycoddle the patient. If he increased the risk to the patient, there is no evidence that his techniques caused more inflammation or failed vaccinations, probably because no one collected such data.

The General Court called for 8 August met as scheduled with 116 present, including Jenner. The original resolution calling for Walker's dismissal was put. Thereupon, his letter of resignation was read to the meeting. It was dated the day before, and mild in tone. The ballot was abandoned and the meeting adjourned.

Jenner wrote to Charles Murray, asking him to call an extraordinary meeting of the Medical Council to replace Walker. On 11 August, he drank tea with his nephew in Berkeley, evidence of a second brief unexplained visit. He had returned to London in time for the extraordinary meeting, which met on 18 August. It passed a resolution that Walker should leave the Central House and be paid his salary, and should hand over books and papers belonging to the Society to a committee of the Medical Council. The meeting also appointed a select committee consisting of Jenner, Ring, Paytherus, Addington and William Blair to redefine the duties of the Resident Inoculator. A further Medical Council meeting a week later heard the select committee's recommendations. The Resident Inoculator was not to accept fees for vaccinations at the Central House, but to vaccinate all who applied. He was to follow printed vaccination instructions exactly, to keep detailed records and 'not publish anything on the subject of vaccination, without being previously authorized to do so' by the Medical Council 'in writing'.

Jenner attended both of these meetings. On 1 or 2 September, a month later than usual, he left London for Berkeley.

The Walker affair now quickly degenerated into farce. From the standpoint of the Royal Jennerian Society, Walker looked dead, but he would not lie down. He and the Board of Directors disagreed on the salary and expenses due to him. Walker had refused to leave the Central House or to hand over records, and he was 'endeavouring to prevent Patients from coming to the Central House'. When he did finally vacate his rooms in the Society's headquarters, not only did he retain the patients' records but he also took a shop at the entrance to the passage that leads from Fleet Street into Salisbury Court, whence he waylaid both new and old patients with enough success to feature several times in the minutes of board meetings.

Walker took his revenge much more effectively, however. On 21 August he organized a preparatory meeting, which launched the London Vaccine Institution four days later. The Lord Mayor of London agreed to become the President. On 30 August, Jenner wrote to Mr S. Leese, another governor of the RJS:

> J.[oseph] Leaper is making a very active and successful canvas I hear for a new Vaccine Institution. So much the better, unless J. W.[alker] is to conduct the practical part of the business – should he have that appointment, with the same train of ideas on the subject as he has at present, much mischief must be the consequence, accompanied no doubt, with positive good. . . .

The new institution battened on the dying body of the old, but by and

1. Jenner vaccinating his son, by Giulio Monteverde. Reproduced by permission of the Wellcome Trust. A second bronze of the same subject is in Rome, and a marble in the museum of fine arts, Genoa.

2. The Chauntry, Berkeley, Gloucestershire. Now the Jenner Museum. Photograph provided by the Jenner Museum.

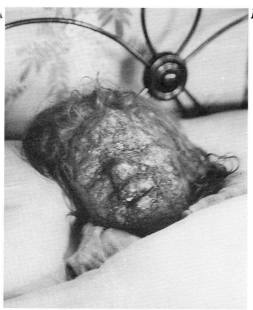 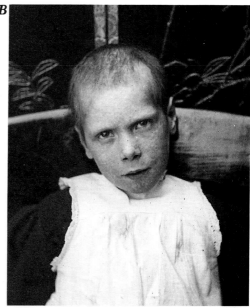

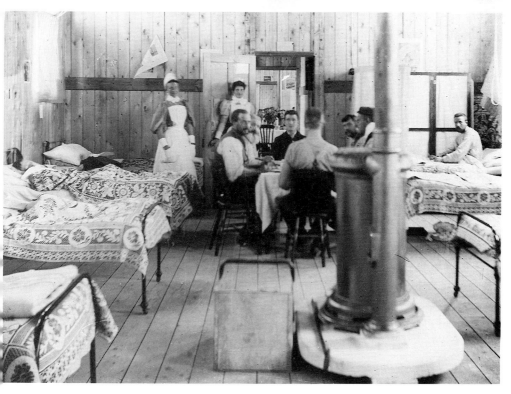

3. A victim of the Gloucester smallpox epidemic, 1896. **A)** during the disease and **B)** after recovery. **C)** Smallpox ward in the Gloucester Infirmary during the epidemic. Note that the epidemic broke out during the centenary year of the first vaccination. Photographs reproduced by permission of the Wellcome Institute Library, London.

4. J Gillray, "The Cow-Pock", 1808. Reproduced by permission of the Wellcome Institute Library, London.

5. G Cruickshank, "The cowpox tragedy", 1812. Reproduced by permission of the Wellcome Institute Library, London.

Cow-Pox Mange Abcess and Ulcers.   *Cow Poxed; Ox-faced Boy.*

6. Imaginative drawings of the 'Mangy Girl' and the 'Ox-faced Boy' published in 1805 by William Rowley, MD. Reproduced by permission of the Wellcome Institute Library, London.

A

above and top right **7.** **A**) "Jenner et le Vaccin", 1820, probably German. One of dozens of continental tributes idealizing Jenner's achievement. **B**) 'Confirmation', by G Hunt, 1831. Reproduced by permission of the Wellcome Institute Library London..

bottom right **8.** The Temple of Vaccinia built by Robert Ferryman in the garden of the Chauntry. Photograph provided by the Jenner Museum.

CONFIRMATION.

CLERGYMEN—First Boy, Have you ever been Confirmed?
BOY —— No Sir but I've been Waxinated.

Doctor Jenner about to Vaccinate a Child.

S Jenner & [?] Represent[?]

Doctor Jenner was below the middle stature
his hair dark and a little inclining to curl
and it was observed at his death he was not the least
gray. He was rather near sighted but never made
use of Glasses, his dress was black, a large Collar to
the coat and loose low trowsers the dress of the day

Chauntry Cottage 1825

9. Stephen Jenner drew and described his great uncle about 1820.
Original in the Jenner Museum.

large it remained a medical charity with almost no medical support. Jenner displayed his usual prescience when he wrote to Marcet late in 1806: 'Walker will be troublesome to our Society as long as he lives.'

On 2 October Dr James Sheridan Knowles, the only candidate, was appointed to the post of Resident Inoculator of the Royal Jennerian Society. Aged just twenty-two, Knowles had studied medicine under Robert Willan and taken his MD at Aberdeen, but he fancied himself a poet and playwright. Two years later he suddenly resigned, having been imprisoned for debt. Jenner wrote to Marcet:

> Poor Knowles, I hear is praying heartily to be reinstated in his situation at the Central House. His late embarrassment appears to have arisen more from misfortune than criminality. He lent money & could not get paid again, & this sent him into temporary durance. I understand out of his slender income, he has nearly maintain'd two little sisters who were destitute. Let this meritorious act plead for him.

Shortly thereafter the Society was to wind up its own affairs.

Soon after his return to Berkeley in September 1806, Jenner hired a tutor for Edward junior. John Dawes Worgan was sixteen, the son of a Bristol watchmaker, and wished to become a minister. After living at a school run by the United Brethren in Fulneck near Leeds, Worgan acted for a short period as tutor to the son of Richard Hart Davis, MP for Clifton. He engaged himself to Jenner for three years.

Toward the end of the month the family took up residence again in Cheltenham, where they remained until the middle of December. Marcet had asked him to write something for a new medical journal he was planning, but Jenner replied in November: 'I fear it will not be in my power to get a Paper ready on any subject for the 1st Vol: of the Medical Society.' Marcet and the surgeon, John Yelloly, had founded the Medical and Chirurgical Society of London in 1805. Jenner became a fairly inactive member of what he called the 'Verulam Socy.' – it met at 2 Verulam Buildings, Gray's Inn. In the event volume I of the *Medico-Chirurgical Transactions* appeared only in 1809, and included *two* papers by Edward Jenner.

At about this time Jenner learned of an heroic triumph for the diffusion of vaccination around the world. On 16 January 1807 he wrote to Richard Phillips, the printer, about 'the very curious & interesting piece of intelligence I recd. from Madrid. . . .What a glorious Interprize!' Upon orders from King Carlos IV of Spain, his physician, Dr Francis Xavier Balmis, had sailed from Corunna on 30 November 1803 aboard a ship bearing medical gentlemen, twenty-two healthy children, and trading goods to help defray the expenses. One of the children had the cowpox when the expedition left port. In the manner that Jenner had proposed to the Admiralty for the shipment of vaccine to India, the children were vaccinated in series. The ship touched at the Canaries, Puerto Rico and Caracas in what is now Venezuela, and at each port the doctors aboard vaccinated some of the inhabitants. At La Guira, the expedition divided. Dr Francis Salvani, after shipwreck in the mouth of La Magdalena river, led a small group to Cartagena, across the Panama isthmus, to Peru, Buenos Aires and Chile, returning to Spain via the Philippines in 1808. Balmis sailed to Havana and the Yucatan. There Professor F. Pastor travelled inland, while Balmis coasted to Vera Cruz where he and Pastor rejoined. They crossed Mexico to Acapulco and sailed for the Philippines with twenty-six children aboard. Balmis stopped at Macao and Canton, returning to Macao to take ship for Lisbon, where he arrived on 15 August 1806. On his return journey the ship called at St Helena, where Balmis 'prevailed upon the English to adopt the astonishing antidote, which they had undervalued. . .although it was sent to them by JENNER himself.' The children had been in the charge of the matron of the foundling hospital of Corunna throughout the voyages. Those picked up at Acapulco had included infants who were later looked after by the Foundling Hospital. Over two hundred and thirty thousand vaccinations were performed during the expedition. Though Britain and Spain were then at war, Jenner told Phillips: 'I have made Peace with Spain, and quite adore her philanthropic monarch.'

On 3 February 1807 Jenner wrote to the Vaccination Committee set up by the Royal College of Physicians in response to the Commons vote. Of the two dates they had proposed for him to be heard, 12 or 19 February, he preferred the latter. The hearings had been set up under the chairmanship of Sir Lucas Pepys, who was no friend of vaccination. On 16 May, after the Committee's report was completed, Jenner wrote to Richard Dunning that Pepys had asked him 'to vaccinate his little grandson. Two years ago the worthy president would as soon have had the boy's skin touched with the fang of a viper as the vaccine lancet.' Sir Lucas held thirteen meetings of the Committee, the first on 23 October 1806, and the last on 5 March 1807. The Royal College had also been charged by Parliament to seek the views of the other Royal Colleges of Physicians in Dublin and Edinburgh and of Surgeons in Dublin, Edinburgh and London. The apothecaries were not yet constituted into a college and were not formally consulted. Jenner himself wrote to Marcet on 30 January 1807, pointing out that John Birch was a member of the committee of the Royal College of Surgeons of London constituted to prepare a report based on replies to the circular letter sent to Fellows asking for their experience with vaccination.

James Harvey, Registrar of the Royal College of Physicians of London, had circulated a similar request to members 'to report their observations and opinions upon that practice, upon the evidence adduced in its support, and upon the causes which have hitherto retarded its general adoption.' The hearings before the Vaccination Committee were open to any interested medical man. Thus Birch, a surgeon, appeared as witness number 155, presenting the drawings of the ox-faced boy and mangy girl from William Rowley's book. Dr Moseley appeared as witness 19. Daniel Sutton himself, witness 52, asserted that in his practice seven out of ten vaccinations were followed by smallpox after five or six years. However, most of those who testified spoke in favour. They included Joseph Adams, Thomas Denman, and Jenner's old friend from Thornbury, Mr Fewster. An even larger proportion of the dozens of written replies supported vaccination, with or without reference to the practitioners' experience with variolation. In a lengthy letter from Berkeley written on 18 January 1807, before his uncle went to London, Henry Jenner mentioned two smallpox outbreaks in nearby Newport during the summer of 1804 and spring of 1806. During both, people vaccinated by his uncle had escaped. 'I mention this chiefly on account of the many years that have passed away from the time some of these persons were vaccinated,' Henry wrote.

Jenner's examination by the Committee elicited the information that he had performed about six thousand vaccinations but had kept no regular journal. The inadequacy of his own records seemed to disturb neither Jenner nor his auditors. Yet he had been one of those who insisted that the Resident Inoculator of the Royal Jennerian Society should maintain complete accounts of his vaccinations. He had submitted his own pamphlet as part of his testimony, but on 19 March he sent in further published material including a pamphlet by Thomas Pruen, a layman.

Jenner had again left his family in Berkeley and had taken lodgings at 15 Bedford Place, Russell Square. On 2 March he had attended a General Meeting of the Royal Jennerian Society, which heard the report of the committee on reorganization. The Board of Directors and Medical Council were to be combined. The new Board would have thirty-six directors, of whom twelve would be medical men. The committee also pointed out that, though the annual income was about £450, the Society's annual expenses amounted to about £800. The new Board met a week later. Marcet and Yelloly represented the physicians. Jenner did not attend. Indeed, he seems to have returned to Berkeley for at least a week from 10 March. The minutes of a board meeting on 17 March contain the following plaintive entry:

> It being stated by the Secretary that there was not a sufficient sum in the hands of the Bankers to pay the several Bills due
>
> Resolved, that the Trustees be desired to sell £500 Stock for the use of the Society.

On 10 April 1807, the Royal College of Physicians submitted its report to Parliament. It was unstinting in its support:

> . . .the progress of Vaccination has been rapid, not only in all parts of the United Kingdom, but in every quarter of the civilized world. . . .the public have, for the most part, received it without prejudice [on a later page: 'The lower orders of society can hardly be induced to adopt precautions against evils which may be at a distance']. . . .
>
> Vaccination appears to be in general perfectly safe. . . .The disease excited by it is slight, and seldom prevents those under it from following their ordinary occupations.
>
> The security. . .if not absolutely perfect, is as nearly so as can perhaps be expected from any human discovery. . . .[The Committee found no evidence for the opinion that protection was temporary.]
>
> . . .it spreads no infection, and can be communicated only by inoculation.
>
> The College of Physicians. . .feel themselves authorized to state that a body of evidence so large, so temperate, and so consistent, was perhaps never before collected upon any medical question. . . .it was not. . .difficult for others to repeat. . .[Jenner's] experiments, by which the truth of his observations was confirmed. . . .

The report concluded that the Royal College 'feel it their duty strongly to recommend. . .vaccination.' To it were added reports from the other Royal Colleges. With one major exception, they came to similar conclusions. In replies to its questionnaires, the Royal College of Surgeons had reports of 164,381 vaccinations which had produced three deaths, fifty-six cases of smallpox after vaccination, sixty-six cases of skin eruptions and twenty-four inflammations of the arm. Despite the overwhelmingly favourable statistical evidence, the Surgeons' report drew no conclusions whatsoever. Birch may have exerted some influence, but the main reason for the churlish silence seems to have been annoyance that Parliament assigned them a role subordinate to that of the Physicians in the matter. 'How unfortunate,' Jenner wrote to Marcet, 'that a Body of Men so respected should have suffer'd resentment thus to have operated.'

The *Medical Observer*'s final account of the report was signed by Dr Charles Maclean, probably one of the editors. It attacked the monopoly of the Royal College of Physicians and observed that vaccination 'may. . .make a very convenient stalking-horse for the College of Physicians, to obtain a renewal of their charter. . . .' Although he doubted the value of vaccination, Maclean disapproved of the excesses of the antivaccinists. His own virulence would in future put other opposition writers in the shade. However, it is interesting that the May 1807 issue of the *Medical and Physical Journal* was the first ever to contain no letters, articles or notices on vaccination, as though the RCP's report had brought peace between the factions at last.

On 4 May Jenner wrote to Dr De Carro in Vienna. He had just received word of a subscription of £4000 from the 'principal inhabitants of Calcutta and its dependencies', acknowledging his contribution to their welfare and success.

> These marks of attention, my dear Friend, are very soothing to my feelings. Without them, I should very shortly have put into execution a resolution I had form'd which many of my Friends, would, doubtless have thought desparate. It was nothing short of retirement from what is called the world. Not that partial exclusion, which admits of occasional visits & correspondence, but a total secession. . . .However I begin to revive again, and hope I shall soon have cause to think as highly of my own Countrymen as of those illustrious foreigners you name to me under the title of Nabobs, Rajah's, Ranees, etc, etc.

Thus he had written to Dunning five years before, while awaiting the results of parliamentary deliberations on his first application. Now he waited a second time, and, as even he knew, the outcome was no more in doubt than it had been when he had written the previous letter. Again the only question was, how much? These curiously megalomaniacal letters imply that Jenner cared less about the answer than he did about the recognition, the approval symbolized by the vote itself.

Two months later Dr James Anderson, President of the Medical Board of Madras, informed John Ring that the Presidency of Madras was raising a subscription for Jenner. It amounted to £1383-1-10. In 1805 or 1806, moreover, he had received £2000 from Bombay. What was perhaps of almost equal importance to Jenner, by the end of 1807 somewhat distorted news of his Indian windfalls was known even to the diarist Joseph Farington.

Two weeks before he had written to De Carro, Jenner heard from Worgan with news of Berkeley. Worgan congratulated him on the Calcutta subscription, 'more desirable. . .than your <u>Liverpoolian</u> honours. . .the merchants of Liverpool themselves, albeit accustomed to <u>curse</u> & <u>revile</u> their <u>African</u> slaves, can occasionally assume an <u>appearance</u> of philanthropy'. Worgan sought Jenner's permission to ask William Hayley the poet to 'compose some Verses for 17th of May', Jenner's birthday and the RJS Annual Festival. On 27 April Worgan wrote again. Mrs Jenner had been writing to her brother, Colonel Kingscote, and had asked Worgan to write her a daily report on Edward. She also wanted to know whether the report could now be every two days because Edward was so much better, '<u>gradually convalescent</u>'. 'Mr H. Jenner tells me that he converses with as much rationality as usual, & his memory continues remarkably tenacious & accurate.' His tongue was well now, he walked about his room and was sleeping satisfactorily. No doubt Edward's health explains Jenner's brief visit to Berkeley in March. Worgan had also been given educational charge of Robert. 'He proceeds as

I could wish.' He repeated his request that Jenner approve his application to William Hayley for celebratory verses. There is no record that they were written.

Jenner remained in London. William Davies attended 'a large party' at the Chauntry on his uncle's birthday, but Jenner attended the Royal Jennerian Society's annual festival.

Perhaps in part to distract himself, he undertook a task that was unique on two counts – a popular article for a non-scientific periodical. *The Artist* consisted of essays by well known artists, writers and politicians. Its editor was Prince Hoare, honorary foreign secretary of the Royal Academy, who was a friend of the portrait-painter, Northcote. *The Artist* had a scientific editor, Tiberius Cavallo, who was interested in electricity and wrote several articles for the magazine, but Jenner was the only physician to make a contribution.

He chose as his subject 'Classes of the Human Powers of Intellect', 'or, to speak more correctly, of the various degrees of intellectual capacity, which distinguish the human animal.' He listed seven classes in all: 'The Idiot', 'the Dolt', 'Mediocrity', that is, 'the large mass of mankind', and 'Mental Perfection'. 'From this point Intellect again diverges' into 'Eccentricity. . . .I have in this class a very numerous acquaintance', 'Insanity' and 'Maniac'. The paper ran to about two thousand words; Jenner proposed to 'throw out a few hints on a subject. . .which I may hereafter treat more copiously'. He did not. Nor does Baron mention the article. It was a fair summary of the common eighteenth-century wisdom on mental attributes, elevated slightly by being ordered into classes. Five years later, Jenner asked Marcet to have the *Philosophical Magazine* sent to Berkeley by his bookseller, but that journal had a strong religious bias. He seemed largely unaware of the philosophical high ground represented by Bishop Berkeley and his Scottish antagonist, David Hume.

At about this time, in more familiar territory, he helped to draft a 'Statement for those Parliamentary friends who were expected to take the most active part in the debate.' It appeared in two forms, one fourteen pages long and the other a six-quarto-page summary. Both present the financial details of his renewed petition. The Statement also compared Jenner's claim to those of others such as Harrison, the chronometer-maker, whom Parliament had supported.

Jenner's social life in London seems to have reinforced his political endeavours. Probably at about this time, he wrote a note to Sir Thomas Bernard, Wilberforce's friend, asking on behalf of Lady Crewe that Bernard attend a small party she was giving. Bernard replied that he was committed to attend a meeting about the slave trade. On 23 June, Jenner reminded Dr Marcet of 'my Conversazione Party this evening. . . .I expect a transatlantic Professor here – '. Unfortunately, the guest of honour is not named. Early in June he asked Marcet whether 'Mrs M. had the kindness to finish her very ingenious work on Vaccination yet? I long to be in possession of it – Excuse my vanity.' The response must have been immediate, for the next day Jenner wrote a note of thanks for the admirable work.

Finally on 29 July 1807, Lord Henry Petty proposed to the House of Commons a further grant to Edward Jenner of £20,000. Windham, Wilberforce, Samuel Whitbread, William Smith and Edward Morris were among those who spoke. The enormous sum was approved without dissent.

Chapter 9

The National Vaccine
Establishment
1807—1809

When Edward Jenner returned to Cheltenham in the late summer of 1807 to settle again with his family at 8 St George's Place, Parliament had gone a very long way toward restoring his financial fortunes. At least two of the Indian Presidencies had contributed substantially to the same end. Parliament together with the royal medical colleges, moreover, had taken substantial steps toward giving a scientific discovery the full weight of their formal approval. The Jennerians had begun to demand legal regulation, if not the banning of variolation, but for the present the comfortable gentlemen of a politely military Britain felt they had done enough about life-saving. Yet it was not their reluctance that delayed Jenner's departure from London.

Jenner wrote to Alexander Marcet on 18 August asking that a Mrs Schmidtmeyer be told 'to bring the young Lady to Bedford Place on Thursday 12 o'Clock, a little one shall be ready to meet her with a Vaccine Pock in the highest state of perfection, & that we can then remove every shadow of doubt respecting the present secur[ity].' He may have seen other patients as well, but it seems unlikely that his disappointing London practice had suddenly burst into life. The month of August intervened between the unanimous parliamentary approval of his grant and his leave-taking, I think, because he was determined this time that firm arrangements for the Treasury to pay the money should be agreed. His neglect of this detail five years before had added greatly to his problems.

Logic rather than evidence underpins my explanation, which has considerable psychological importance. Jenner more than most of his contemporaneous great names has suffered from the tendency of History to convert a person into a legend. Pitt and Fox had political opponents who kept their outlines sharp while whittling them down to size. The poets and writers – Austen, Coleridge, Wordsworth and their friends – left literary work that provides their biographers with vats of nutritious psychological soup. Jenner's opposition, unlike the politicians', was demonstrably wrong in its major thrust if not in much of its detail, and in any case rarely dared to attack him personally. Including his letters, furthermore, Jenner left barely twenty thousand written words – a chapter in an ordinary novel, or one epic poem. Against these comparisons towers his single unalterable achievement: the introduction of a technique that has eliminated a dreadful plague. Later biographers who tried to criticize focused on the achievement rather than the man; since the achievement proved to be unassailable, even his would-be critics reinforced Baron's worshipful estimations. No wonder Jenner emerges from two hundred years of adulation as a boring country doctor for whom serendipity worked overtime. On the other hand, a person grown rich by ukase, who could threaten at least twice to cut himself off because he so unjustly lacked public approval and then haggle (if that is what Jenner did) with Treasury officials over the exact timing of payments to his bankers, takes on some features of human reality.

In 1807 Jenner was fifty-eight. Judged from our viewpoint, his career had been a ladder of cumulative success. Orphaned at five, a spoiled and probably difficult child; early educational failure followed by the discovery of surgery, expansion of his horizons through Hunter; the establishment of a medical practice accompanied by the development of research habits and techniques; success in love followed by marriage; success in original research, admission to the Royal Society, successful vaccination and the achievement of its professional acceptance; monetary acknowledgement by a grateful nation – what more could the youngest son of a country vicar have expected?

From inside his life, the question was probably never asked. Events were related 'sideways', chronologically; for example, work on the cuckoo was followed immediately by marriage and admission to the Royal Society. In the third dimension, what we see as success might instead have been failure. For ten melancholy years he and Catherine Kingscote maintained their plighted troth against all reasonable expectations. Similarly, Jenner realized just in time that his own slipshod procedures could cost him his first original scientific achievement. What if something similar had happened in the summer of 1796 when Phipps had undergone variolation? Jenner knew he had never completed the paper on the migration of birds that he had promised Joseph Banks when he submitted his observations on cuckoos. He knew better than most the risks of failure in vaccination due to spurious cowpox, inflammation, and, as he believed, prior herpetic infections. These risks had to be exposed to the public, thus exposing himself to blame. Other self-doubts and uncompleted projects could be held inside, with inchoate risks only to himself. Jenner lacked Catherine's religious strength to pass the burdens on to God. They were his to shoulder, and they caused him to be inconsistent, arrogant and self-pitying.

At their worst these traits were downright destructive. They operated

most violently whenever Jenner became involved with vaccination organizations. He had to choose between enforcing his role as Intellectual Leader
and Safeguard of the Public Welfare, and leaving others to get on with the
routine operations while he gained a living, promoted the vaccination cause
around the world and played the civic role that he preferred, of family man
and landowner. Making the choice seemed to trigger the worst. Had he
joined Pearson's Vaccine-Pock Institution, he could easily have dominated
it. Instead, he effectively killed it. By foolishly humbling Walker, Jenner
phlebotomized the Royal Jennerian Society and brought the London Vaccine
Institution into existence. These schisms certainly did nothing to advance the
cause of vaccination in Britain. In that sense undoubtedly Jenner's confusion
of roles impeded his own dearest aim. It was about to operate once more, for
the last time.

During his final weeks in London in 1807, Jenner may have discussed with
professional and political acquaintances a new official organization supported
by Parliament to take over the functions of providing free vaccinations in the
capital and free vaccine of good quality to practitioners in the provinces.
James Moore, who was to become the Director of the proposed institution,
later explained how the idea emerged:

> Jenner often communicated to me his distress [about Dr Knowles,
> the new Resident Inoculator of the RJS] confidentially. . . .It was
> evident that a Society thus conducted could do little good. . . .I there-
> fore suggested, that, instead of trusting any longer to a subscription
> society. . .he should endeavour to make the business of Vaccination
> a national concern. With this view, the President of the College of
> Physicians should be consulted, and a proposal made to him to com-
> bine in an application to Government to erect an establishment under
> the control of the College of Physicians and Surgeons of London.
> Delighted with this scheme, he assembled some of his most faithful
> coadjutors. . .who. . .drew up a digested plan. . . .This was carried
> by Dr. Jenner to Sir Lucas Pepys, the President of the College of
> Physicians, who warmly approved of it. . . .

One of the prime movers from the government benches was George Rose,
a junior minister under Shelburne, Pitt, Portland and Spencer Perceval.
According to a letter to Rose drafted by Charles Murray, Secretary to the
Board of the RJS, the two men had discussed 'the intended national Vaccine
Establishment' as early as June 1807. No evidence has come to light on when
Jenner and Rose met.

In Cheltenham, meanwhile, life had returned more or less to normal.
Jenner had become a member of the Cheltenham Commissioners, the
town's co-opted governing body, in 1806 and officially played the role

of local legislator until 1821. His practice continued, of course, as did his correspondence. He wrote to Murray about the Royal Jennerian Society's financial problems on 20 September 1807, but a second letter on 4 December inquiring about Robert Ferryman and a Dr Marshek was written on Jenner's behalf by Thomas Pruen. A few days later Jenner wrote to Marcet, whom he addressed for the first time as 'My dear F[rien]d' rather than the more formal 'My dear Sir', used in all the earlier letters. 'I have sent you a little Game, & a Couple of Woodcocks,' he said, supplies which must have come from Berkeley. 'Our Ladies seem to have laid aside their knotting and netting, & are all becoming Chemists in consequence of two little Volumes in the form of Dialogues which have lately got among them. It is said, these nice-looking Twins were born either at Clapham [Marcet's home] or St Mary Axe [his office].' Jane Marcet, author of the paper on vaccination which Jenner so highly approved, was a practising chemist who evidently prepared prescriptions for her husband. In 1806 she published *Conversations on Chemistry, intended more especially for the Female Sex*. Eight years later during his last visit to London, Jenner and Marcet planned an outing to distant Enfield. 'Perhaps Mrs. Marcet would not dislike a little country oxygen,' Jenner wrote to her husband; 'we should then be just the right number for Chemical conversations.' Clearly the book impressed him.

Just now Jenner was asked to lead the investigation of what at first appeared to be the most serious mass failure of vaccination yet reported. The Royal Jennerian Society received word in December from George Rose that some fifty-six people in the parish of Ringwood near his home at Cuffnells had caught smallpox after vaccinations performed between three years and six weeks before. Of these at least seventeen had died (the figures are extremely confusing), and two more were reported to have died of cowpox. Of twenty vaccinated in the neighbouring parish of Ellingham, eight had died from the smallpox. The vaccine for these vaccinations had come from both the RJS and other sources. Understandably, Rose wanted the whole matter investigated, and suggested that Jenner be called in. On behalf of the Board of Directors Charles Murray wrote to Jenner explaining the circumstances. The day after Christmas Jenner replied that Edward had recently fallen ill again, and that he could not leave him.

On 27 December 1807, a deputation consisting of Knowles, John Ring and William Blair, a surgeon and one of the RJS directors, arrived at Rose's home. The next morning the deputation met William Mills, the local MP, Dr Fowler of Salisbury, S. Tuncks, magistrate of Ringwood, three local clergymen, Messrs Westcott and Macilwain (or McIlwain), local surgeons, and others in the town hall, although a meeting two days later seems to have been held at the White Hart Inn, Ringwood.

Smallpox had appeared in the town, when 'one Hodges a Muffin man' fell ill on 11 September. On 16 October, seventy people had been variolated by

Westcott and Macilwain, who seem to have carried out all the inoculations, both variolation and vaccination. In an attempt to isolate them and prevent the spread of infection, this large group was confined to one part of the town 'surrounded by an open railing, which admitted of the freest intercourse between the Townspeople & the Patients'. According to Mr Macilwain, about two thousand people 'had the S.P. in Ringwd. & neighbourhood, of whom about 70 have died.' On the 22nd, the parish meeting instituted a general inoculation, leaving the choice of vaccination or variolation to the individuals. The majority preferred variolation, but in the rush no one seems to have kept accurate count. Mr Macilwain told the RJS deputation that he and Mr Westcott had inoculated about two thousand since October. He himself had inoculated some twelve hundred, of whom he saw 'no more than 7 or 800' a second time to examine whether their inoculations had taken. About two hundred people had been previously vaccinated and escaped the smallpox.

On 30 December, Mr Westcott submitted the following draft advertisement to William Blair for approval by the RJS:

> After a most careful and Minute Investigation of those cases in which the Small Pox occurred subsequently to Inoculation for the Cow Pox it appears that such Inoculation had not taken effect or that when an effect had been produc'd the progress of Vaccination was interrupted & the Patients render'd Insecure. The Result cannot fail to be highly Interesting to the Inhabitants of Ringwood & of the neighbouring Parishes inasmuch as it must remove the feelings of Alarm which had been excited & must restore & confirm the Confidence of the Public in Practice affording Protection against a Pestilential disease Justly esteemed the scourge of the Human Race – . . . .

In substantially this form, the advertisement appeared in the Salisbury and Winchester newspapers. Obviously, it was directed at the local gentry and business people, who had the money to buy newspapers and the ability to read them.

The formal report by the deputation, probably written by John Ring, began by stating 'that no instance occurred. . .of the Small Pox where the process of Vaccination had been complete'.

> . . .all those persons who were vaccinated, had been previously exposed to the contagion of the Small Pox. . . .
> In various instances, dry Cow Pock matter. . .was dissolved in water almost boiling. . . .
> It was asserted, that the Small Pox was more fatal. . .to those persons who were inoculated for the Cow Pock, than to others. This report appeared to be totally destitute of foundation. The mortality was indeed considerable owing in some instances to want of air and cleanliness, and in others to the immoderate use of spirituous liquors. . .which had been recommended by a Thresher, who inoculates for the Small Pox.

Westcott and Macilwain agreed that the two alleged deaths from cowpox were in fact due in one case to apoplexy, the old name for a stroke, and in the other to self-starvation by a man of seventy-four. Dr Fowler, Messrs Westcott and Macilwain and Mr Rose concurred in the report.

Leaving aside the allegation that the populace, no doubt terrified by an epidemic that exploded *after* the medical man went to work, drank too much because of incompetent advice, the report seems accurately to have reflected the facts. The two surgeons, themselves operating under great pressure, denied that they had declared secure any of the vaccinations they performed at the time. 'The anti-vaccinationists were put to shame,' records Ring's biographer in the *Dictionary of National Biography*, 'but party feeling ran so high that the deputies carried pistols to defend themselves in case of need.' I wonder whether it was the antivaccinists or the townspeople who occasioned this disquiet amongst the three London practitioners.

Although Jenner refused on account of Edward's health to come to London on 26 December, on the last day of the year he wrote to Mrs Black: 'It affords me extreme pleasure still to go on with my comfortable communications respecting dear Edward.' This could mean that he had been improving for some time, but now his father considered him much better though very weak. Edward had asked for 'a Berkeley Sparerib – Perhaps you may not much dislike sending him one next week.' Edward junior may well have been a favourite with his childless Aunt Mary, but her relationship with her youngest sibling seems to have been much more businesslike. On the other hand, surviving correspondence gives the impression that there was warmth between Jenner and Anne Davies.

The next day Jenner told Mary Black that Edward junior had said he was hungry, and had eaten roast beef washed down with cider and water. It was then the '13th. day since he first took to his Bed.' On 2 January 1808, Jenner acknowledged the hamper that had just arrived from Mrs Black. Jenner's man-servant, Richard, 'is his chief Nurse, but his Mother takes the command in these departments', nursing and cooking.

This letter went on: 'I should be obliged to you to make this communication to Mr W. Davies, who will with as little delay as convenient remit me what he can of the Michaelmas rents. This I fear wont be much, as the Taxes etc swallowed up a great deal.' William's response illustrates the dangers and difficulties of sending money, especially cash: 'I have enclos'd the halves of six ten pound Bills, wch. I hope you will receive safe, the other halves shall be sent by to Morrow's Post, & as you will then receive a letter from the Secy. of the Royal Berkeley Lodge, they will be enclosed in it.' I do not know whether he was then himself the Lodge Secretary. He goes on to report that timber on Ham Field cut down by Jenner's direction fetched £35-14. He had paid Jenner's annual subscription, £2, to the Grove Infirmary, Gloucester, and had received from Jenner's new lawyer, Mr Croome, an evaluation of 'your Estate at Berkeley', a copy of which was enclosed for Jenner's 'opinion'.

While Edward junior slowly convalesced and his father carried on his practice in Cheltenham, the worsening affairs of the Royal Jennerian Society imposed themselves upon Jenner. On 18 February he wrote to John Ring, having been informed that

> our Society is in a most deplorable state as to its resources. This was no news to me. I am sorry also to find that the indefatigable zeal and industry of Walker and some of his adherents have so far succeeded in the establishment of a Rival Institution that it is patronized by many names of distinction and that the subscribers to it are already numerous.

To retrieve the Society's finances, he recommended publication of a 'Memorial' restating the purposes and auspices of the RJS. The straitened circumstances probably explain why such a document was never published. '. . .I would appear myself among you on this emergency, but cannot do it without putting myself to the most distressing inconveniency. . .with regard to the intention of my own Subscription I shall be ready to come forward in any way the Society may think proper. . . .'

The Board of Directors established committees to report on the Society's finances and to look into the recruiting practices of the London Vaccine Institution. The committee on the LVI discovered evidence of what it considered fraud by Walker's group. It claimed that several vice-presidents of the LVI had been listed without their consent or were under the impression that the Royal Jennerian Society supported the new body. The committee recommended a letter to all LVI supporters, clarifying the facts. Such a letter was indeed sent. Inevitably a few sponsors, especially members of the peerage, it seems, had misunderstood, and resigned from the LVI forthwith. Most important was the defection of the Lord Lieutenant of Ireland who had accepted the presidency of the new body. Even so, the fallout was much less than the Jennerians had hoped.

When the London Vaccine Institution applied to Parliament for a grant, the RJS formally objected. The LVI had been established, it argued, not to promote vaccination but for the advantage of John Walker. Money and support had been gained by fraud. In the event, the plan for a National Vaccine Establishment intervened. The Society's direct and indirect successes *vis-à-vis* the LVI neither seriously weakened the latter nor strengthened its own position.

On 1 March Jenner wrote again, this time to Charles Murray, defending himself against the urgency of the demand by 'some of my Fds.' that he come to London. 'Their language is – "come to Town immediately or the Jennerian Socy. is for ever ruin'd". . . .they ought to consider that there are other Duties which I am imperiously called upon to perform. And they must be perform'd, or from increasing perplexities I shall become unfit for any kind of exertion.' Jenner had written from Cheltenham. The 'Duties' and 'perplexities' remain uncertain, but were probably creatures of the noisy opposition to vaccination, particularly by the *Medical Observer*. With claims of objectivity, its March 1808 number attacked Jenner:

> The cow-pox appears: it seems to prevent the small-pox infection. Mother's fly to it, as they have done to Ching's Lozenges for the cure of worms. Every young doctor, who can condescend, for the sake of notoriety, to obtrude himself upon the public in plumage not his own, writes upon the cow-pox. . .the legislature thought proper to reward a discovery, which, far from being accomplished by any great efforts of the mind, did not require three steps of induction, with the sum of 30,000l. . . .It is absolutely cramming the cow-pox down our throats. . . .
> . . .We disclaim all ideas of prejudice against the cow-pox . . . . Neither do we possess any of that inveteracy which characterizes those who go from one extreme to the other. . . .but we also consider it incumbent on us to record every well-attested instance of its failure.

Except to Jenner and his partisans, this is not an unreasonable statement, but in one particular it is revealing. The anonymous editors of the *Medical Observer* were medical practitioners, probably doctors. Their understanding of Jenner's role is summed up in the clause, 'did not require three steps of induction'. Indeed, it had taken only two. Observation of a series of experiments permitted induction of two facts: (1) arm-to-arm vaccination protects against smallpox; (2) protection is permanent. From these inductions Jenner deduced a general rule, that cowpox transmitted arm-to-arm protects permanently against smallpox. Incidentally, from an induction with respect to the occasional failure of cowpox to protect, he deduced the notion of spurious cowpox, and from a fourth induction concerning the apparent contiguity of grease in horses and cowpox, he deduced the alleged origin of the latter. Neither of these is central to Jenner's contribution. The editors were either speaking elliptically – 'not. . .three steps' = two steps – which I doubt, or they were utilizing sarcasm. Sarcasm often masks incomprehension – never more clearly, I think, than in this instance. The editors represented classical medicine. Show us a discovery requiring lots of inductions, and we may believe it, even if it flies in the face of authority. What they omitted, not yet having grasped the significance of the new science of Hunter, Priestley and Lavoisier in France, was the role of *de*duction. Science grows in part through induction, in part through linking together inductions by means of a general rule, a theory or deduction. Further inductions then test that theory, and frequently show that it is faulty and must be replaced by a new deduction. In the promotion of vaccination Jenner's deduction governed.

Jenner had learned all of this at Hunter's knee. 'All medical facts begin in theory, unless stumbled upon by accident. Theory is the bud and fact the fruit,' he wrote in his notebook. I have no doubt that he perceived the editorial misunderstanding, though it may have irritated him less than the implied criticism of vaccination. He certainly favoured further attempts at 'cramming'. 'In my opinion', he wrote to Richard Dunning a month later, 'a proclamation from the King, founded on the Report of the College of Physicians, universally dispersed, and recommended to the attention of the magistrates, the clergy, etc. would produce a striking effect. This would be greatly aided by allowing some pecuniary acknowledgement to those who vaccinated the poor.' Only the last sentence achieved limited embodiment in the National Vaccine Establishment.

In the matter of his attending board meetings, Jenner was surely right. His presence could do little to halt the decline. On 17 March the Board heard that in the year May 1807–May 1808, its estimated expenditures were £850 and its receipts £504-7-1. Its estimated income from subscriptions for the coming year was £350. Subscription arrears amounted to £139-11, of which the bulk was owed by 'Town' as against 'Country' subscribers. Free vaccinations, the Society's *raison d'être*, had fallen. During October 1807 the Resident Inoculator performed 246 vaccinations and dispatched 667 charges of vaccine. During November the respective figures were 37 and 329; December, 80 and 1085; January through May, 97 and 943. The London Bills of Mortality listed 1937 dead of smallpox in 1807, more than three times the number in 1804. Little wonder that Jenner sought the help of an organization supported by government.

Just at this time, the Society and Jenner were embroiled in yet another investigation into alleged vaccination failures. A tailor, William Howard of Bledlow, Buckinghamshire, had taken up work in London when his wife and two of his three children contracted smallpox. All four had been vaccinated by a Mr John Norris of Princes Risborough some two years earlier. The two children recovered, but Ann Howard died. Norris said that he had seen the patients four times after they had been vaccinated and had no doubt that the vaccinations had taken. However, the vicar of Bledlow, William Stephen, and the churchwarden, Joseph James Harper, sent Dr Knowles evidence of a letter written by Howard to William Fryday, governor of the poorhouse in Bledlow where the family were confined before they moved to London, stating that his wife and one child had not caught the cowpox. The London surgeon, Rees Price, who attended the Howards during the smallpox, said that Mrs Howard knew that her vaccination had failed to take, and in a letter to the *Medical Observer*, quoted Norris as now doubting the certainty of his earlier diagnosis.

Howard described the family disaster in an open letter to Dr Jenner published by the *Morning Advertiser*. It later transpired that Benjamin Moseley paid him one guinea when the letter appeared. Howard had met Dr Moseley and John Birch after his wife's death, possibly through a debating society called the British Forum, one of the few centres of disaffection in London allowed to escape the harsh laws suppressing all so-called Jacobin opposition to the status quo. Quite apart from his recent stint in the poorhouse, Howard's participation in the British Forum marked him out for Rees Price as antisocial, if not unstable. Worse still from the standpoint of the Royal Jennerian Society, Howard was literate and outspoken. William Blair threatened to inform his employer of Howard's attack on Jenner. Howard replied on 5 April 1808 'your great condescenscion in writing to one so far beneath your notice demands my acknowledgements, but I must beg leave to say that when you speak of an abusive Letter recd from me it certainly comes with a very ill grace from you. . . .be assured I will oppose Dr Jenners Quackery as long as I have an existence.' In a later letter to Blair, Howard incorporated his own poetry:

> Weep Jenner weep and hide your head
> Or blush in crimson like the Sun
> Visit the mansions of the dead
> And see the mischiefs you have done
>
> Then view the falling pearly tear
> That gushes from each orphan's eye
> Ask them the cause and soon you'd hear
> Jenner and Cow Pox they'd reply

Jenner refused to become involved in the hurly-burly, leaving it to Knowles and Blair in this instance. Doubtless the vaccinations had failed, although it is just possible that Ann Howard was one of that small minority whom no form of immunization would protect because she remained subject to reinfection. Whatever the facts, the behaviour of the RJS displayed precisely those class prejudices which made it extremely hard to gain the confidence of the Lower Orders. If Moseley and Birch exploited a semi-subversive organization like British Forum, to say nothing of William Howard, for their own dubious ends, at least they seemed to comprehend how to win over public opinion. However well he understood the importance of the media, Jenner failed to exploit it because he and his partisans lacked the common touch.

He withstood pressure for the inevitable trip to London until his friends, probably led by George Rose, urged that parliamentary consideration of a National Vaccine Establishment be contemplated. In April his finances had recovered sufficiently to make possible a loan to his Gloucester medical friend, Charles Brandon Trye, of the proceeds from selling £1000 in 3 per cent government Consols. The loan was still outstanding in 1810. On

6 May he and Catherine, along with their two boys and George Jenner and his first wife Mary, dined in Eastington with Anne and William Davies. On that day Jenner also wrote to Thomas Pruen. He began with a complaint: 'These things would affect nerves less irritable than mine.' What things is unstated, doubtless because Pruen knew well enough what they were; I think the Howard case a likely referent. Certainly the antivaccinists loomed large at the moment, because he continued: 'I have lately recd. a most impertinent letter from that detestable Fellow Lipscombe', a lesser antivaccinist. At the end of the short note, Jenner wrote: 'If you send me a line by return of Post, I shall get it before my sentence of transportation to Town is put into execution.' The time had come at last.

Thomas Pruen and Jenner had been friends for many years, but perhaps because Pruen had settled in Cheltenham, their lives became much more intertwined from this period. The Pruen family was almost as widely distributed around Gloucestershire as the Jenners. On 3 July 1782, William Davies noted that he 'Recd. of Mr Pruen a Year's Tithes due at Michs last 1/17/6'. This Mr Pruen could have been Thomas's father. The boy went to school in Reading, where he met Thomas Dibdin to whom he introduced Jenner in due course. The *Glocester Journal* for 12 June 1797 recorded the marriage of Pruen of Gray's Inn, London, to Miss Andrews of Cheltenham. Evidently, Pruen had taken up the law before becoming a clergyman. At this stage of his life, however, he was contemplating another change of career. In May 1809 he founded a newspaper, *The Cheltenham Chronicle & Glostershire General Advertiser*. It was not a success, and he sold it in January 1811. At the outset Jenner had annoyed Pruen by advising caution: 'In the heyday of Life, everything appears so clear to our Conceptions that we act without hesitation. As we advance, we look back with Surprise & sorrow on our past inadvertencies'. Almost exactly a year later, Pruen knew he was in trouble. Jenner chided him for poor management, urging that good management would provide 'a Rock, from which you must never move again till you have ascertained by the Plumet the depth of the water which surrounds you.' One difficulty, he wrote, 'there certainly is, & I not only foresaw it, but foretold it. Into this you were seduced by your love of literature & the hopes of gain. . . .Have done with it immediately, or as soon as the season for advertising ceases,' Jenner concluded with characteristic acumen. Let us cringe before this overdose of sanctimonious friendship, and pass on.

In 1812 Pruen obtained a living at Aldbourn, Wiltshire. Apparently, this too was a disaster. Pruen had written two books the laborious production of which, Jenner believed, among other factors, had brought on a 'seizure'. 'I am glad you have made your escape [to London] tho' it should be but temporary, from that detestable place Aldburne. You have found that you can do the people no good, & that they can do you a great deal of harm.' Four months later in April 1817 Jenner wrote to Pruen in Cheltenham, but the letter was readdressed to Dursley, in the foothills of the Cotswolds near Berkeley.

Pruen seems to have been a man weak in the ways of the world but strong in his attachments and varied, not to say diffuse, in his interests. He had expected to be asked to write the official life of his boyhood friend who had become a great man. Imagine the shock he must have felt when he received a letter from Jenner's executors, dated eight days after Jenner's death, informing him that his friend had asked John Baron to be his biographer and that Baron had accepted.

Jenner and Baron met that summer of 1808. Jenner had again come to London without his family, intending a short stay, and taken a room at Fladong's Hotel on Oxford Street. There they were introduced by a Dr Maton. Baron had recently come from Edinburgh, where he had undertaken his medical education. He noted that Jenner was dressed in a blue coat, white waistcoat, nankeen breeches and white stockings, but made no observations on his person. Although neither recorded the actual date, it was probably May or June. Baron later recalled that the day before, Jenner had had an interview with the Princess of Wales, who gave him a watch. Throughout the summer he bounced back and forth between London and Berkeley. No explanations have survived, but the most likely have to do with the health of Catherine and his sons. In any case, in August and September he was certainly staying again with Thomas Paytherus at 109 Great Rupert Street.

He addressed almost his unique surviving comment on Baron to Pruen in April 1810, calling him 'one of the first men in point of Talent the county has to boast of.' The praise was apropos of a letter on vaccination that Baron had published in the *Glocester Journal*. Baron became Jenner's friend and confidant as well as his student. Under Jenner's influence, he established his practice in Gloucester and remained there for the rest of his life. Baron was a physician with direct experience of both the art and the politics of medicine. Objectively, his professional knowledge enhanced his role as candidate biographer. Understandably, Jenner would have considered him steadier than Pruen, added to which a younger man inevitably appeared to sit at the feet of his master. Two months before Jenner died, Baron's book, *Illustrations of the Enquiry Respecting Tuberculous Diseases*, appeared. It was dedicated to Jenner, and bound into the presentation copy are the critical editorial notes that Jenner had written when Baron submitted the proofs to him. Such subtle flattery had to be heartfelt. In his isolated old age Jenner correctly sensed and deeply appreciated Baron's respectful affection.

Jenner had departed for London on or about 10 May 1808. He was immersed in politics from the outset, having submitted a plan to Sir Henry Petty. A meeting with George Rose, Treasurer to the Navy in Spencer Perceval's new ministry, established that the government favoured a nationally funded body to promote vaccination. Rose's views 'were almost exactly the same as my own', Jenner wrote to Pruen on 26 May. He had been asked 'to lay before him [Rose] a plan for the management of Vaccination in this country.' The letter continued: 'I prevail'd upon Mr Fuller to put off the reading of the Bill for a week, as you may have seen by the Papers, for [to tell?] the truth I thought his restrictions [unreadable words] were or rather more severe than the People would have immediately submitted to'. This was a bill, also supported by government, which would have outlawed variolation after 1 August 1808, 'where infection can be communicated therefrom within the distance of three Statute Miles'. It provided for various quarantine measures, including a provision that any place where variolation was practised must be clearly marked 'Small Pox Hospital' or 'Pest House'. The first of several bills with similar objectives and provisions, it was allowed to die, as Jenner's letter implied, because the ministry preferred the more positive approach to regulation embodied in the National Vaccine Establishment.

Very few people now denied that, without proper quarantine, variolation spread smallpox. The Nottingham General Hospital and the Whitehaven Dispensary had acknowledged the danger at the end of 1800, and had abandoned smallpox inoculation. On 1 January 1803, Sir Henry Mildmay reported to Jenner that 'some of our friends' intended to introduce a bill to restrict variolation. He opposed it because he sensed that prohibition would alarm people, whereas vaccination would win the day in any case. The Board of the Royal Jennerian Society voted in favour of some such legislation on 5 June 1805, and appointed a committee led by the Duke of Bedford, President of the Society, and Jenner. A year later Wilberforce spoke in the House, recommending the formation of a committee drawn from both Houses of Parliament to investigate the possibility of restrictive legislation. He could not agree to compulsion, but felt that Parliament could impose quarantines. In support of this proposal, Sir Edmund Carrington, a noted lawyer, published his opinion that a precedent for legislation imposing quarantine had been created by restrictions on leprosy patients imposed in 1468. This was the background to Mr Fuller's bill, but even the medical authorities could not agree. William Blair asked Dr J. C. Wachsel, resident apothecary at the London Smallpox Hospital, for his support. Wachsel replied: 'I cannot agree perfectly in your opinion. . .while Vaccination continues so uncertain in its Prophylactic Powers'. Three more years passed before the London Smallpox Hospital finally stopped variolating in-patients, and it was not until 1841 that the practice was forbidden by law.

Toward the end of Jenner's letter to Pruen of 26 May 1808, he wrote: 'Cobbett, I find, sides with Moseley – This will prove fatal to thousands of little Innocents.' William Cobbett's attitude probably had more to do with the behaviour of the RJS during the Howard case than with Moseley's medical opinions, but he was an influential enemy. It apparently never occurred to Jenner or his partisans that Cobbett might respond to face-to-face discussion, such as was frequently applied to uncertain peers, gentry and Members of Parliament. Indeed, Jenner's failure to perceive the value of such a simple political step vividly demonstrates the fateful division between the ruled and their rulers, exacerbated now for a decade by Pitt's repressive anti-subversive Acts. Cobbett was beyond the pale.

By the end of May the plan for the new organization was well advanced. Charles Murray, who was still Secretary to the RJS, wrote privately to Jenner complaining that both the new Resident Inoculator and the new Secretary were to be medical men, leaving him out in the cold. He argued that a non-medical man could undertake most of the secretarial duties, and pointed to his experience. In the event Murray got the job, probably through Jenner's influence.

On 9 June Rose proposed to the House that Parliament authorize the creation of 'a central institution in London, for the purpose of rendering Vaccine Inoculation generally beneficial to his Majesty's subjects, to be superintended by a certain number of the Royal College of Physicians and of the Royal College of Surgeons in London'. Rose estimated that the cost of the institution would be £2500 to £3000 per year. The House approved, again without dissent. Despite this unanimity, the Home Secretary, Lord Hawkesbury, did not issue the formal warrant authorizing Sir Lucas Pepys, President of the Royal College of Physicians, to set the machinery in motion until 28 December 1808, more than six months later. No reason for the delay has come to light. Of course, there was a war on. The bloody Iberian campaign reached a climax during the summer and autumn. On 29 November Jenner wrote to Pruen from Berkeley, 'Great news from Spain, if it is but true.'

Meanwhile, the Home Secretary had been expected to act at any moment. Sir Lucas Pepys was eager that Jenner should be in town when the President and censors of the Royal College of Physicians first met with the Master and governors of the Royal College of Surgeons to establish the National Vaccine Establishment. It was understood that Jenner was to be its Director. The fate of the Fuller bill had not been finally decided, furthermore, and Jenner may have felt that his presence might be useful if it went forward. The fact that he thus found himself compelled to return again and again to London that summer may explain the surprising fact that a comparatively innocuous letter in the *Medical Observer* finally drew blood.

It was written by Dr Richard Reece, author of the medical dictionary that attacked vaccination. He undoubtedly went beyond the usual reticence of the antivaccinists and attacked Jenner personally. Jenner and Dr Marshall were alleged to have sought 'to monopolize' the practice of vaccination. They had been well paid for their efforts. When Reece had asked for vaccine matter, Marshall had agreed to send it by post, but then had used vitriol on the arms of his patients so that their pustules afforded no lymph. Jenner refused to use his own money on a 'wild goose scheme' of general vaccination, 'nor, after his speculations in Bond Street, is it likely that any person would have advanced it.' Because Jenner had been unknown before vaccination, moreover, his practice could not have been damaged by the time he devoted to the new therapy, as he had claimed in his first petition to Parliament. Jenner consulted Sir Edmund Carrington. Charles Murray prepared a fair copy of the claims for Carrington, and added a note of explanation: 'Dr. Jenner's reputation stands perhaps generally too high in this Country to be injured by this attack; but as these medical publications are circulated throughout the Continent of Europe, he feels it incumbent upon him to notice it, if it be possible, by a legal prosecution.' Sir Edmund advised against. He held that the attacks were 'not so scandalous in' themselves, nor did they 'reflect such moral turpitude on the character of Dr. Jenner, as to warrant the institution of criminal proceedings against Reece'.

The summer began as it meant to continue, however. No sooner was one libel dealt with than another threatened. Again the source was the *Medical Observer*. This time the offender was none other than John Walker, who had written a 'Jenneric Opera'. It began 'from the first movements of the great Hero. . .among the Cow-doctors in Gloucestershire, to the formation of the Royal Society, and the wars and rumours of wars which arise in that *wonderful* Institution.' Thence it continued in poetic vein through four acts published in the August, November and December issues of the periodical. Act I opened with:

> There was a jolly Potiker [apothecary], liv'd near the
> Severn side,
> He mounted on a good fat cow, and a begging he did ride.

Act II:

> Now to Glostershire, I hie,
> To my rural habitation,
> To my native field and sky. . . .
> Ring and Blair are a pair, *par horribile fratrum –*,
> More cunningly they attacked Mordecai's [the author's] fame;
> With Sec. and some others, conspiring *ad Paytherum*,
> They strive to destroy him, or bring him to shame.

Jenner felt sufficiently aggrieved to consult Sir Edmund Carrington once more. He told Pruen that 'Murray. . .inform'd me he forgot to tell you that Dr E. Carrington pronounced the Ballad to be decidedly libellous; but thought it best to postpone prosecution till more of the same kind of stuff appeared.' To the distanced observer, it appears that both Murray and Carrington were trying to let him down easily.

Such sensitivity to the slings and arrows betokens a mounting paranoia.

'I have no heart, no spirit to set about anything,' he cried out to Pruen on 11 August.

> Both seem broken from the cruel privations I have experienc'd in being pent up for so many months in this lonely place, and subjected to constant harassings – Banish'd from my Wife & family; in short deprived of all comforts. I wait not[w?] for the organization of the new Vaccine Establishment, which is to be call'd the National. Our intended arrangement has been more than a month in the hands of the Ministry for their approbation or the contrary, & I cannot stir till they are pleas'd to return it at least without the risk of being ordered back again as soon as the Paper is return'd by Lord Hawkesbury.

There was more, much more, to oppress him. Not satisfied with one attack, the editors of the *Medical Observer* also published in its August issue an item by 'W.B.' – John Birch, according to Jenner – 'exhibiting four heads diseased by vaccination', he wrote in his notebook. 'How easily he might have added a fifth by giving his own.' So taken was he by this witticism that he repeated it twice, in letters to Pruen on 1 September and to Marcet the next day. It continued: 'These attacks upon me keep up a Clamour, and tho' I know from good information that my person is not in safety here, yet I do not feel the least dread of assassination. This is not to be accounted for easily. The Medical Journal thro' the chicanery of Dr Adams, has turn'd upon us. . . .Now what is to be done?' The *Medical and Physical Journal* had merely published a letter from Adams pointing out that some vaccination failures had undoubtedly occurred.

Dr Adams's observations concerned the London Smallpox Hospital, but during this same nightmare month of August, the issue impinged much more directly on Jenner. He chaired a meeting of the RJS Board of Directors on 3 August, which sent William Blair and John Ring to Cambridge to investigate more 'Reports unfavourable to Vaccination'. The source of these complaints was none other than the eminent Professor of Medicine at Cambridge, Sir Isaac Pennington. Blair and Ring requested that Pennington accompany them during their investigations, or if he could not, that he supply a list of those 'cases he thinks most necessary to be inquired into.' Pennington refused to cooperate, but two local surgeons, Frederick Thackeray and a Mr Farish, assisted them in investigating seventeen cases of apparent vaccine failure. They concurred in the diagnosis of smallpox in ten cases, but two of these, including the only death, had been variolated, and four had had vaccinations that did not take for various reasons. The remaining four cases had been mild. Seven patients were said to have had chicken-pox, not smallpox. Not surprisingly, Pennington disagreed with at least two of these disputed diagnoses; he had seen the patients when they were ill. In October he communicated six cases, including the disputed diagnoses, to the Royal College of Physicians to support his original charges. At best, the outcome can be seen as proof that the Jennerians were prepared to accept that vaccinations could fail, their critics such as Adams and Robert Willan to the contrary notwithstanding.

As his 11 August letter to Pruen indicated, Jenner's instability in the face of these vaccination problems stemmed from his sense of uprootedness. His daughter had been living in south London but had had little contact with him. On 28 August, he wrote again to Pruen: 'You will be sorry to hear that poor Catherine has been so ill with a fever at Balham Hill, that I was greatly alarm'd for her safety. She is still confined to her Bed; but I trust the danger is over.' Four days later Jenner reported to Pruen: 'My poor dear Catherine is getting better; but still too weak to quit her Bed.' If the rarity of references to his daughter in correspondence can be taken as an indication, they were not close. His wife and sons remained in Berkeley.

Pruen was acting as overseer and steward for the planning and construction of a new stable and coach house at 8 St George's Place. A servant, James, was to proceed at once with the work. A friend (whose name is not legible in Jenner's letter to Pruen) 'and I think it wd be most suitable to have the Coach House 11 Ft. wide instead of 10, which wd. admit of the Harness being hung on the side of the Carriage. The gain wd. be a longer room in the front – and such a room wd. be useful as a Laundry, Brewhouse etc. The Pump might go to some other part of the Court.' Jenner also directed Pruen to supply James with money 'from some of my stores in Cheltenham. I have some cash in Ferndale's Bank, but my Acct. Curt. [current account] is not here. Will you be good enough to ask Drayton [the manager?] how it stands?' Three weeks later he again asked Pruen to 'enquire the present state of my Funds at Ferndale's Bank.' At the bottom of the letter in a different hand, probably Pruen's, is a note: 'Cr £103.8.7'. In another letter to Pruen dealing with domestic matters dated 2 September, Jenner demonstrated his practical interest in the fixtures and fittings of his home. Some person (name again illegible) 'has made so great an improvement in the oven that I cd wish to dispose of mine to the best Bidder. Mr Stephensons Pipe entirely removes the noisome smell.' In December when he had returned to Berkeley, Jenner wrote to Pruen, now in London, asking him to look at a grate 'which struck my Fancy much'.

At about this time, late 1808, his notebook contains two builders' receipts which are perfectly useful today. Dry rot is not something new: 'The destructive visitant in dwelling houses generally, grows and originates in cellars. If persons white-washing cellars will mix as much copperas (fer;sulph) with the wash as will give it a clear yellow hue & repeat this every year the dry rot may be prevented; or its progress stopped, if it has already appeared.' The second is for 'Strong Cement, Scarcely Inferior to Stone': 'Lime well slacked, sand. Temper it with linseed oil to the consistency of mortar. Beat it well on a floor or a trough & then spread it on a dry wall. It will last for ages.' These notes, like the instructions to Pruen and Davies, are reminders of the life of a country gentleman from which Jenner was interminably separated during this tedious waiting for bureaucrats and ministers to act.

Since he had to be in London, he continued to meet with the Royal Jennerian Society. On 22 September the Board examined the Society's expenditures, before proposing an address to the public for funds to maintain its functions until it 'shall be superseded by the Measures of Government.'

Jenner was also preparing a new contribution to the vaccination debate, focusing on the phenomenon of repeated smallpox infections. *Facts, for the Most Part Unobserved, or not duly Noticed, Respecting Variolous Contagion* was published on 18 November 1808. This sixteen-page pamphlet repeated several cases from *Further Observations on the Variolae Vaccinae or Cow Pox* and *A Continuation of Facts & Observations Relative to the Variolae Vaccinae* of patients who had had smallpox a second time, either after the natural disease or after variolation. To these he added two cases of smallpox that had affected the foetus without infecting the mother. His object was to reiterate the warning that had appeared in *Further Observations*: 'the constitution cannot by previous infection be rendered totally unsusceptible of the variolous poison; neither the casual nor the inoculated Small Pox. . .can perfectly extinguish the susceptibility'. He believed that the foetal cases demonstrated the variability of infection. Like so much of Jenner's deductive work, *Facts* was ahead of its time. Though it will not always assure immunity to both parties, the placenta often protects the mother against the child, and vice versa. Smallpox, furthermore, is far less contagious than Jenner and his contemporaries believed. Whether exposure produces disease depends in some measure on factors such as the health of the exposed person. Before vaccination, and while variolation was restricted to a small minority, the question whether smallpox could occur twice in the same person was largely irrelevant. Nothing could be done about the universal plague, so a second dose had been ignored; besides, the second illness was almost always mild.

Widespread vaccination and its apparent failures created a new problem in epidemiology. The antivaccinists capitalized on it. Yet Jenner's prescient pamphlet failed to stem the tide. There were two reasons: the antivaccinists insisted that if vaccination suffered from the same fault as variolation, it was better to stick with the established protection. Against the weight of evidence, they denied that vaccination was safer. But they had also raised the question of permanence, and it would not go away. Even Jenner admitted that most people caught smallpox only once, they argued. Most people were protected by variolation for life. Could vaccination make the same claim? Elsewhere, Jenner wrongly insisted that it could. The correct response, had he but realized it, lay in an analogy with his argument in *Facts*: the permanence of the protection afforded by vaccination varied with the individual. The safety of vaccination meant that it could be repeated almost without personal or social risk as often as seemed desirable.

On the day that *Facts* was published, Dr Knowles resigned as Resident Inoculator of the Royal Jennerian Society because of the criminal charges of debt default against him. A Special General Court under Jenner's chairmanship had allowed him leave of absence only a week before. Knowles recommended Mr Richard Kennedy to fill his place, and the Board confirmed Kennedy's appointment. The same meeting approved a move to rent out the larger part of the Central House by Christmas. When Knowles asked for his job back, with Jenner's sympathy, he was told that it was to be abolished by the same date.

The Society's disintegration took another eight months. Dr Lettsom chaired the last board meetings, the most important of which, on 16 March 1809, resolved not to dissolve the organization formally – with unforeseen results. Dr Jenner was to be informed of the decision 'when he comes to Town'. The last minutes were dated 3 August 1809.

During October 1808, perhaps in order to spare Jenner yet another bruising problem, Charles Murray became involved as middleman between Mrs Jenner and her nephew, Henry, in a bizarre family scandal. Henry's wife, the former Susannah Pearce, had died at Thornbury near Berkeley in August 1798. The following year Henry was elected Mayor of Berkeley. He and his twin brother, George, were then assisting their uncle in his practice. Henry had written *An Address to the Public on the Advantages of Vaccine Inoculation*, published at the end of 1799 in Bristol. In a postscript to this pamphlet, he offered to vaccinate free any 'families, or individuals, who shall come forward with a proper recommendation from any reputable person.' The respectability of his career seemed beyond doubt.

Within the next year Henry set up practice in Bristol. Jenner wrote to Mary Black: 'Tell Henry I recd his Letter. He certainly has a road now opend for him that may lead to fortune if he will pursue it, & suffer Industry & Attention to be his travelling Companions. In their Society he may yet flourish.' On 20 January 1802, Henry published a leaflet asking support for the Bristol Vaccine Institution for the Inoculation of the Poor. He also established in his home one Charlotte Fryer, previously named Cross. On 6 November 1802, after the banns had been properly called, the couple were married, but with the full knowledge of his bride Henry had signed his name, Harry Hedgenar. They lived together quietly in Bristol for three years, and Charlotte bore a son who was named William and survived into adult life. Then, however, the marriage broke down. Whether for that reason or because of other pressures, Henry left, probably returning to Berkeley.

It occasions little surprise to learn that news of Henry's adventures returned with him. On 5 October 1808 he wrote an astonishing letter of explanation. Though the addressee is not named, the letter was found amongst Charles Murray's papers.

In compliance with Mrs. Jenner's desire, I have written such particulars as I deem sufficiently necessary, and which I beg you will give or relate to her with any observations or remarks you think proper.

The case is this: – After keeping the young woman sometime, I certainly had a great affection for her, and thinking, she behaved herself in a kind and constant manner, and (laying aside the consideration of money and Family) she was all that could be required. After directing her to get educated, and conduct herself in the most prudent manner, I was resolved to marry her, when I had obtained her solemn promise not to mention the marriage for three years. In order, therefore, to keep it secret, and that it might not appear in the papers, I put up the Banns in a fictitious name, conceiving that the ceremony if performed in a Church by a regular Clergyman, would be good and lawful, however it might be brought about [?] being asked three Sundays we were married. Some time after seeing in a paper (I think the Sun of the [?] of June 1805) a marriage render'd void owing to one of the [?] party being asked and married in a wrong name, I began to think our's was void also; and upon hearing & suspecting inconstancy and want of affection, I mentioned the [?] circumstances to her; and upon perusal of Burn's [a popular legal manual] still my opinion seemed strengthen'd: – But not satisfied with this, I bought the Marriage Act, which appeared more clear and decisive; and after quarrelling with her, I told her that it would be my duty to take care of her and the Child, but that the marriage was not valid.

Hearing that such case would be decided by a law of equity and not by common Law, and that circumstances would establish the validity of the marriage, or render it void, I chose rather to allow I supposed it not good, and subject myself to what I supposed would be a fine, (till after seeing the Act) than by allowing it to be good, and have it so established.

She consulted a Lawyer, and gave him a very unjust statement of the case; and being informed by him that it was her intention to prosecute me, he proposed that I should pay her £100 per annum, as she had represented me to be in ample circumstances, but this I absolutely refused to do. In a subsequent conversation with her, and in the presence of two respectable witnesses, I told her she had falsely represented the business, that she was more to blame than I was, and that she did not deserve, nor would I pay such a

sum of money – She said "agree to it"; the Lawyer will make me
have it, tho I know 'tis too much, and I will give you a portion
back; but said she would retain 60£ – at last I consented to allow
her 59£ by which means I should save the Tax on her income. I
have nearly paid her this sum, with which she seems satisfied, as
I have peremptorily refused paying more. She now seems, I think,
quiet and satisfied, and will, probably continue so. With respect to
the Law of the case, the statement I before gave Mrs. Jenner, which
I believe will be found correct, was the opinion of an eminent Coun-
sellor, but be the Law what it may, nothing will induce me, after the
treatment etc I have received, to take her as my wife. Yr obt fd. &
sert

Charlotte Fryer was probably not too far off the mark in the matter of the
compensation she demanded. She must have known that Henry was a man
of some property. In addition to an estate at Halmore in the tithing of Hinton,
part of Berkeley parish, he owned three houses on Church Lane, around the
corner from the Chauntry. These he leased to his uncle in January 1810, and
Edward gave one to James Phipps, now married with small children, for the
latter's lifetime. However, Henry seems not to have been overburdened with
common decency.

The next year he concluded two agreements which his uncle must almost
certainly have concurred in. The first, with the tithing of Ham, presumably
a contract with the Berkeley parish council, paid him twenty-five guineas
for attending the poor with medicines and surgery, but not variolation or
lying-in, from 6 April 1809 for one year. Under the second, the town of
Berkeley paid him twelve guineas to attend the poor and to supply medicine
to those outside the parish, for a year from 19 April.

The consequences of Henry's illegitimate marriage continued to surface.
At the end of 1809, contrary to his hopes and expectations, Charlotte Fryer
brought a presentment against him in the Ecclesiastical Court of Gloucester
Diocese. Nothing happened until 1814, when she sued him in the Ecclesiastical Court for 'restitution of Conjugal Rights.' In his sworn reply, dated two
years later, Henry denied they had accepted each other as man and wife or
were thought by their friends to be married. Because the marriage had taken
place in the Diocese of Bath and Wells, the case was finally transferred to
that jurisdiction in 1817. It was then irrelevant. Charlotte Jenner, otherwise
Fryer, aged thirty-five, was buried at Berkeley on 23 December 1816.

Jenner made no explicit comment on these events, but in a letter to
William Davies junior written in January 1813 he wrote: 'Pray have some
conversation with him [Mr Pearce, the lawyer, Henry's brother-in-law] on
the subject of the new freak of H. J. and say how much obliged we should
be if Mr. P would once more have some serious conversation with him on this
subject.' In 1789 when Henry was twenty-two and just starting out, Jenner

had written to the Revd John Clinch, 'his general appearance and manner is so very <u>fifteenish</u>, that a poor mortal on the bed of sickness will hardly look up to him with that eye of confidence and hope that might safely be placed in him.' Almost exactly thirty years later, Edward commented to his friend Richard Worthington:

Henry Jenner, who, though he has seen nearly half a century fly over his head, has not yet begun to <u>think</u>, perched himself in the midst of a poor family pent up in a small cottage. It was the abode of wretchedness, had the addition of pestilence been wanting. He was infected, of course; and his recovery is very doubtful.

Henry Jenner died in 1851. He seems to have been a kind doctor, but his uncle's strictures were no doubt soundly based.

As November advanced, still with no word from the government, Jenner suddenly decided to leave London anyway. The immediate cause was almost certainly the health of his eldest son. 'Poor Edward is again going through one of his dreadful Fevers', he wrote to Pruen on the 21st. 'My letters today from Henry Jenner & [my] poor Wife are soothing to my feelings. God grant on my arrival, I may find him better.' He reached the Chauntry in the evening of 23 November. Edward *was* better, he reported to Pruen. 'I write to tell you that I once more feel myself in the only place a man has any chance to find comfort in – home.' 'As I have brought my Daughter from Town, I should be obliged to you to send by Hooper's Waggon on Saturday the Piano Forte. There is a Case for it in St George's Place – James wd. pack it carefully.'

Jenner had addressed this letter to Pruen's home in Cheltenham, but it had been readdressed to Kensington. Either Pruen had remained in London most of the autumn, or he had returned in November, possibly in connection with his newspaper. By mid-December he was back in Cheltenham where Jenner wrote to him about a mutual acquaintance, Dr Thomas Charles Morgan of Peterhouse, Cambridge, whom Jenner considered a suitable candidate for a post at the Gloucester Infirmary. In London during October, Morgan had worked with Jenner, perhaps in the preparation of *Facts*. 'Morgan is just the same good humor'd [illegible word] as you found & left him. I work him hard, but cannot reform him. He has kept bad Company I fear. Tis pity among so much amicability one shld. not find one spark of religion.+ But it may be struck off yet by some unlooked for stroke from Heaven.' Jenner had shown this to the young man, who wrote below it: '+Dissentient – because I have (modesté loqum) [modestly speaking] at least two J.C.M.', to which Jenner added: 'As he had plenty of Virtue Time & reflection I trust will set all to rights.' Such playfulness is rare indeed in Jenner's correspondence, and reveals not only his intimacy with Pruen but the special regard that he must have felt for Morgan. On 20 December 1808, he wrote to Morgan: 'It affords me great pleasure to assure you that your pamphlet is much liked. . .and by no one more than myself. A few trifling alterations will be necessary for the next Edition.' Morgan's pamphlet, published anonymously, was *An Expostulatory Letter to Dr. Moseley*, answering some of the criticisms made by Moseley in *A Review of the Report of the Royal College of Physicians of London, on Vaccination*. A year later Jenner asked Morgan what expenses he had incurred for printing and advertisements, presumably of the 'next Edition'. 'Enclosed is a Draft on my Banker for the discharge of Murray's Bill. I not only pay it cheerfully, but with a thousand thanks to you for your kind exertions.'

In the letter of 20 December to Morgan, Jenner had also criticized his most zealous defender, John Ring.

> Alas! poor Ring! He has been too daring, & I tremble for his fate. The Scourge is out, and I don't see that he erased a single line that was pointed out to him as dangerous. This venomous sting will produce a most troublesome reaction, & injure the cause it was meant to support. You know the pains I took to suppress it; but all would not do.

The Vaccine Scourge: Part II. . .in Answer to Dr. Walker's Jenneric Opera . . . was published anonymously, perhaps to mollify the criticism its potentially libellous vituperation courted. Jenner had written in much the same terms to Pruen a week earlier: 'These things injure the Vaccine Cause far more than the productions of Moseley & Birch.' Yet it was his nomination of Ring to the position of Principal Vaccinator of the National Vaccine Establishment that was to lead directly to Jenner's ill judged desertion of the new institution.

Sir Lucas Pepys had begged Jenner to come back to London for the first meeting of the National Vaccine Establishment Board, held immediately after the warrant was issued by Lord Hawkesbury on 28 December. Jenner refused, citing the health of his two sons. 'I should be unworthy of the name of father were I to stir from my children,' Jenner wrote to Mrs James Moore. 'Indeed, nothing could make me, not even a royal mandate, unless accompanied by a troop of horse.' Edward junior had evidently come down with typhoid fever in November, and although he was better by the time Jenner returned to Berkeley, Robert had caught it. Meanwhile, Jenner in his putative position as Director had supplied Sir Lucas with his nominees for vaccinators, both for the position of Principal Vaccinator, Ring, and seven others who would man the London vaccination stations on the pattern of the Royal Jennerian Society. On January 9 1809 he wrote to Pruen:

> The affairs of the National Vaccine Establishment go on badly. . . .The Board appointed me Director of course but they have contriv'd to let me know that I am the Director directed; for out of the eight names

I nominated to fill the Vaccinating Stations, they have taken only
two; the others are fill'd by men who are utter strangers to me,
and what is still worse (indeed is it not insulting?) one of them
who is appointed the Vaccine chief, & to superintend the other
Stations is sadly taken from Pearson's Institution to which he was
Surgeon. Keate, the very man who linked himself with Pearson to
form his Institution & the very man who made a base attempt
to upset me in the Committee of the House of Commons, is one
of the Board. The question is then, shall I immediately resign &
shew them a little of the indignation I feel, or wait till I have
cooly taken the opinion of my Friends? At all events. . .I must
be embroil'd. . . .

His two acceptable nominees were Charles Aikins and Joseph Leese, both
formerly directors of the RJS. During the hearings in 1802 John Keate,
formerly Surgeon-General of the Army, had merely transmitted papers to
Pearson concerning an alleged prior claim to cowpox inoculation. As for
the appointment of J. C. Carpue as Principal Vaccinator, perhaps Pepys
understood what Jenner did not, that the success of the new institution
would depend to some extent on binding together the pro-vaccination
elements divided by Jenner's blind refusal to accept any questioning of
his authority over the past seven years. Baron wrote, 'there is reason to fear
that his feelings would have been wounded' had he attended the first board
meeting, as Pepys had urged. On the other hand, had he gone, there is reason
to hope that gentlemen seeking the same objectives could have talked sense
to each other. Surely, he could no longer seriously have advocated Ring's
appointment? Might he not have been induced to shake hands with Carpue
and Keate, both perfectly respectable medical practitioners committed to
vaccination? But he refused to go, perhaps suspecting another subversive
'Flag of Truce'.

In its February 1809 number, the *Medical and Physical Journal* announced
the Board of Directors and the officers of the National Vaccine Establishment.
The Board was made up of Sir Lucas Pepys, Doctors Mayo, Heberden,
Satterley and Bancroft and the surgeons, George Chandler, Keate and Sir
Charles Blicke. The officers: Jenner, Director; James Moore, Assistant Direc-
tor; Registrar, Dr Harvey; Principal Vaccinator, Carpue; Secretary, Charles
Murray. In January news arrived from the bloody Spanish battlefields that
James Moore's eminent brother, General Sir John Moore, had been killed.
There was talk of James receiving honours which would have caused him to
withdraw from the NVE. 'This blow will fall heavy on me let things go how
they will,' Jenner wrote to Pruen, 'for I know not who can well supply his
place.'

Marcet urged him to complete his paper on dog distemper, because
plans for the first number of *Medico-Chirurgical Transactions* were well

advanced. On 17 January he replied that he was doing his best, 'but such have been my incessant occupations since my arrival here, that I have had no time to bestow on anything not immediately professional, or what was connected with the business of the National Vaccine Establishment, which I may say to you is by no means fashioned to my liking'. However, there was also time for domestic matters. Pruen visited him briefly. His Eastington friend, Henry Hicks, and Catherine's brother, Colonel Kingscote, came to dinner on successive days. At the beginning of February, he described to Pruen progress with the new laundry at the Chauntry. But how, he asked, does one put up the boilers?

> Baker, <u>cute</u> as he is, seems at a loss on this point. If you have any [illegible word] Pamphlet on the subject I will thank you for it by the first Coach (as we are at a stand still) or any plain instructions you can convey in a Letter. . . .Has Rumford [Count, founder of the Royal Institution?] any new Ideas on the subject of conveying heat into a Room distind for the purpose of drying Linen? I mean as to the placing of the stove, or anything else.

Clearly his friendship with Pruen was grounded on the latter's practical knowledge. Jenner was also doing his best to recruit customers for Pruen's newspaper: 'In my own family I have one Recr: – The Revd. Wm. Davies, Rockhampton', but he also promised to show the prospectus at Berkeley Castle.

On 1 March in a letter to Dr Morgan, he reported, 'My Boys are better – '. The letter also conveyed the first surviving indication that he had at last reached a decision with regard to the National Vaccine Establishment. He had 'informed the Gentlemen in Leicester Square, that I cannot accept' the office of Director. He wrote to Pruen with the same information two days later, adding: 'my conduct being reported to Government, I am likely soon it seems, to be had up before the Privy Council.' Was this a little joke between friends, or paranoia? Supporting the joke hypothesis: no record of such a remark being made to other friends. Supporting paranoia, his next letter to Pruen:

> I am to be torn limb from limb it seems by Government & the College of Phys. but I hope my Executors will collect my scattered remains and give me Christian burial. Hostilities are about to commence, & the odds against me would be fearful if my heart was not well shielded. . . .the new Institution is disgraceful to the Nation & degrading to me.

The image of the governmental lions may be a bitter joke, but the astonishing final clause is not so pleasantly explained.

Baron defensively quotes a letter written by Sir Thomas Bernard on 6 March: 'I am glad you have resigned, and have confidence, that when the Board is noticed in Parliament, the treatment you have received will be properly censured'. Three more of Jenner's letters defending his decision have survived. He wrote to Marcet on 15 March: 'I hope my Friends in Town will contradict a rumour, wherever they find it, (& it is put about with considerable industry) that I seceded from the new Institution, because its whole management was put into my hands. Nothing was ever further from my thoughts or wishes.' In a letter to the Wiltshire MP, T. J. Estcourt, on 25 March, he acknowledged that he had expected to be in town for the NVE, 'but things have taken a turn that has quite astonish'd me, & hurt my feelings so much that I have been under the unpleasant necessity of withdrawing from it entirely.' The last was addressed to William Blair on 26 April:

> . . .you know how this business was managed; & how I was insulted (was it not an insult?) by their selecting one, & appointing him the Chief, from an Institution that had always most wantonly opposed me. . . .The Colleges in thus inadvertently degrading me, will undoubtedly injure themselves. But, my good Sir. . .I think it would be most prudent for me at present to remain silent.

Jenner's hurt feelings ought no longer to surprise us. Nor should his sense of persecution; six months earlier he had discovered 'that my person is not in safety here'. His belief that the Royal Colleges had shot themselves in their respective feet passes beyond mild paranoia to megalomania, but in the circumstances he could not have been expected to undervalue his great contribution. Nor was he completely isolated; some like Bernard and Blair appear to have understood and sympathized with his position. A public statement might have gained further support, but it was unlikely to change the Board's mind and would certainly have damaged the NVE at the outset. On this occasion Jenner's reluctance to write and publish served the nation well.

The Board promptly appointed James Moore Director. This enabled Jenner to keep up 'his communication with the Institution', as Baron put it, because he had no quarrel with Moore. On the other hand, it would surely have put Moore in a difficult position had he not had the tacit agreement of the Board, especially of Pepys, that he should act as a conduit for Jenner. Perhaps they worried that Jenner might still make some pronouncement that had to be answered, and preferred to keep the peace. In any case, Moore himself wrote in 1817 that he had drawn up instructions to the seven vaccination stations after he had 'consulted Dr. Jenner'.

The National Vaccine Establishment, as constituted in 1809, remained in charge of the distribution of vaccine to the Army and Navy throughout Britain, until 1861 when its functions were transferred to the Privy Council. With the Smallpox Hospital, the Finsbury Dispensary, the London Vaccine Institution and other organizations, it also offered free vaccinations at seven, later expanded to nine, stations in the capital. It circulated handbills and cards amongst the poor and letters to medical practitioners and the clergy, and within the first three months had performed 733 vaccinations and dispatched 2580 charges of vaccine.

Jenner's resignation isolated him from the medical establishment in London, a fact which he recognized by reducing even further his visits to the capital. His support amongst City magnates such as Angerstein had been dissipated by the Walker affair. Whatever chance he might have had to obtain the formal honour he craved now disappeared. He approached his sixtieth birthday with much reduced opportunities to influence either political events or public opinion, but with more leisure to renew research interests long set aside and to enjoy what time remained for family affairs. On balance, he thought himself the gainer.

Chapter 10

Deaths
1809–1815

Jenner's paper, 'Observations on the Distemper in Dogs', was read to the Medical and Chirurgical Society in London on 21 March 1809. He was in Berkeley. His observations of a 'large number of foxhounds belonging to the Earl of Berkeley' had been conducted over 'several successive years'. Jenner's interest began with the hypothesis that cowpox might prevent distemper. He and his nephew George Jenner vaccinated about twenty of the royal staghounds in June 1801, producing a mild form of what he believed was dog distemper. He communicated this experiment to De Carro in Vienna. De Carro repeated the test on a few dogs; at first he was reported as agreeing with Dr Jenner, but in his own letter published by the *Medical and Physical Journal* more than a year later, he said that his results differed from Jenner's.

Probably during 1808 while the discussions concerning the Fuller bill were proceeding with Rose and others, Jenner showed a rough sketch of the paper to someone connected with a medical publication, possibly Dr Bradley of the *Medical and Physical Journal*. 'It has been promised to the Med: & Chir: Socy.,' he wrote, 'therefore you must not make me commit myself by taking Extracts – at least this must be managed with proper delicacy – '. Jenner was neither the first medical scientist nor the last to sip the wine from several bottles, if an alternative publisher expressed interest. In the event, his slight treason toward Marcet led nowhere.

The paper traced the disease back to 1750 and earlier on the continent. He described the symptoms in detail, and added descriptions of the organs from his own dissections conducted during the brief illness as well as *post mortem*. An anonymous reviewer in the *Medical and Physical Journal* called it 'a truly valuable paper, inasmuch as it describes a canine epizootic with great accuracy'.

The first volume of the *Medico-Chirurgical Transactions* also contained Jenner's short article repeating the clinical data on 'Two Cases of Small-Pox Infection, Communicated to the Foetus in Utero', which he had first reported in *Facts. . .Respecting Variolous Contagion*. It was dated 18 November but had been read to the Society on 4 April 1809. One of the two cases was a patient of a Dr Croft. The other was communicated to Jenner by Henry Gervis, a surgeon at Ashburton in Devon. This patient had been successfully vaccinated during pregnancy, but her infant had been born five weeks late and had died of smallpox. 'My principal object. . .is, to guard those who may think fit to inoculate with variolous matter, after vaccination, from unnecessary alarms' due to 'slight eruptions' that may follow. However, instead of using variolation as a test of vaccination, he recommended revaccination because it was 'less hazardous'.

That variolation was to be avoided was nothing new, nor was the idea of revaccination as a test, especially if any doubt existed. At most, Jenner had, without realizing it, changed the emphasis. 'One perfect Vaccine Vesicle is sufficient', according to the instructions of the National Vaccine Establishment published in April 1809; 'but for various reasons, it may often be prudent to make two or three punctures, especially when the danger of receiving the Small Pox is imminent, the Lymph dry, or the patient's residence distant'. In January 1810 Jenner revaccinated Henry Jenner's three children after they had been exposed to smallpox; the twin girls, Susan and Caroline, had been vaccinated between a year and two years and their older brother, Stephen, twelve years before. A few years later, Jenner revaccinated a surgeon, Francis Hands, first vaccinated fifteen or sixteen years before, because he had been attending a man with smallpox in Hinton Workhouse near Berkeley. 'Dr. Jenner told me if I had not been Revaccinated I should have had a severe case of Smallpox'. 'Whenever there is a shadow of doubt upon the mind respecting a child being perfectly vaccinated, I always recommend the insertion of a little vaccine fluid,' Jenner wrote to a patient. In his completely pragmatic approach to revaccination, whether the risk of smallpox infection arose from exposure or was secondary to doubt about the original vaccination, he undoubtedly confused two clinically distinct situations both of which he made the subject of one deduction: if in doubt, revaccinate. Unfortunately, the confusion, productive though it may have been of safer procedures, neglected the issue of whether the risk of infection from exposure increased statistically through time – a fact which Jenner denied, perhaps in part because he never separated it from his immediate clinical experience.

Toward the end of 1810 he wrote to James Moore from Cheltenham about a problem that Moore was experiencing with the 'points' or quills coated with vaccine fluid being sent out by the NVE:

The complaint against your points is partly just and partly unjust. Knowing that four times out of five, those I send out will pass into the hands of a bungler, I give them a double dipping; that is, when one coating is dry I dip again; and when they are to go beyond the seas, I put on a third coating. By this means I very seldom hear of failure from the points. However, I am persuaded this would rarely happen even from a single dip, if the operation was conducted properly. . . .In general, <u>doctors</u> don't make a puncture sufficient to admit a due length of the point, they bring its extremity only in contact with the wounded cutis [skin].

This perfect example of a clear technical description combined with a precise clinical direction demonstrates that, even after a decade of official acceptance, Jenner's first consideration was detail, the detail that guaranteed his patient's safety. Generalizations, scientific deductions, followed from such detail. Precisely this ordering of experience made him a medical scientist in the modern sense of the phrase.

He faced an omnipresent incentive: 'Numerous instances of the small-pox have lately occurred', warned an official document at the end of 1809.

In a few cases. . .the small-pox has appeared on subjects that have regularly gone through the process of vaccination. . . .These facts, which have been but very few. . .have nevertheless so far increased the prejudice of some, and produced such doubt and hesitation. . .as to lessen the inclination for using the salutary means of prevention.

Apart from the two papers in the *Medico-Chirurgical Transactions*, Jenner now entered that state of retirement he had vowed to adopt for so long. With one very brief exception, he and his family even abandoned Cheltenham during 1809. The reason was Edward junior's deteriorating health. The 'typhus' in December no doubt hastened his physical decline. Nor would his mental outlook have been improved by the health of his tutor, John Worgan. In April Jenner wrote to Pruen: 'Poor Worgan has for some time been confined with symptoms that portend approaching consumption. Nature dislikes the burthen of a premature Head & is too apt to shake it off – '. Jenner admired Worgan's poetry as a recapitulation of his younger self, but perhaps also because its seriousness reflected a philosophical mien approved by the eighteenth-century gentleman. It compensated for his poverty and almost explained his illness. One love sonnet from a collection made by William Davies junior in 1809 will suffice:

> No, – to thy shrine no suppliant strains I bring,
>> Imaginary Queen of soft desires!
> Nor shall my chords with lawless ardor sing
>> Of Cupid's Darts, and Passion's treacherous fires.
> To pure affections holy shrine I bow, –
>> There the fond feelings of my heart proclaim,
> There for Eliza breathe th' unhanging vow,
>> While soften'd love inspires a mutual flame.
> To thee, Omniscient Father! I resign, –
>> Almighty Guardian of my doubtful way!

If such thy will, Oh make Eliza mine,
      Yet – let my heart thy sov'reign doom obey.
And oh! how blissful shall our moments roll,
      When Love inspires, and Heav'n directs the soul.

A dying seventeen-year-old boy could have hoped for little more than an 'Imaginary Queen', but what effect had he on his moribund twenty-year-old pupil?

Worgan had written a poetic address for the annual festival of the Royal Jennerian Society in May 1808. Jenner was in London and presumably attended. At the end of the year he paid £21 for printing and binding 'Worgan's little Poem', but the work is not further identified. The next year Jenner's birthday was celebrated by a gathering of family and friends for dinner and tea at William Davies's house in Stone. Davies listed those present: Dr and Mrs Jenner, their son Robert, Mary Jenner, youngest sister of Henry and George, Henry Hicks, Mrs Worgan and William Smith, possibly the MP. Within a day or two Mrs Worgan took her son back to Bristol. Jenner wrote to Pruen: 'Poor Worgan left me. . .in so bad a state of health that I almost despair of his recovery.' A month later after acknowledging Worgan's decline, he reverted to his curious belief that 'When the mind ripens so early, the vital functions are always weak. . . .The Bird-peck'd Cherry is the soonest red.' Curious, not because it is particularly surprising – we still say, 'The good die young.' On the other hand, in his beloved son Jenner had evidence to the contrary. Though good no doubt, Edward was admittedly no genius. Yet 'Poor Edward remains in statu quo,' he said in the same letter. Worgan died in Bristol on 25 July. On that day Jenner wrote at length to Pruen:

> I fear it is all over with my coming to Cheltenham this Season. Poor Edward's complaint which remained so long enveloped in obscurity, has at length shewn itself in a most alarming shape. Within this last fortnight he has been repeatedly affected with Haemorrhage from the Lungs. . . .Death is a terrible visitor in whatever shape he approaches us, and this is a frightful one indeed. But God's will be done!

Only a father's love for his damaged eldest son could have protected even an ignorant layman, let alone a physician, from seeing the cold fact that poor Jenner now admitted. He asked Pruen to re-let the house on St George's Place for another month from the end of July, and sought the help of Pruen's brother, 'my Attorney at Cheltenham', to explain to the Cheltenham Commissioners that he paid their assessment of '£40 for my professional income' at Berkeley. 'Your Paper seems to flourish beyond all precedent; & I rejoice in it', he concluded. At the beginning of September he informed Pruen that he intended to ride to Cheltenham, and hoped they could meet. 'As I shall stay with you but a few hours, it is my wish to be as much Incog as possible; so, say nothing of my intention.' He probably intended to have a careful landlord's look at his Cheltenham house before re-letting it.

On Friday 15 September Jenner noted, 'Went to Gloucester with Lord Berkeley to visit his R.H. the Duke of Sussex. Spasm; Asthma, opium & ipecac.' Two days later the Duke had improved sufficiently to be moved to Berkeley Castle, where Jenner visited him again. 'There was certainly an honor in being called to [visit?] His R.H. the Duke of Sussex,' he wrote to Pruen the next day. 'Had the Paragraph in the Gloster Herald or Journal, just added this simple sentence, I shld have been fully satisfied "His R.H. was attended by Dr Jenner".' He asked Pruen to do so in the *Chronicle*, 'but not puff me higher.' 'The Duke of Sussex is now here & much better. He was so extremely ill at Gloster that he was about to send an Express to Town for his Physician just as I arrived. The Prince [of Wales] is expected today or tomorrow.' By the end of the month, the patient was well enough to leave the castle. 'He has been having a grain of epecacuani two or three times a day and occasionally the extract of Colocynth comp,' Jenner wrote in his notebook; 'He smokes three or four pipes of Turkish tobacco daily.' Jenner's reward from the Duke was a 'very handsome hookah'.

While Jenner attended the royal duke, William Davies junior wrote in his diary on 18 September: 'In the morning at an adjourned Quarter Sessions of the Peace, at the White Lion Berkeley, when the oaths of Allegiance, Qualifications etc were severally administered to Dr. Jenner & me by the Earl of Berkeley, the Chairman, to enable us to act as Magistrates for the County of Gloucester'. The acceptance of a post that would certainly have been offered to him long before indicates more than anything else could how, in his mind, Jenner had retired from London's politics and other strains. Not only was the magistracy the symbol of stability, it was also, of course, the actual weapon of authority. Only landowners and the clergy could be magistrates. It was a duty not just to his class and status, however, but to the people of England that Jenner at last acknowledged.

Magistrates had to be communicants of the Church of England, to be doubly sure of which they were required to take Holy Communion after their appointments. George Jenner administered the sacrament to both his cousin and his uncle on 1 October. Two days later both Edward and William made note of the fact that together they had gone to Gloucester – 'in a chaise', added the latter – to take their magisterial oaths.

Toward the end of September Jenner took up his correspondence with the Revd Richard Worthington, now living at Southend near Upton, where there had been a 'prevailing ophthalmia'. Diseases of the eye had interested Jenner since Hunter had involved him in experiments with colours. As long ago as 1783, he told Worthington, he had introduced the use of setons to combat acute eye inflammation. A seton is a fine thread that was drawn through a channel introduced, in this case surgically, through the skin 'about an inch from the outward angle of the eye.' It was intended to provide a route along which drainage could take place. Barbarous though the procedure now seems, especially in the absence of anaesthesia, Jenner believed that it had 'given sight to thousands'. From June through November 1812, he conducted a correspondence with a Mrs Meade, wife of a fossil-collecting friend near Bath, directing her treatment of her husband's ophthalmia. She was to introduce a seton in his temple, to be changed 'Once in a day or two. . .otherwise the smell will be offensive', and to apply various ointments and effusions to the eye. He would not prescribe medicines, 'not being sufficiently acquainted with the general state of his [Meade's] Constitution.' The last two letters acknowledged that there had been improvement, continuation of which would afford yet another demonstration of our animal healing powers. To Worthington, however, he recommended the use of an ointment based on hydrated nitrate.

Worthington had developed a superior hoe. Jenner recommended he read a paper on it to the Agricultural Society, 'of which I have the honour to be a member, and should be proud to transmit it.' In December he wrote again to Worthington, principally about Edward's failing health, but the subject of Worthington's paper revealed Jenner's confusion: 'if my letter is not destroyed, and you can refer to it, I believe you will find that I told you I was a member of the Board of Agriculture, meaning that in London. If I said the Agricultural Society, you have certainly been led into an error.' He nevertheless sent the paper to Lord Somerville, still the head of the Board of Agriculture as he had been when Joseph Banks consulted him about Jenner's draft *Inquiry*. I have not determined when Jenner became a member of the Board, nor found evidence that he participated in its useful activities.

The Board of Agriculture may have provided the venue for his meeting with a rising scientific star, Humphry Davy. Davy had been Superintendent of Thomas Beddoes's Pneumatic Institution in Bristol, where he discovered the properties of nitrous oxide gas. As a result, he was appointed Assistant Lecturer in Chemistry and Laboratory Director of the newly organized Royal Institution. In 1802 he began work on agricultural subjects at the request of the Board of Agriculture. Davy's brother recorded in his biography of Sir Humphry a conversation with Jenner about the uses of earthworms that took place in 1809. Davy

> was more disposed to consider the dunghill and putrefaction as useful to the worm, rather than the worm as an agent important to man in the economy of nature, but Dr. Jenner would not allow my reason. He said the earthworms, particularly about the time of the vernal equinox,

move much under and along the surface of our moist meadow lands, and whereever they move they leave a train of mucus behind them, which becomes a manure to the plant. In this respect they act as the slug does in furnishing materials for food to the vegetable kingdom; and under the surface, they break stiff clods in pieces, and finely divide the soil. They feed likewise entirely on inorganic matter, and are rather the scavengers than the tyrants of the vegetable system.

Jenner was an active gardener as well as what would now be called a farmer.

On 4 October he wrote to Charles Murray, now Secretary to the National Vaccine Establishment. He asked Murray to supply a 'medical Gentleman at Lisbon' with vaccine and instructions pursuant to a request from Admiral Berkeley more than a year before. Then he reverted to a favourite theme, the importance of the popular press:

> You have heard me say fifty times, the minds of the People, high & low, can only be brought to bear on the Point [vaccination], thro' the medium of the Newspapers. Do what you will in any other way it wont avail. This I shewd clearly to Mr. Rose, & <u>endeavord</u> to show it to Sr. L.[ucas] P.[epys] but perhaps he thought the money it would take up might as well go in <u>another direction.</u>

Grist for this particular mill was supplied by Dr John Thomson of Halifax, whose pamphlet, *A Plain Statement of Facts, in Favour of the Cow-pox, Intended for Circulation through the middle and lower Classes of Society*, had been published recently. Jenner wrote to Thomson warmly commending the tract: '<u>all</u> who read it must understand it. . . .Allow me to suggest the [pro]priety of your sending it to the Reviews – the most popular of the Magazines.' While one must admire the candour of Dr Thomson's title, surely the question arises, whether his simplified advocacy of vaccination got through to the poor and semi-literate to whom it was addressed.

About this time Jenner asked Dr Thomas Morgan to send him the annual *Medical Register* 'with my next Parcel of Books' from his bookseller, W. Harewood, 21 Great Russell Street. That Harewood continued to supply most of his literary needs appears from a letter to Marcet dated 26 March 1812, asking him to instruct the bookseller to send 'Tilloch's Journals [the *Philosophical Magazine* established by Alexander Tilloch in 1797] & with them the last three numbers of the New Medical Journal'. Interesting that Jenner had neither a standing order for the *Medical and Physical Journal*, despite its importance in the struggle to assure continued acceptance of vaccination, nor the need to read it fresh off the press. Harewood was not alone in supplying Jenner's literary needs, however. In August 1812 he paid Wood of Covent Garden £4-15-5 for newspapers supplied, presumably, over several months.

Perhaps the most important and permanent of the researches to which Jenner returned after his retirement was the study of fossils and geology. He became a gifted amateur, responsible for at least one major contribution in the field. This interest may have been a legacy from his father. Certainly he had begun collecting fossils by the time he attended school in Cirencester. During the intervening years, Hunter had helped to keep Edward's prospecting alive, but the great events that held Jenner in London made collecting hard, if not impossible. That he had never abandoned the field entirely, the letter to Morgan demonstrated:

> Do you recollect my exhibiting some curious Pebbles, which I had collected during my stay in Town. . .By some mishap, they were left behind me. They were good Specimens of Wood & Bone converted into Silex [flint]. I don't think there is a Corpuscle of the Globe we inhabit that has not breathed in the form of an animal or a vegetable.

He returned to the theme of ancient movements that created our world in a note about the macrocosm written at the same period.

> It is possible that the surface of the earth or more than the mere surface, forming the Berkeley District, may by one of those vast convulsions (wct. it is plain at distant periods threw the globe into the utmost disorder) has been covered with materials brought from very distant regions. The shells & corals found in the Rocks of Gibraltar are similar to those found in the Rocks of Thornbury, & so are the fragments of some of the stones. The Coral so abundant in a range of many miles was never probably generated in the spot on which it now reposes, nor any of the <u>Families</u> of stones wct. lie about the surrounding country. All might have been impelled forward at the same period, driven by the mighty, the irresistible torrents of the great deep. . . .

Jenner had not only observed and collected with care and persistence, but by 1809 he had acquired considerable sophistication in his understanding of the geological theories of his contemporaries. On 2 November he wrote in his notebook: 'Rec'd the books of the Geological Society of London & a letter acquainting me that I was an honorary member.' Marcet, who was also a member, may have nominated him. Membership of course provided a focus for his interest as well as contacts with many others like himself.

In mid-December Jenner acquired a small property, the boundaries of which remained to be settled by his man, Stibbs. Pruen paid him a visit in Berkeley, but increasingly the health of his eldest child blocked out every other concern. 'My poor dear Edward is much as you left him', he wrote to his friend. 'As I am commonly either sitting with him or within the sound of his hollow Cough, I am at times most miserably depress'd.' William Davies dined or breakfasted with his uncle on several days, including 30 January, but Jenner almost certainly did not sit with him that morning at the Petty Sessions held at the White Hart. The next day Edward junior died.

He was twenty-one. Four years before, he had grown taller than his father. He was mentally retarded. He died of tuberculosis, pulmonary consumption. We know nothing more, other than that his parents loved him and grieved. On 3 February his sister Catherine wrote to inform Charles Murray, because their father was 'labouring under such a depression of spirits from. . .the death of my poor brother'. Two days later Murray received a letter from Robert Jenner containing a draft with which he was asked to pay Wood, the newsagent, '& desire him to exchange the Pilot for the Globe –'. Of such grey events is the black of mourning composed.

Edward was buried on 7 February in Berkeley church. Jenner's first letter after the event appears to have been written on the 10th, to Henry Hicks: 'I had no conception till it happened that the gash would have been so deep; but God's will be done!' Two days later he thanked Pruen 'for your kind soothing letter. Poor dear Edward – He is gone, & with him much of my earthly comfort.'

Even Robert's letter of 5 February to Murray, however, contained signs that the living world had begun to reassert itself. He 'begs you. . .to hold your post even if the Board should further insult you, by offering you a still smaller stipend – '. Later in the month Jenner himself wrote to James Moore, asking for ivory points which he used to send out vaccine. 'I am now reduced to bits of quills. . . .The combmakers who prepare the ivory points are apt to make them too small and narrow towards the extremities, unless instructed otherwise.' He also asked Moore to call on his bookseller, Harewood, and to 'Remember all parcels must come by the Gloucester mail coach.' His mourning appears to have been neither excessive nor surprising, but what is perhaps a little unexpected is the absence from this correspondence of any reference whatsoever to Mrs Jenner's feelings or state of health.

Early in March he called on his niece Sophie Davies, wife of William's youngest brother, Edward. She had given birth prematurely in January, and had suffered since then from violent pains in her legs '& many other Complaints which I cannot describe,' wrote her father-in-law. Edward Davies farmed at Ebley on the valley road to Stroud. His wife was to be safely delivered of three more children.

Pruen's affairs now became intertwined with Jenner's professional worries. The *Chronicle* faced a cash-flow crisis. Jenner replied to Pruen's plea for help:

> I will with great pleasure assist you, but cannot go beyond the sum you first specify, being in hopes of changing ere long my funded property into Land. Some fine estates belonging to Lord Sherbrooke [possibly Sir John Coape Sherbrooke, later Governor General of Canada] I hear are soon to be sold in the Neighbourhood of Standish [the Jenner family

seat]. . . .You shall have it when you want it. With regard to security, we must comply with old Forms, as there are more eyes upon me than my own.

Two weeks later Jenner instructed Messrs Ladbroke to deposit £1000 at the bank of Messrs Fisher, Wells & Co, Cheltenham, in Pruen's account.

The earlier letter continued: 'I can say nothing at present about coming to Cheltenham – I mean as to <u>when</u>. I don't fear a Man, but I detest a Viper; and in Cheltenham this noxious Reptile is supported.' 'Could you find out Walkers motives for this kind of conduct?' I think this viper was the Walker referred to in a letter from Jenner to Paytherus dated 1 October (1809?): 'I have seen Walker the Printer of the [Cheltenham] Journal & had a long conference with him at Ruffs – all present agreed that the Resident Physician alluded to was myself.' Walker had probably reopened a vexatious group of failures affecting Cheltenham children, some of whom Jenner had vaccinated.

The *Medical Observer*'s campaign against the vaccinists had led its editors to publish a sequence of letters to Sir Lucas Pepys, demanding an answer to the question: '*Whether the Cow-pox be, or be not, a permanent protection against Small-pox.*' In its July 1809 issue, a letter from James Freeman, surgeon and apothecary of Cheltenham, called attention to five cases of smallpox after vaccinations, four of which had been performed by Jenner. Jenner complained to Dr Morgan that he had ordered one of the children to be revaccinated because of an irregular pustule, but the mother disregarded his advice. 'Between 3 & 4000 persons have been vaccinated there & in the circumjacent Villages <u>who remain'd in the midst of the Epidemic untouch'd</u>. This <u>trifling</u> circumstance these worthy Gentlemen did not think worth their while to mention.' Basing it on an investigation by Mr Wood, a Cheltenham surgeon, and Thomas Pruen, James Moore submitted a report to the NVE on 29 July 1809. There appear to have been only three siblings, not four, and they had been vaccinated about four years earlier. Two had very mild cases. The third, whose vaccination Jenner had doubted, suffered severe smallpox. The family had been under the care of Dr Thomas Jamieson (or Jameson) of Cheltenham, who wrote a letter to the *Cheltenham Journal* on 22 August. He agreed substantially with Moore's findings, but said that the mother denied she had been told to return with one of the children. James Freeman also now added to his testimony five more failures in one family vaccinated by Jenner, all of whom Freeman had variolated in July.

Jenner responded warmly to two 'good Vaccine Letters' published by the Gloucester newspaper on 26 March 1810, in reply to the *Cheltenham Journal*. 'Who is Publicola? The matter seems to come from [Jenner's close friend, Dr Charles Brandon] Trye, but the manner is not his. J– – – will I imagine, draw up his Forces & open a Fire upon him. We must prepare for

Battle.' A few days later Jenner seems to have lost the will to fight. He wrote again to Pruen about Publicola:

> It wd have been a much better thing if nothing had been said about Cheltenham, as it was sure to rouse from their slumbers the spirits of the antivaccinists. I fear the controversy can now never end, without a full & candid investigation. The result of this would be most triumphant & consign the Snarlers to disgrace & contempt. Moore must come down to Cheltenham, & make his arrangements in the way he may deem most prudent.

The Cheltenham medical practitioners, he suggested, should write to the NVE proposing such an investigation. 'I don't think it should be noised about that an Investigation is likely to take place at Cheltenham, till you and Wood have again seen the young woman (Dodeswells nurse) who gave an evidence to Jamesson & Freeman totally opposite to the real facts she laid before you.' No further NVE investigation seems to have taken place.

After an outspoken career, the *Medical Observer* now rapidly approached its demise. The last issue appeared in January 1811. Jenner wrote to Baron: 'There is another *Med: Observer* come out. This poor Object, now upon Crutches not stilts, is to crawl forth, it seems, quarterly all right.' It ceased forthwith. It should not be allowed to die, though, without notice of a challenge to a duel in which one of its editors, Dr Charles Maclean, was involved to his cost. Maclean was also Lecturer to the East India Company. William Blair, surgeon turned satirist, published a verse in which Dr Maclean appeared as 'I':

> Who'd peruse their dull books, or, for medical skill,
> To their fountains of learning repair?
> If my practice is bold, I have licence to kill,
> By a vote of the East India chair.
>
> Tho' the King, Lords, and Commons, the State and the Church,
> To expel dread contagion unite,
> With brave Campbell, and Moseley, Reece, Lipscomb and Birch,
> I'll diffuse it from envy and spite.

Maclean challenged Blair, but Blair ignored him. He said Maclean was neither a gentleman nor a 'man of honour'. Maclean replied by applying brute force to lock Blair in a room, threatening him with assault. Blair brought a criminal prosecution. Maclean was found guilty, 'ordered to give security to keep the peace for twelve months – himself in 200 l. and two friends in 100 l. each.'

The magazine's failure was largely due to its stridency. Questions it raised, like the permanency of vaccination, were entirely reasonable. Nor would vaccination have a clear and untroubled future, with severe smallpox epidemics ahead. Naturally, Jenner feared and disliked the periodical, but had it achieved a better editorial balance and perhaps maintained its original stance against quackery, the *Medical Observer* could have become a useful whetstone for establishment knives.

Jenner wrote to Sir Thomas Bernard on 1 April 1810 that he still felt 'that state of dejection which renders me unfit to perform my ordinary duties'. Toward the end of April, nevertheless, he described to James Moore a Gloucestershire scheme to put an end to variolation in the county. The idea was 'to place every man in a questionable point of view who presumes to inoculate for the smallpox. . . .Some of the variolo-vaccinists have already abjured their old bad habits, and joined the standard before it was half hoisted.' The Gloucester Vaccine Association agreed not to sanction variolation except in extreme situations, such as an outbreak of smallpox when no vaccine was available. Its thirty-one signatories included Baron, Trye and Charles Cooke in Gloucester; Charles Parry, elder son of Jenner's old friend, and Mr Newell in Cheltenham; Henry Jenner and J. C. Hands in Berkeley, and sixteen others from various communities. Why Edward Jenner was not a signatory I cannot imagine.

Mrs Jenner was again confined to her bed, this time by severe rheumatism. Pruen paid them a visit and arranged for his wife to go to Berkeley. Now Jenner thought her visit must be postponed for 'about a month, when perhaps the weather may be warm enough for Mrs J. to go out with her into the open air, a gratification I believe she has not once enjoyed since the autumn.' But on 5 May Catherine was still confined to 'her apartments up stairs'.

Plans for new building in Berkeley were under way in April. Robert Ferryman had designed a brewery house for Jenner, who approved of some building he had done for Colonel Kingscote. He wrote to Pruen that he did not like Ferryman's plans for his own house, however.

In May he told Pruen he would be pleased to buy Thomas Newell's stables and coach house. Newell was not only his neighbour in St George's Place, but one of Cheltenham's leading surgeons. Jenner thought that if he needed still more space he could build on his own land, but questioned whether he had not in fact already bought a small adjoining tract. A fortnight later he had had a favourable report from his man Stibbs: 'I shall certainly accept of Mr. Newell's offer.' The money was available for immediate payment. Pruen appears again to have acted as Jenner's agent in these transactions. Jenner knew Newell, who was one of the pro-vaccinists. They could certainly have dealt with each other directly. Perhaps it was awkward because of their professional status. There is no indication whether Pruen received a fee or acted simply in recognition of the material support he had had from his friend.

On 10 May the diarist William Davies married Sarah Buckle of Chepstow, an event which his uncle would have missed, though with regret. The next day William Davies senior noted in his household accounts that Jenner called on his youngest son, Edward, who had been ill. But Jenner's own health was troubling him. He had complained to Sir Thomas Bernard of the lasting effects he felt from Edward junior's death. They were neither simple nor slight. Cascades roared in his ears, and he felt a heaviness in his head. 'The constant disposition to drowsiness is a lamentable tax upon me,' he wrote to Baron. 'I feel lively from breakfast time till about one o'clock, when the signal of acidity in my stomach is the signal also for nodding.' Finally, he asked Baron to accompany him on a consultative visit to Parry in Bath. Baron agreed, but then could not. Jenner went on his own, about 5 June. 'I have been cupped, calomeled, salted, etc etc,' and he thought himself somewhat better, he told Baron. Immediately after his return in the evening of 9 June, he wrote to Pruen: 'My sentence is as follows. Cupping, blistering, purging, water drinking, a long journey thro' untrodden regions, & a cessation of all mental concerns.' Where these untrodden regions may have been remains a mystery, because, in the event, he decided to accept Bernard's invitation to spend a few days amongst his friends in London.

This was the first sign of the nervous illnesses that were to afflict Jenner from time to time for the rest of his life. It recalls his abnormal response to 'imaginary noises. . .and sudden jars' following his long convalescence from variolation at the age of eight. Whether there was any connection between these symptoms and the stroke that finally killed him thirteen years later, no one can say. Strokes are physical events, of course, in which a group of nerve cells in the brain are suddenly deprived of nutrients and die. The symptoms that Jenner experienced in 1810 – roaring in the ears, heaviness, stomach acidity and uncontrollable drowsiness – reflected the depression caused by the death of his son. The pressures he had felt from the quarrel with John Walker, his sense of betrayal by the National Vaccine Establishment and the opposition to vaccination may all have added to the severity of his symptoms, but they were nothing new. They were public pressures arising from Jenner's public responsibilities, and they involved him in actions that left him uncertain: 'was it not an insult?' he had asked William Blair about the behaviour of the NVE. Yet he had weathered these storms and his own misgivings, drawing strength through the family umbilicus.

In a sense he was freed from the amorphous and ambivalent stresses of the recent past by the immediate, all-embracing, simple grief of Edward's death. It was a godsend, forcing his mind back to the verities of family love, life and death. If he had doubts about his behaviour in the professional arena, he had none about his relationship to his son. But he was Edward Jenner and could never dodge the responsibilities imposed on him by his own discoveries. Was his mourning extended and his depression deepened by the added stress engendered by the release from ambivalence brought to him through Edward's death? He had lived with the conflict between family and public duties for fifteen years, but this new dimension to the conflict made him ill.

In the midst of his depression he may have felt another factor working. Not only was Mrs Jenner unwell, but she lived in isolation. Whatever the exact level of sympathy between husband and wife, Edward's death does not appear to have enhanced it. Could that rootlessness, sensed so strongly while he waited in London for government to act on the NVE in 1808, now be reaching into his family relationships too? If that were true, then his anomy was understandable, and the physical symptoms reflected an emotional dislocation much more profound than the grief that had triggered it.

Jenner's letter to Baron written shortly after he returned from Bath contains an unexpected analogy which may be relevant. He had enclosed a letter 'from Filkin, surgeon of the Gloucester regiment of Militia. We must not repine at the ill success he has met with. He is on that barren kind of land where science has not yet begun to vegetate. Poor Chatterton, by accident, sprang up on this soil; but he was soon rooted up and flung away like a weed.' There could have been some other Chatterton, a scientist or doctor, but I think Jenner meant Thomas Chatterton, the Bristol poet who had committed suicide in 1770, aged eighteen. Worgan had been a poor Bristol poet. Filkin's 'ill success' almost certainly had to do with the spread of vaccination, and Jenner saw a parallel between his own striving and that of the two unfulfilled poets who had died young, like Edward – a complex, three-element equation: Poets <> Edward junior<> Edward senior.

Judging from the dates on which William Davies drank tea with his uncle at the Chauntry, Jenner went to London on or about 19 June and returned by 2 July. No details of the visit have survived, with one exception. The Earl of Berkeley had fallen ill in London. Sir Gilbert Blane, Physician-in-Ordinary to the Prince of Wales, was his doctor, but Blane implied in a note to the Countess that he had enlisted Jenner, doubtless because he knew Jenner would return to Berkeley at about the same time as the Earl. On 17 July Parry and Jenner signed a bulletin sent to Carlton House, residence of the Prince of Wales: 'Lord Berkeley has pass'd a better night, and has had no return of Fever this morning'. The Earl died early in August, and his *post mortem* examination was signed on 9 August by C. H. Parry, E. Jenner and Henry Jenner.

During July Jenner had arranged for Pruen to meet the Countess of Berkeley. Since Pruen was then contemplating the demise of his newspaper, it is possible that Jenner set up the interview in connection with a living that her husband had at his disposal.

William Davies welcomed Dr and Mrs Jenner, Catherine and Robert to tea on 23 July, the first indication that Catherine senior had recovered her health. From 28 August to 11 September he and his uncle sat with the magistrates' court in Berkeley. Soon afterward the family returned to Cheltenham for the first time in about eighteen months. Their house was no doubt made ready for them by the housekeeper, a Mrs Larner.

On 12 September James Moore wrote to Jenner acknowledging a letter, now missing, to the NVE Board. He urged that Jenner come to London for the board meeting on 17 September, and commented on Jenner's observations on hydatids in relation to the origins of tubercles. Moore himself was engaged in recruiting medical personnel for the Life Guards, still battling in Spain, and wondered again whether he would have to volunteer. The letter concluded on a dour note: 'The increased mortality by Smallpox is a sad Sting; our Stations improve yet Deaths have augmented lately. This I trust will not continue.' According to the London Bills of Mortality, smallpox deaths were then running at about thirty per week. During the next year, 1811, Baron said, deaths had fallen to five or six a week, an improvement which seems to be borne out by figures for the parish of St Leonard, Shoreditch:

Year	Total deaths	Smallpox deaths
1809	1453	65
1810	1867	159
1811	1569	34
1812	1679	143

What stands out from these very partial statistics, however, is the fluctuations in smallpox deaths, which was much more extreme than fluctuations in total deaths although they rise and fall together. In 1813 a Glasgow doctor, Robert Watt, published figures for that city showing that smallpox deaths amongst children under ten – the majority of deaths from smallpox – had fallen from 19.85 per cent of all deaths in 1783 to 3.9 per cent in 1813. Deaths from other causes had risen (for example, measles from .93 per cent of all deaths to 10.76 per cent in the same period), so that total mortality remained about the same. Perhaps the Shoreditch figures reveal similar trends, but that does not explain the fluctuations. Possibly a decline in deaths meant that fewer people were frightened by the risk to themselves or their families of smallpox and so neglected to have their children vaccinated, a course of events that could be reversed when smallpox deaths rose.

Jenner did not accept the invitation to attend the board meeting, but went to Cheltenham. On 23 September he described the season and his own outlook in a letter to his sister, Mrs Black:

> Cheltenham is still full of good company, and the usual round of dissipations are going forwards, such as Plays, Balls, Routs, Public Breakfasts, Concerts etc, but these things have lost their relish with

me. However my professional Calls keep both my mind & Body in activity & I find myself the better for being forc'd to rouse myself.

He was seeking lodgings, he said, for their nephew, Edward Davies. The young man, recently a father, had placed himself in his uncle's care. Jenner does not name his illness, but the tone implies consumption: 'I ardently hope his Journey may be productive of every advantage, but these hopes are certainly blended with Tears'. The nephew survived for many years, suggesting that his uncle's fears were groundless.

On 4 October William Davies junior breakfasted with his uncle in Cheltenham, no doubt to discuss Dr Jenner's business affairs. Two weeks later Jenner wrote to him. Some land at Rockhampton was for sale on which Jenner had an informal prior claim. Because he had not had the opportunity to inspect it, he had decided to forgo his option. 'Notwithstanding Lord Berkeley's premature Draft on his Tenants, I hope you will bring me a good lump of Money, and the Accounts that we may settle everything of this sort. Has H.[enry?] J.[enner?] liquidated any more of the debt at the Berkeley Bank? I fear not.' There was more about property, this time in Berkeley, in a letter dated 1 November to Mrs Black. He had resolved to reclaim a house recently occupied by a 'troublesome Fellow' who had taken it after the departure of Jenner's 'old Neighbour.' A year later, however, the man was still in occupation: 'out with him – ', Jenner directed William Davies.

He was also delighted to tell Mrs Black how well Cheltenham suited Mrs Jenner: 'She has not been once on the Invalid List since She has been here. A Walk of two miles seems nothing to her, and sometimes she walks three miles before dinner [that is, in the morning].'

At 4 a.m. on 13 November 1810, William Davies senior received 'An Express from Henry Jenner'. Mrs Black had fallen downstairs, cutting her head and knocking herself insensible. Anne Davies left Eastington at 4.30, but her sister never regained consciousness. She died in the evening of the 14th, aged seventy-nine. Jenner received word on the same day 'of the death of my beloved sister, Mrs. Black. . .in her 80th year.' It is ironic that the two letters which provided some information about these months in Cheltenham were amongst the few addressed to Mrs Black, as she was always called in the eighteenth-century manner. Although after the death of her husband, she lived in Berkeley, she appears to have kept herself to herself. William Davies junior stayed with her occasionally on his trips to Berkeley, but neither her brother Edward nor his wife were close, nor did she often attend family parties of Jenners and Davieses. Yet little Ned Jenner had looked upon her, with their brother Stephen, as the authorities *in loco parentis* from the age of five. Baron said he was much affected by her death, and he did return briefly to Berkeley for her funeral. He and William Davies senior were her executors.

Later that November Jenner suggested to James Moore that the district around Berkeley would provide good evidence of the value of vaccination. The NVE should send questionnaires to all medical men asking when they had first practised vaccination, the number they had vaccinated, their opinion of its value and whether it was harmful, the longest period that had transpired between vaccination and exposure to smallpox, and their estimate of the effect of vaccination on smallpox mortality. Had the survey been done, the results might have provided a useful contrast to experience in London and other cities. Jenner was gratified to receive a letter from Professor Thompson of Edinburgh on 15 December, which praised the role of vaccination in controlling a recent outbreak of smallpox and congratulated him on his work.

William Davies visited his uncle in Cheltenham from 29 November to 13 December, though he probably did not stay at St George's Place. A stay of two weeks suggests a holiday, possibly in the company of his new wife. Sophia Davies, his sister-in-law, was also in Cheltenham at the time, under Dr Jenner's care. During the first week of December she suffered a miscarriage, but again she seems to have recovered well. At the end of that week Jenner accepted the office of godfather to Edward Jenner Murray, Charles Murray's sixth son. In December he was also elected to a Masonic office for the coming year.

Beginning in February 1811 with a handful of earlier notations dated simply '1810', William Davies junior kept detailed accounts of payments he made for his uncle and of income he received on Jenner's behalf. The entries under 'Dr. Jenner to the Revd. W. Davies [that is, money owed to Davies]' began at the first page and continued chronologically until the month of Jenner's death. In the manner of a period when paper was expensive, moreover, 'The Revd W. Davies to Dr. Jenner' began at the back upside down and continued forward through the book. William Davies paid out for his uncle advances to workpeople and tradesmen, annuities as an executor of family wills, interest on loans or investments to George Jenner among others, highway assessments, land and borough taxes, poor-rates, church rates and tithes, rents, subscriptions such as two guineas annually to the Gloucester Infirmary, and payments to dinner funds set up by the Masons and the Gloucestershire magistrates to pay for their social occasions, plus dozens of miscellaneous disbursements for wine, cheeses, groceries and household needs. On the other hand, Davies collected on Jenner's behalf interest on loans – for example, £27 half-yearly during 1810, 1811 and 1812 on a loan he had had from his uncle; rents from Jenner's tenants; and a limited number of miscellaneous receipts, such as 'Arrears for the House in the Lane 5/5/0' and for cider from Jenner's apples received by himself and his two brothers, at £4-14-6. At suitable intervals, usually in January each year, the accounts were balanced. Like Davies's diaries, his meticulous account book unveils the details of Jenner's life. Jenner lacked the orderliness, the time or the desire to keep records. Baron said he had 'a peculiar horror of arithmetical questions', especially those having to do with money. He was blessed with William Davies junior, truly a clerk with an affectionate family tie and the honesty ascribed to his cloth often more in hope than happenstance. Everything indicates that Jenner appreciated his luck.

For the present he carried on his practice in Cheltenham. On 5 January 1811, he wrote to a patient who lived in Bristol on terms that would have graced a travel brochure about his adopted town:

> I am almost tempted to say, will not Miss Wait be benefitted by a change of scene, at least by that of changing the air of Bristol, a murky City for the Æther of Cheltenham? Our Springs too might prove salubrious. In days of old you know, we could reckon but on one, now we boast of eleven. Our Chalybeate Spring rivals that of Tunbridge, and our Sulphurated Spa, the famous Water of the North. It is really a very extraordinary Fact, that all the Medicinal Waters of any celebrity in the Island are to be found concentrated in this little Spot, Bath excepted, & to this I attach no more value than that which flows from my Tea Kettle.

This chosen retirement came to an end in March, when he answered a summons to appear briefly in London. The House of Lords had begun its hearings into the succession to the Earl of Berkeley's title and estates. Jenner was asked now to testify on the signatures in the Berkeley parish marriage registers. 'In an enquiry of such importance nothing could equal the carelessness of the Person who was appointed to shew me the Registers previously to my appearing before the House,' he wrote to Caleb Parry on 19 March, just after his return to Cheltenham; '. . .every night since, I have been summon'd to the Bar in my sleep and, awoke trembling before the Wig of the Lord Chancellor. Such nerves as mine are not worth owning.' He told Parry that he would soon have to go again in response to 'a kind of Demi-royal intimation'. Some time during the spring he was ill, perhaps with a heavy cold. It was the first week in June before his next journey, but it lasted about five weeks.

On 25 March, according to the dating of William Davies junior, Jenner wrote him a cryptic note:

> Dear William
>
> The Bearer Wm. Clarke, has made out a Case to me which I think if he has stated it fairly, entitles him to the consideration of a Magistrate. Being imperfectly acquainted with matters of this kind, I turn the affair over to you, for which favor you will of course return your best thanks.
>
> Truly Yrs.   E Jenner

The note is weighted with irony. William Clarke was a Berkeley labourer, probably illiterate and, one suspects, a rogue. Two years earlier, Jenner had wanted to buy some timber from him, but he was 'unwilling to set a price upon it alleging frivolous pretences for so doing. This Mr Clarke is a fellow newly risen from the mud. My late Brother kept the Family from starving, & he being now beyond the reach of his insolence, the Puppy takes every opportunity of shewing it to me.' On this occasion perhaps he had approached Jenner for money, under circumstances, known also to Davies, connecting Clarke with some villainy, if not overt blackmail. Jenner's note was intended as evidence that Clarke was indeed guilty. He could be less than amiable when crossed.

The Clarke note may have been connected with another, also dated 1811 by Davies, written from Berkeley. Jenner returned to Berkeley only during April and May 1811, and the abrupt departure was probably his second journey to London. This note was addressed to Davies as magistrate:

> My Orchard & Garden have been plundered unmercifully last night – & the young Trees torn sadly. Having some scent of the property I shd. be glad to pursue it with a search Warrant, if Your Worship's Honor would have the goodness to grant it. I am necessitated to leave Berkeley at one o'clock but hope to see you here in good time.

This time the irony has become mere playfulness, but perhaps betokens a chase after the same alleged culprit. The trees in question may have been more precious because they had been obtained with some difficulty. In January 1810 Jenner had written to Paytherus: 'I shall not let you alone till you have procured for me some of the Apple Trees that bear the transparent Apples such as you brought to your Table. . . .They seem to be a Breed from the Siberian Crab'.

Mrs Jenner remained at Berkeley when Edward went up to town the second time. His daughter and Robert were with him in London, at 9 Cockspur Street.

Jenner gave evidence on the Berkeley succession before the House of Lords, but his nervous state had deteriorated since his rather lighthearted letter to Caleb Parry in March. 'For many weeks before the meeting I began to be agitated, and, as it approached, I was actually deprived both of appetite and sleep: and when the day came, I was obliged to deaden my sensibility and gain courage by brandy and opium.' Jenner's behaviour recalls his inability to give evidence to the Committee on Vaccination of the House of Commons in 1802. It may have been exacerbated by his sympathy for the Countess of Berkeley, who hoped against all probability that her eldest son would be declared the heir. He also had personal cause for distress just then, of which more in a moment, but the major factor was his neurotic stage fright.

By this time, however, following the bout of nerves after Edward's death, he was beginning to see these nervous afflictions as parts of a whole cloth, a diagnosis with which it is hard to quarrel. The stage fright only confirms that conflict between public persona and private uncertainty underlay the whole syndrome. Jenner ought to have spoken out like the Old Testament God of William Blake, finger pointing to sin, but his omniscience hesitated and his voice quavered before mere mortal authority.

Later that year the Committee of Privileges of the House of Lords named the Berkeleys' fourth son, Thomas Moreton, the first born in wedlock, as the legal heir. Out of loyalty to his eldest brother William, the Earl's favourite as well as the Countess's, he never assumed the title. It fell into disuse until, a century later, it passed to a grandson of Admiral Berkeley. William inherited Berkeley Castle and the estates, and later became Earl Fitzhardinge, a new title.

Jenner's personal distress rose out of yet another apparent vaccination failure involving a patient of his. The Honourable Robert Grosvenor, eldest child of the Earl of Grosvenor, was then ten. Jenner had vaccinated him along with two siblings in infancy. On 26 May 1811, Robert fell ill with a severe dose of smallpox. Jenner visited him on 8 June. He was attended by Sir Henry Halford and Sir Walter Farquhar, and recovered 'more rapidly than usual', according to these eminent physicians. The other two children remained healthy.

The fact that this child was heir to an earldom gave the case great prominence. Several other similar failures at the same time added to public alarm. The National Vaccine Establishment undertook a special investigation and prepared a report on the subject. The Board stressed the milder, shorter course of the disease – a result of prior vaccination, as they quite rightly pointed out. The report also called attention to the growing body of evidence, now it was being sought, that smallpox itself could occur a second time. Undoubtedly, the Grosvenor case further disrupted the halting progress of vaccination, with inevitable results.

Jenner wrote about the case to several correspondents. To a patient, Miss Calcraft, he said:

> take a wide, comprehensive view of Vaccination & then ask yourself what is this Case? You will find it a speck, a mere microscopic speck, on the page which contains the History of the Vaccine discovery. . . .now this single, solitary instance has occurr'd, all my past labors. . .are forgotten, & I am held up by many, perhaps the majority of the higher Classes, as an object of derision & Contempt. . . .

Grosvenor was not a 'single, solitary instance'. Nevertheless, Jenner's self-pity went only a degree or two over the top. Most of the assertions – the mildness of the smallpox, second cases of smallpox – were valid. Toward the end of the letter he wrote, 'the safest & best test is re-vaccination'. What a tragedy that he could not break free of his early conviction that, excepting the rare individual subject to smallpox after cowpox, vaccination lasts a lifetime. From a purely personal standpoint, his inability to see even such a prominent failure in its proper perspective was perhaps a greater tragedy. Dr Parry had written a few months earlier: 'The great business is accomplished, and the blessing is ready for those who choose to avail themselves of it; and with regard to those who reject it, the evil be on their own heads'. But Parry had not the responsibility of invention and could no more feel its weight than can the sane person comprehend jealousy.

At the end of June Jenner wrote from Cockspur Street to Pruen that the Berkeley case had ended. 'The Sol[icito]r General paid a compliment to your discernment. . .by coinciding in opinion with you, that Lady B.[erkeley] had been cajoled.' The purpose of the letter was to offer a subscription 'for two or three hundred, or so' to the turnpike roads then being advertised in the Cheltenham paper. Meanwhile, he had attended a levee at 'Charlton House', residence of the Prince Regent: 'I was one of those who had temerity to risk the squeeze. . .& who had the good luck to come off with uncrack'd ribs. Great was the splendour, but the sight of the Paintings delighted me most. Such an assemblage from the Pencils of the best Masters, my eyes never beheld before. You should have been there.'

William Davies junior called on him in Cheltenham on 19 July. Mrs Jenner had already come from Berkeley to join her husband. Davies called again on 2 August, and then until October the record is blank.

On 3 October, Jenner travelled the eight miles to Gloucester. His friend Charles Brandon Trye had become seriously ill, and he died four days later. Trye had been senior surgeon to the Gloucester Royal Infirmary, a post filled by vote of the subscribers who included both William Davieses, members of the Berkeley clan, Colonel Kingscote, Henry Hicks of Eastington, Mr Bromedge on whose farm Jenner had observed the behaviour of cuckoo chicks twenty-three years before, and several other small landowners near Berkeley. Jenner favoured the election of a Mr Fletcher. He asked William Davies junior to canvass locally on Fletcher's behalf. In November he told Baron that he would 'do what I can to keep the Berkeley Men at home, if they will not vote with us.' A few days later Fletcher was duly elected, with 101 votes to 95 for his only rival, a Mr Cother.

The Jenners returned to Berkeley in early February 1812 after 'an anxious. . .residence at Cheltenham', which Baron also characterized as 'unusually protracted'. The latter phrase was overstated, and he gave no explanation at all for the former. On 12 February, Jenner told Pruen that he 'was again seized with the Influenza which has handled me much more severely than on the first attack'. Perhaps Mrs Jenner had also been ill in

Cheltenham, but there was more to it. Eight months later Jenner told Pruen:

– I have no longer a relish for Cheltenham – on the contrary I nauseate it. At the instigation of a man who is under considerable obligations to me, a building has been erected on the corner of Paceys Garden, close to my front door on St. G. Place. It bears all the appearance of a necessary House [a public lavatory], though used as a Tailor's Shop. Not a Creature could step forward & tell me anything about it till it was finish'd; but when they want the Money to expend on the improvement of the Town, then I can hear from them fast enough.

He repeated his distaste for the town, founded apparently on disgruntlement with its rapid and unplanned growth, in a letter to Pruen dated 25 February 1813: 'Cheltenham does look uncommonly dull & gloomy. Its Physiognomy is totally chang'd. Every man you meet looks as if he were going to be hang'd.' In any case, he did not take up residence in Cheltenham again until late August 1813.

Shortly after he returned to Berkeley, the National Vaccine Establishment claimed Jenner's attention. He wrote to Moore:

I rejoice at seeing so distinguished a person as Sir F[rancis] M.[ilman] at the head of vaccine affairs. We wanted firmness and decision, and I now see that we shall have it. . . .when I go to town I shall have the honour of waiting on him, and hope he will indulge me with a full conversation on the subject, particularly that part of it which relates to the conduct of the first Board, the cause of my seceding, etc, etc.

Sir Francis Milman had succeeded Sir Lucas Pepys in the presidency of the Royal College of Physicians of London and, therefore, ex officio, at the NVE. To Jenner any change would have been welcome, no doubt. He either did not realize or would not believe that the medical establishment now preferred to have him on the outside. They were prepared to be polite, as Oxford soon demonstrated, but unbending, as the Physicians themselves revealed. Baron suggested that his relations with the NVE improved, however, and he supplied reports on vaccination progress in Havana, Caracas, Milan, Vienna, Madras, France and Russia for the 1812 annual report. If so, the improvement was short-lived. On 17 October he wrote in his diary, 'The New Institution in L.[eicester] S.[quare, address of the NVE] bears every mark of a power arbitrarily assumed & capriciously applied.' The nature of this tyranny has not come to light.

Twice during February Jenner called on Anne Davies. They were probably professional visits, but on the second, he and the Davieses attended the christening of Stephen, son of Edward and Sophia Davies. William Davies and Edward Jenner were godfathers and Mrs Davies, godmother. Mrs Jenner was not mentioned.

Jenner's old affection for the local beauty spot, Barrow Hill, revived just now, perhaps partly at the instigation of Baron. In any case Baron was one of the members of what Jenner called the Barrow Hill Club. Edward Gardner, Dr William Hickes and a relative newcomer, Revd Robert Halifax of Standish, met with Jenner and Baron to climb the hill, undertake a little casual fossil-collecting and enjoy the view. Afterward they had a meal at the Bell Inn, Frampton. Or at least that seems to have been the intended programme, but there is no evidence of how often it unfolded.

Later in March Jenner complained to Marcet that being a magistrate took time away from 'other purposes'. Yet there was little to compel his attention. Naturally, vaccination claimed some time. In February a nineteen-year-old recruit in the Gloucester Militia, Robert Stevens, had come to him for vaccination. He had a prior skin infection which, Jenner wrote in his notebook, prevented both cowpox and smallpox when he was later exposed to it. He prepared a package of points bearing dried vaccine for Dr Sacco, Director of Vaccination for the Cisalpine Republic, and arranged with the London art dealer, Colnaghi, to transmit them to his agent in Milan.

In May he asked William Davies junior for a 'few specimens of the Gibralter Rock', adding, 'We held a conference & it is thought that it will be most prudent to postpone the Investigation till Monday next.' Without more information, I cannot guess whether this was a serious reference to some weighty secret or, as seems more probable, a jokey characterization of a forthcoming discussion on geology. Years before, Jenner had compared the Thornbury strata to those at Gibraltar. The letter also referred in passing to the senseless assassination of the Prime Minister, Spencer Perceval.

On 26 June Jenner and his younger son, Robert, dined with William Davies senior. Robert may have been travelling to or from the home of his tutor, Mr Joyce, in Henley with his father for company. Joyce had been curate of Rockhampton and had tutored Edward as well as Robert before obtaining the living at Henley. Robert was now fifteen. When he was eight, Jenner had called him a chip off the old block. The next year in a letter to Joyce, he wrote: 'Your old Pupil Bob is become. . .a very wild Boy'. He was then planning to 'consign him', Jenner said, to the care of 'a Mr Bayley, a Clergyman at Gloster'. The next glimpse of Robert proved to be a prognostication. It consists of a draft drawn by his father on John Croome, his Berkeley lawyer, for £50, payable to the eleven-year-old boy. Perhaps the money was to be delivered back to his father, but in light of their future relationship, dominated by Jenner's excessive if understandable concern for the boy's health and their conflicts over money, it is at least possible that Robert had been given the responsibility of paying this large sum to his tutor. During the summer of 1811 Jenner had given Robert a holiday in London during which he enjoyed 'all the sights from the Hut of the poor Hottentot in Picadilly to the splendor of Prince Regents Palace in Pall Mall.' In his diary Jenner wrote a quatrain to Robert:

> To B.[ob] J.[enner] on hearing him say he should like to go into the army or navy.
>
> > You'd better learn Mens lives to save
> > and Bobus Draught or Pill them,
> > Than seek the bloody Field or Wave
> > and like a Savage kill them.

In the sense that he too was prepared to drift through life, Robert was a chip off the old block, but in no other way. He had none of that powerful inner call to duty that had characterized his father. Edward Jenner had found a vocation by the time he was fifteen. For both the call and the vocation Robert, like millions of others, was prepared to substitute authority. But of course it was wartime; the old world that had shaped his father had disappeared, added to which they were divided by almost fifty years. Conflict and distrust were almost inevitable.

Later that summer of 1812, Colonel Berkeley suffered from what was almost certainly a severe case of gonorrhoea. 'The discharge fm. the Urethra, after a suspension of days, is again become copious,' Jenner noted in his diary on 18 August. The next day he was 'free from pain & every unpleasant Symptom – discharge continues copious'. But then the Colonel, having eaten and drunk normally, again suffered 'spasm about the Neck of the Bladder' and retention. Jenner noted a further prescription in October, and the Colonel paid him £50 on 2 November 'for attendance during his late illness'.

In September he travelled to Gloucester to call on a Mrs Colchester: 'She has a large Tumor'. When he called on the lady again a week later, he had enlisted Mr Naylor, a local surgeon. This time he noted, 'She has an immense abcess on the right side which appears encysted & to originate from an Hydatid on the surface of the Liver.' For these calls he received eight guineas.

His principal concern during these weeks, however, must have been the health of his sister, Anne Davies. On 7 August she suffered the first of a series of strokes. Mr Darke of Eastington was in attendance, but Jenner called that day and on the 19th and 27th. On 5 September he went to Stonehouse to visit Louisa Davies, wife of the eldest son, Robert. In the evening he stopped at Eastington, where Mrs Jenner had spent the day with her sister-in-law. Five days later he and Catherine called, and she kept poor William Davies company for the day. Anne Davies died on 25 September. Her husband noted the death of 'My dearest Friend'. She seems to have been a warm-hearted, hospitable and kindly woman, perhaps because some record of her was left by her husband, perhaps because she had three sons each of whom formed stable and apparently loving families, perhaps because Catherine Jenner liked her. Jenner felt her death more because she was the last of his brothers and sisters.

Her death was the fifth reason he gave Pruen why 'my spirits suffer the lowest ebbings you can conceive'. Fourth was the apparent success of Napoleon's invasion of Russia; third, the delicate state of Mrs Jenner's health; second, his dislike for Cheltenham. But the first reason for his depression really raises the eyebrows: '. . .by nature I was never framed' for the solitude of retirement to Berkeley. What had he cried out for during the London years? Where had he dreamed of being, felt his roots to grip, his life? I hope Pruen replied with reference to his modest inconsistency, but somehow I doubt it. Jenner suffered because he was no longer at the centre of things. For the wrong reasons and without intending it to work that way, he had cut himself off from events that concerned him most. 'Two persons dead of Smallpox here!' he fairly shouted at Baron from Cheltenham in November 1811: 'One thro' the inattention of Mr. Freeman who is spreading the disease from a total indifference about the Parish Poor over whom he presides as Doctor.' Charles Murray had received a letter dated 14 September 1812 from Edward Rigby, a Norwich doctor, about an outbreak of smallpox caused by an amateur variolator – 'not a Norwich Man. . .He comes from London'. Perhaps Murray passed the information to Jenner because he knew Jenner had corresponded with Rigby, but Jenner saw that he now circled at the periphery of great events that he had originated, like Pluto flung off by the sun.

In fact, he had again been less than fit for several months. He wrote to Murray on 30 July 1812 (the letter in which he mentioned correspondence with Rigby): 'This langour, of which you have often heard me complain; and corresponding depressions of mind, with aversion to everything like application pursue me so closely, that I have now but short intervals of comparative ease & comfort. My mind I fear has been a little overdone.' Dyspepsia played an ill defined role in his acedia. It 'has been the constant resident of [my stomach] these thirty years', he wrote to Pruen, 'bidding defiance to all attempts at ejectment.' That would have been as long ago as 1782, and would connect dyspepsia to the early frustrations of his affair with Catherine. Early in 1813 he gave Dr Parry several colourful details:

> I don't know that there is much the matter with me, but if I look at my Tongue in a morning before breakfast I am sure to find it highly tinted with yellow. I first perceived it at Cheltenham & shewd it to Dr. Charles [Parry?] – Pho! said he, this is nothing but a dye from the oranges you were sucking yesterday. Well – when I came home, I look'd again & beheld it just the same; tho' I had eaten no oranges; and still it goes on without any diminution. I am cautious as to diet; but

even with this caution, Dyspepsia haunts me. Whether this is simply the cause, or whether this yellow secretion arises from any incorrect action in the Hepatic System I know not.

Jenner was not simply hypochondriacal. Back in 1789 he had written to John Clinch: '. . .it has long been my creed that stomach is the governor of the whole machine, the mind as well as the body.' And to Parry he wrote again in 1816: '. . .you know it is a doctrine in my School, that the Stomach is the first – the root, the foundation, the Governor of the whole family.' His view was not strikingly original, but it was a theory, not merely a complaint. In June 1813 he wrote to Murray:

For some months I have been in very ill health. Low, nervous, debilitated & incapable half my time of attending to my ordinary occupations. But what annoys me most is a palpitation of the Heart. My medical attendants assure me that all my symptoms arise from indigestion & that I must go to Cheltenham.

Today he might be told that he suffered from stress, the pressures of everyday life like job dissatisfaction (worries about vaccination), family problems (a sick wife, restless children), bereavement, and that he needed a holiday (Cheltenham). The diagnosis is not in question. Jenner's bears comparison with that of modern medicine. He suffered from depression and indecision, associated with indigestion and mild palpitation. The causes were a complex mismatch between roles and self-image.

Jenner's medicine, in that vast arena beyond the infectious diseases, lacked the sophistication that has come with 150 years of technological improvements in the laboratory, but it sought for cause and effect in the same way. In his mind he approached every medical problem as subject to experimental solution, eventually. Hunter had taught him, and he could no more ignore observation and hypothesis in general practice than he could with vaccination. His doubts about his own liver functions reflect a broader awareness of this common and persistent disorder. On 26 September 1812, the day after the loss of his sister, he wrote to Alexander Marcet:

We talk of Chronic inflammation of the Liver. This is vague kind of language – How it commences, what system of Hepatic Vessells it first attacks, how it makes its progress & leads on to Scirrhus [literally: scarring visible in diseased liver at autopsy], has not, as far as I know, been yet explain'd. I think I have made something out. . . .

He proposed to write a paper for publication, a task he never performed.

I will just mention that there are two causes of scirrhosity each having a distinct source; the one arising from Hydatids, the other from inflammation of the internal Coats of the biliary Ducts. My observations have been drawn from the dissection of diseas'd Quadrapeds; but the general appearance of the Liver & its effects in exciting other diseases. . .will not I believe be found to differ from the human.

The hydatids proved to be a will-o'-the-wisp. Inflammation was more to the point, but what was its cause? Jenner could not have known of chemical poisoning, for example by alcohol, let alone of bacteria and viruses. Marcet replied in October, but the letter did not survive. Jenner's diary records another reference to the subject from a Mr Mountjoy, Surgeon, of Wotton, and six months later he wrote again to Marcet that he had been making 'Inquiries into the origin of Tumors & schirrhosities of the Liver'.

Diabetes was another disease that he was called upon to treat, almost always without success. In September and again in November 1812 he called four times to see a Mrs Hale, a woman of about thirty. Jenner's diagnosis was *Diabetes insipidus*, a less common form of the disease in which urine volume increases substantially but blood sugar is not elevated. Following the September calls he wrote:

> What part of the animal Machine is deranged to occasion this strange disorder – Where shall we fix the point? The Sympathies [symptoms] are numerous, but where is the origin of the disease? – Is it in the Brain? This organ is evidently affected in the case before me, Mrs Hale's, & even her limbs are sometimes affected with torpor, sometimes with convulsive motions. In Hysteria, where the brain is evidently affected, we see Diabetes Insipidus, tho' recurring at intervals only. Is it in the Stomach? Its habits become changed & are preternatural – Mrs Hales appetite & thirst are insatiable. Is the Chyme or is the Chyle [products of digestion prior to absorption from the intestines, but Jenner meant also secretions of stomach and intestines] imperfectly form'd? Is it in the Lacteals [ducts also now called lymphatics, which carry away absorbed fat]? Do they devour their food <u>raw</u>, that is, before it is properly prepared for them [the Lacteals]? Have they in themselves a digestive power, (considering them as animals or part of an animal) which is defective. Are the Kidneys themselves defective in their secretory offices?

Some of these questions remain unanswered today.

Diseases of the skin were among the most common medical problems. Jenner had a general theory which he explained in October to the Wiltshire MP, T. G. Estcourt. The patient was Mrs Estcourt.

> . . .diseases of the skin are often call'd into existence for the protection of some vital organ which is dispos'd to go into decay. The Lungs & the Liver seem to be those which require the protection most frequently. Erysipelas, among a great variety of others, is one of these Shields, & when it has appeard & disappeard, and finally has been lost, at the

same time other maladies coming on, I have commonly found pleasant results from exciting some artificial disease of the Skin, by blistering, the opening of [?] absesses etc etc.

If they had any beneficial effect at all, blisters worked as counter-irritants. They might be especially useful, for example, if the patient suffered a pain in the chest from inflammation of the lungs, when rest might conceivably help nature. Any itchy or painful skin eruption might serve the same purpose. Although Jenner's theory was otherwise wide of the mark, it did propose rational explanations linking two disease states, erysipelas and lung complaints, and an important and popular form of treatment.

His diary for December 1812 lists his cases day by day. The first, on 27 November, included two vaccinations and a woman, Charlotte Roberts, whose trouble was not specified. On 2 December he saw Roberts again, and Mrs Hale. More vaccinations followed. On the 9th, he sent vaccine to a Dr Woodyett and wrote to Mr Newell, his Cheltenham neighbour, about a patient. He revaccinated several of the children done earlier, and their mother. On the 12th he saw William Banks Lyttleton, who had 'short breath', excess water in the tissues and shoulder pains. Lyttleton paid a guinea. More vaccinations, after which Jenner wrote: 'N.B. The small pox has broken out among them at Cambridge [a hamlet about four miles from Berkeley].' He called on Mr Lyttleton again on the 20th: 'Dyspnoea [short breath] continues.' The vicar at Frampton had dropsy, then an unexplained condition which could often be controlled with foxglove, a discovery announced in 1776 by another English physician, William Withering. Foxglove contains digitalis, and dropsy is swelling of the tissues caused by low blood pressure and heart disease. Jenner did not note his treatment, if any. The Honourable Miss Coventry at Berkeley Castle, aged eight months, suffered a violent catarrh – probably a cold and cough, this being December. Finally, on Christmas Day he performed three more vaccinations. Jenner was a busy doctor, much in demand by his neighbours. The chances are that the vaccinations were done at no charge, but his fees should have been substantial. If other months were as busy – and there can be little doubt of it – he would seem to have been capable of controlling his inertia and apathy.

Had he seen the need and found the energy, he might have published a book of household medicine which could have enhanced his practice and perhaps his fame. In fact, such a volume has survived. Titled 'Directions & Observations etc.', the flysheet carries the inscription: 'These Prescriptions given to Mrs Pruen by Dr Jenner her respected fri[end]'. The hand-bound booklet runs to about forty-eight pages and is undated. It could have been copied by Mrs Pruen before she moved with her family from Cheltenham to the Wiltshire village of Aldbourn, as the introductory note implies:

Although medical & surgical professors are not very thinly scattered through our island, yet now and then, invited by some pleasing peculiarity to see a Family making choice of a residence remote from their immediate assistance. To a parent of sensibility, a Mother for instance, surrounded by a numerous Offspring, perpetually subjected, in spite of every tender protection, to the common little accidents of childhood, this must prove a constant source of alarm & disquietude. . .To one of this description, the possession of the following instructions will probably be in some degree soothing – On sudden emergencies they will tell her, what ought to be done; they will likewise point out where, her exertions ought to stop: The latter, to one unacquainted with the Science of Physic, is as essentially useful as the former.

The table of contents that follows is arranged alphabetically: 'Arteries, wounds of'; 'Boils'; 'Burns & Scalds'; 'Cough', and so on to 'Stomach – pains in'; 'Tooth ach' and 'Worms'. So eminently sensible are many of the procedures recommended in this little book, and with such unusual brevity, that the Pruen children and servants must have benefited greatly. Here is the beginning of the entry called 'Head – Blows in': 'When children fall down & receive hard blows on the head, if they become Sick, or appear stupid after the accident, even tho' they shou'd not complain of the pain, the enquiries of a Surgeon will be necessary. . . .' On worms: 'Whether Worms do much hurt the constitution, I know not. Certain I am, that great numbers of them have existed in the Bowels of Children, who have enjoyed the most perfect Health.' Hardly acceptable in our homes, but so common were they then in every class that the doctor's principal concern was to warn an overanxious mother against extreme treatments that might really injure the child. For ascarides, which can irritate and cause itching of the anus, he recommended lime water: half a pound of quicklime to twelve pints of boiling water. Let stand and pour off clear water for use. Jenner's hints in his own hand at the end of the book covered burns and fits – 'Rub the upper gum with Salt. This application recovd a Servant of Mine. . .after every other means had failed'. He concluded with what looks like an excellent recipe for lemonade: 'Pour 1 quart of boiling water on the juice of 6 lemons add nearly 1 lb of Sugar [Cool.] add a pint of boiling skim milk [Pour through] jelly bag till clear.'

The man who introduced vaccination is seldom seen as the Dr Spock of his age, but Mrs Pruen's little book demonstrates the breadth of his practice. Even now at the age of sixty-three, Jenner went out in all weathers. On 14 October he noted: 'Wind – N.E. Stormy – Glass down to much rain. Visited Mr Loyd at Ashmead & met Mr Taylor. His symptoms are still alarming'. As a countryman, Jenner paid close attention to the weather. Mid-October 1812 must have been extremely unsettled, as he observed in marvellous detail five days later: 'Wind S.W. A dreadful tempest during the night. It continued during the greater part of the morning with such heavy rain as to inundate the meadows surrounding the town. A rainbow in the evening – remarkably vivid. Flies crawling into the house in great abundance half drowned.' It was evidently the beginning of a long winter. 'Frosty morning,' Jenner noted on 24 April 1813. 'Snow storm at 12 oclock. Wind East.' On 1 September 1812 he had listed in his diary the names of those to whom letters were due: Ring, Murray, James Moore, Mrs Cumming, a neighbour and patient, Mr Graham at India House, Dr Parry and others. The appearance of John Ring's name is revealing. Toward the end of the previous year, Jenner told Baron that word had reached him from London 'that my honest friend poor John Ring has pass'd the boundaries of mere irritability and is actually deranged.' Ring had furnished the issue over which he had resigned from the National Vaccine Establishment. Perhaps by now Jenner had learned he was not mad, merely a little overwrought like himself. However, on 18 November he wrote to only two from his list, Murray and Moore, as well as to Dr Harvey.

On the same day he sent to Mr Darke, the surgeon at Eastington, vaccine to be used for the poor. His messenger was Henry Hicks, who had come to Berkeley to pay Jenner £150, probably the principal of a loan. Hicks must have been growing old now, and his business may have been adversely affected by the war. A few days earlier, Jenner had written to his nephew on business, a letter which is worth reading complete:

Dear William

As neither my Man nor my Horse have much to do, I have dispatch'd them with this note to bring back an answer to the following Question. When do you think of coming to Berkeley? I want to know for this reason. Evans Stibbs's Brother in law, I find is a good practical Farmer, and as such would be a fit Man to go over the Tan-House grounds with you, ascertain their quality and condition, and form an estimate whether Stibbs would be competent to the management of the Farm and be likely to receive a profit equal to his labors. There is another view also to be taken of this business, namely, the sum requisite to stock the Farm. All these points, you & the farmer will easily adjust, when he has notice to meet you.

Mastr. Cole, who never looked to anybody but himself in the management of the Premises, has destroyd the roof of the Brewhouse, by the constant exposure of the wood work to the steam of the Potatoe Pot, which was ever fuming to fatten his immense Herd of filthy Swine.

With our best regards truly Yours Edw. Jenner

Stibbs had been Jenner's manservant for many years and now wished to become a tenant farmer. Perhaps his marriage had been recent. The

Tan-House was one of the properties left to Jenner by his father. Two months later he wrote again to his nephew about the property:

> Cole ought to consider (if he is capable of thinking honestly for five minutes together) that it was for his accommodation that I fitted up the House in the first instance, & secondly that I extended his conveniences at a great expense at a time when Lady Berkeley had sent him to seek for shelter. The Lands would certainly have let for as much as they did without any house. Think then what a heavy Tax this man has brought down upon me.

The tax was no doubt a burden, but in the nature of things Cole's side of the story is not available. Stibbs did take over the tenancy, as the account book kept by William Davies indicates.

At the very beginning of 1813 Jenner provided a list of his annual contributions and subscriptions: first he named the Bible Society, the predecessor of the Society for the Propagation of Christian Knowledge, a straightforward fundamentalist missionary body; then the Cheltenham Chapel, presumably the Methodist church, reflecting Mrs Jenner's influence, and the Clergy Charity. The Bloomsbury and Cheltenham Dispensaries, the Fever Institution – probably the Fever Hospital founded in 1802 in a building beside the London Smallpox and Inoculation Hospital – and the Gloucester Royal Infirmary encompassed his professional commitments. The Cheltenham Club, the Gloucestershire Society and 'Plough – Dr. Fleece', presumably two pubs, received contributions for the social functions they performed. The Society for the Relief of Foreigners in Distress may have been a wartime charity, perhaps directly related to Jenner's efforts on behalf of French prisoners in England, about which there is more to say. The Philanthropic Society was a Cheltenham charitable institution, and the Berkeley School of Industry was an organization operated by the parish in an effort to employ some of those made landless by enclosures. At least two industries had operated in or near Berkeley at the turn of the century: a linseed oil mill which belonged to George Jenner's father-in-law, and a pin manufactory at Ham. Some cottage industry may have existed in connection with the Gloucester textile trade. Finally, Jenner's annual subscriptions included the Alfred Royal Institution. The list ends with 'etc', which may stand for three omissions from it: the Medical and Chirurgical Society, the Geological Society and the Royal Society.

His investments also continued. 'I know not what to do about the Gas Light Company,' he wrote to Charles Murray in February, '& I fear they know not themselves. I have not sent any more money.' Perhaps appropriately, this PS was added to a long letter offering his contribution to the 'sum required for the <u>Illuminats</u> in Pall Mall.' In March Jenner wrote to Baron about an important new venture, a Gloucester fish market, being set up by a group of Gloucestershire entrepreneurs led by Lord Somerville:

> He has sent out a second circular Letter more explicit than the first – he gives a list of the fish they shall bring up from the Coasts & the mode of preserving them – Ice is the antiseptic to be employ'd & a good one too. By the way is not this the mode by which Fish are conveyd from the north shores of Scotland to the London Markets?

As cities grew and agricultural reforms began to produce surpluses, land-owners such as Jenner became as interested as the manufacturing and mining entrepreneurs in improving transportation. His brother-in-law, Revd William Davies senior, kept the earliest available records of his family's involvement. He may have been a Commissioner of the Stroudwater Navigation, the earliest canal in the region built to connect the Kennet and Avon Canal to the Severn. Its route passed through Eastington. On 21 April 1788, Davies listed properties in the parish that had been valued or already sold to the canal proprietors. He noted payment for his own canal shares in July 1795, at a time when the Stroudwater was increasing its capitalization by selling two hundred shares at prices ranging from £30 to £250. Amidst several other similar entries, Davies senior noted on 25 May 1813 'Dr Jenners Turn[pike]: Chippenham – 3/3 – ' (possibly also including a contribution to the poor), and on 16 July, 'Turn[pike]. to Berkeley [and others] 0/5/11'. His eldest son was a Commissioner for Turnpikes, and possibly for the new Gloucester and Severn Canal. William junior's accounts with his uncle include regular disbursements for road taxes and turnpike subscriptions.

During the first half of 1813 Jenner became closely involved in the exact terms of a new bill designed to regulate the use of variolation. It became known as the Boringdon Bill after its principal sponsor, Lord Boringdon. The National Vaccine Establishment report for 1812 contained two alarming figures. Whereas there had been 761 cases of smallpox in London during 1811, the number rose to 1287 in 1812. The report attributed the increase 'to the inconsiderate manner in which great numbers are still every year inoculated for the Small Pox, both by private persons and public charities'. For this reason the NVE decided to back regulation. At the end of 1812, Sir Francis Milman set forth in a letter to Charles Murray the kind of bill the NVE would support: 'it should be styled a Bill for regulating and not for the Prevention of Inoculation for the small Pox', and it should avoid terms such as 'pest house', which were offensive.

Soon afterwards Murray sent Jenner a copy of the draft bill. With the help of the Berkeley lawyer, Thomas Pearce, Jenner made detailed comments. For example, the draft provided that quarantines and other regulations should be the sole responsibility of members of the Royal Colleges and selected apothecaries. Jenner pointed out: 'Few country practitioners come under the description there specified, although many have attained high professional eminence.' In an attempt to soften the language, the author of the draft, probably Murray, had omitted the word 'quarantine', merely providing equivalent conditions such as a sign on the infected premises. Jenner urged that the word should be used, 'as it would associate an useful idea with the object of the present Bill, & soften its rigor, as it will doubtless be considered as severe by many an honorable Gentleman.' He even suggested that because many of his countrymen could not read, the sign of quarantine should be a 'yard of red Tape or riband' stuck out of a window on a pole, as in the United States, he said. In the covering letter returning the amended draft bill to Murray, Jenner summed up his attitude toward it:

> . . .how strange it is that such a Bill should be necessary. The records of Society, in modern times at least, afford no example of such a dereliction of common sense in any matter respecting self preservation, & in this particular matter before us, we the inhabitants of good old England stand alone, for it would be a libel to include our Neighbours the Scotch & Irish. Take a survey of Europe and you will find that while we are fighting our Battles with the antivaccinists, they have been fighting with the Smallpox & have vanquish'd the Monster.

Angrily, he wrote to Baron two weeks later on 1 March: 'Mr G. Rose says that nothing but the actual existence of the Plague amongst us wd. make such restrictions necessary. Including the Parishes out of the Bills of Mortality [which covered only inner London], 3000 persons perished in the year 1812 by the S. Pox. Is not this a plague Mr Rose? Plague on you for your want of feeling!' When the bill was at last introduced into the House of Lords in July, Lord Ellenborough, the Lord Chancellor, said that the Common Law provided adequate safeguards against anyone introducing smallpox, and it was thrown out. The National Vaccine Establishment published a circular pointing to the risks of exposure following variolation, which Jenner thought was of much too 'tame and insipid a nature'.

In a slightly modified form the bill was reintroduced during the summer of 1814. Jenner was in London for other reasons and did not become involved directly. Ellenborough again spoke against it during the Committee stage. This time he argued that vaccination was less effective than had been hoped. The bill was withdrawn.

The Boringdon Bill and its predecessors afford a marvellous opportunity for intellectual hindsight. Of course Jenner was right, as he so often was, and the Lord Chancellor was wrong. Unfortunately, their respective opinions were less clearly labelled at the time. On this occasion the gentry who governed England held views much more closely aligned to those of the Lower Orders than did Jenner and the medical profession. Their mutual deep suspicion of medical men rested on the age-old perception that, at best, medicine might soften or postpone death. Why should these professional partners of the rich and powerful be given the authority which only parents had the right to exercise over their children? Even many doctors agreed, not least John Walker who opposed an unsuccessful attempt by the National Vaccine Establishment in 1815 to grant licences for vaccinators. The reluctance to regulate variolation, like the refusal to make vaccination compulsory almost a century later, had less to do with the rights of freeborn Englishmen than with the conviction that professional men were the servants, not the masters, of the people. We have lost that conviction.

As to Lord Ellenborough's argument that the Common Law gave adequate protection against those who might spread the smallpox, two indictments were brought in London during 1815. A Sophia Vantudillo carried her infant child, who had smallpox, through the streets and was convicted and sentenced to six months' imprisonment. An apothecary of Marylebone, Gilbert Burnett, was indicted 'for causing and permitting persons to bring children to his house to be inoculated for the Small pox and then to be inspected while the disease was upon them to the danger of infecting others', and was also imprisoned for six months. Charles Murray described these cases to a Margaret Legan or Lagan of Cork, who had complained to the NVE about a local practitioner. Murray asked for reports from the Cork Vaccine Institution and Fever Establishment. A further case was reported in 1816 involving one Taunton, a subscriber to Walker's London Vaccine Institution, who performed variolations if the patient preferred. After the trial of Burnett, he issued a printed bill warning any variolated patients against exposing others. Information was supplied by Murray, among others, but the case was abandoned by the Attorney-General. The Common Law was used, but as Jenner and the NVE realized, by the time the crime had been committed, others had been exposed. It was not that the Lord Chancellor misunderstood the freedom of the person, but that he failed to understand the nature of infection.

On 7 April 1813, the Royal College of Surgeons of London had issued a circular signed by the Master, Thompson Foster; two governors, Sir Everard Home and Sir William Blizard; Henry Cline; John Keate, whose presence on the first NVE Board so offended Jenner, and thirteen other Fellows, declaring that they would no longer variolate their patients, that they would promote vaccination and urge their colleagues to do likewise. Not surprisingly, Jenner was so pleased that he wrote to Pruen and to two of his patients about it. The London Smallpox Hospital had stopped variolating out-patients in 1808, but although variolation was performed on in-patients at their request until 1822, the number fell dramatically, to twenty-seven, in 1814. According to the annual report of the NVE for 1815, variolation was no longer being used in Edinburgh, Glasgow or Norwich. Smallpox had disappeared entirely, furthermore, from the country around Aberystwyth and

Bawtry in Yorkshire. Unfortunately, the reverse was true around Portsmouth, Bristol and London.

By the midsummer of 1813 when the first Boringdon Bill was rejected by Parliament, Jenner's attitude toward the National Vaccine Establishment had undergone a sea change. No doubt that the departure of Sir Lucas Pepys had provided the *sine qua non*, but Jenner's own extended retirement to Berkeley created the conditions, and the flattery implied in sending him the draft Boringdon Bill for comment seemed to indicate a reciprocal acknowledgement of past errors on the part of the NVE itself. As the summer progressed, furthermore, his health slowly improved.

Another factor may have contributed to his feeling of isolation, and at the same time driven him toward friends like Moore and Murray in the NVE. On 17 and 27 July, advertisements had appeared in the London papers 'summoning the Governors and Life Members' of the Royal Jennerian Society to a meeting on 4 August 'to consider what could be done to resuscitate the Society.' They were signed by John Walker as Pro Secretary. His London Vaccine Institution had flourished partly because of the financial control exercised by his friend, Andrew Johnstone. The RJS had never been dissolved, and someone, possibly Johnstone, conceived the idea of connecting the name of Jenner to the LVI as a means of strengthening it in the face of the threat posed by the National Vaccine Establishment, funded by the Treasury. Dr Bradley chaired the meeting at which Jenner was elected President and Walker, Director.

Toward the end of August the Jenners returned to Cheltenham for the first time in eighteen months. On 3 September, having just received Bradley's letter addressed to him at Berkeley, Jenner replied briefly, refusing the proffered honour. Two months later he told Moore that he could see no good in cooperating with Walker and Joseph Leaper. But the resuscitated Society kept him as President, nevertheless, and indeed revived the annual festival dinners on his birthday.

Jenner's annoyance with Cheltenham had begun to moderate as Berkeley palled. On 15 June 1813, he wrote to Pruen: 'In about a month we think of going there <u>for good</u>. The place looked very different from what I found it in February. The visitors appeared gay & the Shopkeepers merry at the thoughts of easing them of any incumbering Cash.' His sense of irony helped restore his balance. Besides, toward the end of the year he became involved in steps to bring culture to this spa. Back in 1805 Jenner had complained to Thomas Frognall Dibdin about 'a great dearth of mind in' Cheltenham. Now preliminary meetings to establish the Cheltenham Philosophical and Literary Society took place at Jenner's house. Baron, who was a member, said that the first public meeting was held at the Assembly Rooms on 3 February 1814, but Dr Charles Parry, also a member, reported toward the end of 1814 that 'The party increased beyond the House and the meeting assumed a more regular form by commencing its sittings this year at the Public Rooms.' Jenner was elected President, and the Society collapsed after he returned permanently to Berkeley, following Catherine Jenner's death.

On 1 October 1813 Jenner had received a letter from Charles Cooke, the Gloucester doctor who had begun by doubting the value of vaccination in Beddoes's volume of medical papers fourteen years before, asking for enough lymph to vaccinate two children. 'I am unwilling to complain of the National Vaccine Institution', he wrote, 'but I can assure you I experience frequent failure in the Virus sent me from London.' Whereas Jenner might have made a song and dance of this a year earlier, there is no evidence that he even reported Cooke's important observation to Moore or Murray. He had criticized the NVE's response to Lord Ellenborough and a year later, when his own prospects had changed, expanded his charge that 'the business is conducted most wretchedly from one end of it to the other'. But on the whole he approved the administration of Sir Francis Milman.

His remark to James Moore on 27 October, nevertheless, comes as something of a surprise. He wrote: 'I have some reason to think that all etiquetical impediments to my becoming a member of the Board will soon be removed.' Enter the University of Oxford followed by the Royal College of Physicians of London, perhaps supported by Napoleon Bonaparte.

Jenner must have heard some talk from friends in Cheltenham to prompt his letter, but it was not until 4 December that he wrote in his notebook:

> Letter from Sir C. Pegge informing me that the degree of Doctor of Medicine has been unanimously conferred upon me by the University of Oxford by Diploma in convocation without one dissentient voice. This is the more honorary as I understand they consider this gift so precious that it is not bestowed twice in a century. E.J.

On the 6th, he reported the news to Moore, asking Moore to meet him in Oxford. 'Pray inquire of Dr. Hervey whether I may not knock boldly at the door of the College of Physicians and gain admittance', he added.

Jenner and Baron left Cheltenham on the morning of 14 December, arriving in Oxford that evening. The next day, having 'reluctantly put on his gown and cap', Baron recalled, he received the diploma from Sir Christopher, now Regius Professor of Medicine, and was presented to the Vice-Chancellor and many of the professors and proctors. Pegge gave a dinner for him, attended also by the Chancellor, Dr Cole. On the 16th he and Baron returned to Cheltenham. A few days later he described the events to Richard Worthington: 'I went. . .to receive my Honors & met with a warm reception there. There is one good shews itself in their coming so late. It proves that the Judgement of the University was fully matured as to the merits of Vaccination.'

Now with an Oxford MD degree, Jenner and his friends considered he was technically eligible to become a Fellow of the Royal College of Physicians, and that this in turn would 'remove all objections to his taking his seat at the vaccination board', as Baron put it. The College governors, however, ruled that they could not admit Jenner without the usual examinations, which included tests of the candidate's facility in Greek and Latin. 'In my youth I went through the ordinary course of a classical education', Jenner wrote on 15 March 1814, to Dr Cooke of Gower Street who was in charge of the matter, 'obtained a tolerable proficiency in the Latin language, and got a decent smattering of the Greek; but the greater part of it has long since transmigrated into heads better suited for its cultivation. At my time of life to set about brushing up would be irksome to me beyond measure: I would not do it for a diadem.' And that was that.

The third leg of the stool supporting Jenner's statement to Moore that he could soon join the NVE Board may have been his genuine, occasionally successful, efforts to free prisoners of war. On 11 December 1813, he wrote to Napoleon requesting the release of 'My Relation Mr Milman Captain of Infantry', adducing as reason that vaccination had benefited the Empire and preserved 'the valuable life of your Son'. Milman was, of course, not Jenner's relative but the son of Sir Francis.

Normal prisoner exchange procedures had virtually disappeared after hostilities were renewed in 1803. In the circumstances many prominent people on both sides tried to use their influence whenever possible. Jenner complained once that whereas he had failed to obtain the release of a French prisoner, John Philip Kemble, the actor-manager, had succeeded with the brother of a French comedian. In 1803 Jenner applied to the French Ambassador to London and wrote to the National Institute of France on behalf of British civilians detained at the outbreak of war. Two years later he told Robert Ferryman that he had written to Napoleon seeking liberation of two civilians, a Dr Wickham, a travelling Fellow from Oxford, and another traveller named Thomas Williams. His first application to the Central Committee of Vaccination had produced no results, and two more years passed before the letter to Napoleon bore fruit. It was probably on this occasion that Josephine was said to have directed the Emperor's attention to the signature, Edward Jenner. According to legend, Napoleon said, *'Ah, Jenner, je ne puis rien refuser à Jenner.'*

During 1807 he wrote to King Carlos IV of Spain, successfully requesting the release of 'Judge Powell's son'. Three years later on 6 June 1810, he recorded in his notebook the release of Messrs Gold and Garland as a result of another petition to Napoleon.

Jenner's most testing and important case was that of Captain E. Husson, the brother of Dr Henri-Marie Husson, a member of the Imperial Medical Society. George Jenner had met Dr Husson at a Paris meeting on vaccination during the summer of 1802. Captain Husson wrote to Jenner on 21 July

1811, requesting that Jenner visit him at Thame, Oxfordshire, where he was confined, and asking Jenner to arrange that his friend, the son of a Senator Bellenger, might be moved from a village near Northampton to Thame. When Alexander Marcet asked for his help with another British captive, he replied that 'in the space of nine years I have been only able to bring away six Prisoners; and not one of these was a Military Man.' He complained of his treatment by the British government, which had refused to release Captain Husson despite his brother's frequent interpolations on behalf of Jenner's appeals to the Emperor. In April 1812 he had still not obtained Husson's release. 'Our government has treated me cruelly', he told Pruen. Eighteen months later Husson was imprisoned on a hospital ship off Chatham. Despondent because of the failure of Jenner's efforts, he had broken his parole at Thame by attempting flight. Jenner wrote to a naval surgeon on the ship, Richard Dobson, explaining the circumstances and asking Dobson to communicate with Husson and perhaps help to obtain his release. At the same time, December 1813, he had petitioned for the release of Milman's son, and promised Dr Husson that 'as soon as Cpt. Milman arrives in England', Captain Husson would be returned to France. By mid-February 1814 the exchange had taken place. Jenner said that Milman was the only military prisoner he succeeded in freeing, but of course he might have added Husson and possibly Judge Powell's son. By way of a coda to the Husson incident, George Jenner wrote to Captain Husson in August 1814, asking for his help in transmitting a letter from London to Malta. Husson agreed as a means of expressing his thanks for Edward Jenner's efforts to end his captivity.

Husson concluded his letter with best wishes for Mrs Jenner's early recovery. Catherine had been ill for several months, making it necessary for Edward to remain in Cheltenham with her through the previous winter. In April 1814 he told William Davies junior that she was 'much better', but a month later he wrote to Baron that she had been so ill that he had 'held myself in readiness to go down on the arrival of the post. My last accounts have been very pleasant.' Jenner had gone to London toward the end of April for reasons which may have been a little uncertain, even to him. They seemed important enough to warrant leaving Mrs Jenner while her health was at best up and down. The occasion was the conference of the allied sovereigns in London, following the fall of Paris and Napoleon's first exile to Elba – an event which proved to be as abortive as Jenner's peculiar journey.

In March 1814 Jenner was introduced to the Russian Ambassador, Count Orloff, by Orloff's physician, Dr Meyer. 'The Count has promised to send me some Siberian fossils.' On the 15th of the same month Dr Hamel, a young man from St Petersburg 'sent by the Emperor of Russia to examine our public institutions & improvements', visited Cheltenham and met Jenner. Two days later Dr Charles Parry met Hamel 'at Dr. Jenner's table'. Orloff and possibly Hamel seem to have suggested that Jenner should address the European heads of state on his own behalf. I can only assume that the implication was that he should ask them for money as an acknowledgement of his contribution to the elimination of smallpox from their realms. Baron said that Jenner 'shrank from such a project', but he apparently felt it worthwhile to make himself available for interviews. Possibly his friends, including Lord Egremont, Moore and Marcet, proposed that if he received signs of favour from the continental crowned heads, our own might find it opportune to add British honours. A year earlier, Jenner had written to Pruen: 'The Prince has at last Gazetted me in conjunction with my Fd [Thomas] Christie [who introduced vaccination in Ceylon and had retired to Cheltenham]. On his account I am glad of it – Feathers are of no value to me.' Jenner's past ambivalence on matters of public recognition suggest that the statement could not be taken as prescriptive of his behaviour in the event that an offer should be made. Another letter to Pruen from London, dated 14 May 1814, gave an explanation which was probably genuine within the limits of his motivational self-perception:

> My visit to the Metropolis at this time was in obedience to many calls of consequence. The Court has a demand upon me, & there I have been, made up of shreds and patches like a Morris Dancer. . . .Another object was to pay my devoirs to some of the great Russians already come, & those who are coming. . . .And next I am come (I feel no melancholy whatsoever in the reflection) to bid a long farewell to the Town & all who are within it.

He took up residence at 7 Great Marylebone Street, accompanied by George Jenner, Robert and Catherine junior. Robert enjoyed seeing the 'mighty Potentates' and 'brilliant illuminations', and Catherine was visiting her friends. He expected Pruen to pay him a visit. By the time of his letter in May, Jenner had already 'been closeted for more than an hour with one who was worth going to Kamchatka to see her Imperial Highness the grand Duchess of Oldenburgh', sister of Tzar Alexander. On 14 June he told Robert's former tutor, the Revd Joyce: 'I have not seen any of these great men & it is possible I may not as I cannot push myself into their presence'; and four days later he wrote to Robert, who was visiting Joyce: 'I have been to the Oldenburgh Hotel no less than three times by the command of the Emperor & Grand Duchess, & was detain'd many hours each time for no purpose.' In the event the Duchess gave him a ring, and he shook hands with the Tzar. He also had an interview with the King of Prussia, the first royal person to adopt vaccination for his family, using vaccine supplied by Jenner in 1799. And he met the Prussian Crown Prince, General Blücher and the Russian general, Count Platoff. Whether this short list, to which must be added the Prince Regent, contributed to the advancement of either vaccination or the name of Jenner, is very doubtful.

As to the valedictory aspect of the visit, he had planned to join the Marcets for a concert on 3 June, but proposed to offer his ticket to a friend because he could not leave a meeting with Lord Egremont in time. Because of this meeting, he was also unable to go to the Geological Society to meet Marcet. He had brought some rocks for the Society but wanted Marcet's opinion of them first. However, he would 'certainly bring my <u>Fragments</u> to your House on Saturday, where I shall be proud to meet that <u>flaming Diamond</u>, Dr Woolaston.' He and Marcet called on Sir Walter Farquhar, and drove out to Enfield with Mrs Marcet to visit Dr William Saunders, first President of the Medical and Chirurgical Society. On 4 July he asked several friends to breakfast, and returned to Cheltenham the next day.

Because this did prove to be his last trip to London, Jenner's letter to Pruen seems again to demonstrate remarkable prescience. The letter must have emerged from his worry following Mrs Jenner's relapse, but of course he might have returned. On 23 September, the crowned heads were the subject of another letter to Pruen. Jenner proposed, if the opportunity arose, that they 'be attack'd in their entrenched Camp at Vienna', where they would have assembled for the peace negotiations. His agent was to be none other than the Foreign Secretary, Lord Castlereagh. Jenner hoped 'to get his ear, & to find that ear harmoniz'd to vaccination.' It would have meant another journey to town, but 'At present I see no opening.' Nor did one materialize.

Probably during this unsatisfactory quarter-year, a movement arose to draw up a testimonial to Jenner signed by mothers and daughters throughout the kingdom whom vaccination had saved from disfigurement and death, and whose children had been similarly blessed. Queen Charlotte had agreed to become the patron. Baron recalled that 'but for the distresses of the country after a long and arduous warfare, it would have been crowned with success.' Perhaps, but Jenner never became a popular hero. He preferred the plaudits of the powerful.

In Cheltenham he found Mrs Jenner improved, though still weak. Late that summer Jenner caught cholera, possibly from the servants; his housemaid, footman and cook were ill. Dr Parry came from Bath, and along with a local surgeon, Mr Wood, attended the servants. By the beginning of November he was well enough to travel to Eastington. William Davies senior had been having severe palpitations and had fainted. Jenner called on him twice. Two days before Christmas he could report to Pruen: 'Mrs J. left her chamber about a week ago for the first time since May. I fear she must return as the weather is so severe.'

'I am still weak,' Jenner wrote to Pruen around the 1st of the year, 'but recovering fast.' His poor health, combined with his wife's, put paid to their seasonal return to the Chauntry. On 11 April he asked William Davies junior to send her the 'elegant Bouquets you used to send'. It was an 'extraordinary season' in which 'nature smiled' on the birth of William's son, but: 'You say nothing about the late disastrous events on the Banks of the Severn – I therefore hope the enraged Lady, Sabrina, thought my portion of the Wall too insignificant for her attack. All the accounts I have heard are vague & unintelligible.' The weather again, I assume, because 'Sabrina' is another name for the Severn. Nevertheless, he went to Berkeley for a few days on his own, in part so that he could go to see his sister-in-law, Harriet Kingscote, wife of Catherine's brother Thomas. She had been very ill, he told Robert, and 'a vast influx of Letters foreign & domestic deranged my plans. . .and I have no assistance from any quarter whatever, except what I derive in the practical part of Vaccination from Friends' Hands.' The pressure of correspondence seems never to have diminished. Occasionally, George Jenner or one of his children might help out, and for a time during his London years Dibdin acted as his amanuensis.

Ultimately, Jenner himself had to deal with inquiries or requests for vaccine but, as he said, assistance with vaccination required no special knowledge. 'Friends' Hands' was a pun. His helper was Francis Hands, a Berkeley surgeon like his father before him, whom Jenner had met the year before. Hands left a good description of his role:

I. . .went to his House several times a day Sundays not excepted to assist in Vaccinating the poor who came from the surrounding neighbourhood of Five and Eight miles. . . .

It was my province to examine each candidate. . .to see that each person was in good health. Also to see that every person who was to be Vaccinated should be perfectly free from Worms of every sort. . . .The Skin Diseases were subjugated by the Ung: Hydr:Nit:Mitius [hydrated nitrate salve] or Ung Linci [linseed oil salve]. The same applications. . .were used for removal of Scratches of thorns, Cats, Needles, Pins, Bruises, Scalds, and all abrasions of the skin. . . .

Jenner's letter to his son was addressed to Exeter College, Oxford. Robert had gone there very recently, evidently with the intention of matriculating. His Latin and Greek seem to have been deficient, however, because after a period 'reading Greek with Mr. Williams' in Cheltenham, which he had found impossible, he wrote to his cousin William Davies on 1 September 'as there are so many interruptions', he had been sent off to Mr Joyce in Wiltshire. According to his father, Robert had also been studying Hebrew in Cheltenham and 'has acquired a tolerably good knowledge of this wonderful language in about three weeks.' Robert neglected to mention to William Davies that he had managed a holiday in Scotland over the Glorious Twelfth; as Jenner wrote, 'it must be a great comfort to the Grouse to find that such a shot as Robert is amongst them.' He was now scheduled to return to Oxford in October.

Robert had probably last seen his cousin when Davies came to Cheltenham in mid-May. On the 18th William had noted that he walked with his uncle to Swindon, a village about two miles north-west of Cheltenham, to call on Revd Worthington. Jenner continued very active with his Cheltenham practice. Toward the end of July his old friend Fewster of Thornbury asked him to see a patient, Mrs Cox, at Almondsbury nearby, but Jenner pleaded that he was 'always extremely harried & fatigued' during the season. He said that he agreed with Fewster's regimen, adding that he might try opium and camphor, a cinchona tonic (quinine) and leeches. Meanwhile, Catherine Jenner 'has been down stairs & once out of doors.' Perhaps on the strength of her improvement, Edward spent some time in Berkeley during the latter part of August. On the 27th he wrote to H. N. Trye of Cheltenham, a nephew of his old friend who had died a year before, about some land Jenner hoped to buy from him. Apparently Trye had suggested that Jenner's dog, Darby, might be of some use to him. 'Darby should be much at your service, could I spare him. He is a capital House dog, & I rely on his vigilance to keep off Thieves, with whom we are terribly beset, having at this time some hundreds added to our old stock, in the form of Canal diggers.' The navvies had been hired to dig the Gloucester-Berkeley Canal, now the Gloucester-Sharpness.

On 1 September he was back in Cheltenham, and wrote to Pruen: 'Poor Mrs Jenner who has been much better in some respects is laboring under a dreadful depression of spirits.' Baron came to Cheltenham on the 12th, probably so that Jenner could consult him about Catherine, who was fast failing. She died at 12.30 in the morning of 13 September.

Chapter 11

In Sum
1815–1823

Catherine's niece, Mary Jenner, had come to Cheltenham a few days earlier, probably to help with the nursing. It was she who wrote to William Davies junior with the sad news, and summoned her brother George 'to come here by the Doctor's desire'.

Almost twenty-four hours after Mrs Jenner's death, her husband wrote a note to Baron:

> I know of no one whom I should like to see here better than yourself; and as often as you can find a little leisure, pray come and exercise your pity. I am, of course, most wretched when alone; as every surrounding object then the more forcibly reminds me of my irreparable loss. Every tree, shrub, flower, seems to speak. But yet no place on earth would at present suit me but this, and I trust my friends will not endeavour to take me away; for, strange and contradictory as it may seem, the bitter cup has a kind of relish in it here, which it could afford no where else.

Catherine Jenner was buried at Berkeley by the vicar, Caleb Carrington, on 21 September. Henceforward, Jenner lived at the Chauntry, 'never, except for a day or two, quitting it again', wrote Baron.

After the arrangements to inform the family, transport the body to Berkeley, and prepare for the funeral, Jenner had time to take stock. The letter he wrote to Thomas Pruen on 23 October shows how his sense of loss had matured and deepened. Gone is the harsh self-pity of a month before, replaced by gentle recollection and real feeling.

> My whole frame is thrown into derangement. What a severe shock have I received. It was the more severe as it was unexpected. Poor dear Soul, but little more than a fortnight before, we walk'd together about the streets of Cheltenham & took a ramble in Mrs Williams's Garden. Never sufficiently attentive to herself, tho' ever mindful of the wants of others, she was inadvertently exposed to a cold current of air from the North, which brought on an inflammation of the Lungs,

too violent for her tender frame to sustain. Her departure was mark'd with that sweet serenity, which I believe ever attends the last hours of those who have spent an [?] in life. Her's is a bless'd gain; mine an irreparable loss. The privation is not to be describ'd.

Of course, these were the customary expressions of grieving, but after thirty-seven years together, the first ten absorbed by a struggle for the approval of her family, they were surely heartfelt. Catherine is too shadowy, and Jenner was too self-absorbed, to allow for certainty. But everything – the attitudes of his family, the children's behaviour, the actions of friends and what little is known about their lives together – is consistent with friendship and love. Jenner's attitude toward religion seems to have been tolerant enough to allow for his wife's more intense views. Indeed, had it not been for his determination that she should be buried at Berkeley, he would have spurned the services of the Revd Mr Carrington, whom he disliked in the same measure as his wife did, if for different reasons. What their marriage lacked was a common interest beyond the hearth. To a great extent, however, sympathy, a trait I think they both possessed, overcame this lacuna.

Their daughter stayed on at Berkeley, but Robert entered Exeter College in October. William Davies junior was a frequent visitor, of course. On one October day his youngest brother Edward joined them for dinner and tea, and on 4 November William brought his wife Sarah and their two children, William and Sarah, to call. Robert came home too over Christmas and the New Year.

'Your intention is to visit Edward Jenner,' he wrote to Pruen on 2 January 1816, 'that being with whom you have spent so many social hours. You will find him not, but only a part of him, and that part, in a sad sad state of decomposition. The Mind & body act reciprocally on each other. In me the qualities of both have undergone a considerable change.' These melancholy *aperçus* were repeated in letters to a medical acquaintance, Dr Thomas Harrison Burder, who had recently received his degree at Edinburgh, and to James Moore to whom he complained of palpitations. They were almost ritualized expressions, expected by the recipient from 'a mind possess'd of sensibility', as Jenner described himself to Burder. Like our own expressions of grief – 'great loss', 'in loving memory' – they did not demean Jenner's feelings, but stylized them in a manner acceptable for social exchange.

Perhaps the external interest that first returned was not medicine but geology. True, on 29 February 1816 William Davies junior brought his eldest son to be vaccinated, and a week later Jenner rode to the Davieses to inspect the boy's arm – 'Every puncture took effect and the pustules are quite perfect' – and used lymph from his grand-nephew to perform another vaccination. But on 23 February, he wrote in his notebook: 'Saw Mr. Hawker's splendid collection of fossils. He has a species of Oolite wct. seems to throw some light on that wct. forms the top stratum of our hills.' Introducing this entry, he speculated: 'might not mountains themselves, be they ever so high, have formed the bottoms of antideluvian seas.' The Revd Peter Hawker was rector of Woodchester near Stroud, and thus provided an outing for Jenner, as well as instruction.

Whenever he had had a few weeks in Berkeley, rocks and fossils had diverted him. During these years he explored the mineral content and organic remains along the left bank of the Severn at Parton, Aust and Westbury, as well as closer to home. During the long residence in 1812, he had asked Davies to 'speak to the Quarry Men to bring me the Fossils they have collected'. At the end of the year, he acknowledged receipt of a 'Basket of Fossils' from Mrs Meade, wife of the patient whose eyes he had been treating. 'Altho' I am not at all scientific in forming arrangements, my Fossils for the most part lying in as little order as in their native Beds, yet I take a vast delight in contemplating this sublime, this aweful subject. Fossils are. . .monuments of departed Worlds.' Four months later he wrote to Parry about a selection of rocks he was about to send to him, and referred to 'Rock- hampton specimens' that bore a resemblance 'to the Rock of Gibralter – but I have not yet decidedly met with Bone in them.' After he had sent the 'Hamper of Minerals', he wrote again to Parry with a less scientific request: 'In Bath, I think you have men of ingenuity enough to split & polish the Pebbles. It wd. be a gratification to me to have a broach, or a Ring, decorated with a thing or two from my own Sod; or what wd. be still more congenial, my Tobacco Box'.

Jenner thought of himself as an amateur, a dilettante, in geological matters, but since early boyhood the pursuit had offered him relaxation within a scientific bailiwick he understood. He wanted the same pleasure to accrue to Robert, completely overlooking the differences in his son's personality. During his brief stay at Exeter College in April before his mother died, Robert had begun to attend lectures by William Buckland, the Professor of Mineralogy. His father was delighted:

> Be assured Robert, that whatever your mind imbibes of this description will be of lasting benefit & will, as you advance in life, afford you more real & substantial gratification than thousands of those baubles which you have frequently [been] seeking for. . . .I hope you will take some Notes on anything particularly interesting that Mr. Buckland developes, especially with regard to our Rocks.

Professor Buckland subsequently became a visitor to the Chauntry. With Jenner and Revd Robert Halifax of Standish, also a member of the Barrow Hill Club, Buckland explored the neighbourhood. In October 1816 Parry's eldest son, Dr Charles Henry Parry, whom Jenner had known in Cheltenham, entered the geological correspondence. He had been examining the oolites which Jenner had sent his father in March by splitting them and using a magnifying glass. 'I find – (stop – I fancy so),' wrote Jenner, 'they are made up of concentric layers; the first crystaliz'd on a small atom, a fragment of stone.' Which is exactly right. 'You really should see, with a geological eye, the country around this place – the diversity it presents would delight you.'

Geology afforded relaxation from Jenner's medical and magisterial duties. On 11 March, he and William Davies junior drove to Eastington to see Davies senior, now in his seventy-seventh year. William junior noted that they returned the next day in Jenner's carriage, the first reference to that vehicle. He had probably acquired it a few years before when the stables in Cheltenham had been enlarged.

Uncle and nephew next made use of the carriage on 4 April, to attend the Assizes at Gloucester. Jenner stayed with Baron during the trial, notorious locally, of fourteen poachers who had been in a gun fight with the game-keepers of Lord Segrave and Lord De Clifford. De Clifford's gamekeeper was killed by a Mr Cassel, himself the brother of the Mayor of Bristol. The case was further complicated by the fact that one of the keepers had actually been part of the poaching party, and the poachers were mostly young, 'sons of respectable farmers'. It was a sign of the times. Prices forced sky-high by wartime shortages had suddenly collapsed, following the peace in 1815. Not only were landowners hit by falling incomes, but the army of landless peasants created by the enclosure movement now faced terrible hardships. Returning servicemen swelled their ranks. The landowners and their tenants could no longer afford to employ labourers, and the urbanizing cottage industries had also fallen on hard times. Poaching was a capital offence. For an increasing minority of the starving rural poor, it became a necessity. The involvement of a relatively well connected man like Cassel with a gamekeeper and other 'respectable' elements suggests a kind of derring-do, like biting your thumb at the big landlords. There was some sort of oath sworn by members of the gang. Perhaps a Robin Hood element operated in Gloucestershire. Naturally, none of these twentieth-century sociological explanations would have occurred to Jenner, who saw only that the law was being broken violently, or for that matter to the poachers themselves.

In February he had written to Robert that a man named Grove had been 'taken in Monmouthshire & I sent him to Gaol. A more harden'd or obstinate young Fellow I never met with. He might have been liberated on bail if he would have confess'd, but I could not get a word to the purpose out of him.' Robert would have known whether Grove was part of the poaching gang. I do not, but the fact that he might have been bailed at the time makes it possible. Jenner outlined the state of the trial in a further letter to Robert dated 2 March. Cassel had fled but the keeper with him 'is taken &

committed. Nothing new has come out respecting the Poachers – They affect
to consider the matter lightly. Sergt. Best, I understand, is engaged as their
Counsel. I do not see how they are to get off for if they be acquitted on the
first Count (the Murder) how are they to escape from the second – the taking
an illegal Oath?' Two of the defendants, Allen, a farmer, and Penny, were
executed. The remaining twelve were transported for life.

It may have been about this time that Jenner wrote to the overseer of the
poor at Ham, a Mr Pearce, that 'Several Paupers. . .are now here making
complaints respecting their inability to support themselves & families. Your
presence [at the magistrates' court in Berkeley] is therefore immediately
neces[sary].' Baron has vividly described the scene on this occasion, or
another very like it:

> I found him one day sitting with a brother justice [perhaps William
> Davies, who was present when the paupers complained] in a narrow,
> dark, tobacco-flavoured room, listening to parish business of various
> sorts. The door was surrounded by a scolding, brawling mob. A fat
> overseer of the poor was endeavouring to moderate their noise; but
> they neither heeded his authority nor that of their worships. There
> were women swearing illegitimate children, others swearing the peace
> against drunken husbands, and able-bodied men demanding parish
> relief to make up the deficiency in their wages. The scene altogether
> was really curious; and when I considered who was one of the chief
> actors. . .I experienced sensations which would have been altogether
> sorrowful had there not been something irresistibly ludicrous in many
> of the minor details of the picture. He said to me, 'is not this too bad?
> I am the only acting magistrate in this place, and I am really harrassed
> to death.'

Jenner went on to say that he had asked the Lord Lieutenant to assign
his nephew to the court permanently, but without success.

Each parish appointed an overseer of the poor to carry out various
duties, such as the administration of relief and the management of the
poor house, where the homeless were segregated by sex. Relief 'to make
up the deficiency in their wages' was raised by a poor-rate paid by all
landowners and tenants and awarded under the notorious Speenhamland
system. Speenhamland is a part of Newbury, Berkshire, where in 1795 the
Berkshire magistrates assembled ostensibly to fix a minimum wage for the
county related to the price of bread. In the event they bowed to pressure
from the landowners and, instead of raising wages, they drew up a scale of
relief to be paid in addition to wages, based on the number of people in the
family and the price of bread. The Speenhamland system forced the smallest
landholder to help the largest, and converted even the employed labourer
into a pauper. In northern counties competition from new manufacturing
industry tended to keep wages up, but the Speenhamland system became

the norm throughout the south, absorbing most of the magistrates' time.

Jenner had little understanding for the poor and unfortunate, but he knew his class duty. A dozen years before, he had highly recommended a pamphlet by his friend Richard Worthington on the care of the sick poor. Worthington had pointed out that the poor-rate produced about £3,000,000 each year but was 'inadequate to the purpose of relief.' By 1816 it was costing double that amount. A parish might contrive to send 'a poor, disabled wretch, tossing to and fro in a common cart, along roads, it may be, so rough and vile, as to render travelling perfectly uncomfortable even in the easiest carriage' up to sixteen miles to a hospital in order to rid itself of the pauper, his maintenance and the maintenance of a surgeon. Worthington urged the extension of the dispensary system, supported both by rates and by charity, to the countryside. Jenner agreed with such reforms.

In the spring of 1812, four years before the Gloucester poaching trial, the country was rocked by rioting and machine-breaking – the brief, hopeless episode known as the Luddite Rebellion. There were food riots in Bristol because, according to one historian, 'People were so hungry that they were willing to risk their lives upsetting a barrow of potatoes.' Disturbances took place in Plymouth and Falmouth. Something similar must have affected Berkeley later in the year. On 13 October, Jenner wrote to Pruen about 'refind Brutes of my own Species, Dancing Dogs & learned Pigs.' 'I had rather see our Island in the possession of the French, than in the hands of our own Rabble'. A month later he confided to his diary: 'B– is a place where the amiable qualities of the Mind – where talent and Genius are chill'd by the repulsive scorn or at least indifference of its ignorant inhabitants, numbers of whom are scarcely elevated above the rank of barbarians.' Events that were national in scope – the record has not revealed what – seemed to have impinged directly on his personal life. But in July 1816 he wrote to the son of his old friend, Mr Fewster of Thornbury, about a report 'that you are threatened with destruction by some persons in your neighbourhood on account of a late unfortunate business. . .[yet] it is well known that not only yourself but your Father signed a Petition in favour of the men who belong'd to Thornbury.' Whether these men were among the poachers sentenced to death or transportation by the Gloucester Assizes in April, I cannot say. Class warfare in the lovely Vale of Berkeley neared the surface, as it did in many other parts of postwar Britain.

At the end of April 1816 Jenner spent a few days in Cheltenham. He may have gone to see patients worried by an epidemic of smallpox in the town, which had disappeared by September. He wrote to Fewster senior that he was 'going to Town for a fortnight a letter would reach me directed at James Moore's Esqr. Surgeon Conduit Street.' This note is baffling. The only two-week break in William Davies's notations of meals with his uncle during almost the entire year occurred between 13 and 27 May, but I have found no positive evidence of a journey to the capital after Mrs Jenner's death.

On 5 May Jenner walked the four miles to Stone to visit 'the Wolfershans, the Hicks and the Jenkins.' Toward the end of June he wrote to Pruen. Robert was still at Oxford but Catherine was at home. 'This country, from the Spring onward, has been overrun with Catarrhs & I have been roughly handed, & am so still. . . .My Spirits are for the most part miserably low, & I must expect they will remain so, till the few verses that remain of the Chapter are ended.' July passed quietly, perhaps the most noteworthy event being the birth of William Davies's third child, a daughter named Anne. On 14 August Davies noted that Jenner came to Rockhampton to see Sarah Davies, William's wife, who was very ill. He wrote a note to Baron saying that Mrs Davies was suffering from an 'epidemic Fever'. 'The House has been full of typhoid Contagion for these two months.' Darke, the local doctor, was expecting Baron the next day. Baron came first to Berkeley, and on the 16th he and Jenner rode to Rockhampton. Jenner went again three days later. Sarah Davies died on the 20th, aged twenty-eight. That his depression should have been reinforced seems hardly surprising. He had agreed to act as godfather to Charles Henry Parry's daughter, but wrote on 31 August that he was unable to make the journey to Bath: 'all hopes. . .gone among the Gas. I am fasten'd to this place by a chain so massy that it is quite impossible for me to move.'

Yet the letter has a positive side. Parry was a newly fledged doctor, aware of the latest advances in medicine. Jenner enjoyed discussing them with him.

> With regard to Pathology. The impression at present on my mind is that somehow or another the Milk, of the Mother is capable of receiving impregnations which affect the child. We have not yet made out all the odd things going forward in the animal economy. Tell me how it comes to pass that if I drink a glass of good Cider my Urine smells as fragrant as the bottle when just uncork'd? I dont give this as a paralel case, but as a puzzle. There must be a short cut from the Stomach to the Bladder. Shall we ask Riddle about these things? What if we were to fill the Stomach of a Puppy with Mercury, first tying up the Intestine, & then give it a good squeeze?

A century later in Petrograd, the great Russian pathologist, Pavlov, was performing just such experiments showing how absorbed food affected all the fluids of the body, including mother's milk and urine. Jenner's prescience must be admired. No wonder Charles Parry's father had written to his old friend almost six years before: 'it is your own fault if you are not still the first pathologist existing.'

Jenner wrote to Charles Parry again on 15 October, a long joyous letter, full of data, sentimental and sad, almost hysterical. He sent points from which

Parry was to vaccinate Jenner's goddaughter, although in his usual way with vaccine for children of the gentry, he recommended that Parry's vaccinator 'had better use the points on the arms of some Cottage Children, & having produc'd a Pustule (Vesicle if it must be so) to vaccinate from that.' This reminded him of cavils by Richard Walker of Oxford and Robert Kinglake of Taunton, who published fears 'in the Yellow Journal' that vaccine matter then available was becoming worn out because of passage through many arms. How significant that he should accuse the honourable and established *London Medical and Physical Journal*, presumably because it dared to publish articles that questioned vaccine practices. Nevertheless, on the matter in question he was largely right, and he ended the first paragraph, ' "The world is in its infancy." ' The letter's second paragraph dealt with the infant's diet. She had apparently failed to gain weight, and Jenner recommended a dilution of cow's milk with added sugar to supplement Mrs Parry's milk. He went on to consider that the absorptive power of the stomach, 'the root, the foundation, the Governor of the whole family', might be improved by vaccination. This led him to hydatids, which might by their appearance and growth damage 'the Lymphatic'. ' "The World's a Baby." ' The final paragraph concerns Parry's oolites, and his father: 'I want too, to write to him; but when I think of setting about it my head seems so full, I know not how & so it is put off till tomorrow, tomorrow & tomorrow. "The world's a Foetus." '

Even a reference to *Macbeth*. This ebullient letter reveals an Edward Jenner much recovered from the depression of bereavement. No doubt Charles Parry was good for him, since he obviously found it possible to write to the father of his goddaughter but not to his old friend, the grandfather. The new mood seemed to persist. When he wrote to Pruen again in December, he was 'almost alone here, Robert being nominally at home only, & Catherine on a visit to the Paytherus's at Woolwich-Blackheath.' The customary self-pity was muted.

Apart from the usual visits from William Davies junior, the New Year began with more poachers and robbers, this time three local villains. Colonel Fitzhardinge, the Berkeley heir to the castle, proposed to attend the hearing at Jenner's convenience, adding 'and I am sure they will confess.' He suggested that the vicar, Mr Carrington, would help to draw up warrants for the arrest of the three, a formal task in which Jenner lacked experience.

Robert had returned to Oxford, where his father wrote to him on 13 February. The early part of the letter dealt with financial matters. He was hoping to complete a property sale that would cover the tenant's debt, 'but as things are sunk in value that is not quite certain. You must not only try, but really make both ends meet with £200 per annum & the addition of 40 for a Tutor – Consider this sum in the present unexampled state of things why it doubles & more than doubles an estate of 400. You may send down the bills when you like.' Money was a constant issue between them, Jenner offering too little and reluctantly giving more in the end, Robert resenting the struggle. After some further details, the letter continued: 'Catherine who is at home, has had a letter from Mrs Taylor. There are some hints respecting your calling on Adml. Manley.' Nothing seems to have come of this opening. Jenner's last paragraph urged Robert to look up fossil-collectors in Oxford; 'you might be able to make exchanges for [th]ose of this Country. Young Shrapnell is indefatigable [?] the Museum begins to wear a scientific appearance.' Henry Shrapnell had helped to arrange Jenner's specimens in trays and cabinets in one of the rooms at the Chauntry. Only the presence of willing hands could have brought Jenner to set to rights the chaos he had described to Mrs Meade.

On 22 February Jenner wrote to Charles Parry that Robert Bakewell, a well known geologist and popular lecturer, 'call'd upon me yesterday'. Jenner showed him fossiliferous rocks from the Chauntry garden, but he had also been conducting experiments. Bakewell reported them in his *Introduction to Geology*. Jenner 'informed me that he had made several experiments upon recent bones, by burying them in the dark mud from the lias clay. . . .The specimens which he showed me, presented the same appearance as the fossil bones in the lias clay', where the specimens had been buried for a year. Obviously, Jenner was applying Hunterian practices in geology too. He mentioned none of this to Parry, but said that Bakewell was on his way to give a course of lectures in Bristol. 'Do beat up for him'. By April he was again complaining to Pruen about his general health:

> The disrelish for anything like exertion increases fast upon me. I strive to the utmost of my power, feeble as it is, to shake off the mists & clouds which almost constantly envelop me, but still they stick close. Your letter has been for some weeks traveling from room to room & plac'd in various situations so that it should be staring me in the face. Now on the mantlepiece in my Library, then in my parlour – put into my pocket to be felt with my most familiar utensils – clap'd into the Quire of letter Paper I am compell'd occasionally to resort to, or into some Book that I am forc'd to read. . . .

Poor Pruen may have been a lightning rod drawing off melodramatic charges of self-pity.

Early in May, Jenner and William Davies junior in their capacities as magistrates visited Hinton workhouse, 'which we found in good order', said Davies. Circumstances must have improved since Jenner had written in his notebook under the heading, 'Hinton Workhouse':

> Sam'l Williams, Master, has a guinea a week to find himself. A.B. reports that he lives on the provisions appropriated for the use of the poor. The house is extremely filthy and full of vermin. Stench intolerable. Covering of the beds insufficient. One family, who sleep

four in a bed, have no covering but a single sheet and an old bag.

These appalling conditions were by no means unique.

On 16 May Baron paid another call on Jenner and spent the night. That evening they walked in the garden and discussed the National Vaccine Establishment. Jenner said that the 'present constitution. . .is bad. The Marquis of Lansdowne and myself had arranged an excellent plan; but the change of the ministry knocked it on the head, and George Rose and Sir Lucas Pepys concocted the present imperfect scheme.' Not only did Baron neglect to describe the 'excellent plan', but he had forgotten that in 1809 Jenner's proposals to Rose had been enthusiastically adopted by Pepys. Baron observed: 'He [Jenner] had neglected himself.' Jenner told him: 'Catherine and Robert. . .think I am shamming'. A few days later his nephew William ate dinner with Jenner and a 'large party' at the Chauntry. On 10 June the elder William Davies died at Eastington. But for Jenner, he was the last within the family of his generation.

Despite his malaise, Edward Jenner remained fit enough to walk with his son Robert and William Davies to the Tan-House Farm to visit Stibbs. A few days later he wrote to a former patient, John Ward of Ryeford near Stroud, thanking him for 'a very fine specimen of the arsenical Pyrites. . .but as nothing is more interesting to me than organic Remains, especially Bones, I hope you will bear in remembrance your promise respecting those in possession of your Father.'

His interest in bones suggests that Jenner had made a logical extension from fossils into regions of learning labelled palaeontology and archaeology. The terms were certainly in use in his day, but I doubt that he thought of his own observations as subjects of separate disciplines. 'Bones found in the grave pits near Wick', he wrote in his notebook about this time. 'Several fragments of the human skeleton, both adult & infantile. . . .Fragments of urns, some like those at Herculaneum of a dark sooty color. Ashes in considerable quantities. Antiquaries conceive this to have been a Roman Cemetery & that some fire must have been near.' He had been brought 'a fine impression of the coin of Alectus' from Wick. Alectus, he noted, had usurped the governorship of Britain in the reign of Diocletian before being 'slain on the banks of the Severn.'

In reply to a query from his old friend William Shrapnell, Henry's father, he recorded the discovery of Whitehall, a 'long lost place' that had stood 'near Edward Clarke's'. He had also advised Thomas Fosbroke about matters of local archaeological interest. 'Dr. Jenner has observed that an avenue of ancient oaks may be traced all the way from Berkeley to Gloucester at the present day.' He pointed out that 'opposite the West window of the Church was a street with a cross in the centre, now lost in the kitchen-garden of the Castle.' Amongst his collections of fossils and stones, moreover, were fragments of pottery found 'on the high road between Newport and Stone', and glazed tiles from the Anglo-Saxon church that had once stood in the present Berkeley churchyard.

Neither the best physical health nor the most far-flung intellectual interests can stave off a summer cold. William Davies called when Jenner was ill on 29 and 30 July, noting on 1 August that he was much better. A day or two earlier, Jenner replied to a letter from Pruen:

> I wish it were in my power to spend the week at Cheltenham with you; not for pleasure altogether but more from the aid you could afford me in arranging some of my secular affairs there. Holdship's is the principal & Ferryman's is the next. . . . I shall endeavor to prevail on Robert to give you the meeting at Cheltenham; for I think it is time for him to know the position of my pecuniary affairs.

To Baron he wrote on 2 August that his health was 'in every respect better', but the details would interest his medical friend:

> The pain gone from my head – my respiration easy – expectoration lessened. . . .eating or drinking anything hastily produc'd palpitation [which]. . .entirely ceases when digestion has gone on to a certain extent. Flatus in the stomach has the same effect. . . .I did not leave my bed till yesterday afternoon & had no conception I cd have suffered such a diminution of muscular strength. Today I feel a great increase of strength but was excessively faint till I took a little animal food & a small quantity of wine largely diluted with water.

Baron came to see him a few days later. In the same letter, however, he noted that 'The Dance was kept up at the Vicar's till near six this morning. Catherine accepted the fascinating hand of the gallant Colonel.' Could this have been William Fitzhardinge, or some other?

He was planning an extension to the hothouse at the Chauntry. Pruen had recently moved to Dursley, where Jenner wrote to him about new arrangements that would 'form a kind of room – which will open into the Grapery, & be itself a Grapery in succession.' Although he had his own brewery, I have found no evidence that he used the grapes except to grace his table. He had always bought his wine, the dealers being principally in London. His wine-dealer friend Edward Gardner was perhaps the only local exception. 'In his house-keeping nothing was gaudy,' reported the *Gentleman's Magazine* after Jenner's death, 'but all was good. The cookery was tastefully and fashionably set out; the wines, commonly five or six kinds, old and of fine flavour.'

His letter to Pruen touched somewhat cryptically on more significant matters. 'We shall have a most furious Vaccine Campaign this winter, & I of course must be in the midst of it. J. Moore, by exposing to the open day, the bad mindedness of the antivaccine Chieftans, will bring them into the field in a state of madness. This, he expects.' Moore's *History and Practice of Vaccination* had just been published. Although the general trend in deaths from smallpox in London probably continued downward, the year 1817 suddenly saw a rise to 1051 over 653 the year before. In Edinburgh too an outbreak of the disease occurred, but its signs and symptoms differed in many ways, especially in being much milder. Some people called it 'modified' or 'mitigated' smallpox. The objective need for a 'Vaccine Campaign' was certainly there, but Jenner's attempt to place himself 'in the midst of it' appears to be a sad recollection of past glory rather than descriptive of reality.

Indeed, taken together with the sudden announcement of a trip to London that almost certainly never took place, this misconception looks unbalanced, like a self-righting doll. Jenner may have suffered brief spells of unreality, perhaps foreshadowing the first unmistakable seizure.

Later in August he wrote to his relative, Elizabeth Hodges, at nearby Arlingham, 'I was happy to find' that a cousin who had suffered from a persistent nervous disorder 'had submitted to the Seton, & trust it may keep her nerves in a state of more composure.' He did not discuss the location of the seton in this case, but it seems certain to have worked by counter-irritation. No country practitioner could escape patients with mental problems. Twenty years earlier he had used his emetic tartar to curb the violence of the insane by making them vomit. Joseph Farington, who recorded this fact from Jenner's pharmacopeia, added, 'Camphor water is an excellent medicine for nervous complaints.' In his notebook, Jenner observed that delirium is 'An irregular & unnatural connection between mind and body.' No doubt true, but hardly a guide to treatment. Though he noticed the various levels of hysteria, and the link to emotion, his medicine gave him little more guidance to the amelioration of this disorder. 'Pure simple hysteria at the onset. . . .may, in many instances, be controlled and even subdued by the mere effort of the will.' 'What is the cause of the pain under the left breast in hysteria?' he wrote in his notebook a few days later. The mystery remains, Breuer and Freud to the contrary notwithstanding, and may be relevant to the bizarre symptoms Jenner would shortly experience.

For the present he seemed to have recovered from the midsummer setback. Early in September he dined with Robert Davies at Stonehouse. On the 24th, after treating a bruised hand belonging to his great-nephew William Davies, Jenner joined Francis Hands, the Berkeley surgeon, Mr and Mrs George Jenner, his son Robert and Henry Shrapnell at dinner provided by the boy's father. The increased frequency of William Davies's visits to Berkeley, on ten days in October, ten in November and nine in December, reflect the recent losses both uncle and nephew had suffered.

During the last months of the year Jenner became entangled in a four-way attempt to settle a debt with a Gloucestershire man named Murray. A lawyer, Mr Vizard from Dursley, had been introduced by Pruen as an arbitrator. The matter dragged on. Jenner told Pruen, 'I feel myself indebted to Murray to a certain extent', and added somewhat later: 'I am desirous of getting out of the hands of Murray'. One senses that it should all have been handled by William Davies, who may have known Vizard, or possibly Vizard's father.

On 18 December Jenner returned from what he told Pruen was an 'Eastington excursion', probably an overnight journey to visit friends. Two days later he was appointed by the corporation to serve for one year as Mayor of Berkeley. It was an honour that seems to have come surprisingly late, but it did not elevate his vision. 'My House has been full of company for this month past,' he wrote to Pruen, 'which does not suit me at all, as I have not spirits to give the required attention – '. Probably they had come to visit his children.

The year 1818 began with a dreadful nursery fire at Kingscote. His niece Caroline, daughter of Catherine Jenner's younger sister, was so severely burned that Jenner feared for her life. He called to see her on 15 January and again five days later. Jenner's daughter helped to nurse the child during her most difficult period. Apparently Caroline did survive, but on 16 March Jenner again went to Kingscote because the older sister, Harriet Frances, was 'alarmingly ill', according to William Davies. Harriet died in May of causes unknown.

Between the two January visits to Kingscote, Jenner was called to Arlingham to see another patient, Mrs Sayer. A few days later in a letter to Richard Worthington, he described his own state of health: 'And now about Corporal Strength & animal spirits. The Corporal is in tolerably good condition & fit for service; but of the latter, if I give any account at all, it must be such a miserable one, that I will spare the feelings of a Friend, & say nothing.' But he qualified even the former: 'You little think what a condition this Swindon-battered Shoulder of mine is in – seldom free from pain by day, & at night it often so terrifies poor quiet Morpheus, he won't come near me.' The Revd Worthington lived at Swindon, so the injury must have occurred during a visit. Neither it nor his general depression seriously affected his epistolary style.

Early in March 'a dreadful hurricane' warranted a record in his notebook. Throughout April, May and June William Davies attended a Petty Sessions in Berkeley followed by a meeting of either the Berkeley Masonic Lodge or the Royal Arch Lodge. Their periodicity varied, though the interval was never less than a week and not more than three. His uncle must have attended one or both occasions with him. For example, on 14 April he and Jenner signed an order of removal, no doubt executing a local enclosure. The unusual regularity of the two events suggests either that Davies, though I think not Jenner, was exceptionally attentive to his duties during these months, or that the local magistracy and Masonry happened to be in the hands of the same person(s).

On 9 June Jenner made a horticultural note: 'Fig trees not to be pruned before May or June. Barberries to be cut down to two or three feet. The vines were planted in the hothouse by Mr. Gold'. In a relatively small garden he had engineered a remarkably varied output. On the purely decorative side, Fosbroke reported that 'the trees are chiefly of the forest kind. . . .This elegant woodlet is inhabited by fowls, the burrow or Sheldrake duck, pigeons, and half-domesticated pheasants, which are never killed for the table, but preserved to give a constant bustle of animation to the still life of wood'. There is today a bosky dell in the quarter nearest to the churchyard. It contains Ferryman's Temple of Vaccinia. But Fosbroke loved his eighteenth-century pictures, somewhat to the restriction of truth. Jenner certainly had apple trees, nor had he been satisfied with the single variety he had obtained from Paytherus. 'I am quite in love with the Flanders Pippin,' he wrote to Richard Worthington, '& must have (not for love but money) half a dozen more grafted Stocks sent to Berkeley'. No doubt he obtained some variety from grafts on to existing trees. He found room for soft fruits too. Soon after Pruen moved to Aldbourn, he asked for cuttings from his gooseberry 'trees'. 'When you plant Cuttings of any kind,' he advised his friend, 'stick them into the ground obliquely, thus / or the wind by constant agitation will prevent them having a due contact with the soil'. Raspberries, he told William Davies, 'should be put into the ground while they remain in a dormant state, that is, before even the buds begin to swell. N.B. a small bundle to be sent here [Cheltenham], & another to Berkeley if Mr. Slade (to whom my Compliments) can spare them.' There was room as well for a kitchen garden, a practical necessity if there was to be any variety on the table. In January 1818 Jenner asked his nephew, Edward Davies, to buy for him 'a few packets of good garden seeds, such as carrot, onion, lettuce, etc etc and the most dwarfish of all the dwarf peas? There is a sort that grows scarcely higher than this sheet of paper, and are excellent bearers.' That May, Worthington, who knew Jenner's garden, seems to have asked for planting advice. Jenner replied: 'I can get nothing but a few spring greens. Ragged jacks and jerusalems [artichokes?] I will show with anybody; but if you want a capital thing, get some Buda kaleseed, and sow immediately. . . .I am daily expecting packets of seeds from Italy and the south of Spain. Nothing, you know, ripened here last year.' It had been very cold. In England, almost nothing could frustrate the gardener like the weather.

Except perhaps the staff. Not surprisingly, Jenner employed men to carry out his plans. He wrote to Worthington:

Old John and I, at last, after about thirty years' association, are come asunder or rather we did separate, and are again forming something like an acquaintance with each other. The <u>old Celt</u> dug up my precious beet-root, just as it was in high perfection, and conveyed it to the dungheap. Within a week old John felt the loss of the pantry so much, that half of him evaporated.

Whether Old John was the same as Mr Gold in the hothouse, I do not know. Jenner's attitudes toward his servants were wholly consistent with others' of his class and period. For the most part servants were invisible. When one grievously misbehaved, as did Old John, he or she might be summarily fired, though it was an uncommon crisis. Jenner's former manservant, Stibbs, on the other hand, had become a tenant farmer, thereby effectively changing both his status and his class. This unusual upward mobility made it possible for Stibbs and probably Mrs Stibbs to entertain William Davies, Richard Worthington and his former employer to tea on 28 July at Tan-House Farm.

On 3 August Jenner called on Davies's youngest child, Anne, who was teething. William then accompanied his uncle in the latter's carriage to a meeting at the Ship Inn, Alveston. With twenty-four other local gentry, they were 'qualified as Commissioners of the Sewers.' These sewers had nothing to do with public health in the narrow sense, but helped to drain the flat land of the Vale of Berkeley into the Severn. The next day they both attended a Petty Sessions in Berkeley.

William Davies noted on 17 August that he was unwell. Nevertheless he 'rode to Berkeley – Dr. Jenner kindly prescribed for me'. They attended Petty Sessions, and that afternoon he and three neighbours, Mr and Mrs Sayer, and Mrs Thomas of Slowwe at Arlingham, 'partook of a haunch of Venison at Dr. Jenner's.' A haunch of venison appears to have been to William Davies what a *tournedos béarnaise* or a cold baked salmon mayonnaise is to some of us today – almost a means of shackling him to the generous and percipient donor. Years before, Jenner had written to Sarah Davies:

My dear Madam

Mr Davies intends making a halt here this afternoon in his way from Eastington & partaking of a haunch of Venison with a few select Friends. He gave me this promise yesterday on condition only that I wd. apprize you of it, as I understand you would otherwise expect him home at dinner. . . .

Early in December 1818, Edward wrote another note:

Dear William

I was sorry to find by Joseph that you have not been quite well –

If you are well enough today perhaps it might be agreeable to you to meet G. Jenner & Mr Hands here at 4 o'clock & partake of that digestable diet Venison.

Of course, the notes reflect Jenner's own delight in food, which underlay and gave meaning to his complaints about dyspepsia. Not unnaturally, good humour accompanied good appetite. 'If you can conveniently spare a Tongue I shd. be obliged to you for it,' he wrote to William a month before the invitation above, 'but shall only take it as a loan to be returned in the form of a salted spare-rib Jennerually prepared – '. Back in 1803 he had asked Elizabeth Hodges of Arlingham for her recipe for 'preserv'd Gooseberry' and cucumbers. Several years later he commented on an item in Pruen's newspaper: 'you have an excellent mode of giving flavour to Soup by a means which lessens the expense of making it. It is the result of an experiment of my own. The fact is, the essential oil of the Celery (the flavourng princip) is extremely volatile, & flies up the Chimney before the Soup is half boild.' I fear the experiment was lost with the flavouring, in the enthusiasm of recollection. About the same time he asked Mrs Black to instruct her cook, Mary Turner, 'to make us some Jelly & Jam. Of the former we shall want not inconsiderable quantity. The last year's Stock was not half sufficient for the year's consumption. We must not regard a few pounds of Sugar.' Mrs Pruen was asked to send 'Rects for Parsnip Wine & a Pud. without an Egg, together with any other little thing from her Book of Domestic Cookery.' After Mrs Jenner's death he entertained more frequently, in part no doubt because her ill-health had restricted them. Food and drink, no less than the company, cheered him.

One more note in the food line suggests that Jenner was a landowner who understood the role that producers played for good or ill in feeding people. Berkeley was known for cheeses called locally 'Berkeleys', but thought to be similar to double Gloucester. In 1819 he wrote: 'The average of every hundred of cheese made in this Parish (Berkeley) costs the farmer one pound four shillings exclusive of house-keeping for the family. Servants go into the general account. There should be at least one servant to ten cows, if the business of the dairy is expected to go on well.' However inefficient he was with his accounts, he understood the practicalities of management in food supply to earn a profit.

Shortly after the dinner party featuring a haunch of venison, vaccine matters again claimed his attention. In a long letter to an American doctor, William Dillwyn of Philadelphia, who had questioned the appearance of smallpox after vaccination, he said, 'Wherever Vaccination has been universally practiced, there the smallpox ceases to exist.' He cited the experience of Sweden. Despite partial vaccination in Britain, furthermore, deaths from smallpox had fallen from about forty thousand per year in

1798 to six thousand. With the letter he enclosed not only his paper on the *Herpetic State of the Skin* but also a copy of the report on the Balmis expedition from the *Madrid Gazette*. The letter itself is not remarkable, but it coincided with another outbreak of smallpox in Edinburgh, characterized by Baron as 'unusually fatal and malignant'. Jenner was devastated: 'What shall I do?' he wrote to Baron. 'This business is too much for me – wd. not the best thing be a Circular, so contrivd as to be a general address to the satisfied & the unsatisfied? In the present state of the Enquiry in Edinb: you will see when you get the [Duncan's] Journal, the nature of the Eruption is involv'd in some mystery.' Jenner was grasping at straws. The disease was smallpox. The only mystery involved epidemiology, and there were probably two answers: imports in the persons of travellers who infected the unvaccinated, and those whose immunity had worn off with the passage of time.

The proposed circular was no doubt the origin of the 'Letter addressed to the Medical Profession generally, relative to Vaccination', published in the *London Medical and Physical Journal* in April 1821. Jenner felt the impact of deaths in Edinburgh because of the correspondence addressed to him personally. 'More letters are come in,' he wrote in a postscript to Baron. Yet nothing could have brought home his powerlessness more effectively. Ageing, unable or unwilling to write for the popular press and severed from the National Vaccine Establishment by his own act of self-emasculation, his sense of frustration must have been enormous.

According to the National Vaccine Establishment report covering the year 1818, Shrewsbury, Faversham, Worksop and Armagh had been without smallpox 'for sometime' – not much of a tally. The Secretary of Addenbrook's Hospital, Cambridge, had reported that eight thousand vaccinations had been carried out during 1818 despite 'every impediment'. Smallpox had been eliminated from the parish of Mickleham, Surrey, in an operation exemplifying the role of the gentry as they perceived themselves in pre-Reform Bill England: Mr Curtis, surgeon of Dorking, had inoculated the poor at the expense of William Lock of Norbury Park and his widow. Despite the signs of improvement, an epidemic in Norwich during 1820 caused three thousand cases of smallpox of which 530 died – about 1 in 6. Most of the dead were children under ten. In the face of such a disaster, however, the vaccinists pointed to ten thousand vaccinated persons of whom only two died of smallpox.

Yet these very facts raise the question of how countries like Sweden and Denmark and cities like Vienna could manage to eliminate smallpox by universal vaccination alone. Despite quarantine, which was none too efficient, imported disease was always a possibility. Before Jenner's death, either these places were lucky or they failed to report outbreaks of smallpox. Between 1824 and 1827, Copenhagen suffered an epidemic which coincided with a general European outbreak, renewed between 1837 and 1840. The latter epidemic at least seems to have been less severe than those of preceding centuries. Neither Faversham nor Sweden could hope to escape an endemic worldwide disease until vaccination was adopted in a worldwide campaign of eradication a century later.

Jenner may have begun to realize something of the magnitude of the task he had set the world, and if he did, he may also have glimpsed the time-scale. In his personal life he contemplated the visible evidence of the future, his own great-nieces and -nephews. His own generation had died; family meant the young.

Neither Catherine nor Robert had yet married, but Henry and George Jenner and all three of the Davies sons had produced offspring. Early in November 1818 Jenner asked William Davies to 'Tell Willy [then seven] as soon as he can read I shall give him some pretty Books.' Later that month William went with his uncle to Stonehouse Court, home of his brother, Robert Davies. Robert's daughter, Louisa, and Emily Worthington, Richard's daughter, required treatment for bilious fever. It was probably about this time, moreover, that another great-nephew, Stephen Jenner, came to live at the Chauntry.

Stephen, eldest child of Henry and Susannah, was born in 1796. When he was nineteen, three years before, he had visited his great-aunt and -uncle Davies, '& shews signs of improvement. I hope he may at least be put out of the road to ruin by being snatch'd away from Berkeley.' Although Stephen's father was still very much alive, Henry's unseemly second marriage under a false name had certainly diminished his family stature. Edward Jenner may have acted as Stephen's guardian. In May 1817 he had noted that 'The money belonging to Stephen Jenner. . .amounts to £730.' These slender references to his great-nephew suggest that Edward Jenner felt an interest. Stephen liked to draw, and when he could be brought to it, produced interesting pencil and charcoal sketches and a few paintings in oil. Fosbroke said he 'possessed talent for comic painting', which was catty. 'I fear the Drawing-job was executed in a Stephenish kind of way', Jenner wrote to his nephew Edward Davies; 'for much of it was done on the morning of the Messenger's departure. . . .What is this about Stephen's Drawings going to Bristol for a Guinea rack? – If I may judge from the present appearance of things, the Market will not be overstock'd.' Jenner found the young man talented, lazy and amusing. Perhaps Stephen's watchful companionship to his ageing uncle was the quid pro quo for his comfortable life at the Chauntry.

The obverse of the youthful coin was death in the family. During their child-bearing years, the women were most vulnerable. Sarah Davies had died after childbirth. At the end of January 1819 Jenner wrote to Baron that he was about to go 'from home to a considerable distance' but would be at the Chauntry the rest of the week. Two days later he visited Louisa

Davies, Robert's wife, who had just given birth to a fourth child. Matters must have been worse than he expected because he called on Louisa again after two more days, accompanied this time by her brother-in-law, William. She died on 5 February, aged thirty-seven.

Early in March William Davies complained of severe, persistent headaches. Jenner prescribed blisters. Perhaps it was then that Jenner urged his nephew, 'Never be without a Small Blister at your command; and apply it when necessary.' He preferred them the 'size of a Crown Piece', because he recognized the relationship between the surface covered by the blister and the probability of suppuration. Their irritant power came from a chemical like cantharidin, that killed skin cells. Not only did the irritation lead directly to inflammatory reactions, but the loss of skin left an open wound that might easily become infected. 'Has not many a one died from the application of a blistering plaster; but still it is as much in use as if this had never happened.'

On 22 March Jenner visited a patient in Tetbury. On the 27th he rode to Stone. After twenty-six hours in labour, George Jenner's wife, Mary, had a stillborn son. 'Dr. Jenner was kind enough to come and see her and will sleep here this night,' George wrote to William Davies. Barely a week later Mary Jenner died.

These tragedies seemed only to strengthen Edward's need for a social life. His old friend Thomas Fosbroke brought his son John to dine at the Chauntry early in April. William Davies was of the party. On the 16th the new William Davies junior, Jenner's great-nephew, arrived for a visit, in company with his father and nursemaid. The four-year-old stayed with his great-uncle for a month, during which his father visited several times, once accompanying Jenner to a Petty Sessions. The next day William Davies noted uniquely in his diary, 'Berkeley Fair'. On 22 May Jenner accompanied his daughter with William Davies to visit Mr Hicks at Eastington. Two days later he and Catherine joined Davies and other neighbours for dinner and tea with the Misses Jenkins at Stone. Jenner and Davies attended court on the 31st and conducted 'Magisterial business at Berkeley from six to nine' p.m. on 5 June. Five days later Davies had a family tea party attended by George Jenner and his daughter Mary; Henry's three children, Stephen and the twins, Susan and Caroline; Henry Shrapnell, Catherine Jenner and her father. Eleven days now intervened before the next meeting of nephew and uncle at breakfast followed by Petty Sessions, and a Masonic lodge meeting, a central feature of which was dinner and tea at the White Hart. The diary entry ends: 'The day was spent most pleasantly in harmony & brotherly love', a formula used regularly after meetings of the Royal Arch Lodge.

During the first six months of 1819 Jenner had once again made contributions to geology. The first concerned the disappearance of a natural feature by human agency: '<u>Our</u> Giant's Cause way at the South eastern extremity of Michael Wood [Woodford] is most magnificent. The Cups and Balls are stupendous. Those of Antrim compared with them are mere pebbles. . . .the workmen now supply the roads with them thro' an extensive district.' The geological portion of this letter to a Bristol acquaintance, George Cumberland, was prompted by some drawings Cumberland had sent to him:

> The teeth of your marine monster are rather indistinct, or I should suspect from large portions of Jaws which were formerly in my possession, that the Rocks of the Severn have ere now turnd out from their Cemeterys, some of this paddling tribe. . . .
>
> The Porpus that so frequently in the Summer season makes an excursion from the Atlantic & comes here to take a roll in the Severn, is a whale. The Bones of the head & Jaws much resemble your etching – The carpal Bones & the Tarsal resemble it also; but the fingers are as dissimilar as any thing can be. These whales by the way are very wonderful animals – They seem to be the human beings of the Ocean & whenever nature could humanize them compatibly with progressive motion & their apparatus for taking their food, she does it. Instead of the small divisions which your Porpus presents for a Paddle, she has given fingers, contained as it were in a glove without any partings; so that these fingers appear only on dissections. There is a fine Skeleton of the Bottle-nos'd whale in the Hunterian Museum which I sent to Mr. Hunter from the Severn. It was shot having got into shallow water – by its side was a young one, to which it was giving Suck. The milk was like that of the Alderney Cow.

This fine mixture of enthusiasm, anthropomorphism and reminiscence demonstrates Jenner's continuing vitality. Some modern geologists maintain that his most important contribution to the science was his discovery, some time before June 1819 at the foot of Stinchcombe Hill, of the fossil remains of a Plesiosaurus, a sea-dwelling sauropterygian reptile. It was the first to be identified in Britain.

On 22 June Robert was about to come down from Oxford. His father asked him to bring 'a little of that Lettuce Seed which the Oxf'd Gardners sew for standing the winter.' But the major object of the letter was to ask for Robert's company. 'I have a Call down to Plymouth & think of going next week – You have never seen anything of Seaports & perhaps you would like to accompany me.' He may well have made the journey, but whether Robert went too was not recorded. On 17 July William Davies brought his seven-year-old daughter, Sarah, to visit her great-uncle. Jenner held 'a grand rout' at the Chauntry for thirty-three Masons and their guests, a few days later, the only such affair noted by Davies in all the years he knew his uncle. On 3 August he accompanied Jenner to

Wotton-under-Edge, a visit that was repeated on the 12th. These were but two of the journeys repeated 'three or four times a week for some time past', which Jenner reported to a Mrs Mary Dyer of Wotton who was then living at Dawlish. On at least one occasion he had visited the Dyers' garden and was shown around by the gardener, though he knew it well. The patient at Wotton may well have been Mrs Dyer's relative.

How long Sarah Davies stayed at Berkeley is not clear, but she was certainly still there on 13 August. Jenner had guests at breakfast on 9 August, William Davies helped to eat a haunch of venison on the 11th, and two days later Jenner joined Henry Hicks and Henry Shrapnell for a neck of venison at Davies's. On 31 August, uncle and nephew dined together and then drove to Cam to call on a patient who died soon afterwards 'in consequence of having taken Arsenic.' After tea with Mr Fryer, the vicar, they returned together to Berkeley. Catherine was visiting in Yorkshire and 'Mr. Fitzhardinge [i.e., Robert Fitzhardinge] is grousing in the Highlands,' he wrote to Worthington on 4 September. 'I am in perfect solitude, and have been so these six weeks.' Which only goes to show that solitude can be relative.

'My hothouse has been beset by a new species of white blight', he wrote to Richard Worthington early in September; 'great has been the havoc it has made among the vines.' Six months later he wrote to another correspondent, Eliza Cox, about the plague of insects he had experienced in the hothouse during the previous summer. 'All this afforded me very frequently a delightful Microscopic repast.' I suspect he meant for the eyes and brain, but not the stomach. Miss Cox had sent him new trees which had died, either because they had been too long out of the ground or 'by meeting with bad gardening when they came here.'

On 13 September, accompanied by William Davies, Jenner dined with Miss Langley Fust of Hill Court, probably the granddaughter of his god-father. There are no other indications, but the families appear to have remained friendly.

Jenner and Davies attended Petty Sessions and Masonic meetings twice in late September and once in October. On 30 October, moreover, Robert was sworn in as a magistrate in the presence of his father, Colonel Berkeley, Henry Hicks and William Davies. The next month Robert qualified as Com-missioner for Turnpikes of the Berkeley and Dursley division of Turnpike Roads. Since 1816 he had been a Mason. At last Robert seemed to be settling into his proper place, but not without cost.

The year before, his father had written to Baron: 'I fear you could do nothing with poor Robert! Many thanks to you for your attention to my request respecting the urgency. I don't exactly know where the young man is at present, but will find him out soon.' Something serious had happened.

Robert had run away. Six months later he was back at Exeter College, where he wrote to Henry Trye:

> I had heard accidentally. . .that you had been at Berkeley lately, but I must say that I am very <u>sorry</u> at the conversation which passed between you and my Father. Edwd Davies wrote to me some short time since & told me many things which you did respecting my Fathers determinations. But what gave rise to them are scandalous untruths. I hope by this time I have convinced my Father & every body that they are so. . . . .I cannot think how I can be supposed to be extravagant as I am sure all my Bills are moderate & all of which will be discharged by me in due time. As for debts of honour I am pretty even on that score. . . . .There was an infamous report spread, that I was involved very deeply & particularly to Tullok. . .when at the same time I was not in debt to him one single halfpenny. In the latter part of your letter you say – There are some persons who will tell me to let my Father have his own way. & not trouble my head with him, but these you say are not my Friends – I agree perfectly with you about it, but at the same time I assure you on my honour that I have never yet had the ill luck to meet with such despicable people. . . .

This remarkably twisted letter leaves one with very little sympathy for a young man who may have had a better case than he made out. The impression is not helped by a letter from his father dated two months later.

> Mr. Hicks was with me some hours yesterday – I find you have had a good deal of conversation with him & in consequence I send the enclosed Drt for £150 – If it is not enough you must have more; but I could wish you to bring your Bills down with you & the Chancellor of my Exchequer (the Doctor) shall see to all this. He tells me he has cash in hand for you.

I believe that various close friends must have tried to interpose themselves between father and son, perhaps more blessed for their efforts by the former than by the latter. In May 1819 in the midst of this correspondence William Davies had called twice to see Robert at Oxford. Because he was Jenner's manager and accountant and because of the very closeness of their family ties, William may have found the role of intermediary impossible. The 'Doctor' must have been Baron. Though Robert might well have distrusted his father's partisan, Jenner could have insisted that there was no one else he would involve in intimate money transactions.

His appointments as JP and Commissioner for Turnpikes seemed to promise that Robert might at last settle in Berkeley in communication, and perhaps some harmony, with his father. In fact another motive had moved him. 'He is unfortunately so attach'd to a neighbour of mine that

I see but little of him – ,' Jenner wrote to Nigel Kingscote in December 1819. 'I shall forbear going into this matter now, but I dare say you know enough to excite pity for Your old & affectionate Fried Edw. Jenner'. The lady thus referred to with downcast eyes was probably Mary Perrington, wife of the local tailor. In his will, Robert left her £160 per annum plus the right to live in or receive rents from the Chauntry and his house at 7 Portland Street, Cheltenham. After Mary Perrington's death, the rents were to go to her daughter, Emily Allen Perrington. Meanwhile, Emily received a legacy of £50 and income from Robert's estate to pay for her 'maintenance, education and advancement in the world'. I have no proof that Emily was the child of Mary Perrington and Robert Jenner, but it seems a fair bet. Nor do I know whether Edward Jenner knew about this grandchild.

Beyond the Jenner household, too, the year 1819 ended in unrest. Indeed, since the Luddite rebellions conflict had continued between the skilled trades in industries such as rope-making and cloth-weaving and the new masters supported by the landowning magistrates. In June 1817 a rising that began in the Derbyshire village of Pentridge seemed for a moment to threaten law and order. It was put down by militia and vigilantes. Pitt's repressive legislation forbidding free speech and association was still in force, and trade unions of any kind were against the law. In August 1819 a peaceful assembly of ordinary citizens in Manchester was fired on by frightened troops in what became known as the Peterloo Massacre. 'What think you of the News from the North?' Jenner asked Baron on 4 December. 'I fear there will be much blood shed before things get smooth again. . . .Here will be more <u>Tales</u> cut out for some future <u>Landlord</u> to unfold [*Tales of a Landlord*, a popular collection of stories, not to be confused with Sir Walter Scott's *Tales of My Landlord*]. I wish Cobbet would change places with Tom Paine – I would travel many a mile in the snow to put him in the Box.' Paine, defender of the rights of man, had had the grace to die in 1809, but William Cobbett could still claim new successes as a campaigning popular journalist.

Jenner took a middle ground. While showing no sympathy for the unrest, he considered extreme measures unnecessary. Two weeks after the letter to Baron, he wrote to his brother-in-law, Colonel Kingscote, mentioning Robert, but the note began with a sarcastic comment on the behaviour of gentlemen in general, moved swiftly to irony, and then to a serious mood:

I think it is possible she [Mrs Kingscote] did not see my last letter to her. It was written on a backpage of Roberts letter to Henry & on this account might escape notice; for it would be an ungentlemanly departure from modern etiquette not to burn a Letter the instant it has been read. The liberty of doing this must still remain, for I do not recollect that the Ministers when sweeping away our Liberties brought in any Bill for its prevention; but tho' I talk at this rate I do not pretend to give an opinion on the late proceedings. The Question is whether the existing Laws were sufficient to keep down that spirit of insurrection which has risen up & spread among a considerable number of our Inhabitants, & whether measures more coercive were not necessary for the well being of the community at large. Bad habits are contagious & when they are dangerous, perhaps it may be best to use preventives I do not imagine with you that the Radical forces will be called out this winter; and for this reason, there is noone to call them out – fortunately they have no leader – so that if tens of thousands were embodied they must be considered merely as a Mob & wd. be unable to move a Stone in the fabric of the Constitution. However they would do a vast deal of mischief before the Corps of Hangmen had finish'd the business.

It was a time of great repression, because even the more moderate were frightened. Only two months later, the Cato Street Conspiracy, consisting of a handful of desperate London artisans, seemed to threaten the overthrow of the state.

Jenner's stance was that of a country doctor with the duties of a magistrate: that is, a mixture of *noblesse oblige* with unalterable commitment to the legal structures that his kind had put in place. In his last published work before his death, *A Letter. . .on the Influence of Artificial Eruptions*, he recalled Richard Worthington's 1804 pamphlet on 'the conditions of the sick Poor.' 'It is to be lamented that the opulent, in most countries, pay so little attention to these abodes of wretchedness [parish workhouses]. When sickness and poverty unite, no uncommon union here, let those who have felt the one (and who has not felt it?) conceive, if they can, the situation of a sufferer, when united with the other.' 'Do the rich support the poor or the poor the rich, or do we each reciprocally support each other?' he asked his notebook. 'Every atom of the creation has an office to perform as a part of one harmonious whole'. Of course the rich and fortunate had a duty to educate the poor, recognizing that the values of the existing order could be understood only by those who possessed the practical skills for life. Back in 1813 Jenner had written to Pruen at Aldbourn, 'I should like to be appointed your village schoolmaster, provided you would allow me to adopt my new system of educating poor children; for I am persuaded the old one is fundamentally wrong.' Unfortunately, he seems never to have written down what Pruen had 'often heard me dwell upon'. However, in 1819 he specified the curriculum:

The intention of Sunday schools, schools of industry and the like, is to impart instruction on the greatest & the least of all mental endowments – Religion & the lowest order of domestic economy. An early knowledge of God cannot be too strongly impressed on the growing mind. . . .in the hour of sadness especially if poverty sho'd add its weight to the load of wretchedness, is there anything can render such soothing consolations as divine contemplations.

For the man who had introduced vaccination to eradicate smallpox, educating the poor had a very special aspect.

The generation which has risen up since the small pox has made so near an approach to extinction. . .know nothing of its ravages & consequently are heedless of giving protection to their children. They hear you speak of the disease & hear you forewarn them of their danger, but as the proofs which come home to their sense are wanting, they exercise that conceit wct. is so predominant in the lower orders of society & listen to you with doubt and suspicion.

He could not have realized that, as the dispossession of the poor increased, their self-awareness also mounted. People who once accepted the designation 'Lower Orders' because they were made relatively comfortable by doing so, now resented it; those whose habits of mind kept them down deserved only doubt and suspicion. In our time, as we approach the topping out of the intricate structure whose foundations were laid with the phrase, all men are created equal, the damaging paternalism that Jenner practised seems all too clear.

Despite worries about the wider world and complaints about loneliness, Jenner prospered during 1819. With the new year came influenza and what he called 'a Typhoid Catarrh, because in every case of any violence, the Brain has been as much disturbed as the lungs; & prostration of strength immediately follows the attack.' In mid-March he told Thomas Fosbroke that he had been ill for about six weeks. Not until 24 April did William Davies note Jenner's participation in any of the events likely to interest him. This was a Royal Arch Lodge meeting followed by dinner and tea with his fellow Masons at the White Hart. In addition to Edward and Robert Jenner, the party included William and Edward Davies, Dr Baron, J. C. Hands, George Jenner, and eight other local gentlemen. The next day Jenner was one of the sponsors at the christening of William's youngest daughter, Anne. Catherine had returned after six months spent visiting Yorkshire friends immediately after the first of the year.

Jenner and his nephew attended a general turnpike meeting at Newport on 20 June, along with three other Commissioners. A week later William noted that the Revd Rowland Hill preached in Berkeley church. The vicar of Berkeley, Caleb Carrington, was in great trouble and possibly unable to conduct services. In December he had been accused before the Consistory Court of Gloucester Diocese of malfeasance in several particulars. The churchwardens of Berkeley complained that Carrington omitted lessons from the services, refused communion, and on one occasion refused to bury one

Peter Grafton unless given a black hat-band. He was alleged to have carried on only after the object had been removed from the corpse and given to him.

Carrington had been presented to the living in 1798, but apart from the Berkeleys, he seemed to have been at odds with a great many of his parishioners for many years. Catherine Jenner may even have threatened to leave the Church of England because of him. In 1812 Jenner had written to Pruen:

> What a curse to Society is a Clergyman who performs no other part of his duty than what is just sufficient to prevent the forfeiture of his stipend. With us the misery does not end here. You know what our Squire is. The profligacy of the common people, particularly the female part, is encouraged to an unlimited extent, & the consequences are deplorable. I wish you had the Living – we want a Giant here.

The Earl had died, but evidently his eldest son was another chip off the old block. A year later Jenner repeated his complaint to Pruen, adding: 'Our Vicar is literally turned Quack Doctor, & vends Pills à la Bedlam with pompous advertisements etc etc!!! – You will see how ingeniously he has avoided the Law, by calling himself the Inventor & making his Son (a mere Child) the vender.'

Early in 1815 some new problem arose with Carrington. Jenner wrote to his neighbour, John Bromedge, 'I had not the least knowledge whatever of the intention of our worthy Vicar till I received your obliging Communication respecting it. It will not be convenient for me to attend on the 17th. but I shall be united heart & hand with my fellow Parishoners in opposing his measures, conceiving them to be extremely nefarious.' Yet Carrington buried Catherine Jenner nine months later. I can only imagine that Jenner acted out of deference to the Berkeleys.

What is more, the unfortunate vicar of Berkeley had undergone a previous suit before the Consistory Court, according to minutes of that body dated 17 April 1817. In 1820 he was called twice to appear, but failed to do so until 13 July. He admitted the charges, made answer to them, and endlessly examined witnesses until 24 January 1822, at which date minutes of the case ended, no action whatsoever having been taken. But on 19 November 1822 Jenner wrote to Baron, who lived in Gloucester:

> If the Bishop will do me the honor to dine with me, & you, or any of your friends will accompany his Lordship, I shall be glad to see you. Pray let me know in time, what there will be for me to do exclusively. I mean with regard to Carrington etc. Someone of course must apprize him of it.

That the Bishop should consult with the leading men in the parish about a troublesome priest had ample precedent, except for the absence of any reference to Colonel Fitzhardinge, whose living it was.

During the early summer of 1820, however, the excitement stirred up by a Methodist preacher in Berkeley church quickly dissipated before the domestic course of events. A month later William Davies brought his children, Sarah and William, to visit their great-uncle. The boy returned home with his father, but Sarah stayed on. William senior attended another meeting of the Turnpike Commissioners at Newport, and the next day Robert Davies came to escort his niece to Stonehouse Court. William Davies junior called on or dined with Jenner on four more days before noting on 5 August, 'Heard that Dr. Jenner was seriously ill.'

According to Baron, Jenner had been walking in his garden when he felt faint and giddy. He fell and was not discovered for some time. Stephen and Henry Shrapnell put him to bed. Baron arrived about 2 a.m. He found Jenner asleep. The next morning he seemed quite well and perfectly lucid. Baron then superintended the usual therapies: leeches, bleeding and blistering. On 6 August Miss Elizabeth Jenkins reported to William Davies that Jenner was 'considerably better, & not much weaken'd by the severe discipline'. Davies breakfasted at his uncle's, and noted a few days later that he was much improved.

Though Jenner seemed relatively unaffected at first, the seizure had its aftermath. 'I am getting better, in some measure from the lameness I mentioned to you; but I feel assured that I am not yet sufficiently sound to bear the motion of a carriage without a great risk. It is my intention ere long to put myself to a test by driving a few miles, & seeing how I can bear the motion', he wrote to Robert Ferryman on 9 November, three months afterwards. Three days later he refused an invitation from Baron to meet the liberal lawyer and MP Sir James Mackintosh at Baron's house in Gloucester, but repeated his intention of attempting a carriage ride shortly. An undated letter to J. Ward, possibly a patient, contains the information that Jenner intended to take his first carriage ride the next day. 'Writing is painful to me,' he added, '& on this acct. you will excuse this scrap – the Seat of my Malady is now in my head.' It was not until 12 January that he revealed his more bizarre symptoms. The letter to Baron began with some comments on the younger man's 'amended health', but then:

> I cannot get my Nerves in good order. Certain sounds, such as I am frequently expos'd to, still irritate them like an Electric Shock. The blunt sounds, such as those issuing from the Bells in the Tower – two pieces of Wood striking each other – indeed obtuse sounds of any kind, do not harm me, but the sharp clinking of Teacups & Saucers, Teaspoons, Knives & Forks on earthen Plates, so distract me that I cannot go into Society which has not been disciplined & learnt how

to administer to my state of distress. But my dear Baron, I will not repine – I have enough & enough to be thankful for, & trust you never will find me ungrateful to the Almighty God who bestowed them.

Gone is the note of querulous self-pity so often evident in the past decade, replaced by resignation.

Six weeks after the seizure, he had written to Baron praising an account of the smallpox epidemic in Norwich by a Dr Cross; '. . .a general vaccination is about to commence in the Clothing Towns of Wotton, Dursley, etc etc.' On 3 October Jenner received a letter from Mr Fry, surgeon at Dursley, concerning a family in which the value of vaccination had been brilliantly demonstrated. The eldest had been variolated, but had caught smallpox many years later. The next four had been vaccinated and in the current epidemic had continued to nurse their youngest four siblings, none of whom had been inoculated. Then one of the latter died. 'About eleven hundred of the poor were then vaccinated at Dursley & at the circumjacent villages & the plague was stayed.' Early in 1821 Jenner referred again to the vindication of vaccination at Wotton in a letter to Edward Davies. 'The Wotton Epidemic turn'd out most famously.' A curious assertion, which underlined the relief Jenner felt at the success on his doorstep.

Although William Davies saw his uncle with the usual frequency during the final months of 1820, Jenner seems to have entertained only once. On 27 November Baron, Henry Shrapnell, and two other gentlemen came for breakfast and stayed the day. He observed New Year's Day, however, by attending a Masonic lodge meeting along with Colonel Berkeley, Robert, George Jenner and William Davies. This is the first time that Davies referred to Robert as Captain Jenner, his rank in the Gloucester Militia.

In February Edward wrote to Richard Worthington about the problems he faced in commanding himself to work normally:

> I rise in the morning tolerably active, and disposed to work with mind and muscle, and actually do work, though scarcely half an hour in the day in the way I could wish, from incessant thwartings and interruptions. . . .though I boast of my strength in a morning, yet evening seems to come before its time. My afternoon is all evening, and my evening midnight. Such are the uncontrollable workings of the old partners mind and matter (body and soul if you will), after the firm has been very long established.

His wit seems unimpaired, a circumstance the more welcome in view of the news he gave Baron three days after the letter to Worthington: 'I find great advantage by setting aside Alcohol altogether, in all its forms. It is a daring Experiment at my time of life'. Nor did it last many weeks.

This letter also carried a complaint about his solitude. 'Catherine has been at Bath for some months; & as for Robert he cares but little for me & less for himself.' Henry Shrapnell had moved to Gloucester. 'Even Henry Jenner is about to leave the place, & Stephen might as well be dead as in the state he is,' Jenner wrote at about the same time; 'so that it seems I must either migrate or spend the remainder of my days in a solitary Cell.' At the beginning of March Stephen had gone to stay with Edward Davies. Jenner was awaiting Catherine's return, but why she

> stays so long at Bath I cannot imagine. I have not a Creature with me, and the solitude of long winter evenings sinks one into the Earth. In 'days lang syne' young people enjoyed a mingling of pleasures; one was the interchange of filial & parental sympathies.
>
>   – but Nature,
>   Is now become a vulgar Creature.

William Davies made only four February visits, and none at all during the two weeks at the end of the month which produced these understandable outcries. Relatively speaking, he was alone, briefly.

On 23 March, however, William paid the Berkeley lawyer, Mr Croome, ten guineas 'for making Dr. Jenner's will, his charge very moderate'. It ran to forty-six pages! Like all wills, it was drawn up to protect those who required protection and to benefit those whom he considered worthy, but in the main it was designed to make an equitable division of his estate between Catherine and Robert. Jenner intended to do this by leaving cash, stocks and government securities to Catherine, and, in the accepted manner, the property to his son; but he did not trust Robert. With the exception of the Portland Street house in Cheltenham and the land called Parslow's Orchard at Berkeley, 'lately conveyed to qualify him for the Office of One of His Majesty's Justices of the Peace', all other property was willed to Robert in trust for his children, or, if he did not marry, for Catherine and her children, if any. Even the county plate, given to Jenner by his grateful Gloucestershire neighbours in 1804, was left to Robert in trust for the same people. William Davies said soon after Jenner's death that his personal property 'did not amount to 35-000 - '. It was more than a little, and Robert must have found the restrictions extremely galling.

The will had two codicils, dated 1 November 1821 and 6 August 1822. The first added to the bequest to Robert to be held in trust, Benson's Leaze, a property near Berkeley, the purchasing and conveyancing of which had been completed after the will had been drawn up. The second took into consideration Catherine's marriage, in recognition of the very substantial marriage portion she had received. The trustees were Colonel Robert Kingscote; Thomas Kingscote, Robert's nephew; Henry Hicks and William Davies. Jenner left to them as trustees his manuscripts, books and papers 'to destroy publish or dispose'.

Surviving Jenners and the Davies brothers were suitably remembered, with bequests and small annuities for Henry, George, Mary and Stephen Jenner. Edward Gardner received an annuity of five guineas for life. To John Baron, Jenner left a ring and his preparation of a hen's oviduct. The choicest specimens from his geological collection were left to Revd Robert Halifax and Henry Shrapnell. The latter had second choice, but was also given Jenner's other anatomical preparations. The Barrett painting acquired for Jenner by John Hunter went to Henry Hicks. Thomas Pruen, John Ring and James Moore were left £10 each. Two of Jenner's tenants who, like Stibbs, also worked for him were left their houses rent-free: George Knight's, for his lifetime and that of his two sons; and James Phipps's, for his lifetime and that of his wife and eldest son.

Jenner may have spent part of this lonely February preparing his circular letter, again warning the profession of the danger arising from herpes infections – that is, skin eruptions. It was published by the *London Medical and Physical Journal* in April 1821. Although the paper contained nothing new, it re-emphasized the importance Jenner ascribed to prior eruptions as a cause of vaccination failure. In point of fact they were his answer to the case now being increasingly heard, that vaccination was not a permanent protection and had to be repeated. His immediate purpose was to obtain information from other practitioners about their experience with the effects of herpetic and other skin eruptions on the course of vaccination. On 3 August he sent a circular to Eliza Cox, with a covering note:

> Dr Jenner on reference to his Memorandum Book perceives that he wrote very fully to Miss Cox respecting the influence of Eruptions over the progress of the Vaccine Vesicle; & conceiving that her vaccine practice, both before & since that period, has been extensively conducted amongst the poor, would be much obliged by any observations she might be kind enough to make to him on the subject.

By the time he finished the second volume of his biography in 1837, Baron knew that the evidence against his revered master had mounted unassailably. He wrote: 'For some time before his death he was employed in reviewing his own opinions, and in comparing them with the facts. . .obtained. . .throughout the world.' Baron also knew that Jenner had not changed his mind, and made the best of it.

Towards the end of March Jenner spent a day or two in Gloucester, where William Davies came to meet him. The Assizes may have occupied their time, and in any case they travelled back to Berkeley together in Jenner's carriage. Some time in April he answered queries from the Norwich Union Life Insurance Company concerning a policy for which his nephew had applied. Jenner said Davies had not had gout, a rupture, spitting of blood, asthma or consumption, fits or 'mental derangements' or any other 'organic or chronic disease' 'except hemorrhoids occasionally.' I am not aware whether William obtained the insurance.

Jenner's health continued uncertain, and there was reason to sympathize with him. 'The streams of nature shall flow undisturbed for me – ,' he wrote to Baron on 7 April.

> Yet I must confess to you that the other day I would have lost some blood when I felt as if these streams would have overflowed their banks & deluged my brain – 'Henry, said I, (Dr Henry Jenner) I wish you would cupp me 'That I would said he but I have lost all my [cupping] Glasses – 'Well then – You must bleed me in the Arm' – Yes but Stephen has broken the points of all the lancets or rusted them.' 'Get some leeches then & put a good cluster of them on each of my Temples' – That I would but I have not one in the world; they all died in the last hard frost' – Thus my dear Doctor am I situated, worse off by far than the Parish Pauper. . . .

He may even have seen the funny side when it happened. Six weeks later he felt less playful. Again, it was to Baron that he described how 'sharp sounds. . .produce an effect like the splash from a stone forcibly thrown into a pool of smooth Water. The propensity to feel this & the violence of the shock, is in proportion to the length of the interval between one shock & another.' This is a new image of his suffering, emphasizing the resonating magnification of sound-feeling within his consciousness. By mid-June, the malign effects of noise seemed to have diminished, though 'clicks still annoy me,' he told Richard Worthington. Following Worthington's advice, he now walked two miles before dinner 'and a pretty long see-saw walk after'. He was enjoying 'larger supplies both of wine and of animal food. . . .My sleep is sound. . . .I go to bed at 11, and rise before 8.' Then in August he complained again to Worthington that clicking cutlery 'gives my brain a kind of death blow. Though I soon scramble out again, I am instantly engulfed. . .in an abyss of misery.' Seldom can a clinical description have more precisely linked a sensation to a pathological mental state.

He was again alone, he told Worthington in the same letter. A few days later he wrote to Mrs Pruen that Catherine was at Bath, Robert at Sidmouth and Susan and Caroline, his great-nieces, were at Burbage, where their grandfather had preached for many years, with their aunt Mary. According to William Davies, he and his two older children were Jenner's sole visitors during July and early August. To relieve his monotony and provide a change of scene, he went on a visit for two or three days at the end of August to Dr Matthew Baillie, John Hunter's nephew, who had a country home at Duntisbourne near Cirencester. Apart from the London medical scene, their mutual interests included rocks and fossils. Baron spent a day with them, probably having accompanied Jenner during his journey there.

The change did him some good. On 14 September he told Charles Parry that his 'Nerves are not quite so susceptible of the sharp noises as they have been.' The letter makes it clear that he had kept himself occupied during his solitude, and despite his symptoms. He had sent the manuscript for a new pamphlet both to John Fosbroke, Thomas's son, and to Charles Parry, the former for stylistic and the latter for medical comment. 'I have a dread about me at the idea of publishing it', he wrote. Even as late as 10 December, he told Parry that he had been finding mistakes in the printed sheets, though publication had been announced with advertisements in *Gentleman's Magazine* and a Bath paper.

A Letter to Charles Henry Parry. . .on the Influence of Artificial Eruptions, In Certain Diseases incidental to the Human Body, with an inquiry respecting the probable advantages to be derived from further experiments was published early in 1822, though it was dated November 1821. Jenner began with nineteen cases, several with mental disorders or a history of heavy drinking and others with physical diseases including consumption, whose symptoms seemed to be diminished or actually cured by rubbing their skins with a salve of emetic tartar. In this form the antimony-based drug is a violent vesicant, causing severe eruptions on the parts to which it has been applied. His rationale was the same as that which underlay the use of blisters: that the creation of a skin disorder can 'check the progress of disease in a vital organ or in a part where it may be unmanageable'. He believed that emetic tartar ointment worked when other vesicants did not because it acted beneath the surface of the skin; his evidence for this would have been the more severe burn produced by emetic tartar.

These hypotheses are almost wholly invalid. A confused old man treated by rubbing a burning ointment between his shoulders might well respond with a shock reaction which was anything but confused. A young man with consumption might return to work after similar treatment, but for how long? Jenner was confusing a sequence of events with cause and effect. He was not alone, and he rightly believed that his series of cases should be brought to the attention of his peers so that they could experiment further with their own patients.

He had also returned to a subject outside medicine that had occupied him since he had observed the murderous behaviour of cuckoo chicks forty years before. One of his central points had been that the mother cuckoos laid their eggs in the nests of other species because the migratory cycles of cuckoos made it impossible for them to tend their own. When he had submitted the paper to the Royal Society, he assured Joseph Banks that another study on the migration of birds was under way. In the early autumn of 1822, he made two entries in his notebooks relating to dissections of martins and swallows to determine their recent diets.

In the wet summer of 1821, when the air was unusually chilled by the long continued rains, they [martins and swallows] were observed to assemble, during some intervals of sunshine, for several successive mornings, as early as the middle of July, & in the present year (1822), I remarked the same on some mornings that were unseasonably cold about the middle of August.

He used further evidence from dissections to show that the gonads of birds shrank before migration, fertilization and the production of young having been completed. From these observations, it followed that the purpose of migration was to lay eggs in a climate and setting damp and green enough to support the food needed for rearing of chicks.

Jenner's major contribution, however, was his argument that birds do not disappear during the winter because they go into hibernation, as had been widely accepted. Some species were thought to lay up beneath the surface of ice covering lakes and ponds. Jenner showed that the movements and conditions of the birds could be better explained by their migration than by the hibernation theory.

Some Observations on the Migration of Birds appeared first in the *Philosophical Transactions* of the Royal Society in 1824, with an introductory letter to Sir Humphry Davy, the President, from George Jenner. The paper had been completed by the end of 1822, but Jenner had not submitted it. His ability to assemble these data and the case histories in the paper on artificial skin eruptions, and to organize them into a clear presentation, demonstrates that his mind had not been damaged by his seizure two years before, however lasting its effects on his sensorium.

Although he told Richard Worthington's daughters that he was 'still in solitude' on 15 September 1821, the autumn began to bring life back to Berkeley. First, Stephen Jenner returned from an extended visit to Edward Davies. In a postscript to a letter to his brother from William Davies, Jenner added:

By what means, moral or physical, did you continue to bring about so great a change in the mind of Stephen Jenner? Since his return, he has conducted himself in every respect in a proper manner. The cold, sour, forbidding trump [obstruction; i.e., obstructive person], is changed into good humour & complacency; and the paralys'd Pencil is perfectly restord to its wonted action – Indeed, it goes beyond it – for a Drawing he shew'd me yesterday, in point of execution, goes far beyond any former production.

Soon after this Jenner wrote a note to his great-nephew, William Davies, who had been ill while at school in Bristol. 'My dear Willy Yr Father dined yesterday with Mr Pruen, Susan, Caroline & Stephen He gets on with his painting surprisingly; and in due time, if he will but stick to it closely, he will be as eminent as Sir Joshua.' And for a time Stephen did stick to it. Probably during the winter of 1821–2, Jenner wrote again to Edward Davies:

> I had a pleasant Letter from Kensington yesterday – Miss Paytherus speaks of Stephens Genius as exhibited in the Lithographers, as exhibiting proofs of talent & Genius. Wilkie is the near neighbour of the Paytherus; & Sr. Thomas Lawrence is often there, Wilkies picture for the present Exhibition eclipses all his former productions. One of the life Guards has arrived at Chelsea with the Gazette Extraordinary of the Battle of Waterloo & the moment selected for the Picture is the reading it to the Chelsea Pensioners.

On 23 October, Robert was elected Mayor of Berkeley. The honour may have given less pleasure to the recipient than to his father.

A day or two later Jenner went to visit Edward Davies at Ebley. His letters indicate that Edward, a successful farmer, shared his uncle's interest in the arts. During the visit, which lasted a week, Jenner sat for a portrait by William Hobday, then also staying with his nephew. The painting was exhibited at the Royal Academy the next year, and became the subject of an engraving begun by William Sharp and completed by William Skelton after Jenner's death. William Davies called the Hobday painting 'a very excellent & correct likeness'.

Like the earlier portraits, Hobday's is grand and formal. Stephen Jenner left only one picture of his great-uncle, a sketch showing him vaccinating an infant sitting on its mother's lap. There is a cat in front of them looking out at the viewer. This may have been the picture for which Jenner offered him five guineas when or if it was completed. Jenner complained to Edward Davies that Stephen had ceased almost entirely to work again, despite the fact that everyone who saw his pictures agreed that he had talent. However deficient his completion-rate, Stephen left a verbal portrait of his great-uncle written below his sketch:

> . . .his dress was a black coattailed coat with a large collar as it was worn in his time, loose black trousers and waistcoat a white neck cloth and white stockings he was a little near sighted, but never made use of glasses. his hair was a dark brown a little curly but not the least grey. he was below the middle stature rather short necked. After dinner he frequently took a nap. . . .he was always pleased to have the family round him.

Despite his complaints, Edward Jenner at seventy-three displayed a remarkable state of preservation. 'Thank Heavens, I have not been in better health for some years than at present,' he wrote to Mrs Pruen at the end of the year.

A few days after leaving Edward Davies's, he went to Bath for a visit, probably to see his old friend Caleb Parry for the last time. Jenner attended his funeral in January.

He still suffered from his aversion to sharp sounds, and had described them to Alexander Marcet in a letter dated 5 March 1822, concluding: 'In a Female I should call it Hysterical – but in myself I know not what to call it, but by the old sweeping term nervous. Will you allow me to call it electrical?' The remark reveals much about Jenner in relation to these interesting and persistent symptoms. Apart from the femaleness of the word, deriving from its Greek origin, to which Jenner may have been referring, he was also right to distinguish his symptoms from hysteria because, then as now, it meant a disorder with no apparent cause, and certainly no physical origin. In so far as nervous impulses consist of a flow of electrically charged particles, something he could not have known, he nevertheless guessed correctly that there was something electrical about his disorder. He introspected the connection between a noise and certain mental states, but he ascribed the connection to the seizure, almost certainly with justice. In sum, he was fascinated by the symptoms. He could not experiment with them, but he could catalogue them in the museum of experience.

He told Marcet that he had had two continental visitors, Dr V. V. Herberski from Vilna, a friend of Marcet, and Dr F. Holst of Christiana, Herberski's travelling companion. These visits were a compliment much welcomed. Even the new physician to the Smallpox and Vaccination Hospital, Dr George Gregory, supposed he was involved with the National Vaccine Establishment. Jenner wrote to deny any connection, though he was 'by no means at variance.' Later in March 1822 Edward Davies told him about newspaper reports of a vaccination conference involving John Walker's London Vaccine Institution, which now incorporated the Royal Jennerian Society. Jenner wrote in reply that he had enlisted Richard Worthington to write to one of the participants, and asked his nephew to inform any MP with whom he was acquainted 'that I have nothing whatever to do with Walkers Society, except that general tie which in some measure unites me with every Society in the world which has through the medium of Vaccination, the eradication of smallpox for its object; nor have I any <u>direct</u> communication with the National Vaccine Establishment.' Marcet remained his only medical friend in the metropolis.

'How goes on Vaccination?' he asked Revd William Pruen, Thomas's brother, who had a church near Evesham. 'I feel under obligations to every one who pursues it with even half the ardor & attention that you do. . . .When you fall in with any of the neighbouring Faculty, convince them if you can of the vast importance of attending to the state of the skin when they vaccinate.' He enclosed a copy of his *Letter to Parry*.

Early that March, William Davies spent the day with Jenner at the

Chauntry. 'Col. Kingscote and the Mr. Bedford's' were also there. This Mr Bedford, who had appeared with his family – perhaps a mother and/or sister – had become a friend of Catherine's. He came from Birmingham, where he was in business, and when or where he and Catherine had met I have not discovered. His visit to Berkeley was almost certainly to meet her father.

At the beginning of June Robert wrote an affectionate note to William Davies, asking him to attend a meeting with Mr Croome and Henry Hicks 'on the business of my Sister's marriage settlements. . . .you know of course – the importance of the matter – '. It was in the end straightforward: Jenner gave his daughter £13,333-6-8 in Consolidated 3 per cent annuities, to be held in trust for her during her lifetime by Colonel Robert Kingscote and Revd William Richard Bedford. It was an enormous sum of money. She was twenty-six years old, perhaps, for her class, a little late for marriage. Knowing nothing of Catherine other than the little that has already been conveyed, I cannot say why her husband-to-be should have expected or been given so much. Perhaps she insisted on thus insuring her own independence within a legal framework that otherwise made her her husband's chattel. Jenner gave her another £1000 on her marriage day.

On 26 June William Davies had a tea party for 'My Uncle Dr. Jenner – My Cousins R.F. Jenner, Cath: Sus: Car: & Steph Jenner, Mr. Bedford, Mr. J. Fosbroke & Mrs Step. Jenner.' This interesting cast list contains not only Mr Bedford but a new character. Mrs Stephen Jenner appears to have entered the play within the last six months, or at least after Stephen returned full of energy from his visit to Edward Davies the previous autumn. She and her husband and their first-born then lived in a cottage belonging to Jenner beside the Chauntry.

Catherine Jenner and John Yeend Bedford were married in Berkeley church by the Revd William Davies on 7 August 1822. They lived at Southbank, Edgbaston, Birmingham, until on 5 August 1833 Catherine died after the birth of her first child, a daughter who was christened Catherine Sarah and survived.

Amongst the guests at Catherine's wedding breakfast were Mr and Mrs H. Marklove. They were old friends, part of a large and respectable Berkeley family. Jenner and Daniel Marklove, probably an uncle, were the guardians of a young woman named Maria Marklove. She and Henry Shrapnell must have met during the latter's employment as Jenner's informal curator. They had eloped to Gretna Green, but then decided to do the whole thing properly. On 17 September Maria's guardians consented to a remarriage, which was performed on that day in Berkeley church by Caleb Carrington. Jenner was one of the witnesses.

He was certainly having his off days. There is occasionally a quaver in his handwriting, and business transactions could be difficult. His twin nieces, Susan and Caroline Jenner, copied letters for him and helped with the pleasure of their company. He worried about Stephen's inability to finish a drawing. 'For a pretty good definition of Genius, see Jenner on the Divisions of human intellectuality,' he told Pruen, and put forward the idea that the artist needed not just a school but firm guidance from a fellow-painter such as David Wilkie. He also asked Pruen to help obtain a copy of Robert Bloomfield's new poem. 'I should be glad to have it & to pay him a couple of Guineas for it.' On 19 December he and William Davies attended a meeting at the White Hart to form a branch of the Bible Society. Robert Davies with his second wife, Mary, and one of his sons dined at the Chauntry soon after the first of the year, and three days later William held a large dinner party, attended by his uncle and various relatives and friends. Jenner was neither alone nor confined.

He wrote to Edward Gardner, whom he called the 'Frampton Watchmaker', on 13 January, sending dried vaccine matter for Gardner's use. This included scabs from drying vesicles, another less effective means of preserving the lymph. The letter conveyed family news. Susan and Caroline were visiting Edward Davies at Ebley. 'Catherine is very well, and I believe very happy. Edward Davies has been on a visit to her, and speaks highly of her situation.' The letter continued in a philosophical vein appropriate between two old friends:

> Never was I involved in so many perplexities – Metaphysics are on the shelf – But mind me – I do not conceive there is a single living particle of matter in the Universe – The Brain, age & the nerves too are dead as my hat – All life is in that something superadded to matter the Anima, diffused through matter if you wish, but to speak like a Chemist, not chemically combined with it, not forming an integrant part but merely influential – 'There is something behind the Throne greater than the Throne itself'

Jenner's God was a chemist who possessed the secret of life in the form of anima, or soul. He had worshipped the same God at least since his education by John Hunter, the God Who made of nature a 'sylvan minstrelsy'. This God allowed him to employ medicine to change diseased chemical structures toward normality and health, but the anima remained beyond his power or that of any man.

A few days later William Davies paid his uncle a visit. William was off to Bristol to take his son back to school after the holidays. Jenner wrote a short, affectionate note wishing the boy well. Pruen was also there that evening, Friday 24 January. Jenner was walking with Stephen in the garden when his butler brought the news that Mr Joyner Ellis, the Berkeley coroner, had been taken ill and wished Jenner to come at once. Stephen was smoking a cigar and reported that his great-uncle suggested he 'go into the Hot House and smoke the red spider'. Jenner returned in time for tea. In response to Stephen's inquiry, he said that Mr Ellis was fatally ill, and indeed he died two days later.

Henry Jenner had come for breakfast the next morning at the usual hour of 8 a.m. His son, Stephen, told him Jenner was not down yet. Henry rang for the servant and sent him to say that breakfast was ready. 'The servant found his Master on the floor in the Library and after placing him on a sofa, hastily returned', according to Henry Shrapnell's account. Henry Jenner realized he had had 'an apoplectic seizure accompanied with paralysis of the right side.' He bled his uncle and applied blisters to the feet. Henry sent for the Berkeley surgeon, Mr Hickes, and Stephen set off for Gloucester to inform Robert and to ask Baron to attend immediately. At 1 p.m. George Jenner wrote a note to William Davies, not yet returned from Bristol, and sent it via James Phipps. Meanwhile, Henry persisted with bleeding and blisters 'and the Doctor seemed to revive, but scarcely a hope could be entertained of his restoration'. He remained unconscious. Baron arrived late in the afternoon and promptly cut the temporal artery to induce greater bleeding, but with no effect; '. . .he expired soon after two o'clock on the following morning', 26 January 1823.

William Davies noted: 'A deep snow. No service at Stone or Rockhampton on account of the death of my revered & ever to be lamented Uncle Dr. Jenner.' George Jenner was curate at Stone, and William the incumbent at Rockhampton. William dined with Robert and George at the Chauntry. The next day Catherine and her husband arrived from Birmingham. At the funeral in Berkeley church on 3 February, Caleb Carrington read the service. James Phipps was among the mourners. The pallbearers included Colonel Berkeley and several of Jenner's tenants, including Stibbs. Edward Gardner, Henry Hicks and Thomas Pruen attended, as did Baron and several other members of the Gloucestershire medical faculty, but no one from London. Edward Jenner was buried beside the altar next to his wife and eldest son, and near his parents and eldest brother.

Notes

ABBREVIATIONS ALS, Autographed Letters Store; *Ann. Med. Hist.*, *Annals of Medical History*; BL, British Library; BLMS, British Library Department of Manuscripts; GCRO, Gloucester County Record Office; GL, Gloucester Library; JM, Jenner Museum; *Med. Hist.*, *Medical History*; *Med. Phys. Jour.*, *Medical and Physical Journal*; RCP, Royal College of Physicians of London Library; RCS, Royal College of Surgeons of England Library; RJS, Royal Jennerian Society; RSM, Royal Society of Medicine Library; Well., Wellcome Institute for the History of Medicine Library.

Chapter 1: Gentry 1749

Page

1 'I hope he will live . . . .': Revd Stephen Jenner, Correspondence and papers. . . . 1720–49, Well. MS5224.

Indigent Blind: Sir Gilbert Blane, *A Statement of Facts, Tending to Establish an Estimate of the True Value and Present State of Vaccination*, London: Thomas & George Underwood, 1820, p. 12 footnote.

Robert John Thornton, MD, *Facts Decisive in Favour of the Cow-Pock.* . . ., 4th edn, London: H. D. Symonds *et al.*, 1803, pp. 7–11.

3 'unprecedented event . . . .': Derrick Baxby, *Jenner's Smallpox Vaccine: The Riddle of Vaccinia Virus and its Origins*, London: Heinemann Educational, 1981, p. vi.

5 dormice: Thomas Dudley Fosbroke, *Berkeley Manuscripts*, London: John Nichols & Son, 1821, p. 222.

Booksellers . . . and . . . Merchant,: William Davies, Household accounts, Vol. III, Well. MS2050.

'Kenelem Jenour . . . .': LeRoy Crummer (ed.), 'Copy of Jenner Note Book', *Ann. Med. Hist.*, N. S. I (1929) p. 421.

T. D. Fosbroke, *op. cit.*, facing p. 220.

Vive ut Vivas: Crummer, *op. cit.*, p. 420. Literally: 'Live in order to live life fully.' I am indebted to Colin Haycraft who corrected the Latin in Crummer's published version of the Note Book (confirmed by reference to a photocopy of the original (40).) and gave me the literal translation.

Bonham Bazeley, *Standish Church*, Gloucester: T. W. Cole, 1984, p. 3

6 cereal prices: Michael Reed, *The Georgian Triumph, 1700–1830*, London: Routledge & Kegan Paul, 1983, pp. 68ff.

'Rode to Slimbridge . . . .': William Davies, 27/5/1805, *Memoranda 1792* (1/1/1792–27/5/1805) (henceforward: Diary 1792–1805), Well. MS2052.

'discharge every thing . . .': Revd Stephen Jenner, *op. cit.*, Well. MS5224(4).

'shall be Glad . . .': *ibid,*. Well. MS5224(3).

'the beauty you admire . . . .': *ibid.*, Well. MS5224(1).

7 curate of . . . Coates,: *ibid.*, Well. MS5224(11).

'Dear Cousin . . . .': *ibid.*, Well. MS5224(6).

'ye Reverd Mr heads . . .': *ibid.*, Well. MS5224(5).

Page
7 inducted: Berkeley Parish Register, GCRO PFC42 1/15–1/39.

came to live there.: Stephen Jenner, Tythe and rent book . . . 1729–55, Well. MS3038.

'Kind expressions of Joy . . .': Jenner family of Standish, Glos., and Seely family of Oxford, Correspondence and papers. . . . Well. MS5222(5).

The marriage settlement . . . 9 September 1729.: Stephen Jenner, Leases, indentures and marriage settlement, 1712–53, GCR0 D873 T100.

8 St Catherine's Hospital,: Fosbroke, *op. cit.*, facing p. 220.

Berkeley . . . population: *ibid.*, p. 64. Dorothy Fisk, *Dr Jenner of Berkeley*, London, Melbourne and Toronto: Heinemann, 1959, p. 2.

'It is seated on a hill . . . .': Joseph Stratford, *Good and Great Men of Gloucestershire*, Cirencester: C. H. Savory, [1867], p. 285.

tower . . . restored: Fosbroke, *op, cit.*, pp. 51, 60.

Berkeley . . . a borough: *ibid.*, p. 38.

9 four valuable tithings: T. D. Fosbroke, *Abstracts of Records and Manuscripts Respecting the County of Gloucester*, Vol. I, Gloucester: Jos Harris, 1807, pp. 462–3. In his history of Berkeley, Fosbroke refers to seven tithings but says they compose the Manor of Berkeley (*Berkeley Manuscripts*, p. 38).

1733 . . . a house and orchard: Stephen Jenner, *op. cit.*, Well. MS3038.

Dayhouse Mead,: *idem.* and Revd Stephen Jenner, *op. cit.*, Well. MS5224(19).

land taxes on parcels: [Stephen Jenner, Account and commonplace book, 1740–55], [p. 19], GCRO P271 IN 4/1.

indenture . . . 2 May 1753,: GCRO D873 T100.

by 1751 . . . land taxes: Stephen Jenner, *op. cit.*, Well. MS3038.

Part of the Hinton lands: *idem.* Stephen Jenner, *op. cit.*, GCRO P271 IN 4/1. Notebook kept by Thomas Jenner: Stephen Jenner, vicar at Berkeley 1729–44, Well. MS3070.

Christmas . . . 1744 to 1746,: Notebook kept by Thomas Jenner, Well. MS3070.

'Recd all rent . . . .': Stephen Jenner, *op. cit.*, Well. MS3038.

purchase . . . of Rockhampton,: Stephen Jenner, *op. cit.*, GCRO P271 IN 4/1.

10 'we must not judge . . . .': Stephen Jenner, '2 Cor: 2d Chapr: prt of ye 17th Verse but as of Sincerity', [1745?], p. 19.

'The Danger of Sin': Revd Stephen Jenner, 'The Danger of Sin', Berkeley, 9/11/1729, Well. MS3032.

'the things appointed for Sacrifices': Revd. Stephen Jenner, 23/5 [1747?], Well. MS3036.

11 'Old Obodiah . . . .': Notebook kept by Thomas Jenner, Well. MS3070.

man named Williams,: Revd Stephen Jenner, *op. cit.*, Well. MS5224(7).

Thomas replied,: *ibid.*, Well. MS5224(8).

school land rents: Stephen Jenner, *op. cit.*, 4/4/1748, GCRO P271 IN 4/1.

Berkeley Lecture Sermons.: Notebook kept by Thomas Jenner, Well. MS3070.

ordinary diary entries: *idem.*

'Cyder House': Stephen Jenner, *op. cit.*, GCRO P271 IN 4/1.

advertisement: p. 3.

12 Sarah gave birth: John Baron, *The Life of Edward Jenner, M. D. . . .*, Vol. II, London: Henry Colburn, 1838, p. 381. In a letter to James Moore from Berkeley, 11/10/1812, Jenner said there were ten in all. I believe he simply miscounted.

she was called Sally,: Jenner family, MS Account book, [1760–97], Well. MS3072.

Mary was baptized . . . biography.: Berkeley Parish Register (1706–1823 baptisms, marriages, burials), GCRO PFC42 1/15–1/39. All of these events are also recorded in the Bishop's Transcripts of the Berkeley Parish Record, also GCRO, being abridged transcripts of parish registers sent to the Gloucester Diocese annually by parish clerks. The dates in the Transcripts may vary by as much as a year either way from the dates in the registers.

Chapter 2: 'a distemper named the Cow-Pox' 1750–1772

13 Pembroke . . . Magdalen.: [Stephen Jenner, Account and commonplace book, 1740–55], GCRO P271 IN 4/1. A Demi was so-called, it is said, because he received half the stipend of a Fellow.

Page

13 'S Jenner July 23rd 1750 . . .': [Stephen Jenner, Tithes and Church House accounts, Rockhampton, 1758–91], Well. MS3039.

'Gave him 20s . . . 5£ 10s'.: Stephen Jenner, *op. cit.*, GCRO P271 IN 4/1.

father signed an agreement: [Rockhampton, Parish of], 'Enclosed in this book are the severall amounts of the severall Churchwardens . . . out of an Old Book now in the Custody of the Revd. Stephen Jenner Clk Rector of Rockhampton . . . 1735 to the yeare 1752 . . .', GCRO P271 CW2/3.

Thomas,: Berkeley Parish Register, GCRO PFC42 1/15–1/39.

Sarah Jenner died,: J. Stratford, *Good and Great Men of Gloucestershire. A Series of Biographical Sketches . . .*, Cirencester: C. H. Savory, [1867], p. 286. He was just fifty-two: *idem*.

14 presented . . . in January.: Revd George Charles and Mary Black . . ., Correspondence and papers . . ., 1750–1810, Well. MS5226(2).

rector of Cranford.: *ibid.*, Well. MS5226(1).

account book: Jenner family, MS Account book, [1760–97], Well. MS3072.

marriage settlement,: Black and Black, *op. cit.*, Well. MS5226(3).

rector of Rockhampton.: [Rockhampton, Parish of], *op. cit.*, GCRO P271 CW2/3.

Its grammar school: E. S. Lindley, *Wotton under Edge*, London: Museum Press, 1962, p. 231.

inoculated . . . by a local surgeon,: T. D. Fosbroke, *Berkeley Manuscripts*, London: John Nichols & Son, 1821, p. 222.

'He was bled,. . . . ever since subsisted.': *ibid.*, pp. 221–2.

15 from Persia and China.: Donald R. Hopkins, *Princes and Peasants: Smallpox in History*, Chicago and London: University of Chicago Press, 1983, p. 46; for the best nineteenth-century account, see Edgar M. Crookshank, *History and Pathology of Vaccination*, Vol. I, London: H. K. Lewis, 1889, pp. 1–2ff.

Lister . . . Lister,: Hopkins, *idem*.

Timoni: John Baron, *The Life of Edward Jenner, M. D. . . .*, Vol. I, London: Henry Colburn, 1827, pp. 230–3.

Robert Halsband, *The Life of Lady Mary Wortley Montagu*, Oxford: Clarendon Press, 1957, pp. 80–1.

Princess Caroline of Wales,: *ibid.*, pp. 104–10. Hopkins, *op. cit.*, pp. 47–8. Derrick Baxby, *Jenner's Smallpox Vaccine: The Riddle of Vaccinia Virus and its Origin*, London: Heinemann Educational, 1981, p. 22.

16 Sarah Chiswell, died: Hopkins, *op. cit.*, p. 48.

Baron . . . said: Baron, *op. cit.*, I, pp. 232–3.

1 in 5 to 1 in 8.: Baxby, *op. cit.*, pp. 34–5.

Onesimus,: Hopkins, *op. cit.*, pp. 173–4.

17 to inoculate the next person.: Allan W. Downie, 'The poxvirus group', in *Viral and Rickettsial Infections of Man*, ed. Frank L. Horsfall Jr and I. Tamm, 4th edn, London: Pitman; Philadelphia: Lippincott, 1965, p. 933.

Sydenham: quoted in Hopkins, *op. cit.*, p. 33.

18 Suttons recommended: *ibid.*, p. 60.

Ingatestone: James Johnston Abraham, *Lettsom: His Life, Times, Friends and Descendants*, London: William Heinemann Medical, 1933, p. 189.

Fourteen thousand people: Crookshank, *op. cit.*, I, pp. 46–8.

£3-15 . . . £20: Abraham, *op. cit.*, p. 191; Baxby, *op. cit.*, pp. 25–6.

1 in 2800.: Baxby, *idem*.

about 12 per cent: Hopkins, *op. cit.*, p. 60.

Dimsdale: Abraham, *op. cit.*, pp. 194–5.

19 London Foundling Hospital: Hopkins, *op. cit.*, p. 59.

Gloucester . . . smallpox hospital: *Glocester Journal*, 4/11/71, p. 2; 30/3/72, p. 3.

variolators: See 8/1/70, p. 3.

'Beneficial Effects . . .': *Glocester Journal*, 27/4/72, p. 2.

twenty Liverpool medical men: [John Ring], 'To the Editors of the. . . .', *Med. Phys. Jour.*, 25 (4/11), p. 305.

Haygarth . . . *Plan*: Hopkins, *op. cit.*, p. 77.

Page

19 Lay people,: Dorothy Fisk, *Dr Jenner of Berkeley*, London, Melbourne and Toronto: Heinemann, 1959, pp. 119–20.

309 people . . . 1795,: Berkeley Parish Register (baptisms May 1787 to Jan. 1810), p. 3, GCRO PCF42 1/15/1/39.

' . . . Dr. Capell': Fosbroke, *op. cit.*, p. 222.

aged about forty: *Glocester Journal*, 22/9/88, p. 3.

20 ' . . . classics',: Baron, *op. cit.*, I, p. 3.

Washbourne . . . 1765,: Paul Saunders, *Edward Jenner: The Cheltenham Years 1795–1823*, Hanover, Vt., and London: University Press of New England, 1982, p. 5.

' . . . my Mother Tongue'.: letter to Dr A.J.G. Marcet, 15/3/1809, in *Letters of Edward Jenner and Other Documents concerning the Early History of Vaccination*, ed. Genevieve Miller, Baltimore and London: Johns Hopkins University Press, 1983, p. 53.

'obtained a tolerable proficiency . . .': letter to Dr Cooke, quoted by Baron, *op. cit.*, Vol. II (1838), p. 192.

also found friends,: *ibid.*, p. 5.

remained with Ludlow for six years.: Fosbroke, *op. cit.*, p. 222.

21 'About the year 1768,. . . .': James Moore, *The History and Practice of Vaccination*, London: J. Callow, 1817, p. 2.

In 1782. . . . Apothecaries.: E. Ashworth Underwood, 'Jenner and the Story of Vaccination', bound MS, p. 25, Well. Contemporary Medical Archives Centre.

John Ludlow's son: Charles Creighton, *Jenner and Vaccination: A Strange Chapter of Medical History*, London: Swan Sonnenschein, 1889, p. 2.

22 Edward formally enrolled: Baxby, *op. cit.*, p. 39.

George Qvist, *John Hunter, 1728–1793*, London: William Heinemann Medical, 1981, pp. 1–18.

'read every winter, . . .': from *European Magazine*, 1782; quoted in Fisk, *op. cit.*, pp. 33–4.

23 'that Mr Edward Jenner, . . .': [Edward Jenner], Diplomas and certificates, 1772–1804, Well. MS5231(1).

Dr George Fordyce,: *ibid.*, Well. MS5231(3). Underwood, *op. cit.*, p. 40.

Denman and . . . Osborne.: Underwood, *op. cit.*, pp. 42–3. [Edward Jenner], *op. cit.*, Well. MS5231(2).

24 £100 a year,: Underwood, *op. cit.*, p. 44.

Edward's income . . . 30: Jenner family, *op. cit.*, Well. MS3072.

25 co-boarders . . . Jenner's letters: Jessie Dobson, *John Hunter*, Edinburgh and London: Livingstone, 1969, pp. 125–6. Baxby, *op. cit.*, p. 40.

26 admired by Burns.: Fisk, *op. cit.*, p. 44.

'My mother bids me . . .': Underwood, *op. cit.*, p. 37.

Hunter started: Qvist, *op. cit.*, p. 38.

Thomas Beddoes: Moore, *op. cit.*, p. 18 and footnote; Beddoes's book is: *Queries concerning Inoculation*, 1795.

Banks and . . . Solander: 22/7/71, p. 1.

report that early in 1772 Banks: [John Coakley Lettsom], *Memoir of Edward Jenner, M. D..*, [London]: I. Gold, 8/3/1804], p. 2. Underwood, *op. cit.*, p. 48, doubts the whole story because the Banks papers do not mention it.

27 Banks . . . scientific officer,: Patrick O'Brian, *Joseph Banks, A Life*, London: Collins Harvill, 1988, pp. 150ff.

'partly guided by the deep . . . .': Baron, *op. cit.*, I, p. 7; see also Moore, *op. cit.*, p. 3.

'one of the literary associates'.: Moore, *idem*.

'was probably the closest friend . . . .': Dobson, *op. cit.*, p. 152.

'dear man'.: Baron, *op. cit.*, I, p. 10.

Chapter 3: Romance 1773–1788

28 Paul Saunders, *Edward Jenner: The Cheltenham Years, 1795–1823*, Hanover, Vt., and London: University Press of New England, 1982, p. 10, states that Jenner returned from London in 1773. John Baron, *The Life of Edward Jenner, M. D.*, Vol. I, London:

Page

Henry Colburn, 1827, p. 28 leaves open the year in which Jenner returned, but dates the first of the surviving Hunter letters (see p. 34), 1773. Jenner's last course certificate is dated May 1772, but he could have stayed on to work with Hunter until after the 1st of the year 1773. No firm evidence has been found.

28 young Ned,: Stephen Jenner to William Davies, 27/3/1775, William and Anne Davies, Correspondence. . . . 1775–1812, Well. MS5229(1).

29 'the ground was deeply covered . . . .': quoted in Baron, *op. cit.*, I, pp. 72–3.

'activity of mind with indolence . . . .': T. D. Fosbroke, *A Picturesque and Topographical Account of Cheltenham . . . to Which are Added, Contributions to the Medical Topography . . . by John Fosbroke*, Cheltenham: S. C. Harper, 1826, pp. 276–7. For later criticism: C. Creighton, *Jenner and Vaccination: A Strange Chapter of Medical History*, London: Swan Sonnenschein, 1889, pp. 5–18.

30 Letter to Revd John Clinch, 7/2/1789, quoted in Baron, *op. cit.*, I, p. 88.

'virtuous . . . excellent sense'.: quoted by Saunders, *op. cit.*, pp. 54–5.

'I fought my way . . . .': Stephen Jenner to William Davies, 23/7/[?], William and Anne Davies, *op. cit.*, Well. MS5229(8).

Revd Stephen Jenner, certificate of institution to the rectory of Fittleton, Wilts. . . . 16/9/1773, Well. MS5225. *Glocester Journal*, 27/9/73, p. 3. Saunders, *op. cit.*, p. 8.

Stephen resigned the rectorate: Revd Henry Jenner and Henry Jenner MD, Papers, 1774–92, Well. MS5227(1 and 2). *Glocester Journal*, 7/3/74, p. 3.

curate of Stone: Baron *op. cit.*, I, *passim*.

Edward 'was extremely happy': William and Anne Davies, *op. cit.*, Well. MS5229(8).

acquired adjacent property: indenture, [Frederick Augustus Earl of Berkeley to Stephen Jenner, 8/9/1781], GCRO 41/8.

'His height was rather under . . . .': Baron, *op. cit.*, I, pp. 15–16.

31 a catch club: *ibid.*, p. 26.

ballads of his own composition.: [W. MacMichael], *Lives of British Physicians*, London: J. Murray, 1830, p. 259.

'Come all ye bold Britons . . . .': 'Ladbroke's Entire', MS in Edward Jenner, [Poems 1], Vol. I, W. Davies, 1794, Well. MS3017. The ballad contains 13 more verses.

Two of her poems: Edward Jenner, Papers 1790–1822 . . . .' Well. MS5235(13).

Marvell.: *ibid.*, Well. MS5255(14). 'How strange the reverses we're doomed to behold —/Why, who can believe what I say, when he's told/That a gallant Commander, who'd die soon as yield/The fight to a Foe on old Neptunes green field,/On our shores has excited our grumbling & wonder,/For now to a Cooper forsooth he knocks under'

'Address to a Robin': Edward Jenner, MS in [Poems 2], Vol. II, W. Davies, Well. MS3016.

32 'To a Lady — with a Woodlark': [Poems 1], Vol. I, p. 48, Well. MS3017.

'By a Negro . . .': *ibid.*, p. 5.

'To a Fellow Sportsman . . . .': *ibid.*, p. 47.

'Epigram': *ibid.*, p. 12.

33 'To Mrs J on her dismal dream . . .': William Davies DD, Correspondence and papers, 1716–1847 and n.d.. . . ., Well. MS5230(110).

'Why Lettsom bid the sculptur'd Pillar . . . .': 'An Unpublished Diary of Edward Jenner', ed. C. Doris Hellman, *Annals of Medical History*, N.S. III (1931), p. 431.

'Epitaph on an Ass': [Poems 2], Vol. II, Well. MS3016.

34 'had a particular dislike for cards. . . .': Baron *op. cit.*, I, p. 26.

William Davies, Household accounts, Vol. II, 1780–98, pp. 37, 46, 52, 55, Well. MS2049.

'a small landscape of Barretts . . . .': *Letters from the Past from John Hunter to Edward Jenner*, [ed. E. H. Cornelius and A. J. Harding Rains], Royal College of Surgeons of England, 1976, p. 7.

Hunter was a collector: G. Qvist, *John Hunter, 1728–1793*, London: William Heinemann Medical, 1981, p. 33.

'Bassani': *From Hunter to Jenner*, p. 20.

'The Landscape by Barret, . . .': *ibid.*, pp. 20–1.

Edward Jenner 1749–1823

Page
34 'bought the print of wright . . .': *From Hunter to Jenner*, p. 37, corrected from original in
   Royal College of Surgeons of England.
   candlesticks,: *ibid.*, p. 19.
   'They all went so dear.': *ibid.*, p. 25.
35 Inigo Jones: 'An Inventory and Valuation of all the Household Furniture, Plate Linen and
   China, Wine and other Liquors, and all other Effects the property of Dr. Edward
   Jenner decd. taken by order of the Executors of his Will . . . the 8th 10th 11th 12th 13th
   & 14th days of February 1823 by John Hall Hunt. . . .', Well. MS3028.
   'on the Cuckow . . . .': *From Hunter to Jenner*, p. 9; corrected, as have been all the
   quotations from this pamphlet, from the original letters held by the Royal College of
   Surgeons.
   'two young animals . . . .': *ibid.*, p. 13.
   'The large Porpois . . .': *ibid.*, p. 15.
   'the Delphinus Delphis . . .': W. R. LeFanu, *A Bio-bibliography of Edward Jenner
   1749–1823*, London: Harvey & Blythe, 1951, p. 7.
   'The bubby's of this . . . .': *From Hunter to Jenner*, p. 16.
   'Black birds nests . . .': *ibid.*, p. 21.
36 'I Have rec'd my Hedge Hogs. . . .': *ibid.*, p. 19.
   'I want you to pursue . . . .': *ibid.*, p. 31.
   'I do not know well . . . .': *ibid.*, p. 27.
   'the Thermometer is a very useful one . . . .': *ibid.*, p. 17.
37 'take care you do not brake . . .': *ibid.*, p. 27.
   'you very modestly ask for . . . .': *ibid.*, p. 34.
   'I thank you for your Expt . . . .': *ibid.*, p. 9.
   Jenner's contribution: Baron, *op. cit.*, I, p. 59. Saunders, *op. cit.*, p. 10.
   'I own I suspected . . . .': *From Hunter to Jenner*, p. 9.
38 offer to Daniel Ludlow,: Creighton, *op. cit.*, p. 5.
   University of Erlangen: [J. C. Lettsom], *Memoir of Edward Jenner, M. D.*, [London]: I.
   Gold, [1804], p. 2.
   'happened to dine . . . .': *idem*.
   Warren Hastings,: 'Edward Jenner', *Annual Biography & Obituary 1824* (n.p.), p. 188.
39 'did not chuse to come . . . .': *From Hunter to Jenner*, pp. 31–2. Baron, *op. cit.*, I, pp.
   66–7.
   they were again in Bath: *From Hunter to Jenner*, p. 19.
40 a blind patient of Jenner's: Hunterian Society, Manuscripts, Vol. I, Well. MS5608(24).
   'if it is Brain . . . .': *From Hunter to Jenner*, p. 12.
   Heberden replied: Principally letters by Edward Jenner to Elizabeth Hodges, Well.
   Photocopies held by Curator of Western MSS (originals in GCRO).
   a patient named Bailey: Thomas Dudley Fosbroke, *Berkeley Manuscripts*, London: John
   Nichols & Son, 1821, pp. 223–4. Baron, *op. cit.*, I, p. 53.
   Fewster had been either a pupil: Creighton, *op. cit.*, p. 144. Edward Leese, *An Explanation
   of the Causes Why Vaccination Has Sometimes Failed to Prevent Small-Pox. . . .*, London:
   Thomas Underwood, 1812, p. 60.
   'Cow Pox and its Ability . . .': C. W. Dixon, *Smallpox*, London: J. & A. Churchill, 1962,
   p. 250.
   'often recurred to the subject . . . .': Baron, *op. cit.*, I, p. 48.
   'As a proof': Davies, *op. cit.*, Well. MS5230(2).
41 'I was told the other day . . . .': *From Hunter to Jenner*, p. 24.
   'I own I was at a loss . . . .': *ibid.*, p. 23.
   possible local heiresses: *Gloucestershire Marriage Index 1776–1800, Brides*, comp. Eric Roe,
   Salt Lake City, Utah: Genealogical Society, 1958 (typescript), GCRO. Edward Jenner,
   An Inquiry into the Causes and Effects of the Variolae Vaccinae. . . , London: Sampson
   Low, 1798, p. 43.
   nineteenth-century romance.: The outline for the scenario that follows emerged from a
   conversation with the leading expert on the Jenner family, Canon J. E. Gethyn-Jones of
   Berkeley, and Mrs Gethyn-Jones in Berkeley on 29 July 1989. The idea that the 'lost
   lover' was in fact Catherine Kingscote herself is theirs, and I am most grateful to them
   for suggesting it to me.

Page
41 *Glocester Journal*: 10/3/1788, p. 3.
   brother, Thomas: *Letters of Edward Jenner and Other Documents concerning the Early History of Vaccination*, ed. Genevieve Miller, Baltimore and London: Johns Hopkins University Press, 1983, p. 24 footnote.
42 'After he had discovered. . . . I feel there influence no more.': Baron, *op. cit.*, I, p. 52.
43 'Jenner appears to have experienced . . . .': *ibid.*, p. 51.
   'Jenner's future mistrust . . . .': 'Edward Jenner: His Life, His Work, and His Writings', *British Medical Journal*, 23/5/1896, p. 1246.
   'the defect of reflection . . .': Fosbroke, *Cheltenham*, p. 258.
   'as a medium of conveyance . . .': 'Copy of Jenner Note Book', ed. LeRoy Crummer, *Ann. Med. Hist.*, N. S. I (1929), p. 408.
   'How wonderfully constructed . . . .': Edward Jenner to Thomas Pruen, 19/1/1809, Well. Photocopy held by Curator of Western MSS.
   'Essay on Marriage': Well. MS3014.
   'that Man is naturally . . . .': *ibid.*, p. [1].
   'The deviation of man . . . .': Jenner, *Inquiry*, p. 1.
   'The most prevailing passions . . . .': Jenner, Well. MS3014, p. [2].
   'Marriage is undoubtedly . . . .': *ibid.*, p. [3].
   'converts the Baseness . . . .': *ibid.*, p. [5].
   'to follow the dictates . . .': *ibid.*, p. [6].
   'can make another . . . .': *ibid.*, p. [7].
   'no one has Ventur'd . . .': *ibid.*, pp. [13–14].
   'all those . . . who make . . .': *ibid.*, p. [15].
44 ' "whistling of a Name" . . . Concern of Life.': *ibid*, pp. [15–16].
   'a path to Misery.': *ibid.*, p. [19].
   'Please to send me by return . . . .': Miller, *op. cit.*, p. 3. This letter is undated; Miller dates it 1785, but the flights took place two years earlier. Parry himself built and let off a balloon in front of his home in Bath in January 1784. *Bath Chronicle*, 15/1/1784.
45 second flight: Baron, *op. cit.*, I, pp. 69–70. Saunders, *op. cit.*, p. 14.
   Cursory Observations on Emetic Tartar.: Wotton-under-Edge: J. Bence, [1780].
   'I have a great deal to say . . . .': *From Hunter to Jenner*, p. 34.
   'I love a new name . . . .': *ibid.*, p. 33.
46 'I am puffing off . . . . stirr for you. . . .': *ibid.*, p. 35.
   published almost a decade later: Edward Jenner, 'A Process for preparing pure Emetic Tartar by Re-crystallization. . . .', *Transactions of a Society for the Improvement of Medical and Chirurgical Knowledge*, 1 (1793), pp. 30–3.
47 'I recollect that I promis'd . . . .': Miller, *op. cit.*, p. 4.
   'When I had the honor . . .': *idem.*
   'Observations tending to show . . .': *ibid.*, p. 6 footnote.
   'By a letter from Mr. Blagden . . . .': *idem.*
   'In consequence of your . . . .': Baron, *op. cit.*, I, p. 77.
48 'to run over the Ph. Trans: . . .': Daines Barrington, FRS, naturalist and lawyer, RCP:ALS.
   Henry, being a lazy boy,: Baron, *op. cit.*, I, pp. 85–6.
   '17. Saw a Hedge Sparrows Nest . . . .': [Edward Jenner] 1787 Notebook [15/1/1787–29/4/1806], RCP MS372.
49 the cuckoo chick's back: [Edward Jenner], 'Observations on the Natural History of the Cuckoo', *Philosophical Transactions of the Royal Society* (read 13/3/1778), pp. 219–37.
   'The contest was very remarkable . . . .': *ibid.*, p. 226.
   'supposing from the feeble appearance . . . .': Derrick Baxby, *Jenner's Smallpox Vaccine: The Riddle of the Vaccinia Virus and its Origin*, London: Heinemann Educational, 1981, p. 43.
   migratory behaviour of cuckoos,: [Edward Jenner], *op. cit.*, *Phil. Trans. Roy. Soc.*, pp. 13–14.
50 sent to Hunter: *ibid.*, pp. 1–2.
   Charles Blagden, . . . Sir William Watson.: Dr Hugh S. Torrens (notes for a lecture): 'Edward Jenner and his circle: their contribution to natural history', (delivered August

Page

1982 to a meeting entitled): 'Edward Jenner and the Early History of Vaccination, Jenner Old & Rare Books, 2nd medico-historical conference, Bath'. I am grateful to Dr Torrens for letting me use these notes.

Chapter 4: Immortalizing James Phipps 1789–1796

51 £600 from Jane Hicks,: Robert Haines, Eric Gethyn-Jones and Arnold Sanderson, 'Edward Jenner: his life and work', *Immunology Today*, 5/1981, p. x.

Thomas Dudley Fosbroke, *Berkeley Manuscripts*, London: John Nichols & Sons, 1821, p. 266.

Edward Robert Jenner was born: William Davies, Household accounts, Vol. II, 1780–98, facing p. 66, Well. MS2049.

'Dear Jenner I wish you Joy, . . .: *Letters from the Past from John Hunter to Edward Jenner*, [ed. E. H. Cornelius and A. J. Harding-Rains], Royal College of Surgeons of England, 1976, p. 39.

a new medical society.: John Baron, *The Life of Edward Jenner, M. D.*, London: Henry Colburn, 1827, Vol. I, pp. 50–1.

Henry Hicks: *ibid.*, p. 45.

'at first instituted. . . . exceeds 40 years.': 'Records of an Old Medical Society: Some Unpublished Manuscripts of Edward Jenner', *British Medical Journal*, 23/5/1896, p. 1296.

52 Original papers: *ibid.*, pp. 1297–8.

sixteen papers in the three years: 'Regulations and Transactions of the Glostershire Medical Society', instituted May 1788, RCP MS736.

An Inquiry into the Symptoms . . .: Bath: Cruttwell.

'the influence of the heart . . . .': *ibid.*, p. 3.

'the Symptoms arising . . . .': 'Regulations and Transactions', RCP MS736.

53 Instead, he wrote to Heberden: Baron, *op. cit.*, I, pp. 38–41.

'Mr. Cline . . .': Henry, also Hunter's student and now surgeon at St Thomas's.

'Mr. Home . . .': Everard, surgeon and Hunter's brother-in-law.

'The first case. . . . to tell me I was right.': Parry, *op. cit.*, pp. 3–5.

54 'a case of Hydatids . . . .': 'Regulations and Transactions', RCP MS736.

'When the natural History . . . .': [Edward Jenner], 1787 Notebook [15/1/1787–29/4/1806], RCP MS372.

'The bake-Apple,': *ibid.*, p. 57.

cysts . . . hydatids . . . tubercles.: *ibid.*, pp. 47–8.

'that encysted Tumours . . .': *ibid.*, pp. 52–3.

'All Tumors truly cancerous . . . .': *ibid.*, p.81.

'on Mrs Jenner's Lip'.: *ibid.*, pp. 54–5, 58.

the case of James Merrett,: [Edward Jenner], 'Report of a case of hydatids. . . .'. fols 3–4, McGill BO, MS1268.

55 'I have just now forgot . . . .': Hunter, letter in Hunterian Society, photocopies: RCS.

'How does Mrs Jenner. . . . extremely ill.': Baron *op. cit.*, I, p. 103.

'The two young women . . . .': 'Regulations and Transactions', pp. 4–5, RCP MS736.

56 Edward junior was variolated again: Baron, *op. cit.*, I, pp. 129–31.

'My two eldest . . .': *The Medical Observer, and Family Monitor. . .* By a Society of Practical Physicians, Vol. VIII [7/1810–1/1811], London: Stockdale (n. d.), p. 379.

'Upon the whole, . . .': 'Regulations and Transactions', p. 15, RCP MS736.

'This was the mild . . .': Edward Jenner, *Further Observations on the Variolae Vaccinae or Cow Pox*, London: Sampson Low, 1799, p. 126 note.

'called by the common people . . .': *ibid.*, p. 9.

Dr William Heberden: Donald R. Hopkins, *Princes and Peasants: Smallpox in History*, Chicago and London: University of Chicago Press, 1983, p. 61.

57 'that infection with one . . . .': Derrick Baxby, *Jenner's Smallpox Vaccine: The Riddle of the Vaccinia Virus and its Origin*, London: Heinemann Educational, 1981, p. 2.

sheep, cats, goats,: Maurice Green, 'Major groups of animal viruses,' in *Viral and*

Page

Rickettsial Infections of Man, ed. Frank L. Horsfall Jr and I. Tamm, 4th edn, London: Pitman; Philadelphia: Lippincott, 1965, pp. 11–19.

57 resident of Bushire: letter from W. Bruce to W. Erskine dated 3/13, published in *London Medical and Physical Journal*, 41 (5/19), p. 451.

'but may be a disease of rodents. . . . vaccinia virus. . . .': Baxby, *op. cit.*, p. vii.

Poxvirus officinalis.: A. W. Downie, 'The poxvirus group', in Horsfall and Tamm, *op. cit.*, p. 932.

58 'Boy that passed . . .': 'Regulations and Transactions', RCP MS736.

59 'no reliance . . . .': Baron, *op. cit.*, I, p. 134.

Idem. See also Joseph Adams, *Observations on Morbid Poisons, Chronic and Acute*, London: J. Callow, 1795.

degree of Doctor in Medicine: The minutes of the Senatus Academicus actually name Mr Edward Jennings; quoted in Dorothy Fisk, *Dr Jenner of Berkeley*, London, Melbourne and Toronto: Heinemann, 1959, p. 106.

'candidate for the degree . . . .': *Letters of Edward Jenner and Other Documents concerning the Early History of Vaccination*, ed. Genevieve Miller, Baltimore and London: Johns Hopkins University Press, 1983, p. 39 footnote; this form was approved in 1802 but is thought to be similar to that used ten years earlier.

'The fatigues . . . .': Baron *op. cit.*, I, p. 105.

called 'Doctor': William Davies, Diary 1792–1805, 19/3/1792, Well. MS2052.

'A man must be guided . . . .': Baron, *op. cit.*, I, p. 89.

'For it is by appearances . . . .': *ibid.*, p. 92.

60 Dr Edward Jenner's Patients' Visiting Book, Well. MS3018.

Catherine, was christened.: Berkeley Parish Register, GCRO PFC 42 1/15–1/39.

'for his Attendance . . .': Davies, *op. cit.*, [p. 119]. Well. MS2049.

Hunter's household.: Davies, 26/1/1792, *op. cit.*, Well. MS2052. 'My Cousin Henry Jenner set off for London. Call'd upon his Father at Burbage.'

'Pupils'.: G. Qvist, *John Hunter, 1728–1793*, London: William Heinemann Medical, 1981, p. 23.

61 Linnaean Society: Fisk, *op. cit.*, p. 105.

Henry married: *Glocester Journal*, 17/12/1792, p. 3.

dower of £1300: Revd Henry Jenner and Henry Jenner MD, Papers, 1774–92, Well. MS5227(3).

'being lame of one leg . . .': *From Hunter to Jenner*, *op. cit.*, p. 40.

'the dreadful fever': Letter to Revd John Clinch, 7/2/1789; Baron, *op. cit.*, I, pp. 90–1.

62 'A severe Frost . . . .': Davies, *op. cit.*, facing p. 123, Well. MS2049.

'so feeble that . . . .': Letter to W. F. Shrapnell (n.d.); Baron, *op. cit.*, I, p. 107.

Revd. Nathaniel Thornbury: Baron, *op. cit.*, I, p. 109.

In April he was able: Davies, *op. cit.*, Well. MS2052.

'is what they call "a watering place;" . . . .': *Selections from William Cobbett's Illustrated Rural Rides, 1821–1832*, introduction and notes by Christopher Morris, Exeter: Webb & Bower, 1984, p. 186.

'great rejoicing': Paul Saunders, *Edward Jenner: The Cheltenham Years, 1795–1823*, Hanover, Vt., and London: University Press of New England, 1982, p.28.

63 in 1788 George III: Robin Reilly, *Pitt the Younger, 1759–1806*, London: Cassell, 1978, p. 156.

'Dined and spent the day . . .': Davies, *op. cit.*, Well. MS2052.

haunch of venison: *ibid.*, 12/9/93.

20 June 1793: *ibid.*

'Mr Fosbrokes Acct': Davies, *op. cit.*, facing p. 118, Well. MS2049.

'Dr. Jenner's Ladies Club'.: Davies, *op. cit.*, 3/1/1794, Well. MS2052.

64 Edward heard the news: William and Anne Davies, Correspondence. . . . 1775–1812, Well. MS5229(2). [Edward Jenner], . . . various correspondents, 1795–1822, Well. MS5232(1). Saunders, *op. cit.*, p. 40.

'I pick up a few Fees . . . .': William Davies, Correspondence and papers, 1716–1847 and n.d. . . . ., Well. MS5230(1). 'this day se'ennight' = 'this day week'; cf. a similar Quaker phrase.

Page
65 Mary Reed: Saunders, *op. cit.*, pp. 20–3.
66 against syphilis and gonorrhoea: Qvist, *op. cit.*, p. 52.
'I do not believe . . . .': [Edward Jenner], *op. cit.*, Well. MS5232(5).
Saunders, *op. cit.*, p. 43 and note.
'The more accurately to observe . . . .': Edward Jenner, *An Inquiry into the Causes and Effects of the Variolae Vaccinae . . . known by the name of the Cow Pox*, London: Sampson Low, 1798, p. 32.
2s to a James Phipps: Stephen Jenner, Tythe and rent-book . . . 1729–55, 16/8/1745, Well. MS3038.
'each about half . . .': Jenner, *Inquiry*, p. 32.
67 'much the same as . . .': *ibid.*, p. 33.
'My Uncle Dr. Jenner . . . .': Davies, *op. cit.*, Well. MS2052.
'As I promised to let you know . . . .': [Edward Jenner], 41 letters (mostly to John Baron), Royal College of Surgeons.

Chapter 5: 'To the King' 1796–1800

69 Joseph Farington, *The Farington Diary*, ed. James Greig, Vol. I, 1793–1802, London: Hutchinson, 1924, p. 165.
'Mr Dolland, . . .': Edward Jenner, *An Inquiry into the Causes and Effects of the Variolae Vaccinae . . . known by the name of the Cow Pox*, London: Sampson Low, 1798, p. 45.
'ought not to risk . . . .': John Baron, *The Life of Edward Jenner, M. D. . . .*, London: Henry Colburn, Vol. II, 1838, p. 168. Baron gives no date. Paul Saunders, *Edward Jenner: The Cheltenham Years, 1795–1823*, Hanover, Vt., and London: University Press of New England, 1982, p. 57, says Jenner sent the MS to Home after the meeting with his friends in March 1797; but see p.   below.
cowpox disappeared: Baron, *op. cit.*, Vol. I (1827), p. 14.
until 7 December,: William Davies, Diary 1792–1805, Well. MS2052.
On Christmas Day,: William Davies, Household accounts, Vol. II, 1780–98, facing p. 139, Well. MS2049.
70 'alone, of all the villagers . . . .': Saunders, *op. cit.*, p. 18.
she had died in 1786.: Jenner family, MS Account book, [1760–97], Well. MS3072, shows that Sarah Hayward's account closed with credit balance carried over on 28/4/1786.
On 24 August 1797,: Davies, *op. cit.*, facing p. 144, Well. MS2049.
'The Doctor & Mrs. Jenner . . . .': Principally letters by Edward Jenner to Elizabeth Hodges, sent by Edward Carter to Dr E. A. Underwood, Well. Curator of Western MSS.
71 Revd Dr Ramsden: Baron, *op. cit.*, II, p. 43.
trumpet the Ramsden version: John Birch, *Report of the True State of the Cow Pox Experiment, At the Close of the Year 1809. . . .*, London: Smeaton, [1810], p. 2. *Medical Observer, and Family Monitor*, VIII, London: Stockdale, [7/1810–1/1811], p. 419. For explanation in Reading newspaper, Edward Jenner to Revd G. Hulme, Weymouth, 2/3/1813: Letters, no. 18, RCS.
two or more very similar: Well. MS3019 is in William Davies's hand with changes and additions by Jenner. Dated Berkeley, 29/3/97. The Royal College of Surgeons MS is in Jenner's hand, probably his fair copy of corrected Well. MS3019, but bearing further corrections by an unknown editor, possibly Worthington. Well. MS3019 must be based on an earlier draft by Jenner, perhaps the one submitted to the Royal Society, which has not survived. Cf. Derrick Baxby, 'The genesis of Edward Jenner's *Inquiry* of 1798: a comparison of the two unpublished manuscripts and the published version', *Med. Hist.*, 29 (1985), pp. 193–9.
'on the Minds of this Society': RCS MS, p. 8; Well. MS3091, pp. 7, 31.
Glocester Journal: p. 3.
'at home to protect . . .: William Peter Lunnell, Bristol, 8/10/97, in *Letters of Edward Jenner and Other Documents concerning the Early History of Vaccination*, ed. Genevieve Miller, Baltimore and London: Johns Hopkins University Press, 1983, p. 7.
following Robert's birth.: *idem*.

Page

72 John Nichols . . . to John Evans.: Evidence is admittedly slender; apart from the fact that they lived near each other in Islington, both men were subscribers to John Nelson, *The History, Topography, and Antiquities of the Parish of St. Mary Islington*, printed by John Nichols in 1811.

By 4 December,: Davies, *op. cit.*, Well. MS2052.

'was rendered unfit . . . .': Jenner, *Inquiry*, p. 37.

workhouse fever.: Edward Jenner, *Further Observations on the Variolae Vaccinae or Cow Pox*, London: Sampson Low, 1799, footnote p. 23.

73 William Summers,: Jenner, *Inquiry*, pp. 37–8, 42–3.

William Pead,: *ibid.*, pp. 38, 43.

Hannah Excell,: *ibid.*, p. 43.

74 'the Small-pox in the usual . . . .': *idem*.

'These experiments afforded me . . . .': *ibid.*, p. 44.

Mrs Ladbroke, in Pall Mall.: Baron, *op. cit.*, I, p. 149.

James Woodforde,: *The Diary of a Country Parson, 1758–1802*, ed. John Beresford, Oxford, London, New York: OUP, 1978.

75 Berkeley peerage scandal.: see below, pp. 284–6.

'My dear Wife . . . .': William Davies, Diary 1805–17, 8/6/1811, Well. MS2053.

'unable . . . to procure . . . .': Baron, *op. cit.*, I, p. 150.

'had some affection . . .': *ibid.*, p. 152.

Glocester Journal.: p. 3.

76 outraged the antivaccinists,: Charles Creighton, *Jenner and Vaccination: A Strange Chapter of Medical History*, London: Swan Sonnenschein, 1889, pp. 78ff.

'The useful terms . . . .': Baron, *op. cit.*, II, p. 336.

'A new species of Inoculation . . .': [Royal Jennerian Society], 'Minutes of the Royal Jennerian Society for the Extermination of the Small Pox', [6/1/1803–3/12/1806], Well. MS4303.

'vaccination': [Royal Jennerian Society], 'Minutes of the Medical Committee. . . .', [23/2/03–21/2/07], Well. MS4304.

'kine-pock': Benjamin Waterhouse, *Information Respecting the Origin, Progress, and Efficacy of the Kine-Pock Inoculation. . . .*, [editor unknown], Cambridge, Mass.: Hilliard & Metcalf, 1810, p. 5, footnote 14.

'bear so strong . . .': Jenner, *Inquiry*, p. 2.

'the *true* and not . . .': *ibid.*, p. 74.

77 a recurrence of cowpox.: *ibid.*, p. 51.

'Although the Cow Pox shields . . . .': *ibid.*, p. 21.

Case 9 . . . Case 14 . . . .: *ibid.*, pp. 9–30.

78 'notwithstanding the happy effects . . . .': *ibid.*, pp. 66–9.

'in which, however, conjecture . . . .': *ibid.*, pp. 74–5.

79 'Shall I, who even in the morning . . . .': Baron, *op. cit.*, I, pp. 154–6.

80 Thomas Tanner,: [Thomas Paytherus], *A Comparative Statement of Facts and Observations Relative to the Cow-Pox. . . .*, London: Sampson Low, 1800, pp. 10–11.

Dr John G. Loy, *An Account of Some Experiments on the Origin of the Cow-Pox*, Whitby: Thomas Webster, 1801, pp. 18–19.

Dr Louis Sacco of Milan,: Baron, *op. cit.*, I, pp. 428–9.

'corrected': Baron, *op. cit.*, II, p. 225.

81 'the Cow-pox protects . . .': Jenner, *Inquiry*, p. 45.

'It seems as if a change, ...': *ibid.*, footnote p. 13.

'being the original, the latter . . . .': Edward Jenner, *A Continuation of Facts & Observations Relative to the Variolae Vaccinae*, London: Sampson Low, 1800, pp. 150–1.

'same diseases under different . . . .': *ibid.*, footnote p. 151.

82 'are always free of the bluish . . . .': *ibid.*, footnote p. 7.

earlier versions of the *Inquiry*,: Edward Jenner, 'An Inquiry into the natural History of a Disease known in Glostershire under the name of the Cox-Pox', 1797, pp. 43–44, Well. MS3019.

four different circumstances: Edward Jenner, *Further Observations on the Variolae Vaccinae . . ., bound with An Inquiry into the Causes and Effects of the Variolae Vaccinae . . .*, London: Sampson Low, 1801, p. 89.

Edward Jenner 1749–1823

Page
82 'A Medical Gentleman . . . .': Jenner, *Inquiry op. cit.*, p. 56.
83 'or even a day or two later, ...': Edward Jenner, *Instructions for Vaccine Inoculation*, London: D. N. Shury, 1801.
'supplies the single deficiency . . .': Thomas Creaser, *Observations on Dr. Pearson's Examination of the Report of the Committee of the House of Commons. . . .*, 2nd edn, Bath: Richard Cruttwell, 1805, p. 29.
Dr Jan Ingenhousz: Baron, *op. cit.*, I, pp. 201–300. Creighton, *op. cit.*, p. 87. D. Baxby, *Jenner's Smallpox Vaccine: The Riddle of Vaccinia Virus and its Origin*, Heinemann Educational, 1988, pp. 70–1. D. R. Hopkins, *Princes and Peasants: Smallpox in History*, Chicago and London: University of Chicago Press, 1983, p. 64.
84 'I cannot understand . . . .': John Birch, *Serious Reasons for Uniformly Objecting to the Practice of Vaccination. . . .*, London: Harris, 1806, p. 40.
'may be occasioned . . . .': Royal Jennerian Society, *Advertisement. . . . Instructions for Vaccine Inoculation*, [London]: W. Phillips, [1807], RCP 108/8.
'Some deviations from the usual course . . . .': Royal College of Physicians of London, . . . on Vaccination. . . ., *Med. Phys. Jour.*, 18 (8/07), pp. 97–111.
85 'Whether the nature of the virus . . .': Jenner, *Continuation*, p. 162.
'the vaccine fluid . . .': [John Coakley Lettsom], *Observations on the Cow-Pock*, London: John Nichols & Son, 1801, p. 27.
modern science did not: C. W. Dixon, *Smallpox*, London: J. & A. Churchill, 1962, p. 119.
'this day return'd . . . .': Davies, *op. cit.*, Well. MS2052.
'first gentleman': Baron, *op. cit.*, I, p. 304.
Mary Hearn,: Jenner, *Further Observations*, pp. 99–103.
86 five of Mr Darke's patients,: T. Hughes, 'The following letter from Mr. Hughes to Dr. Jenner. . . .', *Med. Phys. Jour.*, 1 (6/99), pp. 318–22. Also Baxby, *op. cit.*, pp. 87–8.
a family called Stanton,: Creighton, *op. cit.*, p. 94.
Dr George Pearson,: Baxby, *op. cit.*, p. 118.
'perusal . . . has afforded me . . .': Dr [Thomas] Bradley, 'An Account of the Publications and Experiments on the Cow-pox. . . .', *Med. Phys. Jour.*, 1 (3/99), p. 6.
'expectation of participating . . . .': London: J. Johnson, p. 38.
nine questions: E. M. Crookshank, *History and Pathology of Vaccination*, Vol. II, London: H. K. Lewis, 1889, pp. 38–59.
87 Mr Fewster of Thornbury: *ibid.*, p. 85.
went to Cheltenham, probably without: William Davies, Household accounts, Vol. III, facing p. 17, Well. MS2050; Davies, *op. cit.*, 19/2/1799, Well. MS2052.
he called on Sir Joseph Banks,: Baron, *op. cit.*, I, p. 308.
vaccinated two hundred people: William Woodville, *Reports of a Series of Inoculations for the Variolae Vaccinae, or Cow-Pox. . . .*, London: Jas Phillips & Son, [1799].
'suggest the immediate propriety . . . .': Baron, *op. cit.*, I, p. 308.
88 'Dr W and myself conclude . . . ': *ibid.*, p. 314.
Ann Bumpus developed: Baxby, *op. cit.*, p. 111.
eighteen in all.: Jenner, *Further Observations*, pp. 130–4.
difference in the air.: *ibid.*, p. 135.
a dairy at Marylebone: Peter Razell, *Edward Jenner's Cowpox Vaccine: The History of a Medical Myth*, 2nd edn, Firle, Sussex: Caliban Books, 1980, p. 47.
89 Woodville received the first: Baron, *op. cit.*, I, p. 322; cf. E. Ashworth Underwood, 'Jenner and the Story of Vaccination' bound MS, p. 143, Contemporary Medical Archives Centre, Well.
'produced so great a number . . .': Jenner, *Further Observations*, p. 122.
'enforce the precaution . . .': *ibid.*, p. 70.
'immediately' to Berkeley,: Jenner, *Continuation*, pp. 151–2. Davies, *op. cit.*, Well. MS2052.
'I had no intention . . .': *ibid.*, pp. 152–3.
90 'In three days . . .': *ibid.*, pp. 160–1.
William Woodville's: London: Jas Phillips & Son (n. d., dedication 16/5/1799 to Sir Joseph Banks), in Crookshank, II, *op. cit.*, pp. 92–154. Baron says Jenner returned on 14 June (I, pp. 322–3), but William Davies noted: 'My Brother Robert & I dined & drank tea

with Dr Jenner' on 3 June *op. cit.*, Well. MS2052).
90 second original contribution: Baxby, *op. cit.*, pp. 95–6.
some sort of eruption after: Woodville, *op. cit.*, p. 154.
'before the constitution . . .': *ibid.*, p. 148.
'in respect to their local action': *ibid.*, p. 149.
not derived from the horse.: Baron, *op. cit.*, I, p. 323.
'I have observed, that the result . . . .': W. Woodville, 'To the Editors of the Medical and
Physical Journal', *Med. Phys. Jour.* 1 (7/99), p. 417.
91 Pearson naturally became head: Baron, *op. cit.*, I, pp. 359–61.
annual migration to Cheltenham: Davies, *op. cit.*, Well. MS2052.
'He says that the generality . . . .': quoted in John Ring, *A Treatise on the Cow-pox*. . . . (2
vols continuous pagination), London: J. & T. Carpenter & J. Johnson, 1801 and 1803,
p. 153.
Francis Knight,: Baron, *op. cit.*, I, pp. 327–9. Cf. Saunders, *op. cit.*, p. 67.
92 'paper . . . thick enough . . .': Thomas Frognall Dibdin, *Reminiscences of a Literary Life*
(2 vols continuous pagination), London: John Major, 1836, footnote pp. 201–2.
first translation of the *Inquiry*: Baron, *op. cit.*, I, p. 339.
Dr Jean De Carro,: Underwood, *op. cit.*, p. 183.
the office of the Foreign Secretary,: Baron, *op. cit.*, I, pp. 333–6.
'in this Island . . . .': Miller, *op. cit.*, p. 11.
Princess Louisa of Prussia: Baron, *op. cit.*, I, pp. 348–9.
vaccinated in Manchester: Baxby, *op. cit.*, p. 122.
W. Finch, 'To the Editors . . . .'. *Med. Phys. Jour.*, 3 (5/1800), pp. 415–20.
93 'the facts which I have . . .': Creighton, *op. cit.*, p. 89.
'until the whole of the facts . . . .': Thomas Beddoes, *Contributions to Physical and Medical
Knowledge* . . .' Bristol: Biggs & Cottle, 1799, p. 469.
'a *bottle-conjuror's* history': Creighton, *op. cit.*, pp. 192–3.
W. Simmons,: I (1799), p. 417.
Dr Benjamin Moseley.: *Dictionary of National Biography*, XIII, pp. 1071–2. Creighton, *op.
cit.*, p. 310. Dorothy Fisk, *Dr Jenner of Berkeley*, London, Melbourne and Toronto:
Heinemann, 1959, p. 153.
'Cowmania': London: John Nichols & Son, pp. 181, 183.
(Review), P., '*A Treatise on Sugar*. By Benjamin Moseley, M. D. . . . .', *London Medical
Review and Magazine*, I (6/99), pp. 311–18.
94 '. . . on the 5th day . . . .': Miller, *op. cit.*, pp. 10–11.
the same explanation.: Jenner, *Continuation*, pp. 147–8.
'May I not with perfect confidence . . . .': *ibid.*, pp. 181–2.
'concerning the Eruptions . . .': *Med. Phys. Jour.*, 3 (2/1800), pp. 97–101.
'. . . at present, I very much suspect, ...': Edward Jenner, 'To the Editors. . . .', *Med.
Phys. Jour.*, 3 (2/1800), pp. 101–2.
'but where it produces . . . .': Woodville, *op. cit.*, p. 153.
'I readily admit . . . .': quoted in review, '*Observations on the Cow-Pox* by William
Woodville. . . .', *Med. Phys. Jour.*, 4 (9/1800), pp. 256–9.
95 'Much, if not most . . . .': Dixon, *op. cit.*, p. 118. Cf. Baxby, *op. cit.*, pp. 105–14; and for
an opposing view: Razell, *op. cit.*, pp. 41–4.
'The controversy . . . ended . . . .': Joseph Adams, *A Popular View of Vaccine Inocula-
tion*. . . ., London: Richard Phillips, 1807. pp. 159–60.
reconciled through the mediation: Baron, *op. cit.*, I, pp. 555–6.
96 'be an extra [ordinary?] . . .': *ibid.*, pp. 360–1.
'It appears to me somewhat . . . .': quoted in *ibid.*, p. 362.
Jenner wrote proposing: *ibid.*, p. 365.
Jenner replied with an account: *ibid.*, pp. 339–46. The letter to Egremont is undated.
97 'make what alterations . . . .': [Vaccine-Pock Institution], *The Report on the Cow-Pock
Inoculation . . . 1800, 1801, 1802. . . .*' London: Hy Reynell, 1803, pp. 12–13, Jenner
Museum.
stayed nine days,: Saunders, *op. cit.*, pp. 86–7.

Page

97 the Duke of York: George III had in all nine sons and six daughters. Frederick, Duke of York, was the second son, at this time in command of the Army. He died in 1827, three years before his eldest brother, then King George IV. The third son, William Henry, Duke of Clarence, became William IV. The fifth, the Duke of Kent, died in 1825 leaving a daughter, Victoria. Ernest Augustus, Duke of Cumberland, was the sixth son and later became King of Hanover. The three remaining brothers were Adolphus Frederick, Duke of Cambridge, Octavius and Alfred, all of whom died in early childhood. Because they played no role in Jenner's life, the daughters need not detain us here.

inscribed to the Prince of Wales.: Edward Jenner, Papers 1790–1822. . . ., Well. MS5235(1).

'the conduct of the individuals . . .': Baron, *op. cit.*, I, p. 370.

'at last said, it was . . . .': [Vaccine Pock Institution], *op. cit.*, p. 13.

John Julius Angerstein,: Saunders, *op. cit.*, pp. 82–3. Baron, *op. cit.*, I, P. 372.

98 withdraw their support.: Baron, *op. cit.*, I, pp. 370–1.

'Great news from St. James's. . . .': *ibid.*, p. 346.

'What will you give . . . .': *ibid.*, pp. 374–5.

Chapter 6: Ten Thousand or Twenty? 1800–1802

99 'marked respect': John Baron, *The Life of Edward Jenner, M. D.*, London: Henry Colburn, Vol. I, 1827, p. 375.

Queen's chamberlain,: *ibid.*, p.379.

'that Dr. Jenner would receive . . . .': Hunter-Baillie Manuscripts, Vol. 5, Well. MS5617(88).

100 fifty-first birthday.: William Davies, Diary 1792–1805, Well. MS2052. Mrs Jenner was still in Berkeley at the end of April, but she remained in London for a short time after Jenner returned to Berkeley in June; cf. Paul Saunders, *Edward Jenner: The Cheltenham Years, 1795–1823*, Hanover, Vt., and London: University Press of New England, 1982, p. 89.

'George . . . went Saturday . . . .': [Edward Jenner], various letters, Medical Center Library, Duke University, Trent Collection.

vaccinate the 86th Regiment.: Baron, *op. cit.*, I, pp. 379–81. Cf. Edward Jenner, *On the Varieties & Modifications of the Vaccine Pustule, occasioned by an Herpetic State of the Skin*, Cheltenham: H. Ruff, 1806.

a farm at North Nibley,: Baron, *op. cit.*, I, p. 379.

'taking the result of a great number . . . .': Richard Dunning, 'To Drs. Jenner, Pearson, and Woodville', *Med. Phys. Jour.*, 3 (5/1800), pp. 436–41. Edward Jenner, 'To the Editors. . . .', *Med. Phys. Jour.*, 3 (6/1800), pp. 502–3.

101 Thomas Denman, 'To Dr. Bradley, etc', *Med. Phys. Jour.*, 3 (4/1800), pp.293–4.

from Lord Derby: *Med. Phys. Jour.*, 4 (7/1800), pp. 1–2.

Charles Cooke,: *ibid.*, p. 21.

Navy adopted: Baron, *op. cit.*, I, pp. 403–4.

criticized Trotter's action: *Monthly Review*, 32 (7/1800), p. 249; quoted in J. C. Lettsom, *An Apology, for Differing in Opinion from the Authors of the Monthly and Critical Reviews. . . .*, London, J. Bryan, 1804, p. 18.

'the Managers of the Publick . . .': Charles Murray and the Royal Jennerian Society. . . . 1803–15. . . ., Well. MS5244(68).

102 'an hundred orphans. . . . by Dr. Heysham.': R. J. Thornton, *Facts Decisive in Favour of the Cow-Pock. . . .*, 4th edn, London: H. D. Symonds *et al.*, 1803, pp. 191–225.

'alternately read . . .': quoted in F. D. Drewitt, *The Life of Edward Jenner, M. D., F.R.S., Naturalist, and Discoverer of Vaccination*, 2nd edn, London, New York, Toronto: Longmans Green, 1933, p. 66.

'variolous-like eruptions . . .': [Vaccine-Pock Institution], *The Report on the Cow-Pock Inoculation . . . 1800, 1801, 1802. . . .*, London: Hy Reynell, 1803, pp. 40–1, Jenner Museum, part of a Report published as late as 1803 when Jenner had triumphed in Parliament and the Royal Jennerian Society was burgeoning.

Page

103 'probably the same . . .': George Pearson, 'On the present State of the Evidence with regard
to the Vaccine Inoculation', *Med. Phys. Jour.*, 3 (5/1800), pp. 399–401.
'Such was the terror . . . .': 'Dr. Jenner', *Public Characters of 1802–1803*, Vol. V, London:
Richard Phillips, 1803, p. 28.
Jenner first wrote: John Ring, 'Remarks on the Cow-Pox', *Med. Phys. Jour.*, 2 (8/1799),
pp. 25–9. John Ring, *An Answer to Dr. Moseley. . . .*, London: J. Murray, 1805,
pp. 28–31.
'poor John Ring': Edward Jenner, Letters (mostly to John Baron), 12/12/1811, RCS.
'He vaccinated vast numbers . . . .': James Moore, *The History and Practice of Vaccination*,
London: J. Callow, 1817, p. 120.
'broken off his correspondence . . .': Baron, *op. cit.*, Vol. II (1838), p. 394.

104 'those persons who have had . . . .': C. Creighton, *Jenner and Vaccination: A Strange
Chapter of Medical History*, London: Swan Sonnenschein, 1889, p. 189.
Catherine and the children: cf. Saunders, *op. cit.*, p. 91.
Doctor of Civil Law: *Glocester Journal*, 25/6/1792, pp. 2–3.
William Fermor, *Reflections on the Cow-Pox illustrated by Cases . . . in a Letter to Dr.
Jenner. . . .*, Oxford: Dawson & Co., 1800, pp. 21–8. Baron, *op. cit.*, I, p. 332.
Saunders, *op. cit.*, p. 76.

105 'insecure, from the appearance . . .': Edward Jenner (7/9/01), 'Dr. Jenner, in Reply to Mr.
Fermor', *Med. Phys. Jour.*, 6 (10/01), pp. 325–6.
his uncle's land taxes.: Davies, *op. cit.*, Well. MS2052.
in Cheltenham,: Saunders, *op. cit.*, p. 91.
'who thought fit to apply . . . .': Baron, *op. cit.*, I, pp. 433–4.
Count de la Roque: *ibid.*, pp. 392–3.
Valentin and Desoteux: *ibid.*, p. 300.
brought lymph. . . .Minister of the Interior.: *ibid.*, pp. 390–2.
Journal de Paris: 'Vaccine Inoculation', *Med. Phys. Jour.*, 4 (7/1800), p. 90.

106 'having little to lose . . . .': Moore, *op. cit.*, p. 253.
['Woodville in France'], *Med. Phys. Jour.*, (11/1800), p. 470. Creighton, *op. cit.*, p. 292.
'this opportunity . . . .': review, '*Sur la Vaccine. . . . By Dr. Careno*. Vienna. 1801.'
London Medical Review, 7 (9/1801), p. 179. *Rapport sur la Vaccine. . . .* by Dr A.
Aubert appears to have been the first book in French on vaccination, a second edition
having appeared in Paris in 1801.
'supported by the lady . . . .': John Epps, *The Life of John Walker, M. D.*, London:
Whittaker, Treacher & Co., 1831, p. 28.
'I am extremely happy . . . .': *ibid.*, pp. 330–1.
island of Malta: Drewitt, *op. cit.*, p. 69.
Walker went on to Egypt: Baron, *op. cit.*, I, pp. 395–401.
'It was not unusual . . . .': *ibid.*, p. 403. D. R. Hopkins, *Princes and Peasants: Smallpox in
History*, Chicago and London: University of Chicago Press, 1983, p. 83.

107 a dinner in honour of Edward Jenner: Baron, *op. cit.*, I, pp. 526–7.
cowpox lymph from a Lombardy herd,: cf. Saunders, *op. cit.*, p. 111.
Royal Economical Society: Baron, *op. cit.*, I, pp. 393–4.
'this malignant design': Edward Jenner, 'Nineteen autograph letters to Alexander Marcet. . . .' (hereafter: 'Edward Jenner to Alexander Marcet'), dated Hertford St, 23/2/03,
RSM.
fifteen hundred citizens: Baron, *op. cit.*, I, pp. 398–9.
The Berlin situation: Moore, *op. cit.*, pp. 144–5.
vaccination throughout Prussia.: Creighton, *op. cit.*, p. 222.
Bohemian priests: Hopkins, *op. cit.*, p. 83.

108 'It consisted of . . . .': T. F. Dibdin, *Reminiscences of a Literary Life*, 2 vols, London: John
Major, 1836, p. 199 and footnote.
Edward replied: [Edward Jenner], . . . various correspondents, 1795–1822, Well.
MS5232(7,8).
'just at the time the small-pox . . . .': Baron, *op. cit.*, I, p. 467.
'I am now so far behind . . . .': *Letters of Edward Jenner and Other Documents concerning the
Early History of Vaccination*, ed. Genevieve Miller, Baltimore and London: Johns

Edward Jenner 1749–1823

Page

Hopkins University Press, 1983, p. 13; Miller supposes this article was E. Viborg, 'Experiments made for the Purpose of proving that the Small-pox is a Disease common to both Men and Brutes,' *Med. Phys. Jour.*, 8 (9/1802), pp. 271–3.

108 Denmark banned variolation: Baron, *op. cit.*, I, pp. 263, 450–1, 475–8. D. Fisk, *Dr Jenner of Berkeley*, London, Melbourne and Toronto: Heinemann, 1959, p. 161.

Vaccination was confounded: Dr De Carro, 'Extract of a Letter . . . to Dr. Marcet, of London.', *Med. Phys. Jour.*, 10 (9/1803), pp. 272–4.

at least by 1808,: Baron, *op. cit.*, I, p. 263.

109 Lord Elgin: *ibid.*, pp. 414–17.

'from her alone . . . .': Bombay Medical Board, 'Report . . . July 2, 1802', *Med. Phys. Jour.*, 9 (6/1803), p. 535. [Bengal, East India Company], *Report of the Progress of Vaccine Inoculation in Bengal . . . by John Shoolbred, Superintendent General of Vaccine Inoculation*, Calcutta, 1804; London: Black & Parry, 1805, pp. 2–3. Baron, *op. cit.*, I, pp. 421–2. Hopkins, op. cit., p. 147.

£1 to equip a vessel: [J. C. Lettsom], *Memoir of Edward Jenner, M. D.*, [London]: I. Gold, [1804], p. 5. Baron, *op. cit.*, I, pp. 408–10.

Thomas Christie,: Charles Murray and the National Vaccine Establishment, Correspondence and papers . . . 1809–29. . . ., Well. MS5245(33). Baron, *op. cit.*, I, pp. 426–7. Hopkins, *op. cit.*, p. 147.

'the successful introduction . . . .': quoted in Baron, *op. cit.*, I, pp. 424–5.

'The Brahmins finding . . .': G. D. Yeats, *An Address to the County and Town of Bedford, on the Nature and Efficacy of the Cow-Pox*. . . ., Bedford: W. Smith, [1803], p. 17.

110 'slight offering . . . .': Moore, *op. cit.*, p. 235. [Bengal, East India Company], *op. cit.*, p. 12.

double the income: Moore, *op. cit.*, p. 236.

Dr George Kier,: Charles Murray, *An Answer to Mr Highmore's Objections*. . . ., London: Longman, Hurst, Rees & Orme, 1808, pp. 59–60.

Clinch vaccinated: Baron, *op. cit.*, I, pp. 532–3. Hopkins, *op. cit.*, p. 262.

Benjamin Waterhouse,: Hopkins, *op. cit.*, pp. 262–3. Baron, *op. cit.*, I, pp. 385–6. Baron calls Harvard the 'University of Cambridge, Massachusetts'.

the first United States citizen: Benjamin Waterhouse, *Information Respecting the Origin, Progress and Efficacy of the Kine-Pock Inoculation*, Cambridge, Mass.: Hilliard & Metcalf, 1810, p. 22 footnote.

a monopoly: E. Ashworth Underwood, 'Jenner and the story of vaccination', bound MS, pp. 166–9; also Benjamin Waterhouse to Dr Lyman Spalding, Wellcome History of Medicine Museum 39826 (photocopy).

111 'under his own eye . . . .': John B. Blake, *Benjamin Waterhouse and the Introduction of Vaccination*, Philadelphia: University of Pennsylvania Press, 1957, p. 14.

One sailor on a ship: Baron, *op. cit.*, I, pp. 387–8.

Jefferson designed: Hopkins, *op. cit.*, pp. 263–6. Baron, *op. cit.*, I, pp. 387–9.

'and the interpreter . . .': Baron, *op. cit.*, I, p. 595.

'that mankind can never . . . .': Baron, *op. cit.*, II, pp. 94–5.

'For Chief of . . .': Hopkins, *op. cit.*, pp. 270–1. Fisk, *op. cit.*, p. 237.

112 produced cowpox by inoculating cows.: Benjamin Waterhouse, 'Extract of a Letter from Professor Waterhouse . . . to Dr. Lettsom. . . .', *Med. Phys. Jour.*, 6 (10/1801), p. 330,

London Medical Review,: 'Discovery of the vaccine Pock among American Cows', 8, pp. 255–6.

Boston Board of Health: Waterhouse, *Information*, pp. 9–22.

Harvard dismissed him.: Hopkins, *op. cit.*, pp. 263–6.

late in the century: Blake, *op. cit.*, pp. 11–12 footnote.

Review, '*The Charleston Medical Register* . . . 1802. By David Ramsay, M. D. . . . .', *Med. Phys. Rev.*, 10 (11/03), p. 471.

'no man who is so much . . . .': [House of Commons], incomplete verbatim report of the debate . . . on a second grant to Edward Jenner, [1807], p. 62, Well. MS3023.

'Vaccine Clerk to the World',: Edward Jenner, letter to Revd Robert Ferryman, 17/2/05, [Berkeley], RCP:ALS. Baron, *op. cit.*, II, p. 53.

Page
113 'expense and anxiety': E. M. Crookshank, *History and Pathology of Vaccination*, Vol. I, London: H. K. Lewis, 1889, p. 174.

'upwards of twenty-five . . .': London: D. N. Shury.

effects were less severe.: Baron, *op. cit.*, I, p. 434. Saunders, *op. cit.*, p. 97.

a party given by Lord and Lady Spencer: Baron, *op. cit.*, I, p. 435.

Mr Evans's school: *ibid.*, p. 435.

'very well at Mr. Moore's',: Edward Jenner to Revd John Clinch, 12/3/1801, RCS. Savory's and Moore's was founded in 1797 (personal communication, Secretary to Managing Director, Savory and Moore, 25/10/1989). The firm was not listed by the *Post Office Directory, 1813*, but does appear in Pigot & Co., *New Commercial Directory for 1826–7*. 'Quite early in the [nineteenth] century the historic house of Savory and Moore were making and selling Dr. Jenner's Absorbent Lozenges': H. E. Chapman, 'A century of proprietary medicines', *Pharmaceutical Journal*, Vol. 146 (4th series, Vol. 92), 12/4/1941, p. 139. My thanks to Dr Roy Porter, Wellcome Institute for the History of Medicine, for directing me to the *Pharmaceutical Journal*. The mention of Mr Moore in the letter to Clinch is the only connection between Edward Jenner and the firm that I have found, and it is circumstantial. Could the Dr Jenner have been Henry, or some other Jenner, capitalizing on the name?

114 'Notwithstanding the immense importance . . . .': RCS 65.

gold medal: Baron, *op. cit.*, I, pp. 404–7.

Lyceum Medicum Londiniense: *ibid.*, p. 449.

115 'My Parliamentary affair . . . .': Edward Jenner to E. Davy, Yoxford, Suffolk, 'Miscellaneous Original Letters', Vol. I, *Mus. Brit. Jureemptionis* 19242, BLMS.

then lived in Worcester: Dibdin, *op. cit.*, pp. 199, 742.

Theatre Royal, Cheltenham,: Saunders, *op. cit.*, p. 103.

'I have a long letter . . .': Jenner, *op. cit.*, Well. MS5232(26).

Rowland Hill, 'To the Editors', *Med. Phys. Jour.*, 17 (4/1807), p. 341.

Mary Tudway,: *Glocester Journal*, 28/6/89, p. 3.

An Oliver for a Rowland . . . .: 2nd edn, London: Longman, Hurst, Rees, & Orme, 1806.

116 'We are very happy . . .': William Davies, Correspondence and papers, 1716–1847 and n.d. . . ., Well. MS5230(34).

'but I trust, if the wind . . .': William and Anne Davies, Correspondence. . . .1775–1812, Well. MS5229(3).

'Mrs Jenner is much reduc'd . . . .': Carter letters, Cheltenham, 14/8/03; Well. Curator of Western MSS.

'My dear Wife on the whole . . . .': Edward Jenner, Miscellaneous Letters, etc., Brit. Mus., Add. MS 36,540, no. 52, BLMS.

'My good Man . . .': William and Anne Davies, *op. cit.*, Well. MS5229(7).

117 Berkeley Sunday School.: Drewitt, *op. cit.*, p. 117.

Manning (1776–1812) had just completed a bust of Jenner for the Royal Jennerian Society. His most familiar work may be a monument to Captain George Hardinge in St Paul's Cathedral.

'Mrs Jenner will add . . . .': William and Anne Davies, *op. cit.*, 11/12/05, Well. MS5229(4).

'wch. contains many great . . . .': *ibid.*, 27/1/09, Well. MS5229(5).

'Grosvenors Mourner, . . .': *ibid.*, 23/11/12, Well. MS5229(7).

a shipment of Bibles: Charles Murray and the National Vaccine Establishment, *op. cit.*, 22/10/13, Well. MS5245(6).

118 'Robert pays you a visit . . . .': William and Anne Davies, *op. cit.*, (n.d.), Well. MS5229(10).

Rowland Hill actually preached: William Davies, Diary 1820–1, 27/6/1820, Well. MS2055.

119 Jenner's Gloucester neighbours: Jenner, *op. cit.*, Well. MS5232(26).

'Respecting Letters . . . .': Miller, *op. cit.*, pp. 14–15.

Fewer than 1 per cent: R. Reilly, *Pitt the Younger, 1759–1806*, London: Cassell, 1978, p. 60.

an opposition party.: Michael Reed, *The Georgian Triumph, 1700–1830*, London: Rout-

Page

ledge & Kegan Paul, 1983, p. 16. A. D. Harvey, *Britain in the Early Nineteenth Century*, London: Batsford, 1978, pp 10–15.

120   admired Fox,: Miller *op. cit.*, p. 21.

a Whig,: Saunders, *op. cit.*, p. 29.

'Every state, from the nature . . . .': C. Doris Hellman (ed., 'An Unpublished Diary of Edward Jenner', *Ann. Med. Hist.*, N.S. III (1931), pp. 433–4.

'as it may facilitate . . .': 7/11/1801, RCS 12.

121   organized the list of subscribers: Baron, *op. cit.*, I, pp. 481–3.

the account was paid: Davies, *op. cit.*, Well. MS5230(121/1).

returned to the trustees,: GCRO D3900/1.

read and corrected the proof: W. R. LeFanu, *A Bio-bibliography of Edward Jenner 1749–1823*, London: Harvey & Blythe, 1951, p. 61.

122   'incessant interruptions': Jenner, '. . . Reply to Mr. Fermor', *op. cit., Med. Phys. Jour.*, 6 (10/01), pp. 325–6.

123   '[a] paper on the cow-pox . . . .': 'Physical Society at Guy's Hospital', *London Medical Review*, 8 (2/02), p. 94.

honorary member: Edward Jenner, Diplomas and certificates, 1772–1804, Well. MS5231(4–5).

Further recognition: Baron, *op. cit.*, I, pp. 537–9.

Fellow of the American Society: Saunders, *op. cit.*, p. 109.

he and Jenner met: Davies, *op. cit.*, 1/3/02, Well. MS2052.

Edward Gardner's child.: *ibid.*

'your petitioner . . . .': quoted in Crookshank, *op. cit.*, I, pp. 173–4.

'the practice of which Dr. Jenner . . .': Revd G. C. Jenner, *The Evidence at Large, as Laid before the Committee of the House of Commons, Respecting Dr. Jenner's Discovery of Vaccine Inoculation; together with the Debate which Followed. . . .'* London: J. Murray, 1805, pp. xxv–xxvi and footnote.

124   'saved human beings . . .': *ibid.*, p. 191.

'for a solvent of the stone . . . .': *ibid.*, p. 186.

125   'A petition of Edward Jenner, ...': Murray and RJS, Well. MS5244(7).

Dr James Currie: Miller, *op. cit.*, p. 16. For some reason the import of this letter has been overlooked.

drawings of the vaccine pustule: George Kirtland (32 watercolour drawings), Well. MS3115. Kirtland had copied Gold's drawings after the hearings.

'He himself was called in, ...': Moore, *op. cit.*, pp. 132–3.

126   'Though Jenner felt . . . .': Baron, *op. cit.*, II, pp. 95–6. See also: J. J. Abraham, *Lettsom: His Life, Times, Friends and Descendants*, London: William Heinemann Medical, 1933, p. 346.

'I am by accident, . . .': *ibid.*, p. 407.

' "Allow me to present . . ." ': J. Stratford, *Good and Great Men of Gloucestershire*, Cirencester: C. H. Savory, [1867], p. 293.

'I think it the greatest . . . .': Revd G. C. Jenner, *op. cit.*, p. 13.

'I doubt not but . . . .': *ibid.*, p. 98.

'*it is the most important* . . .': *ibid.*, pp. 93–4.

'considering the apparent . . . .': *ibid.*, p. 89.

127   'the propriety of examining him',: [House of Commons], 'The Evidence relative to Dr. Jenner's Petition', *Med. Phys. Jour.*, 8 (8/1802), p. 142.

Sir George Baker,: Revd G. C. Jenner, *op. cit.*, p. 161.

called him Justin.: Thomas Creaser, *Observations on Dr. Pearson's Examination of the Report of the Committee of the House of Commons. . . .*, 2nd edn, Bath: Richard Cruttwell, 1805, pp. 6–7.

Dolling had acknowledged: *ibid.*, p. vi footnote.

Benjamin Jesty: Revd G. C. Jenner, *op. cit.*, pp. 156–8. Creighton, *op. cit.*, pp. 23–4. Fisk, *op. cit.*, pp. 189–90.

Thomas Nash: Revd G. C. Jenner, *op. cit.*, pp. 140–2, 155. Creaser, *op. cit.*, pp. x–xi. Crookshank, *op. cit.*, I, pp. 101–2.

128   *Observations of an Eruptive Disease*: Sherborne: J. Langdon.

Page
128 reported this news to Jenner.: Murray, *op. cit.*, Well. MS5245(70). Cf. also 'La Vie Exemplaire et L'Oeuvre de Jenner', *Archives de l'Institute Claude Bernard*, Vol. 4, Part I (1973), pp. 175–85. I am grateful to Dr Hugh Torrens, Department of Geology, Keele University, for showing me his copies of this article and of three letters from Ireland to Rabaut-Pomier dated 1811 which deal with information the latter had given to Pew. Dr Torrens also showed me a copy of Pew's pamphlet.

less well authenticated candidates: Revd G. C. Jenner, *op. cit.*, pp. 135–6. Fisk, *op. cit.*, pp. 190–2.

129 'safety of infant inoculation'.: Revd G. C. Jenner, *op. cit.*, pp. 130–1.

an infant of six months,: p. 36. Henry Hicks, *Observations on a Late Publication of Dr. Pearson. . . .*, Stroud: W. S. Wilson, 1803, p. 8.

twenty hours before.: Crookshank, *op. cit.*, Vol. II, p. 137.

'Since my return . . . .': Miller, *op. cit.*, p. 24.

'if Dr. P. could atchieve . . .': Creaser, *op. cit.*, p. v.

a convenient shorthand,: [House of Commons], *op. cit.*, pp. 3, 4, 35, 80, Well. MS3023.

130 half a year before the Committee: L. H., 'A Proposal', *Med. Phys. Jour.*, 6 (11/1801), p. 422.

'National Subscription': Thomas Beddoes, 'To the Editors. . . .', *Med. Phys. Jour.*, 8 (7/1802), p. 7.

'What was my surprise . . . .': quoted in Crookshank, *op. cit.*, I, p. 205.

'the original inventor': [House of Commons], 'Report from the Committee. . . .', *Med. Phys. Jour.*, 7 (6/1802), pp. 488–9.

'The difference of ten and twenty . . .': [Thomas Creaser], *Observations on Dr. Jenner's Parliamentary Reward & its probable Effects on the Progress of Vaccine Inoculation* (n.p., n.d., probably 1802), [p. 6].

'June 2 1802 . . . .': William Davies, Household accounts, Vol. III (facing p. 48), Well. MS2050.

Chapter 7: The Royal Jennerian Society 1802–1803

132 twenty-five-guinea fee: [Plymouth Medical Society], 'The case of the almost identical twins. . . .', signed 1/1959, Bernard J. Peck, Hon. Sec., Well., Jenner Folio Reproduction. A second portrait by Northcote was thought to exist but is here shown to be a copy.

'a fine engraving . . .': J. J. Abraham, *Lettsom: His Life, Times, Friends and Descendants*, London: William Heinemann Medical, 1933, p. 358.

'Lawrence catches . . . .': Edward Jenner, [Pruen papers], Well. MS5240(10).

'Many catch the mind . . .': L. Crummer (ed.), 'Copy of Jenner Note Book', *Ann. Med. Hist.*, N. S. I (1929), p. 407.

'I never knew a man . . . .': T. F. Dibdin, *Reminiscences of a Literary Life*, 2 vols (cont. pag.) London, John Major, 1836, p. 199.

133 They portray the squire: Lawrence's portrait hangs in the Royal College of Physicians, London. Various other portrayals were done at this time. In 1800 John Raphael Smith painted a standing three-quarter portrait showing a bucolic background with Berkeley Castle. The figure is more ample than in Northcote's painting, and the features more pronounced and uglier. It is owned by the Wellcome Institute for the History of Medicine. The portrait by Hobday (1822) hangs in the main reception hall of the Royal Society of Medicine. Also in 1800, Samuel Medley painted a group portrait of the members of the Medical Society of London which was finished before Jenner's rise to prominence. Medley added Jenner's head behind the President, James Sims. (Abraham, *op. cit.*, pp. 336–8.) In 1805 Charles Manning obtained permission to dedicate a sculpted bust of Jenner to the Royal Jennerian Society, which paid him for it. Jenner called Manning 'a young Artist of merit' (Genevieve Miller (ed.), *Letters of Edward Jenner and Other Documents concerning the Early History of Vaccination*, Baltimore and London: Johns Hopkins University Press, 1983, p. 26), and selected him to do the monument for his brother Stephen.

'While the vaccine discovery . . . .': quoted by J. Baron, *The Life of Edward Jenner M. D. . . .*' Vol. I, London: Henry Colburn, 1827, p. 140.

Edward Jenner 1749–1823

Page

133 opium-based reverie: Richard Holmes, *Coleridge: Early Visions*, London, Sydney, Auckland, Toronto: Hodder & Stoughton, 1989, p. 162.
'Vaccination draws upon me . . . .': Edward Jenner, letter to Revd Robert Ferryman, 17/2/1805, [Berkeley], RCP:ALS.
'Notwithstanding the extraordinary . . . .': Crummer, *op. cit.*, pp. 415 (36).

134 'nothing could exceed . . . .': review, '*The Life of Edward Jenner*. . . . By John Baron. . . . 1827', *Med. Phys. Jour.*, 57 (1827), p. 545.
a house on Hertford Street.: 'Dr Jenner's Claim', [1807], Well. MS3022, p. 4.
the son of Lord Holland,: Baron, *op. cit.*, Vol. II (1838), pp. 327–8.
Edward Jenner (to W. T. Cobb), Miscellany 1960, Add. MS 50483 A–U BLMS (7).

135 'with a sort of pious fraud, . . .': Charles Murray, *An Answer to Mr. Highmore's Objections*. . . ., London: Longman, Hurst, Rees & Orme, 1808, pp. 28–9.
20,323 vaccinations,: Joseph Adams, *A Popular View of Vaccine Inoculation*. . . ., London: Richard Phillips, 1807, pp. 152ff.
'to my very great disappointment, . . .': Mr Thomas, 'Observations on Vaccine Inoculation. . . .', *Med. Phys. Jour.*, 8 (8/1802), p. 169.
There Edward received: Baron, *op. cit.*, I, p. 565. Franck also visited Beddoes's Institute for Preventive Medicine while he was in the west country. D. A. Stansfield, *Thomas Beddoes M. D. 1760–1808*. . . ., Dordrecht, Boston, Lancaster: . Reidel Publishing Co., 1984, p. xviii.
'dined and spent the day': William Davies, Diary 1792–1805, 9–12/8/1802, Well. MS2052.
'Dr and Mrs. Jenner, ...': Catalogue of the Witts Family Papers, N. W. Kingsley, 1984 [Upper Slaughter, Stow-on-the-Wold, Gloucestershire], GCRO, EL429, p. 32 (2nd page in, begins 28), Appendix 1.
'for the purpose of considering . . . .': [Royal Jennerian Society Board of Directors], 'Minutes of the Royal Jennerian Society for the Extermination of the Small Pox' [3/12/02–4/12/05], Well. MS4302, pp. 1–2.

136 'after an absence of some years'.: *ibid.*, pp. 7–9.
Jennerian Society,: *ibid.*, pp. 3–10.
'by spreading the contagion,. . . .' . . . adjourned for a week.: *ibid.*, pp. 11–13.
'The idea of the formation . . .': *Royal Jennerian Society*. . . ., London: Jas Swan, 1816, pp. 29–30.

137 at a public meeting: [RJS Board], *op. cit.*, pp. 14–16. Well. MS4302.
6 January 1803: [Royal Jennerian Society], 'Minutes of the Royal Jennerian Society for the Extermination of the Small Pox', [6/1/1803–3/12/06], Well. MS4303. (Henceforth: [RJS, General].)
seventy-six signatories: [RJS Board], *op. cit.*, pp. 18–20, Well. MS4302.
'other Noblemen and Gentlemen': *ibid.*, pp. 29–30. [RJS, General], *op. cit.*, Well. MS4303.
It resolved to invite. . . . Dr Edward Jenner.: [RJS Board], *op. cit.*, pp. 23–4, Well. MS4302.

138 The meeting of 26 January. . . .*ex officio* directors too.: *ibid.*, pp. 23–7, 32.
on 10 February.: *ibid.*, p. 28.
overnight journey: Baron, *op. cit.*, I, p. 575.
Dr Edward Jenner's Patients' Visiting Book, Well. MS3021.

139 Edward Jenner to Dr De Carro, 30/3/1803, Hertford St, RCP:ALS.
'generally prevailing sickness',: [RJS Board], op. cit., pp. 76–7, Well. MS4302. [Royal Jennerian Society], 'Minutes of the Medical Committee. . . .', [23/2/03–21/2/07], Well. MS4304. (Henceforth: [RJS, Medical]). Of the instructions Jenner wrote to John Ring in 1807 agreeing that 'Too Many Cooks Etc.' and blaming himself as well as the other members of the drafting committee: Ring, John Addington and Samuel Merriman, obstetrician connected with Middlesex Hospital and Westminster General Dispensary. (Miller, *op. cit.*, pp. 41–2.)
'since I saw you . . . .': Edward Jenner, 'Nineteen autograph letters to Alexander Marcet. . . .' (hereafter: 'Edward Jenner to Alexander Marcet'), 6/4/03, RSM.
'We have all had it . . . .': Edward Jenner to T. Pearce, Hertford St, 14/4/03, Jenner Musuem.

Page
139 'Honours certainly fall . . . .': Miller, *op. cit.*, p. 20. The connection, if any, between T. Cobb of Cheltenham and W. T. Cobb of Banbury is unknown. Jenner to Pearce, *op. cit.*, JM.
140 'Elated and allured . . .': Baron, *op. cit.*, II, p. 4.
'The London smoke . . . .': *ibid.*, p. 5 footnote.
'your liberality and disinterestedness . . . .': *ibid.*, p. 6.
141 annual festival: [RJS, General], *op. cit.*, 17/2/03, Well. MS4303.
Medical Committee met: [RJS, Medical], *op. cit.*, Well. MS4304.
vaccination instructions.: *ibid.*, 28/2/03, 10/3/03.
'had not yet had sufficient . . .': [RJS Board], *op. cit.*, p. 86, Well. MS4302.
John Birch, *Serious Reasons for Uniformly Objecting to the Practice of Vaccination. . . .*, London: Harris, 1806, p. 24.
with Drs Denman and Bradley,: [RJS Medical], *op. cit.*, 31/3/03, Well. MS4304.
'mode of obtaining and preserving . . . .': [RJS Board], *op. cit.*, pp. 88–91, Well. MS4304.
142 'scabby Face, . . .': 'Edward Jenner to Alexander Marcet', *op. cit.*, 23/2/03, RSM.
143 'Don't you observe . . . .': Edward Jenner to Dr De Carro, 30/3/03, *op. cit.*, RCP:ALS.
£500 from the Corporation: [RJS Board], *op. cit.*, p. 73, Well MS4302.
a gift of £100: *ibid.*, p. 146.
'a free benefit there . . .': *ibid.*, p. 106.
twelve inoculation stations,: *ibid.*, p. 68.
Society signed a lease: *ibid.*, pp. 80–1.
asked six members: *ibid.*, p. 93.
144 'persons of all ages' 'or oftener if desired': [RJS, Medical], *op. cit.*, 14/4/03, Well. MS4304.
election by the Council: *ibid.*, 28/4/03.
its first two publications: [RJS Board], *op. cit.*, pp. 107–9, 118–19, Well. MS4302.
145 with three directors: *ibid.*, pp. 236–7.
first annual festival,: *ibid.*, p. 125. D. Fisk, *Dr Jenner of Berkeley*, London, Melbourne, Toronto: Heinemann, 1959, p. 206.
'I was all but overcome . . . .': William and Anne Davies, Correspondence. . . . 1775–1812, Well. MS5229(3).
franking privilege: [RJS Board], *op. cit.*, pp. 130–1, 140, 173, Well. MS4302.
15 June: [RJS, General], *op. cit.*, Well. MS4303.
Jenner attended: *ibid.*, 15/6/03.
between the Board and the Council: [RJS Board], *op. cit.*, pp. 128–9, 133–4, 136, 143–4, Well. MS4302.
146 'Preservative against the Small Pox': *ibid.*, p. 142.
Thirteen stations. . . . Dimsdale at Drury Lane.: *ibid.*, pp. 104–5. [RJS, Medical], *op. cit.*, 5/5/03, 12/5/03, Well. MS4304.
2701 inoculations.: [RJS Board], *op. cit.*, p. 148, Well. MS4302.
'that the prejudices. . . .': *Monthly report* 03, pp. 373–4.
147 'It appearing that a small . . . .': [RJS, Medical], *op. cit.*, 9/2/04, Well. MS4304.
In March 1805 the General Meeting heard: [RJS, General], *op. cit.*, 6/3/05, Well. MS4303.
'whether some additional Plan . . . .': [RJS Board], *op. cit.*, [p. 270], Well. MS4302.
[John Ring], *The Vaccine Scourge: Part II. . . .* London: J. Callow, 1815, p. 37.
'In London my practice . . . .': Edward Jenner to Dr De Carro, *op. cit.*, RCP:ALS.
Freedom of the City: Edward Jenner, Diplomas and certificates, 1772–1804, Well. MS5231(7).
Royal Humane Society: *ibid.*, MS5231(9).
'has recommended Him . . . .': J. Farington, *The Farington Diary*, ed. J. Greig, Vol. II, London: Hutchinson, p. 146.
since the previous January.: Davies, *op. cit.*, Well. MS2052.

Chapter 8: . . . so large, so temperate, and so consistent. . . 1804–1807

148 deficit of nearly £6 : John Baron, *The Life of Edward Jenner, M. D. . . .*, Vol. II, London: Henry Colburn, 1838. p. 9.
'I have to thank my stars . . . .': *ibid.*, p. 330.

Edward Jenner 1749–1823

Page
149 'a large party': William Davies, Diary 1792–1805, Well. MS2052.
   Jenner's excuse.: D. Fisk, *Dr Jenner of Berkeley*, London, Melbourne, Toronto: Heine-
      mann, 1959, pp. 215–6.
   'went to Berkeley . . .': William Davies, Household accounts, Vol. III, Well. MS2050.
150 'I wish I cd transfer . . .': Edward Jenner, [Pruen papers], Well. MS5240(1).
   'If a Catholic peer,. . . .': L. Crummer (ed.), 'Copy of Jenner Note Book', *Ann. Med.
      Hist.*, N. S. I (1929), p. 413.
151 'I dread the consequence . . . .': Jenner, *op. cit.*, Well. MS5240(29).
   'How often do we say . . . .': Crummer, *op. cit.*, p. 403.
   'To an observer . . . .': Edward Jenner, *Some Observations on the Migration of Birds*. . . .,
      in *Philosophical Transactions*, London: Wm Nicol, 1824, p. 29.
   'I learnt from him, ...': Richard Holmes, *Coleridge: Early Visions*, London, Sydney,
      Auckland, Toronto: Hodder & Stoughton, 1989, p. 36.
   'The highest powers . . . .': Crummer, *op. cit.*, p. 413.
152 'On the Varieties and Modifications . . .': 12 (8/04), pp. 97–102. Published as a pamphlet,
      On the Varieties & Modifications of the Vaccine Pustule. . . ., Cheltenham: H. Ruff,
      1806.
   'Varieties' 'in the character . . . .': Edward Jenner, Autographs from the Morrison
      collection, Vol. I, Add. MS 39, 672, BLMS.
   Robert Willan, *On Cutaneous Diseases*, Vol. I, London: J. Johnson, 1798.
   'I am greatly deceived . . . .': Edward Jenner, letter to Revd Robert Ferryman, 17/2/1805,
      [Berkeley], RCP:ALS.
153 'the herpetic and some . . . .': Jenner, *Vaccine Pustule*, p.3.
   Even after smallpox inoculation,: John Ring, *An Answer to Mr Goldson*. . . ., London: J.
      Murray, 1804, pp. 14–15.
   'Respecting the principle, ...': Robert Willan, *On Vaccine Inoculation*, London: Richard
      Phillips, 1806, p. viii footnote. Willan died in 1812.
   'by far the most useful . . . .': Underwood papers (photocopy in Catalogue 62, Martin
      Breslauer, 7/1947, p. 45), Well. Curator of Western MSS.
   'My paper on Herpes . . . .': John Walker, 'To the Editors. . . .', *Med. Phys. Jour.*, 13
      (6/1805), p. 541.
   'my experience warrants . . . .': J. Wood, 'To the Editors. . . .', *Med. Phys. Jour.*, 15
      (1/1806), p. 136.
   'There is no evidence . . . .': C. W. Dixon, *Smallpox*, London: J. & A. Churchill, 1962,
      pp. 141–2.
154 'It is unaccountable, ...': Edward Jenner, Letters. . . ., 1794–1822, Well. MS5236(16).
   'Dandriffe': Edward Jenner to Thomas Fosbroke, 13/3/1820, Berkeley; Well., photocopies
      of letters held by Curator of Western MSS (orig.: Edinburgh University Library).
   'a speck behind the ear . . . .': [Edward Jenner], 'Presuming that you are conversant. . . .',
      2 printed pp. (n.d., hand-dated: Berkeley, 31/1/21), Well. MS5240(79).
   Medical flavour.: Paul Saunders, *Edward Jenner: The Cheltenham Years, 1795–1823*,
      Hanover, Vt., and London: University Press of New England, p. 99.
   '*So great has been the scramble* . . . .': Jenner to Ferryman, *op. cit.*, RCP:ALS.
155 *Glocester Journal*: 13/9/1790, p. 3.
   'a refuge for faun . . .': [J. C. Lettsom], *Memoir of Edward Jenner, M. D.*, [London], I.
      Gold, [1804], p. 6. Fisk, *op. cit.*, p. 99.
   Ferryman: Brian Frith, 'Robert Ferryman, Clergyman Extraordinary', *Gloucestershire
      Record Office Annual Report, 1982–83*, Gloucester County Council, 1983, pp. 25–6.
   'I have just got a letter . . . .': Jenner, *op. cit.*, Berkeley, 19/12/1817, Well. MS5240(66).
156 separated angrily.: Dr Hugh Torrens, Centre for the History of Science and Technology,
      University of Keele, suggested this explanation. He has painstakingly collected
      biographical data on Ferryman.
   'in the skirts of the Town. . . .': Edward Jenner to Miss Sheppard of Uley, Berkeley,
      11/11/1822, no. 36, RCS.
   Dibdin's poem, *Vaccinia*,: T. F. Dibdin, *Reminiscences of a Literary Life*, 2 vols, London,
      John Major, 1836, p. 201 footnote.
   John Ring, *A Translation of Anstey's Ode to Jenner*. . . ., London: J. Murray, 1804.

Notes pp. 156–165

Page
156 'Do me the favour . . . .': quoted by Baron, *op. cit.*, Vol. I (1827), p. 39.
Thomas Campbell,: Crummer, *op. cit.*, p. 413.
Thomas Moore . . . and . . . Coleridge.: T. D. Fosbroke, *A Picturesque and Topographical Account of Cheltenham* . . ., Cheltenham, S. C. Harper, 1826, p. 281.
'His offer to me . . . .': Jenner, *op. cit.*, MS5240(71).
157 'he was not only fond . . . .': Fosbroke, *op. cit.*, p. 279.
'I show everything . . . .': *ibid.*, p. 282.
158 *A Practical Dictionary of Domestic Medicine*: London: Longman, Hurst, Rees, and Orme.
favoured vaccination: 'Letter from Mr Stewart to Dr Remmett', *Med. Phys. Jour.*, 3 (3/1800), pp. 234–8.
alleged fatality: 'Case of Erysipelas followed by general Anascara, succeeding the Vaccine Inoculation, and terminating fatally', *Med. Phys. Jour.*, 6 (8/1801), pp. 131–3.
a London surgeon,: Mr Brown, 'The following Cases of Small-pox subsequent to Vaccination. . . .', *Med. Phys. Jour.*, 29 (3/1813), pp. 281–5.
Walker of Oxford.: See especially 'On the Cow-Pox. . . .', *Med. Phys. Jour.*, 32 (9/1814), pp. 211–16; cont. in (10/1814), pp. 189–94; and other articles by Richard Walker in the same journal during 1815 and 1816.
William Goldson, *Cases of Small Pox subsequent to Vaccination.* . . ., Portsea: William Woodward, 1804.
159 *An Answer to Mr Goldson*: London: J. Murray, 1804.
Some Recent Cases of Small Pox: Portsea: W. Woodward, 1805.
'I hope it will teach him . . . .': *ibid.*, p. 127.
'it has been represented . . . .': quoted in Baron, *op. cit.*, II, p. 25.
160 23 October,: Davies, *op. cit.*, Well. MS2052.
A week later,: *ibid.*
'All the Petty opposition . . .': Edward Jenner, Berkeley 16/1/1805, Underwood papers 62, (photocopy in Catalogue Martin Breslauer, 7/1947, p. 45).
'You don't like my style . . . .': Baron, *op. cit.*, II, p. 370.
161 'As I so much wish . . . .': Genevieve Miller (ed.), *Letters of Edward Jenner and Other Documents concerning the Early History of Vaccination*, Baltimore and London: Johns Hopkins University Press, 1983, pp. 25–6. The letter is dated only '4th February' in a PS. Miller dates it 1805 on the basis of other internal evidence. The first of the drafts following is dated 27/12/1805. Perhaps the second, undated, draft is actually earlier. Miller also supposes the letter to have been written at Cheltenham, but William Davies's Diary shows that he dined with his uncle at the Berkeley Masonic Lodge on that date.
'It has been a question . . . .': Edward Jenner, Papers 1790–1822. . . ., Well. MS5235(5).
162 'I lately made a digression . . . .': *ibid.*, (6).
163 *Observations Addressed*: London: W. Smith & Son, 1805.
'are the only men . . . .': *ibid.*, pp. 2–3.
An Examination of That Part: 2nd edn, London: J. Callow, 1805.
'The first fatal case . . . .': *ibid.*, p. 17.
'this case, I think, . . .': *ibid.*, p. 20.
Cow Pox Inoculation No Security: London: J. Harris, 1805.
164 'From motives of liberality . . . .': *ibid.*, p. v.
'Why leave a certainty . . . .': *ibid.*, p. 4.
'There is no danger . . . .': *ibid.*, p. 9 footnote.
'The Small Pox is a visitation . . .': *ibid.*, p. 8 footnote.
'I could pardon this kind . . . .': Robert John Thornton, *Vaccinae Vindicia; or, Defence of Vaccination. . . . and the Debate in the House of Commons (July 2, 1806)*. . . ., London: H. D. Symonds *et al.*, 1806, pp. 97–8 footnote.
Serious Reasons for Uniformly Objecting: London: Harris, 1806.
'unfounded or grossly misrepresented': John Ring, *An Answer to Mr. Birch Containing a Defence of Vaccination*, London: J. Murray, 1806, pp. 26, 28.
'scarcely any': *ibid.*, p. 30.
165 'ambiguous expressions': Birch, *op. cit.*, pp. 4–5, 7.
'Dr. Rowley's *placards* . . . .': *ibid.*, p. 161.
'More Proofs. . . .': *ibid.*, p. 170.

[315]

Edward Jenner 1749–1823

Page
165 'Coercion, in a state . . . .': [Edward Jenner], [4 letters to T. J. Estcourt MP. 13/3/
1805–25/3/1809], GCRO, D1571 F222.
On 23 February: Davies, *op. cit.*, Well. MS2050.
Masonic lodge meetings: Davies, *op. cit.*, Well. MS2052.
'The Treasury still . . .': Baron, *op. cit.*, II, pp. 4–5 footnote.
£1000 had been deducted: *ibid.*, p. 9. Fisk, *op. cit.*, p. 218.
'Statement for those Parliamentary friends': 'Dr Jenner's Claim', [1807], Well. MS3022,
pp. 12–13.
166 returned to the capital: Baron, *op. cit.*, II, p. 55. Baron says Jenner left Berkeley on the 9th,
arriving in London the next day, but the minutes of the RJS Medical Council show that
he chaired the Council meeting on the 9th.
appointed a new committee: [Royal Jennerian Society Board of Directors], 'Minutes of the
Royal Jennerian Society for the Extermination of the Small Pox' [3/12/02–4/12/05],
Well. MS4302, pp. 243–7, 252.
167 'and Morpeth, and they will . . . .': Baron, *op. cit.*, II, p. 56.
'Lady Crewe happened . . . .': *ibid.*, pp. 55–6.
'your Brother too, . . .': Edward Jenner, Letters to . . . from various correspondents,
1805–20, Well. MS5233(1).
'& 3 children . . .': Davies, *op. cit.*, Well. MS2050.
'to consult Mr. Pearce . . . .': *idem.*
168 19 June: Davies, Diary 1805–17, Well. MS2053.
disposition of his property.: Davies, *op. cit.*, Well. MS2050, contains the following cryptic
entry.

No W 9230 Dr. Edward Jenner Decr 14. 1802 –
A. 4. Post Bank. F. Hensall

213
113/10/0
106/ 0/0
12/10/0

445/ 0/–

Each of the amounts is written in a different pencil as though at different times. Is this a
record of loans made to Jenner by William Davies senior over a period of years, possibly
beginning in 1802 and extending to 1805? In any event I think these family matters may
have indicated Jenner's somewhat overdramatic sense of desperation.
4 and 15 July 1805,: [Royal Jennerian Society], 'Minutes of the Medical Committee. . . .',
[23/2/03–21/2/07], Well. MS4304.
where he remained: Thornton, *op. cit.*, pp. 274–7.
She wrote to reassure: Charles Murray and the Royal Jennerian Society. . . .
1803–15. . . ., Well. MS5244(1).
'Schweppe's Soda water': *Medical Observer. . . .* Vol. I, London: S. Highley, 1806, pp.
159ff.
'Of the Practice of Medicine . . .': *ibid.*, pp. 219; article: pp. 177–206; vaccination: pp.
196–200.
169 'In the *Med: & Phys: Journal* . . . .': Miller, *op. cit.*, p. 29.
'drank tea with my uncle . . . .': Davies, *op. cit.*, Well. MS2053.
'Godfather to Mr Hickes' son . . .': Crummer, *op. cit.*, p. 414.
'has been four or five years . . . .': 'Medical and Physical Intelligence', *Med. Phys. Jour.*,
15 (6/1806), p. 588. John Ring, 'To the Editors. . . .', *Med. Phys. Jour.*, 17 (1/1807), p.
12.
30 May,: Edward Jenner, 'Nineteen autograph letters to Alexander Marcet. . . .' (hereafter: 'Edward Jenner to Alexander Marcet'), RSM.
a month later.: Miller, *op. cit.*, p. 30.
Great Rupert Street,: In a letter to Paytherus from Cheltenham dated 1 Oct., no year but
probably 1806 (paper watermarked 1805), Jenner wrote: 'With respect to the House, I
can only repeat what I wrote before "do with it as if it were your own & I shall be

satisfied" '. I believe this referred to the Hertford Street house – according to available evidence, the only London house that Jenner owned. If that is so, his inability to recover the money he had invested in it would certainly have exacerbated his financial difficulties. However, it is possible that he had taken a lease on 27 Great Russell Street, and that it is that house to which the letter referred. Jenner, *op. cit.*, Well. MS5236(7).

170 John Bedwell: Murray and RJS, *op. cit.*, Well. MS5244(65, 66).
 in a letter to the Medical Council, ... 'confidence of the Council.': [RJS Medical], *op. cit.*, 17/10/1805, 7/11/1805, 2/1/1806, 15/1/1806, Well. MS4304.

171 'The first thing that Dr. Walker . . . .': John Epps, *The Life of John Walker, M. D.*, London: Whittaker, Treacher & Co., 1831, pp. 120–1.
 'I am ashamed to send . . . .': Edward Jenner to Rowland Hill, 1/8/1822, Various correspondents 1795–1822, Well. MS5232(21).
 'You pass by . . . .': Z. Z. [Henry Jenner?], 'Of the Late Dr. Jenner', *The Monthly Gazette of Health*, no. 93 (1/9/1823), London: Sherwood & Co.
 'After our conference . . . .': Edward Jenner to E. Davy, 19/6/1801, 'Miscellaneous Original Letters', Vol. I, *Mus. Brit. Jureemptionis*, 19242, BLMS. George Evans, Baron Carbery, died London, 31/12/1804, aged 38, 'from the bursting of a blood vessel'. *The Complete Peerage of England*. . . ., Vol. I, Gloucester: Alan Sutton, 1982.

172 September 1804,: Vol. 12, p. 243.
 'Matter may be taken . . . .': [Royal Jennerian Society], *Address . . . and Instructions*. . . ., London: W. Phillips, 1803, pp. 42–3.
 'From the constant demands . . . .': Vol. 13, p. 456.

173 'we beg leave to call . . . .': *ibid.*, pp. 542–7.
 'In the numbers which . . . .': 'To the Editors. . . .', *Med. Phys. Jour.*, 15 (3/1806), p. 256 footnote.
 'If no case can be secure . . . .': Med. Phys. Jour., (4/1806), p. 320.

174 'for the purpose of enquiring . . . .': [RJS, General], *op. cit.*, 7/6/06, Well. MS4303.
 a vote of 158 to 6: *ibid.*, 25/6/1806.
 23 June 1806,: Davies, *op. cit.*, Well. MS2053.
 'the subject of vaccination': Baron, *op. cit.*, II, pp. 56–7.
 an inquiry into the practice,: *ibid.*, p. 64.
 Joseph Farington, *The Farington Diary*, ed. James Greig, Vol. III, London: Hutchinson, pp. 264–5.

175 'my opinion that Dr. Walker . . .': [RJS, Medical], *op. cit.*, 3/7/1806. Well. MS4303.
 'That he has from time to time . . . .': . . . 'To Dr. Jenner's charge. . . .': *ibid.*, 17/7/1806.
 Special General Court: [RJS, General], *op. cit.*, 25/7/1806. Well. MS4306.

176 thirty new subscribers,: *The Vaccine Scourge, in Answer to . . . Mr. Birch*. . . ., London: J. Murray, 1808, p. 58.
 'I think the conduct . . . .': John Walker's *Reply to James Moore, on his Mis-Statements*. . . ., London: Highley & Son, 1818, p.107.
 'Another Flag of Truce . . . .': 'Edward Jenner to Alexander Marcet', 4/8/1806, RSM.
 353 who voted,: [RJS, General], *op. cit.*, 5/8/1806. Well. MS4306.
 'It would be supposing you . . . .': [RJS, Medical], *op. cit.*, 7/8/1806. Well. MS4304.

177 'In his *History and Practice*': London: J. Callow, p. 213.

178 11 August,: Davies, *op. cit.*, Well. MS2053.
 on 18 August.: [Royal Jennerian Society], Directors [16/12/05–3/8/09], minutes: 2/9/1806, Well. MS4305.
 'not publish anything . . .': [RJS, Medical], *op. cit.*, 18/8/06, 25/8/06, Well. MS4304.
 On 1 or 2 September,: Miller, *op. cit.*, p. 30. Davies *op. cit.*, 1/9, Well. MS2053. Tea 'with' his uncle.
 'endeavouring to prevent . . .': [RJS Board] 1805–, *op. cit.*, 9/10/06. Well. MS4305.
 London Vaccine Institution: Epps, *op. cit.*, pp. 95–6.
 'J. Leaper is making . . . .': Jenner, *op. cit.*, Well. MS5236(6).

179 'Walker will be troublesome . . . .': Miller *op. cit.*, p. 32.
 'Poor Knowles, . . .': *Ibid.*, p. 45.
 John Dawes Worgan: John Dawes Worgan, *Select Poems*. . . ., London: Longman, Hurst, Rees & Orme, 1810, pp. 23, 97. Baron, *op. cit.*, II, pp. 71–2.

Page

179 in Cheltenham,: Davies, *op. cit.*, 15/9, 6/10, 15/12, Well. MS2053. Miller, *op. cit.*, p. 34.

'I fear it will not . . . .': Miller, *op. cit.*, p. 32.

'Verulam Socy.': *ibid.*, pp. 5, 6 footnote, 33 footnote.

'the very curious and interesting . . . .': Edward Jenner to Richard Phillips, Cheltenham, RCP:ALS.

Dr Francis Xavier Balmis,: Baron, *op. cit.*, II, pp. 78–81. John Ring, 'To the Editors. . . .', *Med. Phys. Jour.*, 17 (1/1807), pp. 9–16. Moore, *op. cit.*, pp. 267–70. D. R. Hopkins, *Princes and Peasants: Smallpox in History*, Chicago and London: University of Chicago Press, 1983, pp. 224–5.

180 'prevailed upon the English . . . .': William Smith MP, in [House of Commons], incomplete verbatim report of the debate . . . on a second grant to Edward Jenner, [1807], pp. 84, 86, Well. MS3023.

12 or 19 February,: [Royal College of Physicians], Vaccination Committee (3 vols: letters and report), Vol. II, RCP MS2321. The RCP Library holds the complete proceedings of the Vaccination Committee and what appears to be a complete file of its correspondence!

'to vaccinate his . . . .': Baron, *op. cit.*, II, p. 358.

thirteen meetings: [RCP], Vaccination Committee 1806–7 (minutes and summaries of all letters), RCP.

John Birch was a member: 'Edward Jenner to Alexander Marcet', *op. cit.*, RSM.

181 Birch, a surgeon,: [RCP], Vaccination Committee, Vol. III, RCP MS2321. Rowley had died the year before.

Daniel Sutton: [RCP], Vaccination Committee 1806–7, (unbound booklets . . . analysis of replies. . . .), RCP MS2309/2.

'I mention this . . .': [RCP], Vaccination Committee, Vol. II, RCP MS2321.

about six thousand vaccinations: *ibid.*, Vol. III.

Thomas Pruen,: *ibid.*, Vol I, II. *On the Mortality of the Small-Pox*, showing no date and no author but with 'Compiled by J. Pruen Esq.' written in pencil at the top, is held by the RCP: T88/10, However, there is also: Thomas Pruen, *A Comparative Sketch of the Effects of Variolous and Vaccine Inoculation. . . .*' [London?]: Phillips, 1807.

committee on reorganization: [RJS, General] *op. cit.*, Well. MS4306.

returned to Berkeley: Davies, *op. cit.*, 10/3, 16/3, 17/3, Well. MS2055.

'It being stated . . . .': [RJS, Board] *op. cit.*, Well. MS4305.

182 'the progress of Vaccination . . . .': 'Report of the Royal College of Physicians of London on Vaccination. . . .', *Med. Phys. Jour.*, 18 (8/1807), pp. 97–102.

'How unfortunate, ...': Miller, *op. cit.*, p. 40 and footnote.

'may . . . make a very convenient . . . .': *Medical Observer*. . . ., *op. cit.*, p. 385 footnote.

183 'principal inhabitants of Calcutta . . .': Baron, *op. cit.*, II, pp. 87–8.

'These marks of attention . . . .': Jenner, *op. cit.*, Well. MS5236(8).

Dr James Anderson,: John Ring, 'To the Editors. . . .'. *Med. Phys. Jour.*, 17 (6/1807), p. 540.

£1383-1-10: Baron, *op. cit.*, II, p. 92 footnote.

£2   from Bombay.: *ibid.*, pp. 87–8.

Farington, *op. cit.*, Vol. IV, p. 223..

'more desirable . . .' . . . 'for 17th of May.': Jenner, *op. cit.*, Well. MS5232(10).

'gradually convalescent'. . . . 'He proceeds as I . . . .': *ibid.*, Well. MS5232(11).

184 Davies, *op. cit.*, Well. MS2055.

The Artist: W. R. LeFanu, *A Bio-bibliography of Edward Jenner 1749–1823*, London: Harvey & Blythe, 1951, p. 84.

'Classes of the Human Powers . . .': Vol. I, London: J. Murray, 1810.

Philosophical Magazine: Miller, *op. cit.*, p. 76.

'Statement for those . . . .': 'Dr Jenner's Claim', Well. MS3022.

a meeting about the slave trade.: Jenner, *op. cit.*, Well. MS5232(15).

'my Conversazione Party . . . .': 'Edward Jenner to Alexander Marcet', *op. cit.*, RSM.

'Mrs M. had the kindness . . . .': *idem*.

Chapter 9: The National Vaccine Establishment 1807–1809

186 late summer of 1807: William Davies, Diary 1805–17, 3/9/1807 Well. MS2055: dined and took tea with his uncle in Cheltenham; 4/9: breakfast and dinner with.

'to bring the young Lady . . . .': *Letters of Edward Jenner and Other Documents concerning the Early History of Vaccination*, ed. Genevieve Miller, Baltimore and London: Johns Hopkins University Press, 1983, p. 41.

187 would-be critics: e.g., C. Creighton, *Jenner and Vaccination: A Strange Chapter of Medical History*, London: Swan Sonnenschein, 1889, pp. 5–18. Creighton cites Jenner's claim in his first reply to Ingenhousz that he had engaged in several 'other physiological investigations' as evidence that Jenner exaggerated his contributions. Creighton asserts that there were only two investigations, of hedgehogs and cuckoos, both of which were deeply flawed. Apart from Creighton's analytical errors, his recitation of Jenner's activities depends entirely on Baron's account.

188 'Jenner often communicated . . . .': J. Moore, *The History and Practice of Vaccination*, London: J. Callow, 1817, pp. 216–17. There is no evidence that Jenner ever questioned Moore's account; he certainly read and approved of the book.

'the intended national Vaccine . . .': Charles Murray and the National Vaccine Establishment, Correspondence and papers. . . . 1809–29. . . ., Well. MS5245(28).

189 'My dear F[rien]d': Edward Jenner, 'Nineteen autograph letters to Alexander Marcet. . . .', 8/12/07, RSM. (Henceforth: 'Edward Jenner to Alexander Marcet'.)

'Perhaps Mrs. Marcet . . . .': Miller, *op. cit.*, p. 87 and footnote.

some fifty-six people: [Royal Jennerian Society], Minutes of the Board of Directors. . . ., 24/12/07. Well. MS4305.

The day after Christmas: G. Rose and others, Ringwood Papers, [1807–8], Well. MS4257(6).

On 27 December. . . . White Hart Inn, Ringwood.: Charles Murray and the Royal Jennerian Society. . . . 1803–15. . . ., Well. MS5244(32) and (16).

190 'one Hodges . . .': Rose, *op. cit.*, Well. MS4257(4).

'surrounded by an open . . .': *ibid.*, Well. MS4257(5).

'had the S. P. . . . .': Murray and RJS, *op. cit.*, Well. MS5244(19).

'no more than 7 or 800': Rose, *op. cit.*, Well. MS4257(5).

'After a most careful . . . .': Murray and RJS, *op. cit.*, Well. MS5244(30).

'that no instance occurred . . .': *ibid.*, Well. MS5244(32).

191 'a Berkeley Sparerib . . . .': Revd George Charles and Mary Black, Correspondence and papers . . ., 1750–1810, Well. MS5226(6).

'13th. day . . . .': *ibid.*, Well. MS5226(7).

'is his chief Nurse, . . .': *ibid.*, Well. MS5226(8).

'I have enclos'd . . . .': [Edward Jenner], various correspondents, 1795–1822, Well. MS5232(3). Unfortunately, Croome's evaluation has not survived.

192 'our Society is in a most . . . .': [RJS, Board], *op. cit.*, 25/2/1808. Well. MS4305.

The committee recommended: Murray and RJS, *op. cit.*, Well. MS5244(93), 133. [RJS, Board], *op. cit.*, 17/3/1808. Well. MS4305.

'some of my Fds.': Murray and RJS, *op. cit.*, Well. MS5244(6).

193 'The cow-pox appears . . . .': *Medical Observer*, Vol. II, pp. 171–2.

194 'All medical facts . . . .': L. Crummer (ed.), 'Copy of Jenner Note Book', *Ann. Med. Hist.*, N. S. I (1929), p. 417.

'In my opinion . . . .': quoted in John Baron, *The Life of Edward Jenner, M. D.*, Vol II, London: Henry Colburn, 1838, p. 359.

On 17 March: [RJS, Board], *op. cit.*, 17/3/1808. Well. MS4305.

Free vaccinations,: *ibid.*, 9/11/1807–20/5/1808.

William Howard: Murray and RJS, *op. cit.*, Well. MS5244(34–47).

195 Charles Brandon Trye,: [C. B. Trye, Documents concerning & by. . . .], GCRO D303 C3.

196 On 6 May: William Davies, Household accounts, Vol. III, Well. MS2050. Davies, *op. cit.*, Well. MS2053.

'These things would affect . . . .': Edward Jenner, [Pruen papers], Well. MS5240(3).

'Recd. of Mr Pruen . . .': [William Davies, Tithes, taxes & dispursements, 1776–1814], Well. MS2051.

Edward Jenner 1749–1823

Page

196 school in Reading,: T. F. Dibdin, *Reminiscences of a Literary Life* (2 vols, continuous pagination), London: John Major, 1836, pp. 157–8.
Glocester Journal: p. 3.
Cheltenham Chronicle: Miller, *op. cit.*, p. 69 footnote.
'In the heyday . . .' . . . 'a Rock, from which . . . .': Jenner, *op. cit.*, Well. MS5240(23, 37).
'seizure'. . . . to Dursley,: *ibid.*, Well. MS5240(46,62,63). I think it likely that Jenner had known about the forthcoming move but had mistaken the date.

197 Imagine the shock: William Davies, Correspondence and papers, 1716–1847 and n.d. . . ., Well. MS5230(96).
probably May or June.: Baron, *op. cit.*, II, pp. 136–40.
between London and Berkeley.: By his use of the preposition 'with' instead of 'at' in connection with various meals, William Davies junior's diary indicates that Jenner returned to Berkeley at the beginning and end of June, on 18 and 19 July, and from 2 to 19 August. He must have been in town during the debate on 9 June and by 28 August. Davies recorded dinner and tea with his uncle on 1 September, but Jenner wrote to Pruen from London on the 2nd.
'one of the first . . . .': Jenner, *op. cit.*, Well. MS5240(35).
Illustrations of the Enquiry: London: T. & G. Underwood, 1822.
about 10 May 1808.: Davies, *op. cit.*, Well. MS2053.

198 This was a bill: [House of Commons], 'An Act for preventing the spread of the Small pox. . . .', Well. MS3025(3). [pp. 2, 5].
abandoned smallpox inoculation.: J. R. Smith, *The Speckled Monster: Smallpox in England, 1670–1970, with particular reference to Essex*, Chelmsford: Essex Record Office, 1987, p. 95.
quarantines.: R. J. Thornton, *Vaccinae Vindicae; or, Defence of Vaccination . . . and the Debate in the House of Commons (July 2, 1806) . . .* London, H. D. Symonds et al., 1806, pp. 436–9.
[Sir Edmund Carrington], *A Letter to . . . Spencer Perceval . . . on . . . the Practice of Variolous Inoculation. . . .*, London: Hatchard, 1807. pp. 31–6.
'I cannot agree . . .': Murray and RJS, *op. cit.*, Well. MS5244(83).
'Cobbett, I find, ...': Jenner, *op. cit.*, Well. MS5240(4).

199 a non-medical man: Jenner, *op. cit.*, Well. MS5232(16).
Murray got the job: Murray and NVE, *op. cit.*, Well. MS5245(28).
'a central institution . . .': *ibid.*, Well. MS5245(29). Moore, *op. cit.*, p. 218.
'Great news from Spain, ...': Jenner, *op. cit.*, Well. MS5240(12).

200 'wild goose scheme': Reece did not explain Jenner's 'speculations'; might they have had to do with Dr Jenner's Absorbent Lozenges later marketed by Savory and Moore?
'not so scandalous in': 'Statement of a Case against Richard Reece. . . .', London, 1808, Well. MS3024.
'Jenneric Opera', *Medical Observer*, Vol. IV (8/1808), pp. 19–24. An undated pro-vaccination drama appeared about this time. It was anonymous but the Wellcome Institute Library copy is bound in a volume of plays by A. Maclaren. *The Cow-Doctor, A Comedy . . . with Prologue by Rev. T. Pennington* [Rector of Thorley, Herts and Kingdown, Kent], London: T. Billing, consists of three acts and a complex plot about country bumpkins who are anti vaccination and a Squire and Cow-Doctor who favour vaccination.
'Murray . . . inform'd me . . . .': Jenner, *op. cit.*, Well. MS5240(14).

201 'I have no heart, . . .': *ibid.*, MS5240(6).
'exhibiting four heads . . . .': Crummer, *op. cit.*, p. 409.
repeated it twice,: Jenner, *op. cit.*, Well. MS5240(8). 'Edward Jenner to Alexander Marcet', *op. cit.*, 2/9/1808, RSM. The latter was written from Great Rupert St, but the letter to Pruen was written at George Rose's house in Grosvenor Square.
'Reports unfavourable . . .': Murray and RJS, *op. cit.*, Well. MS5244(48–59). J. Ring and W. Blair, 'Report on . . . Vaccination at Cambridge', [15/8/1808], Well. MS4220.

202 'You will be sorry . . . .': Jenner, *op. cit.*, Well. MS5240(7).
'My poor dear Catherine . . . .': *ibid.*, Well. MS5240(8).

Page
202 'think it wd be . . . .': *ibid.*, Well. MS5240(7).
    'enquire the present state . . . .': *ibid.*, Well. MS5240(9).
    'has made so great . . . .': *ibid.*, Well. MS5240(8).
    'which struck my Fancy much'.: *ibid.*, Well. MS5240(13).
    'The destructive visitant . . . .': Crummer, *op. cit.*, p. 407.
    'Strong Cement, . . .': *ibid.*, p. 420.
203 'shall be superseded . . . .': [RJS, Board], *op. cit.*, Well. MS4305.
    Facts, for the Most Part Unobserved,: London: S. Gosnell, 1808, p. 15.
    'the constitution cannot . . .': *Further Observations on the Variolae Vaccinae or Cow Pox,*
        London: Sampson Low, 1799, p. 116.
204 Special General Court: [RJS, General], *op. cit.*, 11/11/1808. Well. MS4306.
    Richard Kennedy: *ibid.*, 18/11/1808. [RJS, Board] *op. cit.*, 18/11/1808. Well. MS4305.
    to be abolished: *ibid.*, 1/12 and 15/12/1808.
    'when he comes to Town'.: *ibid.*, 16/3/1809.
    elected Mayor: William Davies, Diary 1792–1805, 18/10/1799, Well. MS2052.
    'families, or individuals, ...': p. 19.
    'Tell Henry I recd . . . .': Black and Black, *op. cit.*, MS5226(9). Dated 26 July; '1809'
        added by William Davies junior. The same letter refers to a letter from the Earl of
        Berkeley published by the *Medical and Physical Journal* in August 1801, however.
    Bristol Vaccine Institution: GCRO 421 X10/152.
205 'In compliance with Mrs. Jenner's . . . .': Murray and RJS, *op. cit.*, MS5244(8). Letter is
        unsigned, but written on the back in a different hand is the date and 'Case Dr. Jenner's
        neph.'
206 estate at Halmore: T. D. Fosbroke, *Abstracts of Records and Manuscripts Respecting the
        County of Gloucester*, Vol. I, Jos Harris, 1807, pp. 462–3.
    to James Phipps,: J. E. Gethyn-Jones, 'New light shed on home of vaccination "guinea-
        pig" ', [Gloucester] *Gazette*, 6/4/1984.
    two agreements: Well. Papers held by Curator of Western MSS.
    Charlotte Jenner,: Berkeley Parish Register, Burials, GCRO PFC 42 1/15–1/39, Gloucester
        Diocesan Records, 4/1/195, B3/46. Her death was brought to my attention by Canon J.
        E. Gethyn-Jones of Berkeley.
    'Pray have some conversation . . . .': Davies, *op. cit.*, Well. MS5230(13).
207 'his general appearance . . . .': Baron, *op. cit.*, Vol. I (1827), p. 92.
    'Henry Jenner, who . . . .': Baron, *op. cit.*, II, p. 420.
    'Poor Edward is again . . . .': Jenner, *op. cit.*, Well. MS5240(11).
    evening of 23 November.: John Dawes Worgan, *Select Poems. . . .*, London: Longman,
        Hurst, Rees & Orme, 1810, p. 87.
    'I write to tell you . . . .': Jenner, *op. cit.*, Well. MS5240(12).
    Dr Thomas Charles Morgan: *ibid.*, Well. MS5240(14).
    'Morgan is just . . . .': *ibid.*, Well. MS5240(10). Note the initials, 'J. C. M'. A
        blasphemous joke? He became Sir Thomas Charles Morgan.
208 An Expostulatory Letter: London: J. Murray, 1808. Miller, *op. cit.*, p. 47.
    A Review of the Report: London: Longman, Hurst, Rees & Orme, 1808.
    'next Edition'.: Miller, *op. cit.*, pp. 64–5.
    'Alas! poor Ring! . . .': *ibid.*, p. 47.
    The Vaccine Scourge London: J Murray., 1808. It was reprinted in 1815.
    'These things injure . . . .': Jenner, *op. cit.*, Well. MS5240(13).
    'I should be unworthy . . . .': Baron, *op. cit.*, II, p. 119.
    'The affairs of the National . . . .': Jenner, *op. cit.*, Well. MS5240(15).
209 'there is reason to fear . . .': Baron, *op. cit.*, II, p. 119.
    February 1809: Vol. 21, pp. 170–1.
    'This blow will fall . . . .': Jenner, *op. cit.*, Well. MS5240(16).
210 'but such have been . . .': Miller, *op. cit.*, p. 49.
    on successive days.: Jenner, *op. cit.*, Well. MS5240(15).
    'Baker, <u>cute</u> as he is, ...': *ibid.*, Well. MS5240(17).
    'In my own family . . .': *ibid.*, Well. MS5240(16,18).
    'My Boys are better − ': Miller *op. cit.*, pp. 50–1.

Edward Jenner 1749–1823

Page

210 'my conduct being reported . . . .': Jenner, *op. cit.*, Well. MS5240(18).
'I am to be torn . . . .': *ibid* Well. MS5240(19).
'I am glad you have resigned, . . .': Baron, *op. cit.*, II, p. 130.
211 'I hope my Friends . . . .': Miller, *op. cit.*, p. 52.
'but things have taken . . . .': [4 letters to T. J. Estcourt MP, 13/3/1805–25/3/1809], GCRO D1571 F222.
'you know how this business . . . .': Miller, *op. cit.*, pp. 54–5.
'his communication . . .': Baron, *op. cit.*, II, p. 125.
'consulted Dr. Jenner'.: Moore, *op. cit.*, p. 223.
to the Army and Navy: Derrick Baxby, *Jenner's Smallpox Vaccine: The Riddle of Vaccinia Virus and its Origin*, London: Heinemann Educational, 1981, p. 179.
212 expanded to nine,: Murray and NVE, *op. cit.*, Well. MS5245(34a).
733 vaccinations: Charles Maclean, *On the State of Vaccination in 1810. . . .*, London: various publishers, 1810, pp. 36–8.

Chapter 10: Deaths 1809–1815

213 'a large number of foxhounds . . .': Edward Jenner, 'Observations on the Distemper in Dogs', *Medico-Chirurgical Transactions*, London: Medical and Chirurgical Society, 3rd edn, Vol. I, 1815, p. 265.
his results differed: John Baron, *The Life of Edward Jenner, M. D. . . .* Vol. I, London: Henry Colburn, 1827, p. 450. *Med. Phys. Jour.*, 6 (7/1801), p. 95. Dr De Carro, 'Observations on the Vaccine Inoculation. . . .', *Med. Phys. Jour.*, 8 (9/1802), pp. 193–4. In the same article De Carro reported French tests with vaccine to combat sheep rot.
'It has been promised . . .': Edward Jenner, Letters. 1794–1822, London, Well. MS5236(39).
'a truly valuable paper, ...': review, 'Medico-Chirurgical Transactions . . . Vol. I.', *Med. Phys. Jour.*, 22 (9/1909), p. 240.
'Two Cases of Small-Pox . . .': *Medico-Chirurgical Transactions*, 3rd edn, Vol. I, 1815, pp. 270–7.
214 'My principal object . . .': *ibid.*, p. 277.
'One perfect Vaccine Vesicle . . .': *Medical Observer*, Vol. V, [1809], p. 280.
In January 1810: L. Crummer (ed.), 'Copy of Jenner Note Book', *Ann. Med. Hist.*, N. S. I (1929), p. 426.
'Dr. Jenner told me . . . .': Francis Hands, *Palman qui Mercuit ferat* (Essay on Vaccination, 1867, MS entered in competition for best essay on vaccination), Well. MS2766, p. 8.
'Whenever there is a shadow . . .': Baron, *op. cit.*, Vol. II (1838), pp. 169–70.
'The complaint against . . . .': *ibid.*, p. 373.
215 'Numerous instances of . . . .': 'An Account of Diseases in an Eastern District of London from October 20, to November 20, 1809', *Med. Phys. Jour.*, 22 (12/1809), pp. 524–5.
'Poor Worgan has . . . .': Edward Jenner, [Pruen papers], Well. MS5240(20).
Sonnets, William Davies, 1809 (copies, by various poets), Well. MS2069, 'By John Dawes Worgan', [p. 1].
216 'Worgan's little Poem',: Jenner, *op. cit.*, Well. MS5240(13).
Davies listed those present: William Davies, Diary 1805–17, 18/5/1809, Well. MS2053.
'Poor Worgan left me . . . .': Jenner, *op. cit.*, Well. MS5240(23).
'When the mind ripens . . . .': *ibid.* Well. MS5240(24).
Worgan died: Baron, *op. cit.*, II, p. 76. Davies, *op. cit.*, Well. MS2053.
'I fear it is all over . . . .': Jenner, *op. cit.*, Well. MS5240(25).
217 'As I shall stay . . . .': Edward Jenner to Thomas Pruen, Berkeley, 2/9/1809, Jenner Museum.
'Went to Gloucester . . . .': Crummer *op. cit.*, pp. 412(37).
'There was certainly an honor . . . .': Jenner, *op. cit.*, Well. MS5240(26).
'He smokes three or four . . . .': Crummer, *op. cit.*, pp. 412(37).
'very handsome hookah'.: Baron, *op. cit.*, II, p. 143.
George Jenner administered: Davies, *op. cit.*, Well. MS2053.

[322]

Page
218 'about an inch . . . .': Baron, *op. cit.*, II, p. 405. T. D. Fosbroke, *Berkeley Manuscripts*, London: John Nichols & Son, 1821, p. 225, gives the date as 1792.
From June through November 1812,: Edward Jenner, Letters . . . to Mrs Meade of Chatley Lodge, near Bath. . . ., 6–11/1812, Well. MS5238(1–6).
'of which I have the honour . . . .': Baron, *op. cit.*, II, pp. 407–9.
'was more disposed to consider . . . .': John Davy, *Memoirs of the Life of Sir Humphry Davy.* . . ., London: Smith, Elder & Co., 1839, Vol. 1, pp. 446–7.
219 'You have heard me say . . . .': Charles Murray and the National Vaccine Establishment, Correspondence and papers. . . . 1809–29. . . ., Well. MS5245(1).
A Plain Statement of Facts,: Halifax: Holden and Dowson, 1809.
'all who read it . . . .': *Letters of Edward Jenner and Other Documents concerning the Early History of Vaccination*, ed. Genevieve Miller, Baltimore and London: Johns Hopkins University Press, 1983, p. 63.
'with my next Parcel . . .': *ibid.*, p. 62.
'Tilloch's Journals . . .': *ibid.*, p. 76 and footnote. The *Medical and Physical Journal* became the *London Medical and Physical Journal* from 11/1810.
Wood of Covent Garden: C D. Hellman (ed.), 'An Unpublished Diary of Edward Jenner' (henceforward: Hellman Diary), *Ann. Med. Hist.*, N. S. III (1931), p. 416.
220 'Do you recollect my exhibiting . . . .': Miller, *op. cit.*, p. 62.
'It is possible that the surface . . . .': Crummer, *op. cit.*, p. 423.
'Rec'd the books . . . .': *ibid.*, p. 420.
acquired a small property,: Jenner, *op. cit.*, Well. MS5240(29).
'My poor dear Edward . . . .': *ibid.*, Well. MS5240(28).
221 Edward junior died.: Davies, *op. cit.*, Well. MS2053.
taller than his father.: Baron, *op. cit.*, II, p. 55.
'labouring under such . . .': Murray and NVE, *op. cit.*, Well. MS5245(2).
'& desire him to exchange . . .': *ibid.*, Well. MS5245(3).
'had no conception . . . .': Baron, *op. cit.*, II, p. 141.
'for your kind soothing letter . . . .': Jenner, *op. cit.*, Well. MS5240(31).
'I am now reduced . . . .': Baron, *op. cit.*, II, p. 368.
'& many other Complaints . . .': William Davies, Household accounts, Vol. III, 6/3/1810, Well. MS2050.
'I will with great pleasure . . . .': Jenner, *op. cit.*, Well. MS5240(32).
222 instructed Messrs Ladbroke: *ibid.*, Well. MS5240(33).
'I have seen Walker . . . .': Jenner, *op. cit.*, Well. MS5236(7).
'Whether the Cow-pox be . . . .': Vol. V (5/1809), p. 311.
James Freeman,: Vol. VI (7/1809), pp. 86–90.
'Between 3 and 4000 persons . . . .': Miller, *op. cit.*, p. 58.
The family had been under: John Birch, *Report of the True State of the Cow Pox Experiment, At the Close of the Year 1809.* . . ., London: Smeaton, [1810]. Thomas Brown, *A Correspondence with the Board of the National Vaccine Establishment*, London: S. Highley, 1810, pp. 70–1.
'good Vaccine Letters': Jenner, *op. cit.*, Well. MS5240(33).
223 'It wd have been a much better . . . .': *ibid.*, Well. MS5240(34).
'There is another *Med: Observer* . . . .': Edward Jenner to John Baron, Letters, RCS. The letter is undated but the watermark, 1811, seems to fix its relationship to the final *Medical Observer* issue.
'Who'd peruse their dull books . . . .': quoted in [John Ring], *The Vaccine Scourge: Part II.* . . ., London: J. Callow, 1815, p. 99.
'ordered to give security . . . .': *Medical Observer*, Vol. V (2/1809), pp. 46–8.
224 'that state of dejection . . .': Baron *op. cit.*, II, p. 144.
'to place every man . . . .': *ibid.*, pp. 369–70.
'about a month, ...': Jenner, *op. cit.*, Well. MS5240(33,34).
'her apartments up stairs'.: *ibid.*, Well. MS5240(36).
did not like Ferryman's plans: *ibid.*, Well. MS5240(35).
if he needed still more space: *ibid.*, Well. MS5240(36).
'I shall certainly accept . . . .': Miller, *op. cit.*, p. 68.

Edward Jenner 1749–1823

Page

225 'The constant disposition . . . .': Baron, *op. cit.*, II, p. 145.
Jenner went on his own,: Davies, *op. cit.*, Well. MS2053. June 4: tea with his uncle.
'My sentence is as follows . . . .': Jenner, *op. cit.*, Well. MS5240(37).

226 returned by 2 July.: Davies, *op. cit.*, Well. MS2053.
The Earl of Berkeley: William Davies, Correspondence and papers, 1716–1847 and n.d.
. . ., Well. MS5230(122).
'Lord Berkeley has . . .': Jenner, *op. cit.*, Well. MS5240(38).
post mortem: Edward Jenner, Papers 1790–1822, Well. MS5235(10).
arranged for Pruen: Jenner, *op. cit.*, Well. MS5240(39).
23 July,: Davies, *op. cit.*, Well. MS2053.

227 Mrs Larner.: Jenner, *op. cit.*, Well. MS5240(34).
'The increased mortality . . . .': Edward Jenner, Letters to . . . from various correspondents, 1805–1820, Well. MS5233(2).
thirty per week.: National Vaccine Establishment, 'Letter . . . to the Governors of the
Finsbury Dispensary. . . .', [25/10/1810], *Med. Phys. Jour.*, 25 [5/1811], p. 459.
five or six a week,: Baron, *op. cit.*, II, p. 163.
'1809 1453 65': 'An Account . . . extracted by Geo Limming . . . dated Febry ye 18th
1813', Murray and NVE, *op. cit.*, Well. MS5245(51).
Robert Watt, *Treatise on the History, Nature, and Treatment of Chincough [Whooping
Cough]*. . . ., Glasgow: John Smith & Son, 1813, p. 375.
'Cheltenham is still full . . . .': Revd George Charles and Mary Black, Correspondence and
papers . . ., 1750–1810, Well. MS5226(10).

228 'Notwithstanding Lord Berkeley's . . . .': Davies, *op. cit.*, Well. MS5230(4).
24 to 26 October.: Davies, *op. cit.*, Well. MS2053.
'out with him' – : Davies, *op. cit.*, 10/10/1811, Well. MS5230(7).
'She has not been . . .': Black and Black, *op. cit.*, Well. MS5226(11).
'An Express from . . .': Davies, *op. cit.*, Well. MS2050. Crummer, *op. cit.*, p. 415.
for her funeral.: Davies, *op. cit.*, Well 2053.

229 The NVE should send: Baron, *op. cit.*, II, pp. 371–2.
a letter from Professor Thompson: Crummer, *op. cit.*, p. 140.
suffered a miscarriage,: Davies, *op. cit.*, Well. MS2050.
godfather to Edward Jenner Murray,: Miller, *op. cit.*, p. 70 and footnote p. 71.
Masonic office: Davies, *op. cit.*, 17/12/1810, Well. MS2053.
detailed accounts: Well. MS2068.
'a peculiar horror . . .': Baron, *op. cit.*, II, pp. 293–4.

230 'I am almost tempted to say, . . .': Miller, *op. cit.*, p. 72.
'In an enquiry of such . . . .': *ibid.*, pp. 72–3.
'Dear William . . . .': Davies, *op. cit.*, Well. MS5230(6).

231 'unwilling to set a price . . . .': Jenner, *op. cit.*, 29/1/1809 Well. MS5240(16).
'My Orchard & Garden . . . .': *ibid.*, Well. MS5240(8)
'I shall not let you . . . .': Miller, *op. cit.*, p. 66.
His daughter and Robert: Edward Jenner to Miss Calcraft, 17/6/1811, RCP:ALS. Edward
Jenner to Mrs. Worthington, Upton, Worcs., 10/7/1811, RCP:ALS.
'For many weeks before . . . .': Baron, *op. cit.*, II, p. 162. The 'meeting' was actually an
annual festival of the Royal Jennerian Society, but Baron and apparently Jenner saw his
reactions there as being the same as his behaviour before the Lords.

232 a diagnosis with which: For those who want names to identify disorders, Jenner may have
been suffering from myalgic encephalomyelitis (ME). His signs already included
tinnitus and dyspepsia. Noise sensitivity afflicted him from childhood and became
much worse after what may have been a minor stroke in 1820 (see p.   ). Against the
diagnosis of ME, however, is the absence of muscle pain. Cf. E. J. Field, 'Darwin's
illness', *The Lancet*, 336 (29/9/90), p. 826.
'more rapidly than usual',: National Vaccine Establishment, Report [18/7/1811], pp. 4–5.
to several correspondents.: Edward Jenner to T. G. Estcourt, 24/6/1811. GCRO D1571
F363. Edward Jenner to Mrs Worthington, Upton, Worcs, 10/7/1811, RCP:ALS.
'take a wide, comprehensive . . . .': Jenner to Calcraft, *op. cit.*, 19/6/1811, RCP:ALS.

233 'The great business . . . .': Baron, *op. cit.*, II, p. 147.

Page
233 'The Sol[icito]r General paid . . . .': Jenner, *op. cit.*, Well. MS5240(40).
then until October: Davies, *op. cit.*, Well. MS2053.
Charles Brandon Trye: Baron, *op. cit.*, II, p. 151 footnote.
on Fletcher's behalf.: Davies, *op. cit.*, Well. MS5230(7).
'do what I can . . . .': Jenner to Baron, *op. cit.*, no. 15, RCS.
101 votes to 95: Davies, *op. cit.*, 14/11/1811, Well. MS2053.
'an anxious . . . residence . . .': Baron, *op. cit.*, II, p. 181.
'was again seized . . .': Jenner, *op. cit.*, Well. MS5240(42).
234 'I have no longer a relish . . . .': *ibid.*, Well. MS5240(47).
'Cheltenham does look . . . .': Well. Papers held by Curator of Western MSS (photocopies).
late August 1813.: Davies, *op. cit.*, Well. MS2053.
'I rejoice at seeing . . . .': Baron, *op. cit.*, II, pp. 376-7.
relations with the NVE: *ibid.*, p. 182.
'The New Institution . . . .': Hellman Diary, p. 421 (88).
Twice during February: Davies, *op. cit.*, 11/2/1812, 18/2/1812, Well. MS2050.
235 Barrow Hill Club.: D. Fisk, *Dr Jenner of Berkeley*, London, Melbourne, Toronto: Heinemann, 1959, p. 253.
'other purposes.': Miller, *op. cit.*, p. 75.
Robert Stevens,: cited in Baron, *op. cit.*, II, p. 270.
dried vaccine for Dr Sacco,: Miller, *op. cit.*, p. 76.
'few specimens of the Gibralter Rock',: Davies, *op. cit.*, Well. MS5230(11).
On 26 June: Davies, *op. cit.*, Well. MS2050.
chip off the old block.: Baron, *op. cit.*, II, p. 55.
'Your old Pupil Bob . . .': Jenner to Joyce in Edward Jenner, 'Nineteen autograph letters to Alexander Marcet. . . .', 30/6/1806, RSM. (Henceforth: 'Edward Jenner to Alexander Marcet'.)
a draft drawn by his father: [Edward Jenner], Robert Fitzhardinge Jenner. . . ., Letters from his father. . . ., 14/2/1809, Well. MS5243(1).
'all the sights from the Hut . . . .': Jenner to Worthington, *op. cit.*, 10/7/1811, RCP:ALS.
236 'To B. J. . . . .': Hellman Diary, p. 431 (159-60).
'The discharge fm. the Urethra, . . .' . . . 'his late illness.': *ibid.*, pp. 415, 423 (104).
Mrs Colchester: *ibid.*, p. 416 (34, 39, 41).
'My dearest Friend': Davies, *op. cit.*, Well. MS2050.
237 'by nature I was never framed': Jenner, *op. cit.*, 13/10/1812, Well. MS5240(47).
'Two persons dead of Smallpox . . . .': Jenner to Baron, *op. cit.*, 10/11/1811, RCS.
'not a Norwich Man . . .': Murray and NVE, *op. cit.*, Well. MS5245(47).
'This langour, of which you . . . .': Edward Jenner to Charles Murray, *op. cit.*, Well. Curator of Western MSS.
'has been the constant resident . . . .': Jenner, *op. cit.*, Well. MS5240(48).
'I don't know that there . . . .': Edward Jenner to Caleb Hillier Parry, 24/2/1813, Jenner Museum.
238 'it has long been my creed . . . .': Baron, *op. cit.*, I, p. 93.
'you know it is a doctrine . . . .': Miller, *op. cit.*, p. 96.
'For some months I have been . . . .': Murray and NVE, *op. cit.*, Well. MS5245(4).
'We talk of Chronic inflammation . . . .': Miller, *op. cit.*, pp. 78-9.
239 Mr Mountjoy,: Hellman Diary, pp. 423 (98), (102).
'Inquiries into the origin . . .': 'Edward Jenner to Alexander Marcet', *op. cit.*, 25/7/1813, RSM.
'What part of the animal Machine . . . .': Hellman Diary, pp. 427-8.
'diseases of the skin . . . .': [Jenner to Estcourt], 11/10/1812, GCRO D1571 F141.
240 December 1812: *ibid.*, pp. 427-30.
'These Prescriptions . . .': Well. MS3027. The handwriting may have been Mrs Pruen's (it was not her husband's) excepting for two pages at the end in Jenner's hand and headed 'I shall add a few hints of my own which I can recommend from experience.' This is puzzling. It seems to contradict the flysheet inscription which must refer to the text because the pamphlet contains very few recipes as such. I can only suppose that Jenner

had recommended the material to her from some source, and possibly recommended changes that she incorporated from his dictation.

240 'Although medical & surgical . . . .': *ibid.*, pp. 1–1a. Obvious mistakes have crept into Mrs Pruen's copying of the first sentence, not mine.

241 'Head − Blows in': *ibid.*, p. 11.
On worms: *ibid.*, pp. 25–7.
'Rub the upper gum . . . .': *ibid.*, pp. 47–8.
'Wind − N. E. Stormy −': Hellman Diary, p. 420(76).
'Wind S. W.': Crummer, *op. cit.*, p. 426.

242 'Frosty morning': *ibid.*, p. 414.
letters were due: Hellman Diary, p. 416(33).
'that my honest friend . . . .': Jenner to Baron, *op. cit.*, RCS.
he wrote to only two: Hellman Diary, p. 426(118).
'Dear William': Davies, *op. cit.*, Well. MS5230(27).

243 'Cole ought to consider . . . .': *ibid.*, 2/1/1813, Well. MS5230(13).
annual contributions and subscriptions: Crummer, *op. cit.*, p. 415.
linseed oil mill: *Glocester Journal*, 16/7/1779, p. 1. Davies, *op. cit.*, 27/12/1799, Well. MS2052.
pin manufactory: Davies, *ibid.*, 5/3/1800, Well. MS2052.
'I know not what to do . . . .': Murray and NVE, *op. cit.*, 11–13/2/1813, Well. MS5245(14).

244 'He has sent out . . . .': Jenner to Baron, *op. cit.*, 1/3/1813, RCS.
21 April 1788,: [William Davies, Tithes, taxes & dispursements, 1776–1814], Well. MS2051.
his own canal shares: William Davies, Household accounts, Vol. II, 1780–98, facing p. 129, Well. MS2049.
by selling two hundred shares: John Westoby, 'Sources of the investment capital of the Stroudwater canal', in 'Some aspects of the historical geography of Gloucestershire and Gloucester in the Eighteenth-century, . . .', second-year students of the geography department, University of Liverpool, 1975, pp. 16–17, GCRO CMS88.
'Dr Jenners Turn . . .': Davies, *op. cit.*, Well. MS2050.
Commissioner for Turnpikes,: William Davies, Diary 1817–20, 20/7/1817, 26/8/1818, 16/1/1819, 27/1/1819, Well. MS2054.
'to the inconsiderate manner . . .': Murray and NVE, *op. cit.*, Well. MS5245(9).
'it should be styled . . .': *ibid.*, 11/12/1812, Well. MS5245(12).
the draft provided: [House of Commons], An Act for preventing the spread of the Small Pox, Well. . . . MS3025.
'Few country practitioners . . . .': Murray and NVE, *op. cit.*, 2/1813, Well. MS5245(16).

245 'as it would associate . . . .': *ibid.*, Well. MS5245(14), Jenner to Murray, 11–13/2/1813.
'yard of red Tape . . .': *ibid.*, Well. MS5245(15–16).
'how strange it is that . . . .': *ibid.*, Well. MS5245(14).
'Mr G. Rose says . . . .': Jenner to Baron, *op. cit.*, no. 17, RCS.
'tame and insipid . . .': Baron, *op. cit.*, II, p. 389.
The bill was withdrawn.: Murray and NVE, *op. cit.*, Well. MS5245(23,24). Fisk, *op. cit.*, p. 257.

246 to grant licences for vaccinators.: John Walker, 'On the rejected Vaccination Bill. . . .', *London Med. Phys. Jour.*, 34 (8/1815), pp. 113–14.
'for causing and permitting . . .': Murray and NVE, *op. cit.*, 27/1/1816, Well. MS5245(55).
'King *v* Taunton', *London Med. Phys. Jour.*, 35 (1/1816), pp. 68–9.
Jenner was so pleased: Jenner, *op. cit.*, 15/6/1813, Well. MS5240(50).
and to two of his patients: Letter to Revd G. Hulme, 7/6/1813, in Jenner to Baron, *op. cit.*, no. 19, RCS. Edward Jenner to Miss Calcraft (n.d., after 7/4/1813), RCP:ALS.
twenty-seven, in 1814.: 'Report of the Hospitals for Small Pox Inoculation and Vaccination', *London Med. Phys. Jour.*, 33 (3/1815), p. 250.
Smallpox had disappeared: 'Report of the National Vaccine Establishment, for the Year 1815. . . .', *London Med. Phys. Jour.*, 36 (8/1816), pp. 167–9.

247 By the midsummer of 1813: Baron, *op. cit.*, II, p. 386. 'Edward Jenner to Alexander Marcet', 25/7/1813, RSM.

Page
247 'summoning the Governors . . .': J. J. Abraham, *Lettsom: His Life, Times, Friends and Descendants*, London: William Heinemann Medical, 1933, p. 348. J. Epps, *The Life of John Walker, M. D.*, London: Whittaker, Treacher & Co., 1831, pp. 98–9.
in cooperating with Walker: Baron, *op. cit.*, II, p. 389.
annual festival dinners: Abraham, *op. cit.*, p. 348.
'In about a month we think . . . .': Jenner, *op. cit.*, Well. MS5240(50).
'a great dearth of mind in': Miller, *op. cit.*, p. 25.
Baron, *op. cit.*, II, pp. 217–18.
Charles Henry Parry to his family, 10/1814, from copies held by Dr Hugh Torrens.
248 'I am unwilling to complain . . . .': [Edward Jenner], various correspondents, 1795–1822, Well. MS5232(18).
'the business is conducted . . .': Jenner to Revd. J. Joyce, 14/6/1814, in 'Edward Jenner to Alexander Marcet', *op. cit.*, RSM.
'I have some reason to think . . . .': Baron, *op. cit.*, II, p. 391.
'Letter from Sir C. Pegge . . . .': Crummer, *op. cit.*, p. 411.
'Pray inquire of Dr. Hervey . . .': Baron, *op. cit.*, II, p. 393.
'reluctantly put on . . .': *ibid.*, p. 190.
Pegge gave a dinner: Crummer, *op. cit.*, p. 411.
'I went . . . to receive . . . .': Miller, *op. cit.*, p. 83.
249 'remove all objections . . .': Baron, *op. cit.*, II, p. 191.
'In my youth I went through . . . .': *ibid.*, p. 192.
'My relation Mr Milman . . .': Jenner, *op. cit.*, Well. MS5235(2).
Normal prisoner exchange: H. D. Harvey, *Britain in the Early Nineteenth Century*, London: Batsford, 1978, p. 305.
John Philip Kemble,: Miller, *op. cit.*, pp. 75, 76 footnote.
applied to the French Ambassador: Baron, *op. cit.*, I, pp. 601–3.
liberation of two civilians,: Jenner to Ferryman, *op. cit.*, 17/2/1805, RCP:ALS. Baron, *op. cit.*, II, p. 36.
According to legend,: Baron, *op. cit.*, II, p. 38. D. R. Hopkins, *Princes and Peasants: Smallpox in History*, Chicago and London: University of Chicago Press, 1983, p. 82.
'Judge Powell's son'.: N. 'Anecdote of Dr. Jenner', *Gentleman's Magazine*, 5/1822, p. 396.
Messrs Gold and Garland: Crummer, *op. cit.*, p. 426.
Captain E. Husson,: Revd George Charles Jenner, Correspondence and papers . . . 1794–1820, 26/11/1810, Well. MS5228(14).
250 asking Jenner to arrange: Edward Jenner, *op. cit.*, Well. MS5232(17).
'in the space of nine years . . . .': Miller, *op. cit.*, p. 75.
'Our government has treated . . .': Edward Jenner, *op. cit.*, Well. MS5240(44).
Richard Dobson,: Miller, *op. cit.*, p. 80.
'as soon as Cpt. Milman . . .': *ibid.*, p. 82.
the only military prisoner: Edward Jenner to Edward Davies, 15/2/1814, Well. Curator of Western MSS.
Husson agreed as a means: Revd G. C. Jenner, *op. cit.*, MS5228(13).
'much better',: Edward Jenner, [Letters], Duke University Medical School Library, 16/4/1814.
'held myself in readiness . . . .': Baron, *op. cit.*, II, p. 206.
'sent by the Emperor . . .': C. H. Parry, [letters to his family], MS Eng. Misc d612, Cheltenham Literary Philosophical, photocopies held by Prof. Hugh Torrens.
251 met Jenner.: Crummer, *op. cit.*, p. 412.
'at Dr. Jenner's table': C. H. Parry, *op. cit.*, Torrens.
'shrank from such a project',: Baron, *op. cit.*, II, p. 209.
'the Prince has at last . . . .': Edward Jenner, *op. cit.*, 15/6/1813, Well. MS5240(50).
'My visit to the Metropolis . . . .': *ibid.*, Well. MS5240(52).
'mighty Potentates': Edward Jenner to Revd J. Joyce, 14/6/1814, in 'Edward Jenner to Alexander Marcet', *op. cit.*, RSM.
'been closeted for more than an hour . . .': Edward Jenner, *op. cit.*, Well. MS5240(52).
'I have not seen any . . . .': Jenner to Joyce, 14/6/1814, in 'Edward Jenner to Alexander Marcet', *op. cit.*, RSM.

Page
251 'I have been to the Oldenburgh . . . .': Miller, *op. cit.*, p. 86.
Prussian Crown Prince, General Blücher: Fosbroke, *op. cit.*, pp. 237–40.
252 could not leave a meeting: 'Edward Jenner to Alexander Marcet', *op. cit.*, RSM.
'certainly bring my Fragments . . . .': *ibid.*, 1/6 and 3/6/1814.
drove out to Enfield: Miller, *op. cit.*, p. 87.
several friends to breakfast: *ibid.*, p. 88.
'be attack'd in their entrenched . . .': Edward Jenner, *op. cit.*, Well. MS5240(53).
'but for the distresses . . . .': Baron, *op. cit.*, II, pp. 210–11.
Jenner caught cholera,: Edward Jenner, Well. MS5240(53,54). Baron, *op. cit.*, II, p. 212.
called on him twice.: Davies, *op. cit.*, 7/11–8/11/1814, Well. MS2053. Davies, *op. cit.*, 29/10, 8/11/1814, Well. MS2050.
'Mrs J. left her chamber . . . .': Edward Jenner, *op. cit.*, Well. MS5240(55).
'I am still weak, . . .': *ibid.*,Well. MS5240(56).
253 'elegant Bouquets you used to send'. . . . 'vague & unintelligible.': Davies, *op. cit.*, Well. MS5230(15).
'a vast influx of Letters . . . .': Miller, *op. cit.*, p. 89.
'I . . . went to his House . . . .': Hands, *op. cit.*, p. 1.
Robert had gone there: Davies, *op. cit.*, 11/4/1815,Well. MS5230(15).
'has acquired a tolerably good . . . .': Edward Jenner, *op. cit.*, 2/8/1815, Well. MS5240(57).
'it must be a great comfort . . . .': [Edward Jenner, letter to Henry N. Trye], in [C. B. Trye, Documents concerning and by. . . .], 27/8/1815, GCRO D303 C6.
254 On the 18th: Davies, *op. cit.*, Well. MS2054.
his old friend Fewster: Edward Jenner, Letters. . . ., 1794–1822, 25/7/1815, Well. MS5236(12).
'has been down stairs . . . .': Edward Jenner, *op. cit.*, 2/8/1815, Well. MS5240(57).
'Darby should be much . . . .': Edward Jenner, letter to H. N. Trye, *op. cit.*, 27/8/1815, GCRO D303 C6.
the Gloucester-Berkeley Canal: Hugh Conway-Jones, *Gloucester Docks*, Gloucester: Alan Sutton & Gloucester County Library, 1988.
'Poor Mrs Jenner who has been much better . . . .': Edward Jenner, *op. cit.*, Well. MS5240(58).
Baron came to Cheltenham: Baron, *op. cit.*, II, p. 220.

Chapter 11: In Sum 1815–1823

255 'to come here . . .': William Davies, Correspondence and papers, 1716–1847 and n.d. . . ., 14/9/1815, Well. MS5230(38).
'I know of no one . . . .': John Baron, *The Life of Edward Jenner, M. D.* . . ., Vol. II, London: Henry Colburn, 1838., p. 221.
buried at Berkeley: Berkeley Parish Register. GCRO PFC 42 1/15–1/39.
'never, except for a day or two, . . .': Baron, *op. cit.*, II, p. 221.
'My whole frame is thrown . . . .': Edward Jenner, [Pruen papers], Well. MS5240(59).
256 William and Sarah, to call: William Davies, Diary 1805–17, Well. MS2053.
Robert came home too: Jenner, *op. cit.*, 2/1/1816, Well. MS5240.
'Your intention is to visit . . . .': *idem.*
Burder, . . . Moore: *Letters of Edward Jenner and Other Documents concerning the Early History of Vaccination*, ed. Genevieve Miller, Baltimore and London: Johns Hopkins University Press, 1983, p. 90. Baron, *op. cit.*, II, p. 400.
brought his eldest son: Davies, *op. cit.*, Well. MS2053.
'Every puncture took effect . . . .': L. Crummer (ed.), 'Copy of Jenner Note Book', *Ann. Med. Hist.*, N. S. I (1929), p. 408.
257 'Saw Mr. Hawker's splendid . . . .': *idem.*
Parton, Aust and Westbury,: Joseph Stratford, *Good and Great Men of Gloucestershire*, Cirencester: C. H. Savory, [1867], p. 287. Baron, *op. cit.*, Vol. I (1827), p. 59.
'speak to the Quarry Men . . .': Davies, *op. cit.*, 8/1/1812, Well. MS5230(10).
'Basket of Fossils': Edward Jenner, Letters . . . to Mrs Meade of Chatley Lodge, near Bath . . . 16/11/1812, Well. MS5238(6).

Page
257 'Rockhampton specimens': [Jenner to Caleb Hillier Parry], Berkeley, 5/3/1813, Bristol
Public Library, SR4 pb Southey/22330. Again, I am grateful to Dr Hugh Torrens who
allowed me to use his copy of this letter.

'In Bath, I think you have . . . .': [Jenner to Caleb Hillier Parry], Berkeley, 24/3/1813,
Jenner Museum. For the benefit of geologists, the letter continued: 'I must not forget to
tell you that among those portions of the Rock which are decisively siliceous, I
sometimes find a small quantity of Chalk, just dusting them over. I have no specimens
of the Derbyshire Loadstone but from its description by Withering, the Woodford Rock
is composed of this Earth, which Cronstedt classes among the argillaceous.'

'Be assured Robert, ...': Miller, op. cit., pp. 88–9.

Buckland explored: Baron, op. cit., II, p. 289.

258 'I find – (stop – I fancy so),': Miller, op. cit., p. 96.

Jenner's carriage,: Davies, op. cit., Well. MS2053.

part of the poaching party,: Miller, op. cit., p. 93 and footnote.

'sons of respectable farmers'.: Baron, op. cit., II, p. 222.

'taken in Monmouthshire . . . .': ibid., p. 92.

'is taken & committed . . . .': ibid., p. 93.

259 transported for life.: Glocester Journal, 15/4/1816. Baron, op. cit., II, pp. 221–2.

'Several Paupers . . . .': Edward Jenner, Letters, 1794–1822, Well. MS5236(21).

'I found him one day . . . .': Baron, op. cit., II, p. 303.

Speenhamland is explained by many historians of the period, but none with greater brevity
and clarity than G. M. Trevelyan, English Social History, London: Reprint Society,
1948, pp. 473–4.

260 costing double that amount.: F. P. Thompson, The Making of the English Working Class,
New York: Pantheon, 1964, p. 592.

'inadequate to the purpose . . . .': Richard Worthington, A Treatise on the State of the Poor
in Sickness. . . .', Ludlow: H. Proctor, 1804, pp. 6, 21.

'People were so hungry . . . .': Thompson, op. cit., p. 592.

'refind Brutes of my own . . . .': Jenner, op. cit., Well. MS5240(47).

'B– is a place where . . . .': C. D. Hellman (ed.) 'An Unpublished Diary of Edward
Jenner', Ann. Med. Hist., N. S. III (1931) (henceforth: Hellman Diary), p. 427(128).

'that you are threatened . . . .': Jenner, op. cit., 10/7/1816, Well. MS5236(14).

a few days in Cheltenham.: Baron, op. cit., II, p. 188.

'going to Town for a fortnight . . . .': Jenner, op. cit., 27/4/1816, Well. MS5236(13).

13 and 27 May,: Davies, op. cit., Well. MS2053.

261 'the Wolfershans, . . .': Crummer, op. cit., p. 408.

'This country, from the Spring . . . .': Jenner, op. cit., 27/6/1816, Well. MS5240(61).

'epidemic Fever'.: Edward Jenner, Letters (mostly to John Baron), no. 1 RCS, undated,
but facts described fit Davies, op. cit., Well. MS2053.

'all hopes . . . gone among the Gas . . . .': Miller, op. cit., p. 94.

'it is your own fault . . . .': Baron, op. cit., II, p. 146.

262 Richard Walker, 'A brief Journal of the ordinary Progress of Natural Small-Pox. . . .',
London Med. Phys. Jour., 35 (6/1816), pp. 439–48, and 37 (7/1816), pp. 14–19. Robert
Kinglake, 'On Vaccine and Variolous Inoculation', London Med. Phys. Jour., 33
(4/1815), pp. 257–61.

'had better use the points . . . .': Miller, op. cit., pp. 95–6.

'almost alone here, . . .': Jenner, op. cit., 8/12/1816, Well. MS5240(62).

'and I am sure they . . . .': Edward Jenner, Papers 1790–1822, 18/1817, Well.
MS5235(20).

'but as things are sunk . . . .': [Edward Jenner], Robert Fitzhardinge Jenner. . . ., Letters
from his father. . . . Well. MS5243(2).

263 'informed me that he had made . . .': 4th edn, 1833, p. 27, quoted in Dr Hugh Torrens
(notes for a lecture): 'Edward Jenner and his circle: their contribution to natural
history'.

'Do beat up for him'.: Miller, op. cit., p. 97.

'The disrelish for anything . . . .': Jenner, op. cit., Well. MS5240(63).

'which we found in good order',: Davies, op. cit., 8/5/1817, Well. MS2054.

Page
263 'Hinton Workhouse': Crummer, *op. cit.*, p. 411.
264 On 16 May: Baron, *op. cit.*, II, p. 224.
'present constitution . . . is bad.': *ibid.*, pp. 223–4.
'He had neglected . . . .' . . . 'think I am shamming'.: *idem.*
29 May . . . . 10 June: Davies, *op. cit.*, Well. MS2054.
to Tan-House Farm: *ibid.*, 8/7/1817.
'a very fine specimen . . . .': Miller, *op. cit.*, p. 98.
'Bones found in the grave pits . . .': Crummer, *op. cit.*, p. 425.
'a fine impression . . .': *ibid.*, p. 408.
a 'long lost place': *ibid.*, p. 413.
'Dr. Jenner has observed . . . .': T. D. Fosbroke, *Berkeley Manuscripts*, London: John
    Nichols & Son, 1821, p. 3.
'opposite the West window . . . .': *ibid.*, p. 39.
265 'on the high road . . . .': *idem.*
from the Anglo-Saxon church: *ibid.*, p. 49.
noting on 1 August: Davies, *op. cit.*, Well. MS2054.
'I wish it were in my power . . . .': Jenner, *op. cit.*, 27/7/1817, Well. MS5240(64).
'in every respect better': Jenner to Baron, *op. cit.*, no. 26, RCS.
Baron came to see him: Davies, *op. cit.*, 6/8/1817, Well. MS2054.
'form a kind of room . . . .': Jenner, *op. cit.*, Well. MS5240(75). In 1989 a thick-trunked
    grape vine stood rooted just outside the wall of the glass house, into which it grew and
    spread out, bearing bunches of white grapes.
'In his house-keeping . . . .': Mr W.[illiam] D.[avies?], 'Anecdotes of the late Dr. Jenner',
    Gentleman's Magazine, 2 (1823), p. 104.
266 1051 over 653: Sir Gilbert Blane, *A Statement of Facts, Tending to Establish an Estimate of the
    True Value and Present State of Vaccination*, London: Thomas & George Underwood,
    1820, p. 18.
'modified' or 'mitigated' smallpox.: Robert Chawner, *et al.*, *Address to the Public, Relative
    to Some Supposed Failures of the Cow-Pox, at Repton. . . .* Burton-upon-Trent: Thos
    Wayte, 1821, p. 16. Richard Harrison, 'An Essay towards a Pathology of Eruptive
    Fevers', *London Med. Phys. Jour.*, 44 (7/1820), pp. 24–5.
'I was happy to find . . .': Jenner to Carter, 24/8/1817, Well. Curator of Western MSS.
'Camphor water . . . .': J. Farington, *The Farington Diary*, ed. J. Greig, Vol. I,
    1793–1802, London: Hutchinson, p. 165.
'An irregular & unnatural . . . .': Crummer, *op. cit.*, p. 413.
'Pure simple hysteria . . . .': *ibid.*, p. 421.
'What is the cause of the pain . . . .': *ibid.*, p. 422.
The increased frequency: Davies, *op. cit.*, Well. MS2054.
267 'I feel myself indebted to Murray . . .': Jenner, *op. cit.*, 14/10/1817, 19/12/1817, 12/1817 or
    1/1/1818, Well. MS5240(65,66,76).
Vizard's father.: [William Davies, Tithes, taxes & dispursements 1776–1814], 1778, Well.
    MS2051.
'Eastington excursion',: Jenner, *op. cit.*, Well. MS5240(66).
Mayor of Berkeley.: Jenner, *op. cit.*, 20/12/1817, Well. MS5235(7).
'My House has been full . . .': Jenner, *op. cit.*, Well. MS5240(76).
The year 1818 began: Miller, *op. cit.*, p. 99 and footnote. Baron, *op. cit.*, II, pp. 416, 430.
    Davies, *op. cit.*, Well. MS2054.
'And now about Corporal Strength . . . .': Miller, *op. cit.*, pp. 98–9.
'a dreadful hurricane': Crummer, *op. cit.*, p. 407.
Throughout April, May and June: Davies, *op. cit.*, Well. MS2054.
268 'Fig trees not to be pruned . . . .': Crummer, *op. cit.*, p. 418.
'the trees are chiefly . . . .': Fosbroke, *op. cit.*, p. 226.
'I am quite in love with . . . .': Miller, *op. cit.*, p. 83.
variety from grafts: Jenner to William Davies junior, [Carter letters], 16/4/1814, Well.
    Curator of Western MSS.
gooseberry 'trees'.: Jenner, *op. cit.*, 14/2/1810, Well. MS5240(31).
'should be put into the ground . . . .': Davies, *op. cit.*, 2/1/1813, Well. MS5230(13).

Page
268 'a few packets of good garden . . . .': Baron, *op. cit.*, II, p. 416.
'I can get nothing . . . .': *ibid.*, p. 419. 'Ragged jacks' were unknown at the Royal Botanical Gardens, Kew, in February 1990.
269 'Old John and I, . . .': *idem.*
On 3 August . . . . on 17 August: Davies, *op. cit.*, Well. MS2054.
'My dear Madam . . . .': Davies, *op. cit.*, 4/9/1812, Well. MS5230(12).
'Dear William I was sorry . . .': *ibid.*, 4/12/1818, Well. MS5230(18).
270 'If you can conveniently spare . . .': *ibid.*, 6/11/1818, Well. MS5230(17).
'preserv'd Gooseberry': [Carter letters], *op. cit.*, 14/8/1803, Well. Curator of Western MSS.
'you have an excellent mode . . . .': Jenner, *op. cit.*, 1/12/1809, Well. MS5240(28).
'to make us some Jelly & Jam. . . .': Revd George Charles and Mary Black, Correspondence and papers . . ., 1750–1810. 26/7/[1809], Well. MS5226(9).
'Rects for Parsnip Wine . . . .': Jenner, *op. cit.*, 1811, Well. MS5240(45).
'The average of every hundred . . . .': Crummer, *op. cit.*, p. 408.
'Wherever Vaccination . . . .': Edward Jenner, letter . . . to William Dilwyn. . . ., Philadelphia: Philadelphia Vaccine Society, 1818, dated: Berkeley, 19/8/1818.
271 'unusually fatal and malignant'.: Baron, *op. cit.*, II, p. 232.
'What shall I do?': Jenner, *op. cit.*, 24/9/1818, Well. MS5236(16).
'Letter addressed to the Medical Profession . . .': Vol. 45, pp. 277–80.
[National Vaccine Establishment], Draft Vaccine Report 1819. . . ., Well. MS3663, p. 2.
an epidemic in Norwich: Chawner *et al.*, *op. cit.*, pp. 20–1.
1824 and 1827, . . . 1837 and 1840.: D. R. Hopkins, *Princes and Peasants: Smallpox in History*, Chicago and London: University of Chicago Press, 1983, pp. 86–7.
272 'Tell Willy . . . .': Davies, *op. cit.*, 6/11/1818, Well. MS5230(17).
bilious fever.: Davies, *op. cit.*, 26/11/1818, Well. MS2054.
'Stephen Jenner . . . .': Davies, *op. cit.*, 11/4/1815, Well. MS5230(15).
'The money belonging . . . .': Crummer, *op. cit.*, p. 408.
'possessed talent for comic painting': quoted in Paul Saunders, *Edward Jenner: The Cheltenham Years, 1795–1823*, Hanover, Vt., and London: University Press of New England, p. 35.
'I fear the Drawing-job . . . .': Edward Jenner, Letters . . . to his nephew Edward Davies, (n.d.; watermark 1818), Well. MS5237(5).
'from home to a considerable distance': Jenner to Baron, *op. cit.*, no. 27, 30/1/1819, RCS.
visited Louisa Davies,: Davies, *op. cit.*, Well. MS2054.
273 prescribed blisters.: *ibid.*, 3/3/1819.
'Never be without a Small Blister . . . .': Davies, *op. cit.*, (n.d.), Well. MS5230(28).
'size of a Crown Piece',: Jenner to Elizabeth Hodges, [Carter letters], 19/10/1811, Well. Curator of Western MSS.
'Has not many a one . . . .': Crummer, *op. cit.*, p. 418.
a patient in Tetbury.: Davies, *op. cit.*, Well. MS2054.
'Dr. Jenner was kind . . .': Davies, *op. cit.*, 27/3/[1819], Well. MS5230(40).
Mary Jenner died.: *idem.*, obverse.
'The day was spent . . .': Davies, *op. cit.*, Well. MS2054.
'Our Giant's Cause way . . . .': [Edward Jenner to George Cumberland], Cumberland Papers Vol. XVII, Correspondence 1819–June 1820, 8/2/1819, BM Add. 36507, no. 38.
274 Plesiosaurus: Torrens, *op. cit.*
'a little of that Lettuce Seed . . . .': Jenner to Baron, *op. cit.*, no. 29, RCS.
made the journey,: Davies, *op. cit.*, Well. MS2054, records no meetings from 28/6 to 12/7.
275 Mrs Mary Dyer: Miller, *op. cit.*, p. 101.
'in consequence of having taken Arsenic.': Davies, *op. cit.*, Well. MS2054.
'fill up by throwing . . . .': quoted in Baron, *op. cit.*, II, p. 422, but sadly minus the artwork.
'My hothouse . . . .': *ibid.*, p. 422.
'by meeting with bad gardening . . . .': Edward Jenner, Correspondence and papers . . . of Miss Eliza Cox. . . ., 18/3/1820, Well. MS5239(1).
Jenner and Davies. . . . had been a Mason.: Davies, *op. cit.*, 5/8/1816, 25/11/1816, Well. MS2053.

Page

275 'I fear you could do nothing . . . .': Jenner, *op. cit.*, 24/9/1818, Well. MS5236(16).

276 'I had heard accidentally . . . .': [Robert Fitzhardinge Jenner, letter to Henry N. Trye. . . .], 7/4/1819, GCRO D303 C6.

'Mr. Hicks was with me . . . .': Jenner to Baron, *op. cit.*, (letter to Robert Fitzhardinge Jenner), 22/6/1819, no. 29, RCS.

called twice to see Robert: Davies, *op. cit.*, 4/5/1819, 12/5/1819, Well. MS2054.

'He is unfortunately so attach'd . . .' Jenner, *op. cit.*, 27/12/1819, Well. MS5236(18).

277 'maintenance, education and advancement . . .': 'This is the last Will and Testament of me Robert Fitzhardinge Jenner. . . .', Dursley, 16/4/1853, Well. MS3030.

'What think you of the News . . . .': Jenner to Baron, *op. cit.*, 14/12/[1819; watermark 1818?], no. 5, RCS.

'I think it is possible . . . .': Jenner, *op. cit.*, 27/12/1819, Well. MS5236(18).

278 *A Letter . . . on the Influence of Artificial Eruptions*,: London: Baldwin Craddock & Joy, 1822.

'It is to be lamented . . . .': *ibid.*, p. 19 footnote.

'Do the rich support the poor . . . .': Crummer, *op. cit.*, pp. 403–4.

'I should like to be appointed . . .': Jenner, *op. cit.*, 3/11/1813, Well. MS5240(51).

'The intention of Sunday schools, . . .': Crummer, *op. cit.*, p. 416.

279 'The generation which has risen . . . .': *ibid.*, p. 409.

'a Typhoid Catarrh, . . .': [Carter papers], Jenner to Thomas Fosbroke, 13/3/1820, Well. Curator of Western Manuscripts. Neither Baron nor William Davies mentions this illness specifically, putting all the weight on the minor stroke in August. Yet although Davies saw Jenner with the usual frequency during January and February, there are no indications of Jenner's usual activities after 10 January. Davies, *op. cit.*, Well. MS2054. Davies, *op. cit.*, Well. MS5230(20).

William's youngest daughter,: William Davies, Diary 1820–1, Well. MS2055.

Catherine had returned: Jenner, *op. cit.*, 27/12/1819, Well. MS5236(18).

Caleb Carrington,. . . . given to him.: [Consistory Court, Diocese of Gloucester, Church-wardens of Parish of Berkeley v. Caleb Carrington], GCRO, GDR B3/1/197.

280 'What a curse to Society . . . .': Jenner, *op. cit.*, 27/6/1812, Well. MS5240(46).

'Our Vicar is literally turned . . . .': [Carter papers], Jenner to Pruen, 25/2/1813, Well. Curator of Western Manuscripts.

'I had not the least knowledge . . . .': [Edward Jenner, 4 letters to John H. Bromedge], 14/1/1815, GCRO.

'If the Bishop will do me the honor . . . .': Jenner to Baron, *op. cit.*, no. 37, RCS.

281 'Heard that Dr. Jenner . . . .': Davies, *op. cit.*, Well. MS2055.

Baron arrived: Baron, *op. cit.*, II, pp. 308–10.

'considerably better, and not much weaken'd . . .': Davies, *op. cit.*, Well. MS2055.

'I am getting better, . . .': Edward Jenner to Robert Ferryman, *op. cit.*, RCP: ALS.

refused an invitation: Jenner to Baron, *op. cit.*, 12/11/1820, no. 30, RCS.

'Writing is painful . . . .': Miller, *op. cit.*, p. 102.

'amended health': Jenner to Baron, *op. cit.*, RCP:ALS.

282 'a general vaccination . . . .': *ibid.*, 20/1/1820, RCP:ALS.

'About eleven hundred . . . .': Crummer, *op. cit.*, pp. 418–19.

'The Wotton Epidemic . . . .': Jenner to Edward Davies, *op. cit.*, [n.d., watermark 1820, probably after 2/3/1821), Well. MS5237(7).

Captain Jenner,: Davies, *op. cit.*, Well. MS2055.

'I rise in the morning . . . .': quoted in Baron, *op. cit.*, II, pp. 423–4.

'I find great advantage . . . .': Jenner to Baron, *op. cit.*, 27/2/1821, no. 31, RCS.

283 'Even Henry Jenner is about . . . .': *ibid.*, (n.d., watermark 1820), no. 3, RCS.

'stays so long at Bath . . . .': Jenner to Edward Davies, *op. cit.*, 2/3/1821, Well. MS5237(1).

'for making Dr. Jenner's will, . . .': Davies, *op. cit.*, Well. MS2055. The document is dated 6/3/1821.

'did not amount to 35-000': William Davies, Diary 1822-4, 20/2/1823, Well. MS2055.

[Edward Jenner], Probate of the Will and two Codicils. . . . Dated 15/3/1823, GCRO D3900/1. Copies are held by the Wellcome Institute Library.

284 'Dr Jenner on reference . . . .': Jenner, *op. cit.*, Well. MS5239(2).

Page
284 'For some time before his death . . . .': Baron, *op. cit.*, II, p. 271.
    Towards the end of March: Davies, *op. cit.*, 28/3/1821, Well. MS2055.
    Norwich Union Life Insurance: Crummer, *op. cit.*
285 'The streams of nature . . . .': Jenner to Baron, *op. cit.*, no. 32, RCS.
    'sharp sounds . . . produce an effect . . . .': *ibid.*, no. 33, RCS.
    'clicks still annoy me': Baron, *op. cit.*, II, p. 425.
    'gives my brain a kind of death blow. . . .': *ibid.*, pp. 427–8.
    wrote to Mrs Pruen: Miller, *op. cit.*, p. 104.
    July and early August.: Davies, *op. cit.*, Well. MS2056.
    to Dr Matthew Baillie,; Hunter-Baillie Letters, Vol. 2, no. 73, RCS. Baron, *op. cit.*, II,
        pp. 306–8. F. D. Drewitt, *The Life of Edward Jenner, M. D., F. R. S., Naturalist,*
        and Discoverer of Vaccination, 2nd edn, London, New York, Toronto: Longmans
        Green, 1933, pp. 126–7.
286 'Nerves are not quite . . . .': Miller, *op. cit.*, pp. 105–6 and footnote.
    finding mistakes in the printed: *ibid.*, p. 106.
    A Letter to Charles Henry Parry: London: Baldwin Craddock & Joy, p. 67.
    nineteen cases: *ibid.*, pp. 5–15.
    'check the progress . . .': *ibid.*, p. 47.
    tartar emetic ointment worked: *ibid.*, p. 29.
    A confused old man . . . . A young man: *ibid.*, pp. 6–8, Cases 2 and 3.
    early autumn of 1822,: Crummer, *op. cit.*, p. 424.
287 'In the wet summer . . . .': Edward Jenner, *Some Observations on the Migration of*
        Birds. . . .' in *Philosophical Transactions*, London: Wm Nichol, 1824, p. 21 footnote.
    'still in solitude': Baron, *op. cit.*, II, p. 429.
    'By what means, moral or physical, . . .': Jenner to Edward Davies, *op. cit.*, 19/9/1821,
        Well. MS5237(1).
    'My dear Willy . . . .': Davies, *op. cit.*, (n.d.), Well. MS5230(128).
288 'I had a pleasant Letter . . . .': Jenner to Edward Davies, *op. cit.*, (n.d.), Well. MS5237(6).
    On 23 October,: Davies, *op. cit.*, Well. MS2056.
    'a very excellent . . .': *ibid.*, 5/11/1821. Baron, *op. cit.*, II, pp. 307–8 and footnote. Davies,
        op. cit., Well. MS5230(26/2).
    complained to Edward Davies: Jenner to Edward Davies, *op. cit.*, Well. MS5237(7).
    'his dress was a black coattailed coat . . . .': Underwood, *op. cit.*, photocopies in 3" file.
    'Thank Heavens, I have not . . .': Jenner, *op. cit.*, 26/12/1821, Well. MS5240(82).
289 to Bath for a visit,: Davies, *op. cit.*, 19/1/1821, Well. MS2056.
    attended his funeral: Baron, *op. cit.*, II, p. 277.
    'In a Female I should . . . .': Miller, *op. cit.*, pp. 108–9.
    two continental visitors,: *ibid.*, pp. 109, 110 footnote.
    'by no means at variance.': George Gregory, 'A Letter to the Editors . . . inclosing
        a Correspondence with Dr. Jenner. '. . . *London Med. Phys. Jour.*, 48 (9/1822), pp.
        193.
    'that I have nothing whatever . . . .': Jenner to Edward Davies, *op. cit.*, 1/4/1822, Well.
        MS5237(3).
    'How goes on Vaccination?': Miller, *op. cit.*, pp. 110–11.
290 'Col. Kingscote and the Mr. Bedford's': Davies, *op. cit.*, 7/3/1822, Well. MS2056.
    'on the business . . .': Davies, *op. cit.*, 9/6/1822, Well. MS5230(46).
    Jenner gave his daughter: Jenner, *op. cit.*, Well. MS5235(12).
    Mrs Stephen Jenner: Underwood, *op. cit.*, photocopies of notes by Stephen Jenner.
    Catherine Jenner and John Yeend Bedford: Baron, *op. cit.*, II, p. 290. Davies, *op. cit.*,
        Well. MS2056.
    one of the witnesses.: 'Consent to Marry', Gloucester Library, red catalogue 7011–8384,
        S10.8. Berkeley Parish Register, GCRO PFC42 1/15–1/39.
    business transactions: Davies, *op. cit.*, 2/9/1822, Well. MS5230(22).
291 Susan and Caroline Jenner,: Baron, *op. cit.*, II, pp. 430, 432.
    'For a pretty good definition . . .': Jenner, *op. cit.*, 26/10/1822, Well. MS5240(69).
    a branch of the Bible Society.: Davies, *op. cit.*, 6/1/1823, 9/1/1823, Well. MS2057.
    'Frampton Watchmaker',: Letter to Edward Gardner, in Jenner to Baron, *op. cit.*, RCS.
        Baron, *op. cit.*, II, p. 433.

Page

291 a short, affectionate note: Davies, *op. cit.*, 24/1/1823, Well. MS5230(127).

Pruen was also there: Miller, *op. cit.*, p. 135. A fact that he later briefly thought to use in order to win over the executors to the idea that he should write the official biography.

'go into the Hot House . . .': Underwood, *op. cit.*, Photocopies of notes by Stephen Jenner.

292 George Jenner wrote a note: Davies, *op. cit.*, 25/1/1823, Well. MS5230(41).

'and the Doctor seemed to revive': [Henry Jones Shrapnell], Correspondence and papers. . . ., Well. MS5241(1).

Bibliography

LeFanu, W. R., *A Bio-bibliography of Edward Jenner 1749–1823*, London: Harvey & Blythe, 1951 (2nd edn, 1985) is scholarly, remarkably complete and highly accurate, but locations of manuscripts may be out-of-date. Although I have used a wider range of secondary sources than he required, this Bibliography makes no attempt to duplicate LeFanu and no claim to completeness. I have listed the sources of manuscripts, Jenner's writings and secondary sources, including contemporary contributions to the vaccination debate, that were useful. An author's articles are mixed in with his books and pamphlets. By and large I have sought to list items of wider interest which are more readily available, both criteria being ill defined and subjective, but sources cited in the Notes may not appear below.

Manuscripts

Manuscript letters from and to Edward Jenner, journals, diaries, notebooks, commonplace books and account books by and referring to Jenner are scattered in libraries around the world. The collections used for this book are held by:

> Wellcome Institute for the History of Medicine Library, London
> Royal College of Physicians Library, London
> Royal College of Surgeons Library, London
> Royal Society of Medicine, London
> Jenner Museum, Berkeley, Glos.
> Gloucester County Record Office, Gloucester
> British Library Department of Manuscripts
> William H. Welch Medical Library, Johns Hopkins University, Baltimore, Maryland
> Trent Collection in the History of Medicine, Duke University Medical Center Library, Durham, North Carolina
> Alfred Taubman Medical Library, University of Michigan, Ann Arbor, Michigan
> Osler Library of the History of Medicine, McGill University, Montreal

By far the largest collection of relevant material is held by the WELLCOME INSTITUTE LIBRARY (abbreviated Well. in the Notes and below). This collection includes one of the extant manuscripts of Jenner's 'Inquiry' (see p. 337), minutes of the Royal Jennerian Society, and correspondence and other records related to the National Vaccine Establishment. I will not attempt a complete catalogue because to do so would be to duplicate the 'list of papers' under the title, 'Edward Jenner (1749–1823)', prepared in 1986 by Richard Palmer, Curator of Western Manuscripts. This spiral-bound book of 77 pages contains a useful introduction to the collection by Dr Palmer and an annotated description of each item. Items are numbered: e.g., MS5222(1–50). Note that these item numbers have been used throughout the Notes to identify references from the Wellcome collection.

The ROYAL COLLEGE OF PHYSICIANS (RCP) houses some letters, the 'Regulations and Transactions of the Glocestershire Medical Society', the minutes and correspondence of the College's Vaccination Committee (1807), and the manuscript of the Drewitt *Note-book* (see p. 336). In the Notes the initials RCP may be followed by ALS, i.e., Autographed Letters Store.

The ROYAL COLLEGE OF SURGEONS (RCS) holds all but one of the extant letters from John Hunter to Edward Jenner. They were published by the College in *Letters from the Past from John Hunter to Edward Jenner*, 1976. The exception is a letter belonging to the Hunterian Society. In addition to Jenner correspondence with Baron, the RCS has several volumes of correspondence involving John Hunter and Matthew Baillie and their families, the Hunter-Baillie Correspondence, and one of the extant manuscripts of Jenner's 'Inquiry' (see p. 337).

The ROYAL SOCIETY OF MEDICINE (RSM) houses many of Jenner's letters to Marcet and the only complete set of the *Medical Observer*.

The JENNER MUSEUM (JM) is relatively new and holds few MSS.

The GLOUCESTER COUNTY RECORD OFFICE (GCRO) contains parish records for the whole county, Jenner's will, many indentures involving the Jenner family and some Jenner correspondence.

The BRITISH LIBRARY DEPARTMENT OF MANUSCRIPTS (BLMS) holds several Jenner letters in various collections.

All letters held by the WILLIAM H. WELCH MEDICAL LIBRARY, JOHNS HOPKINS UNIVERSITY, have been published in a well researched, annotated volume edited by Genevieve Miller, *Letters of Edward Jenner and Other Documents Concerning the Early History of Vaccination*, Baltimore and London: Johns Hopkins University Press, 1983.

The TRENT COLLECTION IN THE HISTORY OF MEDICINE, DUKE UNIVERSITY MEDICAL CENTRE LIBRARY, contains the manuscript of the Hellman 'Diary' (see pp. 336–7) and a small number of Jenner letters, some of them copies of letters in other collections.

The TAUBMAN MEDICAL LIBRARY, UNIVERSITY OF MICHIGAN, holds the manuscript of the Crummer 'Note-book' (see p. 336).

The OSLER LIBRARY OF THE HISTORY OF MEDICINE, McGILL UNIVERSITY, houses two letters by Mrs Catherine Jenner and Robert Fitzhardinge Jenner, and a paper by Edward Jenner, 'Report of a case of hydatids of the kidney, successfully treated with oil of turpentine', 28/7/1790.

The inner two pages of a letter from Edward Jenner to Caleb Hillier Parry, 6/7/1808, are displayed at Sudeley Castle, Winchcombe, Glos., the only Jenner letter I know of still in private hands.

Jenner manuscripts and publications

Baron John, *Illustrations of the Enquiry Respecting Tuberculous Diseases*, London: T. & G. Underwood, 1822: critical notes by Edward Jenner, bound into presentation copy.
'Classes of the Human Powers of Intellect. . . . By Dr. Jenner', in *The Artist: a Collection of Essays*. . . ., Prince Hoare (ed.), London: J. Murray, 1810, Vol. I, number XIX.
A Continuation of Facts & Observations Relative to the Variolae Vaccinae, London: Sampson Low, 1800. The third vaccination pamphlet.
Crummer, L., (ed). 'Copy of Jenner Note Book', *Annals of Medical History*, N. S. I (1929), pp. 403–28.
Cursory Observations on Emetic Tartar. . . ., Wotton-under-Edge: J. Bence, [1780].
'Directions & observations etc', inscribed on the flysheet, 'These Prescriptions given to Mrs Pruen by Dr Jenner her respected fri[end]' (n.d.), MS. Well.
Drewitt, F. D., *The Note-book of Edward Jenner*, Oxford University Press, 1931.
'An Essay on Marriage', 1783, MS. Well.
Facts, for the Most Part Unobserved, or not duly Noticed, Respecting Variolous Contagion, London: S. Gosnell, 1808.
'Dr. Jenner, in Reply to Mr. Fermor', *Medical and Physical Journal*, 6 (10/1801), pp. 325–6.
Further Observations on the Variolae Vaccinae or Cow Pox, London: Sampson Low, 1799. The second vaccination pamphlet.
Hellman, C. D., (ed.) 'An Unpublished Diary of Edward Jenner' (Hellman Diary), *Annals of*

Medical History, N. S. III (1931), pp. 412–38.

An Inquiry into the Causes and Effects of the Variolae Vaccinae . . . known by the name of the Cow Pox, London: Sampson Low, 1798. First vaccination pamphlet.

'An Inquiry into the natural History of a Disease known in Glostershire under the name of the Cow-Pox', [Berkeley, 29/3/1797], MS. Well.

'An Inquiry into the natural History of a Disease known in Glostershire by the name of the Cow-pox' (n.d.), MS. RCS.

Instructions for Vaccine Inoculation, London: D. N. Shury, [1801].

'A Legendary Tale', [c.1790], MS probably in hand of William Davies junior. (Cf. 'The Highwayman', [Poems 1], pp. 22–36.) Well.

'Letter addressed to the Medical Profession generally, relative to Vaccination', *London Medical and Physical Journal*, 45 (4/1821), pp. 277–80.

A Letter to Charles Henry Parry, MD., FRS etc on the Influence of Artificial Eruptions, In Certain Diseases incidental to the Human Body. . . ., London: Baldwin Craddock & Joy, 1822.

'Notes from Dr. Jenner Respecting the preceeding Facts on Cow-pox', in *Contributions to Physical and Mental Knowledge . . . Collected by Thomas Beddoes MD*, Bristol: Biggs & Cottle, 1799.

'Observations on the Distemper in Dogs', *Medico-Chirurgical Transactions*, London: Medical and Chirurgical Society, 3rd edn, Vol. I (1815), pp. 265–70.

'Observations on the Natural History of the Cuckoo', from the *Philosophical Transactions* (read at the Royal Society, 13/3/1788).

On the Varieties & Modifications of the Vaccine Pustule, occasioned by an Herpetic State of the Skin, Cheltenham: H. Ruff, 1806.

The Origin of the Vaccine Inoculation, London: D. N. Shury, 1801. Fourth and last vaccination pamphlet.

[Poems 1], Vol. I, most but not all by Edward Jenner, copied by W. Davies, 1794, MS. Well.

[Poems 2], Vol. II, all by Edward Jenner but two repeated from [Poems 1], copied by W. Davies (n.d.), MS. Well.

'Presuming that you are conversant. . . .' (n.d. (1821?)). Printed circular letter on influence of herpes infections on vaccination.

'A Process for preparing pure Emetic Tartar by Re-crystallization. . . .', *Transactions of a Society for the Improvement of Medical and Chirurgical Knowledge*, 1 (1793), pp. 30–3.

Some Observations on the Migration of Birds. . . ., from the Philosophical Transactions, London: Wm Nicol, 1824.

'To the Editors. . . .', *Medical and Physical Journal*, 3 (2/1800), pp. 101–2. Response to Pearson, 'A Communication . . .' (see p. 340).

'To the Editors. . . .', *Medical and Physical Journal*, 3 (6/1800), pp. 502–3. Reply to Dunning, 'To Drs. Jenner. . . .' (see p. 338).

'Two Cases of Small-Pox Infection, Communicated to the Foetus in Utero. . . .', *Medico-Chirurgical Transactions*, London: Medical and Chirurgical Society, 3rd edn, Vol. I (1815), pp. 270–7.

Waterhouse, Dr B., *Information Respecting . . .* (see p. 341): letter to Benjamin Waterhouse, 4/3/1801, bound with book.

Secondary sources
(including contemporary contributions to the vaccination debate)

'Dr. Jenner', *Public Characters of 1802–1803* (Vol. V), London: Richard Phillips, 1803. The first published biography.

'Edward Jenner', *Annual Biography & Obituary 1824* (n.p.), pp. 186–217.

'Edward Jenner: His Life, His Work, and His Writings', *British Medical Journal*, 23/5/1896, pp. 1245–61. Centenary memorial issue. This article states that Jenner had a disappointed love affair before he met his wife.

Abraham, J. J., *Lettsom: His Life, Times, Friends and Descendants*, London: William Heinemann Medical, 1933. One of Jenner's most influential early supporters.

Adams, J., *Answers to All the Objections hitherto Made against Cow-Pox*, London: J. Johnson, 1805. Cautious approval by an open-minded physician.

—— *Observations on Morbid Poisons, Chronic and Acute*, 2nd edn, London: J. Callow, 1807. An influential textbook.

Addington, J. *A Comparative View of the Natural Small-Pox, Inoculated Small-Pox, and Inoculated Cow-Pox*, London: Medical Council of the Royal Jennerian Society (n.d.). A wall-chart showing the official view.

Aikin, C. R., *A Concise View . . . concerning the Cow-Pox*, London: R. Phillips, 1801. Favourable report by a London surgeon.

Aubert, A., *Rapport sur la Vaccine ou Traité sur Cette Maladie. . . .*, Paris: Richard, Caille et Ravier [1801]. First pro-vaccination tract from abroad.

Baron, J., *The Life of Edward Jenner, M.D. . . . with Illustrations from His Doctrines, and Selections from His Correspondence*, 2 vols, London: Henry Colburn, Vol. I, 1827; Vol. II, 1838. The official life.

Baxby, D., 'A death from inoculated smallpox in the English royal family', *Medical History*, 28 (1984), pp. 303–7. Death of Prince Octavius.

—— 'The genesis of Edward Jenner's *Inquiry* of 1798: a comparison of the two unpublished manuscripts and the published version', *Medical History*, 29 (1985), pp. 193–9.

—— *Jenner's Smallpox Vaccine: The Riddle of Vaccinia Virus and its Origin*, London: Heinemann Educational, 1981. Excellent scientific detection by a practising virologist.

Coxe, Dr [J.R.], 'History of a Case of Tinea Capitis cured by vaccination. . . .', *Medical and Physical Journal*, 18 (10/1807), pp. 340–1. A Philadelphia supporter of vaccination with a case that seemed to invert Jenner's fears about herpetic diseases.

Creaser, T., *Observations on Dr. Pearson's Examination of the Report of the Committee of the House of Commons. . . .*' 2nd edn, Bath: Richard Cruttwell, 1805.

Creighton, Dr C., *Jenner and Vaccination: A Strange Chapter of Medical History*, London: Swan Sonnenschein, 1889. Creighton believed Jenner had acted fraudulently.

Crookshank, E. M., *History and Pathology of Vaccination*, Vol. I: *A Critical Inquiry*; Vol. II: *Selected Essays*, London: H. K. Lewis, 1889. Crookshank also believed that Jenner had practised variolation, perhaps unwittingly. Vol. II contains a number of pamphlets which contributed to the early vaccination debate.

Davy, John, *Memoirs of the Life of Sir Humphry Davy. . . .*, London: Smith, Elder & Co., 1839.

De Carro, Dr J., 'Observations on the Vaccine Inoculation. . . .', *Medical and Physical Journal*, 8 (9/1802), pp. 193–6. Favourable report from Vienna.

—— 'To Dr. Jenner', *Medical and Physical Journal*, 9 (5/1803), pp. 450–7. Transport of vaccine to Bombay.

Dibdin, T. F., *Reminiscences of a Literary Life*, 2 vols, London: John Major, 1836.

Dobson, J., *John Hunter*, Edinburgh and London: Livingstone, 1969.

Drewitt, F. D., *The Life of Edward Jenner, M. D., F. R. S., Naturalist, and Discoverer of Vaccination*, 2nd edn, London, New York, Toronto: Longmans Green, 1933.

Dunning, R., *Minutes of Some Experiments to ascertain the permanent security of Vaccination. . . .*, [Plymouth] Dock: E. Hoxland, 1804.

—— 'On Vaccination', *Medical and Physical Journal*, 7 (1/1802), pp. 2–8. Note early use of word.

—— 'To Drs. Jenner, Pearson, and Woodville', *Medical and Physical Journal*, 3 (5/1800), pp. 436–41. Questions to which Jenner replied (see p. 337).

—— 'To the Editors. . . .', *Medical and Physical Journal*, 13 (6/1805), pp. 542–7. The reply to John Walker, expressing alarm at Walker's procedures.

Epps, Dr J., *The Life of John Walker, M. D.*, London: Whittaker, Treacher & Co., 1831.

Farington, J., *The Farington Diary*, ed. J. Greig, 8 vols, London: Hutchinson, 1924–8.

Fermor, W., *Reflections on the Cow-Pox illustrated by Cases . . . in a Letter to Dr. Jenner. . . .*, Oxford: Dawson & Co., 1800. Favourable reports by a layman.

Fisk, D., *Dr Jenner of Berkeley*, London, Melbourne, Toronto: Heinemann, 1959.

Fosbroke, T. D., *Abstracts of Records and Manuscripts Respecting the County of Gloucester*, Vol. I, Gloucester: Jos Harris, 1807.

—— *Berkeley Manuscripts. Abstracts and Extracts of Smyth's Lives of the Berkeleys . . . and Biographical Anecdotes of Dr. Jenner. . . .*, London: John Nichols & Son, 1821.

—— *A Picturesque and Topographical Account of Cheltenham . . . to Which are Added, Contributions to the Medical Topography . . . by John Fosbroke*, Cheltenham: S. C. Harper, 1826.

Gardner, E., *Miscellanies, in Prose and Verse*, 2 vols (bound in 1), Bristol: Biggs & Cottle, 1798. Jenner's old friend from Frampton.

Goldson, W., *Some Recent Cases of Small Pox subsequent to Vaccination. . . .*, Portsea: William Woodward, 1804. The first notices of vaccination failures.

Griffin, J., *The Jennerian Discovery: or Testimonials in Favour of the Cow-Pox-Inoculation. . . .*, Portsea: J. Horsey, 1804. Griffin was a Dissenting minister in Portsea.

Haines, R., E. Gethyn-Jones, A. Sanderson, 'Edward Jenner: his life and work', *Immunology Today*, 5/1981, pp. vii–x. Written to promote the work of the Jenner Society.

Halsband, R., *The Life of Lady Mary Wortley Montagu*, Oxford: Clarendon Press, 1957. The woman who introduced variolation into England.

Hammond, J. L. and B., *The Village Labourer, 1760–1832*, Gloucester: Alan Sutton, 1987. Essential background reading. Reprint of a classic.

Harrison, Dr R., 'An Essay towards a Pathology of Eruptive Fevers', *London Medical and Physical Journal*, 44 (7/1820), pp. 16–27. Important contribution to description of smallpox after vaccination.

Harvey, A. D., *Britain in the Early Nineteenth Century*, London: Batsford, 1978. Useful for political background.

Hopkins, D. R., *Princes and Peasants: Smallpox in History*, Chicago and London: University of Chicago Press, 1983. Entertaining and scholarly, written to show how the disease has been exterminated by the World Health Organization.

Jones, E., *Vaccination Vindicated against Misrepresentation and Calumny, in a Letter to His Patients*, Welshpool; reprint London: J. Murray, 1806. Published by a Welshpool surgeon to warn his patients.

Lane, J. M., D. R. Hopkins, W. R. Dowdle, J. D. Millar, 'Razell and Jennerian vaccination', *Bulletin of the History of Medicine*, 55 (1981), pp. 273–6. A reply to Razell (see p. 340).

[Lettsom, J. C.], *Memoir of Edward Jenner, M. D.*, [London]: I. Gold, [1804].

Lettsom, J. C., *Observations on the Cow-Pock*, London: John Nichols & Son, 1801.

Lipscomb, G., *A Dissertation on the Failure and Mischiefs of the Disease Called the Cow-Pox. . . .*, London: Geo. Robinson, 1805. A surgeon who believed in variolation.

Loy, J. G., *An Account of Some Experiments on the Origin of the Cow-Pox*, Whitby: Thos Webster, 1801. Supports Jenner's grease theory.

[MacMichael, W.], *Lives of British Physicians*, London: J. Murray, 1830. Contains a biography of Jenner.

Merriman, S., *Observations on Some Late Attempts to Depreciate the Value and Efficacy of Vaccine Inoculation*, London: J. Murray, 1805. Cases from a London surgeon.

Monro, Dr A., *Observations on the Different Kinds of Small Pox, and especially of that which sometimes follows Vaccination*, Edinburgh: Archibald Constable, 1818. An attempt to classify the moderate symptoms of 'varioloid disease'.

Moore, J., *The History and Practice of Vaccination*, London: J. Callow, 1817. Moore was Director of the National Vaccine Establishment.

[Morgan, Sir T. C.], *An Expostulatory Letter to Dr. Moseley. . . .*, London: J. Murray, 1808. Moseley was the most persistent anti vaccinist.

Moseley, B., *An Oliver for a Rowland; or, a Cow Pox Epistle to the Reverend Rowland Hill. . . .*, 2nd edn, London: Longman, Hurst, Rees, & Orme, 1806.

—— *A Review of the Report of the Royal College of Physicians of London, on Vaccination*, London: Longman, Hurst, Rees & Orme, 1808.

—— *A Treatise on Lues Bovilla; or Cow Pox*, 2nd edn, London: John Nichols & Son, 1805.

—— *A Treatise on Sugar. with Miscellaneous Medical Observations*, London: John Nichols & Son, 1799. Contains the remark on 'Cowmania'.

Murray, C., *An Answer to Mr. Highmore's Objections to the Bill before Parliament to Prevent the Spreading of the Infection of the Small Pox. . . .*, London: Longman, Hurst, Rees & Orme, 1808. Murray was then Secretary to the Royal Jennerian Society.

(National Vaccine Establishment) 'Copy of a circular letter addressed by the Board . . . to regulate the Affairs of the National Vaccine Establishment', *Medical and Physical Journal*, 23 (2/1810), pp. 114–15. The 'constitution' of the NVE.

(Norwich) Rich. Lubbock *et al.*, 'A Memorial of the Medical Committee, addressed to the Inhabitants of the City of Norwich, and of the County of Norfolk . . . for . . . a general inoculation for the cow-pox', *Medical and Physical Journal*, 14 (9/1805), pp. 277–82. Similar efforts in several towns and cities.

(Nottingham) *Proceedings for Establishing a Plan of General Cow-Pock Inoculation with a View to the Extinction of the Small-Pox in the Town of Nottingham*, [Nottingham]: S. Tupman, [1805]. As for Norwich.

O'Brian, P., *Joseph Banks, A Life*, London: Collins Harvill, 1988. A good read and highly informative.

Parry, Dr C. H., *An Inquiry into the Symptoms and Causes of the Syncope Anginosa, Commonly called Angina Pectoris. . . .*, Bath: Cruttwell, 1799. Quotes a letter from Jenner about his own work on this disease.

Pearson, Dr G., 'A Communication concerning the Eruptions resembling the Small-Pox, which sometimes appear in the Inoculated Vaccine Disease', *London Medical Review and Magazine*, 2 (12/1799), pp. 393–9. *Medical and Physical Journal*, 3 (2/1800), pp. 97–101.

—— *An Inquiry concerning the History of the Cow Pox. Principally with a View to Supersede and Extinguish the Small Pox*, London: J. Johnson, 1798.

—— 'On the Progress of the Variolae Vaccinae', *Medical and Physical Journal*, 2 (9/1799), pp. 97–8. The first of several similar reports.

Pew, Dr R., *Observations of an Eruptive Disease Which Has Lately Occurred in the Town of Sherborne, Dorset, after Vaccination. . . .*, Sherborne: J. Langdon, [1808 or 1809]. Pew later claimed to have told Jenner about reports of cowpox in France.

Porter, D. and R., *Patient's Progress: Doctors and Doctoring in Eighteenth-Century England*, Cambridge, Polity Press, 1989.

Pruen, T., *A Comparative Sketch of the Effects of Variolous and Vaccine Inoculation. . . .*, [London?]: Phillips, 1807. A lay contribution to the debate by one of Jenner's oldest friends.

Qvist, G., *John Hunter, 1728–1793*, London: William Heinemann Medical, 1981. Recommended to the reader who wants a brief, well rounded biography.

Razell, P., *Edward Jenner's Cowpox Vaccine: The History of a Medical Myth*, 2nd edn, Firle, Sussex: Caliban Books, 1980. Unsuccessful attempt to prove that Jenner 'vaccinated' with smallpox, a century after Creighton.

Reece, Dr R., *A Practical Dictionary of Domestic Medicine*, London: Longman, Hurst, Rees, and Orme, 1808. Antivaccination entry. Evidence that DIY medicine has a long history!

Reed, M., *The Georgian Triumph, 1700–1830*, London: Routledge & Kegan Paul, 1983. Good social and political background.

Reid, L., *Charles James Fox: A Man for the People*, London: Longmans Green & Co., 1969. Emphasis on his supremacy as a public speaker.

Reilly, R., *Pitt the Younger, 1759–1806*, London: Cassell, 1978. Readable and scholarly, if uncritical.

Ring, J., *An Answer to Dr. Moseley. . . .*, London: J. Murray, 1805.

—— *An Answer to Mr. Birch Containing a Defence of Vaccination*, London, J. Murray, 1806.

—— *An Answer to Mr. Goldson, proving that Vaccination Is a Permanent Security against the Small-Pox*, London: J. Murray, 1804.

—— 'Mr. Ring on Inoculation', *Medical and Physical Journal*, 14 (11/1805), pp. 401–9. A continuation of the next entry: successful cases in England and reports of successes abroad.

—— 'To the Editors. . . .', *Medical and Physical Journal*, 14 (10/1805), pp. 355–61. Unjustifiable attack on Dr Adams (see p. 000). Almost every issue of this periodical carried articles of between two and ten thousand words by Ring for more than a decade.

—— *A Treatise on the Cow-pox. . . .*, 2 vols, London: J. & T. Carpenter & J. Johnson, 1801 and 1803.

[Rogers, W. R.], *An Examination of that Part of the Evidence Relative to Cow-Pox, which was Delivered to the Committee of the House of Commons, by Two of the Surgeons of St. Thomas's Hospital. To which is added A Letter to the Author, from John Birch, Esq.*, 2nd edn, London: J. Callow, 1805. Antivaccination, by a surgical colleague of John Birch.

Rowley, Dr W., *Cow-Pox Inoculation No Security against Small-Pox Infection*, London: J. Harris, 1805. Contains drawings and case descriptions of the 'Oxfaced Boy' and 'Mangy girl'.

Royal College of Physicians of London, '. . . on Vaccination. . . .', *Medical and Physical Journal*, 18 (8/1807), pp. 97–111. Report prepared for Parliament.

Saunders, P., *Edward Jenner: The Cheltenham Years, 1795–1823*, Hanover, Vt., and London: University Press of New England, 1982. Much early newspaper and municipal-records research, gossipy and a good read, but filled with inaccuracies.

Smith, J. R., *The Speckled Monster: Smallpox in England, 1670–1970, with particular reference to Essex*, Chelmsford: Essex Record Office, 1987.

Squirrell, Dr R. [Jones, J. G.], *Observations Addressed to the Public in General on the Cow-Pox, Showing it originates in the Scrophula. . . .*, London: W. Smith & Son, 1805. Influential antivaccination tract.

Stansfield, D. A., *Thomas Beddoes M. D. 1760–1808. . . .*, Dordrecht, Boston, Lancaster: D. Reidel Publishing Co., 1984.

Stock, Dr J. E., *Memoirs of the Life of Thomas Beddoes, M. D.*, London: J. Murray, 1811.

Stratford, J., *Good and Great Men of Gloucestershire. A Series of Biographical Sketches. . . .*, Cirencester: C. H. Savory, [1867].

Thompson, E. P., *The Making of the English Working Class*, New York: Pantheon, 1964. Essential for the social and economic background.

Thomson, Dr J., *A Plain Statement of Facts, in Favour of the Cow-pox, Intended for Circulation through the middle and lower Classes of Society*, Halifax: Holden & Dowson, 1809. Simple and straightforward.

Thornton, Dr R. J., *Facts Decisive in Favour of the Cow-Pock. . . .*, 4th edn, London: H. D. Symonds et al., 1803. Influential, by the author of the textbook description of smallpox quoted in chapter 1.

Tudor, M., *The B. . . . . . y Family: A Narrative*, London: J. Green, [1823?]. Mary Tudor was sister-in-law to the Countess of Berkeley and felt she had been hard done by following the fraudulent marriage.

Walker, [Dr] J., *Reply to James Moore, on His Mis-Statements. . . .*, London: Highley & Son, 1818. Regarding Moore's *History* (see p. 339).

—— 'To the Editors. . . .', *Medical and Physical Journal*, 13 (6/1805), pp. 539–42. Defence of his procedures, citing Jenner.

Walker, R., 'On the present State of Vaccination in Oxford', *London Medical and Physical Journal*, 35 (2/1816), pp. 93–8. This and several other *Journal* articles by Richard Walker at roughly the same time indicate that he favoured vaccination despite its failures.

Wallace, E. M., *The First Vaccinator: Benjamin Jesty. . . .*, [Swanage: 1981].

Waterhouse, Dr B., *Information Respecting the Origin, Progress, and Efficacy of the Kine-Pock Inoculation. . . .* (editor unknown), Cambridge, Mass.: Hilliard & Metcalf, 1810.

—— 'The following Letters are extracted from the Independent Chronicle, published at Boston, on the 15th Day of July, 1802', *Medical and Physical Journal*, 8 (12/1802), pp. 543–5.

Watt, Dr R., *Treatise on the History, Nature, and Treatment of Chincough [Whooping Cough] . . . to which is subjoined an Inquiry into the Relative Mortality of the Principal Diseases of Children. . . .*, Glasgow: John Smith & Son, 1813. Useful statistical material and therefore rare.

Willan, Dr R., *On Cutaneous Diseases*, 4 vols, London: J. Johnson, 1808. Parts I–III first published 1798–1808, but revised when republished with Part IV. The standard text on the subject for a generation.

—— *On Vaccine Inoculation*, London: Richard Phillips, 1806. Pro-vaccination.

Woodforde, J., *The Diary of a Country Parson, 1758–1802*, ed. J. Beresford, Oxford, London, New York: Oxford University Press, 1978. The abridged paperback edition; thoroughly enjoyable and informative.

Woodville, Dr W., *Report of a Series of Inoculations for the Variolae Vaccinae, or Cow-Pox. . . .*, London: Jas Phillips & Son, [1799]. The first major clinical trial of vaccination at the London Smallpox and Inoculation Hospitals.

Worthington, Dr R., *A Treatise on the State of the Poor in Sickness. . . .*, Ludlow: H. Proctor, 1804. The pamphlet by Jenner's friend on improvement of hospital facilities for rural poor.

Yeats, G. D., *An Address to the County and Town of Bedford, on the Nature and Efficacy of the Cow-Pox, in preventing the Small-Pox . . . to which is annexed, A Letter from Dr. Jenner. . . .*, Bedford: W. Smith, [1803]. Another pro-vaccination tract by a local practitioner.

Acknowledgements

For a total of three years I worked two or three days a week at the Wellcome Institute for the History of Medicine Library. My gratitude is properly extended to the entire staff. They made the facilities of a great library accessible and comfortable to use. I thank them all, but at risk of appearing to slight their colleagues, it is necessary that some contributions to this book be acknowledged by name. For fifteen years Robin Price, Deputy Librarian, has made it possible for me to use the Library for various projects, especially this book. Dr Richard Palmer, Curator of Western Manuscripts, prepared the 'list' of Jenner papers before we had an opportunity to meet, but without it, my job would have been much harder. He has also read difficult handwriting for me, looked out special sources and relevant papers in disparate collections, and obtained copies of manuscripts held in the United States and Canada so that I could use them in the first instance. John Symons, Curator of Early Printed Books, frequently helped me with difficult references and in the location of books. Julia Sheppard, Archivist of the Chemical Medical Archives Centre, brought the Sudeley Castle letter to my attention. William Schubach, Curator of the Iconographic Collection, showed me the rich pictorial resources relating to Jenner held by the Library. Judith Barker, Elizabeth Doctor and Caroline Peck, Reader Services Department, and Brenda Sutton, Department Head, held research material for days, guided me through the catalogue and saved me myriad minutes by helpful suggestions, fetching and carrying. They demonstrate that even the richest collection is no better than the people who make it available to the public.

For my purposes the other libraries I used had fewer resources, though they were none the less of major importance to the book. Geoffrey Davenport, Librarian, allowed me to use the Library of the Royal College of Physicians of England and delivered vital manuscript material as required. Ian Lyle, Librarian, and Mrs Tina Craig, his assistant, at the Royal College of Surgeons of London also made my research work fast and as easy as possible. Once I had made my purposes clear, Mr David Stewart, Librarian of the Royal Society of Medicine, gave me assistance in locating material and a comfortable carrel in which to use it. The staff of the British Library Department of Manuscripts are, I am afraid, nameless to me, but they were helpful and patient with a novice to the use of their vast and complex collection. The Gloucester County Record Office was perhaps the one library where I could have used more time. In part that was because Mrs K. Haslem, the Searchroom Supervisor, gradually opened out to me the wealth of material in the library as I made clear to her what I needed. My thanks to her and her colleagues, both in the Record Office and in the Gloucester Library on Brunswick Road. Mrs Denise Rawlinson, Custodian, and the staff of the Jenner Museum at Berkeley welcomed me to their growing collection on more than one visit. R. A. Jamieson, Archives Assistant, British Waterways South-West, directed me to materials on early canal construction.

In the Notes I have acknowledged specific contributions to this book by Dr Derrick Baxby, Canon J. E. Gethyn-Jones and Dr Hugh Torrens. I wish to thank them here as well for their help with various aspects of their respective fields of interest. I am also grateful to Jim Connell, Editor, *Illustrated Islington History Journal*, for information about the schoolmaster, John Evans. Professor Michael Neve arranged for me to read a paper to a research seminar on medical lives and practice at the Wellcome Institute. I thank him for the opportunity to try out and subsequently modify some ideas when the writing had just begun.

Helpful, often beyond the call of duty, though all of these people have been, this book has only one author, for better or worse. Any errors of omission or commission are of course mine.

RBF
London
April 1990

Index

EJ = Edward Jenner; CJ = Edward Jenner's wife, Catherine

225, 233, 258; marries EJ's sister Anne
24; as rector of Eastington 25; and
games of chance 34; EJ performs
minor surgery on 60; describes winter
of 1794 61-2; surgical treatment by
Cline 74; and EJ's first petition 130-31;
on son Edward 149; and death of Mary
Black 228; and wife's death 236; and
canals 244; illness 252; death 264
Davies, Rev William (EJ's nephew; main
references); and enclosure 6; as EJ's
unofficial business manager 9, 100,
191-2, 228, 229, 230, 242, 243, 244,
276; diary 63-4, 67-8, 70, 85, 149-50,
160, 169, 174, 217, 273; receives living
of Stone 70; and Berkeley peerage
scandal 74-5; and freemasonry 149-50,
165, 169, 191, 267-8, 273, 274, 275,
279, 282; and Henry Jenner's
illegitimate marriage 206; becomes a
magistrate 217; marries Sarah Buckle
224; attends poachers' trial 258; EJ's
treatment for headaches 273; visits
Robert at Oxford 276; and EJ's will
283; and insurance policy application
284-5; and Hobday paintings of EJ
288; officiates at Catherine's wedding
290; and death of EJ 292
Davies, William (EJ's great-nephew)
256, 266, 272, 273, 281, 287
Davis, Richard Hart, MP 179
Davis, William, of Slimbridge 8
Davy, Sir Humphry 218, 287
De Carro, Dr Jean 80, 92, 94, 107, 108,
109, 139, 143, 147, 183, 213
De Clifford, Lord 258
De la Roque, Count 105
degrees; in 'physic' 21; of Doctor of
Medicine 21, 59; selling of 59
Delambre (correspondent of EJ's) 112
delirium 266
Denman, Dr Thomas 23-4, 71, 101, 103,
126, 138, 141, 174, 176, 181
Denmark 108
Derby, Lord 101
Desoteux (author of book on variolation)
105
Devonshire, Duke of 167
Diabetes insipidus 239
Dibdin, Thomas Frognall 92, 108, 115,
132-3, 153, 156, 160, 161, 162, 196,
247, 253

digitalis 240
Dillwyn, William 270
Dimsdale, Dr Thomas 18, 79, 146
'Directions & Observations etc.' (Jenner)
240-41
Dissenters 10, 21
distemper, dog 209, 213
Dobson, Richard 250
Dolland, Mr (surgeon) 69
Dolling, W. 127
Domeier, Dr William 144
Downe, Mr (witness at petition hearing)
127
Drew, Rev Herman 127
dropsy 240
Ducie, Lord 60
Duncan, Jonathan 109, 271
Dunning, Richard 76, 100, 101, 132,
145, 148, 159, 160, 172, 173, 176, 180,
183, 194
Durham, Bishop of 137
Dusthill, Anna 109
Dyer, Mary 275

East India Company 143, 223
École de Médecine 105
Edgar, Robert 64, 65
Edinburgh Public Dispensary Vaccine
Institution 101, 145
efflorescence 83, 121
effluvia 2, 17, 78, 100, 122
Egremont, George O'Brien Wyndham,
3rd Earl 91, 96, 97, 98, 137, 145, 155,
166, 252
Ehrmann, Dr 107
86th Regiment 100
Elford, Sir William 127
Elgin, Dowager Countess of 24
Elgin, Lady 108
Elgin, Lord 109
Ellenborough, Lord 245, 246, 248
Ellis, Joyner 291, 292
emetic tartar 45-6, 79, 168, 266, 286
engrafting 15, 16, 93
epidemiology 80, 81, 203, 271
Erlangen, University of 38
erysipelas 72, 82, 239, 240
escharotics 73
    see also caustics
'Essay on Marriage' (Jenner) 43-4, 45
Estcourt, Mrs 239
Estcourt, T.J. 165, 211, 239

Oldenburgh, Grand Duchess of 251
*Oliver for a Rowland; or a Cow Pox
Epistle to the Reverend Rowland Hill,
An* (Moseley) 115-16, 163
'On the Chicken-Pox' (Heberden) 56
'On the Variety and Modifications of the
Vaccine Pustule' (Jenner) 152
Onesimus (slave) 16
ophthalmia 217-18
Origin of the Vaccine Inoculation, The
(Jenner) 113
Orloff, Count 250, 251
orthopox virus family 57
Osborne, William 23, 24

Paine, Thomas 277
Paris 123, 147; institute for the
promotion of vaccination established
105; Marshall in 106-7; vaccine sent to
Madrid 107
Parkinson, Sydney 26
Parry, Caleb Hillier 20, 44, 45, 51, 52,
53, 59, 60, 61, 71, 75, 89, 96, 98, 129,
225, 226, 230, 231, 233, 257, 289
Parry, Dr Charles Henry 224, 237, 238,
242, 247-8, 251, 252, 258, 261-2, 263,
286
Parry, Mrs C.H. 262
Pasteur, Louis 76
Pastor, Professor F. 180
Pavlov, Ivan Petrovich 261
Paytherus, Miss 288
Paytherus, Thomas 51-4, 71, 89, 100,
104, 155, 169, 174-7, 197, 222, 231,
262, 268
Pead, Mary 73, 74
Pead, William 73
Pearce, Mr (overseer of poor at Ham) 259
Pearce, Thomas (lawyer, father of
Susannah Jenner) 35, 61, 100, 140,
167, 168, 206, 244
Pearce, Thomas (Case 13) 77
Pearson, Dr George 86-9, 91, 92, 94-7,
99, 100, 102-5, 107, 112, 123, 127,
128, 129, 136, 149, 209
Pegge, Sir Christopher 104, 248
Pembroke College, Oxford 6, 13
Pennington, Sir Isaac 201-2
Pepys, Sir Lucas 157, 180, 188, 199, 208,
209, 211, 219, 222, 234, 247, 264
Perceval, Spencer 188, 197, 235
Perrington, Emily Allen 277

Perrington, Mary 277
Peterloo Massacre 277
Petty, Lord Henry 167, 174, 185
Pew, Mr (surgeon) 128
Philanthropic Society 243
Phillimore, John (EJ's uncle) 6, 63
Phillimore, Mary (EJ's aunt) 6
Phillimore family 5
Phillips, John 77
Phillips, Richard 168, 179, 180
Phillips, William 138
Philosophical Magazine 184, 219
Philosophical Transactions of the Royal
Society 69, 287
Phipps, James 9, 66-8, 69, 76, 78, 85,
128, 187, 206, 284, 292
Phipps, Susan 85-6
'physic' 68; degrees in 21
Physical Society (Guy's Hospital) 123
physicians; training of 21; gulf between
physicians and surgeons 28; and
variolation 68
picotte, la 128
Piguilem, Francesco 107
Pitt, William, the Younger 91, 99, 113,
115, 119, 120, 134, 137, 140, 150, 167,
186, 188, 199, 277
*Plain Statement of Facts, in Favour of the
Cow-pox, Intended for Circulation
through the middle and lower Classes of
Society, A* (Thomson) 219
plant manures 46-7
Platoff, Count 251
Platt, Peter 128
Plymouth Medical Society 132
Pneumatic Institution, Bristol 218
Portland, Earl of 51, 188
Portlock, Sarah 77
Portsmouth Medical Society 158
Powell, Judge 249, 250
pox diseases 57
Poxvirus officinalis 57
*Practical Dictionary of Domestic Medicine,
A* (Reece) 158
Price, Rees 194
Priestley, Joseph 35, 193
Prince of Wales *see* George IV, King
Privy Council 210, 211
Pruen, Mrs (née Andrews) 240, 241, 270,
285, 288
Pruen, Rev Thomas (main references)
121, 181, 189, 196, 197, 202, 203, 207,

210, 216, 217, 220, 221, 222, 224, 226, 237, 265, 267, 268, 270, 284, 287, 291, 292
Pruen, Rev William 289
Prussia, King of (Frederick-William III) 251
psoriasis 152
Pulteney, Dr R. 127
purification technique 45-6

quarantine 271; the Suttons and 18; and variolation 198; control of 244-5

Rabaut-Pomier, Jacques-Antoine 128
rabies 76
Ramsden, Rev Dr 71
Reece, Dr Richard 158, 199, 200
Reed, Mary 64, 65
Reed, William 64, 65
Reflexions on . . . the Caesaerean Operation. To which are added . . . Experiments on the Supposed Origin of the Cow-Pox (Simmons) 93
Rendell, Mrs 128
Rensmett, Dr 132
Report on the Vaccine-Pock Institution 97, 102
Report of a Series of Inoculations for the Variolae Vaccinae . . . with Remarks and Observations on this Disease, considered as a Substitute for the Small-Pox (Woodville) 90, 91, 94
Review of the Report of the Royal College of Physicians of London, on Vaccination, A (Moseley) 208
Riddiford, Abraham 77
Rigby, Edward 237
Ring, John 103, 104, 123, 126, 135, 136, 138, 141, 144-7, 153, 156, 159, 172-6, 178, 183, 189-92, 201, 208, 242, 284
ringworm 142, 152, 153
  see also tinea capitis
Roberts, Mr (antivaccinist,? Rogers, W.R.) 158
Roberts brothers 44
Rodway, William 77
Rogers, W.R. 158, 163
Rose, George 188, 189, 191, 195, 197-8, 199, 213, 219, 245, 264
Rous, Sir John, MP (later Lord) 41, 126
Rowland for an Oliver, A (Hill) 116

Rowley, Dr William 126, 158, 163-5, 169, 181
Royal Academy 288
Royal Botanical Gardens, Kew 47
Royal College of Physicians 15, 17, 21, 84, 126, 168, 174, 180, 181, 182, 188, 194, 199, 202, 210, 234, 248
Royal College of Surgeons 27, 126, 180, 182, 188, 199, 246
Royal Economical Society (Spain) 107
Royal Humane Society 147
Royal Institution 210, 218
Royal Jennerian Society 104, 156, 188; establishment of 76, 135-8; Medical Council 76, 138, 139, 141, 143-7, 164, 168, 170, 172, 174, 176, 178; on spurious pustules 84; Annual Festival 126, 145, 149, 183, 184, 216, 247; destruction of 136; Board of Directors 137, 138, 141, 143, 145, 146, 147, 166, 170, 172, 174, 178, 192, 198, 201, 203; delayed reply to Earl of Hardwicke 139, 141-2; adopts by-laws and regulations 141; receives substantial contribution 143; inoculating stations 143, 144, 146-7; and post of Resident Inoculator 143-4; issues first publications (1803) 144; appearance of free vaccine institutions 145; quarrel between the Board and the Council 145; Woodville becomes an inoculator for 149; committee appointed to investigate EJ's vaccination expenses 166-7; EJ threatens to resign from Medical Council if Walker remains 174, 175; Special General Court (June, 1806) 174; Special General Court (July, 1806) 175-6; Walker's letter of resignation read to meeting 177-8; Resident Inoculator's duties redefined 178; Board of Directors combined with Medical Council 181; EJ concerns himself about financial problems of 189; objects to LVI's application for grant 192; last minutes 204; resuscitated 247
Royal Medical Hospital, Chelsea 93
Royal Society 16, 25, 26, 47, 48, 50, 56, 71, 187, 200, 286
Rumford, Count 210

Sacco, Dr Louis 80, 107, 112, 235